DOMINANCE IS EVERYTHING...
To A Monster Whitetail Buck!

BOB J. MERCIER

Copyright © by Robert Joseph Mercier 2011

All rights reserved. No part of this book may be used or reproduced in any manner whatsoever without the prior written consent of the author.

Published 2011
Printed in the United States of America
ISBN 978-0-9840403-0-8

Author/Self-Publisher/Inventor/Instructor
Robert Joseph Mercier
Mindful Of Nature LLC
P.O. Box 511302
New Berlin, Wisconsin 53151

Photographs by
Scott Anderson, Brookfield, Wisconsin
Dick Ellis, New Berlin, Wisconsin
Robert Joseph Mercier, New Berlin, Wisconsin
Jerry Mercier, Madison, Wisconsin (Cover Photo) see more of Jerry's photos at www.pbase.com/jmercier

"Dominance Is Everything" Logo Art by
Tom Earle
Antler Bound Enterprises
Palmyra, Wisconsin

First News Article by
Dick Ellis, Publisher
On Wisconsin Outdoors
New Berlin, Wisconsin

Cover Design by
Composure Graphics, Nashotah, Wisconsin

Cover Layout by
Karen Cluppert, Not Just Words, Menomonee Falls, Wisconsin

Interior Design and Composition by
Composure Graphics, Nashotah, Wisconsin

Printed by
Quad/Graphics, Dubuque, Iowa

D.I.E. Hunter Testimonials by
Tom Earle, Artist, Sign Painter, and Shed Antler Expert, Palmyra, Wisconsin
Matt "Rhino" Rynearson, Wisconsin Pro Staff Hunter, West Allis, Wisconsin

Taxidermist of Mercier's 17-point non-typical whitetail buck
Dan Trawicki
Northwoods Taxidermy, Waukesha, Wisconsin

Special thanks to:

God. Thank you, God! You are the one who has given me the passion to be the best at everything I do, the faith that I can achieve anything I attempt, and the will to move forward even when I fear there are tough times are ahead. I hope and pray that you will grant me many more seasons to be hunted by dominant bucks with D.I.E.!

Michele Mercier. Michele, you are the love of my life. Thanks for appreciating that I was a hunter before we met, and that I will be hunting as long as I live. Thank you for marrying me on opening day of the Wisconsin archery deer season (September 14, 1996), and for promoting that I go deer hunting opening weekend, on our first two anniversaries. I think God has rewarded us both with D.I.E., because now I do not hunt deer until October 29 and we can spend each anniversary together as we intended. Thanks for always helping me set up my D.I.E. system, rain or shine, with a smile on your face. I love you, and I could not have written this book without your support.

Dick and Judy Mercier. Dad, thanks for teaching me all you know about deer hunting, and for always giving me good advice when I asked for it. Mom, you praised my abilities when I was a boy, and you have always made me feel special. Mom and Dad, thanks for being supportive of me, and for telling me how proud you are of me. You have been the best parents a person could have. Mom and Dad, I am proud to dedicate this book, "DOMINANCE IS EVERYTHING... TO A MONSTER WHITETAIL BUCK!" to you!

Scott Anderson. Scott, thanks for taking the great winter scouting photos. Whether we are hiking, snowshoeing, target shooting, filming bucks, or just hanging out together, we always have a great time! Thanks for dedicating so much of your time to helping me promote my system, and for committing to working on this project in the future. We will have some of the best times of our lives together in the years to come. Thanks for being such a good friend.

Paul Dallmann. Paul, thanks for taking time away from your family to help a good friend. In 2009, you trudged through a foot of standing water and waist-high vegetation to help me set up my D.I.E. system in no-man's land, where only a monster buck would enjoy living! It takes a dedicated sportsman and a great friend to volunteer for a job like that! I enjoyed hunting ducks, geese, and deer with you while we could find the time to spend together. All you need to do is call when you want to go hunting! I will be there for you, man!

Bryan Van Laarhoven. Bryan, thanks for personally financing my right to hunt Wisconsin deer in 2009. Without the fifty bucks you lent me to buy my deer hunting licenses, I would have missed the best bow hunt of my life—and I would have never seen the monster 17-point buck. Times got tough because of the economy and I could not even come up with the $50 it cost to hunt Wisconsin bucks. Can you believe it! You are a very generous man and a great friend to Michele and me. Thanks for caring about my passion to hunt monster bucks, and for keeping this buck hunter in his stand, where he belongs the first week of November!

Ann M. Mercier. Ann, I appreciate your love and dedication for doing a job the only way it should ever be done (the right way) the first time. You helped me a great deal, paving the way for me to get this book published. Without your patience, guidance, and tutoring, I might not have been able to see the big picture here. Thanks for making personal sacrifices to help me achieve my goals. Your selflessness and your desire to work through the mountain of rough drafts I put before you, proved you are a patient, respected, gifted, and very talented woman. Thanks for everything you have done to help me succeed in my life. Your help and support means a lot to me. I am very proud that you are my sister.

Jerry Mercier. Jerry, you inspire me! I admire your love of nature's beauty. You are an incredible wildlife photographer, an author, and a wonderful father to Josh and Zach. Through the lens of your camera, you have given many people a glimpse into the wonders of the wild. You have amazing skills that allow you to be one with nature. I am looking forward to working with you in the future. Brother, I am very proud of you. Thanks for your insight and your guidance, and most of all thanks for keeping me focused on "The Big Picture!"

Mike Mercier. Mike, thanks for all the mornings that we walked into our stands together under the moonlight—including that time you left me alone in my stand with a timber wolf nearby. I still think that was funny. Thank you for all the $3 gut jobs, and for always showing up when I could use a hand dragging my deer out. Mike, I always have great times hunting with you. I am very proud that you are my brother!

Dick Ellis. Dick, thanks for taking the time to get to know me as a man and as a hunter. Thanks for dropping everything and coming right over to help me drag out my monster 17-point buck. The article you wrote, in your news column in November 2009 and the article and cover story in the September-October 2010 issue of *On Wisconsin Outdoors* magazine about my incredible D.I.E system, have helped me launch this book and brought me nationwide exposure. I cannot thank you enough. I want you to have the first copy of my book. Thanks a ton, Dick! I welcome you to hunt with me anytime.

Tom Earle. Tom, you have been an awesome friend! You have kept my D.I.E. system a secret for 11 long years—thank you for that! You are an amazing artist and you did an amazing job drawing the DOMINANCE IS EVERYTHING logo. Way to make me look bad in the pictures showing off your nice camouflage! Thanks for teaching me how to find shed antlers. I wish you many years of monster buck hunting, my friend!

Matt "Rhino" Rynearson. Rhino, you kept my system a secret for three years and that means a lot to me. I wanted to teach you, my then-secret DOMINANCE IS EVERYTHING system, because you already had an expansive knowledge of hunting big whitetail bucks. Having your testimonial (that of a professional hunter), and knowing that D.I.E. works every time, regardless of the level of hunting experience a hunter has before learning it, has made it easier for me to teach my system to the public. I am glad you love hunting with my system! Thanks for inviting me to hunt with you in the future! I am going to take you up on that!

Table of Contents

Special thanks to: iii

Testimonials 3

Preface 9

Chapter 1 How I developed my "DOMINANCE IS EVERYTHING" system 11
    The type of rub behind a D.I.E. scrape makes it unique 14
    What I can teach you that no other person can 15

Chapter 2 How I learned about whitetail bucks 27
    Attend a D.I.E. seminar to get hands-on instruction from me 33

Chapter 3 My opinions are my own 35
    Doubting the fact that D.I.E. has never failed is human nature 39

Chapter 4 What "DOMINANCE IS EVERYTHING" does for you 49

Chapter 5 Whitetail deer and their behavior 57
    The most dominant buck—how to identify him 77

Chapter 6 Reading the signs of the most dominant buck 99
    How to analyze dominant buck rubs 110
    There are 9 different types of rubs a dominant buck makes 116
    How to identify dominant buck scrapes 129

Chapter 7 Dominant bucks behave predictably 133

Chapter 8 Understanding the whitetail buck pecking order 141

Chapter 9 How deer identify danger 145
    The dominant buck knows what trail camera users are up to
    —because they tell him 153
    Pretend you are a deer for success with D.I.E. 155

Chapter 10 Becoming invisible to deer is easy—follow these steps 163
    Look in the mirror: Do you see a human? 172
    Adolescent and mature deer see things differently 174

Chapter 11 How to walk like a deer. 181

Chapter 12 The wind—check it, understand it, and adapt to it 195
    The wind does not lie—it only persuades 199

Chapter 13 Three lures that have never let a D.I.E. hunter down. 203

Chapter 14 Get into the head of the most dominant buck. .211

Chapter 15 You are pretending to be a doe in heat, going into estrus. 215
    How the dominant buck goes from doe to doe during the rut. 219

Chapter 16 The 4 continuous phases of the whitetail rut. 225
    D.I.E. works anywhere deer live as long as the rut is on. 228

Chapter 17 Stay away from the land until you need to scout it 235

Chapter 18 Scouting. 239
    21 Questions to help you see "The Big Picture". 239
    Scouting for a D.I.E. Set Up location 256
    Take notes when you scout, so you can remember what you find 260

Chapter 19 Set Up Day. 269
    Here are the set up rules to live by for 100% results with D.I.E. 269
    Choose the best stand site and expect to be hunted there 272
    Using a portable tree stand is the best bet 282
    Setting up the stand on set up day. 285
    Equipment and things to remember when preparing to set up 287
    Do not use drippers as the manufacturer suggests—listen to my advice to
    succeed on a D.I.E. hunt. 298
    How to make a D.I.E. scrape and a D.I.E. rub 301
    Step-by-step lure use process 302

Chapter 20 The Waiting Period. 313
    Choose to hunt with OPTION 1 or OPTION 2. 321
    OPTION 1 makes the buck hunt the scrape only. 322
    OPTION 2 makes you the "hunted" and the scrape is also an attraction. 322

Chapter 21 The Rundown – Step-By-Step D.I.E. Hunt Instructions 325
    Here is the timeline of an entire hunt with D.I.E.. 331

Chapter 22 Freezing temps require you to modify your D.I.E. hunt 335

Chapter 23 "SAFETY FIRST" while gun hunting with D.I.E. .341
    Never risk your safety when gun hunting with D.I.E. 343

Chapter 24 How to talk like a deer 345
    What a grunt call was made to do 347
    You can opt out of making any calls 353
    If you want to call to the buck—learn to master these three calls. 353

Chapter 25 D.I.E.—a system that allows you to role-play with the king 359
    Role-playing every day is important—stay with it 366

Chapter 26 Always live by the rules—here are the "NEVER DO" lists 369
    "NEVER DO" list for Walking Like A Deer 369
    "NEVER DO" list for Scouting & Setting Up 369
    "NEVER DO" list for Days 1, 2, 3 and 4 of your hunt. 370

Chapter 27 Cramming the D.I.E. system (optional) 371

Chapter 28 Important lessons to avoid being busted 377
    Have faith in the D.I.E. system 379

Chapter 29 My secret to 100% success—I always keep him guessing! 381
    Getting busted stinks—avoid it happening to you by not breaking any rules. 382

Chapter 30 Stories of my most memorable hunts with my D.I.E. system 387
    Bullwinkle—A 12-point monster buck that got away 387
    My 2009 Wisconsin bow hunt for the 17 point buck 391

Summary 393

Glossary 395

Hunting Notes 401

Here is a recent photo of myself. If you are interested in being hunted by the king of deer, on public or private land, I am willing to teach you. I will be touring the United States teaching D.I.E. seminars to people who want to learn how they can become the 'hunted' instead of being a hunter.

Thank you

I would like to thank everyone who contributed to the publishing process of this book. It was a long and arduous journey but it was well worth the effort we made. I could not have done it without your help. Thank you for supporting me and my dream to become a published writer who is able to teach people a new way to hunt mature whitetail bucks. I would also like to thank the first 700 people who registered to buy my book, for patiently waiting for their copy, while I got the book published. God bless you all!

Bob J. Mercier (right) – inventor of DOMINANCE IS EVERYTHING, along with Tom Earle (left) – 1st hunter in the world to be taught the D.I.E. system, displaying their D.I.E. bucks.

When a person uses DOMINANCE IS EVERYTHING as directed, the most dominant buck in the herd walks or trots within 35 yards of their tree stand while they are in it. He is searching for an invisible pair of breeding deer that he is brainwashed to believe are real. The buck will always be 2 ½ years of age or older, and he will show up in broad daylight on 1 of 4 consecutive days. DOMINANCE IS EVERYTHING to all breeder bucks. That is why my system doesn't fail. The most dominant buck must show up, because the D.I.E. system forces him to in order to remain the most dominant buck of the herd.

Testimonials

This is Tom Earle of Palmyra, Wisconsin with his 3 D.I.E. bucks. He took the 7 pointer on the right with a muzzleloader on the first day of his first D.I.E. hunt in 2002. He got it on public land in Walworth County Wisconsin. Tom is holding a 13 pointer he shot in 2006 on private land in Jefferson County Wisconsin with a bow, and the middle buck is a 9 pointer taken in 2004 on private land with a bow. Tom is the first person I ever taught my secret system to, and he has been hunting with it ever since.

Here is a close-up photograph of Tom Earle's 7-point monster buck. The buck's rack scored 150-inches. The buck walked across the middle of a snow-covered field in a snowstorm to get to Tom's D.I.E. scrape and rub. What an amazing animal. My congratulations go out to Tom for his continued success with DOMINANCE IS EVERYTHING.

Tom Earle's Testimonial

"My name is Tom Earle and I am a devout follower of Bob's "Dominance Is Everything" system... I am married with two adult children and I live in the small town of Palmyra just 45 miles West of Milwaukee... I have a sign and mural business. Some might recognize my name from the Shed Antler seminars I put on throughout the state since 1998.

I have been bow and gun hunting whitetails since 1974 of which I had to learn everything through trial and error. Shed hunting has definitely honed my skills as a deer hunter. I believe everything happens for a reason and that is how I met Bob. I was working at Dresser Industries in Waukesha in 2001, when a co-worker introduced me to Bob. The common denominator we had was deer hunting and shed hunting of course...

Bob was good enough to share his system with me, which I took notes on while we were at lunch one evening at work. I could not wait to try it! Being a seasoned deer hunter myself, I knew it made total sense.

Following Bob's directions to the tee, I had success! Gun season 2002 hunting state ground, I shot with my .50 cal muzzleloader a 150-inch class buck! In 2004 early bow season, I harvested a 120-inch class buck and in 2006, again in early bow season I took down a 130-inch class buck. The last two bucks mentioned were on private land.

I found that if a hunter follows Bob's system step-by-step they have a great chance of tagging a nice buck with bow or gun. If a hunter can find an undisturbed piece of land and hunt it according to the wind, they will succeed with the help of Bob's system. To be honest, I have had some outside variables interfere with my hunting plans, which spoiled a few of my hunts. Since those bad experiences, I have done everything possible to search out undisturbed areas to implement Bob's system. It has worked every time!

Of the three nice bucks I have shot, the last one I mentioned in 2006 has a notch in my memory log.

It was a warm 65-degree day, November 5, 2006 and I had Bob's set-up 20 yards away. No one would think deer would be out moving, but at 1:23 p.m., a nice 130-inch class buck walked right in. I double-lunged the buck at five yards and had made one of my quickest kills with a bow that I could remember. The buck traveled just 75 yards and piled up. Thanks to Bob's system, another one for the wall!

In closing, I would like to say this: There are no "magic bullets" out there. To be successful one must put in a lot of time and effort. Having a system like Bob's will cut out a lot of the wasted time with trial and error. Bob has already done that for you. Follow it and have your gutting knife ready, is all I have to say! Good luck and happy hunting."

Tom Earle
Antler Bound Enterprises
Palmyra, Wisconsin

Matt Rhino Rynearson of West Allis, Wisconsin, with his first D.I.E. buck. A 9 ½ year old 10-pointer he shot with a bow in Minnesota in 2008 on private land. Rhino is a Wisconsin Pro Staff Hunter, who I granted a wish for. He wanted to become the third person in the world to be hunted by the king of deer with DOMINANCE IS EVERYTHING, and that he is. This buck has two sticker points on the back of the G2's that cannot be seen in either photo, but Rhino states they are there. It is a dandy buck, and I am proud of Rhino for being 2 for 2 on his bow hunts with D.I.E. His other buck was a 7 year old 11-pointer taken in 2009 also in Minnesota. Congratulations go out to Rhino for his efforts in the field with Dominance Is Everything.

Rhino's 2008 D.I.E. bowbuck.

Matt Rhino Rynearson's Testimonial Dated Sunday May 16, 2010

"I have used this system for the last two years and I will not hunt whitetails without using it. I successfully used it last year (2009) and bagged a low 140-inch, 11-point buck that was 7 years old, the most dominant in the area. This great secret will work for anyone if following each step exactly. Bob introduced this system to me two years ago (2008) and I was very excited to see it work, and it did perfectly. The first year… paid off with a very nice old 10-pointer. As I said before, this system will work if followed exactly."

"Hunt Hard - Hunt Safe"
Matt "Rhino" Rynearson
Wisconsin Pro Staff Hunter

November 5th 2009, I was posing with my 17-pointer for Jerry Mercier, my brother, and Dick Ellis, publisher of *On Wisconsin Outdoors* magazine, at the same time.

This is where the 17-pointer lived his life, and where he retreated when I shot him. He was not the most dominant of the herd, but he was mature and he was a magnificent buck. I found him laying in 4 inches of standing water, in the wettest end of the nearest swamp. It was downwind and crosswind of my D.I.E. stand site, over 80 yards away. You have to make the buck come to you.

Photos of the author 7

The author admiring his latest D.I.E. buck.

If you have never seen a monster buck before and you decide to become a D.I.E. hunter, you can count on seeing more than one of them in your future. Every person who has hunted with D.I.E. more than three times has told me that they saw the biggest-racked buck of their life while hunting with my system. DOMINANCE IS EVERYTHING changes everything for a deer hunter. It makes you invisible to all deer, and it makes all bucks believe you are the "hottest doe" in the area. Every monster buck, dominant buck (monster or not), swamp buck, and intruder breeder buck that encounters a D.I.E. scrape and D.I.E. rub in the rut will search for you as their next mate. There is no stopping a breeder buck from pursuing a doe in estrus.

Thanks to the 33 years I spent researching whitetail deer behavior (learning directly from deer), I have been able to establish my own tactics for analyzing how every deer herd lives. Now that I invented DOMINANCE IS EVERYTHING, future generations of hunters and nature lovers will be able to encounter the majestic king of any deer herd within 35 yards during the rut, just by learning how Bob J. Mercier, Tom Earle, and Matt "Rhino" Rynearson, have been hunted by kings. Each of us was able to master using D.I.E. our first time out, and I am confident you will master it just as quickly as we did. Stay safe and remember…always expect that the king of deer is watching you when you are in his territory. Always keep him guessing! When you have D.I.E. you don't need luck!

Dominance Is Everything... To A Monster Whitetail Buck!

Photos of my 17-point non-typical monster whitetail buck, taken at 10 yards with my bow in New Berlin, Wisconsin on November 5, 2009. This buck fought another monster buck 50 yards downwind of my stand which was 35 yards downwind of my D.I.E. scrape and rub, one minute before he rushed in on a one-way buck trail to my D.I.E. scrape. I missed a bigger buck at less than 3 yards 2 hours earlier that morning. My arrow grazed the buck's far shoulder. I am glad I missed, for the opportunity to tell the story of the two bucks fighting for the right to become the mate of the invisible doe in estrus. Three monster bucks hunted me that morning! Dominance Is Everything is amazing!

BEFORE AND AFTER

BEFORE I learned how to be invisible to deer and before I learned to make the most dominant buck hunt me the buck antlers on the top row and the set I am holding in my hands were the biggest bucks I ever shot in Wisconsin with my gun and bow. AFTER I invented D.I.E. I shot the three shoulder mounted bucks. All were taken with a bow, and all at less than 35 yards during daylight in the rut, using my Dominance Is Everything system. I am proud of what deer have taught me, and I am looking forward to teaching D.I.E. to everyone who wants to have a before and after wall like I do.

Preface

In November 1998, I invented a whitetail buck hunting system that I named "Dominance Is Everything" or D.I.E. for short. It makes the most dominant buck, monster intruder bucks, and swamp bucks hunt for its user for one to four consecutive days during the rut. If you use it as directed, the most dominant buck will walk or trot to within 35 yards of your stand during daylight hours. You should not see yearling bucks, fawns, or any pecking order bucks from that herd within 35 yards of your stand. The dominant buck keeps them all away. He commands the area. He is there waiting for you each morning and if you are quiet he will advance on your stand site. He hunts you down because the D.I.E. system brainwashes him to believe that you are a breeding pair of deer, and that you are mating in his front yard. The dominant buck fights off any intruder breeder bucks that attempt to advance on your stand site, because being dominant of his herd is all that matters to him. He feels it is safe to come in, because I teach you to behave as a deer would, and to forget you are a human. You will have options when you hunt with D.I.E., you can "walk like a deer", "talk like a deer", and "leave a scent trail like a deer" or you can opt not to do any of those things. The dominant buck will be hunting you. All you have to do is show up with your gun, your bow, or a hand-held camera and you will be able to take the memories of your first D.I.E. hunt home with you. You have never hunted like this before!

I hunted with D.I.E. on eleven hunts and each time the dominant buck hunted me. It is uncanny to see a majestic (often monster-racked) buck walking into a D.I.E. set up thinking he owns the place, when you (a D.I.E. hunter) are sitting 10 to 18 feet off the ground observing his every move, and he never knows you are there. No deer can find a D.I.E. hunter, because we are invisible to deer. Most people that hunt mature whitetail bucks have only dreamt of having hunts like that, but I have learned to expect them. The D.I.E. system changes people's lives, when they learn how to use it and implement it where they hunt during the rut. When a mature buck shows up within 35 yards of your stand while you are using the D.I.E. system, then the system has succeeded. So far, D.I.E. has never failed to bring the dominant buck to every D.I.E. hunter who used it as directed.

I learned many of my tactics for getting close to whitetail deer when I filmed them in the wild for a 16-month period from 1991 to 1993. I learned what makes mature bucks tick. I know what the rut is, when it turns on and off and how and when bucks meet up with does to breed. I know what a hunter has to do to get a dominant buck or a monster buck to walk right up to them during daylight. They have to hunt with D.I.E. and refrain from telling any deer in the area that a human is there. You have to convince them you are not a human, or they will never show up.

In this book, I am showing you what I know about the whitetail deer herd structure, the rut, the pecking order, the way bucks communicate with one another and how they communicate with does. I explain how deer live, and what makes them move from point A to point B. Where they go when a hunter jumps them from their bed, and how to avoid pressuring the deer where you hunt. I explain the entire herd to you from the deer's perspective. In order to outsmart a dominant buck you have to know what he is thinking.

Deer live very structured lives, and a human can predict the movements of the entire herd if that person, knows how to do it. I am just the man to teach you. I can tell where the entire herd is on your hunting property just by observing one doe eating on a food source in early evening, or by analyzing any fresh buck rub, made on a 2-inch or larger diameter tree. I will teach you how to do it in this book.

I wanted to write this book, and offer it to you for two reasons. The first reason is because, I promised God if he would allow me to learn how to get within 35 yards of a mature buck on every hunt I would share it with the world. I am doing that by writing this book and conducting seminars. The second reason is even more personal. It is because we only live once! Deer hunters everywhere give it their all every season, and many of them are still coming up empty handed in the monster buck category. I invented something special, a system that anyone in the world can use to change the outcome of his or her next deer hunt, and all a person has to do in order to succeed with it, is to have faith in it, and to use it as directed. What can be easier than that? This is my gift to you. Be safe and considerate of others while hunting.

Always keep him guessing with D.I.E.!

Chapter 1

How I developed my "DOMINANCE IS EVERYTHING" system

"DOMINANCE IS EVERYTHING... To A Monster Whitetail Buck!" is meant to be your handbook for brainwashing the most dominant whitetail buck in any area, into believing you are a pair of mature breeding deer from outside his herd. The D.I.E. system works only during the *rut* when deer are mating. It has extraordinary power! It forces the *dominant buck* to alter his normal behavior, in order to deal with the situation that the DOMINANCE IS EVERYTHING system has put before him. That is an immediate threat to his dominance. He will move into the area and bed downwind of your *stand site*, so he can be the first deer to find you (the pair of breeding deer) when you return to the *D.I.E. scrape*. He expects you to come back that night, but you throw him for a loop by only hunting from your stand during daylight. When Day 1 of your hunt arrives you give him what he wants, but until then you make him wait.

The D.I.E. system is comprised entirely of my own hunting tactics that I learned from deer while I was filming them. I learned why dominant bucks would get out of their beds during daylight and I emphasized using as many of those reasons as I could in the D.I.E. system so that the dominant buck could not ignore my stand site. A D.I.E. stand site is the place where you install a *D.I.E. rub*, a D.I.E. scrape, and one tree stand.

All deer avoid humans, but even the most dominant buck can only avoid them when he can detect them. When you hunt with D.I.E., you are invisible to deer. The first step to becoming invisible is washing your hunting clothes (before every hunt) in scent free laundry detergent that is U-V-brightener-free. The second step is bathing in scent free body wash and using scent free shampoo every morning before you get dressed for your hunt. The third and final step is making sure that you wear camouflage clothing with a tree limb and leaf pattern on it, so your body form blends in with the terrain, whether on the ground, or in your tree stand. Then you will be invisible to deer. In a later chapter you will learn how and when to walk to and from your stand without disrupting the dominant buck.

The D.I.E. system creates a situation that deer have to deal with. Each deer in a herd has a different duty. If the deer is a doe or a doe fawn, then her duty is not to mind the buck's business. Her job is to take care of her offspring. If the deer is a buck then he has a job to do.

Depending on his rank, he will either notify higher ranking bucks of the existence of your D.I.E. scrape or if he is a high ranking buck he may go to the scrape and pursue does in the area. My system only works in the rut because you are pretending to be a breeding pair of deer. A dominant buck will not allow any buck to breed with a doe from his herd if he does not have a *doe in estrus* of his own to breed at that time. *Monster bucks* and *swamp bucks* do exist and they are interested in breeding too. They will run in and out of the D.I.E. stand site at all hours of the day until the dominant buck moves in and beds in the nearest available cover downwind of the D.I.E. scrape. Then he can control which bucks enter the area, and if the dominant buck is a monster buck, then you better believe he will end up bedding close to the D.I.E. scrape because he fears no other buck in the area.

I play the role of an *intruder buck* and make a D.I.E. scrape and rub at a comfortable shooting distance from my stand (never more than 35 yards). The dominant buck in the area will check this scrape each day so he can dominate it. I learned from watching deer through two consecutive ruts that dominant bucks do not allow any insubordination within their ranks. If an intruder *breeder buck* from another dominant buck's herd challenges them, they will not back down from the challenge.

I was hunting traditionally for big bucks before I invented D.I.E., but the only time I would see them was early in the morning or late in the day. They were either headed into a swamp to bed (morning), or *staging* in cover before heading out to feed (evening). When I filmed deer, I learned that the most dominant buck would bed in water and stay in his bed for extended periods just to avoid humans. I was not going to be a human anymore. I learned to be invisible to deer and I was going to use my filming tactics on a bow hunt for the first time. That was the best decision I ever made. I forgot about being a hunter, and pretended I had a camera on my shoulder. At the time I did not know where the dominant buck bedded, all I knew was that only *yearling bucks* bedded on our property. The only way I could get a breeder buck to come to my stand site would be if he thought there was a *doe in heat* visiting my scrape.

I knew I needed to challenge the dominant buck and his *pecking order bucks* by acting like an insubordinate buck that was willing to fight for territory. I did that by making the D.I.E. scrape and rub. I needed to challenge the dominant buck for breeding rights to any does that visited the D.I.E. scrape. The only way I knew I could do that was to use lure. I had to persuade the bucks in the area that there were does in heat, and does in estrus visiting my scrape during the hours that I was in my stand. That meant using a scent dripper was necessary. I read up on them a bit and I went out and purchased one. I needed more if I was going to convince a dominant buck that he had to come to my stand site while I was sitting in my tree stand. I needed more than an attraction. I needed a distraction.

I had to become a *monster intruder buck* in the mind of the dominant buck, and I had to become a single doe in heat that was nearing estrus so that the dominant buck could identify those deer by their scent. I went out and searched two counties before I found a pure doe in estrus urine. At the time, I did not know what it was capable of, but now I am hooked on using the stuff. The scent dripper became the messenger, sending signals to all the deer in the area, telling them that there was a breeding pair of deer visiting the D.I.E. scrape each day. This hunt was going to be exciting! I had a plan and I knew it would work if the deer never saw me, heard me, or smelled my scent (as a human). I knew I was capable of achieving invisibility when I was filming deer, so there was no reason why I would not be able to do it while hunting them. I considered using a doe decoy, but that was not necessary. Making a D.I.E. scrape and maintaining it like a real intruder buck and a doe in heat was the answer.

A D.I.E. scrape consists of pawed up dirt with a rub behind it, and a licking branch hanging over it. In the real world, the dominant buck is the only buck alive that ever makes a scrape like this, so you can probably understand why the most dominant buck in the herd would be aggressive toward the maker of the D.I.E. scrape and rub. In most cases, he tears the area up, and he takes the scrape over. From then on, he owns it. The first time I made a D.I.E. scrape, it looked exactly like the ones I make today. I never varied it, because it made the dominant buck start hunting me.

On my first hunt with D.I.E., a 9-point buck approached my stand just after 4 p.m. and he came all the way to the scrape. He stuck his nose in the scent dripper and I shot him with my bow at 3 yards. His rack was 20 inches wide on the inside and he weighed 210 pounds (*dressed weight*). I had his jaw aged and he was only 2 ½ years old. He scored 121 ⅝-inches missing the mark to get into the Pope and Young record book by a little less than 4 inches. I sure was excited when that *mature buck* walked right up to me. I had dreamt of a hunt like that one, but I never imagined that a buck would actually hunt me. It is an incredible feeling when you can command mature deer and make them come to you. With DOMINANCE IS EVERYTHING, you do not have to wish or dream for it to happen; all you have to do is have faith in yourself and in the D.I.E. system, use it as directed, and it will happen.

That 9-point buck was an intruder breeder buck that spent his whole summer five miles away from our property. I would have never known it but when I took the buck to the registration station later that day, another bow hunter that was there looked at my buck and recognized him by his rack. He said he had trail camera photos of my buck taken two days earlier. He showed me some photos of my buck feeding on a soybean field five miles north of our property in New Berlin, Wisconsin. There were a series of photos and each one had a date and time stamp on it. The man showed me aerial photographs of the fields and the woodlots all around the trail camera so I could positively identify them. The field bordered two major streets on the edge of town. I knew those field's well and believed the photos were authentic. The date stamps on the photos were indeed two days prior to the day I shot him. The man said the buck was a middle ranked buck in that herd's pecking order. We agreed that the buck's breeding options were limited in his home herd so he must have decided to roam to find a 'hot' doe that would offer him the opportunity to breed. It is amazing how far a mature buck will travel during the rut for the right to breed. That buck was not dominant, but he was on a mission to find a mate, and he was willing to fight for the right to breed my invisible doe in estrus if he had to. At the time, I invented D.I.E. I was only hunting half days, and I was unaware that the most dominant buck and his challengers were hunting me until I sat in my tree stand all day.

The type of rub behind a D.I.E. scrape makes it unique

As I stated before, a D.I.E. scrape is a mock scrape that a D.I.E. hunter makes to the specifications I set as the D.I.E. hunter's standard. A D.I.E. scrape and D.I.E. rub is nearly identical to a real *dominant buck's primary breeding scrape* and rub. The only differences are a real dominant buck's primary breeding scrape does not have a shredded rub with a smooth center on the tree directly behind it. It has a smooth rubbed tree behind it with no shredded bark anywhere on it, and in the case of a D.I.E. scrape the dominant buck did not make it, we let him believe an invisible monster intruder buck did.

Every D.I.E. scrape must have a D.I.E. rub behind it.

The D.I.E. scrape and D.I.E. rub are unique because I invented them. No buck makes a rub like the D.I.E. rub and places it behind a primary breeding scrape of the most dominant buck. Non-dominant bucks (monster bucks, swamp bucks, and intruder *challenger bucks*) do not mess with the dominant buck's primary breeding scrapes. If they want a scrape they make their own, and none of their scrapes have rubs behind them. I advise you not to disturb any real scrapes or rubs. If you do, then you will be sending signals to the whole herd that a human was in the area. I know that, because no buck, not even an intruder monster buck, would rub a tree behind a dominant buck's primary breeding scrape. The D.I.E. scrape and D.I.E. rub are unique, yet believable to every dominant buck that finds one. They are the most powerful tool a D.I.E. hunter has to convince a dominant buck that he or she is not a human. No dominant buck would ever make a primary breeding scrape and rub within 200 yards of a human or a tree stand that humans were using.

I learned from deer that all shredded rubs are territorial, and that no buck has the right to make *territorial rubs* in the territory of the most dominant buck except the dominant buck and monster bucks. That is one reason why the most dominant buck gets so riled up when he finds a D.I.E. scrape (and rub), he has to take it over right away, or he is giving up his dominance of that piece of his territory, and he is giving up his breeding rights to all the does that visit the D.I.E scrape (and rub).

Not all dominant bucks will actually take over a D.I.E. scrape, but most of them will. The dominant buck may rub the tree (enlarging your rub), he may urinate in the scrape, and if he does, he will leave a track in the scrape from one of his front hooves. He may work the licking branch, which he does by nibbling on it, then he sticks the branch into the corner of his eyelid so his unique scent is deposited on it. From then on, he owns it. He does not always work the rub or take over the scrape so do not worry if you never see his track in the scrape. Some dominant bucks do not like to mess with the scrape you make, those bucks will usually make a new scrape of their own right next to the D.I.E. scrape, or they will rub a nearby tree within view of the D.I.E. scrape. When the dominant buck owns the scrape, his scent is all around it and in it. There is a 35-yard (radius) bubble around the dominant buck's primary breeding scrape. No other buck can go within 35 yards of a D.I.E. scrape without challenging the dominant buck. Every pecking order buck knows the rules so they do not come in when you use the system as directed. Your D.I.E. scrape will be like a deserted island during your one to four day hunt, until the dominant buck shows up. That is because the pecking order bucks are obedient to the dominant buck and they will not challenge him at the scrape. Intruder bucks from other herds might come in, but if they do, they will bed downwind or crosswind of the scrape at least 35 yards away from it. If the buck you see walks or trots in he is the king, and if the buck runs in then he is an intruder.

The best part of a D.I.E. hunt is being there in the tree to witness the dominant buck's arrival. Once you establish yourself as the breeding pair of deer, that herd's most dominant buck, any monster bucks or swamp bucks living in the area, and the highest-ranking bucks from each neighboring herd are in pursuit of you for up to four consecutive days. It is a win-win situation for every D.I.E. hunter. When bucks compete, the strongest buck wins, and the rack of the most dominant buck is usually flawless (having no broken antler tines).

The D.I.E. system convinces the entire herd that you are not their enemy (a human) when you walk into their territory. They believe you are a real deer, and because you let the D.I.E. system tell them there are two deer, the most dominant buck sets out on a mission to find them, one at a time. He has to run the buck out and breed with the doe. You are those two invisible deer on a D.I.E. hunt, and he will not be able to find either one of them because they do not exist, but he will continue to look for them anyway until he knows that they are no longer a threat to his dominance, which is always in less than four consecutive days. The only place he gets their scent is in the D.I.E. scrape, on the D.I.E. rub, or on the trail that you take to and from your tree stand, so you can be sure that his mind is on your stand site all day long while you are there.

The dominant buck will not go within 200 yards of a human at any time day or night if he knows the human is there, but he will come within 35 yards of a D.I.E. hunter any day of the week, because D.I.E. hunters are invisible to deer! In order to role-play with the dominant buck you need to know how deer react to human actions, and how deer react to the actions of other deer. I will teach you to "walk like a deer", "talk like a deer" and to how to "think like a deer". I hope you are convinced that you are a deer, by the time you finish the book!

What I can teach you that no other person can

I will explain to you how whitetail deer use their keen senses to positively identify humans (behaving normally) as being a danger to them, from the first moment a human steps foot into their territory. I will show you what deer do to elude humans, and how a human can become a D.I.E. hunter.

D.I.E. hunters are invisible to deer. Deer will not run from you. They cannot see you, smell you, or hear you. You do not exist in their world, unless you are moving. I teach you to be two deer whenever you are moving. That way the dominant buck never knows which one you are, and his reaction to your actions allows you time to get into your tree stand unseen by any deer.

I will teach you how dominant bucks react to other deer during the rut. I do not hunt whitetail bucks outside of the rut anymore, because **DOMINANCE IS EVERYTHING** to all mature whitetail bucks. Once you understand what being the most dominant means to every mature buck, you will see that there is no better time to hunt dominant and monster bucks than when they are pursuing does in estrus, and that can only be during the rut.

I learned all about whitetail deer behavior by filming them in the wild and then watching the video on a TV without sound. I learned incredible facts about deer behavior that most people do not know, and learning it all from deer changed my life. Looking at deer is one thing, watching deer is another, and observing their behavior, taking detailed notes, analyzing their actions and learning from them is taking it one-step further.

I learned to walk among deer and I learned how to command the king of deer to come to me at my location during the rut. I can bring him in by talking to him, or by playing with his mind. No matter what gets his attention it is his duty to show up no matter what he was doing before I called him out. I could not outsmart deer as a human, so I decided to do all I could to become a deer in the mind of deer. Now I do not need to outsmart them, I just walk among them and do not tell any of them I am a human. I can do that and so can you if you are willing to take my advice.

I am sharing my knowledge of whitetail deer behavior with you because I think you should know there is more to a deer herd than meets the eye. Dominant bucks behave quite a bit differently than all the other deer in the herd. Deer have daily routines, and I know now that their travel patterns are predictable. The most dominant buck has a routine too, it is easy for a hunter using my D.I.E. system to find the buck's haunts, and to alter the buck's routine, so he has to make a stop at the D.I.E. scrape at least once a day during your hunt. A dominant buck travels at night to avoid encountering humans, but he doesn't think you are a human, he thinks you are a deer, and he figures out that you only come to the stand site during the day so he changes his routine so he can meet you when you are actually there. The buck will eventually show himself within 35 yards of you during daylight and you will have an opportunity to harvest the animal if all goes as planned.

I know a lot about mature buck behavior and I have in-depth knowledge of what makes dominant bucks tick. The two hunters that have used D.I.E. prior to 2010 have told me, that my system works because it makes total sense. I personally think it makes total sense because it works. It worked the very first time I set it up. Since then I have only tried to find what its capabilities are. I have always set it up the same way, and I have always had the *king of the herd* hunting me. I think outside the box. No one else I know of puts themselves in the head of the dominant buck and actually knows what he will be thinking. I do not have E.S.P. but my system makes every dominant buck that encounters it behave in a precise manner that a D.I.E. hunter can predict. So far, the D.I.E. system has been a sure thing for everyone who used it exactly as I directed.

There is just one dominant buck in every whitetail deer herd, when he dies the highest-ranking pecking order buck under him (#2 buck) instantly becomes most dominant and becomes the king of the herd. As you can see, there is an endless supply of dominant bucks.

A D.I.E. hunter that follows all the rules has a 50% chance of seeing a monster buck. They will have a chance to harvest a monster buck on every hunt, if they hunt near a herd territory boundary. I teach you what those look like and how to find one on your scouting day, if one exists on your property. I have yet to meet a deer hunter that would turn down an opportunity to be hunted by the most dominant buck in the herd, and have a chance at monster bucks.

I developed my D.I.E. system in 1998 while attempting to attract mature bucks to my stand site during the rut, in daylight hours, without using bait. Well I got more than I bargained for because it does all that and even more. For the past 11 deer seasons, I have been hunted by the king of the herd, and attribute my perfect record to the fact that I always set it up exactly the same way as I did the first time. I hunt in the exact same manner no matter when I am hunting during the rut. I have experimented with the hunt part (your behavior in the stand) of the system through a trial and error process. I wanted to find out what options a hunter had at his or her disposal while on the hunt, and I have learned that you can call, decoy, or rattle antlers and still have 100% success with D.I.E., but there is a time and a place for each of those things. I find it to be much easier to succeed at not being seen by deer on a D.I.E. hunt if you just sit still in your stand being quiet and invisible to them. The results I have gotten have been perfect on every hunt, and I would never ask for more than that. D.I.E. is a miracle system and I thank God for it.

The DOMINANCE IS EVERYTHING system succeeds when a 2 ½ year old or older buck, walks or trots into the set up location within 35 yards of the hunter during daylight, on one of the four days of the D.I.E. hunt. That is what to expect from D.I.E., what you do from that point forward is totally up to you. If you want to snap a few photos of him and not kill the buck, so be it. If you want to shoot him, then take your shot. In my personal experience, the king of the herd has only showed up one time during each D.I.E. hunt, and I have attempted to take the buck at that time. He will not come in every day during daylight because he is smarter than that. It is wise to make the most of your first encounter with him, because it may be your last. If he figures out that, you are a human or he sees another human in the area near the D.I.E. scrape he will never come in within 35 yards of you. In fact, he will stay 200 or more yards away from any human being that he has positively identified. You have to follow my instructions in order not to be *"busted"* by the buck as he makes his way to you. He will come in if you let him.

D.I.E brings in the most dominant buck in the herd at that moment in time. He is always the first buck to approach the scrape or to come within 35 yards of it. Many times, you will not see any other deer on your entire hunt. If you see multiple bucks approach at the same time then only one will be the dominant buck, the other is his challenger. Challengers have large racks of antlers and a body size comparable to that of the dominant buck, and they are willing to fight him to win the rights to breed with the (invisible) doe in estrus. The dominant buck has to deal with one (invisible) challenger from the time you leave the woods on set up day, and with other real intruder challenging bucks from then on, until he makes his appearance at your stand site. It is a win-win situation for you as a hunter. The winner of any fight at the scrape will remain there to hunt you. All mature bucks believe you are a pair of breeding deer. I have only seen multiple intruder bucks compete downwind of the scrape one time in my eleven hunts, so

I do not count on it, and do not hold out for it to happen; I am just happy if it does. I shoot to kill the first buck that comes in within 35 yards of my stand, and over 50% of the time, that buck has had a rack of antlers that was bigger than the antlers of the 17-point buck on the cover of this book. With D.I.E., you should hunt all day and not move around much in your stand. Just sit back and let the dominant buck search for you. The system will perform at 100%, if you set it up properly and have faith in it.

In order to start a D.I.E. hunt with 100% odds for success you need to plan your hunt and you need to follow the rules. The D.I.E. scrape needs to be set up 2 ½ days before you go into the area to hunt it. The D.I.E. system consists of a Scouting Day, a Set Up Day, a 2 ½ day Waiting Period, and Day 1, Day 2, Day 3, and Day 4 of the hunt. How many days you have to hunt is up to the king of the herd. He will decide when to come in but you are in charge of where he will have to go when he gets there. You get to choose a tree stand location that suits you well. You will go in during daylight after legal shooting hours open and be leaving before dark. What could be easier than that?

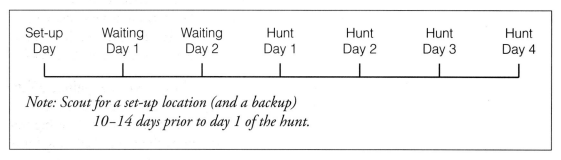

FIGURE 1 Everything revolves around Day 1 of the hunt. Scout 10–14 days prior to it, set up 3 days prior to it, then wait 2 ½ days after set up day before hunting on Day 1.

The D.I.E. system works on any property where there is not a trail camera installed during the hunt, where you are not interfered with, where you are at least 150 yards away from other hunters and where there is a deer track within 35 yards of your stand. If you see a deer track that is 3 ½ inches long or longer from the front to the back of the toe pad. That large track is a track of a mature deer. The dominant buck splays his front toe pads every step he takes all year long. Hunting near large deer tracks will always increase your odds of seeing a monster buck. You can hunt with a gun or bow, on private or public land, and rely on my ingenious system to work rain or shine. If you succeed at harvesting the dominant buck, you can hunt from that location again later on in the season, but I advise you to pull the stand out of the tree immediately after you complete a hunt, and re-install it on your next hunt. You need the element of surprise each time you hunt. Leaving a stand in the woods for longer than a week takes away your element of surprise.

November 8, 1998 was the date I invented my D.I.E. system. I was hunting in New Berlin, Wisconsin on my family's farm. It was the first time in my life that a mature buck crossed my trail and did not flinch. He could not smell me and I walked in on that trail just 2 hours earlier dragging lure. He could not see me, because I was hidden in a large oak tree, twelve feet off the ground, wearing full camouflage, and he could not get my scent because I was 99% scent free that day. In fact, I was invisible to him. I still remember the first moment I saw him, as if it was yesterday. I had set up the system four days prior, and I first hunted it one day earlier. The first day no deer were close enough for a shot, but I saw a large racked buck chasing a doe on a neighboring parcel. The second day proved to be a hunt to remember. I thought about it later and I realized it was the easiest hunt I ever went on. Mature bucks were breeding does in the area, and intruder bucks were roaming looking for does in estrus. There was a heavily used deer trail 5 yards away from my stand and deer used it every day during daylight. They walked or trotted through the area they did not run. I built a mock scrape (D.I.E. scrape) and a rub and made the herd aware of a new pair of deer in their territory, and then I became those two deer. I used the D.I.E. scrape and rub as an attraction to the deer and as a distraction at the same time, it allowed me to slip into the herd without being noticed as a human. I was invisible to deer, while hunting them, for the very first time. I learned to role-play with mature breeder bucks. I was able to convince them that I was their next mate, and their only competition both at the same time, without ever letting them see me, smell me, or hear me. I had learned to brainwash mature breeder bucks into believing they had to meet me, in order for them to be the most dominant buck inside their herd. **Dominance Is Everything** to every breeder buck, and knowing that is a fact, changed my life on that day. Up until that day, I was a traditional deer hunter, but after that day's hunt, I emerged as "one who is hunted by mature breeder bucks".

I attempted to join the deer herd as a pretty doe in estrus, and I succeeded at pulling off the charade. Every mature buck that encountered my D.I.E scrape welcomed me, because they thought I was their next mate. I had not been able to outsmart any mature bucks hunting traditionally, so I decided to step it up a notch and to try to brainwash them into believing I was a real pair of breeding deer. I wanted to fit in with the deer herd in order to get the attention of their king. Using the D.I.E. scrape and rub along with the lures I chose to use, allowed me to slip into the herd structure without being detected as a human.

Deer tolerate the presence of other deer for the most part but they never tolerate having a human being in their bedding area, or hanging around one of their *core breeding areas.* When a human intrudes into deer habitat, the mature deer in the herd sense the presence of the human, and they immediately go on alert, warning the rest of the herd that there is an immediate threat to their survival in the area. Once on alert a deer will notify all the other deer in the area of the apparent danger and they will group up and get out of harm's way as the threat approaches. Alert deer travel in an upwind or crosswind direction heading straight for the nearest heavy cover. They eventually will end up in one of their other two core bedding areas, where it is safe for them to hide from you. They will not return to that area until after the threat leaves which is usually after sunset (when hunters leave). The first deer to return is always the most dominant buck. He will return to that area within three days to investigate the scent, and signs left in the woods by the threat. He will always do so in total darkness.

If the dominant buck identifies you as a human, you will not see that buck or any of his high-ranking pecking order bucks from that stand location. Some traditional hunters have had to deal with this exact situation every deer season for as long as they can remember. I used to have trouble with it happening to me too, until I invented this system and quit traditionally hunting deer. Now deer do not positively identify me as a human, and when the buck comes in, he thinks he is alone there every time. That is because I walk like a deer and he is expecting me to arrive. He is waiting for me. He is expecting one of two deer to arrive, and I represent both of those deer.

With D.I.E. (when you are in your tree stand), you are the two deer that are breeding in the dominant buck's front yard. Whenever you walk in or out of the area, you are making the sound of only one of those two deer, but he can never tell which one, so he sets out on a personal mission to find out for himself. That is what makes the D.I.E. system so great, the fact that you can control the most dominant buck's behavior, by using the system as I direct you. D.I.E. brainwashes the most dominant buck. You are keeping him guessing and he cannot figure out which deer it was that came in and stopped near the base of your tree stand. He does not care about the stand all he cares about is the breeding pair of deer.

What he heard walk in was a deer from another herd, and he knows it was either an intruder monster buck ready to challenge him or a doe in estrus that has come to meet him to breed. It bothers the dominant buck that he can smell them both and hear them enter and leave the area but he cannot catch up to them after dark when he normally would be able to find them. They come and go and he keeps missing them. He is too late each time that he approaches the scrape so he does what you would do if you were always late and missed your appointments; he comes in earlier the next time. Eventually he approaches your stand within 35 yards during daylight. I train you to be invisible to him the entire time you are hunting so he will never know a human is there. He beds closer and closer each day so he does not miss you the next time you arrive at the scrape. You do not actually go to the scrape on Day 2, Day 3, or Day 4, of the hunt, but the buck thinks you do. He does not pay any attention to your tree stand. Your arrival triggers him to get up out of his bed and go downwind of the scrape to conduct a *scent check* on the air current that is drifting toward him from the scrape, and that is where you will most likely see your first glimpse of him.

You have his undivided attention from the first moment he hears you walk like a deer. No bucks from the dominant buck's pecking order can be within 35 yards of the most dominant buck or within 35 yards of his primary breeding scrape during the rut. He has a 35-yard (radius) invisible bubble around his body and it travels with him at all times. A D.I.E. scrape becomes his core breeding scrape after he finds it and takes it over. A real doe in estrus would show herself to him when he calls or she would go to meet him when she heard him come in. You are not making any human sounds, and you are not going to him, so you are invisible when you are in the tree stand. He cannot figure out which deer you are and he has to in order to disrupt the breeding pair, otherwise his hierarchy is in jeopardy. That is why D.I.E. will never fail. He will come in if you wait for him. You have to be patient.

D.I.E. gives a hunter an identity as a real deer, but the dominant buck never knows exactly which one you are, because he never meets either of the two deer. They are not part of his herd, and he knows they are together most of the time. The set up procedure is precise and it makes the buck believe that these two deer from a neighboring herd are here to stay for a while. Location of the stand is your choice but always consider where the buck beds to be the place where he lives. I ask you to stay away from his sanctuary and let him live in peace on his own property all year long. That way when you do set up the D.I.E. system and hunt it, he will not have a clue that a human is anywhere around.

I knew the mature bucks in the area I was hunting in 1998 would be attracted to the scent at my D.I.E. scrape once they got wind of it. Little did I know that the dominant buck would react to the scrape in an unwelcoming manner, but I soon found out! Dominant bucks do not allow any other buck to be insubordinate to them, whether the other buck is part of his herd or not, does not matter. Any insubordination by *lesser bucks* toward the king of the herd is responded to with a physical response, and once the king finds your scrape he will, most often work it up and take it over. If he doesn't work up your rub and paw up your scrape, then he will make his own scrape right next to yours in most cases, as if to call you out of hiding to fight for the right to breed in that area.

I made the decision to role-play with all the mature bucks in the herd, and I was able to accomplish that with the three specific sexual attractant lures I use with my system, in combination with walking like a deer and talking like a deer when I felt I needed to. When I walked to my stand, I pretended I was a doe in estrus and that I had a monster intruder buck as my companion. When I left the stand at closing time I rushed out of the area, so no bucks would follow me. I learned later on during my third hunt with D.I.E. that I should never approach my stand site in the dark. I only hunt in daylight hours. Deer tend to bed, at the time of day I choose to make my way to my tree stand, so I am not interfering with their daily routine. Not even the slightest bit.

The goal was to get multiple mature bucks interested in the does in heat at the D.I.E. scrape and then to keep their interest up on meeting these does until I returned to the stand to hunt it, but there was a catch. They had to come to see the does during daylight, and they had to come in close in order to see if they had been there lately. All does in heat eventually go into estrus and when they are in estrus, they are receptive to mating. They want to get pregnant when they are in estrus. With my system, you become multiple does in heat when you set up the system, but none of the does in heat go into estrus until you arrive at your stand with weapon in hand on Day 1 of your hunt. Then you become one single doe in estrus, by changing the scent in the dripper above the D.I.E. scrape. The dripper starts emitting her urine into the scrape, when you walk away from it. It shuts off with a 10° temperature drop at night. The dripper restarts the next morning with a 10° temperature increase, letting all deer in the herd know she is nearby the scrape only during the day. The D.I.E. system tells them that she is not alone. The monster intruder buck that made the scrape is nearby too. Regardless of that apparent fact, they will all pursue the doe, which they can only find at the scrape, or so they believe. From the day you set D.I.E. up through the last day of your 4-day hunt, the bucks in the area think the doe is real, and that the intruder buck is real too. They cannot find the doe no matter where they look, but she is calling to all of them and she is telling them that she wants one of them to come over to the D.I.E. scrape to breed with her. D.I.E. brainwashes all the mature bucks in the area to believe that any deer they can hear the footsteps of, and they can smell the unique scent of, even if they physically cannot see them must be real.

Deer do not have the slightest clue that humans are capable of making real scrapes. They do not know that we can bring deer urine into the woods with us and lay down a scent trail. The only way a deer could even figure that out would be if you made them in the dark when deer could watch you. I scout, set up, and hunt only during the day with D.I.E. and I do not hunt in deer bedding areas, so I do not encounter any deer when I am setting up. You will not either if you do what I tell you. I took all the guesswork out of hunting with DOMINANCE IS EVERYTHING when I developed it. You can expect the dominant buck to behave in the exact manner I tell you he will behave once he dominates a D.I.E. set up. Just follow my instructions and watch with amazement at how the whole hunt develops in front of your eyes.

All mature bucks will follow a doe in estrus' scent until they find the doe, until a higher-ranking buck or a stronger intruder buck puts a stop to their advances, or until it is not possible for the doe to be in estrus anymore. I believe does are in estrus for 1 to 1 ½ days. No matter when a buck finds the D.I.E. scrape it will be the first time he has identified the scent of the invisible deer in the area. All bucks will try to find the does that visit the scrape (invisible or not), but once the dominant buck finds the D.I.E. scrape he takes it over and he commands the area. He will expect one of the does visiting the scrape to go into estrus in two to three days, and that is when you show up. Dominant bucks do not chase does in heat, they breed with does in estrus. With D.I.E., you show up after the 2 ½ day waiting period as a doe in estrus, and up until then the scent dripping in the scrape was that of multiple does in heat. You will have the dominant buck's attention because of the territorial intrusion (the D.I.E. scrape and rub), but up until you come in to hunt it you will not have his undivided attention. Once you show up to hunt on Day 1 of the hunt, you are one single doe in estrus, he can smell you, and hear you, but he cannot see you. He is willing to fight for the right to breed with you (as the doe in estrus) at the D.I.E. scrape. All he has to do is come in when you are there. I find it amazing that humans have the power with DOMINANCE IS EVERYTHING to make the most dominant buck in any area come to their stand site during the day when they are there. Even better than that is the fact that he will fight other (real) bucks for the right to breed with your (invisible) doe, and that he will not give up unless four days pass or he discovers that there is a human or another threat in the area.

The dominant buck is used to trailing does in estrus for a few hours before finding them, but he is not used to having to find a doe that has come to his primary breeding scrape, and he is certainly not used to having any competition for does inside his own territory. He knows that a doe is only in estrus for one to two days, but he will come into the scrape for up to four straight days to prevent other bucks from neighboring herds from trying to take over his territory. He has to make sure no other buck intends on challenging him at the D.I.E. scrape, so he beds down in the nearest available cover downwind or crosswind of the scrape and waits to see if any deer approach the scrape. If they do then he will know about it.

Sometimes the dominant buck finds the scrape on set up day, but not every time, that is why I installed a 2 ½-day waiting period in my system right from the start. The waiting period is there for the buck to find the scrape and to give him enough time to overcome his fears of entering the area around the scrape during daylight. He will not be familiar with the area you choose to set up in, and he has to explore it night and day before he will feel comfortable bedding down there. It is best if he finds the scrape while you are gone. He needs to find it and take it over or at least control the area around the scrape for a day or two before he will be comfortable approaching it during daylight. I find that the majority of dominant bucks will find the scrape during the waiting period before Day 1 of your hunt, and you will know he found it by looking in the scrape on Day 1 and seeing his front hoof print in it. If you do not see a track in it then the buck has not found it yet, but he will before you enter the woods on Day 2. He cannot stay away from a doe in estrus, and you introduce her to him on Day 1. Always build the scrape at a distance of less than 35 yards from your stand, so the buck will always come in close enough to offer you a shot opportunity with a bow. Every gun hunter I know can shoot well at 35 yards, so I was not concerned about shooting distance for gun hunters when I developed the system.

Remember a doe in heat is an attraction for all mature bucks, but a doe in estrus is one-step better. A doe in estrus is looking for a mate whenever she does not have one, and she needs to breed within one day or two or she will not get pregnant. All mature bucks know that, so the presence of a doe in estrus in the area triggers a breeding frenzy among the herd's pecking order bucks, the area's monster bucks, swamp bucks, and all intruder bucks that can catch a whiff of the doe in estrus' scent.

If the dominant buck is in the area, he will track down the doe in estrus immediately and breed with her. Lesser-ranked (pecking order) bucks will move away as the dominant buck approaches them and the doe. They show subordination to their king. Maybe now you are seeing the brilliance to my D.I.E. system. I needed all the mature bucks that traveled through the area where I chose to hunt, to believe that I was a doe in estrus, a doe that was seeking out a mate, one that came into this herd's territory intent on getting pregnant by the most dominant buck. All mature bucks will pursue a doe in estrus. I learned that while filming deer.

I had to move into the territory later in the day than normal so the buck(s) that were watching my scrape would not see me as I walked into my hunting area. It was obvious to me that I had accomplished my goals and that at least one mature buck in the area was very upset with the challenging scrape I had built inside his territory. He had torn the rub I made behind the D.I.E. scrape to shreds, and he left a 4 ½ in long front hoof print in the center of the scrape, as if to tell any deer that come to it, that he owned the scrape from that point forward.

I was very excited to see I had ticked a breeder buck off, and I sat as still as I could that day in my stand anxiously awaiting the arrival of the buck that I had fired up. The biggest difference between traditional hunting and hunting with the D.I.E. set up is that with D.I.E., the deer believe you are one of them at all times, when you are in the woods, without D.I.E. they know you are a hunter. D.I.E. gives you a positive identity, as a single doe in estrus that is seeking male companionship, one that is only going to be there for a day or so. It forces the dominant buck to respond to her call. He tracks her by her scent, and when he arrives at the scrape, he goes berserk. He has to find her right then so no other bucks can breed with her. You and I both know he will never find her, but he does not know that, so he commits to finding her for the next two days. Those days are most often Day 2 and Day 3. On those days, the buck is in a frenzied breeding mode, and he will stop at nothing to meet your doe in estrus, nothing except encountering a presence of danger.

All the while you also represent one single monster intruder buck, that has come into his territory, made a challenging primary breeding scrape and has attracted some of the herd's does to it before the dominant buck found it. The most dominant buck will be riled up to say the least. He will not leave the area until he meets this intruder, until he breeds the doe in estrus, or until 4 days pass at which time he knows that something is up and that no doe could be in estrus that long.

Do not let the deer in the area see you as a human or identify you as a possible danger to them because you walk like a human or you smell like a human, that way the buck will not sense any danger around the scrape. Stay in your stand all day or you could fail because the buck will bust you if he sees you get out of your stand.

D.I.E. is unique because it places you in the hunt with the deer, not outside the hunt looking in at the deer. The first time I hunted with it, I felt a power come over me that I was not accustomed to feeling. I felt like I was a pair of invisible deer on the ground in front of my D.I.E. scrape, and that every animal in the woods was convinced of that being true, the entire time I was up in my tree stand looking down on the set up. I was one single doe that day, and I was a doe that no buck in the area had ever laid eyes on before. They would search for me but not find me in the obvious places, so they would have to come back to the source of the doe's scent (the D.I.E. scrape). That was where I was waiting for them, up in a tree, above their line of sight. That is the only place a human can be in a deer's territory without them knowing a human is there, and without alerting deer as they go about their daily lives. I was still a hunter and I was still a man, but I never told any deer that a hunter or a man was there, and they never knew it. I was invisible to them, both as a pair of breeding deer, and as a hunter. They could smell two real deer and they believed I was one of them, and nothing I was doing was going to change their minds. I am confident that you cannot be in a better position as a hunter of monster bucks than to be invisible to them and have them hunt for you when you are in your tree stand. It cannot get any better than that!

On the second day of my first D.I.E. hunt, I saw a 9-point buck heading in my direction, from over 140 yards away. I was hunting northwest of intersecting tree lines and he was southwest of the intersection headed straight east toward it. He was coming in at a steady walking pace. He was determined to get to my scrape to meet the doe, and I am sure to combat the buck if he would find the intruder monster buck there. When he got 35 yards away, he walked across my scent trail and never lifted his head. I called to him with my voice by letting out one lone deep sounding grunt, and he turned 90 degrees and walked right to me. He pushed his way through the briars and brush inside the tree line, and he did not stop walking until he was six feet away from me, standing in my mock scrape. I was at full draw at that moment and I let the arrow fly. Right through the ribs it went (a double lung shot). That was the biggest buck that had ever come within 40 yards of me while bow hunting, and he was the first mature buck that I had outsmarted while I was armed and hunting. I did not outsmart him alone. I give all the credit to my D.I.E. system.

The buck was a 2 ½ year old 9-pointer weighing 210 lbs (dressed weight), with a 20" inside spread. I did not properly care for the rack and it shrank to 18 ½-inches wide during the 60-day drying period. I was hoping its rack would score above 125 inches but it came up short at 121 5/8 inches. It was a season of firsts for me and because the hunt was so extraordinary, I decided to repeat the steps I took to set the system up, and hunt over it, on the exact weekend one year later. I wanted to see if I was just lucky the first time, or if I was on to something bigger. One year later to the day, I was sitting in my stand overlooking my secret system and another 9-pointer came in. He ran across the middle of a plowed field to get downwind of my scent, when I grunted he stopped and I took my shot. That buck turned out to be a 3 ½ year old that weighed about 185 lbs (dressed weight). I definitely knew then that I was on to something, and it was something very big! Of course, I kept my system a secret from everyone back then. I did not even tell my family what I was doing. I wanted to make sure no one else was doing things my way and that this system was truly something I could call my own. I knew after my second hunt with it that my tactics brought in the buck and that he was indeed hunting me. Neither of these bucks were dominant and they were not monster, but both of them were mature and they were well deserved after all the years that I hunted for mature bucks using traditional hunting tactics and had come home with an unused back tag.

In 2000, I bow hunted with D.I.E. for mature bucks again on the same field edge. I chose the same days to hunt, and was busted by a monster buck on the way to my tree stand on Day 2. He was laying down 35 yards downwind of the D.I.E. scrape and I jumped him on my way into the stand. I still had my bow in the case so I never could take a shot. That buck was over 250 lbs on the hoof. He had at least 12-points on his rack and it was at least 34 inches wide on the outside spread. After that experience, I started hunting with D.I.E. from daylight to dark and I have encountered the king of the herd on every hunt since. He will always be the first buck to walk into a D.I.E. set up. If you do not hunt all day, you will never know when the first buck comes in.

I hunted eight more times with D.I.E. and each time a dominant buck hunted me. I do not always make the shot, but a dominant buck always hunts me. I want every person to be able to join me as "one who is hunted by monster bucks". You will have the opportunity to become a D.I.E. hunter if you put my system to work on your next hunt. I decided to write this book to show people around the world what an amazing dominant buck hunting strategy I have developed. After reading it, you will be a changed hunter. You will be able to pass all the tests deer conduct on you when they try to identify you as a danger to them. That way you can become one with deer, and they will accept you walking among them. Really… it is true! You will have the ability to walk among deer in the wild and you will know how to behave so they think you are one of them (a wild whitetail deer). They will follow you rather than run away from you. You will know that a deer hunter should never walk with the wind in his or her face during the rut, and you will understand why. You no longer will focus on staying quiet on the way to your stand in the morning; instead, you will focus on making the sounds that deer make as they move through the terrain you are hunting. The most dominant buck will hear you come in, but only when you want him to hear you. You will walk in and out of your hunting area on a precise time schedule from now on, and you will know how to act at all times whether you are in a tree stand or on the ground going to or coming from it. You will know how to stay safe in your tree stand and how to lay down a scent trail that every mature buck will follow. You will know how to read scrapes and rubs and how to sort out a herd's bucks to determine if they are the most dominant or not, just by looking at them. You will know how to scout your property for dominant buck sign and you will know what monster buck sign looks like. You will be an expert on bedding areas and you will know not to enter one if you wish to meet the king of deer on your terms. You will have an image in your mind of your hunting property, as if you were looking down on it from space. That image is "The Big Picture", and once you can see it you will know where to scout for a set up location and where not to bother to go. Most likely you will sell all your trail cameras (if you have any) to your neighbor so the dominant buck moves off his or her land and back into yours and you will have a better understanding of what being "busted" means than the other hunters in your deer camp. You will find out fast that hunting successfully with D.I.E., is as easy as following the steps and being committed.

D.I.E. is a precise system that takes timing your hunt during the rut to a new level. You will get the results that you expect from it. It will sort out the bucks for you. So put your trail cameras away, if you use any, and leave it up to the hierarchy of the buck pecking order to decide which buck is truly the king of the forest in your area. You will be hunting only that one buck, and at the same time, he will be hunting you! It is an incredible way to hunt dominant bucks!

I am certain you are going to learn to plant yourself in the brain of the dominant whitetail buck using my system. You will dream of your next day's hunt in the stand, and your dreams will come true when you first encounter the king of deer and you cannot help but notice he is searching for you. You must follow the set up and hunt instructions exactly in order for the system to provide you the results I have gotten with it. It does not have anything to do with luck. It is your destiny! Remember, to continue to keep him guessing with **DOMINANCE IS EVERYTHING**! Always be safe and have fun hunting with it.

Chapter 2

How I learned about whitetail bucks

Like many other whitetail deer hunters I have had many dreams of harvesting Pope and Young caliber bucks with my bow and Boone and Crockett record book bucks with a gun. I started hunting Wisconsin whitetail deer when I was 12 years old, and I am proud to say that I finally reached my goal of shooting a record book buck with my bow on November 5, 2009. He is not the first monster buck I have seen while hunting with my system, in fact, he is the 6th one, but he is the first one I have successfully hit and recovered. He has the smallest rack of the six bucks. I know many people are better shots with a bow than I am. I admit I need new equipment and I need a lot more practice but one thing I do not need is to learn any more about hunting with my **DOMINANCE IS EVERYTHING** system. I am now an expert with it.

Deer hunting is a tradition in my family, and as soon as I turned twelve, I got to go on my first deer hunt with my dad (Dick) and my older brother (Mike) who was 13 at the time. My younger brother (Jerry) joined us in the hunt in 1981 when he turned 12, and the four of us guys hunted deer together for quite a few years. I had some of the best times in my life hunting deer with my dad and my brothers, but until I learned about dominance and whitetail buck behavior during the rut, I was not able to be successful at getting close to or harvesting mature bucks.

I knew what deer sign looked like but I had no idea how to decipher its meaning. I used to scout in August when the deer were actively feeding on crop fields near dusk. I watched as bucks walked single file onto a field planted with nutrient rich soybeans. The younger bucks showed up first and then as if according to their rank in the pecking order they kept on coming. The last buck to arrive there was the dominant buck, but I did not know him by that name then. I called him 'a monster buck'. I scouted to find big buck staging areas, and I walked my hunting land looking for fresh signs of mature bucks such as tracks, tree rubs, scrapes, and large buck beds. Once I found fresh buck sign, I installed a tree stand, and poured out some shelled corn, to help attract the deer. I would hunt some mornings and some afternoons, but rarely all day long.

I was a traditional deer hunter, and so was everyone else. My dad and my grandpa taught me most of what I knew about deer when I was a kid. I saw lots of does and fawns and yearling bucks on my hunts, but I did not see a mature buck for many years.

As a traditional hunter, I failed, but as a D.I.E. hunter, I have succeeded beyond my wildest dreams. I used to hunt from a tree stand that allowed me to view the the surrounding area 360-degrees around my stand. I could see 200–300 yards in each direction. For the life of me, I could never see what I was doing wrong. Now when I look back, I am amazed at how unaware of my surroundings I really was. I did not scout for big deer. I scouted for big deer tracks. I thought all a person needed to do to kill a big buck, was to be in the right place at the right time, and I thought I had to intercept a buck in the morning or early afternoon, when (I assumed) the biggest racked bucks would be traveling to meet up with some does in heat. Boy was I missing the mark!

First of all, I didn't know anything about deer, other than the fact that for 9 days in November my dad, my brothers, and I would all go 'up north' to hunt them. I knew deer liked to eat corn, and that they hung around heavy cover during the day, but would go out to feed on fields at night. I was not sure when they would get water but I knew they needed to get a drink every day. I thought the bucks only mated on neighboring property, and that monster bucks were not anywhere on the property I was hunting. I thought you had to have special skills to encounter monster bucks on a regular basis. Well in that case I was right, but for the most part, I had no idea what made breeder bucks tick!

Every gun-deer season for as long as I can remember, I hunted all day long with my dad and my brothers making drives and posting on them. We saw deer but they were always running away from us. Each night I dreamt of big bucks. Some nights I could not sleep because I could not stop dreaming about monster bucks. I prayed night after night that God would grant me one wish, and send a monster buck right up to my stand while I was hunting. I had seen a few pictures of monster bucks on the covers of deer hunting magazines and I thought it was only a matter of time before I would get my chance, to shoot one of them. Back then, the chances of me seeing a monster buck were rare. The only monster bucks I ever saw while hunting were walking away from me over 200 yards away, or they were doubling back on one of our deer drives. I always kicked them up out of their beds in a swamp. I was usually up to my armpits in yellow grass, and ankle deep in muck when they took off. All I could see was the buck's huge basket rack, as he galloped away running at a slight crosswind angle. Monster bucks have a way of disappearing before a hunter can get his or her gun up to their shoulder. I was not slow to get my gun up. Those bucks were incredibly fast!

As a kid most of the time I hunted with a gun and I would hike through the woods driving deer toward my cousins or my brothers. We always drove deer from downwind into the wind or at a crosswind. I saw many deer bust out of heavy cover and then stop right in front of me before heading back into heavy cover, but those deer always turned out to be does with their fawns, or yearling bucks. It seemed like I was never ready to shoot when a deer finally did come along. Deer always surprised me. They came in when I least expected it. I did not care for deer drives, but I did not care to hunt alone at the time either. Making deer drives was fun in the beginning because my whole family took part in them, but after many years of making deer drives and never succeeding at filling my back tag while on one, I opted to stay in my stand rather than joining the group to drive deer.

My dad always gave us kids' options. We could hunt however we wanted to, and for me sitting in my stand (waiting for a monster buck) until I got too cold to stay, was the game plan from there on out. Most of my cousins ribbed me and told me I was wasting my time hunting monster bucks where none existed. They had fun telling me that filling my back tag with a doe was better than going home empty handed. I felt differently though. I wanted a mature buck, and I was willing to hunt to the last minute of the last day if that is what it took. I was tired of walking up and down hills all day, never getting a buck in my sights. I was frustrated to say the least. I was an inexperienced buck hunter with the best intentions but I could not succeed in taking mature bucks the traditional way. I realized it early on, but at that time, I did not have any other options.

I liked to take the easy way out. I liked to sleep in late and only hunt a few hours before quitting for lunch, and then I would take a short nap and finally return to my tree stand to hunt the last three or four hours left in the day. I remember hunting year after year in the same woods that my family would be making daily deer drives in and I remained in my stand until they passed by me. Then I packed up my gear and headed back to the cabin, hoping there was some of mom's homemade chili or venison stew on the stove. After eating my fill, I went back to my tree stand (near a doe bedding area) and when I got back I would always come upon a set of fresh buck tracks that told me I just missed my opportunity to see the monster. I sat all day until closing time and headed home empty handed again. I had fun, but I did not get what I went there for.

After the deer drives were over for the day, we sat in our tree stands for a few hours waiting for the deer to settle down, and move back into their bedding areas. After a few hours, some of them would work their way back into our property. I did not like hunting in the low light hours, but the rest of my family did not have a problem with it. My brother Mike would always get a buck while gun hunting. He sometimes would walk a half mile or more just to be alone in the woods. He was and still is a very successful traditional deer hunter.

I know now that being alone with the deer herd is the best way for me to hunt deer. Back then, I never wanted to go very far from the road or from the cabin to hunt. I was unsure what I would do if I was all alone and I experienced a situation for the first time that I did not know how to deal with. I used to worry about everything, even if it was nearly impossible for it to happen, believe me I worried about it.

I hunted deer with a gun until I was 19 without ever seeing a buck with more than 8 points on a hunt. Once I started seeing bucks it was because I moved toward heavier cover and I stayed in my stand until closing time instead of leaving it to get back to the cabin before dark. In 1991, when I was 24 years old I wounded a huge monster buck with a rack twice as wide as his rump, during gun season. He was an 11-pointer. I hit him twice and the shots were fatal but they were both high in the back above his vitals. The buck bedded in a cedar swamp and I lost his blood trail and could not find him. I tracked him until dark that day and the next one too. Seven other people in my hunting party helped me look for that monster buck, because he was my dream buck, and they all knew the buck would be dead when we found him. No one ever wants to lose the buck of a lifetime. After two days of searching, I was feeling sick about the whole thing so I decided to quit deer hunting. I felt I did not deserve to be hunting deer if all I was capable of was wounding the first monster buck that I ever saw in my sights, and then not being able to recover him. I wished at that point in time that I had never shot him. I wished he were still running free.

I love going deer hunting with my brothers and my dad, because we all enjoy each other's company, so quitting that day was a tough choice for me to make. My brothers (Mike and Jerry) and I call hunting and fishing together "spending some quality time with dad", and that it truly is. Instead of finishing the 1991 deer hunt with my family, I drove home to New Berlin, Wisconsin, and there I decided to set out to learn all a person could know about whitetail deer behavior. I was determined to learn all I could from wild deer. I needed to know what made mature whitetail bucks tick and what better way to do it than by following around a few hundred deer in the wild, in an area where they could not be legally hunted.

I was eager to learn all I could in a year so I could go back to hunting deer again the following season, but as it turned out; I did not hunt deer at all in 1992. I was determined to learn how to get close (15 to 35 yards) to mature bucks during the rut without having them run away from me, and videotaping deer in the wild was the answer.

I wanted to know what deer did all day. I had many questions like; what times of day do deer sleep? When deer bed, do they sleep, eat, or just rest? Where do they bed? How many different bedding areas do deer have in one territory? How do deer choose a bedding area? Do they sleep in groups or all by themselves? I wanted to know where monster bucks lived, and if I would ever be able to see one on my parent's 40-acre hobby farm in Waukesha County Wisconsin. I thought big bucks only lived 'up north', and I wondered how far I would have to travel in order to find a woods full of them. I knew there was a difference in the behavioral traits of young bucks compared to older ones, and I wanted to know why 10-point and bigger bucks were so elusive? I wondered if I could get close enough to big bucks to be able to take some still photographs, or if they would charge me, if I approached them during the rut with a camera in hand. I found out all the answers to my questions, and all the hours I spent filming deer were well worth my effort.

I literally spent the next 16 months following five separate whitetail deer herds on their daily routines. I took a VHS video recorder with me and recorded every deer I saw, from the time I first saw it until it went out of view. I wanted to see what deer did when they were not being driven out of a piece of property by hunters (making a drive), and how they lived during the rut in an area where they were not hunted. I wanted to understand how deer detected danger, and what their ways of communicating with one another were. I wondered if deer were friendly toward other deer, and under what circumstances that would change.

I also wanted to understand the rut. What it actually is and how deer act when they are sexually aroused. I wanted to know if *bachelor buck groups* stayed together after they shed the velvet off their antlers, and I wanted to be able to walk among the herd without alerting them to my presence as a human. I knew they had predators other than humans, and I wanted to see if they feared any of them as much as they feared humans. I also wanted to know whether they would run or fight if confronted by a pack of coyotes. I got all my answers and more.

I learned more than I expected to learn during that fall rutting season, so I continued my videotaping into the winter months and on into spring of 1992. I filmed deer all summer and through the entire next rut too. I needed to know when the rut actually started and how it started, and there was no way of learning that if I was in the woods hunting deer, so I made the decision to stay home and film the entire 1992 rutting season. That I did, and after I was done, I was a new man. I knew whitetail deer behavior better than any of my friends and family, but I did not tell anyone what I had learned, because I believed that nobody cared what I knew about deer, all they cared about was how successful or unsuccessful I was as a deer hunter. I had not gotten any better at hunting deer I just got better at understanding them. I was a man with a dream, I was living it, but I was not finished fulfilling it yet.

I filmed deer from daybreak to dusk for the better part of a year and a half, and when I finally put the video camera away and decided I was ready to go deer hunting again, I had recorded deer for more than 500 hours. I had 200+ hours of video with both bucks and does in it, and I had compiled 80 hours of film of just 8-point bucks and bigger during the rut. The biggest buck I filmed was a 14-pointer. He first showed up after dark during the chase phase of the rut. It was the first week of November. I only saw him twice. Once I found him bedded under a cherry tree in a core breeding area that three herds shared. He arrived there an hour after sunset, and the other time I saw him he was leaving an area 200 yards upwind of the first spot, this time he was walking among 8 or 9 other bucks that I was convinced where his herd's pecking order. Every buck he walked past turned his head away to show subordination. He disappeared within 10 days of the time he arrived there and I never saw him again. Filming deer 3 to 6 hours a day 3 to 5 days a week during the day and once or twice at night was a workout. At times, I thought I had learned enough and I wanted to quit, but one thing kept me at the edge of my seat wanting to go out into the woods with the deer for another day. It was the fact that I had a good chance to find another huge-racked monster buck, and that I was skilled enough that I could get within 30 yards of him to film his behavior. I do not believe any person can ever get tired of seeing monster bucks!

I filmed deer throughout Whitnall Park. It is located in Southwestern Milwaukee County. It is a heavily wooded park and it borders some private farms. The park was loaded with whitetails at the time, and to this day, a healthy herd still lives there. I learned about herd structure and deer dominance from watching deer in Whitnall Park. I saw multiple breeder bucks there during the rut. I recall there being one 14-pointer, one 12-pointer, five 10-pointers, three 9-pointers, fifteen 8-pointers, and 23 yearling bucks with 2 to 6 points. The average doe herd had five or six mature does in it, along with their twin fawns (in most cases), and anywhere from 7–10 yearling does. I learned how big bucks rationalize different situations. I learned what they do when a human pressures them out of their hiding place, where they go after being jumped from their bed, and where they go right after you vacate the area. I tracked mature bucks in mud, in sand, and in snow. I tracked them in grass covered with dew. I did not pressure the deer. I followed most of them from a distance of 80 to 200 yards and used the 6-power zoom lens on the video recorder to take me closer. Later on, I started filming without using the zoom lens. I have gotten within 5 yards of over one hundred deer in my life. I was able to do it because I learned how to be invisible to deer.

It was great fun for me. I had spent more than a year within the territory boundaries of a huge whitetail population. There were over 240 deer in the five herds (combined) at that time. All of the things I learned from deer I wrote in this book. I walked among deer and I learned how to think like them. I watched deer watch people, and I learned that you could not be a human and expect the king of the herd to walk right up to you during daylight. It just is not going to happen! Since then I have gained more knowledge of their predictable behavior during the rut by hunting successfully with my D.I.E. system 11 consecutive times. Whitetails cannot identify a human as a human if the human is dressed in full camouflage, is scent free, and is not moving. To top that, if you are walking in snowshoes and dressed in camouflage from head to toe a herd of deer will let you walk right through the middle of them. They do not see anything but some brush (your camouflage pattern) moving and they cannot get your scent if your feet are not touching the ground. Wearing snowshoes will give you a huge advantage when deer hunting.

I learned that there were five deer herds in that 3-mile area x 6-mile area, and each of the 5 dominant bucks held his own territory. They were like kings. Each king had a herd of 40 or more deer that lived in the area with him. I never witnessed a pecking order buck confront the king of his own herd, during the rut. They had the pecking order all worked out before the rut started.

I witnessed some enormous bucks with huge racks going head to head in battle, but I am convinced that those battles were between a dominant buck and an intruder buck every time. Dominant bucks fight for three important reasons:

1. For the right to breed a doe in estrus.
2. For the ownership rights to a scrape or other piece of territory.
3. For the right to rule the herd. For dominance over the other buck.

Pecking order bucks fight one another for different reasons:

1. To challenge a higher-ranking buck for his position in the pecking order.
2. To defend their rank in the pecking order
3. For the right to be the lead buck chasing a doe in heat.
4. For the right to stay with and breed with a doe in estrus (when the king is not there).

I noticed that yearling bucks, does, and fawns were free to move from herd to herd, leaving one herd and joining another without repercussions from the dominant buck in either herd. I was privileged enough to watch as pecking orders were established, and I witnessed hostile takeovers. In one such takeover a monster intruder challenging buck in his prime (4 ½ - 5 ½ years old) took on an 8 ½ year old or older dominant buck and took away the older buck's right to be dominant. I have 200 hours of amazing video footage of deer showing dominance, and someday I might share some of it with you.

I am a self-taught monster buck hunter with a secret system that I invented that changes the way dominant bucks act while in the presence of human beings. D.I.E. is a one-of-a-kind system that I developed through trial and error. I can teach it to any open-minded person in as little as 45 minutes, (granted they do not ask any questions). I currently teach people how to use it and how to understand what deer think in 4 to 5 hour seminars. DOMINANCE IS EVERYTHING makes the king of the herd hunt for the user of the system. There is nothing on earth like it!

God blessed me with a will to succeed at everything I attempt to achieve, and in this case, ladies and gentlemen, I had the will to invent a means to get close to mature whitetail bucks during the rut, and I succeeded when I invented DOMINANCE IS EVERYTHING. My new goal is to teach my DOMINANCE IS EVERYTHING system to every man, woman, teenager, and child that wishes to learn it. Where there is a will there is a way! I have the will, and self-publishing this book is my way. I welcome you to join me as "one who is hunted by kings of the herds".

Come along with me now on a trip into the private life of every dominant buck on the continent. Give your hunt with D.I.E. your best effort and it will reward you with an opportunity of a lifetime each time you decide to hunt with it. I wrote this book for you so I could teach you all I know about whitetail deer, and it is my hope that along the way you will begin to see the deer herd the way I see it, from the deer's perspective.

Attend a D.I.E. seminar to get hands-on instruction from me

Becoming a D.I.E. book buyer has its benefits. You are now eligible to attend D.I.E. seminars. Anyone wishing to attend a seminar must provide proof of purchase of a copy of this book along with paying all applicable fees, and they will be welcomed into a D.I.E. seminar. I am not willing to teach my system to anyone who is unwilling to purchase the book.

You can attend a private or a public D.I.E. seminar. If one-on-one instruction is more to your liking, get in touch with me, and I will be glad to instruct you. I am willing to travel to your hunting land whether it is on public or private property, to teach D.I.E. to you for a fee. I offer seminars in cities all across the upper Midwestern United States, based on the amount of book buyers with interest in attending them in your area. I offer private seminars for one person, or for your entire hunting party. I also do seminars for groups of up to a few hundred people at one time. Recently I started doing outdoor group seminars for 15 to 20 people.

A one-on-one consists of 1 to 2 hours of classroom-style instruction. That is when I teach you how the system works and how the deer herd operates on your property. After that, we scout the land and determine where the deer are at that time, in relation to the place we are standing. I will show you how to track the dominant buck's movements, how to walk like a deer, talk like a deer, and how to pretend you are a deer, by reading deer sign just like a deer. In less than five hours, you will learn all you need to know to be successful with the D.I.E. system.

We set out on a mission to learn where the herd lives, once we do that we focus on finding two D.I.E. set up locations, one to hunt from and the other to have on hold in case you need it. I will show you how to set up a D.I.E. scrape, how to make a D.I.E rub, and how to position your tree stand so you never feel the urge to get out of it until your hunt is over. If the rut is on at the time, all the buck sign that we find will be fresh, and I will teach you how to read it (like a deer) so you will know where the king of the herd is watching us from. He is always watching his enemies when they are in his territory. Then I will show you how to move through the terrain like a deer, and how not to be busted, by refraining from telling any deer that you are a human.

You and I will take a walk down the same path that you will take on Day 1 of your hunt, and I will teach you to lay out your timelines for entering and exiting the property without be busted by the buck that hunts you. Then we will shake hands and we will be done. You will then be a DOMINANCE IS EVERYTHING V. I. P., and I will be proud that you have joined the ranks of the others, who I have personally trained before you. You will be a D.I.E. hunter! I will be proud of you when you use what you learn, to become "one who is hunted by kings".

Anyone who reads this book and implements the D.I.E. system (as directed), will become "one who is hunted by kings". The V. I. P. status gives a D.I.E. hunter the option to attend seminars (for free) for as long as I am giving them.

Bob J. Mercier teaching a D.I.E. hunter how to set up the D.I.E. system during a 5-hour outdoor seminar in 2011.

Chapter 3

My opinions are my own

My name is Robert (Bob) Joseph Mercier and I am the only person in the world (to my knowledge) that has invented a system that commands the attention of the most dominant whitetail buck in any herd, for up to four consecutive days during the rut. I do so by brainwashing all the deer in the area into believing I am a real pair of breeding deer that have traveled more than a mile to arrive here, at this place. The user of my system chooses the exact place and the exact time of the rut for this pair of mature deer to visit. The dominant buck's world changes as soon as one member of the herd finds the D.I.E. scrape and D.I.E. rub. The breeder bucks in the herd cannot help but notice the intrusion that the (invisible) deer have made and they are intent on getting this matter handled as quickly as possible. This is a job for only one deer to become involved. It is the job of the dominant buck!

No matter where you hunt deer there is a buck that ranks the highest in the pecking order, that buck is the most dominant buck. He has a territory, and he keeps the rest of his herd safe from predators and up to date on where any unknown or known threats to their lives are coming from. The most dominant buck is the first and last buck to breed in the rut. He is the herd's king. He is smarter than most other deer, and he shows it by not rushing into risky situations. He is a survivor.

You will see throughout this book that I mention some things repeatedly. Those things are the most important tactics a D.I.E. hunter has to memorize. I take for granted that 90% of my customers have hunted deer before and that they are set in their ways. I have to change the way you think. This is nothing like traditional deer hunting, and you cannot think like a traditional hunter and succeed with D.I.E., you have to become a D.I.E. hunter, believe in the D.I.E. system, and use it as directed in order to succeed with it.

The first time you read about one of my concepts you may wonder if I am right or not, but later on in another chapter when I bring it up again, it should make sense to you. I have been teaching the D.I.E. system (the contents of this book) for nearly one year now and I never had a person who attended a D.I.E. seminar say they did not want to be a D.I.E. hunter, or that they did not understand what I was teaching them. My concepts and the way I go about achieving success with my DOMINANCE IS EVERYTHING system make complete sense to all my customers. I am glad it turned out that way.

This book will make it easy for you to use the D.I.E. system whether you attend a seminar or not. The first two men that ever hunted with this system only had 45 minutes of instruction, and they both had the best hunt of their lives on their first hunt as a D.I.E. hunter. My style of writing may be new to you. I hope you find it easy to follow and easy to understand. I tried to write the book as if I was talking face-to-face with you. This book is my first attempt at becoming an author. I hope you enjoy reading it and I hope you love hunting with D.I.E. as much as I do.

All mature bucks in the area you hunt with D.I.E. will take notice of your set up but only the most dominant buck and his challengers will ever approach it. Until I went public with my theories on October 23, 2010 (when I taught 30 hunters how to use my **Dominance Is Everything** system), I was just a monster buck hunter with a secret. Now I am an inventor, an author, an instructor, a consultant, a publisher and a public speaker. The best part of it all is that I am teaching my own system to the world. I am not selling someone else's ideas. I am teaching the world how to hunt the way I do for dominant bucks, monster bucks, and swamp bucks.

My thought process when developing my **Dominance Is Everything** system was completely different from the thought process a traditional deer hunter uses to get a chance at a mature buck while hunting. My system puts you in the head of dominant buck, before you head into the hunting parcel to set the system up. I learned all I know about whitetail deer behavior first hand from spending time in the wild watching and filming deer. I learned how to think like a deer and how to mimic their behavior so well that deer do not identify me as a human when I am in their territory. The way I overcome being detected as a human is one of my secrets, and so are the methods I use to make the most dominant buck in any area hunt me in a four-day period, whenever I am using the **Dominance Is Everything** system. In this book, I am sharing my secrets with you.

The system is a solid one. There are no variables in a hunt with my system. Deer believe that the user is a real pair of breeding deer, and that the only time this (invisible) pair of deer is in the area of the user's tree stand is when the user is there (during daylight) for one to four consecutive days.

Setting the D.I.E. system up is easy, but knowing how to behave (as a deer) so you can get to and from your tree stand without being patterned by the king of the deer herd is very difficult. I have mastered the means to accomplish it, and so far every hunter I have taught my system to, that used it as directed, has been able to achieve success, by being able to become invisible to deer. I was able to teach them to bypass the keen senses of the most dominant buck in the herd and all of his challengers (during the hunt) because the people learning my system believed in my theories about how deer think.

I put myself in a deer's position and I look at the parcel of land from the perspective of the deer. You can learn a lot from thinking like a deer. The first thing I learned is that people are the number one enemy of deer, and adult deer avoid contact with humans at all times. If you are human (which I know you are) then deer avoid you. I learned to brainwash deer into believing what I want them to believe. I found a way for a human to pass all the tests that deer conduct on the area the human is hiding in, and I learned how to behave differently so deer do not see a human when I walk into their territory. All they see is some bushes moving in the wind. When deer hear an unusual sound they go an alert and test the air for danger. Because I behave differently in the woods than a traditional hunter, I convince deer from the sound of my feet and the way I move through their territory, that I am absolutely no threat to them. They relax (go off alert) and go about their daily lives as if they were never alerted. Deer are not afraid of D.I.E. hunters, instead deer want to meet them. I have learned what it takes to be invisible to deer. I call it having an invisible deer suit. Once you have mastered wearing your invisible deer suit, deer will not be able to detect you as a danger to them, or positively identify you as a human.

Deer are not afraid of me. Some of them never know anything is there, and others know something is there but they are sure it is not a danger to them. Deer are not afraid of other deer that walk through their home territory. I "walk like a deer", I "talk like a deer", and I "read sign like a deer" so that all deer that encounter me by sight, sound, or smell, believe I am a real deer.

I used everything I learned about whitetail buck hierarchy, to my advantage when I developed my DOMINANCE IS EVERYTHING system. I combined different behavioral traits that dominant bucks display during the rut (that I am capable of mimicking) to form a life-like situation for the most dominant buck to encounter. The D.I.E. situation messes with the mind of the dominant buck by intimidating him (which believe me is not an easy thing to do without D.I.E.), and by attracting him (sexually) to the place the user of the system is hiding, at the same time. Some dominant bucks have had to deal with a situation like this one during past ruts, but not all dominant bucks have ever run into one as serious as this. When a dominant buck experiences what goes on before his eyes at a D.I.E. set up, he gets very aggressive, and is determined to put an immediate stop to the mating behavior of the (invisible) breeding pair of deer. I counted on that happening, and to this day, I believe I have control of the dominant buck's mind from Day 1 of my hunt until he we have our one-on-one meeting within 35 yards of my tree stand, which has always occurred within four consecutive days.

D.I.E. is a brainwashing technique that I invented. It starts brainwashing the entire herd from the moment a person sets it up within 35 yards of a real deer track (during the rut). D.I.E. makes all deer aware of the presence of a monster intruder buck, and at least two does that are interested in hanging out with him. The intruder buck is not welcomed by any of the bucks in the herd, but herd does are content with him being there. My DOMINANCE IS EVERYTHING system takes advantage of bucks, because it messes with their minds and tells them that there is a new buck in town and he is not checking into rank in their pecking order. I know there is not a dominant buck on earth (nor will there ever be one), that would ever allow that type of behavior to continue inside his territory. Dominant bucks dominate all the other bucks in their herd. Intruders are not from this herd but they cannot stay in the territory of a dominant buck without either confronting him and beating him in a fight, or checking into ranks under the dominant buck. There is no other option for an intruder to remain inside the herd's territory. They can come and go but they cannot stay overnight.

Anyway, deer believe the set up is a real situation and that you are a real pair of breeding deer. They believe it because I know how to display dominance just like a monster intruder buck does, and I am grateful that I never had to show up wearing a real deer hide on my back and hoisting a set of massive antlers over my head.

As you can see, I have done my homework. I have taken all the guesswork out of hunting with D.I.E. and I have now fine-tuned it so I can teach it to anyone. You can expect to have success with it the very first time, no matter where you hunt, as long as whitetail deer exist on that property. Understand that I lived these moments that I am writing about. I tell you how I believe the deer herd works, and how I believe deer think. I tell you how I believe the rut works, and which days I believe that the rut is "on". I tell you how to behave so that deer will not be able to identify you as a human (their #1 enemy), and I tell you how the deer will react to you when your behave that way. The deer that live there notice everything a human does in a deer country. I believe deer can detect human scent and any intrusions made in their territory for up to 48 hours after the intruding person or animal leaves the area, unless it rains, then all the human scent washes away.

I do not know anyone who ever told the public how deer think or what to do to talk to the king of deer. I am telling you what I know is true. You will not be able to verify my opinions in any library or from any wildlife biologist. My opinions are my own. I decided now is the time to show you how easy it is to have the king of any deer herd hunt you, with my DOMINANCE IS EVERYTHING system, because waiting as the years passed by was not helping anyone learn the things I know. I am only one man, and I am only here for one lifetime. There are millions of people who hunt whitetails and there are millions more that do not want to hunt them, but only want to take their picture. I have met over ten thousand of them already and I have taught 250 people how to hunt with D.I.E. before this book went to publication. I know of 31 people who hunted with it in 2010, and 28 of them saw their herd's most dominant buck on their first hunt with D.I.E. The 3 others were busted by the buck their first time, but next year they will have a second chance.

In 2009, there were only three people in the world hunting with my system, and that is when I started writing this book. This book is all about my D.I.E. system; how I learned it, what it does for you, how it works, and what I think you should know about deer behavior so that D.I.E. will make perfect sense to you. At the last minute, I added two topics to the book that were not originally part of it. They teach you about rubs, and about deer bedding areas. Some of the things I know about deer, that I teach in my seminars have left some of my customers speechless. I see more jaws drop in one D.I.E. seminar than a dentist sees in a week. You will be able to read about a few of my most memorable D.I.E. hunts, as well as read the testimonials of the first two hunters I taught the system to (prior to 2010). I know there will be critics of my methods, and I am all right with that. If they use my system (as directed), they too will see the king of deer up close and personal during their hunt with my system. I do not care if you kill the buck or not. I just want you to be able to see at least one king of the herd at least once in your life, and not have to pay thousands of dollars to do it.

I am not trying to say that it is my way or the highway, but for a D.I.E. user it is the D.I.E. way or the highway. I formulated the DOMINANCE IS EVERYTHING hunting system so it can never fail. I am teaching it to you because I promised God I would not be selfish if he helped me learn how to get close enough to mature bucks that I could shoot them with my bow on every hunt. I asked God to help me learn about deer, so I would know what they were thinking, then I could communicate with them and they would not be afraid of me. I worked hard, for over 30 years to master the skills I am teaching you today. I am proud to be able to self publish this book. It is my first book in a series of books. I hope you enjoy reading it and that you enjoy using the tactics I teach you so you can enjoy many hunts in the company of the king of deer.

As I mentioned in an earlier paragraph, I am not a wildlife biologist. Nonetheless, my opinions and theories about the behavior of deer, specifically those of does in heat and in estrus, and those of bucks during the rut have made sense to everyone I have explained them to so far. I do not know if they are proven facts or not, and it is not important to me whether anyone with expertise in deer biology ever contradicts my findings. I write what I know, and what I know has always worked when using my DOMINANCE IS EVERYTHING system. I learned that I could brainwash all deer making them believe what I want them to believe, and exactly when I want them to believe it. By analyzing the actions of the deer that I filmed over the years and by learning to mimic their behavior, I have been able to convince them that I am not human. How many people in the world can do that? Today, I could name 250 people that I know are capable of it, because I taught them how to do it. Now I am teaching you. Ever since I figured out how the heat cycle of a doe worked with estrus being part of it, and the whole thing being timed to less than four consecutive days, having the most dominant buck hunt me has become a predictable event. If I hunt with D.I.E., then he will come. That is a fact. Therefore, if you are a believer in D.I.E. and the power it gives you as a hunter or a photographer, then you will have the same results with it that I have had. I am not a college educated deer expert. What I am, is the only man on earth to ever develop a deer hunting system that makes the king of deer into the hunter and makes the hunter into "the hunted". With my heart of hearts I believe that I deserve the respect that all my customers have given me, as an expert in the field of hunting dominant whitetail bucks, and as the only expert in the world at hunting with my invention "DOMINANCE IS EVERYTHING". My goal is to teach it to everyone who wants to learn it, and I will pursue my goal for the rest of my life. Thank you God!

Doubting the fact that D.I.E. has never failed is human nature

Many people tend to doubt things that they do not fully understand that is why I wrote a book instead of just putting out a pamphlet with a step-by step process in it. Hunting with D.I.E. is an in-depth process that is only easy to understand if you see "The Big Picture" the same way I do. We have to look at your land the same way. I teach you how I look at it so you can see it the way it is (from the deer herd's perspective). Seeing "The Big Picture", means you can look at your hunting land and see more than trees and crops. It means when you look at a doe or a buck that you see more than a deer. It means that you understand that deer have a house and a yard and a bunch of neighbors like you do. When you see "The Big Picture" for the first time on a property, it is as if a light bulb just went on in a very dark room. You will be amazed at it all when you take the time to analyze the ways deer move through your hunting property, and make sense of it all. I have learned that I can change a doubting person into a believer in hunting with D.I.E. in as little as ten minutes one-on-one (on the phone or face-to-face) just by talking with them. Once they see "The Big Picture" their eyes open wide, their jaw drops, and their tone of voice improves. That is when I know that the person has become a believer in D.I.E.!

You may have some doubt that hunting with D.I.E. is as easy as I say. That doubt will go away as soon as you become part of your D.I.E. hunt. When you are sitting in your stand, you are the invisible pair of deer, and when you are moving in and out of the area, you are one of those two deer. The way I teach you to behave is the secret to becoming invisible to deer. Once you know that you are invisible to deer, and you have confidence that you can remain invisible, your world is going to change. You will be more comfortable role-playing with the deer herd. Remember invisible deer or invisible hunters are not there. Deer do not view your actions as a D.I.E. hunter as threats to their survival, they see the result of your actions, not the actual acts, and because of the way you act like a deer instead of a human, deer perceive your movements inside their territory as occurrences, not as threats. Deer expect normal occurrences to happen every day. When they move through their territory, the view they have of it today may seem a bit different from how they remembered seeing it the last time they were there. Wind and weather elements can change the landscape of a parcel overnight. Wind and storms down trees, wash tracks away on trails, and knock down vegetation that deer once bedded in and no longer can. Lightning starts fires, and flooding changes the course of rivers and creeks. Deer adapt to their ever-changing environment because they have to in order to survive in it. D.I.E. hunters slip into and out of a herd in less than a week, making very little impact, and never putting any deer on alert, when they use DOMINANCE IS EVERYTHING as directed.

D.I.E. hunters slip into and out of a herd in less than a week, making very little impact, and never putting any deer on alert, when they use Dominance Is Everything as directed.

A threat of a human or another predator (of deer) in the area is identified by deer and avoided immediately, but not so obvious threats (made by invisible humans) cannot be identified (as threats) therefore deer do not automatically avoid them. Deer write them off as occurrences because they cannot detect their source.

D.I.E. hunters are not threats to deer, they are invisible to deer and our actions while scouting, setting up, and hunting with the DOMINANCE IS EVERYTHING system are viewed as normal everyday occurrences in a deer's territory. The way we do things set us apart from traditional hunters. We consider what the deer are going to think about our actions (in their territory) and how the deer will react to them, before we change anything in their world. We adapt to thinking like deer so we are accepted by them, instead of being rejected by them.

In my opinion, there is no easier way to get close to dominant and monster bucks on a daily basis then by using my self-taught tactics. When a person uses the knowledge base I give them about how deer think, and combines it with using the DOMINANCE IS EVERYTHING system, there is no limit to how close that person will be able to get to dominant and monster bucks during the rut. In 2009, a 180-inch class 10-pointer walked under my tree stand while I was in it on Day 3 of my hunt. His antler tips were just 5-inches under my tree stand platform. I was sitting only 95-inches (nearly 8 feet) off the ground at the time. It was my first day in that stand. I had to move there after the same buck busted me from 80 yards away on Day 2; he saw me move but did not know I was a man. It was an incredible hunt, and I did not even get the dominant buck. A 17-point monster-challenging intruder buck came in and fought another huge-racked buck for the right to dominate the D.I.E. scrape and to breed the doe in estrus that they believed was there (me). I am master at using my system, and you can be too!

Deer travel into different parts of their territory on different days because of the ever-changing wind direction. When they see a change in the terrain, they stop to check what happened while they were away. From a downwind position, they process every bit of information that they can gather about the objects that seem to be out of place. The oldest deer (smartest) know that manmade items do not belong in the area, and they know how they got there (a human put them there). They stop to decipher the objects, and they run three tests on them to determine whether the items are threats. **See Chapter 9 - How deer identify danger.** When deer can make sense of an occurrence, they move on and stop worrying about it being there, but when the object moves, makes unfamiliar sounds, or is identified as a predator (animal or human) then the deer goes on alert and sounds an alarming wheeze. All the other deer in the area take notice of the location of the wheezing deer and they avoid that area completely until the threat is gone. They will meet up with that deer later and he or she will tell them what it saw, heard, or scented. Deer do not want to go on alert. They do it as a response to an action that was made inside their territory. You know you are invisible to deer when you do not see any deer going on alert near your stand site, or when they cross your scent trail to and from your stand, and never hesitate or flinch when doing so.

When you hunt with my system, the deer observe the changes you make inside their territory but they do not assume that a human made them. You never tell any deer that you are a human, so they do not think a human is there. Deer know human behavior but you are not displaying any so even if they see the work (tree stand) of a human they will adapt to it being there while they deal with the signs (the D.I.E. scrape and rub) of a territorial intruder. When you set it up as directed no deer will see a human where or when you are setting up, (away from their bedding and breeding areas). When deer encounter the D.I.E. scrape and rub, and your tree stand for the first time you are not there, so they see them as real occurrences.

Deer recognize occurrences, accept them, and get used to them being there. Actions on the other hand, are most often dangers to deer, they have to understand why they are there, and if they cannot make sense of them, they will never accept them. Humans that install tree stands on the edge of a nearby deer bedding area, or on the edge of a food source, are performing actions when they install them. It is the location where you set up, that first gives your identity as a human away to the deer. You took your hunt to the deer. You went where you knew deer congregated. A tree stand showing up in a deer bedding area is not discovered by deer, the human putting it in makes it known by announcing it to every deer in the herd, by taking it to them. Deer are in their bedding areas during the day, so why would anyone think they could outsmart the smartest buck in the herd if they walked right up to him in his house and told him they were going to install a tree stand there, while he watched them do it. Many people have been doing that all of their lives and never had anyone put it in those words before. I am the man to do it, because I do not think like a human on my hunts, I think like the deer.

Those acts do not just happen! A human (deer's #1 enemy) just came in and put it there. Now the deer are forced to accept it being there, and the human never took into account that the deer need to bed in that area when the wind tells them to. I learned from deer that every human action is obvious to them, they notice our behavior as humans, and they learn from it. No mature deer will ever adapt to a tree stand being built in one of its bedding areas. They will avoid it. Instead of the hunter getting closer to adult deer he or she has sent them away packing. Adult deer change their travel routes to avoid being there, when a human is known to be in the area. They still live on the property, but human actions force them to move in the areas where permanent tree stands are erected, only during nighttime hours. Only young deer will approach risky situations without fear. They approach out of curiosity, and many of them lose their lives because of it.

Deer hunters that use traditional tactics do not know how to make their actions into occurrences. Deer are taught by their parents and their peers to become alerted when they encounter the actions of humans. Deer react to actions by going on alert and warning other deer of the possibility of danger in the area.

It is not hard to become invisible to deer or to role-play with them, when you are open-minded and willing to adapt to the situation that the most dominant buck is faced with when he finds a D.I.E. scrape and rub. I will show you the way to a successful D.I.E. hunt. If you are a traditional hunter and you want to become a D.I.E. hunter you need to start thinking like a deer. You need to commit to sitting quietly and waiting patiently in your tree stand until the buck comes in or until closing time arrives. Learn to think "like a deer", and how to "react like a deer", and forget about everything else. D.I.E. hunters must concentrate on remaining invisible to the king of the herd, while he makes his way to meet you face-to-face, while you are in your tree stand. Most traditional hunters have shot some nice bucks, and they are set in their deer hunting ways. I love teaching them that there is another way. It is the D.I.E. way! It takes some getting used to but there is nothing better than D.I.E. once you have hunted with it.

If you want a monster buck to hunt you no matter where you decide to hunt deer, and you are tired of seeing immature deer all over the place, then you should try my system. I have seen a monster buck on more than 50% of my D.I.E. hunts. DOMINANCE IS EVERYTHING changes all the rules you are used to living by as a traditional deer hunter. It does that because dominant bucks do not live by rules, they make their own. In order to be successful at taking a dominant buck using D.I.E. you have to challenge his dominance at your stand site. Doing so makes him follow your rules, the rules you live by (the ones I taught you) when you hunt with DOMINANCE IS EVERYTHING.

I never wish any hunters luck with my system because it does not require any luck. All it requires is hunters having faith, being patient, trusting it, being dedicated to it, and having a willingness to learn as they hunt. If you believe in it then you have 100% odds of having a successful hunt using my D.I.E. system, right from the start. Stick to my set up and hunt procedure and the buck will not be able to bust you. Some hunters want to add their own flare. I do not recommend that you change any part of the set up or the buck will not hunt you 100% of the time. That goes for the hunt too.

The system works every time the same way. It always makes the most dominant buck in the area approach, take over, and protect the scrape from all intruder bucks. It makes him dominate the area where I put the D.I.E. scrape and rub. I teach you to think like a deer when you walk to your stand site, because that is what is required of you in order to have the dominant buck hunt you. Once you can think like a deer you can walk among them, and then you will know how to get to and from your tree stand without any deer seeing you. They can never tell that you are a human. Hunting with DOMINANCE IS EVERYTHING is fun. Everyone who hunts with it will love it, I am sure.

The book would not be complete without me showing you some of the errors I made when I used the system. I had eight hunts that I messed up on, where my mistake(s) cost me the chance to harvest the dominant buck that hunted me. I also need to show you what type of "hunter errors" will occur if you fail to follow my instructions. The buck will bust you if you break the rules. All hunter errors can be avoided by following all the instructions, and staying alert in your stand.

Everyone who has ever used the system prior to 2010 has failed at least once. The reason is they thought the way they used to hunt would work with D.I.E. and that is a false assumption. When you hunt with D.I.E., you have to brainwash deer into believing you are one of them at all times. If you can get into your stand each morning unseen by the buck that hunts you, and you never tell any animals that you are a human when you are there, then you are home free. Stay safe by following the rules. Review the "Never Do" lists before going out to scout, before walking like a deer, and before heading out to hunt. I wrote those lists to protect you. It is important that you never risk your life on a hunt with DOMINANCE IS EVERYTHING, or on any hunt for that matter.

Up until now I never let a hunter I taught the system to, write it down in detail. I feared they would get so excited on their first hunt when the buck showed up that they would be like me, and want to tell all their friends what they learned. The first two men I taught D.I.E. to understood my fear and they promised never to share my secret system with anyone. I wanted to have it perfected before the public became aware of it, so I would be able to answer any questions people who use it might ask me. I broke my silence a few months back when I told my story of being hunted by the king of deer to a good friend and amazing journalist Dick Ellis - Publisher of *"On Wisconsin Outdoors"* magazine. Dick wrote a full-page newspaper story about my 2009 bow hunt in New Berlin, Wisconsin when I arrowed the 17-point non-typical buck (on the cover and on my logo). It officially scored 172 4/8" to Pope and Young record book standards. Dick Ellis came out to the woods that day to help me drag out the monster buck. That was my eleventh hunt with DOMINANCE IS EVERYTHING, and my most exciting action packed hunt ever. The hunt started out a little rough, but it had a wonderful ending. If you would like to read the story that Dick Ellis wrote, you can do so by downloading it (in .pdf format) from his website www.onwisconsinoutdoors.com. Dick published the original article on November 19, 2009 in the WATERTOWN DAILY TIMES, and in 41 other syndicated newspapers across the state of Wisconsin. Dick then honored me by making my story explaining my DOMINANCE IS EVERYTHING system, the cover story of the September/October 2010 issue of *"On Wisconsin Outdoors"* magazine. Here is a direct link to the article http://onwisconsinoutdoors.com/pdf-files/OWOSept-Oct2010WEB.pdf.

Since the running of that cover story, I have now pre-sold more than 700 copies of my book. I attribute more than half of my sales to the articles that Dick Ellis wrote about my DOMINANCE IS EVERYTHING system and me. Those articles informed hunters that there is more to know about big whitetail bucks than meets the eye. Hunters in sixteen states requested a copy of this book before I had it published. They did so because they believe in my theories, and in the fact that I can prove that my system will work anywhere a person hunts whitetails as long as they follow the system's rules. They agree with me that hunting with D.I.E. is the most efficient way of having a close encounter with a trophy whitetail buck during the rut, season after season. It will prove to be the most exciting way you have ever hunted mature dominant bucks, in your entire life. I am quite sure of it and I am very proud of my D.I.E. system.

I was not always an optimist. I became one when I realized that I am on this earth for a reason, a reason that is bigger than I am. I am here to accomplish something great. To be known for something. I am here to contribute to humanity in my own way. I believe every person is on earth to try to make a difference. All people are here to accomplish things, and what you decide to accomplish is up to you. Some people reach their goals and others do not. When I became an optimist, I drew a line in the sand so to speak. I put my past behind me and I started looking forward to the future. Now I always look at what is good in a situation and I build from that, instead of looking at the negative aspects of a situation and giving up on it.

My future is bright because I believe that tomorrow can be better than yesterday was, and today is what I make of it. I am looking forward to spending every waking minute enjoying the things I am most passionate about, and one of those things is teaching people how to use DOMINANCE IS EVERYTHING the right way. Now that I have made my D.I.E. system available to the public, I have found that I get a lot of satisfaction from teaching it to others. Not one student of mine has ever failed to see the most dominant buck in the herd within 35 yards of them during daylight on a 1 to 4 day hunt with my system. That is of course true for those people who followed my set up and hunt instructions and did not break any of the "Never Do" rules. That is good news for you because you are my next student.

I established my theories after many personal trials and errors. I have spent thousands of hours in the woods observing whitetail deer all the while focused on learning how to get close to them. I was an unwelcome guest in the herds when I first started filming deer in 1991, but the more I learned about their behavior the more I realized how they perceived my presence in their territory, and I learned how to overcome it. I was not welcome to walk among them as a human. I did not fit in. I took it upon myself to learn to think like a deer. I rationalized every situation that I witnessed deer having to face, and I learned to predict their next move based on the information I gathered in my observations. Much to my amazement, I was accurate about 90% of the time with my predictions. Then I set my goals higher. I wanted to walk among them, and not have them be afraid of me. I started to think like a deer, I moved like a deer, and then I learned to talk like a deer. The toughest thing to learn was how to look at every situation from the perspective of the deer.

I was able to learn all of those things because I was an optimist. I did not give up when I did not have the answers. I pressed on, because I believed God was leading the way for me. I believe God created heaven and earth, and all creatures everywhere. I have never-ending faith in myself, and in my ability to learn new things. I have the will to move forward, pressing on past any roadblocks I encounter. Where there is a will, there is always a way my dad always told me, and he was right.

Twelve years of deer hunting without seeing a mature buck was long enough

After my first twelve years of deer hunting with a gun, I thought I was a failure as a buck hunter. I had yet to see a mature buck in the woods within 100 yards of me while I was hunting. I pray to God every time I walk into the woods, whether I am hunting or not. I thank him for giving me life and for allowing me to experience nature. I prayed that God would help me improve my hunting skills, and I asked him to teach me how to get close to mature whitetail deer. I was frustrated with my failure to harvest a mature buck during hunting season so I decided to quit hunting, put down my gun and pick up a video recorder instead. I hunted deer in the rut so filming them during the rut made the most sense to me. Picking up that video recorder in 1991 changed my life!

I know now that I was not a failure; I just lacked the skills needed to succeed. Those two seasons away from hunting helped me gain a new outlook on what it takes to be a successful hunter.

A hunter does not have to kill to be a successful. Hunters have to do their best to respect nature, to respect the quarry they seek, to maintain their own safety, and to protect the safety of others while afield. Hunters are discoverers. Successful hunters enjoy every minute they are in the woods, exploring this amazing world, and discovering new things as we experience them for the very first time. Every single hunter who returns to the woods for another hunt is a successful hunter. I will never give up hunting whether I carry a weapon or not.

My recollection of the most amazing day of my life

I experienced one extremely rare moment in my life that I want to share with you. It was the first moment I realized that a human was capable of being invisible to deer. I was filming a herd of deer in the late rut in Wisconsin. No deer had been able to identify me as a human in over a year. I was spending nine or more hours a week in the woods walking among them. I knew where a herd of deer was bedding, and a snowstorm had just passed so I headed out there to their bedding area to do some filming a few hours before dark. I walked in dressed in white camouflage, wearing snowshoes. The snow was 8 inches deep at the time, and about 4 inches of it fell fresh from the sky that day. I headed into the middle of a bedded down family group of does, expecting to see six or seven of them. When I got there, the does stood up in their beds. They looked at me as I approached them from downwind and crosswind. They trotted upwind about ten yards and halted there, looking in my direction but not sounding any alarms. I continued walking forward into the bedding area until I could see four empty deer beds from the place I was standing. I held my VHS video recorder on my right shoulder, pressed record, and then I closed my eyes and waited.

When I closed my eyes, the thought of me being part of my surroundings came over me. I could hear the deer moving through the cover and I could tell that they were circling around me from all directions. They were walking toward me not running away, and I stood motionless in their midst. Wearing Mossy Oak Hardwoods® snow camouflage from head to toe, I could not even see myself. I wore matching gloves, a matching hat, and a matching facemask. Those deer were bedded in four-foot high bushes with thorns on the branches.

Two minutes later, I opened my eyes and I looked around, as if I was looking for someone to share my good news with. It was incredible news to say the least! I had been wearing an invisible deer suit for more than a year and I never realized it before that moment. The fact is that deer cannot see me when I walk among them during daylight, no matter what the terrain is like. There was not a person in sight. Of course, I expected that to be the case, but what I saw when I opened my eyes was even more amazing. I saw that I was standing in the middle of a group of 18 does and they were moving in closer and closer. They assembled in groups of three or four and approached me from both (crosswind) sides. Upwind 5 yards away was an adult doe and she was staring intently in my direction, while all the others surrounded me.

I knew the dominant buck would be among this group of does because the rut was still on, and no pecking order bucks were anywhere nearby. Sure enough, I located him off to my left. He was standing 20 yards away in a patch of heavy cover staring upwind at me, (in amazement, I am sure). He was a heavy beamed 12-pointer with a caramel colored rack. I could sense that the deer knew something moved into their bedding area but they did not know what it was. It is as if they respected me (as a human) being there, but I know that was not the case. Deer avoid humans at all times. These deer were not avoiding me they were trying to discover what I was. These deer were observing me! I had reversed roles with the deer and it was amazing. Now I was 'the hunted' and they were the hunters. Three does walked within four feet of me, and they went right on by me without ever flinching. I just stood there taking it all in, on that December day in Whitnall Park (Franklin, Wisconsin), very amazed at what had just occurred. I looked up in the sky and I said aloud. "Thank you God". I had done it folks. I had finally achieved my goal and I had become a friend of deer. From that point forward, I was confident that I could go into any deer habitat and walk among deer without alarming them. I am invisible to deer no matter what time of the year it is.

I believe that my being able to invent the DOMINANCE IS EVERYTHING system was a gift from God and because of that, I am sharing that gift with you, and with every other person on earth, who decides they want to use it. I will teach you how to get your own invisible deer suit in the pages of this book, and you will know when you have it on because you will see that you are invisible to deer.

Chapter 4

What "Dominance Is Everything" does for you

Dominance Is Everything is a unique system used to hunt only mature whitetail bucks during the rut. I am talking about dominant whitetail bucks, intruder breeder bucks, monster bucks, and swamp bucks. Although pecking order bucks are mature, it is not likely that any of the pecking order bucks from the dominant buck's herd will be commanding your scrape once you arrive there to hunt it. They would have to beat the dominant buck in a fight in order to win the right to dominate the D.I.E. scrape. Pecking order bucks will not walk within 35 yards of the king of the herd or go within 35 yards of one of his scrapes if he is nearby. All the pecking order bucks in the herd know the scent of the dominant buck and they avoid him completely during the rut. Pecking order bucks hang out in groups and the dominant buck is never in a buck group (with pecking order bucks) during the rut. Pecking order bucks from other herds (intruder bucks) will advance on the D.I.E. scrape but only if the dominant buck is not in the area, and only if they are willing to fight with him if he confronts them there. All the bucks that visit a D.I.E. scrape will be at least 2 ½ years old and whichever one comes in first after the 2 ½ day waiting period, is the most dominant buck in the herd at that time.

Dominance Is Everything makes the most dominant buck in any area, search for the hunter for up to four consecutive days straight. The system produced a mature 9-point buck for me in each of my first two seasons using it, and I only had to hunt three days to take each of those bucks. They came to my location looking for an invisible doe in estrus and an invisible intruder buck, both of which I brainwashed them into believing were there. I only hunted in the afternoon back then, and I know now that neither of those bucks were the most dominant of the herd. They were pecking order bucks from other herds that were roaming around looking for a doe in estrus to breed. I call them intruder bucks because they left their home territory and moved into this area just to find a mate. They are not part of this herd. Most intruder bucks will return to their home territory after a few days away from home, but while they are away, they owe no allegiance to any king. My system attracts mature bucks, whether they are the most dominant or not. When you set it up exactly as I teach you to the dominant buck takes the scrape over and he prevents lesser bucks from coming into it. If you set it up too close to deer bedding or breeding areas then the dominant buck will not come in during daylight, in those cases you will see that intruder bucks that are not dominant will be the ones willing to come in. Set it up as directed and you will be amazed at the size of the dominant buck's rack. I always am!

In 2000, I learned that the most dominant buck in the herd would stake out my stand site and come in to the D.I.E. scrape most likely in the morning hours, so I changed my hunting tactics from hunting only partial days to hunting all day. It improved my hunts enormously. I immediately started seeing monster bucks coming in to my stand site. The only way for you to have 100% odds of seeing the most dominant buck in the herd is if you are in the stand from morning until night.

I have experienced 11 hunts so far using my "DOMINANCE IS EVERYTHING" system, and each time a dominant buck was hunting me. I can all but guarantee you that a buck will be hunting you. He will make his presence known within 35 yards of you during daylight. I hope you understand that because I am not there, in the woods with you, I cannot guarantee your results, but I can prove the D.I.E. system has never failed anyone who followed my instructions and used the system during the rut. See the hunter's testimonials in Chapter 31, along with photos of the bucks that Tom Earle of Palmyra, Wisconsin, and Matt "Rhino" Rynearson of West Allis, Wisconsin have taken while hunting with my D.I.E. system. They are the only two people on this planet other than me that ever had the privilege to hunt with DOMINANCE IS EVERYTHING before I started teaching it in October 2010. Tom is an expert shed antler collector, a sign painter, an incredible artist, and a monster buck hunter. I tell you he is a truly talented man. Tom is the artist that hand-sketched and helped design my DOMINANCE IS EVERYTHING logo. I am proud to say, "Thanks Tom for a spectacular job". He drew the 17-point buck on the cover of this book coming through my system name, and what a beautiful job he did! Rhino is a Wisconsin Pro Staff hunter. Rhino asked if he could use D.I.E., that way he could tell you what a professional deer hunter thinks about using my DOMINANCE IS EVERYTHING system. See Tom and Rhino's testimonials in the back of the book.

When hunting with my system during the whitetail rut you can count on the most dominant buck in the area staking out your stand site, bedding down nearby, coming in during daylight, and offering you a standing or walking shot, always at less than 35 yards. That is not all! In most cases, the buck will stand broadside in front of you or he will be quartering away from you—offering you an ideal shot. The buck will not give up hunting you for up to four consecutive days.

These are the only reasons why the buck will end his pursuit of you:
- He positively identifies you as a human. You are busted!
- Someone else enters your hunting area during your hunt. You are busted!
- You break one of the "Never Do" rules. You are busted!
- You place your shot well and you successfully harvest the mature buck. You did it!

There has never been a fifth day. In fact, I have only needed to hunt on Day 4 one time, and that was an extraordinary circumstance. No one else to this day has ever needed Day 4 to see their herd's most dominant buck on a D.I.E. hunt, but I want you to know that disregarding my rules and not planning to have a Day 4 can cost you the whole hunt. In order to have 100% odds from the start on a D.I.E. hunt you need to be in the tree stand all day long, for up to four days. The dominant buck is coming in but you cannot determine when, it could be anytime during daylight on any one of the four days. It is never up to you when he will come in, you have to be patient and wait for him to show up.

I will never forget my one and only four day hunt because I had a monster 12-pointer at 10 yards broadside. He had the widest rack I have ever seen. I believe that buck's rack had a 36-inch inside spread! He lowered his head and turned his neck toward me when I grunted to him to stop, and when he did the inside of his main beam was blocking my ideal shot. His rack was like armor, it was massive, and the inside curl of the main beams lined up with the second rib (that showed through his hide) behind the buck's right shoulder blade. The measurement of the 36-inch inside spread was a guess, but I am confident that what I witnessed was reality. My plan was a good one and well thought out, but I neglected to trim all of the tree limbs between the point on the trail I stopped the buck on and me. The arrow deflected off a branch six feet in front of me and hit gravel in the creek bed under the buck's belly. That was a lesson learned the hard way.

You should see the dominant buck on Day 1, Day 2, or Day 3, but if you do not, you need to hunt Day 4. If you do not see him by the end of Day 4, then it is likely that he identified you as a human and busted you!

Remember that each dominant buck is very smart. He did not live as long as he has by pure luck. You are hunting in his front yard, and he is aware of your intrusion into his territory; that is why he has stayed hidden while you hunted deer there in previous seasons. That will change if you are willing to learn the tactics of DOMINANCE IS EVERYTHING, the art of commanding dominant bucks, and put it to use in your hunting territory.

When hunting with the DOMINANCE IS EVERYTHING system you have to be careful not to put yourself in harm's way. Many of the D.I.E. system's rules are common sense tactics. The rest are safety tips to help you avoid getting hurt. Sometimes a person needs to know what not to do (ahead of time), just so they know what the limits are. Just as it is unsafe to climb a tree with a loaded weapon, it is detrimental to use any trail cameras in your hunting area when you intend to hunt with DOMINANCE IS EVERYTHING. The king of deer can learn hunters' routines. He is an expert at it.

The D.I.E. system does not work flawlessly if you break the rules. DOMINANCE IS EVERYTHING is a role-playing system used only during the rut. When set up properly, D.I.E. will always change the natural behavior of the dominant buck and all other bucks at least 2 ½ years old from being "unpredictable" to being 100% predictable for up to four consecutive days. After that, they lose all interest in protecting the D.I.E. scrape and in pursuing the two invisible deer. While you are in the woods, you have to behave the way I teach you to; then you can count on the buck coming in close. D.I.E. has many steps. None of them is complicated, but you need to take each step in the order I specify to get the results I have always gotten.

The system never fails because the buck can never figure out exactly what is going on. Every day that you hunt, you send him different signals. He has to guess which deer you are. When it gets the best of him, he comes in within 35 yards showing his dominance and *posturing* the whole way to your scrape. It will happen the same way every time. You can rely on the outcome being the same if you always set up and work the system the same way. Using DOMINANCE IS EVERYTHING is easy. For the price of three bottles of lure each season, every D.I.E. hunter can have the hunt of a lifetime.

I am a realist. I know that not every hunter will pick up my book or come to one of my seminars, but the ones who do will be paving the way into the future for all the hunters of monster bucks who follow them. You can be one of those hunters—one of the first to try, then trust, then recommend my amazing DOMINANCE IS EVERYTHING system—and one who each season has an opportunity to harvest trophy whitetail bucks on a regular basis.

The release of my previously secret system can only help the sport of deer hunting. For those of us who have a great passion for it, may it take us forward, teach us new things, and make us better hunters, so some day we can pass on all we have learned from it to a kid who is dreaming the same dreams we did. May God bless you and keep you safe on all your buck hunts with DOMINANCE IS EVERYTHING.

D.I.E. differs from traditional deer hunting

Clearly understanding dominant whitetail buck behavior enables a person to outsmart them. Like many of my fellow deer hunters I mistakenly believed that in order to be a successful hunter of dominant and monster whitetail bucks, you had to be lucky, you had to know the right people, you had to get the right permission, and you had to have all the right gear. Prior to inventing my system, I believed I was doing something wrong every year I set foot in the woods because I never saw a dominant or monster buck when I was armed and hunting. If you love to hunt whitetail deer, DOMINANCE IS EVERYTHING will change the way you think about deer hunting! If you have hoped and prayed that a monster buck would walk right into your stand site, stand still in front of you, and proudly display his dominance over his entire herd, your prayers are about to be answered! I have the system!

I developed DOMINANCE IS EVERYTHING in 1998, during my sixth year of bow hunting whitetail deer in Wisconsin. My system has gotten 100% results each time Tom, Rhino, and I have used it without error. Anyone who is willing to sit in a tree stand for 9 to 10 hours a day (during daylight only) for up to four straight days will love having monster bucks hunting them down. My system works for the average Joe. There is no need to upgrade your equipment—unless it is falling apart. No need to call or use a decoy either, but calling and using decoys are options. All a hunter or photographer needs to do is set aside a day to scout for a set up location 10–14 days before Day 1 of your hunt. Set up your stand and your scrape 2 ½ days before Day 1 of your hunt then wait for the third sunrise before going back to your stand to hunt it. The day of the third sunrise is Day 1 of your hunt. You must hunt each day as if it is your last. At most, you will have to hunt four consecutive days in your stand to see your area's most dominant buck. More than 80% of the time, you will see the buck on Day 2 or Day 3.

The DOMINANCE IS EVERYTHING system will not fail you, but you have to adapt to the system so the buck that hunts you will not be able to identify you as a human during your hunt. I want you to think like the dominant buck in your area. All dominant bucks think alike, and you will learn from me (through my trials and errors using D.I.E.), how to outsmart every dominant buck in every area you choose to hunt for the rest of your life. Let this be your handbook to mastering the skills needed to take dominant whitetail bucks with a bow or a gun from this day forward.

To get a buck to hunt you, you need to follow some rules. The first one is this: **Forget the way you used to hunt bucks.** I know many things about dominant buck behavior that you may never have heard before. I ask you to open your mind and let me show you a completely new way to hunt. The D.I.E. way is the opposite of what you have learned before, but D.I.E. is easy to learn.

To achieve 100% results, you must hunt alone. You need the woods all to yourself for 150 yards around your stand site. This is important to adhere to, from the time you set the system up until you get your buck or until you hunt all four days, whichever comes first. You have to use common sense when setting up and hunting over the DOMINANCE IS EVERYTHING system. If another person is within 150 yards of you while you are in the stand, then the buck may see that person and avoid your set up completely. Hunters who do not know how to be invisible to deer are completely visible to them. The important thing is that you are invisible to deer on a D.I.E. hunt, so the dominant buck will come to you thinking you are a deer. He may have to pass by or go around another hunter to get to your D.I.E. set up, and although he will do what it takes to get there, why not separate yourself from other hunters and make it easy on him. Your odds of success will be less than 100% if another hunter can see you, or if the buck can see another hunter, while he (the buck) is on his approach to you. Always set up in within 35 yards of a deer track or next to a heavily used deer trail, and away from all other people.

Being busted by the buck is bad enough, but getting located by another hunter is even worse for you. You can make the buck listen to you, but another hunter is something else. You have no control over other hunters in the area, so do not use the system where you know you are not all alone, or you will be wising up the buck that you are trying to hunt, and he will avoid you there for the rest of the season. Dominant bucks move away when human pressure gets too great, they still maintain the herd, but you do not ever see them because they only move in the dark.

The D.I.E. system has not failed because it preys on the two most powerful natural instincts of the area's most dominant whitetail buck: to mate with a doe in estrus, and to fight with an intruder buck that challenges his authority. Either way, the buck will come in within 35 yards of your tree stand, and because he is king of the forest, he fears nothing when he is on his way. If you stay quiet, scent free, and hidden—so he cannot hear, smell, or see you—then you can count on a hunt of a lifetime every time you hunt with my amazing system.

The dominant buck is going to come in looking for a deer or a pair of deer and he will not know that you (the hunter) are there unless you announce it to him. You are going to have a close encounter with a mature buck few if any people have seen. A mature buck in the prime of his life that is behaving normally, walking through his own territory looking for a doe in estrus that he is aware has come to his scrape (the D.I.E. scrape) attempting to find him to mate with him. If you have never had a dominant buck or a monster buck within 35 yards before, you are in for a thrill. Be sure to keep your safety in mind at all times. The buck has no clue a human is present, so he will not believe his eyes if he does see you, and positively identify you. Always be watching—but do not move unless you have to. Have faith that I know what I am talking about when I tell you, "Dominance Is Everything . . . to a monster whitetail buck!"

A dominant buck will fight other bucks to keep the D.I.E. scrape to himself, and he will wait for you to arrive and get quiet in your stand before he makes his appearance. Once you hunt with the D.I.E. system, you may not want to hunt any other way for a dominant buck ever again! If you follow my directions exactly, you will not fail. I walk with you, systematically, through the scouting trip, set up day, and the four days of your hunt. If you learn the system and implement it in your hunting area during the rut, then the most dominant buck in that area will be hunting you for one to four days straight. I have said this before and I will say it again because it is the number one reason why a person who is just learning my system will make a mistake that costs them the hunt. They try to change the system by adapting it to the way they hunted in years past. That is the reason for their failure. You must adapt to D.I.E., it will not adapt to you.

I know it is hard to change something you have been doing for many years, but in order to succeed with my system you have to use it exactly as directed. Using trail cameras anywhere within a half mile of your set up will tell the buck, that a human is hunting him. Telling the buck that you are a human and that you will be back is the worst thing any D.I.E. hunter can do. If you ever do that, your hunt will be over. Only pecking order bucks and yearling bucks will come in during the day if you use a trail camera. That is because the dominant buck abandons his mission to meet the doe in estrus at the scrape during daylight, because he knows a human was in the area. If you see pecking order bucks coming to the D.I.E. scrape it means he busted you and that only happens if you break one of the rules. They come in because they want to find the doe in estrus that the dominant buck gave up on. They will not approach a D.I.E. scrape or rub if the king of the herd is guarding it.

You need to make a choice whether you want to hunt with my system or not. If you hunt with D.I.E., give it your all and have no regrets! It does not matter if your neighbors use trail cameras, I am talking about a D.I.E. hunter (you) using them. The dominant buck avoids any humans that intrude into his territory. If you do not use a trail camera, he will not know a human was there, or that a human will be back. If you want to succeed at seeing a dominant or monster buck within 35 yards of you, take my advice and use D.I.E. only as directed.

You should trust me that dominant bucks are the smartest of all deer. My system brainwashes one particular buck (the king of the herd in that area) into believing that a situation in his home territory needs his immediate attention. There is absolutely no better way to harvest a dominant buck season after season than this. Anyone can learn to set up the D.I.E. system successfully, just by reading this book. So get your bow or gun—and camera—ready.

Becoming a master at hunting with D.I.E. will take you a little time and some practice, but once you know the system, hunting with D.I.E. will become second nature to you. Are you ready to learn to understand big, mature, dominant, and sometimes monster whitetail bucks? The most exciting part of this experience is that you will learn to think like a dominant buck, look at the circumstances of the hunt from his perspective, and see why the king of the herd behaves the way he does. I hope you enjoy reading my book, and I hope you enjoy being "the hunted" and no longer, the hunter on your future buck hunts!

The DOMINANCE IS EVERYTHING system is not a system of pursuit. It is a system of role-playing and of mind games. The D.I.E. system tells a dominant buck that a single doe in estrus, came into his territory from a different herd, and she is calling him out to breed with her. At the same time, D.I.E. tells the dominant buck that a monster intruder buck is present and ready to breed with the doe. This intruder buck is way out of line. In real life, an intruder that made a scrape like a D.I.E. scrape would hang around that scrape and challenge the dominant buck, and any other buck that came along to a fight for the right to mate with the does that visit the scrape. However, in the case of D.I.E. the intruder buck is make believe and is only a figment of the dominant buck's imagination. The intruder is invisible but the dominant buck thinks he is real. The dominant buck is obligated as the king of the herd to show up at the D.I.E. scrape, take it over, and maintain it from the minute he finds it. The dominant buck will not rush in at the sound of a deer walking into the area (when you come in to your stand site each morning), instead he beds down, and stays hidden as you pass by him. He is not sure how big of a rack the (invisible) intruder buck has, and he does not want to challenge the intruder without seeing him first. The dominant buck has no choice but to go to the scrape on a daily basis, to try to coerce the intruder buck out of hiding. The sooner the intruder monster buck disappears the quicker the herd will settle down, and the sooner the dominant buck can get some rest. He is losing lots of sleep when a D.I.E. scrape is in his territory, and the more tired he gets, the more aggressive he will act as he approaches your stand site. If he did not show up he would be abandoning his position as king of the herd, and he would be surrendering the doe in estrus and his territory to his opponents. Because DOMINANCE IS EVERYTHING to a monster whitetail buck, he will never give up his position, nor will he waiver in any way because that would convince other bucks that the king no longer cared about dominating his own territory. Instead, he will live up to his reputation as the biggest, toughest buck in the area, one that no lesser buck or intruder buck should ever go into battle with.

An old dominant buck is much more aggressive than a young one, because he has more years of experience being dominant. Every whitetail buck grows up seeing how the king of deer lives among his herd, and he sees that the king has it made when it comes time to breed. I believe that the dominant buck has an earned right to breed with every doe that goes into estrus within his territory boundaries. The king of deer is the only one that can hold territory of his own, and he has to fight before, during, and after the rut to maintain it.

I believe that every whitetail buck strives to become the king. Once a buck achieves that status, and feels the power that goes along with it, he will never willingly relinquish it. If another buck wants to take control of that territory, then he will have to fight the dominant buck and beat him decisively to get it.

Chapter 5

Whitetail deer and their behavior

Each deer in a whitetail herd behaves predictably depending on its sex, its age, and its rank (if it has one). Once bucks are mature (2 ½ years old) they focus on becoming the most dominant. After they get their chance to be dominant, which can span for a couple of years, the ones that survive retire to the wettest part of their territory to live out their lives as a monster buck or a swamp buck.

I believe every word that I wrote in this book is a fact, because it all makes sense to me. I have learned to analyze whitetail deer behavior and I am able to mimic it, at any time of the year so that deer will allow me to walk among them.

The deer living in a herd can be grouped like this:

- Does
- Fawns (buck and doe)
- Yearling bucks
- Pecking order bucks
- One dominant buck

On average, a whitetail deer herd includes between 20 and 60 deer.

Two other groups of bucks can live in a dominant buck's territory but not be part of the herd structure there. They live among the herd but they do not hold rank in the pecking order, and they do not control any territory other than their own bedding areas. These are non-dominant monster bucks, and swamp bucks. If you thought all bucks were in a pecking order, you were mistaken. I believe a mature buck can choose to compete for the throne or can yield to it and focus on surviving instead of breeding.

Wherever a whitetail doe is there is a dominant buck that will pursue her during the rut. In fact, no matter where a person hunts whitetails, as long as there is deer sign there, there is a dominant buck controlling the herd and the territory that his herd lives in. That territory includes the exact location of your tree stand. Therefore, wherever you have hunted in the past and wherever you choose to hunt in the future, there was, is, and forever will be a buck that is king of the herd.

Dominant buck's territories abut one another. They do not overlap, and there are not any gaps between them. My DOMINANCE IS EVERYTHING system will produce the dominant buck for you no matter where you set it up in whitetail habitat during the rut. The first buck to walk or trot in is the most dominant buck.

I want to explain a concept of mine that I teach in seminars and I passionately believe in that may confuse some of my readers if I do not explain it right up front. Brace yourself now. Here we go. I believe some bucks do not live in the herd. They all live in a dominant buck's territory, but not every deer is part of a herd. Members of a herd support each other, and live together. I know that a herd of whitetails consists of does and fawns, yearling bucks, pecking order bucks, and their king (the most dominant buck), but I do not believe that 80-percent of monster bucks and 100% of swamp bucks are members of a herd. They certainly can live within a herd's territory, but swamp bucks do not hold rank in the pecking order of the herd, and whether or not the monster bucks were ever within the herd's ranks is unknown to me. Some dominant bucks and pecking order bucks are monster bucks (because they have monstrous racks), and in that case they are part of the herd of course, but not all monsters are, and neither are swamp bucks. I haven't done enough research on monster bucks or swamp bucks to prove whether they were kings before or not, and whether they are subordinate to the king of the herd or not. I am telling you what I believe is true about deer behavior based on what I have seen with my own eyes. I am open-minded and I am not teaching you a bunch of made up stuff. I am telling you all I know about deer, because knowing it makes it easier for you to understand deer the way I see them, and that is the way you need to see them in order to be 100% successful hunting with DOMINANCE IS EVERYTHING.

I believe that mature bucks get to choose whether they want to compete for the right to be the most dominant buck of the herd that they live in. I know that pecking order bucks can leave their home herd and join another herd of bucks by sliding into ranks with them. That means when they join the ranks of the buck pecking order (at age 2), it is not a lifelong decision. They only stay in that herd as long as they want to. If a pecking order buck is not getting to breed very much, or if he is getting into some fights and cannot win any of them, then he may move into another herd's territory and join the ranks of that pecking order. He first has to yield to the dominant buck of that herd, after that he can see where he fits in. The higher a buck ranks in the pecking order the more does he will be able to mate with in the rut.

I know that 3 ½ year old and older monster bucks choose to detach themselves from having to live with 2 ½ year old pecking order bucks, in order to survive. Pecking order bucks are at a higher risk of being killed, by a hunter than monster bucks. I believe the reason is that pecking order bucks hang out together, and because of that fact, many of them do not live through the rut. Hunting season coincides with the rut, and mature bucks know they are being pursued by humans when they are breeding. Monster bucks and swamp bucks want to survive more than they want to hang out with other deer, so they retreat to the wettest end of a swamp, and live there, where their predators are unlikely to follow. Their predators of course include humans. We are a whitetail deer's number one enemy.

Some monster bucks are the kings of the herd. I believe that about 20% of them are. What I am saying is that each mature buck has a choice. Monster bucks live (bed) away from the pecking order bucks at least 80% of the time. A deer lives where it beds. The bigger the rack gets on a buck the surer of himself he gets, and the more aggressive he gets toward other bucks. DOMINANCE IS EVERYTHING to a monster whitetail buck all right! It surely is!

In order for a person to understand whitetail deer behavior they need to have a clear understanding of what goes on in a deer herd each day. Whitetail deer live in a herd that consists of bucks and does of all ages. I am not sure how old deer in the wild can live to be, but the oldest buck that a hunter harvested with D.I.E. was 9 ½ years old. Matt "Rhino" Rynearson shot that 11-point buck with his bow while hunting with DOMINANCE IS EVERYTHING in 2009 in Minnesota. Unfortunately, I do not have a picture of that buck to publish in this book, but what an amazing animal he must have been.

When you hunt using my DOMINANCE IS EVERYTHING system, the most dominant whitetail buck will come to you, and so will all of his challengers. These are monster bucks, swamp bucks, and mature breeder (pecking order bucks) from other herds. There is no way that a pecking order buck from the dominant buck's own herd (other than the one that ranks #2) will step out of ranks to challenge him for this invisible doe in estrus, at your D.I.E. scrape.

Does and fawns

Does and fawns live in family groups that consist of mature does, yearling does, and all their fawns (both buck and doe fawns), that were born in the current year. A buck fawn is less than a year old. A buck fawn that has just two points on his antlers is called a nubby buck or a spike buck, and those with four points are called forked-horn bucks. Many doe and fawn family groups exist within a deer herd. Does group together to shield their fawns from predators.

A doe is sexually mature at 1 ½ years old, and can become pregnant then. Doe fawns go into heat and estrus for the first time when they reach 6 months old, but I do not know if they can get pregnant so young. I have seen dominant bucks chasing young doe fawns in late December, but I have never seen a small doe with its own fawn in the spring. All the does I see with fawns are big, healthy, older does.

When a doe is in heat, she will lead bucks around the territory. It is a game for a doe to have more than one buck trailing her. Yearling bucks and pecking order bucks will trail a doe in heat, even in daylight away from heavy cover, but dominant bucks, monster bucks and swamp bucks will not. Once she goes into estrus and is ready to breed, the most dominant buck will run the lesser buck(s) off and claim the hot doe for himself. If a more dominant buck never comes along while a lesser buck is mating with a doe in estrus, then that buck has breeding rights at that time. It can all change in an instant, because DOMINANCE IS EVERYTHING to all bucks in a herd. A lesser buck is a buck of lesser rank or a buck with no rank such as a yearling buck.

Doe bedding areas

Does can bed down anywhere, but most of the time they bed with their fawns or other does. All deer bed down at all different times of the day and most will bed while feeding at night as well, but the primary bedding time for whitetail deer is from a half hour after sunrise until two or three hours before sunset. To a deer hunter that means deer are bedded during most of the day. Does like to lie down and hide under evergreen trees, in grassy areas, on dry ground, on ridge tops, or on south-facing slopes. Doe bedding areas are found near their source of water, on moss-covered ground, in thickets or brushy areas, and in open hardwoods. An adult doe will choose a place for her family group to bed that offers security, water, and multiple escape routes. A place where the wind comes through the foliage about 3 feet off the ground, so all the deer bedding in that area will have advance notice when danger approaches. Does and fawns are in constant danger from all predators, including hunters.

Core-doe bedding areas are the daytime homes of does, yearlings (both bucks and does) and fawns. They offer privacy and seclusion from mature bucks. There are always three core doe bedding areas inside every dominant buck's territory. See **Figure 2**. Sometimes one of them overlaps the border of two dominant buck's territories. Does can leave the herd whenever they want to, they come and go as they please. Core-doe bedding areas are places where more than five does, fawns, and yearling bucks bed at one time. During the rut, every buck in the pecking order positions his bed in direct relation to the core bedding area of the herd's does that day. When the

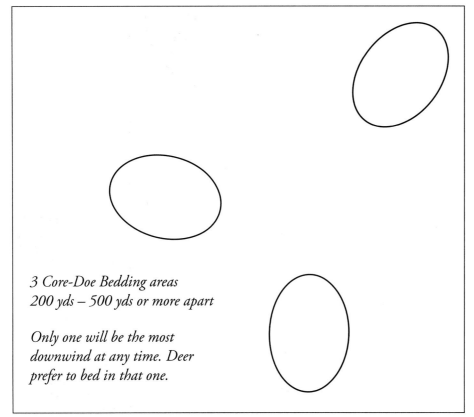

*3 Core-Doe Bedding areas
200 yds – 500 yds or more apart*

Only one will be the most downwind at any time. Deer prefer to bed in that one.

FIGURE 2 Every deer herd has 3 core-doe bedding areas. They are oval and are positioned like this.

wind direction changes, deer move from one bedding area to another, that way they can always bedded on the downwind side of their territory during daylight.

All deer choose a bedding site each morning based on the weather, which way the wind is coming from, whether or not there are any threats to their survival inside their territory, and where they want to go the next evening to feed. Every herd that I have scouted has had 3 core-doe bedding areas in it. I have never seen less than three or more than three.

Any doe, yearling buck, or fawn can bed in any of the three core doe bedding areas at any time, but they tend to prefer to bed in the one that is furthest downwind on any given day. The three bedding areas are always offset from one another and in a triangular pattern. It makes perfect sense to me because I know that they always need to bed as far downwind of their food source and of their known enemies as they can, in order to have the best chance at surviving each day. No matter what direction the wind is coming from you can be assured that the does, fawns, and yearling bucks will be hanging out in their furthest downwind bedding area. I call the preferred (downwind) bedding area core-doe bedding area #1. The closest one upwind of #1 I call #2, and the core-doe bedding area that is furthest upwind in the herd's territory is #3.

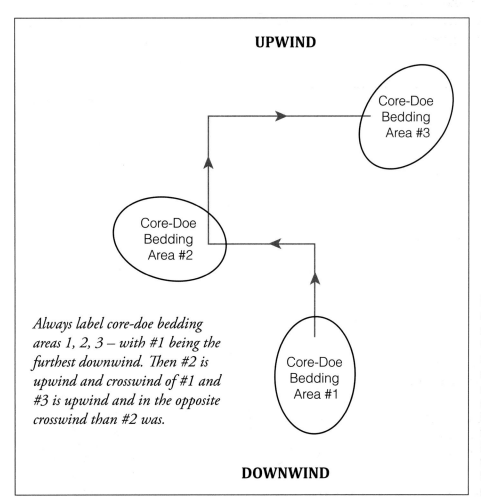

Always label core-doe bedding areas 1, 2, 3 – with #1 being the furthest downwind. Then #2 is upwind and crosswind of #1 and #3 is upwind and in the opposite crosswind than #2 was.

FIGURE 3 Scout for a core-doe bedding area on the land you want to set D.I.E. up on. If you find one enter it from downwind (only on scouting day), and if deer run out of it, then that is core-doe bedding area #1, whenever the wind is from the same direction.

When the wind direction changes the numbering of the core-doe bedding areas change, but the locations of the three core-doe bedding areas never change. If you place a permanent tree stand on the edge of a core-doe bedding area or inside one of them, then your actions force the deer to move to one of their other core-bedding areas when you are there. Deer avoid all contact with people and your presence inside their private bedroom is unacceptable to them. They may even move the herd to avoid you all together. I believe deer will move away permanently if you place tree stands, in every one of their bedding areas. I advise you not to hunt deer in their sanctuaries. In fact if you have tree stands inside bedding areas the best thing you can do for your herd is remove them from there as soon as possible, that way the deer will come back and live on your land where they want to, instead of where they have to, in order to avoid confronting you.

I learned about the structure of the deer herd by following deer, by taking notes, by filming their behavior, and by learning to analyze it from a deer's perspective. Everything deer do makes sense to me. I want to share my knowledge of these amazing animals with you so you will better understand them. Just knowing the facts I know about deer will change the way you think about them in the future. I am thrilled to be the person to teach you these things.

Anytime you are scouting between 10 a.m. and 2 p.m., the does, fawns, and yearlings bucks will be in core-doe bedding area #1. Some of them could be in core-doe bedding area #2, which is upwind, and crosswind of #1, but it is highly unlikely that there will not be any deer in core doe bedding area #3.

I do not think that many hunters have ever figured out or analyzed deer bedding areas the way I have. It gives a deer hunter a huge advantage to know where the deer are at any time of the day on a parcel. I want you to know where the deer are at all times so you can set D.I.E. up as far upwind and crosswind of them as you can. I want you to learn to find deer and leave them alone, so they do not know where you are when you are using DOMINANCE IS EVERYTHING inside their territory. That way the dominant buck will hunt you instead of hiding from you.

Their daily survival depends on the wind current carrying the scent of danger to them wherever they are. Deer do not want to bed in the core-doe bedding area that is furthest upwind in their territory because it exposes them to being attacked by predators, and they will not have anywhere to run except into another herd's territory upwind or crosswind of that bedding area. Deer never want to be forced to leave their own territory. When you see deer double back on your position that tells you that you are near their furthest upwind border of their territory. They will not cross into another herd's territory without being pressured by predators.

Carry a scent free powder bottle with you at all times, and you will always be able to read the deer herd where you are. Deer that are fleeing from danger will run into the wind or at a crosswind, and they will head for the nearest available cover to hide in. They will not run far without stopping to check the wind. Once they get their bearings, they head for the core-bedding area that is farthest away from the danger and they hide there for a while. No deer likes to be forced out of its home territory. Danger awaits deer in the neighboring herd's territory too. When they stay home they can escape danger much more easily.

Deer move from one bedding area to another whenever the wind direction changes because they find themselves bedded on the upwind side of their herd's territory. They most often move from one bedding area to another when a storm is moving through the area. They do so in order to have the wind in their favor when they are making their way to food and water later on that day. If danger approaches them while they are in their most downwind bedding area they can run into the wind to escape it, and then move crosswind to one of their other two bedding areas, rather than be forced to leave the herd's territory like they would have to if they had never moved. Adult deer only move from point A to point B for a reason, not just for the heck of it.

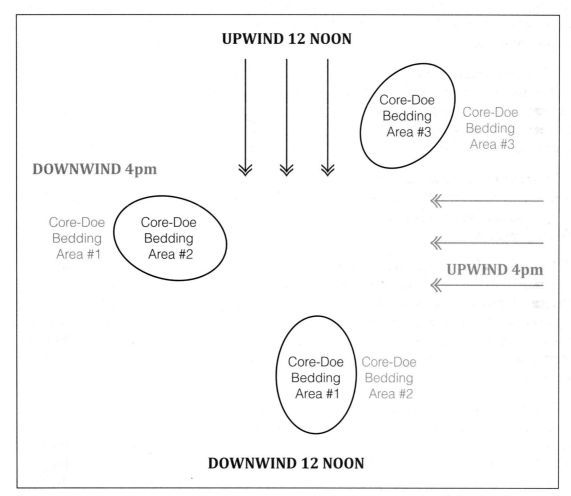

FIGURE 4 Deer move from their current bedding area to the one that is furthest downwind in their territory whenever the wind shifts enough that their current bedding area is no longer the furthest downwind.

For anyone who is not familiar with reading the wind I will explain the basics here. Downwind is where the wind is going **(see Figure 5)**, and upwind is where the wind is coming from **(see Figure 5)**. Crosswind is best described as any direction of travel that crosses the wind current **(see Figure 6)**. Look at it this way. Stand up and face into the strongest wind **(see Figure 5)**. You are looking upwind. Downwind is the direction behind you and crosswind, is any direction that crosses the wind.

LEGEND (for figures 4 through 8)

- ⇐⎯ = Wind direction
- - - - - = Crosswind direction of travel
- ◂- - - = Directions deer travel when there is a Northeast wind
- ⬅⎯ = Deer traveling into the stongest wind
- ◂- - - = The one direction whitetail deer will never travel
- △ = Person facing north

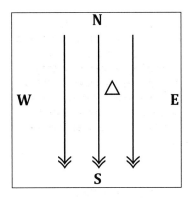

FIGURE 5 In this example, the wind is coming from straight North, and is traveling straight South. Upwind is where the wind comes from. Downwind is where the wind goes. The person in this example is looking into the wind current. The person is facing upwind. If the person moved North they would be moving upwind. If they turned around and moved South, they would be moving with the wind, in a downwind direction, and if they turned their body and faced any other direction, other than north or south, they would be facing crosswind. Walking crosswind means walking at an angle across the wind. Deer walk at crosswind angles when they are not being threatened.

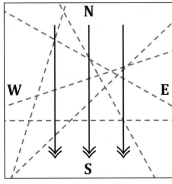

FIGURE 6 In this example, the wind is coming from straight North, and is traveling straight South. The dotted lines are directions a person or an animal can travel that are not upwind or downwind. They are all crosswind. If you always walk slowly at crosswind angles deer will not go on alert when they hear you move.

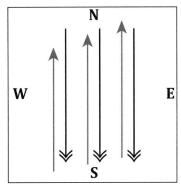

FIGURE 7 In this example, the wind is coming from straight North, and is traveling straight South. The lighter shaded arrows going against the wind (upwind) represent deer travel. Deer travel directly into the strongest wind when their lives are at risk, when climbing up inclines (hills), and when a buck is following a doe in heat or in estrus he will head straight upwind to her location. Otherwise deer do not go directly into the wind.

Whitetail deer and their behavior 65

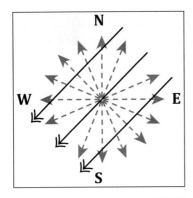

FIGURE 8 In this example, the wind is coming from the Northeast, and is traveling Southwest. The dashed lines crossing the wind, have arrows pointing in opposite directions, to show you that deer will travel at any crosswind angle of the wind. Some crosswind angles head upwind, and some head downwind, none of them head straight upwind or straight downwind.

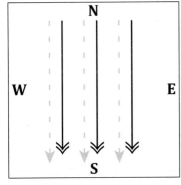

FIGURE 9 In this example, the wind is coming from straight North, and is traveling straight South. The dashed lines going along side of the wind, with arrows pointing straight downwind, represent the direction that no deer on earth will ever travel. Deer have a hard time detecting danger when they are facing downwind, and for that reason whitetail deer do not walk, trot, or gallop in a straight downwind direction. No deer will do it, not ever! You will never see a deer trail that heads straight downwind. If you come upon one that you think does, you should immediately realize that the deer only use that particular trail when it takes them crosswind.

Some deer run from danger by going head on into the strongest wind **(see Figure 7)**, or by heading away from the danger at a crosswind **(see Figure 8)**. That is because danger usually comes from downwind of deer. Deer can easily detect danger that is upwind of them because the scent of their enemies drifts downwind to the deer as they approach an area where an enemy is hiding. Deer never travel directly downwind **(see Figure 9)**. Enemies often approach deer on their downwind side because deer cannot identify them by their scent when they approach from there. That is the same reason why traditional deer hunters enter their hunting area from downwind. Deer can only identify the scent of danger if it approaches them from upwind or at a crosswind. I train all D.I.E. hunters to be deer. You are not a human in deer country. So do not do what humans do. You are always an invisible deer when you are hunting with D.I.E. so you have to do what deer do. It is a lot easier and more fun too. D.I.E. hunters always enter their hunting area from upwind, or crosswind and upwind, and they never worry about deer smelling their scent as a human. They are scent free and the only scent a deer can smell is the scent of the invisible pair of breeding deer that lingers around the D.I.E. scrape and near the D.I.E. hunter's tree stand. Remember the wind is your friend when you are an invisible deer.

If it is not with the wind or into the wind it is crosswind.

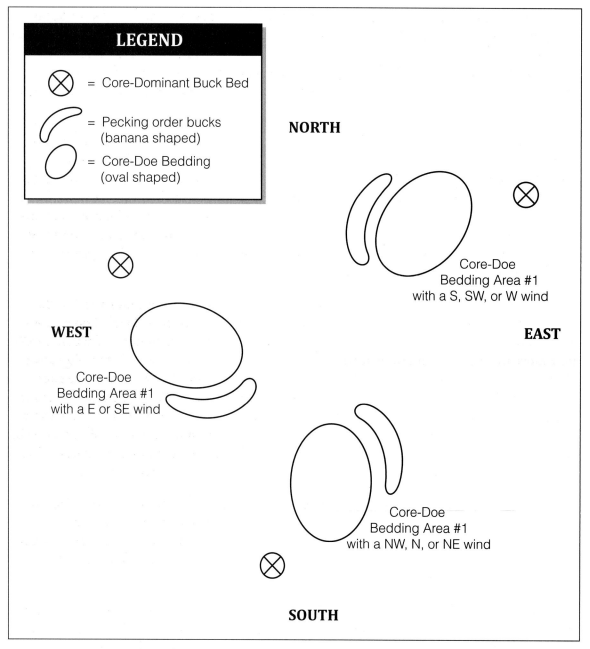

FIGURE 10 Notice how the pecking order bucks bed away from the dominant buck, on the opposite side of the core doe bedding areas.

I teach people one-on-one, how to use D.I.E. on their own property, and every single time I start scouting land with a new customer I start by teaching them about the three core-doe bedding areas that exist in each herd. You should be able to locate at least two of them on our scouting trip. They do not have to be (physically) located on your hunting parcel; you just have to know which direction the deer come from in the evening, that is where they bed during the day. Core-doe bedding areas are 200 to 500 yards apart (sometimes more). Most often, we are able to locate all three. Knowing where the does bed will tell you exactly where the dominant buck is bedded, and where all the pecking order bucks are bedding. Pecking order bucks bed on the opposite side of the core-doe bedding area, than the dominant buck beds on. Pecking order bucks bed in a banana shaped area (if you were to draw and outline around their beds). They are always the furthest upwind of all the deer in the herd. Sometimes they bed crosswind of the does that is why I draw a banana shaped object to represent pecking order buck bedding areas.

It is easy to see what your herd is doing, once you know where they are bedding. You should never hunt in a deer bedding area. You can go eighty yards or more upwind and ten or more yards crosswind and succeed with D.I.E. there, but never hunt inside a buck or doe bedding area. Deer know they are being hunted by a human if you go into their bedding areas or if you hunt closer than 80 away from them. You cannot get a dominant buck to hunt you at a D.I.E. scrape if he knows a human is hunting him. He will bust you every time. As long as you move 80 yards (upwind or crosswind) in at least one direction and then move off to one side a few yards, so your treestand and D.I.E. setup are not straight upwind of deer bedding areas, then you can succeed there with my system.

Does and bucks typically bed down with the wind to their backs or at a crosswind so they can turn their neck and head both upwind and downwind from the same bedded down position. If the wind direction changes while deer are bedded, all the deer in the herd will immediately move to keep the wind to their backs. Does walk straight into their beds and plop down. That way the wind and any bad weather elements like rain or snow hit the does in the back. Their thick hide and fat layer protect them the best in that position. When alerted or after getting up from a bedded position all deer turn and face into the wind, then they conduct a scent check. If there is no danger detected, they will move at a crosswind. If the scent of danger lurks upwind, they will sense it and move away in a crosswind direction, heading toward other deer or toward a place they know is safe for them to hide from the danger until it is gone.

Does choose where to establish *core-bedding areas* by focusing on providing a safe place for their fawns to rest, eat, and exercise during the day without being threatened by predators. During the rut, does spend most of each day in or around one of their core-doe bedding areas, which always have at least two escape routes, and usually are within a few hundred yards of a year round source of water.

Each day, does travel in groups from their core-bedding area to a feeding area. They usually start heading there within the last two hours of daylight. They travel a trail that goes directly from their bedding area to their food source. There is no stopping along the way except to check the wind for danger, which they do once every 30 to 50 yards or so. They always stop on the edge of a terrain change and make sure there is not any scent of danger in the air before proceeding on their way into the new type of terrain. They can get water from the moisture content of their food, and they stop briefly at water crossings to drink water when they are traveling. They feed all night and head back to their bedding areas early in the morning just as the sun is rising.

A dominant buck walks his crosswind corridor everyday during the rut in order to scent check all his herd does without having to go to them in daylight.

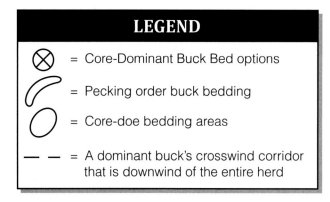

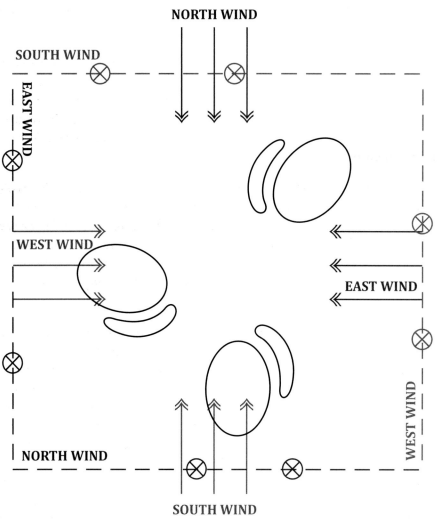

FIGURE 11 When the wind changes the does, fawns and yearling bucks move, the pecking order bucks move, and the dominant buck moves, so they all are bedding in their downwind core beds. The dominant buck has two bedding choices with each wind direction. Both of which allow him to remain downwind of his entire herd during daylight hours. A ⊗ represents his bed. He chooses the one that he is the safest in. From there he can scent check his entire herd, and he never has to endanger his life with hunters that hunt in deer bedding areas. He watches their every move.

Not all does bed in the same areas. They choose where to bed and then they follow the leader into their choice bedding area. On calm days there will be does bedded in the two furthest downwind core bedding areas, but on windy days they will group together and bed in the bedding area that offers them the best wind break.

If you look behind a doe when she first arrives at a food source it is a safe to say she came straight from her bedding area to get there, so she was bedded in the direction opposite the direction she is facing. That is important to know because with D.I.E. you should always try to set the D.I.E. scrape and your stand up in a position that is upwind and crosswind of a doe bedding area. A dominant buck will always bed downwind of his does, so their scent drifts on the wind current to him at his location, and he can identify which does are in heat or in estrus, right from the comfort of his own bed. He will walk back and forth downwind and crosswind of all three core doe bedding areas during the day.

When a storm approaches, the deer go to the bedding area that offers them the best protection from the elements, and from their predators. They stay on their feet until they know it is safe there. Sometimes on windy days, the deer do not bed for more than a few minutes at a time inside their bedding areas. Bedding for longer than one a half hour can be dangerous for a deer that cannot hear well, see well, or get scent well, which is the case for all deer in a storm with high-speed wind gusts.

You want the dominant buck to smell the scent of the lure you put out (of the two invisible breeding deer) when he makes his way to that core-doe bedding area searching for does in estrus. A dominant buck visits every core-doe bedding area in his territory at least once every three days during the rut. The D.I.E. scrape makes him into a daytime visitor of your stand site with the help of the scents and the scent dispensing equipment. He will come in as soon as he smells the scent of the single doe in estrus. There is no exception, as long as you never tell him that he is in the presence of a human.

You should know what a core-doe bedding area looks like and know not to walk through them if you intend to hunt with my system. The dominant buck knows that area, and he may even be there when you find it. He does not bed there; he is not allowed to. He only visits the core-doe bedding areas in search of does in estrus. Leave the deer alone when they are in their core bedding areas, and they will never expect you to be hunting them from upwind or crosswind of those sanctuaries. Deer expect hunters to come in from downwind, because traditional hunters do. D.I.E. hunters never approach a set up from downwind. Deer watch for danger downwind, and they scent check for danger upwind. You are scent free when you hunt with D.I.E. so it does not matter if they do a scent check on you, because you are going to pass the test. Does with fawns do not come into the area if you do it right. Only the dominant buck comes in and he is not going to do a scent check. He will be doing a *lip curl*, because the D.I.E. system brainwashed him into believing that you are a doe in estrus, and no real doe in estrus would ever hang around an area with danger lurking. He has no clue a human is there. The safer your herd feels when you are in the woods with them, the sooner the dominant buck approaches your stand site, so please do what I say and never go into a bedding area to hunt with my system. You will be busted 100% of the time if you do.

Does on the move

Whitetail does usually walk in a single-file line when they are on the move. In a doe line, you will usually see a yearling doe first, next is a fawn or two, then a mature doe, and then the pattern repeated. I have seen doe groups traveling from their food source back to bedding with as many as 18 deer in that line. Sometimes a yearling buck or two will be among the does. Sometimes pecking order bucks will be seen with does leaving a food source. If that is the case, the mature bucks will branch off when they get near heavier cover (unless a doe is in estrus). If a mature buck is in a doe line, he is not the dominant buck 100% of the time.

The dominant buck may trail a line of does at a distance but he will not join one. He will crisscross the trail the does are traveling on, and he will run whenever he is in the open, because does travel in mostly in open areas, and the dominant buck will not feel safe there during daylight. The most dominant buck will hold up in cover and then burst from it, headed to the bedding area where the does are going. I have witnessed this behavior only once; it was during the rut.

Heavily used deer trails—the well-beaten trails you see in the woods as you walk through your hunting area—are trails used primarily by does. Most of the time these trails have tracks going both directions on them. If you scout your hunting parcel and you find one that deer only travel one-way on, then you have found a near perfect place to set up my system. Do not overlook the confidence you will have on your hunt knowing the buck will always approach your D.I.E. set up from the direction that the tracks are coming from. A hunt with D.I.E. can be the easiest hunt of your life! Take advantage of the signs you see and analyze why the deer only go one-way on that trail, then set the D.I.E. system up, upwind of the trail.

Although you may see some bucks using heavily used trails, dominant bucks will not follow them if they are out in the open. If you see big deer tracks on them then you must be in a breeding area or near some *transitional cover*. Many bucks use heavily used *doe trails*. The dominant buck uses them but only for short distances at a time, and only in cover or near core breeding areas. Core breeding areas are where bucks make scrapes year after year, their hooves tear up the ground in the area because many deer congregate there before going to feed at night. Core breeding areas are easily found by looking at aerial photographs. Look for mixed cover, a heavily used deer trail, and dead trees. Bucks kill some trees when they rub them with their antlers, and when a heavily used deer trail runs through an area with new growth trees, those trees get rubbed by bucks and some die. After years of rubbing soft bark trees in the area there sometimes are no live trees, (less than 4 inches in diameter) left to rub within 10 yards of that trail. These areas are the predominant location for all breeder bucks to fight, breed, and stage. All deer will use a trail that leads through an area like this. Do not hunt inside a breeding area or within 80 yards of it, or you will be busted and the whole deer herd will know you are there. Position yourself 80 to 240 yards upwind and slightly crosswind of it. A set up like that has never failed me.

A dominant buck will cross heavily used doe trails, but rarely will walk a long distance on one. A dominant buck is smarter than any deer in his herd. He knows exposing himself to his enemies at any time (day or night) is too risky, so he will always stick to heavy cover until near dark, unless there is a doe in estrus nearby. He cannot resist going to a doe in estrus, no matter where she is or what time of day it is.

Does and fawns are not stealthy when they move from one place to another. They break quite a few branches under their hooves as they walk, and a hunter can very easily (just by listening) identify a line of does walking through an area. Sometimes a doe line is like a small train passing, as ten or more deer walk single file through the woods. They are headed to a food source or to a bedding area, and until they reach their destination—or until they are shot at—they will not break out of that line. When you see them disperse into separate areas on a field or headed into cover, you should know that they have reached their destination.

Lesser bucks will chase does in heat—a dominant buck will not!

Pecking order bucks, and yearling bucks (lesser bucks) will sometimes hang out with does during the rut whether the does are in heat or not, because they do not know any better. Most of these bucks have not been shot at before, and many of them will not live through their first experience of it. Mature pecking order bucks hang around close to one another throughout the rut. They keep constant tabs on one another, so they always know how they rank in the pecking order. Many times, I have witnessed multiple mature bucks chasing multiple does through the woods or across a field during the rut. Those bucks are pecking order bucks 100% of the time. A dominant buck will never chase does with another buck. He will always be 35 or more yards away from other bucks when a doe in estrus is with him. You are a doe in estrus from the first minute you step foot on the land on Day 1 of your hunt. That means no pecking order bucks and yearling bucks from that herd are allowed within 35 yards of the scent of the invisible doe in estrus. That is why I have never seen a pecking order buck near my D.I.E. set up. The dominant buck commands the area. He keeps his pecking order bucks in ranks under him and he makes them stay away from you when you are there. He is protecting his (invisible) doe in estrus from all other bucks. You seek only one buck, and there is only one buck that seeks you. Keep him guessing and he will fight over the right to breed with (the invisible doe in estrus) you.

When the rut begins, all mature bucks look for does in estrus to mate with, but only the most dominant buck has earned the right to breed with every doe in estrus inside his territory. The dominant buck will show up within 35 yards of you whether he is with a doe in estrus or not. He will bring a doe in estrus with him to your stand site if he is with one. He will never be walking along with a doe in heat. He avoids does in heat and lets the pecking order bucks and the yearling bucks chase them until they go into estrus. Then he comes out of hiding, scares the lesser bucks away and he and the doe mate.

I have never seen a dominant buck in the open in daylight (during the rut) without also seeing a doe in estrus in a stationary position (usually bedded down or feeding), in front of the buck. He will commit to going out in the open to a doe in daylight, but only if she is in estrus. Estrus is the period of time when she is willing to let any mature buck mate with her. I believe a doe is in estrus for only a day to a day and a half. A doe in heat will not willingly allow any buck to mount her. She will run from them until she goes into estrus, then she searches the dominant buck out because she wants him to breed with her. That is why non-dominant bucks chase does in heat, because does will not let bucks have sex with them while they are in heat. Heat is a two day period right before the one to two days that a doe is in estrus. I believe a doe's heat cycle is only four days in length, and estrus is the tail end of it.

Most heavily used doe trails meander through open areas on high ground or dry ground. A dominant buck will always stick to heavy cover to hide himself during daylight, whether traveling 10 yards for a drink of water or traveling half a mile to get away from a hunter who shot at him. A dominant buck only moves for a reason, and when he does he keeps to heavy cover or moves after dark. The only things on earth that will bring him from cover in daylight include a D.I.E. set up, a doe in estrus, or a challenging buck with a doe in estrus.

Fawns

A whitetail deer's senses are very keen. A deer relies on its senses to survive. Buck and doe fawns are born with sharp senses, but they need to learn how to use them, before heading out on their own. Does teach fawns how their senses work, but fawns are far from experts at identifying potentially dangerous situations all by themselves. Fawns rely on their mothers to teach them to become adults, to feed them, and to protect them from all types of danger. For the first three months of their lives they know only the basics, they lack the skills needed to elude predators, and many of them get killed by one before they ever get a chance to mature.

Buck fawns leave their mother's side during their first winter. They are cast away by their mothers when the rut starts (in mid October here in Wisconsin). They wander off and try to make friends with mature pecking order bucks. Mature bucks do not want anything to do with buck fawns, so the fawns are sent back to their mothers. After their mother has mated and is no longer in estrus she will allow her buck fawn(s) to move back into the doe bedding area with her and remain living there until the rut starts the following year. Buck fawns do not take part in the rut. They do not get a chance to breed and I have never seen a buck fawn displaying any signs a mature breeder buck displays during the rut.

Doe fawns stay with their mother's family group until they are mature, then they are free to go anywhere they want to. Some will stay in that area forever, but others will choose to leave. When a buck fawn is entering his second rut, he is a yearling buck. Yearling bucks are cast out by their mothers in mid-October just like buck fawns are, but yearling bucks cannot go back to their mothers after the rut. She refuses to take care of them again. They become wanderers, and outcasts. Dominant bucks will not allow any yearling bucks or fawns to follow them.

Buck fawns do not understand how to sense danger, because they do not have much experience avoiding dangerous situations. Many young bucks fall to hunters because of their inexperience with survival techniques. I consider buck fawns and yearling bucks to be young and dumb, and compared to the most dominant buck, they certainly are. Up until I invented D.I.E., yearling bucks were all I could count on seeing within 35 yards of my stand. Now I never see one. The dominant buck will not allow them to come near him when he is with a doe in estrus, or when he is bedded, and he is convinced that bedding downwind a D.I.E. scrape will bring the invisible doe in estrus to him. You will not let him down will you.

Yearling bucks

Yearling bucks are 1 ½ years old; they usually have antlers with 2 to 8 points. In areas where deer get more than the average amount of minerals in their diet, some may have even more than 8 points as yearlings, but I have never seen that.

In Wisconsin, a buck with antlers at least 3 inches long is considered by the state DNR (Department of Natural Resources) to be an antlered buck, and a buck with antlers less than 3 inches long is considered an "antlerless" deer. Yearling bucks can breed, but I do not believe they are in the pecking order and I certainly do not believe they are capable of controlling a herd. In order to be in the pecking order they have to be able to win fights with other bucks their own age as well as older bucks, and they have to be able to hold down territory. I think it is impossible for a yearling buck to be the most dominant, because he would be easily beat by the first mature buck that came along.

Yearling bucks seek a "Big Brother"

Yearling bucks are cast away from their mothers during the month of October, right before the rut starts. They are not part of the pecking order, and cannot become part of it until they have survived two winters. Yearling bucks are loners; they wander the herd's stomping grounds looking for a place they can fit in. Some yearling bucks meet a high-ranking pecking order buck and they are lucky enough to get an "apprenticeship" with the mature breeder buck. I call these yearling bucks "satellite bucks" because they follow the mature buck around the territory, watching and learning from him how to survive. The satellite buck orbits the mature buck constantly, and learns what breeding is, what fighting is, and what being dominant means to a mature buck. If they both survive the rut, the deer-hunting season, their predators, and the winter elements, then they will still be hanging around together the following spring, summer, fall, and winter. In the next rut, the yearling buck will no longer be a yearling. He will become a member of the pecking order and hold rank. If all the bucks ranking higher than him are harvested by hunters or killed by other predators, he could become the most dominant buck in the area that year. That would be when he turned 2 ½ years old. It happens, but it is more likely that the king of the herd you are hunting is 3 ½ years old or older. Most of the dominant bucks I have seen were at least 4 ½ years old, based on their massive antlers and heavy (200 or more pound) body weight.

Yearling bucks are not in the pecking order.

Yearling bucks are not members of the pecking order

Buck fawns and yearling bucks are still not mature enough to hold territory of their own, so they are not threats to any mature buck, including dominant bucks and monster bucks. They do not hold rank in the pecking order and they cannot possibly beat a breeder buck in a fight. Yearling bucks group together in their own bachelor buck groups in the summer. In their first two ruts, they are not leaders within the herd. They are always followers.

Yearling bucks get the urge to mate, and during the rut, they do mount does and attempt to breed, but I am not sure if anything comes of it. Any mature buck that witnesses a yearling buck mounting a doe in estrus will confront that yearling buck and run him away from the doe. Then the mature buck will breed the doe.

Yearling bucks and buck fawns, however, often fight or spar with other bucks their own age for fun. I do not believe that yearling bucks or buck fawns have a rank in the pecking order. The pecking order only includes mature breeder bucks from the same herd and the dominant buck is the highest-ranking pecking order buck.

Yearling bucks and lesser ranked bucks must show subordination

I once witnessed a yearling buck licking the neck of a full-bodied decoy I was using. I had an 8-point real rack of antlers and a real tail on a *Carry-Lite* buck decoy. The young buck was missing half of his rack; he had 4 points on one side of his antlers, and nothing on the other. This buck came out on a soybean field jumping around and acting crazy (shaking his head left and right) while he ran past a huge 12-pointer that was feeding in the field 80 yards in front of me. That was the herd's king.

The yearling buck did not hold a rank in the pecking order. He ran right up to my decoy, circled around it, stood parallel to it, and started licking its neck. He did not look eye-to-eye with the 12-pointer, and he did not look at my 8-point buck decoy face-to-face either. I was watching the big buck and ignoring the yearling when I heard what sounded like a paintbrush going up and down on vinyl siding. I looked down. To my amazement, that yearling was grooming the decoy. I wish I had a camera. The yearling was showing subordination to the decoy, which had a bigger body and rack of antlers than he did.

All bucks in the pecking order (under the most dominant buck) show subordination to the bucks that rank above them. It is normal behavior for a mature pecking order buck to look away from the eyes of a higher-ranking buck as a show of respect for his position. Bucks that behave this way are content in their rank and bucks acting the alternate way (looking into the eyes of a higher-ranking buck) are asking for a head-to-head fight. That is how bucks challenge each other for does, for rank, or for territory. They stare one another down, and if one does not back down, a fight will occur. It was amazing to see that the immature buck fell for the decoy trick but the king of deer knew the decoy could not threaten him because the rack I had on it was much smaller than his own. I learned a lot about buck behavior that day.

Mature breeder bucks

All mature bucks want to breed during the rut, but not all of them will get a chance to. Nevertheless, I call all mature bucks "breeder bucks", because they are capable of breeding. Almost every mature breeder buck will roam out of his home territory at least one time during the rut, but of course some bucks stay at home through the entire rut. The most dominant buck is a mature breeder buck.

Whitetail bucks are herd animals and they have an established pecking order. Every buck ranked beneath the dominant buck envies him and wants to run the dominant buck's territory someday. During the rut, breeder bucks will not fight every other buck they meet. They will posture toward one another and have stand-offs, but they will not always fight. Remember, each herd has an established pecking order. During the rut, bucks fight only over territory, a doe in estrus, or over a doe that is nearing estrus. Breeder bucks fight to establish dominance in the ranks and outside of it. A non-dominant breeder buck will pursue any doe in estrus that he can find during the rut. If the doe is receptive to him, then he will breed with her, and if she is not receptive (in estrus) yet, he will follow her around until she is in estrus—or he will move on to another doe in heat that is nearing estrus. Either way, a mature buck will only spend two or three days with any doe during the rut. Dominant bucks will not chase does in heat out in open areas during the day, but they will chase and stay with any doe in estrus, even if she is out in the open.

Pecking order bucks tend to bed 40 to 80 yards apart from one another on dry ground usually in thickets or on the outside edges of marshes where they have an easy route to the doe bedding areas. Unlike dominant bucks, swamp bucks and monster bucks (which prefer to bed on the wet end of a swamp for their safety), pecking order bucks bed on the outside edges of heavy cover or alongside a water source. I think they do it so they can escape any threat, and avoid being in the way of the dominant buck. Pecking order bucks try to avoid the dominant buck whenever possible. He is on a mission when he is on the move, and they know better than to mess with him. Once he has a doe in estrus with him, then the pecking order bucks go into a frenzy chasing all the does in heat they can find. They will get to breed with some of those does because the dominant buck can only breed and remain with one or two does at a time. Twin does go into estrus at the same time and I witnessed a 12-point monster buck *tending* a pair of does in the same brush line for three days straight. That monster buck came in on Day 4 to my D.I.E. set up. He would not leave those two does on Day 2 or Day 3, because they were both in estrus and allowing him to breed with them. On Day 4, he came over to see what was going on at my D.I.E. scrape. I think those does went out of estrus then, but I am only speculating.

Intruder bucks

I learned while filming whitetails that any intruder buck that enters the home territory of a dominant buck has to do one of two things to be allowed to stay overnight in his territory:

1. The intruder buck can stay and join the herd's ranks under the dominant buck if he yields to the dominant buck by showing subordination to him, he acknowledges a rank of a lesser buck, and he always avoids making direct eye contact with the dominant buck.

2. He can choose to stand and fight the dominant buck to win the highest rank in the herd. If a intruder buck defeats the dominant buck, then the intruder buck becomes the new dominant buck. He then owns the territory, and he is in command of the pecking order bucks unless one of them beats him in a fight. His first task is to run the formerly dominant buck out of the territory immediately. Dominance can change in a minute.

If the intruder buck does not check into ranks, or challenge the dominant buck to a fight, then the dominant buck will search for the intruder until he finds him. He intends to run the intruder out, but until he can locate the intruder, his focus is on getting a glimpse of how big the intruder's rack is. The dominant buck will not run from any intruder's challenge but he has to know how big an intruder buck's body and rack of antlers are before he can make a decision on how to handle his challenge. I know this is a fact in the hierarchy of every herd's pecking order, it is their code of conduct, and the bucks stick to it as if it was life or death. My behavior at the D.I.E. scrape and while putting lure out, resembles the behavior of a monster intruder buck moving into the area to challenge the most dominant buck's dominance there. The dominant buck is led to believe I must be a monster buck that is smarter than he is, otherwise I would not be able to avoid meeting him every time he approaches the scrape. The dominant buck wants me to check into ranks or come out to fight him. He takes back the scrape I make at the D.I.E. set up, because he has to in order to regain control of the herd in that area. He will hunt me at the scrape for two reasons, and one of them is that I am acting insubordinate to him. That is never allowed by any dominant buck. You can count on him showing up just to deal with that, but I want to be sure that he is not distracted so I give him a second reason. I tell him that a doe in estrus is with this (invisible) monster buck. Now he cannot ignore the scrape until the (invisible) doe in estrus is bred, and he is determined to be the one to do it.

All ranked bucks show respect to the dominant buck

Within the pecking order, only one-buck law is upheld by all the breeder bucks. **No buck (in or out of the ranks) shall ever look directly into the eyes of a more dominant or higher ranking buck.** When a buck stares at another buck, he is challenging the buck he is staring at to a fight. They will fight for dominance! Whatever status the losing buck had is lost to the winning buck in an instant. If the challenger is taking on the most dominant buck, he must be willing to fight to the death in order to become king of the herd, because the dominant buck will not give up in any fight until he has won it, he is very exhausted and cannot go on, he is badly wounded, or he dies.

Dominant bucks will never confront a challenging buck by advancing toward him by more than a few feet. Dominant bucks hold their ground and make the challenger bring the fight to them. If the challenger does not approach the dominant buck, then the dominant buck will lower his head and grunt or growl toward the challenger. He will posture and rake brush, or make a scrape with a rub behind it right then and there as if to tell the challenger that he is the king of the herd, and the challenger should leave the way he came. When you hunt with D.I.E., you will experience the dominant buck doing some of those things, on almost every hunt. The king is in charge and he lets you know it. Never talk to him when he is calling out to the invisible buck and doe. Invisible deer are not ever there. Only the scent of them is, so do not make any sounds when he is vocalizing. Just get ready for a close shot opportunity because you are only seconds or minutes away from one when you hear the buck calling to the two invisible deer. Do not call or rattle. Trust me. Wait him out and he will come in close to look for those two deer, which he will always believe are upwind of the scrape. Grunt one time to him when he is in the open and he will stop in his tracks offering you a clear (standing) shot opportunity.

The most dominant buck—how to identify him

The most dominant buck is the king of a whitetail deer herd. Being the most dominant has its privileges. Did you ever wonder what a dominant buck thinks about all throughout his life, what his goals are, or what gives him the will to survive? I think you should know the behavioral traits of a dominant buck before you go out to meet him, so I am going to go into detail about the behavioral characteristics of the most dominant buck in the herd.

Many factors determine whether a buck will become dominant buck or not. Some of those factors are his age, his demeanor, his attitude, his body weight, and the overall size of his antlers. A dominant buck has to have a large body size or a massive rack in order to have the ability to command the attention of all the other deer in the herd, but most dominant bucks rank at the top in both of those categories.

A dominant buck has to meet the following criteria:

He is always mature. A dominant buck must be at least 2 ½ years old. Most dominant bucks are at least 3 ½ years old.

He establishes, maintains, and defends his territory. Every time a buck becomes the most dominant, he is replacing the previous one. When dominance changes, the new dominant buck moves into the three bedding areas of the previous dominant buck, and lives there like the king before him did. The preferred hiding places of a dominant buck are special. They are away from the pecking order buck's bedding area by at least a few hundred yards. He has one bed that allows him to be downwind of all of the other deer in the herd, no matter which way the wind is coming from that day. When the wind switches, the buck moves with the wind.

Dominant bucks mark the boundaries of their territory by making rubs on trees that are 2-inches or larger in diameter. Territorial rubs are always shredded, and the larger the tree trunk the older the buck. When you see an 8-inch or larger (diameter) tree rubbed up, it is the work of a monster buck. Monster bucks also rub small brush and saplings, so it is tough to tell which buck was rubbing brush or saplings, but you can always tell that it was either the dominant buck or a monster buck rubbing a tree that is 2 inches in diameter or larger (if the rub is shredded). Dominant bucks also mark their staging areas, the outside edges of their bedding areas, and their primary (core) breeding areas with rubs. They only make scrapes where does frequent.

When a dominant buck makes a territorial marker (a shredded rub), he always shreds the bark so other bucks know the rub was made by the king. Challenging bucks sometimes rub trees and leave them in a shredded state. If the dominant buck locates a shredded rub that he did not make he will immediately rub the same tree with his antlers and tear the bark off it all the way around the trunk. When you see a tree rub that is smooth all the way around (not shredded) it means that a challenger buck made a territorial rub inside the dominant buck's territory and the dominant buck found it, took it over, and now owns it.

Any buck that leaves his own territory and crosses into a dominant buck's territory becomes an intruder buck instantly; he remains an intruder buck until he returns to his own territory. If a dominant buck leaves his territory and a monster intruder buck (moves in) while he is away, when the dominant buck returns, the two bucks will likely fight to determine which buck will be king there. If the new dominant buck has a bigger rack, the old dominant buck could give up the herd and retire to a swamp to live as a *neutral buck* if he chooses. If not the returning buck will challenge the new dominant buck to a fight for dominance, to regain his position as king.

A dominant buck lives inside his home territory boundaries most of the year. He will not leave unless his life is in danger or if he is looking for a doe in estrus and there are not any in his own territory. The dominant buck will grow old in his territory as long as he is able to elude hunters, wolves, bears, and cougars. In most cases, he will not give his territory up to another buck without losing a hard-fought battle first.

There are three core-doe bedding areas inside every dominant buck's territory. During the rut, the does will remain in the dominant buck's territory until they are bred, unless the dominant buck is away. If a doe comes into estrus in a dominant buck's home territory and he is nowhere to be found—because he is either dead or he is out roaming other areas looking for does in estrus—she will roam into another dominant buck's territory looking for any mature buck to mate with her. Does have freedom to come and go in and out of a dominant buck's territory all year round.

He shows no fear during the rut. During the rut, a dominant buck is not afraid of anything: not other deer, not predators, and not hunters either. He is smart and he is a survivor. He will go where he pleases as long as he does not sense any danger around him.

He accepts any intruder buck's challenge. A dominant buck will never back down or refuse to show up when he is challenged by an intruder buck. He has to show up and be willing to fight in order to remain being the most dominant in the herd.

He wins all his fights. A dominant buck must win all his fights with other bucks to remain being dominant. When bucks fight the loser instantly loses everything he has. Dominant bucks fight to establish dominance. Dominant bucks fight only when they have to, not just for fun.

They fight for three reasons:
- The right to breed with a doe in estrus.
- The right to a command a piece of territory.
- The right to eat or drink where and when they want to.

He maintains his health and actively breeds. If he does not mate or has trouble keeping does in estrus to himself he will not be dominant very long. A healthy buck in his prime years (3 ½ to 6 ½ years old) can maintain a herd well, and can keep the lesser bucks in line.

Which buck is the most dominant can change by the minute during the rut. So do not get it in your head that you think you know which buck is the most dominant, because of the size of his rack, or the number of points that are on it. Those things do not determine dominance. It is up to the deer herd to decide which buck is their king. Once one or more deer find your D.I.E. set up, they inform the king of its existence. He will make sure he goes over there to meet you within the four days of your hunt. Most likely you will meet him on Day 1 or Day 2, but if not it will be Day 3 or Day 4. Know that any mature buck that comes within 35 yards of you is the most dominant buck in the herd at that place and at that time. The first buck that comes in is the king of the herd 100% of the time. I do not care if you shoot him or not.

It is important that you know that waiting for a bigger buck, is not part of the D.I.E. system. The system succeeds when a 2 ½ or older buck comes in. If you see more bucks than that one, it is a bonus. For me on 11 hunts I only saw multiple monster bucks one time, on my 2009 bow hunt, but that was because I missed my shot at the king early in the morning. The first buck in had the biggest rack of antlers of the three bucks. I attempted to shoot him while he stood 8 feet away from me but I aimed too high and my arrow grazed his back. He walked away never knowing I was there or that he had been shot. It was Day 3 of my hunt and he still wanted the doe in estrus, so I decided to stay there to wait for him to come back, or to see what other bucks might come in. The dominant 10-pointer had a rack that would have scored over 180 inches. It was a monster dominant buck. He did not know I was there as a human, because I never told him. I was still invisible to him even after the shot.

If you do not like the size of the dominant buck, when you see him, then I think you should pull your stand and move to a new area, at least a quarter mile away, and set it up there with new bottles of lure. That way you might be hunting a different dominant buck from a different herd, and his rack may be more appealing to you—just a thought!

A dominant buck's territory

The size of a dominant buck's territory depends upon how many bucks are ranked in his pecking order and how many does he has living inside his territorial boundaries. My guess is that the average dominant buck here in Wisconsin has a core home territory of one-half mile square to three-quarters of a mile square. I have never hunted deer in any other state or country so I will not guess the size of a dominant buck's territory in those places. Once I go on tour and meet hunters across the country, I will learn by scouting with them, how much acreage a dominant buck controls in other parts of the continent. You should know that the deer herd in your hunting area might consist of multiple deer herds. Each dominant buck has his own herd of deer. When a person sets up one tree stand and hunts exclusively from it, they are only hunting in one herd's territory. The deer that live in the neighboring herd do not frequent that stand site normally, but after a D.I.E. scrape and rub are installed, the breeder bucks will show up looking for the doe.

Because each dominant buck has a particular home territory, he has to stay there to maintain his status as king. The older a buck gets, the more likely he is to stay in his own territory during the entire rut. A dominant buck in his prime years (3 ½, 4 ½, 5 ½, or 6 ½) will breed with as many does as he can inside his own territory and then he will leave the safety his home territory provides, and roam into another dominant buck's home territory in search of more does in estrus. He fears nothing, so he goes where he wants, whenever he wants. I know that a dominant buck will travel over 5 miles in one direction just for a chance to mate with a doe in estrus. He will return within three days so he can walk his territorial boundaries, refreshing his rubs, so all the deer in the area know he is still their king.

Dominant buck beds

Dominant bucks, monster bucks and swamp bucks all bed in the same type of areas. I was able to locate three separate core beds that one dominant buck favored back in 1992. I went back to the same woodlot in April 2011 and discovered that the current king of the herd is using the same three beds that the king used in 1992 (19 years earlier). Deer territories do not change as drastically in two decades as our own neighborhoods do. Does will always bed where they did the year before, pecking order bucks, and the dominant buck too, granted the land still offers the deer ample cover, water, food, and the ability to breed successfully there.

Dominant bucks have three core bedding areas just as does do, and they choose which one to occupy each day depending on the weather and the direction of the wind. One bedding area is in a swamp or lowland area. He goes there on windy days or when he is feeling pressured by hunters. Another bed is located on a vantage point in loose cover, on the edge of wet ground and near heavy cover. This bed will be very shaded, offering the buck a place to hide during stormy weather, and the last one is usually high up on a hill overlooking hundreds of yards of grazing area, and it is from that bed that the buck will keep track of what his herd is doing on days with a calm wind. If the terrain you are analyzing is not hilly, then use the wind to find the dominant buck's core bedding areas. He has one core bed, on the downwind side of all the other deer bedding areas in the herd, no matter which direction the wind is coming from.

During daylight hours of the Wisconsin deer season (both gun & bow); the dominant buck will be in or around one of the core doe bedding areas, alone or with a doe in estrus as a companion. That is because the rut is on and he is the primary breeder buck in the herd. If the area is heavily hunted then they will not be moving around except to mate and to drink water, feeding during daylight only while they make their way to the water source. If it is not a pressured hunting area then the dominant buck will hang out with a doe in estrus in an open area inside a woodlot or along a field edge (in a core breeding area), without fear of being seen by a hunter.

Dominant bucks and monster bucks love to bed down on the wettest end of a cattail marsh or a swamp. I have found through my research that when a dominant buck positions himself in his primary bed (also known as a core dominant buck bed), he positions himself in tall cattail grass that is 6 feet high or higher, and his bed location will be within 40 yards of the outside edge of the swamp in most cases. Big whitetail bucks love to bed in water. I find many core buck beds with 1-2 inches of water in them. These beds are in areas where bucks can stay concealed and avoid contact with humans, and all their other predators 24 hours a day 7 days a week.

Most core dominant buck beds are 5 to 6 feet around and they do not have any distinctive trails leading to or coming from them. A dominant buck's core bedding area is considered his home turf. If you find one or more of these beds in a lowland or swampy area, you are in the

Dominant buck bed in cattail grass appeared during my 2009 Wisconsin bow hunt. The buck moved in and bedded 35 yards downwind of my D.I.E. scrape. His bed was 15 yards downwind of my stand. See the impression in lower right corner, under green spruce tree.

Close up of a dominant buck's core bed. He made this bed during my waiting period on a D.I.E. hunt. He moved in and bedded 35 yards downwind of the scrape to hunt me.

The dominant buck beds downwind and crosswind of his does. You have to look for his (3) beds to find them. The arrow points to the dominant buck's bed.

This is a close up of the dominant buck's body impression in the bed under the pine tree in the previous photo

midst of greatness. Dominant bucks and monster bucks gallop (jump) into their beds, and likewise they jump out of them when leaving the area. Most often, they jump three times and then plop down into the grass. That allows them to leave very little sign for a human or a predator to discover, and more often than not, we walk right by one of their beds never realizing that a huge buck was bedded there.

The only core dominant buck beds I have found outside of wet areas were on vantage points. A dominant buck will often choose a bed where he has a view of more than 100 yards. A vantage point that is downwind of the intersection of two or more heavily used deer trails lets a whitetail buck keep tabs on his herd. The buck watches the other deer as they cross a field or another semi-open area. Those trails are main travel ways that does, fawns, and lesser bucks use every day. There is no better place for a dominant buck to be!

A vantage point core bed usually is on a hillside with heavy cover, but it can be located any place that has vegetation that is a foot or two higher than the surrounding area. Re-growth timber offers good spots for a dominant buck to hide. New trees are close together and less than 2" in diameter. They are thick enough to keep a buck hidden from predators, yet easy for him to see through. A south-facing slope or a high point above the junction of two or more trails heading into and out of doe bedding, are good locations for a vantage point core bed. Remember he always beds downwind.

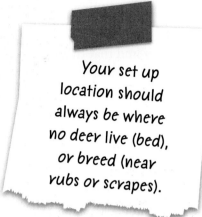

I have also seen vantage point buck beds in alfalfa fields. A buck in short cover will lay his head down on the ground and try not to be seen by passersby. Finding a big-racked buck in one of these beds is easy; just look for his antlers to move around above the height of the crops in the field. Bucks mostly use these beds during July, August, and September, before the rut begins. Once the field is cut, the bed will be no more.

You cannot find a core dominant buck bed on every single property, but when you do find one, be sure to memorize its location, and if possible set up the DOMINANCE IS EVERYTHING system 80 to 240 yards upwind of it and 80 yards off to one side (crosswind of it).

In Figure 12, the wind is coming from the Northwest, and is traveling Southeast. The dominant buck in this herd would be bedded in the wet end of the swamp (in this case it is the West end). Your set up location should always be where no deer live (bed), or breed (near rubs or scrapes). That place is always upwind and crosswind of the herd's bedding areas.

Anytime I locate a swamp on my scouting trip I walk around the upwind side of it in order to read the mature buck and doe sign there. You can tell if the dominant buck lives in the swamp by following his tracks (splayed front hooves). He will enter it on the dry end and bed just downwind of the X-pattern of deer trails. His tracks never go all the way through it. The ground is not dry where he beds, it will be always be wet. I do not walk on the wet end of the swamp because I do not want to tell the buck I am a human and that I will be back. I know dominant bucks and they all would live in a swamp if they had the chance.

If you are like me you are hunting for monster bucks. I find that all monster bucks live in swamps, so I hunt upwind and crosswind of the swamp with the biggest buck tracks going into it. I'll teach you how to set up in relation to a dominant buck's core bed in a swamp, so you can easily get his attention with the D.I.E. system, but take into account that you have to do this exactly as I instruct you to in order for you to be in the same place I would be. I succeed because I trust the system, you will succeed if you trust me.

Scout your land, looking for lowland or a swamp. If you find one then analyze it to determine if you can set up D.I.E. upwind and crosswind of its dry end. If so, then scout the area upwind and crosswind (going away from the wet end) and try to find the X-pattern of deer trails inside it. Sketch what you find on a pad of paper so you can remember it. Walk around the swamp on the upwind side (the side that will be upwind when you plan to hunt that area), and find a deer trail that comes out of the swamp and heads upwind and crosswind, in the direction you parked you vehicle or where you entered the area.

Once you find that trail stand still there with your back toward the the upwind edge of the dry end of the swamp and look upwind and crosswind of that spot for a stand site. Start walking, go 80 or more yards on that trail. If you have the option to walk further than 80 yards, do it. You do not have to stay on the deer trail. Try to get upwind out of sight of the buck's favorite bedding area. You are not hoping for a glimpse of the dominant buck, you are counting on a wide open shot opportunity at him within 35 yards of your stand. The further you go away from his bed and the bedding areas of the rest of the herd, the better your chance is that he will be the only buck you will see. That is what you should want. Seeing more than one buck is common when you set up near deer bedding areas, and setting up near bedding is not advised, it can get you busted. I never hunt within 80 yards of any deer beds.

You need to convince him that you are a stealthy monster buck that has been able to avoid meeting him at the D.I.E. scrape because you keep coming in on his upwind side during daylight. By hunting upwind of him and off to one side you are making it known that you are not interested in meeting him. He figures that out very quickly and he goes on a mission to meet with you where you are (at the D.I.E. scrape).

The most amazing D.I.E. hunts I have been on, took place from a portable tree stand that I set up 300 or more yards upwind and crosswind of the active herd. Seeing other deer is not

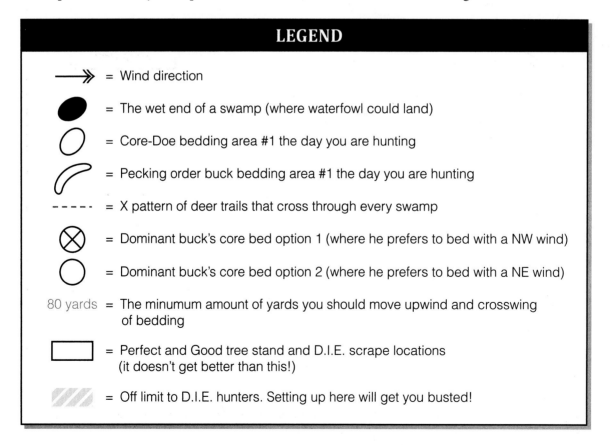

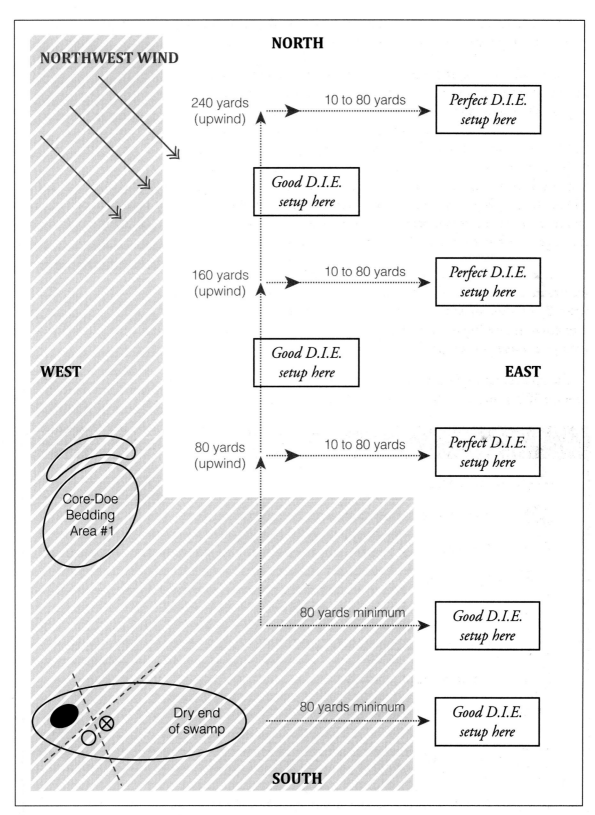

FIGURE 12 If you have the opportunity to hunt upwind or crosswind of a swamp that bucks bed in, you will see monster bucks on over 50% of your D.I.E. hunts (like I do).

normal for me on a D.I.E. hunt. In my experience, the king of the herd always comes in alone. It is just him and me.

Do not crowd the buck. Whether you are gun hunting or bow hunting does not matter here, what matters is that you stay at least 80 yards upwind or crosswind of the closest edge of the buck's bedding cover. If you go closer to it than that he will detect your presence there (as a human) and you will be busted before you get in your stand to hunt on Day 1. When I am scouting for a D.I.E. hunt and I find a core dominant buck bed, I immediately look for a tree to sit in that is at least 80 yards upwind of the grass the buck beds down in, and at least 60 yards off to one side of his bed. When he is in his bed he cannot see me, and when he is coming out of the grass on his way to my D.I.E. scrape there is plenty of room between him and me. He needs a wide-open area to approach from and then some staging cover to hold up in before coming all the way in. One patch of brush 5 yards wide and 3 or more yards deep will be adequate staging cover for the buck, but be sure you have staging cover like that in at least three directions around you.

Only giving the buck staging cover on one side of your D.I.E. scrape and rub, can get you busted. As you know the wind direction can change in an instant, and the dominant buck is smart enough to know that he may be in danger if he does not conduct a thorough scent check of the area from a downwind staging area before coming into an open area that he is not familiar. He will always stage straight downwind of the scrape or of your stand before making his final approach out in the open to the scrape. A mature buck can stand still for over 45 minutes without ever taking a step. Be patient when the buck is in his staging cover, he will come when he is ready, do not get nervous, just give him the time he needs to know it is safe and he will be yours for the taking.

When you scout, make sure you choose a set up location that offers staging cover on at least two sides of the rubbed tree, three or four sides are even better. That way no matter which direction the wind is coming from when you are hunting you are assured that the dominant buck will hold up in whichever piece of cover happens to be downwind of the scrape at the time.

Once you find a good tree to sit in you need to make sure there is a live tree within 35 yards of it that has what it takes to build a D.I.E. scrape and rub. Remember there has to be a licking branch hanging over the scrape 5 to 7 feet off the ground. If you look for that type of scenario on your property, you may find it, but if you never look for it, how do you know that it does not exist. That would be a perfect set up because it will allow him to feel comfortable and look over the area on his approach.

Dominant bucks prefer to walk into an area they can see into, but prior to going out into the open they will always stop in some light staging cover. From there they attempt to view the terrain ahead of them, looking for other deer in the area as well as any predators or other dangers that may be waiting to ambush them in the clearing ahead. You need to make sure the rub on the tree behind the D.I.E. scrape cannot be seen by the buck if he is bedded in the staging cover, or if he could see it that there is ample cover (5 to 10 yards behind the scrape) that is thick enough to hide a bedded down doe. Because the wind is

bound to change direction while you are on a D.I.E. hunt, you need to make sure there is ample cover within 5 or 10 yards of the scrape on at least 3 sides of it. That way the buck will believe the doe he seeks is bedded upwind or crosswind of the D.I.E. scrape no matter what direction the wind is coming from that day.

Dominant bucks need to be able to see ahead of themselves 30 yards or more in order to feel comfortable. They will not rush into an area that is thick with cover. They just will not! You have to make this set up seem real to him, and make him comfortable there, without letting him bed in his normal bedding area. You have to pull him out of his core bedding and breeding area and make him come to you upwind and crosswind of it. You can do that if you follow my set up instructions. Then you will not have to worry about the buck busting you on the way in.

Dominant bucks show dominance 365 days a year

Dominant bucks always do things in a big way. When they enter an area where other deer are present, they always make a noisy entrance and they posture and show off their large rack of antlers. A dominant buck's neck will be massive and his hair may be standing on end. These are all signs of aggression. Dominant bucks are not friendly toward other bucks during the rut. They will be nice to the does but any mature buck is a threat to them and they will try to run all intruder bucks out of the area, when a doe in estrus is nearby.

Whenever a dominant buck encounters lesser ranked bucks, the lesser bucks must show subordination to him, or he will put them in their place immediately. The dominant buck will not tolerate any insubordination from lesser bucks in his herd. All pecking order bucks know their rank in September before the rut starts. Any bucks competing for the same rank will fight when they meet and the winner then ranks one-step higher in the pecking order than the loser. All pecking order bucks must stay away from the dominant buck or he will address their intrusion into his home territory with a show of dominance. A dominant buck will not take the threats made by intruder bucks lightly. You are an intruder buck to him right from the start, because you made a dominant buck's primary breeding scrape and rub inside his territory. He is angry with you for trying to take over a piece of his territory, and he wants nothing more than to put a stop to your coming back into the area!

Dominant whitetail bucks live inside their home territories, but of course, you already knew that. What many hunters do not know is where the dominant buck beds down, where he gets his water, when he likes to travel, how he marks his territory, why he makes rubs and scrapes, and why he is so elusive that they have never seen him before. I have taken understanding dominant buck behavior to a completely new level. I will take you a step closer to the buck, by putting you in a mindset that allows you to relate to him and his daily needs during the rut. I will show you all you need to know about the one buck that will relentlessly be hunting for you when you hunt with DOMINANCE IS EVERYTHING.

All dominant bucks live the same type of lifestyle no matter where they live on our continent. No matter what the terrain is where you hunt whitetails, there is a dominant buck of each deer herd at any given moment. Outside of the rut, my system will not work for attracting the buck because it plays mind games with the boss buck when he is actively breeding, and he is not actively breeding outside of the rut.

Breeding

During the rut, a dominant buck wants to survive, and he wants to breed with as many does as he can find. Achieving dominance in his herd has given that buck the earned right to breed all the does in his own territory. No other buck in the herd has that privilege. A lesser buck does not have a right to maintain a territorial scrape in the dominant buck's territory. Territorial scrapes are scrapes with a rub on a tree behind the pawed up ground. We call it a scrape because the ground is scraped up by the buck's front hooves as he digs down to the dirt. Lesser bucks will make scrapes, but they are not allowed to make any with rubs behind them. If they do, then they are trying to take that piece of real estate that the scrape and rub are situated on, away from the dominant buck. If the dominant buck is nearby, and he discovers any scrapes made in his territory with rubs behind them he will take them over immediately, by rubbing the tree (sometimes all the way around). He also urinates on the ground in the scrape and he nibbles off the end of a branch that over hangs the scrape. It is called a licking branch. He rubs his own scent on that branch from secretions around his eyes. A dominant buck will not allow any other buck to control even one foot of his territory nor will he tolerate any buck being insubordinate in his territory at any time.

Fighting

Once a buck is dominant, he has to win all his battles—against challengers from his own herd and against intruder bucks from other herds—to maintain his dominance. He will not give up his rank without a fight, sometimes to the death. Dominant bucks have proven fighting records, and sometimes—or maybe even always—they think that they are invincible.

Monster bucks

A monster buck has lived at least 3 ½ years, and he has a massive rack of antlers. You will know a monster buck when you see one. The body size and rack mass is massive on a monster buck. Occasionally a monster buck may have a smaller-than-average body, but he will always have a huge rack. I do not believe that all monster bucks hold territory. Sometimes a dominant buck will allow a monster buck to bed near him. They will rely on one another's skills to help them both survive the rut, and the deer-hunting season. I witnessed a dominant buck and a monster buck rise from their beds in 2 inches of standing water once. They were bedded in a cattail marsh on November 7 one bow season. I was tracking one of them when I jumped them from their beds. They both stood there looking at me. The dominant buck was a 10-pointer that I had wounded and tracked for more than a day before rousting him from his bed. I expected him to be alone, but he was with a bigger 12-pointer; they were bedded within 6 feet of one another. The two bucks had retreated into an area of tall cattail grass that was in the wettest end of the swamp. They probably never expected me to push on through that hard-to-maneuver-through snow-covered ice to find them bedded on the only high spot in that swamp. I had shot the 10-pointer in the neck at very close range the day before, but the arrow did not exit his body. I tracked him for two days before giving up. He stopped bleeding, and lived on. I was amazed by all I learned about monster bucks and what they will do to survive while I was tracking that wounded deer. I did not hunt with D.I.E. yet when I shot that buck. I snuck up on him in his bed and shot him at 3 yards. I will never shoot another deer in the neck, because it was not a fatal shot.

Half the time a monster buck does not have to fight another buck to be able to breed with a doe. All he does is show up with his attitude. If the dominant buck is not around—then the monster buck easily claims the doe in estrus. On the other hand, if the dominant buck is home, then the two will go at it, and whichever one prevails is the dominant buck at that minute in that area. If a monster intruder beats the dominant buck, he may stay for a day or two to breed the doe in estrus, but he may not want to claim the territory so he then leaves the area. In that case, the formerly dominant buck can try to reclaim his rank and his territory, by re-establishing his dominance over the pecking order bucks. You can never tell how it will all turn out.

Defeated but respected and accepted

The longer a buck lives the smarter he gets, and the more set in his ways he becomes. If a dominant buck gets beat in a fight he is not always forced by the new king to leave the herd. He can refuse to leave the area, but he must yield to the new king whenever they encounter each other. In some cases, a losing dominant buck has a huge rack but is no longer dominant and is reluctant to leave the territory. He can stay in the territory and live out the rest of his life in a small (1-2 acre) core area in a swamp without holding any territory. Then he is a non-dominant monster buck. In that case, he has earned the respect of the new dominant buck, and he is allowed to remain there for the rest of his days without having to check into ranks.

I believe that was the scenario of my 17-point buck (shown on the cover of this book). I believe he lived in the core area of the swamp where he died. I had never seen territory marked up that way before. All the rubs were on tag alders (tree/shrubs), but the rubs could not be seen by anyone or anything passing through the area on dry ground. The rubs were in the waterlogged part of the swamp, and they faced out of it, not into it. A deer inside the swamp could see all the rubs—20 or more in that immediate vicinity. Outside the swamp, no rubs were visible. I have more to learn about monster buck bedding areas and their territory boundaries. I do not think I will ever know all the whitetail habits that a person can learn, but I surely will try to learn all I can in my lifetime. That site intrigued me.

D.I.E. attracts monster bucks

Monster bucks live long lives because they are very smart! Most deer hunters have never seen a monster whitetail buck while they were hunting. Monster bucks have huge racks that are nothing short of WOW!

I know it sounds crazy, but in my past eight years of hunting with D.I.E. I have seen six monster bucks, and five of them were on the same 12-acre parcel in New Berlin, Waukesha County, Wisconsin. During the first week of November, each of the monster bucks came within

35 yards of me during my four-day bow hunt. Each one came directly from their bedding area that was in the wettest end of a nearby swamp. Each one approached my D.I.E. scrape from directly downwind of my scrape. All six bucks had mammoth typical antlers. Each rack was larger than that of the 17-point non-typical buck on the cover. I believe that the D.I.E. system is capable of pulling a monster buck from the security of a bedding area every single time you hunt with it close to the place he calls home. I prefer not to get any closer to the wet end of a swamp than 80 yards upwind and at least 60 yards crosswind of it. I assume that the dominant buck is bedding in the wettest end of the swamp, and so far, I have always been right with my assumptions. I may go upwind of it as far as 240 yards to find a place that offers the buck staging cover within 50 yards downwind of my scrape. You should try to give the buck some staging cover in at least three directions away from your D.I.E. set up in order to make him feel comfortable and completely in command in the area. The buck will hold up in the staging cover that you leave for him. In my experience, he beds in that cover over 75% of the time.

My system has called 11 bucks to me on 11 hunts. It has been perfect for me. It can be perfect for you too. That is if you do not deviate from my set up and hunt instructions. I have said this before and I will surely say it again because the number one thing a person does that gets them busted by the buck, is they fail to follow my 'Never Do' Rules. I would prefer that everyone would be able to be hunted by the king of deer each time they use D.I.E., but I cannot be with them all when they set it up, and I cannot control what they do, so it will never be perfect for everyone. I know it will never fail anyone who follows the rules.

- Two of the bucks held up in cover within 35 yards of me in gun season, and I never saw them, because I only had two or three days to hunt. If you do not hunt until the buck arrives for whatever reason then your failure is your own. During gun deer season, I have had to quit hunting the morning of Day 3, to go back home and work. My dad drove out the nearest available cover downwind of my scrape on my last day; each time he found a basket racked buck bedded downwind of my scrape. The buck burst from cover and doubled back to his core bedding area. They always do, whenever they are confronted by a human. Do not chase them or they will leave the area for the rest of the week.
- The two bucks with the smallest racks were the first two bucks I got with DOMINANCE IS EVERYTHING, in 1998 and 1999. They were both 9-pointers.
- The buck with the biggest rack is a 17-pointer, a true monster buck. His picture is on the cover of this book. That buck was the sixth biggest racked buck that came in during my 11 hunts.
- Five bucks had wider racks than the 17-pointer, and three of the five had more massive (larger diameter) antlers.
- The other buck hung up 35 yards downwind of me. I could see him, but had no clear shot to his position. He busted me. He was a swamp buck with a 24-inch spread and 12 points. He had a black coat of hair. I think I saw him again in 2009 when a swamp buck fought the 17-pointer and lost. I think it was likely the same swamp buck, but there is no way to tell. Swamp bucks are rare.

DOMINANCE IS EVERYTHING is made to call dominant bucks, intruder bucks, monster bucks and swamp bucks to your stand site. Which one shows up, is up to the deer, but if you were not busted then he will always be the most dominant buck in the area. Often an intruder buck will be a monster buck. The first buck you see within 35 yards of the scrape, is the most dominant buck in the herd at that very minute.

Bucks can be monsters and not be dominant

Non-dominant monster bucks do not hold territory. I do not think they care about it. They have huge racks and even bigger attitudes. They are the ultimate whitetail buck fighting machines! The only things they want are to live and to breed. Because of their age, their size, their strength, and their expertise in winning confrontations with other bucks, they know they can go wherever they want at any time and get any doe away from any buck. Some dominant bucks have monstrous racks, but my point here is that there are monster bucks that do not belong to a herd but live inside the territory of a dominant buck.

Some monster bucks were likely dominant bucks at some point, but they left their territory in search of does in estrus, and when they returned home, another mature buck was holding down their territory. Upon his return home, the former king may have fought the new dominant buck and lost. If a dominant buck loses a battle, but will not leave the area, the new king has a choice to make:

- He can run the former dominant buck out.
- He can let the former dominant buck stay but not rule the herd or hold territory anymore.

I have seen both occur in the wild. I have video of two bucks fighting and dominance passing to the new champion. The formerly dominant buck will still breed, but only at opportune times when his life is not in jeopardy and when the new dominant buck is already with a doe in estrus of his own.

Monster bucks may be neighbors

Multiple monster bucks can live in the same swamp and deal with each other's presence all throughout the year, but in the rut, that harmony is lost. Monster bucks have to travel to find does in estrus, but they mostly travel at night, and hunters rarely see them except near their core bedding areas.

Monster buck core bedding areas

Most deer hunters do not know what a monster buck's core bedding area looks like. It is an amazing place. The buck rubs many large-diameter trees there, and he tears to pieces many saplings or bushes near the main deer trail leading into his swamp. I have only seen monster bucks near water, it is for that reason that one of the first things I ask a D.I.E. hunter when teaching a one-on-one is: "Do you have a water source on your property?" If they say yes, then I tell them that monster bucks and the most dominant buck likely live on their hunting land, and they are going to love being hunted by monsters! He will hunt you no matter if you have water on your land or not, but when you have water and a marshy area you have a better than 50% chance of seeing a monster buck. Those kind of odds will drive a deer hunter to the nearest water source and rightfully so. Dominant bucks, monster bucks, and swamp bucks go to water twice a day (during daylight), usually 3 to 4 hours after daylight and then again just before sunset. Water gives them energy and sustenance. I am not sure how many times they go to water at night.

These bucks are too smart to show themselves to a hunter in an open area during daylight. Just like a dominant buck, non-dominant monster bucks will not leave cover during daylight, except to breed with a doe in estrus. If a monster buck can find a cozy swamp to live in where no hunter bothers him, he will hole up and stay there through hunting season. That area is his core bedding area. Non-dominant monster bucks only have one or two core bedding areas, but dominant bucks always have three.

Let me ask you this. How can a monster buck be a dominant buck (a buck that holds territory for breeding rights there) if he never leaves the sanctuary of his core bed during daylight hours? In my opinion, he cannot.

Monster bucks are survivors

Monster bucks have been hunted each year of their lives, and they have seen hunters kill other deer. Each time monster bucks witness a deer getting shot—or hit by a car—they learn a valuable lesson: be cautious, and identify every sound, scent, and movement nearby or far away, before even thinking about moving out of cover and into the open. If a monster buck makes one mistake, he could end up dead.

Monster bucks, dominant bucks, and swamp bucks love breeding, and they love existing—more than they want to feed on bait piles during the rut. They see other deer die at bait piles, while grazing at food plots, and on the way to and from their bedding areas. They know main trails are hunted by humans, so they know better than to expose themselves in places like those. They crisscross doe trails looking to catch the scent of a doe in heat that is nearing estrus or better yet one that is in estrus. They avoid taking risks. They hold tight in cover during the day, and many of them only come out at night, that is only until they find a D.I.E. set up. DOMINANCE IS EVERYTHING changes everything.

When a doe is in estrus, she will seek out the dominant buck in the area, they will stay together to mate for a day or a day and a half. If she cannot find a mate when she goes into estrus, she will follow deer trails in search of a mature buck. If she finds a scrape, she will urinate in it, bed upwind or at a crosswind of it, and wait for the buck that has been maintaining that scrape to find her scent in the scrape, and then follow it to her. Bucks maintaining scrapes check them often. Both day and night, by going downwind of the scrape into staging cover where they are safe. There he scent-checks the air, he discovers the scent trail of the doe in estrus and he follows it. Then they finally meet. Once a doe is in estrus she constantly deposits her scent everywhere she goes. All mature bucks understand the signals she is sending out to them. It is as if she is wearing a flashing neon sign on her back that reads, "Come, and get it!"

Monster bucks are breeder bucks until death

When a doe is in estrus, she is ready, willing, and able to breed, and every mature buck can sense it. They use the wind to check the area for danger, and then they rush into the area of their scrape to find the doe in estrus. She will allow one buck to breed with her at that time. If more than one buck comes in, then a fight will break out. More than one buck can breed and impregnate a doe while she is in estrus, which I believe is a 24 to 36 hour period that's part of a doe's four-day heat/estrus cycle. Twin whitetail fawns do not always have the same father.

Most monster bucks live solitary lives after they reach 3 ½ years of age. Monster buck numbers are higher in areas where the buck to doe ratio is higher on the buck side.

Dominant bucks are not always aware of the presence of a monster buck in their area, because many monster bucks are intruders during the rut. They may have multiple bedding areas miles apart from each other. Herd structure does not matter to a monster buck that does not dominate a herd. Monster bucks have the most aggressive demeanor of any bucks I have ever seen, and I believe it is because they carry around those huge trophies on top of their heads for nine months each year. Each year that his rack grows bigger and more massive, the buck's attitude grows bigger too. Carrying a heavy and burdensome rack requires a monster buck to reserve all the energy he can, just to survive the rut. Chasing does can take a lot out of a buck. If he burns off too much fat, he will not make it through the winter. In addition, chasing does gets bucks killed, that is why I believe some older bucks do not want to be in kings for more than a few years. There is too much risk of being killed in all that competition. Older bucks just want to live. At least I think they do.

Most dominant bucks retire as monsters

I believe all two-year-old bucks enter the pecking order and move up the ranks for at least one year before they make a descision. They dominate if they can for a day, a week, a month, a year or maybe two before they are beaten in a fight, or they leave the pecking order to become neutral bucks that do not rank, and do not want to be dominant of the herd. These bucks are always intruders when they are breeding, and many of them become monster bucks during their fourth year of life.

If a dominant buck is beaten in a fight by another buck, he is no longer the most dominant in the herd. If he is unable to win fights with every pecking order buck, he will likely slip out of ranks and retreat to one of his favorite core bedding areas, to live out his life as monster buck or as a retired dominant buck. I believe all bucks have the potential to become monster bucks if they live to the age of 4 and I know that non-dominant monster bucks still dominate, but not the herd. They dominate over other bucks that intrude into their core bedding area. They really just want to be left alone to live in peace. Not many bucks can live to be monsters where there is heavy hunting pressure. They need to live past 3 years of age to achieve their biggest rack. I am not an antler expert, so I will not go into that subject any further. To me, the best place to hunt deer is where no one has hunted before. There are sure to be monster bucks there.

Swamp bucks

A swamp buck is a monster buck that lives in a swamp from the time he is 2 or 3 years old until the day he dies. The hair of a swamp buck is always a shade darker than the hair of average deer. His hair will look dark grayish black. I am not sure why, but my guess is it results from the lack of sunlight in a dark, canopied swamp. A swamp buck's core bedding area is a very small area and he will only come out of the swamp at night, unless he is driven out by people pressuring him or by a predator chasing him. Both are unlikely to happen. I do not know much about swamp bucks, but I plan to study them in the future.

Always avoid pressuring a buck in his bedding area

Here is the story of how I learned about mature buck bedding areas, and how dominant bucks do not always bed with the pecking order bucks. In June of 1989, I decided I was going to find a bachelor group of bucks. I set out on a mission to locate them in the morning in their bedding area. I planned to watch them all day (with binoculars) until dark. I wanted to see where they bedded and how often they moved around during the day in the summer when their antlers were covered with velvet. I planned to watch the first bachelor group of bucks that I could find, for two or three days straight so I could get to understand their daily movements. After finding a group, I decided to cut my trip short to allow the bucks to live without human encroachment in their territory. I think you will agree that it was the right thing to do at the time.

On the first morning, I headed for a 5-acre patch of tall green grass that was surrounded by a forest. There was a river flowing along the outer edge of the woods. I knew bucks bedded in grassy cover in the summer to avoid doing any damage to their antlers while they were growing so it made sense to me to look for the bucks there. I had never scouted this area before so everything I was going to learn about it was going to be a new experience for me. I started at first light and I entered the woods from downwind, following large deer tracks (3 ½ inches and longer). The biggest tracks were in the shaded areas so I made a note of that as soon as I realized it. It did not take me long to locate a bachelor buck group with five mature bucks in it. When I first came upon them it was just after sunrise, maybe an hour, or so, and they where bedded down in saw grass. If you never walked through saw grass in the summer, you do not know what you are missing. It feels like razors are cutting your arms. Saw grass cuts you up pretty bad. The pain is as if you got a hundred paper cuts all at once. Talk about heavy cover—it does not get any better than that for deer. The grass is green and it grows at least 5 to 6 feet tall. When deer bed in tall grass it is very hard to see them. You should always assume that a dominant buck would bed in tall grass in the summer if it were available.

The bucks all had a reddish rust colored summer coat of hair and each of them had started growing their antlers. I saw two 8-pointers, a 6-pointer, a 5-pointer, and a 4-pointer. All of their antlers were just starting to grow outside of their ears. All of these bucks were 2 ½ or older. These were some of the area's pecking order bucks. It really amazed me to find three big-racked bucks and two medium-racked bucks hanging out together. In the past, I had only seen mature bucks in the fall and I had never seen more than three in one group. I walked in on the bucks and jumped them out of their beds. They got up, bunched up, looked at me, and then they ran straight away. I proceeded forward to inspect their beds. I took notes so I could document their behavior and I could try to learn how to predict where I would find them the next morning. They bedded apart from each other by about 15 yards. Their beds were in a circle formation and the biggest bodied bucks were bedded in the heaviest cover.

When I happened upon them, they herded up in front of me until I pushed through the tall grass and could see them. They immediately identified me as a human because I didn't stop moving when I saw them, I just pressed on toward them and they galloped away. They ran 40 or so yards flagging their tails briefly before lowering them as they slowed to a trot and entered a thicket of thorn bushes. I knew there was a river about 200 yards in front of me, in the direction the bucks went, and I figured I would be able to follow them to the river and see which trail they used to cross it, so I pushed on… following the bucks. It was 80 degrees that day, I was sweated up, and soaking wet from head to toe from all the dew on the saw grass soaking me as I walked through it. Into the briars I went. There was a deer trail right through the thicket and I could see their hoof prints on that trail so I followed them. That stuff is terrible to walk through and it is impossible to get through it without being jabbed by a few thorns.

After I was 20 yards in I stopped to catch my breath and to look around to see where the bucks were and all of a sudden they burst out of the cover about 40 yards in front of me and they trotted single file into a hardwood forest. The river was immediately on the other side of the forest, and I could not wait to get there because it was bound to be easier to walk in there and much cooler temperature-wise under the shade of the tall oak trees. Anything was better than crawling through that thorn and briar patch. When I got to the edge of the woods, I snuck from tree to tree looking with binoculars for any movement ahead. I caught a glimpse of a flash from a deer tail. I looked around and I saw nine deer now, not five. The bucks had mixed in with some does. The bucks continued to take turns looking back at me, but the does never seemed to notice me. They were walking directly into the wind feeding on acorns. I had not noticed the wind direction before.

I thought back to where I jumped the bucks and I did remember the wind was coming from the NW and I was walking to the East when I found them bedded. Then they ran away from me in a northern direction (crosswind) and they met up with these does and were now feeding right into the wind. They did not see me now because I had my back to a tree. I waited there for nearly 15 minutes and watched as the bucks grouped back up and headed north again toward the river. They were using all their senses. Their ears were rotating like radar and their heads where turning left and right. They were very skittish. One of the does (a little one) bedded 40 yards in front of me and started chewing up some food. Then another doe bedded down near that one and the other two does kept on feeding on twigs and buds. I did not want to spook them so I decided to circle downwind to the SE and get past them, so I could get another glimpse at the bucks if they were still in the area. I was successful. I found a hiking trail and I followed it along the West riverbank toward the place I had last seen the bucks. There they were. Much to my surprise when they caught sight of me this time they headed straight south away from the river, and back to the security of the cover and the other deer.

I walked up to the spot where they were standing and I noticed the river was in view there. I proceeded to its western bank only to see that there was a trail crossing it. I noted the direction the tracks went on the trail. They were all going south. I crossed the river, which was only a foot deep at that spot, and I tracked the trail backwards to the North. After the river, there were 20 yards of hardwoods and then a blacktop road.

I analyzed the actions of the bachelor buck group and tried to look at their movements and their decision making from their point of view. I had cornered the bucks at the river, and they had to make a decision which way to go. They had waited nearly ½ hour for me to arrive. They chose to go back to cover rather than run across a road and expose themselves to people and traffic. The other side of the road offered them no cover at all, and within 80 yards of it was a subdivision. I bet they were hoping I would go back and leave them alone, but I was on a mission to learn about buck habits and to find monster buck bedding areas, and I did just that.

That day in Whitnall Park in Franklin, Wisconsin, I learned many things that I feel every hunter needs to know about bucks, especially big bucks. I learned that in the summer, bachelor bucks are all friends and they tolerate each other and depend on one another for safety when bedded. I learned that older (bigger bodied bucks) are smarter and stay hidden in cover when they bed. When big bucks are pushed by a human, they do not leave the county they just move out of the danger zone and into the next available cover. From there they look back to see if the human is still pursuing them. Alert deer head to a core-doe bedding area to find safety and to warn other deer of the danger a human brings to a herd. They use their eyes and ears, just as much as their nose to detect approaching danger, but if they can see you (the danger) they do not wait around to scent check you, they just run away. They move to safety first and figure out what the danger was from there. They are more cautious than other deer in the herd.

The does just bedded down in front of me but the bucks kept moving. They are patient animals, and their safety is the most important part of their life to them. They must have been tired after I pushed them half a mile through rough terrain, but they didn't go to the river for water, instead they waited in a tight group at the water's edge for the danger to approach and then as soon as they knew it was safe they bolted back to their safety zone. The road was dangerous for them and the trail showed that deer only used it when traveling south into the bedding area, not north when leaving it. I learned that deer have one-way trails and that no matter what they will not go the opposite way on one of those trails. I learned a ton of valuable knowledge about mature bucks that day and I locked that memory into my brain so I could remember it first thing the next morning when I tried to find those same bucks again.

The next morning I headed into the same woods, but this time the wind was from the East. I started on the West side of a wooded hill and worked my way east up over the top of it. I wanted to circle downwind of the place the bucks were bedded the day before. This woodlot was situated on a high hill between two homesteads. I was sure that neither homeowner could see me walking into the woods or out the other side for that matter. It was windy that day and there was a lot of dead timber on the ground. I could not help but step on brittle branches as I went. Just as I turned to head downwind to the South, I jumped a solo buck off the East side of that hill. He was bedded with his chest facing south and his head was facing east (away from me). He did not know I was there until a branch snapped under my foot and that got him up from his bed about 20 yards away. He had antler growth outside his ears and he had 3" diameter antlers at the base. He had 8 points already and would likely be a 10 or 12 -pointer when his rack was done growing. His body was bigger and his rack was taller than the 5 bucks I had seen the day before. This was a new buck, not one of them. He ran in a clockwise direction down the hill and shot across the blacktop road that I had parked my car on to the West. He ran another 200 yards and headed into a heavy thicket where he slowed to a trot and then stood still there for a few minutes. I watched him with binoculars as he slipped into the tall tag alders and disappeared. That buck was in my opinion the dominant one from the year before. He had his own private bed up on a hillside, and it offered him a great view of the lowland, and of the river. He could see over 150 yards to the North and to the East from his bed. To the South was a fallen tree about 3 feet in diameter which gave him cover and to the West, the woods was cluttered with dead branches and other forest debris that made it impossible for anyone or anything (including me) to approach him without sending the buck an audible warning. After I jumped that dominant buck from his bed that day, I made the decision to quit following bucks around during the summer months.

Now I never intentionally go into buck bedding areas from May to February. I never want to disturb them in their sanctuary. Once their antlers drop, I do not see any harm in walking through their bedding areas looking for shed antlers. I have found sheds as early as January 16, and as late as April 28. Other than looking for sheds there is no reason for a D.I.E. hunter to enter the bedding areas of bucks or does. You will have better hunts if you never pressure the deer in your hunting area out of their beds.

Chapter 6

Reading the signs of the most dominant buck

This chapter is jam-packed with many astonishing facts (that I discovered) about dominant whitetail buck behavior, that you probably have never heard anyone talk about or write about before. I have learned to read every sign that a dominant buck leaves in an area before he vacates it. In this chapter, I am going to show you how to read the signs of the dominant buck the same way deer do. I mastered these skills, by studying the mannerisms of every deer I encountered for the past 21 years.

People who have not been taught how to "think like a deer", or how to "read sign like a deer" have a hard time believing that a human can become invisible to deer. In this chapter, you will learn a lot about buck dominance and herd structure. How a dominant buck marks his territory, and what each sign a dominant buck leaves for other deer to read really means to the deer that encounter it. I am going to teach you to look at dominant buck sign as if you were a deer. You have to forget that you are a human for a few minutes and let me show you the way deer think! You represent a pair of breeding deer when you become a D.I.E. hunter. You are a mature doe and a monster buck, neither one of which is a member of the dominant buck's herd.

I am able to prove that my tactics for reading and understanding dominant buck sign do indeed work. I am able to teach anyone how to "think like a deer" by showing them how to analyze fresh sign left by the king of the herd, and by teaching them to comprehend the reasons why a dominant buck makes rubs and scrapes, in strategic locations throughout his core living area. Each rub and scrape sends a message. The message pertains to where the dominant buck is at that moment in time, in relation to the position of the rub on the tree, or the pawed up area of the scrape.

Deer can read dominant buck sign all year long and we (D.I.E. hunters) can too, but in order to make the king of deer approach to within 35 yards of your stand during the rut with D.I.E., you have to make an effort to leave the dominant buck alone. You should not disturb him while he is living his normal life on the land you are going to hunt. On a D.I.E. hunt, no deer ever see you (as a human), so not one deer knows you are there. By scouting and setting up away from deer while they are bedded, you are keeping your human intrusion into their territory a secret from the entire herd. The dominant buck makes his rounds once every three days, and when he does, he finds your D.I.E. scrape and D.I.E. rub. He leaves the core living space of all the deer in his herd and looks for any danger that may have moved in close to them over the past two days. No other deer routinely travel along a dominant buck's territorial boundaries the way he does. He travels at night and beds during the day. The rest of the herd lives in groups found in or around doe bedding areas for their safety. He is not afraid of anything that he can see, and he never knows you are there, when you do what I teach you to, so he is never pressured by a human (D.I.E. hunter) at all. You can only be invisible to deer if you stop acting like a human, stop thinking like a traditional hunter, and start thinking like a deer. Let me show you how it is done!

Do not ever follow the dominant buck's tracks if you want to have him hunt you. Scout for dominant and monster buck sign (rubs and scrapes) one day only, and make sure that the deer are already mating on the day you are going to be scouting. I prefer not to scout for a D.I.E. set-up location before the rut has started. If you do, the data you gather will no longer be accurate information once the rut kicks into gear. You need to know where the dominant buck is living (bedding) one to two weeks before you intend to hunt him, not before that.

I always scout 10 to 14 days before Day 1 of my hunt, and I never sit in my stand before October 29 each year. I only spend time in the woods between 10 a.m. and 2 p.m. on scouting day or on set-up day, because I know that most deer will be bedded down during those hours, and I will not be disturbing any of them, when I scout the areas upwind and crosswind of their beds. I hunt with D.I.E. exclusively from upwind and crosswind of all deer bedding areas, so I am far away and completely out of sight of them when they are bedded.

The dominant buck has to be allowed to travel 80 or more yards from the nearest edge of deer bedding cover, into the wind or at a crosswind, on his approach to your stand site, so he will not feel pressured. If you always allow him to have 80 yards or more of undisturbed space between you and his bedding cover, he will never get nervous or expect that something is up! Give him the room he needs (80 yards minimum) to assure himself that he will be perfectly safe when he is walking out in the open, making his way to your scrape, and he will come in close every time.

Hunting too close to his living room (near deer bedding areas) pressures him, and doing so will cause you to fail. Every dominant buck is smart enough to know when a human is near. That is because humans do not think like deer, or behave like a deer. Humans announce their identity to deer. Their behavior in the territory of the dominant buck, announces to every deer the fact that they are human and that they are coming back. D.I.E. hunters are invisible to deer so I do not consider a D.I.E. hunter to be a human.

Humans act and deer react. Humans (non-D.I.E. hunters) go where they want, whenever they want, and do whatever they want to do, once they get there, without ever stopping to read the signs (the rubs and scrapes) that the dominant buck has left for all deer to see. Members of his herd will read his signs and will live by his rules when they are in the areas where the signs exist. They are required to, as a condition of being allowed to remain living in his territory.

Breaking the rules is not an option for any deer that encounters the signs of the most dominant buck in the herd, and because you are trained to be a deer, you must live by deer rules in order not to call attention to yourself while you are in their territory. Breaking any of the dominant buck's rules on your way to your stand will get you busted more often than not. I learned that the hard way a number of times. Now I always hunt out of view of all rubs and scrapes, so I can be positive that the dominant buck does not live where I am setting up. He always lives downwind and crosswind of my location, and I would like to think he will be living downwind and crosswind of yours as well.

I never worry about having to read his signs on my D.I.E. hunts, because I never set up or hunt with D.I.E. within view of any rubs or scrapes that the dominant buck made. You only have to react to a buck rub (like a deer) when you encounter one. I only read rubs when I scout, that way I know where he is and I can make a good decision on where I want to be, so he will have to come to me there.

I hunt away from all active buck sign on purpose, so I do not have to live by his rules. Worrying about him seeing me as I walk in would be too much for me to think about on a D.I.E. hunt. I make sure he is not bedding where I am hunting, so I am alone when I go to my stand, and I am alone when I leave it. What could ever be better than that for any deer hunter?

Wondering where the dominant buck is coming from is not one of my issues, as it is for most traditional hunters. He will always be headed into the strongest wind when he approaches my stand site. He may walk in from my left, or maybe from my right. Sometimes he will come in from straight ahead of me, but no matter what, he will never come in from upwind of me! Upwind of my set up (200 yards or more) is the upwind boundary of the dominant buck's territory. That means there is another king that lives upwind of my D.I.E. scrape at all times. I can be sure that is the case because I always find all three core-doe bedding areas before I set up my D.I.E. system. I know that he owns the land upwind of the furthest upwind bedding area for at least 200 yards, but more likely 300 to 400 yards when wild land exists that far upwind. His border is up there somewhere, and I am closer to it, when I hunt upwind of all three core-doe bedding areas, than I would be if I hunted 80 yards upwind of his furthest downwind bedding area.

The further you hunt away (upwind) from the buck sign you find, the closer you get to another dominant buck's territory. Having more than one king interested in breeding your invisible doe is a wonderful issue for a D.I.E. hunter to have. Hunting upwind of every deer bedding areas on my hunting property has raised my odds of seeing a monster buck up from 50% to near 90% on every one of my hunts. A normal deer hunter's odds of seeing a monster buck within 35 yards of him or her on a traditional hunt are less than 3% from what I gathered from the information hunters who attended one of my seminars, have shared with me. A first-time D.I.E. hunter has a 50% chance of seeing a monster buck within 35 yards if they do everything exactly as I do. An expert D.I.E. hunter has a better than 50% chance of seeing a monster buck on every D.I.E. hunt for the rest of their lives. Experts at hunting with D.I.E. have hunted successfully with it at least two times and had the king of deer hunt him or her on each hunt.

Currently there are three experts with my D.I.E. system, but that is soon to change. You may be an expert before deer season ends.

Forget what your friends are doing if you intend to succeed with my system this fall. Your friends (traditional hunters) are not trained to be invisible to deer, to read deer sign like deer, or to think like a deer. They are humans and unless they bought my book, they do not know what to do about changing that. You now have an advantage over any traditional hunter, because you are skilled in the art of becoming a pair of invisible deer. Just knowing what I know is not enough, you have to make a conscious decision to give up all the tactics you used on your last traditional hunt, and rely on using the skills that I teach you, to be in control of what the dominant buck will be thinking when he encounters your D.I.E. set up. If you hunt upwind and crosswind of all buck sign you will become "one who is hunted by the king of deer." Traditional hunters will have a hard time breaking the bad habit of hunting where all the deer sign is. If you can overcome the urge to be a traditional hunter, you will do fine with **Dominance Is Everything**.

If you have never seen a dominant buck before, the most likely reason is that your behavior in his territory sent him signals that you were a human. Humans are his biggest threats! If you ever tracked, a big buck and you were never able to catch a glimpse of him I am sure it was because he was watching you before you ever found his tracks. He left the area as you were entering it, and he stayed away from you until he was sure that you were gone!

Dominant bucks know when humans are there, because their behavior in the woods tells him they are not deer. When traditional hunters drive deer they push them out of their beds and force them to hide from the immediate danger that they are facing. Deer hunters, who make deer drives, walk through the entire herd's territory kicking deer up as they go. If they keep at it long, enough they will eventually pressure the dominant buck out of his favorite bed. Their human actions force him to react, and his reaction is to get out of there as fast as possible, usually by galloping away in the opposite direction.

Dominant bucks have to hide from humans (during daylight) in order to survive each day and remain dominant. A dominant buck knows that any moving thing (animal, human, or machine) that does not acknowledge his presence, by changing its course when it encounters one of his signs, is a threat to his survival. Now you know it too! He does not wait around to identify the threat! He escapes danger and then figures out what it was later after dark (when he is in control again). He believes that any human that he can physically see intends to do him harm. For that one reason, once he knows humans are in his territory he disappears like a ghost, never to be seen again during daylight. That is another reason why I never scout before the rut. To avoid making the dominant buck aware of my presence inside his territory.

Are you thinking like a deer now?

If you read this chapter up to this point, then I expect you are now thinking like a deer. If you are, that is good news! If you are not quite there yet, that is all right, you will catch on in the coming pages. I want you to think like a deer as you read the rest of my book. Thinking like a deer takes some practice. I recommend that you use my system the way I do.

Every aspect of a hunt with DOMINANCE IS EVERYTHING has to do with knowing where the bedding areas are and what other areas deer frequent during the day on the land you intend to hunt. Deer hunters can only legally hunt during daylight, so all that should matter to you as a D.I.E. hunter is where the herd is during the day, and how are you going to get in and out of their territory, without being seen by any of them during daylight. This is easy to accomplish if you move upwind of all buck sign, before you set the system up.

The king will find you, if you read his signs. The signs tell you where he will go once he discovers your D.I.E. scrape, and you can predict which piece of cover he will be bedded in the day that he decides to visit your stand site. Your hunt should be easy and fun. All of mine are!

Let me be perfectly clear. A deer hunter that scouts their hunting land before the rut begins, but intends on hunting the most dominant buck with D.I.E. during the rut, is gathering information about the herd's whereabouts that will not be applicable during the rut. You hunt the king of deer during the rut with D.I.E., so you must read (scout for) the dominant buck's sign while he is in rut, in order to know where he is bedding, breeding, getting his water, and sleeping. He gets food after dark so I never worry too much about finding that. I want to know what he is up to when I am in the woods, which is always during daylight.

I hope my opinions makes sense to all those who read them, because frankly too many people walk all over their property at all different times of the year, and they are hurting their chances of seeing the herd's king on a deer hunt by doing so. With D.I.E. he will come out when he knows he is alone, but how will he ever be convinced that he is alone if you are intruding into his core living areas leading up to the four days of your hunt? I know that the most dominant buck will not ever come in during daylight if you tell him a human was there, and that the human is coming back. Trail camera users beware! You are guilty of doing just that!

It is imperative that you learn to read buck rubs like deer do, so you can locate at least one of the dominant buck's three core-bedding areas, without ever walking into any of them. Each dominant buck rub tells you where he likes to bed in relation to it. When you locate a real buck rub, face the side of the tree that is ripped, or rubbed and call that the downwind side of the rub. Trust me that the backside of a rub (un-rubbed area) is always upwind, or at a 45-degree angle to the wind, at the time the buck made the rub. That is very important because it tells you that whenever the wind is hitting that tree on an upwind or crosswind side (with the bark still on it) that the dominant buck will approach that area from downwind of that rub! On the same note, he will always bed downwind or downwind and crosswind of a D.I.E. scrape and rub. Draw it out on paper and see for yourself, which directions downwind and crosswind of a rub really are.

Most rubs face downwind, some face crosswind, and very few face upwind. The ones that face upwind are always part of a rub line.

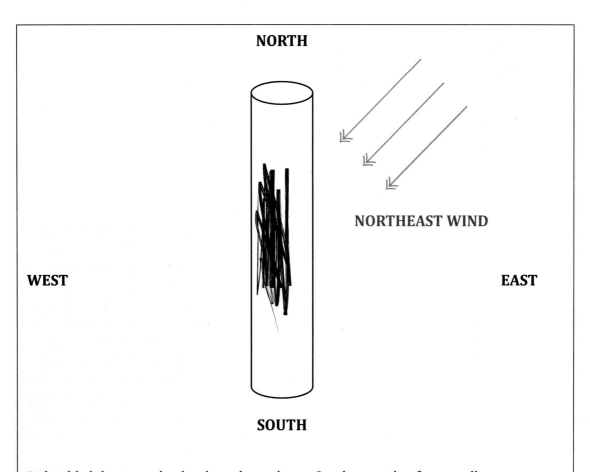

A shredded dominant buck rub made on the on Southwest side of a tree tells you:
① The wind was from the Northeast, the North, or the East when the buck made the rub.
② The buck approached the rub from the South or the West and he tilted his head and shredded the bark off the tree with only his G2 antlers.
③ That tells you that the dominant buck beds Southwest of that tree when the wind is from the Northeast. His bed is not visible from the rub.
④ The rub also tells you that does, fawns, and yearling bucks will walk past the rub on its upwind side, usually 2 to 10 yards upwind of the rubbed tree.
⑤ One of the core doe bedding areas is upwind and crosswind of his bed 100 to 300 yards away.
⑥ The pecking order bucks bed on the opposite side of the does when the wind is from the Northeast.

FIGURE 12 You can learn a lot from a shredded (territorial) dominant buck rub.

By never walking into any area that you expect the dominant buck to be bedding in, you are assured that he is not going to feel pressured by a human being there. That means he will not know you are hunting him when you are in your stand. No deer would ever approach a dominant buck while he was in his bed. Do not ever pressure him out of his bedding area or he will immediately know that you are not a deer. Anything other than a deer that is moving toward a dominant buck is a threat to his survival. If you are a threat, he will not hunt you.

Find his bedding area by analyzing rubs

You can find his bedding area by analyzing the rubs and scrapes that you find when you scout for a D.I.E. set-up location. Freshly made rubs and scrapes tell you everything about the most dominant buck in the herd, so once you find one get to analyzing it as soon as possible. There is always a chance that the dominant buck is watching that rub or scrape at that very moment from his bed downwind of it. You should always step away from the rubbed part of the tree or away from the pawed up dirt in the scrape and try to stay on the upwind side of the marker when analyzing it, always making sure you never stand in front of it. Once you are there squat down immediately so you can look the area over, from the same eye-height that deer do. When you squat down your eyes should be 36 to 44 inches off the ground to be at deer eye-height. From that position you can see the same distances a deer can see and you will notice the terrain looks much different from the eye-level a deer sees it, than it does from the eye-level that a (standing) human views it. Every time I squat down to read deer sign, I say to myself "If I was a deer?" By reciting those words repeatedly in my head, I can convince myself that I am thinking like a deer at that very moment. It helps me see things from a deer's perspective. It is impossible to think like a deer if you do not see the world from a deer's eye-height.

Dominant buck sign is the most important deer sign that a deer hunter can find. Every deer hunter should know how to differentiate between dominant buck sign and other deer sign. The herd is run by the dominant buck and everything that goes on inside his territorial boundaries is brought to his attention immediately. All deer communicate with one another, and small animals and birds often communicate with deer too. Every creature in the woods looks for danger every minute of every day, and they tell each other what is going on in their part of the woods by changing their behavior, from normal (at ease) to alert (at risk). A seasoned deer hunter will know what I mean. The point is that you need to be invisible to all the animals,

Always look for the king's tracks.

all of the time, while you are in their territory on a D.I.E. hunt. They are looking for humans. Behave like a deer so they will not see a human when they get close to you.

Look for the signs that the dominant buck leaves for all deer to see

The most dominant buck leaves signs for all deer to read that inform them of his current whereabouts at all times. Those signs are rubs and scrapes. He also leaves tracks and feces.

Rubs and scrapes tell you more about the dominant buck than tracks and feces do. I believe the number one reason that most deer hunters have never had a dominant buck in their sights, is because they have ignored the signs that the dominant buck left for deer to read. Until now, you probably did not know that humans were capable of reading all deer signs, but we are! When I first mastered the skills needed to locate any herd, I was astonished at how different the two ways of looking at deer sign were. Looking at a rub from a human's perspective told me that a buck was in the area some time ago, but looking at it from a deer's perspective made me aware that I was now standing in the living room of the most dominant buck in the herd. I also know that depending on the wind direction at that moment there is at least a 33.33% chance when I stood in front of one of his rubs, that he was right there watching my every move. I always assume he is watching me whenever I find a rub. Doing so prevents me from being busted for acting like a human and being caught in the act.

The wind direction determines where exactly the dominant buck beds during the day. He has three core bedding areas, and he will always be using the one that is furthest downwind at any given moment. If the wind changes he will move to another bedding area and watch a different rub, that faces a different direction. The rub he watches always faces downwind.

Deer hunters have scouted for dominant buck sign season after season for centuries, and surely, they have been able to find plenty of it, but I am sure that many of them never knew that the buck sign they found, was made by the herd's most dominant buck. The most obvious types of dominant buck sign are tree-rubs, scrapes, tracks, feces, and a single body impression found in a dominant buck's bed. The difference between finding dominant buck sign and understanding what it means is a significant one.

Most deer hunters and outdoor photographers do not know what the messages are that a dominant buck is sending to all the deer that come across one of his rubs or scrapes. I want to be the first person to tell you that I am not like most deer hunters! I know why a dominant buck makes rubs and scrapes, and I know what each one of them means. I know how every deer thinks! It took me 32 years to master the skills needed to become any deer, anytime, anywhere, but it was certainly worth it. No matter where I am inside a dominant buck's territory, I am welcome to stay. I am able to step out of my human mindset, and into the mindset of any deer that I want to pretend to be at any given time. I am so good at it that I can convince every wild deer that I am one of them, even though they can never see the body of the (invisible) deer I am pretending to be. Now I find myself teaching people around the country how to think like a deer, and how to brainwash deer into believing they are one of them. I believe I am the first person in the world to claim that there are nine different types of dominant buck rubs. I am going to prove there are nine types by explaining to you where each one can be found, and what each one of them means to all real and invisible deer (D.I.E. hunters), who know how to read them. I have named some of these rubs with names I thought people could easily understand when they are spoken. The rest of the rubs already were commonly known.

Reading dominant buck sign and knowing how to behave like a doe would, when she encounters dominant buck sign, will keep your real identity (as a human) hidden from the herd. In order to be 100% successful on every hunt with DOMINANCE IS EVERYTHING you need to forget that you are a human and allow yourself to think, act, and react like a whitetail deer from daylight to dark.

Dominant bucks make rubs for a reason

Dominant bucks rub trees from the day they start shedding the velvet off their antlers, until the day their antlers fall off their heads. Rubs are a dominant buck's primary means to communicate with every deer that enters or leaves his territory. If you find lots of rubs on trees greater than 1-inch in diameter, in an area of about 160 acres that tells you that the dominant buck has a lot of competition to breed in that particular area. That is great news for D.I.E. hunters like you and me, because it tells us that his pecking order has multiple (large-racked) mature bucks in it, and that those bucks are constantly getting in confrontations with one another when they come upon does in estrus. The more competition he has to breed, the sooner you will meet him on a D.I.E. hunt! Finding just a few rubs in an area of comparable size tells you he is clearly in charge of the herd there, and that he has been for some time. That is also very good news for a D.I.E. hunter! That means he is likely 3 ½ years of age or older and that he has a big rack of antlers. That dominant buck is a standalone champion. He has no real competition to breed inside his territory. There will be very few (5 or less) bucks in the ranks of his pecking order. In that case, I cannot predict whether he will come in right away or not. I can however tell you he will be much older than the average aged bucks you see.

Monster bucks get very vocal when they enter the core breeding area of a dominant buck. They let it be known that they are there to challenge and conquer. Be prepared to hear the buck announcing his presence in the area straight downwind of your D.I.E. scrape.

No matter where you find rubs, or how many of them exist, be sure to analyze each one of them until you figure out what part of the dominant buck's territory they are positioned in. Draw out a map of his house, and make note of the location of all the dominant buck sign that you find. Then no matter what you are used to doing, move away from all the fresh rubs and scrapes in a crosswind direction and get upwind of the area if you can. Make sure you never intentionally set up a D.I.E. scrape within view of any buck rubs or scrapes, otherwise you will be setting yourself up to be busted by the buck. It would be as if you walked through the front door of his house, made your way into his living room and once you got there, you built a D.I.E. scrape and installed a tree stand in it, even though you knew that the dominant buck was home. Do not ever do that! He lives (beds) where he makes his scrapes and rubs, and he is always watching them. You should never hunt within view of a dominant buck's rub or scrape, because he will refuse to come out of his bedding cover to approach the D.I.E. scrape in daylight if you do.

Find his sign and move away from it (as I do), to increase your odds of seeing a monster buck. Train yourself to stick to the set up procedure no matter how much buck sign you find. You are not a traditional hunter anymore so do not think like one, you are a D.I.E. hunter, and in order to be hunted by the king of deer you have to be far away from the place that he will be coming from. You need to scout for the signs of the dominant buck, and then to move 200 or more yards away from all the sign, as soon as you discover it. Lingering inside the king's house at any time will get you busted. By moving away you are leaving him alone, to live there in peace. That way he does not ever know he is being hunted. It doesn't matter how far you go away from his active sign, what matters is that you are not any closer to it than 80 yards, and that you stay on the upwind side of it, to raise your odds of having multiple dominant and monster bucks fighting for you.

The dominant buck beds as far away from his competition as he can so they are not in constant contact. He always beds downwind of his herd so you should always set D.I.E. upwind of them, that way you will be hunting on the upwind side of one dominant buck's territory and at the same time, you are on the downwind side of another dominant buck's territory just across the border!

Trust your ability to take educated guesses to where you think he is bedded, and use the information you gather while scouting to support your theories. You will learn that finding a dominant buck's rub on your scouting trip is a better for you than finding the dominant buck. You do not want to meet him face-to-face until you are in your stand on Day 1 of the hunt.

When a dominant buck hunts me he has to meet me in his front yard, side yard, or backyard and I get to decide where he is going to bed for the next 4 days. The entire set up revolves around the D.I.E. hunter's ability to read deer sign the way deer do. You need to know where the buck's bedroom and guest bedrooms (doe and pecking order buck bedding areas) are in order to know how to stay away from them. Let the rubs that you find paint the picture for you. Let them show you where he beds, and where his does and pecking order bucks bed in relation to his bed.

All dominant buck rubs are strategically placed inside the core living areas of the herd's king. I can make sense out of the placement and meaning of each of the 9 different types of rubs that are made by the dominant buck, and by doing so I can tell where the whole herd lives just by looking at one single dominant buck rub. Lesser bucks make rubs that do not tell you anything about the whereabouts of the herd. Because lesser buck rubs have no meaning to the dominant buck or the rest of his herd, they mean nothing to me and they should not mean a thing to you either. They are single rubs made on saplings with a tree trunk diameter of less than 1-inch.

Dominant bucks freshen (re-rub) some of their territorial rubs every few days throughout fall and winter so that every deer in the area knows that the king is still alive and well. Bucks deposit their scent on rubs, by rubbing their forehead and antlers on the tree trunk. Every deer can positively identify the buck that owns a rub by inhaling his scent he left on the rub or by identifying the buck's scent left on the licking branch if there is one. Deer approach rubs from crosswind angles so they can look for the owner of the rub while making their way to it. They can only see two dimensions (length and width) so in order to see depth they need to walk around objects. They walk around other deer in order to size up their competition.

Being able to find and analyze dominant buck rubs plays a crucial role in telling D.I.E. hunters where the dominant buck feels safe and where he does not. He makes rubs in areas that he controls. Those are areas that he feels comfortable living in during daylight. He does not make any rubs or scrapes in areas he is not familiar with, and because of that, those are dynamite areas to scout for a D.I.E. set up location.

As a D.I.E. hunter, you need to find his rubs and analyze their meaning so you know what the "Big Picture" looks like for your area's most dominant buck. The big picture is something you can see once you scout a property and find some of the fresh buck and doe sign there. It is the framework of the structure of the deer herd's territory, where they bed, eat, drink, travel, and breed. It is also the location of at least one of the most dominant buck's territorial boundaries. Once you can see the "Big Picture" you should move upwind and crosswind of the dominant buck's stomping grounds to an area he is unfamiliar with, and set D.I.E. up there.

The most dominant buck is the only buck in the pecking order that makes territorial rubs. When the dominant buck dies the No. 2 pecking order buck instantly becomes the most dominant, and he aggressively starts raking brush near the location that the king met his demise. He goes there to show off his new rank and when no buck is there to battle him, he becomes the new king instantly.

DOMINANCE IS EVERYTHING to all pecking order bucks too, and when a new king gains title to the herd, all the lesser bucks in the herd grow restless. They behave both excitedly and aggressively, and they show it by combating each other to attempt to climb up a notch or two in the ranks. When lesser bucks are fighting for rank, they rub their antlers on small saplings and brush while their opponent is watching in order to intimidate him. That is when lesser bucks make rubs, and to me those rubs have no meaning.

When bucks rake brush, they are standing their ground and calling out their competition. They are saying "Bring it!" or "Here I am!" The buck that is raking brush has no fear, just pent up aggression. When you witness a dominant buck raking brush on his way to your D.I.E. stand site, you should immediately realize that he has no idea a human is there. He is calling the invisible intruder buck out to fight (downwind and away from the scrape). He wants the scrape for himself and he is trying to get the invisible monster-challenging buck to leave it, and bring the fight to him (to the king). Dominant bucks know better than any other deer that raking brush is a show of dominance. A buck raking brush is showing his dominance and is on his way to a challenge. He is willing to fight for his territory, and if you wait patiently for him to stop raking the brush, he will make his way to the D.I.E. scrape immediately after he calms down.

Therefore, when you find rubs made on small saplings or brush (less than 1-inch in diameter) and they have a shredded appearance (resembling territorial rubs), know that they are not all territorial rubs automatically. Territorial rubs are shredded and are made on trees that are more than 1-inch in diameter. Small sapling rubs are found throughout a dominant buck's territory. Do not waste too much time trying to analyze small sapling rubs. If you do discover some of them, what they are telling you is that the buck herd in your area is a healthy one. The bucks that made them are competing for the right to be king.

Dominant bucks make territorial rubs and lesser-ranked bucks do not. Monster bucks and swamp bucks also make territorial rubs but only inside their personal bedding areas. Pecking order bucks rub saplings and rake their antlers in brush, but they never make territorial rubs, because they do not have the right to. Only the dominant buck can make territorial rubs throughout his territory that is because he owns it. He tolerates the rubbing that monster bucks and swamp bucks do inside their bedding areas because he respects them living there. After all, they are not competing with him for the territory, or for the right to run the herd. All bucks rake brush to remove the dried up velvet from their antlers in the fall, and pecking order bucks rake brush when they are challenging another buck to a fight to gain a higher rank. Rubs on saplings are not important markers made by a dominant buck unless they meet the definition of a territorial rub. I define all dominant buck rubs in detail later on in this chapter.

How to analyze dominant buck rubs

The brow tines are the first two tines closest to the buck's forehead; they always make the deepest gouges in the bark of the tree trunk when a buck is making a rub. The heavier his antlers, the more momentum he needs to swing his neck into the tree trunk and do enough damage to the tree to rip the bark from it. That is one reason why dominant buck's necks are so big during the rut. They are always rubbing trees to mark their territory, to intimidate other bucks, and to be able to catch a doe in estrus at a primary breeding scrape during the day or at night. When a dominant buck rubs a tree, he is telling every deer that comes along that he is in command there.

The larger the diameter of the tree that is rubbed, the more space there is between the buck's antler tines. The wider the spacing between tines the older the buck is and the more massive his rack is. Dominant buck rubs are not just signs that a buck was there, they are much more than that, they tell the dominant buck's story to every deer, (D.I.E. hunter), and animal that can read them. His story is a complex one, because his intentions are to be king of the herd forever! He makes rubs so there is no doubt in any other deer's mind that he is their king. When he makes each rub, it is for a specific reason. He lays down the rules that the entire herd lives by, and his rubs tell deer in which rooms of his house the rules apply. Being able to read buck rubs will allow you to think like a deer, and read deer sign like a deer. Those are both very advantageous skills to have if you are a dominant buck hunter.

I have seen a few dozen bucks making rubs, and they always rip the bark up and down and get more aggressive on the tree trunk as the bark starts falling off. They approach the tree at a crosswind angle. That means that when a buck rubs a tree with his antlers, he turns his head to one side, and the top of his head or the bottom of his chin, faces directly into the strongest wind current at the time. The buck pushes his main beam into the tree and he forcibly moves his head and neck in a raking motion up and down the tree trunk.

The main beams are responsible for the smooth rubbed part of a buck rub. Some rubs have a smooth area and a shredded appearance. To make one of those rubs he uses the front of his G2 or G3 antler tines to rip and shred the bark off the side of the tree while at the same time he is pushing forward with his main beam and lifting and lowering his head to rub it. Bucks antlers are named so official scorers can document the characteristics of each tine on a buck's rack. I am not an expert at scoring buck racks. I am very far from it actually, but I do know that a buck's brow tines are called G1 tines and that the next tines forward from there are the G2's. A six-point buck only has G1's, G2's, and his main beams. An eight -pointer typically has G1's, G2's, G3's, and his main beams, and 10-pointers have all those and G4's too.

A dominant buck only rubs one of the four sides of the tree trunk when he initially makes a rub. I know trees are round, but I look at them as having a front, a back and two sides. The front is where the rub is, and if there is a scrape under that rub, then the front of the scrape is in front of the pawed up dirt and the rub on the tree. They always face the same direction.

All rubs have a direct correlation to the direction the wind was coming from the moment they were made. A dominant buck usually rubs one of the two crosswind sides of a tree, or the downwind side. He will not rub a tree on the direct upwind side, but he will rub a crosswind and upwind section of the tree trunk (as is the case with rubs in a rub line).

A rub faces the direction that the torn up area of the bark faces. If you find a rub that is facing upwind, then you should know that the wind was from the opposite direction when the dominant buck made that rub (unless it is part of a rub line), and he will only bed down in that area when the wind is hitting the back side of the tree.

Learn to read a rub by analyzing the way that the buck that made it approached the tree trunk. I always carry a set of shed antlers along with me when I scout, so I can use them to help me analyze buck rubs. Hold a set of shed antlers up to the rub but do not make contact with it. Determine which direction the buck was headed when he made the rub, and gather as much information about it as you can before walking away. If he was headed to the left, then he must have come in from the right. That means he was bedding to the right, and that the rub faces to the right. He walked away from the rub heading left looking for a mate, so there must be a doe bedding area off to the left. Pecking order bucks would be bedding on the other side of the doe bedding but never upwind of it. They always bed at a crosswind to doe bedding areas. Dominant bucks are active all day especially during the rut, and they make rubs on their way to their destination. During the rut their destination is usually a doe bedding area, but if not it is a water source.

As you get more experience reading rubs, you will be able to know if he has competition in his territory or if he is the stand alone biggest monster buck that lives in the area. In addition, you will know how big his track is, where the nearest doe bedding area and pecking order buck bedding areas are, and how big his rack is. You cannot find out how many points it has but you can determine the space between his G2 and G3 antler tines, and that will tell you if he is a monster buck or not!

Continue to analyze the rub until you are able to unlock its secrets. You should be able to determine what the dominant buck's mood was while he made the rub. To accomplish that I analyze the characteristics of the rub to determine which of the 9 types of dominant buck rubs I am looking at. Then I figure out what that rub means to all the deer that encounter it. From that point forward, I think like the buck. I put myself in the frame of mind the buck was in when he made the rub. I face the direction he did, and I see the deer herd as my own. I know I am king and I can go wherever I please without fearing for my life. I think like the buck and I figure out why he made the rub there. Once I know why, then I automatically know where he is bedded at that moment in time! I also know where his does are, and where the pecking order bucks will be. They are all in their bedding areas.

The wind direction is the most important factor I use to determine where exactly the deer will be bedded on any given day. This is great knowledge for any deer hunter to have. Knowing that rubs are made by a buck making contact with the tree at a crosswind angle, and knowing where to look for a rub made by the king will help you paint *"The Big Picture"*. Being able to read any one of the dominant buck's rubs will tell you where the whole herd is bedding, therefore any person who can read rubs the same way I can, will be able to see their area's herd structure clearly, just from locating one single rub made by a dominant buck. The more rubs you find the closer you are to his bedroom or his guest (doe) bedrooms and the more likely he is to bust you if you hunt there.

Being able to read buck rubs will help you see the land from a deer's perspective. You will be able to lay out the rooms in the buck's house and see them as separate places. You will understand why the dominant buck has always been so elusive, and how he lives a completely different life than the pecking order bucks. Once you understand all that, then the land will be easy for you to hunt with my system because you will know where to use it and where not to use it. The dominant buck walks into every room of his house, every 24 hours, and checks his yard for intruders once every three days all year long. You need to slip into his front yard or one of his side yards undetected (as a deer) while he is in his bedroom, and you need to get out of his yard (as a human) before the sun sets so he does not ever discover that you were there in the first place.

The main thing is that you find out which type of rub you are looking at and what it can tell you about the herd. Dominant bucks make rubs when they are away from their own bedding areas, and they travel at crosswind angles most of the time. I know that dominant bucks always bed downwind and crosswind of doe bedding areas, so my next step is to sketch what I have found, and determine where his normal bedding area must be in relation to where I am standing (at his rub). Remember to start by analyzing which buck made the rub and determine which type of rub it is. Then all the pieces will start falling into place for you. You will be able to tell which room of his house you are in, and where you have to go to get out of his house and into his front yard.

The dominant buck's front yard is always upwind and crosswind of his core living area, it is from there that I have never been busted by a dominant buck on a D.I.E. hunt! To locate the dominant buck's front yard you first have to look at the land from above. Look at an aerial photograph of your hunting land if you can get one, or just draw it out on paper, and determine which room or rooms of the dominant buck's house your hunting land encompasses. The rooms in a dominant buck's house include: three core doe bedding areas, three core dominant buck beds, a core breeding area, three pecking order buck bedding areas, one primary food source, the junction of deer trails, and a year round water supply. If you hunt less than 10 acres, you may only have one or two rooms on your hunting property. It is all right, you do not even need to be in a room to have D.I.E. work for you. You could hunt a travel corridor. I call them hallways, to the rooms in the most dominant buck's house. The main thing is to know what options you have to choose from, before you set the D.I.E. system up and wait for a miracle to happen. Do your homework and concentrate on giving the buck a sense of always being in control of what goes on in his house. If you can hunt from outside his core living areas, and avoid all the places deer congregate, then you will be invisible to all the deer there. If not, you will be taking risks of being detected.

Analyze your hunting land to realize where in the house or yard of the dominant buck you have been hunting, and where you have to go in order to be out in his front yard away from the herd.

Your most exciting D.I.E. hunts will take place when you pick a stand site that is upwind and crosswind of:

- his bedroom (his core downwind bed)
- his guest rooms (all doe bedding and pecking order buck bedding areas)
- his living room (a food source where deer congregate)
- his kitchen (year round water source)
- his recreation room (a core breeding zone)
- and his backyard (the place that is furthest downwind in his territory that you can go)

When you are upwind and crosswind of all of his active sign, and of all the individual bedding areas (9) of the herd, then you are in a place that I would hunt if I was you. I search for the herd and the dominant buck's sign, so I can get away from it all, and I can set up in a place where I know I will be hunted by two competing dominant bucks on every hunt. The only thing that can prevent a hunter from having that option is land limitation. If you currently hunt a small acre parcel, either hunt on its upwind side 80 or more yards from buck sign and deer beds (or completely out of view of it), or consider hunting on public land, where there will not be any restrictions to how far you can go upwind of deer to set the D.I.E. system up. Public land holds monster bucks too! I am going to back up Tom Earle's proof that monster bucks live anywhere they are not pressured by hunters, when I hunt public land with a gun and a bow in Northern Wisconsin in 2011. I am documenting my hunts for entry in my next book.

Before setting up always, determine where the dominant buck lives. Where his front yard is, where his side yards are, and certainly, where his back yard is. In order to have 100% odds of success with D.I.E. you should always set up in his front yard, one of his two side yards, or in a hallway (crosswind an upwind of all deer bedding) where a heavily used deer trail crosses a water source. If you can be in one of those places go there and start enjoying the fact that you are going to be hunted by the king of deer. Hunt where deer walk not where they run, and hunt safe! No matter what, always put your safety and the safety of others first!

Hunting in his back yard is what most traditional hunters do. The dominant buck has 90% or higher odds of busting you anytime you hunt from downwind of his core living areas even if you are using my system. I know because I have been busted by 3 of the 4 bucks I hunted downwind of since I invented DOMINANCE IS EVERYTHING. Remember he comes from his bed to you, and he always beds downwind of your scrape in the nearest available cover. Coming in from downwind is the wrong way to hunt with D.I.E., never come in from downwind on a D.I.E. hunt! If you do, your odds of success will be less than 100% from the start. All you will be doing is telling the herd that you are a human and that they are being hunted. You may get close to pecking order bucks that way but getting close to the king of the herd is another story!

When a dominant buck beds downwind of a rub he watches it intently

A dominant buck rub has a use. It performs as if it was a motion sensor light. When a deer passes in front of the rub, the buck (if bedded downwind) will notice the rub is not showing and he will stand up in his bed and conduct a scent check to determine the identity of the deer that is visiting his territorial marker. If it is a doe in estrus, he will immediately call out to her and advance to meet her near the rub no matter what time of the day it is, or how terrible the weather has become. I knew that when I developed my D.I.E. system.

Smooth (polished) buck rubs are a lighter color than the regular bark on a tree, and day or night a buck rub of this sort will shine like a beacon that all deer can see. Dominant bucks make smooth rubs so they can watch them from their bedding area which always faces the rubbed part on the tree. All smooth rubs tell a dominant buck when another deer is entering or leaving his breeding territory. It is ingenious!

Shredded buck rubs are not always seen, because only some of them have both a smooth rubbed area and a shredded appearance. Smooth rubs shine but shredded rubs do not. Deer see black, white and grey. Dominant bucks bed downwind of rubs during the day, not so often at night.

Territorial rubs do not shine, but all deer know what they mean. Keep Out!

Shredded rubs are always territorial. Shredded rubs border the places the dominant buck frequents during the day. We hunt during the day, so when we scout we need to look for shredded rubs to find where the buck is bedding down, and look for smooth rubs to see where he goes to breed. He watches smooth rubs at night when other deer are in the area.

With D.I.E. you do not hunt where you see active buck rubs or scrapes and you never pressure a buck near his bedding area. You could succeed that way with my system but not 100% of the time. I know this is a fact, and for that reason I always hunt upwind and crosswind of a dominant buck's core breeding area if I have an option. I like hunting that area of his territory the best because other bucks come there to breed too, and where there are multiple bucks and multiple does in estrus, there is a better than 50% chance I will see a monster buck on my D.I.E. hunt.

Whenever I see a buck rub, I try to decipher it. First, I want to know if the dominant buck made it. I look for the damage his brow tines would have done. I try to find out how far apart the brow tines were on the rack of the buck that made it. The greater the distance apart, the bigger the rack is in most cases. Also, the deeper the gouges from the brow tines, the sharper those brow tines are; and the sharper the brow tines, the older the buck is. Some bucks do not have two brow tines; they may have only one or perhaps none at all. Other bucks have sticker points and other points coming out of their heads near the pedicles (bases) of their antlers. I do not know how whitetail buck's antlers grow, but it is my belief that the shape of a buck's antlers is inherited.

A fresh buck rub always marks something important to a dominant buck. His rubs can mark a territorial boundary, one of his bedding areas, a core breeding area, a doe bedding area, a food source, or the dominant buck's staging area. A dominant buck may make a rub to intimidate other bucks or to show off to a doe in estrus. A shredded rub on a 3 to 12 inch diameter tree is a warning to intruder bucks that a big dominant buck lives here! If rubs could talk, most of them would say "Keep out—or else!"

Weathered rubs were made the previous year or prior to that by the buck that was most dominant then. When a dominant buck is killed, or is no longer dominant because another buck beat him in a fight, then he can no longer make dominant buck rubs, so his rubs from last season dry up and grow old. If the dominant buck survived and is dominant the next year, then he will work (re-rub) the same territorial rubs, but he will always make new breeding area rubs when he starts mating, because the old ones were made on saplings, and most saplings die after getting shredded and broken down by an aggressive dominant buck. Buck rubs are always made on live trees and brush. If there is a new king of the herd in the area, he will choose new trees to rub and ignore the trees that last year's king had marked before him.

You should never set up or hunt with my system within view of authentic buck rubs or scrapes. If you do, the system will still work, but the buck will know that you are a human and that he is being watched. D.I.E. will still bring in the dominant buck in, but he will know something is wrong because a real intruder would not build a challenging scrape within view of the dominant buck's rubs or scrapes, so in that case your odds of success would be less than

100%. I teach you to avoid setting up where there is active buck sign, so you will not be faced with lower than 100% odds of success, but what you do is up to you. The system performs every time, it is up to you to prevent deer from knowing a human is there, or that a human will come back. By setting up near active buck sign, you took the D.I.E. system to the buck's core living area. Some folks have succeeded like that but they see multiple bucks and some does and the hunt is not as easy as it is if you get upwind of it all. If you fail to see the buck during daylight in this case, the cause of failure would be human error. I like 100% odds from the start that way I am a winner every time.

If you scout property the way I do, then you will know where the dominant buck lives (beds) in relation to your hunting land, and where you will have to set D.I.E. up in order to have a near perfect hunt. Rubs are great storytellers. Read on to learn what story the most dominant buck in the herd is telling all who are willing to listen. Open your mind so you can hear his story from a deer's perspective. Allow me to teach you what I know about rubs so you can learn to think like a deer, and you will see what rubs mean to every deer that encounter them. I am sure you will enjoy being in the territory of the king of your herd when your scouting day arrives. It is going to be fun for you to discover what the dominant buck is doing on your hunting property, and all of his sign will be fresh so you will be able to analyze his every move.

There are 9 different types of rubs a dominant buck makes

1. **A buck rub behind the primary breeding scrape of the dominant buck**
2. **Core breeding area rub**
3. **Core dominant buck bedding area rub**
4. **Territorial boundary rub**
5. **Meeting place rub**
6. **Staging area rubs**
7. **Rub line**
8. **Broken off sapling rub**
9. **A row of three or more rubs parallel to the same number of scrapes**

Non-Dominant bucks do not make any of these rubs and they will not rub any trees in the same locations where these rubs are found. Over 90% of all buck rubs that are made on 2-inch diameter trees or larger are made by the dominant buck. You can count on that!

Pecking order bucks are not allowed to mark territory because they do not own it. Only the king of the herd owns the territory, so only he can mark it with territorial rubs. A territorial rub has a shredded appearance. It is not rubbed smooth, down to the bright yellow colored part of the tree trunk. It has ripped bark that hangs off the tree. All non-dominant bucks will rub brush and sapling tops, and some of the rubs will have a shredded appearance, but lesser bucks are not marking territory by doing so, they are just trying to get the attention of other nearby deer when they make a rub like that.

Rubbing a tree trunk is a territorial instinct that all bucks get the urge to act upon, but inside the pecking order, only one buck has the right to make rubs on trees larger than one inch in diameter. That is the dominant buck. All mature bucks rub trees but the dominant buck immediately takes over territorial rubs made by insubordinate bucks whenever he finds them. Non-ranking monster bucks, make territorial rubs in their core bedding areas and the dominant buck will not take them over, because they respect one another, and they have agreed to coexist on the same property without having territorial conflicts. A non-dominant monster buck does not make territorial rubs to intimidate the king of the herd, or as an attempt to challenge him for dominance of his herd, he makes territorial rubs to let all the deer in the area know where the boundaries of the small piece of land that he beds down in are.

Most buck rubs are made on trees in areas where deer tend to be walking (not running), or in places where deer congregate. A dominant buck needs to communicate on a daily bases with every member of his herd, and every intruder buck or doe that passes through his territory. Because he cannot be in more than one place at one time, he makes buck rubs and each type of rub sends a different message to the deer that encounters it. I know what the messages say, and I am going to teach you how to read any dominant buck rub that you encounter.

Dominant buck rubs to deer, are like street signs to people. When we see street signs, we know we have a choice. We can either obey the signs, or ignore them and break the law. Every deer that sees a buck rub can read the sign, and know what the dominant buck is telling them. They know they have a choice too. They can obey the sign, or they can ignore it. Members of his herd (including pecking order bucks) will usually obey his signs, but intruder bucks usually will not. In our world police enforce the law and deal with the people who decide to break the rules. In the deer world, the most dominant buck is the enforcer! He will show up whenever a deer ignores the message that he has left for them. When breeder bucks post signs of their own, inside his territory, it means trouble for the dominant buck. Those actions trigger an immediate response from the king. He takes the rub over as soon as he discovers it so all the deer that encounter it know he is still their king! It has to be his way or else!

Dominant bucks maintain (re-rub) some of their rubs from early October through late February, and others they let fade away. The ones that fade away were temporarily placed in areas that the king spent time during the rut. Re-rubbing a rubbed tree tells all the deer in the area that the message is the same now as it was before, and that the same buck is in charge. Dominant bucks re-rub trees so their sign posts (the trees) and the messages on them are always clear, and easy for other deer to understand.

Any D.I.E. hunter can read buck rubs just as well as any deer, as long as they have completely read this chapter, or have attended one of my seminars. Being able to read and analyze buck rubs will change your world as a deer hunter or as a person who wants to get close to mature whitetail bucks. Once you have mastered the skills of reading buck sign, I think it is best if you practice reading a herd on property you do not intend to hunt. As you walk through the parcel you will feel a bit strange, because you will be aware of where the king of deer is at that given moment, and you will know he is watching your every move. He knows something is there, but if you do what I teach you, he will never know what exactly you are, because he will never lay eyes on you as a human.

A D.I.E. hunter can be successful without scouting for buck sign, but not 100% of the time. Being able to see the herd structure from the eyes of a deer that is a member of that herd, rather than looking at it from your own (a human) point of view, will open your eyes to what is really going on inside that herd each and every day. Imagine that you are the dominant buck when you find a buck rub, and try to analyze which direction he approached it from, and why he made it. Why did he make it there rather than somewhere else? Once you have that figured out, you will know where on that property you will find other rubs. You will know what type of rubs you will find there, and you will always know where the dominant buck is in relation to his rubs at all times of the day.

1. **A buck rub behind the primary breeding scrape of the dominant buck,** a rub that can only be made by a dominant buck. He will make it on a 1 to 4 inch diameter tree directly behind his primary breeding scrape. The rub always will have a smooth appearance, it will be 12 to 30 inches in height, and when the dominant buck makes it, he only rubs one side of the tree. There is always a licking branch hanging over a scrape (with a rub behind it). A rub like this sends three messages from the dominant buck, to all the deer in the herd. First, it announces that he is king of the herd. Second, he is telling every deer that this scrape is his primary breeding scrape. Third, he tells them all he will be watching the rub day and night from his nearby bed on the downwind side of the rubbed part of the tree. These rubs are rare and not every hunter will find one, but if you do then you can be sure that the dominant buck lives on your hunting land, and he will visit your D.I.E. scrape sooner rather than later.

    A dominant buck will always be close by, watching the rub on the tree behind the scrape from the security of his bedding cover (downwind or crosswind of the scrape). The rub on the tree appears to be white in a deer's black, grey, and white world, while the rest of the tree trunk is dark grey or black. The buck purposely watches the rub until a deer or other animal blocks his view of it, at which point he rises from his bed and scent checks the area. He identifies the animal that is visiting his scrape, by looking at it, getting its scent, and hearing it move. The dominant buck can have two or three of these scrapes with rubs behind them inside his own territory, but he can only maintain one at a time. You can tell which one he is using at the time by looking in the dirt for a single front hoof track. The deer track always has splayed toes and dew points showing. I fashioned the D.I.E. scrape to look exactly like one of these scrapes with a territorial rub behind it, minus the presence of a deer track. A dominant buck cannot ignore a scrape with a rub behind it, because it is a sign that an intruder monster buck has moved into his territory and is stealing does in estrus away from him there. He is forced to take it over and he is convinced that does are visiting it already, so he stays there and waits for them. You are one of those does when you hunt with DOMINANCE IS EVERYTHING.

Never hunt with D.I.E. within view of any real buck rubs or scrapes, and never touch a real buck rub or scrape on a D.I.E. hunt otherwise the buck will know a human is in the area. Not one deer living in a dominant buck's territory would ever mess with one of his core breeding scrapes, so he will be instantly on to you, as a human in the area, if you mess with any of them in any way. Subordinate bucks (pecking order bucks) will not rub any trees behind scrapes and they never bed down on the downwind side of scrapes with rubs behind them. Those scrapes belong the king of the herd and only he has the earned right to make them or maintain them. The existence of the rub behind the scrape makes it a territorial marker, and only the dominant buck can mark his territory. All deer know that, and now you do too, so do not make the mistake of altering a real dominant buck's rub or scrape while on a D.I.E. hunt. That type of behavior will get you busted.

2. **Core breeding area rub,** finding a rub like this will tell you that you are standing in the dominant buck's core breeding area. Usually less than 200 yards long and 80 yards wide, the breeding area attracts all breeding deer. Bucks chase does and breed does in this cover 24 hours a day during the rut. A core breeding area rub will most often be on a soft bark tree that is 2 inches in diameter or less and all the branches on the bottom 3 feet of the tree will be broken off. Most of the trees where you will find these rubs are less than 10 feet tall. There are instances where the rubbed tree will be closer to 4 inches in diameter. If that is the case then you can be assured that the dominant buck is a monster buck. The tree looks as if it was attacked! Usually just the branches on the top of the tree will remain intact. The integrity of the tree is no longer there. This is a shredded rub, not a smooth rub. It can have smooth areas but you will see shredded bark hanging off at the top and the bottom of the smooth part of the rub. The buck rips and rubs a tree to make a core breeding area rub.

    Look for one, two, or three rubs of this sort in a dominant buck's core breeding area. They are made 40 to 70 yards apart, and they will be laid out in a line-going crosswind of the area's predominant wind. A dominant buck makes a rub like this one all by itself without any scrape. It stands alone in a semi-open area. The buck stands at the rubbed tree and is able to watch does as they travel from bedding to food, or from bedding to his core breeding area. There will always be two or more doe trails crisscrossing within 80 yards upwind of that location. One of the dominant buck's core beds is always downwind of a rub like this, 100 to 200 yards away just inside the edge of some cover. Oftentimes a water source is nearby, and sometimes the rub is actually made in standing water.

This is how the deer view a core dominant buck's scrape. In this case, it is a D.I.E. scrape complete with a licking branch, a D.I.E. rub, a Scrape-Dripper and pawed up dirt in the scrape. Deer do not notice the dripper.

Downwind side of a "core-breeding area rub."

Upwind side of the same "core-breeding area rub."

This core-breeding area rub was located 40 yards to the left of the rub shown in the last two photos.

Dominant buck core-bedding area rub. The buck's bed was under a pine tree 40 yards downwind and crosswind of this rub.

When the dominant buck is a monster buck, he most often makes his core bed in a swamp. This is a "dominant buck core-bedding area rub." It tells you he beds in front of the shredded bark in the closest cover.

The same dominant buck that made the rub in the previous photo made these two. He owns the area 360° around these two trees and he beds wherever he wants to. The rubs tell all deer to stay out!

3. **Dominant buck core bedding area rub,** these rubs are not made inside dominant buck bedding areas. They are made on the outside edge of the cover that the dominant buck uses to bed in. They are made on the edge of a terrain change. Rubs like this are often made 150 to 200 yards at a crosswind from his bed and normally they are made 3 to 10 yards downwind of a heavily used deer trail, on a 3-inch or larger diameter tree. Core dominant buck bedding area rubs never face upwind. The face of a rub is always the torn up side. I look at these rubs as meaning the same thing as a "Do Not Disturb" sign on a hotel doorknob. We all know what that means. Stay Out! These rubs are made on tag alders or other soft bark trees and they are shredded in appearance at the top and bottom but smooth in the center, just like the rub we make on a tree behind a D.I.E. scrape. Where there are no soft bark trees a dominant buck will rub a tree with hard bark. There could be one, two, or three of these rubs right next to each other. If you find one of these rubs, you should know that the dominant buck beds directly away from the ripped bark.

4. **Territorial boundary rub,** a lone rub often found out in the open, in the middle of one type of terrain. This rub is made by a dominant buck on the border of his territory where it abuts another dominant buck's territory, and then it is located and rubbed by the neighboring herd's king. Here is an explanation of how a rub like this is made. The first dominant buck (Buck A) rubs the tree. He makes a (territorial) shredded rub on a substantial sized tree, usually four or more inches in diameter. The rubbed side faces the side the dominant buck (Buck A) owns. The backside of the rubbed tree is not rubbed by Buck A because Buck B owns the land on the other side of it. Buck A does not have a right to rub it. He makes a territorial rub to draw a line between his territory and that of the neighboring buck. Territorial rubs are always shredded (when they are made), and the shredded side is the side the dominant buck that made it is living on.

   The land on the opposite side of a territorial rub belongs to Buck B, the neighboring herd's dominant buck. Within 3 days, Buck B comes along and he discovers the scent of Buck A on the tree trunk with the rub on it, so he investigates the shredded rub. Apparently, Buck B is unhappy with the placement of the marker that Buck A has identified as his territorial boundary, so Buck B takes ownership of the tree rub back by ripping the bark off the same tree but not just on his side, he rubs it all the way around the tree. He will not leave the bark in a shredded state, because that would mean that only one herd's dominant buck owned it. You will see in each case where you find one of these rubs, that the second buck always rubs the tree smooth all the way around its trunk.

   Now Buck B owns the tree and he is dominating that particular boundary marker. That is until Buck A comes back and finds his boundary rub has been taken away by Buck B. Again, this will happen within 3 days. Dominant bucks (like Buck A and Buck B) will visit their boundary markers once every three days all year long. When each buck discovers that his neighbor has stolen his marker away, he is furious about it. He rips and rubs more of the bark off the tree and he marks the rub with his scent repeatedly. From that point forward, the last buck to rub it owns it again.

   In reality both bucks own it but I know from witnessing two dominant bucks working a tree rub like this while one another watched, that neither one of them is willing to share the tree. The last one to rub it owns it at that moment. A person walking past such a rub can smell the scent of the glands of those two dominant bucks in the area around the rub.

After both bucks have worked, the tree over a few times, the tree starts looking like a shiny new penny. You cannot miss seeing it!

The rub will not have a shredded appearance after both bucks have rubbed it, but it will still be a territorial rub, it is one of the most sought after rubs a hunter can find! There is never a scrape near a rub like this and that is because dominant bucks make scrapes on the edges of cover where they do not have any competition, and a territorial boundary rub is always made out in the open in the center of a clearing so all the deer in both herds can see it. Two kings are competing for dominance of that boundary, and neither one would be dumb enough to make a scrape nearby inviting their does to be distracted by another dominant buck.

Each dominant buck tries to dominate the other by rubbing that tree while the other one watches, and neither one will quit rubbing that tree as long as they are both alive and both are dominant (each in their own herd). Eventually it looks as if a beaver had chewed into it. Most often, you will find a rub like this on a tree trunk that has rough (hard) bark. It takes a buck with a monstrous rack to be able to rip bark off a hard bark tree. Finding one of these rubs is always a good thing for you.

I get excited when I find a territorial boundary rub because I can set up D.I.E. just out of view of it on the upwind side and I will have two monster bucks competing at my D.I.E. scrape on Day 1 of my hunt every time. The bigger of the two bucks will likely be a monster buck and he will be hunting me. I am thrilled when I am being hunted by monster bucks. Search your hunting land for a territorial boundary rub, and be sure to hunt upwind of it, if you have a chance to hunt with D.I.E., on that parcel of land.

5. **Meeting place rub,** is a rub commonly found on a 2 to 5 inch diameter tree but it could be on bigger trees where monster bucks live. It will always be rubbed smooth. The rub is not shredded. The most common place to find one of these rubs is where two or more heavily used deer trails meet. The dominant buck marks a tree at the intersection of 2 trails or downwind within 20 yards of the intersection. He will be very aggressive when rubbing the tree and he will polish the rub so it shines in the moonlight. He beds or stages (stands up waiting) downwind of a rub like this in the nearest available cover, waiting for does in heat and in estrus to pass by on one of the trails. There will only be one meeting place rub upwind of each of the dominant buck's core bedding areas.

Of course, the wind direction can change daily, but that never affects a D.I.E hunter, it only determines which bed the dominant buck will be coming to you from. The dominant buck beds in his furthest downwind bed every morning, so you will be able to find out which of his core beds is downwind of your stand each day, just by drawing the location of any meeting place rubs that you find out on a piece of paper. Once you find the three core dominant buck bedding areas you will know which bed the dominant buck prefers to use depending on the wind direction. The dominant buck usually beds 100 to 200 yards away from a meeting place rub in a downwind or crosswind direction of it. Meeting place rubs are made in places where the dominant buck does not have much competition. Unlike breeding area rubs that are shredded in appearance, and are made in areas where other bucks breed during the rut, meeting place rubs are always smooth and cleaned up in appearance, and you should know the dominant buck is the only buck breeding in that area. These rubs are usually quite tall (20 to 30 inches) and they are rubbed 180° to 270° around the tree. That is done on purpose so that deer approaching the rub from three sides can see it clearly. The backside is never rubbed.

He can see the meeting place rub when he is standing up in his bed, but not always when he is laying down. During the rut, the dominant buck makes a rub like this to attract does in estrus to his core bedding area, and to keep track of his entire herd from this one location. I have always found a water source within 100 yards of a meeting place rub. Hunt upwind and crosswind of a meeting place rub, but make sure you are completely out of view of it, so you do not find yourself trying to watch the buck come to you. If you can see him he can often see you, and that is never good on a D.I.E. hunt. Have confidence that the dominant buck will smell the scent you are using and that he will approach you when he is convinced nothing is there to hurt him.

6. **Staging area rubs,** these rubs are always found on the outside edge or on the corner of one type of cover (usually a swamp edge), where the buck stages before heading out into the open to meet does after sunset. There are usually 3 to 12 or more shredded rubs right next to each other, rubbed only on one side of some 1 inch to 3-inch saplings or on tag alder brush. The buck is saying, "I stand here when my does are going out to feed and I will not tolerate any other bucks hanging around this area". He stages to avoid being shot by hunters. A buck that is staging is hiding. When it is dark, he will move out of his staging cover and meet up with the does. It is as if he has his own parking space and that is it. Staging area rubs are made to warn other bucks to "Stay Out!" They are territorial and they are very close to the dominant buck's bed (within 50 yards).

7. **Rub line,** A rub line is a row of rubs made by a dominant buck that leads from one of his core bedding areas to one of his core breeding scrapes and beyond it. The buck rubs at least three and up to ten, 2-inch or

Meeting place rub, this one was rubbed on 3 sides and had thick cover on the backside where the bark remained. This rub is on the public land I am hunting in 2011 archery season. The king that made it will be hunting me.

larger diameter trees, about 10 yards apart from each other in semi-open terrain. All the rubs will be made on the same side of the tree trunk usually as the buck makes his way up an incline. Rub lines can be found on flat ground too, but most often they are made on high ground. Dominant bucks like to bed in lowland areas, therefore you will see that rub lines most often start out low at the base of a hill and go up the slope to a plateau and then beyond it. On the plateau, there will be a core dominant buck scrape. It will be a real scrape made by the most dominant buck that looks exactly like a D.I.E. scrape. Sometimes the scrape is on top of a hill but most often, it is on the side-hill where the ground flattens out. Look for the scrape within 20 yards of one of the rubs. If he is using it there will be a single front hoof track with splayed toes in it, pressed into the dirt of the scrape. The dominant buck stays in his bed at the base of that rub line most of the day and night as he watches the rub line from there. When a deer or other animal passes by one of the rubs, he becomes alerted to it being there and he stands up and conducts a scent check. If he identifies the movement as a deer then he will approach it, if it is a human he will avoid it. Dominant bucks make rub lines where they have food, water, and safety all around. They always have a core dominant buck scrape within a few yards of one of the rubs in their rub line and the reason they make the rub line there in the first place is that they prefer to bed in that particular area during the rut.

Most often, his bed there is nearly straight upwind of one of the three core doe bedding areas, and he places a primary breeding scrape between his bed and theirs. In this case the buck does not bed downwind in the nearest available cover, instead he is bedded upwind facing the polished rub that backs one of his core breeding scrapes. A rub line is needed to see all approaching animals because the dominant buck cannot use the wind to detect any danger that approaches him from his downwind side. He cannot discover what he cannot smell, hear, or see. That is why you can be invisible to him. He makes a rub line so he can see approaching animals. He cannot hear or smell anything that is downwind of him, but because he is being pressured in his other two bedding areas he has chosen this one to hide in for a while. He watches the rubs on the rub line as if they were the lit up markers on an airport runway at night. The closer he is to them the more obvious they are. When an animal or a person walks in front of a rub in the line, he is able to detect it being there, because the animal or person blocks the light that the rub emits.

Dominant bucks are very smart but not all of them are smart enough to make rub lines. If you find a rub line, you are dealing with a buck that knows how to avoid traditional hunters during the rut. He moves upwind of them and allows humans the opportunity to hunt on the downwind side of his does. From his upwind position, he is still in command of his herd, and from there he is one buck that will never be caught in the sights of a traditional hunter. Not until traditional hunters read this chapter anyway.

Dominant bucks like to bed downwind and crosswind of areas where does frequent, but sometimes due to the terrain being logged off, due to lack of cover, or due to hunting pressure on the downwind side of doe bedding areas the dominant buck is forced to bed upwind of his does. When that is the case, he uses a rub line to be able to watch every living thing that moves around downwind of his safest bed. Making a rub line is the safest way for a monster dominant buck to survive being hunted in the rut. Until now, I do not believe anyone in the world has ever printed anything close to my description of what rub lines are, what rub lines mean, and what rub lines can tell a human about the buck that made them. I decided to add this section about rubs to the book in June 2011. That is why it took me two years to get my book published. I hope you feel it was worth the wait. I certainly think that D.I.E. hunters are going to be the most educated deer hunters out there, but I will wait for your results to see if I am right. I want you to succeed. That is why I am sharing all my findings with you.

If you do not believe what I am telling you, that is ok with me, but if you do believe, then you are about to become a very happy dominant buck hunter. Believe in D.I.E., and welcome to my world!

If you find a freshly made rub line, you can be sure that on the upwind side of it, you will find the dominant buck's core bed at the time, and that he is maintaining a primary scrape with a rub behind it along that rub line, ½ to ¾ of the way down the line away from his bed. You will be able to go from tree to tree following the rub line downwind and you will be able to smell, and eventually see his primary breeding scrape, once you get close to it. He will always make at least one rub downwind of his scrape so he can see any deer that approaches it from downwind. He will watch all the rubs in this row (rub line) as he is bedded upwind of his scrape and he can work his way to the scrape day or night with the wind hitting him in his hind flanks as he moves from rub to rub, staging along the way. The dominant buck is king and he fears no animal. He moves upwind of his does to avoid being detected by humans, during the rut.

Most traditional hunters go about hunting a scrape line all wrong and the dominant buck moves away because of their intrusion in his bedding area. Never hunt a scrape line with D.I.E., let the buck breed there in peace and pull him upwind and crosswind to your hiding place where you are the hunted and he is the hunter. Yes it is exciting to find a rub line but one of the worst things a D.I.E. hunter could do, would be to hunt over one of them. I avoid walking rub lines or hunting near them because I know the dominant buck is watching from upwind and he will know I am there if I walk the line. As the inventor of DOMINANCE IS EVERYTHING, I know that nothing is worse than telling the dominant buck that I am a human. Walking a rub line before I harvest the dominant buck would be like announcing to him on a loud speaker that I am a human and I am there to hunt him. System or no system no dominant buck is stupid enough to come in during daylight if you tell him a human is there. I will never do anything that could jeopardize my invisibility and you should not either.

8. **Broken off sapling rub,** when a dominant buck is in one of his breeding areas or hanging around a staging area, he often times spends a few hours in a small area and he gets restless there. A dominant buck leaves his bedding area and stages on the fringe (outside edge) of the cover where he beds. He will rake brush and make small staging type rubs in the corner of a field or on the edge of a swamp or clearing. Sometimes when he sees other mature breeder bucks heading out to join his does on a food source, he breaks one or more saplings down in an aggressive show of force. Dominant bucks live by very strict routines and one thing they rarely do is rush out to a food source to feed before the sun has set completely. They will often work over a small sapling with their rack, until they break the top off, just about four feet off the ground. Rubs you find on broken off saplings

are shredded in appearance 100% of the time. Finding weathered rubs of this sort, tell you that the dominant buck spent many hours in that exact spot last fall during the rut while he was waiting to go out to meet the herd at their favorite food source.

9. **A row of three or more rubs parallel to the same number of scrapes,** it is rare to see this sort of thing but I have seen it, and so far, two of the 188 people I taught the D.I.E. system to have claimed they have seen it where they hunt. The rubs are all made by the dominant buck that owns the land under the rubs, and the scrapes are all made by the neighboring herd's dominant buck. He builds them on his side of their property border. When you find a scenario like this at least one of the bucks will turn out to be a monster buck.

None of these scrapes will have a rubbed tree behind them. The dominant buck that owns the scrapes will rake his antlers in the pawed up ground in the scrape instead of rubbing a tree. You should see two or three drag marks in the dirt of one or more scrapes. They are made by the longest tines on the buck's antlers. Some of the scrapes will have a licking branch overhanging the pawed dirt, but not all of them.

The row of rubs will always have a smooth appearance. They are made on trees at least 3 inches in diameter, just a few yards from one another. The line of rubs and line of scrapes will be separated by 5 to 15 yards. Each tree is rubbed all the way around and the rub is polished clean. Seeing these signs where you hunt tell you that you are on the fringe of more than one dominant buck's territory.

Two or more kings are competing to breed the does in one bedding area that most likely is divided by a roadway or another human obstacle. Each dominant buck is a bruiser. They bed on their own side of the territorial boundary within view of the main deer trails that lead to the scrapes and rubs. In Chapter 5, I taught you that there are three core doe bedding areas in every herd and that one of them is often overlapping the border of two dominant buck's territories. This is one such case. The does come and go into and out of both buck's territories on an everyday basis. They have to in order to find food, water and shelter. It just so happens that the two kings that breed there are in constant competition for the breeding rights of the does that bed there. It is an ongoing battle, year after year until one of the bucks is killed. If the herd boundary is still intact the following October when the rut kicks in, you will know it by noticing that the same rubs are being worked again and that the scrapes are being made in the same place as the year before. These rubs and scrapes are visited by the bucks that made them on a daily basis during the rut sometimes more than once a day, during daylight.

Look for this scenario to exist on the outside edge of a core-doe bedding area on an old logging road that is no longer used by vehicles. Close to a black top road or a dirt road that is traveled by cars and trucks on a daily basis. The scrapes are often discovered by hunters under pine trees or beneath willow trees. The scrapes are always situated on a high point sometimes on one side of an old logging road. The ground will be 3 to 10 feet higher where the scrapes are than the ground under the rubs. There is always a core-doe bedding area within 50 yards of these rubs and scrapes, normally at a crosswind. Doe bedding areas can overlap dominant buck territorial boundaries and during the rut, all dominant bucks are willing to do just about anything to maintain peace and order within the herd. If that means fighting for the right to breed the does in estrus, in that area, then so be it.

The rubs are made and maintained by the most dominant buck that owns the territory on the rubbed side of the trees. The scrapes are worked and maintained by the other dominant buck that beds (owns the territory) on the other side behind the scrapes. It is as if there is an invisible line drawn between the rubs and the scrapes, and the area is a constant battle zone. Dominant bucks do not budge on property borders, and when two kings clash, there are no winners, because neither king is able to run the whole territory of the other dominant buck. They avoid each other in that area, but each one visits their side of it each day to be sure the other one is not breeding a doe in estrus in the other buck's territory. If you find this sort of thing on your hunting land, you should not overlook it. You just hit the jackpot! You have a great opportunity to meet a true monster buck upwind of this area. Move away from the rubs and scrapes 100-200 yards upwind and crosswind, and set a D.I.E. scrape up in a place where you cannot see any buck rubs or scrapes. I would choose to hunt on the side that had the biggest buck tracks.

Never hunt inside a buck or doe bedding area. By placing the D.I.E. scrape upwind and out of sight from the rubs and scrapes, you will pull both of those kings to your ambush point. Do not ever overlook a set up like this one! I hunted one like this and saw the heaviest buck of my life on Day 2 of my hunt. He was a monster buck, standing still at 15 yards doing a lip curl, in gun season. He weighed more than 300 pounds on the hoof. I shot too quickly and hit him in the front leg. I lost the buck to some other hunters after I trailed him for over one mile. I wish I could take that shot back. His main beams were as big around as my forearms! What a hunt, D.I.E. worked but I made two costly mistakes that cost me that buck. I did not have see-through scope mounts on my rifle, and I had my scope turned up to 12x (power) when I aimed at the buck and fired. All I could see was his chin, neck, shoulder, and I fired. I hit him in the front leg, and I never regretted a shot that I fired more.

How to identify dominant buck scrapes

Dominant bucks maintain one or more scrapes inside their home territory. A scrape is a pawed-up area where the buck has dug down into the soil with his front hooves, and then urinated to leave his scent deposited there, in hopes does in heat and does in estrus will pay him a visit there. He is leaving his calling card for them. Dominant bucks always have a licking branch above their scrapes, but a rub behind a scrape is optional. When you find a scrape with a rub behind it and a licking branch above it that is nibbled off, you have found a core dominant buck-breeding scrape. No other buck makes a scrape like that! If there is a huge track in it with splayed toes then the dominant buck is using the scrape and he is bedded in the nearest available cover on the downwind or at a crosswind of the scrape (in front of the polished rub) at that very moment. You will only find a scrape like that with a fresh track in it if the rut is on. If there is a doe track (closed toes) in it but no buck track, that tells you that there is a doe in heat or a doe in estrus searching for the dominant buck. Does in estrus go to a dominant buck's scrape and urinate in it, because they know the dominant buck will visit the scrape once or twice daily, and when he does he will be able to identify that doe, by the scent of her urine. He will stay nearby downwind in cover, if she is in heat, and he will immediately track her down to mate with her if she is in estrus.

You can assume that the rut is on if you see a fresh doe track in a freshly made scrape (whether there is a rub behind it or not). Dominant bucks make multiple scrapes in areas they can watch from the security of cover. Lesser bucks also make scrapes but not any with a rub behind them, and a licking branch above. I have even seen does pawing up the earth and urinating in the scrape they made. When you find a freshened scrape (urinated in by a buck, a doe, or both) you should know that the dominant buck is breeding and the rut is on.

I have learned to recognize when a scrape was made by a mature intruder buck and then was taken over by the most dominant buck in the herd. It looks just like the D.I.E. scrape I teach you to make, except the rub on the tree behind the scrape is rubbed all the way around. That is a scrape that the dominant buck now owns and controls. It must have an overhanging licking branch to make it the core scrape of the most dominant buck in the herd. I fashioned my D.I.E. scrape after one of these scrapes. I always make my D.I.E. scrape exactly the same way and by doing so I tell the dominant buck that I am a monster intruder buck (not a man) and I am trying to take over a bit of his territory. When he finds it (which has always been within 3 days), he is forced by instinct to take it over and control it until I (the intruder buck) return to fight him for dominance at the scrape. I also tell the buck I am a doe that came to the D.I.E. scrape as a doe in heat and after 2 ½ days returned there as a doe in estrus, looking for him to breed with her. If a dominant buck did not take over the intruder monster buck's scrape on a D.I.E. hunt, he would be yielding the territory the scrape is in and he would be giving up on the doe in estrus. **DOMINANCE IS EVERYTHING** to every dominant buck. That is why I do not believe there will ever be, a dominant buck that yields to another buck. A territory is something worth fighting for and the earned right to breed is worth fighting to the death for therefore every dominant buck will fight if challenged at his core scrape.

If you find a real scrape with a rub behind it and a licking branch overhanging it and you notice the rub is all the way around the tree, you are in heaven my friend. That is a sign that two bucks are fighting to maintain that scrape. These two bucks are not lesser bucks by any means. They are both huge racked bucks. One of them is dominant of the land under the scrape and the other one may or may not be dominant of the neighboring herd. If not, he is going to turn out to be a monster buck more than 50% of the time. Do not hunt near a scrape like this with my system, because both of the bucks will be on to you in a heartbeat. Move upwind and crosswind in the direction you entered the property from and set up 150 or more yards away. There you will see your dominant buck within 35 yards of your stand in one to four days, and I would be willing to bet he turns out to be a monster buck more often than not under circumstances like that.

A dominant buck makes scrapes near his primary bedding sites, around the edges of food sources, and at water crossings. He leaves fresh signs (rubs) of his presence on all sides of the doe bedding areas. He will always choose to bed within view of one of his core scrapes and he will always face the rubbed side of the tree trunk, when he beds down.

Real scrapes range from one to 7 feet in diameter. I have seen circular, oval, and triangular buck scrapes. I like to make my D.I.E. scrape in the shape of a trapezoid. Bucks make scrapes in many different types of terrain.

A scrape is a meeting place for a dominant buck and a doe in heat—or better yet, a doe in estrus. Scrapes are the location where breeding deer deposit their scent to communicate with one another. A buck makes a scrape, and then a doe in heat visits it and urinates in it to let the buck know how close she is to being in estrus (ready to breed). Sometimes a doe will make a scrape, and she wants a buck to move in and go to her there. The scrapes that does make do not have rubs behind them and dominant bucks do not bed down within view of those scrapes to the best of my knowledge.

During the rut, the dominant buck breeds with every doe in estrus that he can find. Finding a doe in estrus can be tough after the peak rut has ended, but that never stops the most dominant buck from pursuing does. He works up his scrapes and makes new rubs, and if he has to, he will go to the does instead of waiting for them to come to one of his scrapes.

When the dominant buck sees an intruder buck near a freshened scrape, he will charge in with his head lowered in the snowplow position and he will aggressively clash antlers with that buck, right then, and right there! When a dominant buck fights with another buck, it is for real. There is no backing out. If the dominant buck loses the battle, he loses both his territory and his earned right to breed. If he wins then the intruder leaves the area, but usually not for good.

The decision is final unless another fight develops after the first one, and the same two bucks go at it again. The second fight can happen the same day or a week or two later. I witnessed herd dominance-changing hands

This is the first dominant buck's core-breeding scrape that one of my clients was able to find on public land in Wisconsin. I was with him when he found it.

before my eyes while I was filming deer. An initially dominant buck could regain his title if he won a second fight. Sometimes a dominant buck will not leave the area after a loss. After a fight involving a dominant buck, the winner is king and the loser could either become second in command (if he was fighting his next ranked #2 pecking order buck), or he could lose it all and no longer hold rank. That happens if an intruder buck from another herd kicks his butt, then the dominant buck loses it all. He is kicked out of the ranks, because the challenger had nothing to lose. If an initially dominant buck loses a fight but refuses to leave his territory, he may become a monster buck, and stay there but not have to check into ranks. I have seen it with my own eyes and I have video of it happening.

Chapter 7

Dominant bucks behave predictably

Whitetail deer need four things in order to survive. They are food, water, safety from predators, and the ability to breed successfully. A dominant buck always prioritizes them in this order:

1. CONCEALMENT (SAFETY)
2. FOOD (NUTRITION)
3. WATER
4. THE OPPORTUNITY TO BREED

They hide from humans 24/7.

Total **concealment** is necessary 24 hours a day, and 7 days a week in order for a dominant buck to survive. He is the most sought after buck in the herd (by hunters) because of his larger than average antlers. Staying invisible to humans is the number one job of a dominant buck every day of his life. By bedding down in a safe place in heavy cover, a dominant buck can spend his entire day unmolested. Heavy cover does not have to be tall enough to hide a standing buck, it just has to be 3 feet tall or taller and offer the buck a place to bed down where he cannot be seen by his enemies from any angle.

Dominant bucks love to bed in marsh grass, and if there is a swamp inside their territory, they will strategically place one of their three core beds in the wettest end of the swamp. Before choosing a bed dominant bucks always consider which direction their enemies are likely to approach their bed from, then they figure out ahead of time how they will escape if they are rousted from that bed.

The home territory of a dominant buck has borders. I do not believe that fences, roads, or waterways define the outside edge of a dominant buck's territory. There is more to it than that. It has to do with dominance among the area's bucks. Every dominant buck's territory butts up against another dominant buck's territory. I am sure of that. You and I cannot see each of the borders, but that is ok because we do not ever need to. No matter where you place a D.I.E. set up, a dominant buck calls that parcel of land under your tree stand home. He is the king of the area's herd, and he will be one of the bucks that will be hunting you. Bucks from neighboring herds will hunt you too, as long as you set the system up along one of their shared territorial boundaries.

Note: If you find a rub on a tree that is more than three inches in diameter and the rub does not have a scrape under it, but it is rubbed smooth all the way around the tree, it tells you that there are two dominant bucks fighting for the right to dominate that exact spot. I have seen these types of rubs many times and I am convinced that they are signs of a border between two dominant buck's territories. If you set up the D.I.E. system upwind and crosswind 150 yards or so of a marker, like this one, your odds of seeing a monster buck on your hunt will automatically increase by 50%. Scout for rubs like this, and note their location if you find any. Whenever two dominant bucks are fighting for territory, there is a higher than 50% chance that one of them will be a monster buck. Only one buck will visit the D.I.E. scrape at a time, and the first one there is always the most dominant of the herd. If any others show up, they are intruder challenger bucks. There is never a guarantee that more than one buck will show up. So do not count on it.

How dominant bucks move through cover

All mature deer conduct scent checks downwind of an area they want to move into, prior to moving into it, and the dominant buck is no exception. If a predator moves in on a dominant buck while he is bedded his first instinct is to stay in his bed until the threat passes by him. He can outwit almost every predator that pursues him, by staying still and hiding, rather than running and exposing himself to the predator.

No mature deer will proceed on its route of travel without first doing a scent check to make sure there are no predators or unidentifiable scents coming from the area they are about to enter. Yearling deer and fawns are different. Most of them are not familiar, with which scents belong to dangerous animals or to humans, so many of them fall victim to predators during their first year or two of life. Deer stand still to scent check the wind. If they sense an unusual aroma the will go on alert.

All deer attempt to detect danger in cover ahead of them while they are on the move. They need to know it is safe before heading into any tall vegetation to bed down for the day. Dominant bucks and most other mature deer move 9 to 13 steps at a time. They hesitate often while walking to their choice food source, and back to their bedding area, finding water along the way. The reason deer do not walk steadily from point A to point B is because the terrain they are moving into is forever changing, and their field of view is altered with each step.

I teach you to squat down to a deer's eye height when you are scouting for a D.I.E. set up location because it is imperative that you see how often the terrain changes in a deer's world. I thoroughly enjoy tracking deer and learning from their movements. I learned what they think about as they move into areas with different types of vegetation, and I learned how to mimic their behavior so I am invisible to them when I walk through the woods on a D.I.E. hunt.

You need to think like a deer in order to pass yourself of as one of them. Dominant bucks will not move one leg forward if there is even a 1% chance that danger is lurking ahead. That is why most people have never seen a dominant buck before face to face. He avoids people because they are his number one enemy.

Dominant bucks are very cautious. They are constantly listening, looking, and using their keen sense of smell to check their surroundings for any threats. They conduct scent checks as they move from place to place. That means all deer on the move stop every 50 yards or so and try to locate (traditional) hunters, but the dominant buck checks the air more often than that, and when he detects any scent that he is unsure about, he stops there and turns around. He wants to live another day more than he wants any other thing. Do not ever forget that!

In a deer's world, danger can lurk behind any type of vegetation. The smart ones (mature deer) never take chances with their lives. If they are concerned about something not being just right, they wait for darkness to fall before proceeding into that area. Deer feel safe moving at night because they can see well in the dark, and because humans cannot see as well in the dark as deer do, I made my D.I.E. system into a daytime only hunt. You do not go out to your stand before the start of legal shooting hours (each day), and you leave your stand before the close of legal shooting hours. That way the dominant buck cannot bust you on your way in or out of the area. He only hunts the scrape during daylight and he is waiting for you to arrive when you get there.

The Dominant buck watches you enter and leave your land

Many people do not think that the dominant buck is constantly avoiding them when they are afield. They assume instead that the dominant buck does not live on their hunting property. That is their misconception. He owns your hunting property just like you do, and he is always aware of what is going in and out of it. Give credit to dominant bucks for being smarter than other deer, and know you are in the home territory of a dominant buck no matter where you are on the property at any time. He is either watching you, scent checking you, or listening to you every moment you are on your hunting land, and you can be assured he is doing so from heavy cover, because his life depends on it. Once you leave the area, he will investigate your scent and identify you as a human. From that point forward he knows what you smell like, where you like to walk, how long you stay in the woods, and what time you leave. With D.I.E., he will never know you are a human, so he never looks for a human when you are in your stand. If the dominant buck is a half mile or more away when you are there, it may take him up to three days to know you were there. Once he finds out, he avoids you and watches you. I always assume the buck is watching me. That way I do not make mistakes that could get me busted.

All deer go on alert—but not all deer will flee

When a deer detects a sound, a scent, or some movement (a possible danger) that they cannot positively immediately identify they go on alert. In alert mode, a deer will either decide whether to flee the area by returning the way it came, or go off alert (after a false alarm) and resume normal browsing activity. A deer on alert raises its tail and stands up as tall as it can, then flicks its tail back and forth, kind of like flagging it. A deer may wheeze to warn other deer in the area that it has discovered, but has not yet identified a sound, an object, a human, or an odd scent in the area. If a deer cannot make sense of the situation, it will flee the area by galloping crosswind at first and eventually straight upwind from the cause for the alarm. A deer that flees will wheeze as it runs away and once it is a safe distance away from the thing that scared it, the deer will stop running, lower its tail, and walk into the nearest available cover. All deer wheeze, but a hunter with a wheeze call can calm down a deer that wheezes by wheezing back. Wheeze only one time. By doing so, you are telling all the deer in the area that you are a deer, and that they should not fear you. Nine times out of ten, the deer that wheezed at you will relax and walk downwind of you to do a scent check, because it can smell the scent of other deer in the area. It is aware that you are not one of the deer in its herd and it can tell for sure by scent checking the air downwind of you. Stop walking if you hear a deer wheeze, and face downwind, the deer will always check you out if you do that. Be ready with your weapon in hand. Point it downwind from the start, because any movement they notice will send them galloping away.

Dominant bucks react to unknown sounds differently than does. A dominant buck will stay in his bed as danger approaches—and he will only flee if he is convinced that the danger means him harm.

A subordinate pecking order buck on alert in August 2009 on a soybean field in Wisconsin.

A 10-point Dominant buck sees a coyote but does not go on alert, he just shows concern. This is the 10-point monster/dominant buck I missed in 2009 before the 17-pointer came to my scrape.

Dominant bucks behave predictably **137**

The same 10-point Monster/Dominant buck is now on alert with two does. Notice his ears are straight out away from his head, his tail is tucked, and his muscles are tense. There was a coyote on the edge of the field and it was coming closer.

He is relaxed again. The dominant buck allows two does to feed nearby.

Dominant bucks are loners. This buck exits to the security of cover in the corner of the field. The two does exited to meet up with other feeding deer. Does stay out of the dominant buck's way.

Deer need daily food and water to survive

After a dominant buck has found a safe place to live and to sleep, he has to focus on getting enough **food (nutrition)**. Getting daily food and **water** is necessary for all deer to survive. When bucks are growing a new set of antlers in the summer months, they spend many hours each day eating. During the rut, dominant bucks get their daily intake of food after sunset when it is safe for them to travel. They travel from doe bedding area to doe bedding area concentrating on finding does in heat, and in estrus.

Mating is the number one priority for all dominant bucks after dark. Of course, they need to eat too. They will eat twigs, grass, and nuts that they find along their travel corridors as they search for does in estrus. Deer love eating farmer's crops. They will head there in a hurry just before dark if a farm field with standing crops is available. Some of their favorite foods are corn, hay, clover, and soybeans. I am newcomer to food plots, but from what I have seen they do a wonderful job of keeping deer on a property throughout the year. If there are no fields where you deer hunt, deer feed on grass, acorns, buds, tree leaves, wild clover, and sometimes they will wade out into streams, rivers, and swamps to eat underwater vegetation. Deer eat other crops that I have not listed here, as well. Deer also need salt in their diet. With DOMINANCE IS EVERYTHING, you are not attracting the buck with food, so having a food source in the area is not necessary in order to have success with my system.

Bucks compete for the right to breed

Every dominant buck needs the **opportunity to breed**. I believe dominant bucks are dominant beyond the end of the rut. They hold the title of king of the herd all winter long, through the next spring, and summer, and right back into the next rut in the fall that is unless they are beaten in a head-to-head battle by a stronger breeder buck. Dominant bucks display their dominance all year long, even at the time of year when they do not have any antlers on their heads (March-April). Their will to survive another year is great. They are focused on one purpose... to keep their right to be the first and last buck to breed the next fall and winter during the rut. A dominant buck is mating with a doe in estrus one or two of every three days during the rut. They will breed with as many hot does (does in estrus) as they can find.

A dominant buck has an earned right to mate with any doe that goes into estrus inside his home territory. That is why all bucks want to be dominant, because lesser bucks do not get as many opportunities to breed as a dominant buck does. Exceptions occur when an intruder buck invades a dominant buck's territory. The dominant buck has to run the intruder buck out of the area if he can. If the intruder does not leave, a fight will develop and the winner will dominate the area from that minute forward. Some dominant bucks will not surrender their dominance after a loss to a stronger opponent. There are times when they will fight to total exhaustion. Sometimes one buck or both bucks will perish from injuries they received from a buck fight. Most of those times the bucks are found dead with their antlers locked together. Having the right to call an area home and having the right to breed with every doe that goes into estrus at home, is what every mature pecking order buck wants. In order to achieve the status as king (primary breeder buck) a buck has to be the most dominant. DOMINANCE IS EVERYTHING to all mature bucks all year long, not just during the rut.

All mature bucks compete for the right to breed with does. Mature bucks will tend (stay with and breed with) a doe in estrus for a period of one to two days. Hunting with D.I.E. has taught me that a doe's heat cycle lasts only four days. The first two and a half days the doe is in heat, and the last day to day-and-a-half is when she is in estrus. That is when she will let any buck mate with her. All bucks except dominant bucks, monster bucks, and swamp bucks will chase does in heat in daylight or after dark. Does in heat are nearing estrus but have not yet reached that final stage of their breeding cycle. A doe has to be in estrus to be willingly to allow a buck to mount her. Estrus is the peak time of a doe's heat cycle. It is the only period during the heat cycle that a doe is able to get pregnant. She cannot get pregnant while she is in heat, only when she is in estrus.

Dominant bucks, monster bucks, and swamp bucks are smarter than the herd's younger bucks. They know that does in heat do not allow any buck to mount them to breed, so they do not endanger their lives like other bucks do by chasing does in heat (not ever). Dominant, monster, and swamp bucks will advance on a doe in estrus day or night, no matter where she is at the time. Whether they walk after does or chase (run) after them is not important. Once they catch up with the doe the fact is that she is willing to let them breed with her, and that is all that matters to them.

Every whitetail buck on earth is drawn (attracted) to every doe in estrus. A buck's rank in the pecking order is the determining factor that relates to how many times that buck will actually be allowed to breed during the rut (inside his own herd's territory). Higher-ranking bucks breed more often than lesser-ranked bucks, and the dominant buck breeds more than any other buck. Mature bucks and immature (yearling) bucks breed with does in estrus, but buck fawns do not breed.

A dominant buck can take any doe in estrus away from a pecking order buck (inside his own territory) by lowering his head and letting out a grunt while charging out of cover, heading directly toward the mating pair. The lesser buck will immediately stop breeding the doe, and veer away from her, trying to avoid a confrontation with the approaching dominant buck. **Dominance Is Everything** to all bucks and all herd bucks know to yield to their king whenever he approaches them, no matter what they are doing at the time. Dominant bucks will breed with a doe in estrus until she goes out of it, which D.I.E. has taught me is within 1 or 2 days of the time she went into estrus, then the buck leaves her to find another doe in estrus.

D.I.E. messes with the dominant buck's mind to make him believe you are an intruder monster buck, hiding in cover upwind or crosswind of the D.I.E. scrape. Your presence within 35 yards of the dominant buck's primary breeding scrape is not acceptable to him, because he is in charge of the scrape once he takes it over, and he has earned the right to breed with any doe in estrus that visits it. Your actions in the woods, combined with the way the D.I.E. system's lures have brainwashed the buck (in advance), make the dominant buck believe that you are calling him out for a fight. He will be determined to show up in short order. As he makes his way to the scrape, he scent checks the air and discovers the doe in estrus is there at that very moment. That is because you are there, and anytime you are there both the doe in estrus and the intruder monster buck are there. They are just invisible to the real deer. No mature whitetail buck is capable of walking away from an invitation to breed with a doe in estrus, because she is ready, willing, and able to mate with him, when she visits his scrape, and urinates in it. That is a fact. The 'DOMINANCE IS EVERYTHING' system proves that to you every time you hunt with it.

Chapter 8

Understanding the whitetail buck pecking order

Within each whitetail deer herd is one group of bucks ranked according to their attitude, aggressiveness, body strength, antler size, level of maturity, and fighting ability. This ranking system is called the pecking order. Every buck in a herd has input into determining which buck will hold the highest rank in that herd. I refer to him as the king also known as the most dominant buck.

Whitetail bucks shed their antlers each year between late January and the end of March. These are the winter months in the Midwest; often a blanket of snow covers the ground then. Most shed antler hunters start-combing whitetail haunts in the middle of February looking for proof that one or more mature bucks lived through deer hunting season.

In April, a whitetail buck begins growing his new set of antlers. His rack reaches full development by middle-to-late August. Herd bucks need big, strong antlers to help them establish their dominance in the pecking order before the rut begins.

Bachelor groups - When the rut is not on

Starting in early spring each year, usually in April, whitetail bucks gather into bachelor groups. Previously deer of all ages and both sexes lived together as one herd from late December through March. Deer live as one group during the winter months in the Northern United States to have better odds of making it through the sometimes very harsh weather conditions that winter brings with it. A herd may have more than one group of bachelor bucks. One bachelor group may consist of only 1½-year-old bucks and another of all mature bucks at least 2 ½ years old. A group of bachelor bucks will run together, feed together, stay together, and defend themselves from danger together. The bucks in a particular bachelor group show mutual respect to one another. Just because they are in a bachelor buck group does not automatically mean a buck is a member of the pecking order. A buck has to be 2 years old to join the pecking order. One-year-old bucks are not allowed to hold rank.

In early August, the bachelor groups break up and the highest-ranking bucks attempt to establish their own home territories. Immature bucks remain in the home territory of the most dominant buck, and they are subordinate to him there. Bucks that cannot retain their own territory will rejoin a herd's pecking order. It does not have to be the one that the buck left. Bucks fight other bucks to establish their pecking order rank.

Not all dominant bucks and monster bucks join bachelor buck groups during the summer. The bigger the antlers on the dominant buck or monster buck and the older the animal gets, the more set in his solitary ways he gets, and the more he sets himself apart from the rest of the herd. Deer are at the most risk of being killed by a predator while they are feeding or bedding, so the older and wiser a buck gets the more he avoids moving with other deer into those areas during daylight. He will be there at breeding time, but otherwise he hides in cover (away from the bachelor bucks) where he is safe.

Dominant bucks that do not have massive antlers will often times join a bachelor group during the spring and summer. They do so in order to keep the other bucks in the ranks in check.

Battles for dominance during the rut

A dominant buck that controls a one-half-mile-square area will likely have 5 to 9 mature subordinate (lesser) bucks in his herd. One will rank second in command, one third, one fourth, and so on. In the two weeks before the rut, or possibly during the rut, the second-ranked buck likely will fight the dominant buck in an attempt to take over the herd. If the second-ranked buck wins the fight, he instantly becomes king of the herd, and the formerly dominant buck moves down a peg to second in command. If the dominant buck wins the fight—which is what usually happens—he upholds his dominance and he remains king of the herd. The second-ranked buck will still hold his rank as number two.

A middle-ranked buck usually will not attempt to fight the dominant buck—not until he has already fought and won all of his battles with the other bucks ranked above him in the pecking order. Subordinate bucks need to climb the ladder to reach the top. They cannot jump up into the ranks.

Once a buck attains the status of king, he has earned the right to breed with any doe in his home territory. His only competition will come from the second-ranking buck or from any mature intruder buck, which challenges him to a fight. Challenging intruder bucks are usually monster bucks from another herd that want to breed with a doe in estrus inside a dominant buck's territory. They usually do not want the territory; maintaining it takes a lot of energy, and monster bucks need to retain energy to survive. Not all challenging intruder bucks are monsters, but they quite often have a rack that is near equivalent to that of the dominant buck.

A dominant buck mates with as many does in estrus as he can find inside the boundaries of his own territory. When all the herd does have been bred the dominant buck makes a choice on whether he will leave and roam into neighboring bucks' ranges to find more does in estrus or not. If you choose a four-day period to hunt and your area's dominant buck is out roaming, you will either see an intruder buck, the second-ranking buck, or—late on the third or fourth day of your hunt—you'll see the dominant buck when he returns from his trip. No matter which buck shows up at within 35 yards of you on a D.I.E. hunt, believe me he is the most dominant buck in the herd at that exact moment in time. Mature bucks are known to roam up to 5 miles in a day or two searching for does in estrus during the rut.

Dominant bucks are continually patrolling their territory during the rut. A dominant buck walks around his entire territory marking his boundaries and looking for intruders and threats to his herd's survival once every three days (all year long).

Look at your deer herd from their perspective

Monster buck numbers are higher in areas where the buck to doe ratio is high on the buck side. My family's property in New Berlin, Wisconsin had a 4 to 1 ratio of bucks to does on it for the last 5 years that I hunted it. Coyotes arrived in the area in 1990 and many coyotes were successful at killing newborn deer fawns. That affected the doe population, but I do not believe a coyote can stop a healthy mature buck. Gun hunting was illegal there, but archery hunting was allowed as long as I had a permit and landowner permission. We had three farm fields bordered by tree lines, and two drainage ditches running through their center. There was a subdivision to the North of our land. I parked my truck a block away on a side street when I was hunting and I walked in from the North property boundary, which was ideal for hunting with D.I.E. in a NW wind. The area was being heavily developed into a commercial business center and the deer numbers were high due to lack of available habitat, all around our land. It was an ideal property to hunt bucks on, and I will surely miss it now that we sold it. Before I invented my system, I never knew that dominant bucks existed. I put all big-racked bucks in one category together. I knew there was a pecking order, but I did not know how it functioned.

Competition among bucks was high and because there were and still are many bucks in that area older than 3 ½ years old, they had to learn how to live in the area with one another, without constant battles. Look at the pecking order like this; twelve breeder bucks are living in one territory, and because they all appreciate the security that this particular piece of property offers them, they are forced to get along. Only one of them can be the leader. It is up to them individually to survive the 85 to 93 day breeding period in each other's company without getting into too much trouble. If that was not tough enough, let us throw in the fact that there are only six adult does, five yearling does, and five doe fawns that live in the territory. These bucks dislike each other and some of them hate one another, but they all know if they can find a way to get along, they will all survive the situation. They all have the same upbringing, and they all know how to survive tough situations. They know if they leave the structure of this herd, they will get into fights when they try to join another one. Most pecking order bucks will stay with their herd all season long, but some higher ranking bucks will leave during the rut to pursue does in estrus on other parcels of land. Wandering breeder bucks become intruder bucks and they instantly become interested in a D.I.E. scrape when they encounter one.

That is how I saw the buck herd on our farm in New Berlin, and by looking at it from the deer herd's perspective; I could make perfect sense of their behavior during the rut. You need to try to understand what your herd is doing before you hunt with D.I.E., simply said you need to see "The Big Picture".

A dominant buck wants to survive first and breed second. He has to live in close proximity with many other bucks, some of which are bigger than he is, but he does not have to be friendly to any of them. He goes about his business silently, and aggressively. He dominates the other deer in the herd with his attitude, and until another buck challenges him on his own turf, the dominant buck has freedom to expand his boundaries and do whatever he chooses, whenever he decides to do it.

A dominant buck will not go out of his way to cause trouble for other bucks, but if a subordinate buck steps out of line, the dominant buck will immediately put him in his place. Dominant bucks will never leave the safety of cover for any reason except the companionship of a doe in estrus, to meet the challenge of an intruder buck, or to escape danger. Does in heat are a dime a dozen, but a doe in estrus is a gold mine. Register that in your memory bank and it will improve your odds of taking monster bucks each deer season.

Not all bucks hold rank in the pecking order

Monster bucks that live inside a dominant buck's territory are known by all the bucks in the area, and their fighting ability is unmatched. Monster bucks and dominant bucks posture no matter what time of year it is, whether they have antlers or not. When a buck postures he splays his front hooves and walks with stiff front legs, barely bending his knee joints as he walks. He drags his front hooves on the ground. In snow, it is easy for a person to identify the dominant buck's tracks for that one reason alone. They tense up their shoulder, neck, and back muscles to show a force to be reckoned with. They walk in at angles always turning their muscular neck toward the animal or other buck that intimidated them. The hair on their entire body may be standing on end too. They flaunt their brute strength throughout the year. Most mature bucks will yield to a monster buck rather than fight with him. Dominant bucks are the exceptions, they never yield to any buck, if they did they would be showing weakness and another buck would remove them from the rank of king.

Buck fawns and yearling bucks do not hold rank in the pecking order. Only a mature buck that is at least 2 years old can hold a rank. Mature bucks fight, dominate, breed, and survive. Yearling bucks and buck fawns have yet to prove themselves in all of those situations. A buck of any age has to be able to dominate more than one other buck in order to gain the respect of the herd, and in order to be dominant.

Chapter 9

How deer identify danger

Deer use three senses to identify danger.

First, deer use their sense of hearing to identify danger. The sounds made by a human talking, coughing, or sneezing are not natural sounds for deer to hear in the wild, so whenever they hear one of those sounds they go on alert. All manmade sounds are signals to deer that a human is in their territory. When deer hear the sound of a metal object rubbing up against another metal object they immediately stop what they are doing, they listen to what the wind is telling them, and they move away from the source of the sound immediately. Metallic sounds, the sounds of tires screeching on a roadway, of a car door being opened and closed, of a human's footsteps as the human walks hurriedly through deer habitat, and the sounds made by a human or an animal that is pushing through a patch of thick brush are all sounds that alert deer.

Second, deer use their keen sense of smell to identify danger. If they smell danger—such as a human, a predator, or smoke from a fire—they will vacate the area immediately, traveling into the wind whenever possible.

Third, deer use their keen eyesight to identify danger. However, deer do not see as people do. I believe that deer are color blind. I have come to this conclusion because deer cannot identify me as a human if I am wearing clothes that have a camouflage pattern on them. It doesn't matter if it's blaze orange, brown, black, green, grey, white, or tan in color as long as the fabrics have tree limb and leaf patterns on them, then deer cannot see the human who is wearing the clothes. Deer mostly see things as a light or dark shade of gray, or as black. Snow appears as a light shade of gray to them. If deer see a human riding an ATV or a snowmobile through their herd's territory, they get nervous, and they slip into some nearby cover to hide, but they do not always leave the area. That is unless the human on the machine either stops the engine, or pursues the deer, in those cases, adult deer know enough about humans to know they are in danger and they will flee the area immediately. Immature deer may stick around to see what is going on, especially if it is their first encounter with a situation like that.

How to avoid being detected by deer as being a danger to them

Always wear camouflage clothing that has been washed in scent free laundry detergent. Wash your body in scent free body wash, and spray down with a scent eliminator, that way no deer will be able to detect you as a human just by detecting the scent of your laundry soap, the scent of your perspiration, or by looking right at you. You will be invisible deer.

The good news for all D.I.E. hunters is that although deer use three senses to identify danger they do not use reason. I can successfully brainwash any dominant buck into believing I am any one of the deer in his herd by messing with his thought process and preventing him from identifying me—or anyone else who uses my system—as a human being. If you can pass the three tests that deer use to identify danger, then you are automatically invisible to deer. They do not rationalize situations to try to discover what else you might be, if you pass all three tests. If you fail one of the tests, the deer goes on alert. You fail two of the tests the deer flees the area, and if you fail all three, they make an effort never to be in that same place, at the same time (that they encountered you there) ever again.

Deer can never find a D.I.E. hunter so they cannot positively identify you as a threat. If you do not smell like a threat, sound like a threat, or look like a threat, then you are not a threat to a deer. Trees and brush are not threats to deer. They are structures inside deer habitat that provide deer with safety and concealment from their threats. A human who is dressed like a tree or some tag alder brush, who smells like a tree or some tag alder brush, and who moves like a tree or some tag alder brush, is a tree or a some tag alder brush to a deer. It is mind over matter. A D.I.E. hunter pretends to be many things on a D.I.E. hunt, so that deer never are alarmed by their presence, none of which is a human.

That's me with a doe decoy. If I was wearing a facemask I would be invisible to deer even if I was holding that Montana Doe Decoy.

If traditional deer hunters became invisible to deer they would have mature bucks and does walking around in close proximity to them during daylight, and the deer would never know that a human, a threat, or any other danger was there. I do not teach you how to hunt deer traditionally, but I want you to know that you can become a better hunter, no matter if you hunt traditionally or with my DOMINANCE IS EVERYTHING system, if you make sure you are invisible to deer at all times. When you are invisible to deer, you can still be seen by humans. That is a good thing, because it helps keep you safe in the woods while hunting.

Solid blaze orange vs. blaze orange camouflage

I never hunted with D.I.E. during gun deer season until 2006, because up until then deer identified me as a human in the woods 100% of the times they encountered me. In order for you to be able to succeed with D.I.E., you have to be able to become invisible to all deer. Having deer identify you as a threat is far from being invisible.

I know now that the only reason deer ran away from me then was that I was dressed in solid blaze orange clothing, instead of wearing blaze orange camouflage with black tree limbs and leaf patterns on it. I used to hunt from the ground in gun season (without using D.I.E.), and whenever I leaned up on a tree, and a deer came running down the trail toward me it would get one look at me, then it would turn around and take off like a rocket, back the way it had come. I know now that the solid color of my jacket blocked out the tree trunk, and when deer looked at me they must have thought they were hallucinating. My standing in front of a tree trunk that they see as black, wearing my solid blaze orange jacket that they see as gray (in sunlight), made it look like the tree trunk was floating 6 feet above the ground, because I am over 6 feet tall. If something strange like that appeared in front of me, I would run too!

My wearing a solid blaze orange jacket made it impossible for me to blend in with my surroundings standing on the ground in a hardwood forest. When I look back now I wonder how I could have overlooked that for the first eight years that I was bow hunting with my system. I wanted to use it gun hunting but I couldn't figure out how to be invisible to deer when I was wearing blaze orange so I never tried it until 2006 when I got my new blaze orange camouflage outfit.

The only difference between what I was wearing on my bow hunts with D.I.E., and what I wore gun hunting without D.I.E. was the color of my clothes and the pattern of my camouflage. Solid blaze orange does not have a pattern, and therefore it can only blend in with the sky or a snow covered clearing. I found out the color orange does not scare deer, but not having a camouflage pattern on your hunting outfit will alert them to you being there every time. The good news for you and I both, is now I know, and I am sharing my news with you.

Do you want to wear solid blaze orange, or do you want to wear blaze orange camouflage? My advice if you have a choice is always wear blaze orange camouflage. With it, you can be invisible to deer, and I do not believe that anyone can be invisible to deer if they wear a solid blaze orange jacket or pants while hunting in a forest or from a tree stand. A hunter using D.I.E. has to be invisible to all deer all the time, because with D.I.E. the king of the herd is looking for you as an invisible pair of breeding deer. If he sees you as a bush, he will keep coming in to try to see past you, but if he sees something strange, he will retreat and assume it is not safe for him to be there during daylight.

After analyzing some photographs in both black and white (what deer see) and in color (what people see), I have been able to understand which things stand out to deer and why they react the way they do, when they encounter certain things.

Deer can always pick out a silhouette of a human hunter in a tree stand or on the ground, if that hunter is wearing clothing that is just one color. It is for that reason that I do not wear hunting jackets or bib overalls that are a solid color any longer. If you see deer running away from you, and you are wearing solid blaze orange, make the change to blaze orange camouflage and then you will be able to use DOMINANCE IS EVERYTHING successfully without being busted by the buck that is hunting you.

I have not hunted in any other state for deer, and it is likely you are not from Wisconsin seeing how it is only one state in our great nation, so I leave it up to you to do the research for your state. Find out if the deer hunting regulations allow you to wear blaze orange camouflage or just solid blaze orange. If they allow you to wear blaze camouflage then wear it. No matter if it is orange, brown, or green, if it is camouflage you are invisible to deer. Then and only then will you be able to hunt successfully with my DOMINANCE IS EVERYTHING system. Do not forget to wear gloves, a hat and a facemask, with a camouflage pattern on them also.

Always put your safety first when hunting. You only get one life and it is not worth taking any chances with it. Never endanger your life or the lives of others. Be safe and do all you can to prevent hunting accidents.

How I like to dress for a D.I.E. hunt

While bow hunting I sometimes wear a knit hat in a solid color, and I prefer olive green, black, or brown to any other colors. They all blend in well with a tree trunk. I do not wear a knit hat while I am on the ground, because it will seem odd to a deer why a solid object is floating 6 feet off the ground. I wear a camouflage baseball hat out to my stand and once I am settled in, I change my hat to a knit hat. When the hunt is over for the day, I change hats again and leave the area wearing the camouflage hat. I also wear a facemask on every hunt. I feel a person should always do what I do if they want to be 100% successful with D.I.E. every time they use it (as I have been). You should wear a facemask. If you prefer face paint, and you cannot be seen that way then go for it, but whatever you do be sure you always cover your face, the whole time you are in the woods. I will only wear camouflage facemasks and gloves.

I like to wear clothes that will keep me warm when I hunt using my D.I.E. system. I favor being warm and comfortable in the stand, over the alternative of dressing light for the walk in, and then getting cold late in the day, as the North winds pick up and the sunsets. If I am too warm and I sweat, I do so inside my one-piece Mossy Oak® camouflage reversible suit and my human scent cannot escape, so the deer are none the wiser. Some days I wear bibs and a parka, it depends on the weather and most of the time the two pieces of clothing do not match. I believe it is good to mix up the patterns on the camouflage clothes you wear, but it is not necessary to do so in order to succeed with my system.

I think it should be your personal preference with regard to what brand of camouflage clothing you decide to wear, but in case you were wondering what brand of camouflage clothing I like to wear, I will gladly tell you. Some days I wear an insulated one-piece suit with Mossy Oak Break-Up® camouflage. Other days I wear Realtree® camouflage bibs and a parka that I purchased at Cabela's® last fall. I love the new outfit because it is waterproof, it is warm, and the material is soft and does not make noise if it brushes against tree branches.

I like to wear a "spandex type" or a "mesh type" camouflage facemask on warm days and on cold days, I wear a wool ski mask that is fully camouflaged and has ear holes cut into it so I can hear the dominant buck when he approaches me. Gloves are mandatory, as are a pair of warm boots with rubber soles. I wear camouflage cotton gloves, and I wear LaCrosse® boots because they are very comfortable, they keep me warm and dry, and every pair I have ever owned has lasted 7 years or more for me.

Things deer do to try to make people move

Adult deer are able to survive because they are experts at identifying danger before they have a face-to-face encounter with the source of it. All mature deer know that humans do not live in the woods, out in the elements as deer do, 24 hours a day and 7 days a week. Even if a deer has never seen a human before, if that deer is an adult, it is capable of determining that you do not belong in its territory and for that reason, alone the deer would assume you must be a threat to its survival. Deer look around constantly searching for any signs of trouble ahead. They know they are safe wherever they currently are, but as a deer moves or as time passes by, situations come up that deer find themselves in, and it is up to each deer individually to be able to get out of harm's way. Mature deer are constantly looking for humans inside their territory, and I have learned that most humans are not aware of what it is that deer see them do, that gets them busted! I like to say you are busted if any deer identifies you as a human. I want to show you what a deer looks for when it is trying to identify a human from something else. I learned how deer think and how they process this type of information by watching deer while they watched people. Deer cannot tell I am a human when I am in the woods, because I am always wearing my invisible deer suit. When I watched (filmed) deer watching people, no deer knew I was there!

When a deer first looks at you, it will identify you as a human if:

1. You are walking, running, or talking aloud.
2. You are wearing clothing that is not camouflage.
3. It is downwind of you and your clothes or body are not scent free.
4. You are standing still but you have your arms up in the air.
5. You are wearing jewelry, a watch, or eyeglasses that glare.
6. You have bad breath, are wearing cologne or perfume.
7. You are in a tree but you are silhouetted in the sky.
8. You move any part of your body while it is watching you.
9. You blink or move your eyeball(s).
10. You are holding your weapon at a 90° angle to your body.
11. You react when it stomps its front leg on the ground.
12. You react when it raises and lowers its head fast.
13. You are chewing food in a tree stand for more than 3 minutes.
14. You walk out on a field while it is there.
15. You blow a deer call from your tree stand more than two times.
16. You raise your weapon while it is looking at you.
17. You load your weapon while it is looking at you.
18. You leave your walkie-talkie on and it hears the static.
19. Your cell phone rings or vibrates in your tree stand.
20. It hears someone approaching you yelling out your name.
21. Someone else is hunting within view of you.
22. You are standing on a deer trail.
23. You are standing in front of a buck rub, blocking its view of the mark.
24. You drop anything out of your stand while the deer is there.

To prevent a deer from identifying you as a human when it looks at you always:

1. Stop in your tracks as soon as you see a deer.
2. If you have one foot off the ground keep it there until the deer looks away. Then put it down quietly.
3. Stare at its back or body, do not ever look it in the eyes.
4. Keep your clothes and your body 99% scent free.
5. Wash your clothes in SPORT WASH scent free wash or Scent-A-Way™.
6. Spray SCENT KILLER® 99% on your forehead, neck, hands, waistline, and ankles.
7. Wear camouflage clothing head to toe (wear blaze orange camouflage).
8. Wear a no-visor hat in your tree stand.
9. Always wear a facemask, & gloves (camouflage preferred).
10. Remain motionless. Do not move a muscle, a limb or an eyeball.
11. Stay perfectly quiet and never talk to anyone.
12. Remember not to call to a deer if it is grunting, snorting, or bleating.
13. Be patient and wait for the deer to look away within 45 seconds.
14. Keep your arms at your side when you are moving through the woods.
15. Only move when the deer is moving its legs.
16. Stay still if it raises and lowers its head, or if it stomps one hoof on the ground.
17. If the deer wheezes, then wait 2 seconds and wheeze back.
18. Do not raise your weapon while a deer is looking in your direction.
19. Breathe through your nose if you can and do not sniffle, sneeze or cough.

As you can see, it is much easier to be seen by a deer and be positively identified as a human than it is to be able to walk into the woods, and remain unseen by them as a deer. Once I train you how to become invisible to deer, you will think it is fun and easy to accomplish.

Why I refer to people as humans

I always refer to people as being humans in the eyes of deer instead of referring to them as people, because deer do not know you have a personality. To deer, all humans are the same.

How you prepare for a D.I.E. hunt will determine whether you will succeed

Dressing in full camouflage alone is not enough to keep a deer from identifying you as a human. You must be scent free as well. That means you should wash your hunting clothes with scent free laundry soap, and wash your body with scent free body soap. Use scent free shampoo and deodorant too. These things are all very important when you want to be successful in harvesting dominant whitetail bucks.

What food you decide to eat in the tree stand and what beverages you bring along on your hunt, can play a big role as to whether or not the dominant buck will be wise to you being a human or not. I have some -pointers that I learned on my hunts that always work for me. A deer has never busted me while I was eating or drinking in my tree stand, and I know some hunters always are caught. So prepare yourself for a long day in the stand and do not plan to leave it until you get the buck or the hunting hours close for the day, whichever comes first.

I recommend you take two bottles of water, a Snickers candy bar, one or two granola bars, and maybe an apple or two. As far as a sandwich goes, it is okay to take a sandwich but make sure it is not a strong smelling sandwich. You do not want to take a corned beef on rye, a roast beef sandwich, or anything with mustard on it into the woods with you. I mean it; do not let the smell of your lunch give your hiding place away to the dominant buck. There is not a delicatessen in the woods you are hunting so do not attempt to bring in foods that have powerful aromas.

You do not want to make noise rustling the wrappers on any of the food that you take with you on your hunt. It is best to take the granola bars and Snickers bar out of the original wrappers and put them in non-zippered plastic bags. That way you will not make crinkling sounds with their wrappers when you open them in the woods. Zippered plastic bags can make noise so I do not use them. You can do what you are used to doing if you have never been busted by a deer while you were eating. All I want you to be able to do is succeed with my system the first time you use it, and I know you can, if you do everything the same way that I do.

If he never identifies you as a danger—expect to be hunted

If you succeed (by not changing my system in any way), the buck will remain bedded down in the morning on the way to your stand. Although he will be bedded in the nearest available cover downwind or crosswind of the D.I.E. scrape, he will not get out of his bed to investigate you, until your footsteps have stopped for about 8 minutes. Then the dominant buck instinctively responds to your actions. Do not linger around the base of your tree stand. Climb the tree in a normal manner, and in a safe manner. Hook up your safety strap as soon as you are standing on the platform of your tree stand, and then proceed to pull up your weapon and hang it in the tree next to you, before you settle in to get comfortable.

If you are hunting with a gun, be sure to load and put it on safe before hanging it by its sling in the tree next to you. If you are hunting with a bow, make sure you nock an arrow and have your release in your hand, before you settle in. If you fail to get your weapon prepared as soon as you get into your stand, the buck may come along and you will not have your weapon ready when needed. I do not think anything worse can happen to a D.I.E. hunter. The worst part of not being prepared on a D.I.E. hunt is that it will be the most dominant buck down there walking toward you. The dominant buck in the area will not tolerate the presence of any other buck within 35 yards of the D.I.E. scrape or of the tree; you placed your stand in.

He will be coming in steadily showing dominance the whole way, in an effort to show you (and the invisible pair of breeding deer) that you have to respect his hierarchy. He is telling you whether he makes a sound on his way in or not that if you are a buck, you must leave, and if you are a doe in estrus, you must breed with him. You see, there is no option for you to be a human being on a D.I.E. hunt, because if he knows you are a human, he will not come in at all. Remain still as he makes his way to you and he will never know you (a human) are there.

Deceiving a deer's senses is easier than you think

Deer can be tricked into believing a make believe situation is a real one, as long as the human pulling one over on the deer is invisible to the deer the entire time. Deer do not know that invisible hunters exist, so when they encounter one on a D.I.E. hunt they do not know that they are being watched. They never know you are there, not unless you tell them.

With D.I.E., the brainwashing begins when you install your tree stand on the same day as you build the D.I.E. scrape. Normally a dominant buck would avoid walking within 200 yards of a newly installed tree stand during daylight but this set up is different. It is in an area that he is not familiar with, and because you waited the 2 ½ days before coming back to the stand, all your human scent has left the area. He is distracted by the existence of a territorial dominant buck scrape appearing inside his territorial boundaries, and he has to take it over and command it to prevent other breeder bucks from other herds from getting the impression that he is weak, and that he can be beat. He comes in and takes the scrape over immediately, and the whole time he believes that no hunter is in the area, because in the deer world it is unheard of for a monster buck to breed in front of a human.

Remember, with D.I.E. deer think they are alone. They do not know you made the scrape. The dominant buck knows that only another dominant buck or a monster buck would make a scrape like the D.I.E. scrape, and he is convinced you are one of them.

He believes it is safe for him to be there at any time of the day because he is the king of the herd, and because a monster intruder buck would never construct a primary breeding scrape anywhere near a hunter's tree stand. Especially if the intruder buck sensed that, a hunter was using it. The dominant buck has met his match and he has to show up there to meet the monster intruder buck on the intruder's terms. You are the monster intruder buck and D.I.E. has set up the terms. He will hunt you from the first minute he catches your scent in the area on Day 1 of your hunt, until you kill him or until he gets wise to the set up being make believe. He will always be able to discover that it is not real by the end of Day 4. Each time he makes an appearance at the scrape while you are in the stand he expects to meet the doe in estrus, for that reason alone, if you do not take your shot at that time, your best and maybe your only opportunity will have passed you by.

The dominant buck knows what trail camera users are up to—because they tell him

Trail cameras are not part of a D.I.E. hunt. I have never used one and I have always succeeded. If there are any trail cameras on the property that you are going to hunt, remove them 15 days or more before hunting there. If you are unable to remove them, you should not use D.I.E. there. No dominant buck will walk up to a human ever! Their territory can span an area that is larger than ½ mile wide by ½ mile long.

Any item that a human leaves inside a deer's territory will get the same response from the dominant buck there, as long as a human keeps going back to it. It does not have to be a trail camera. The buck usually moves downwind to some heavy cover to bed in. He will return to the area the camera was in, once all the cameras are removed from the property. He wants to live where he was living before the person installed the camera, but he will refuse to live there (bed there) during daylight if cameras or the like, are anywhere in on the property.

I teach my customers in seminar that the best thing a trail camera user can do is remove their cameras immediately, to allow the dominant buck to move back into the area that he used to want to frequent during the day. That is the area where the trail cameras were installed. Better yet, give the cameras to your neighbor on the downwind side of your property to use for the season, granted that neighbor knows nothing about **Dominance Is Everything**. That way the dominant buck that was forced to move off your land when you installed the cameras will be willing to come back and live there in peace, not knowing you are going to set up D.I.E. in the area during the rut. It is a win-win situation for both you and the dominant buck!

You should know that it does not matter what your neighbor is doing on his or her property, even if he or she is using trail cameras, because if they are, you can be sure they are not hunting with D.I.E. and therefore they are not invisible to deer. As a user of D.I.E., you need to take care of what you are doing in the woods, not worry about what other traditional hunters (out of view of your stand) are doing. Concentrate on never telling any deer that you are a human or that they are being hunted while you are on the property, whether deer season is, open or not.

As a D.I.E. hunter, you must learn to think about what the buck will be thinking when he surveys the D.I.E. set up, on his way to you. He is looking for any hints of danger. Why give him anything to wonder about? I want the dominant buck to walk in during daylight not knowing I am there. That is what I expect to happen on all of my D.I.E. hunts. He is convinced that he is alone in the area because I do not use any trail cameras.

If you have trail cameras out on your hunting property and you intend to hunt with (harvest a buck with) my system this fall during the rut, then I advise you to remove all trail cameras immediately. Be sure you remove the cameras and the camera supports. Dominant bucks avoid all human intrusions in their territory. They will not return to any area (during daylight) where trail cameras were placed, until all the signs of the human intrusion are no longer evident there. If you remove the trail cameras, and leave the property undisturbed for at least two weeks before hunting with D.I.E. there, you should be in good shape.

I know that my **Dominance Is Everything** system does not fail to bring the dominant buck in within 35 yards of the user's tree stand whether the person using D.I.E. uses a trail camera or not. If the person uses a trail camera the most dominant buck will still come into the

D.I.E. set up, but he is forced to visit only after dark. The human placing the camera is forcing the buck to avoid the D.I.E. scrape during the day, and for all D.I.E. hunters that defeats the purpose, but in turn, it may be acceptable to D.I.E. users, who are just seeking a photograph of the herd's most dominant buck.

Wondering why people see lots of mature bucks on their trail camera photos

Pecking order bucks do not avoid trail cameras because they do not care about human intrusions into their herd's territory. They do not own the territory, nor do any of them maintain it, so they do not have any reason to care about it. Pecking order bucks will revisit a trail camera location because they are in competition for breeding rights, and they have to go where the does are in order to get a chance to breed. Many times a person will place a trail camera on a food or water source because those are places deer congregate. The pecking order bucks will show up there day and night to find does in heat and does in estrus, whether there is a trail camera installed there or not.

A dominant buck will never go out in daylight to any place where he knows a human has been within the past 48 hours. He never chases does in heat, and when does go into estrus they seek him out, so he never has a need to take any risks with his life, like entering areas known to him as places humans frequent. Humans mean death to a dominant buck, and he knows that, so he avoids all humans 100% of the time. I know that I have said this before. The reason I often repeat myself is so you do not forget the facts.

Knowing the way deer think will set you apart, from the mindset of traditional hunters in the future. It is my hope that you appreciate learning everything I am teaching you. I do not have a hidden agenda, I just want you to be able to succeed using my system the first time you try it. You might have some questions and I want to provide you with the answers, so please attend one of my seminars if you have a question to ask. I will be happy to answer it there.

Pretend you are a deer for success with D.I.E.

You have to pretend you are a deer when you hunt with my D.I.E. system. That way when you enter your hunting parcel the deer in the area will not be alerted to the presence of a human. Instead, they assume you are one of two deer. In turn, you will be able to get to your tree stand without scaring any deer away or alerting any of them to the fact that you are their enemy. Once you are settled into your stand, you will be invisible to deer. They will go about their business as usual, as if you (a human) were never there. When you leave your stand just before closing time, you will represent the invisible monster intruder buck. It keeps the dominant buck's interest up at the scrape as he tries to find the doe in estrus, and he will not follow you out to your car.

Never walk like a deer on the way out of the area, only walk like a deer on the way into it. If you do not want to walk like a deer, then walk quietly like a human, but first be sure to read the chapter on walking like a deer, so you know how to pace your steps, where to put out lure (optional), and when to stop walking. The cadence of your steps is important even if you are taking human steps to get to your stand. Knowing when to pause, how long to wait, and when to start up again helps you keep from being busted even though you walk in only making the sound of two feet hitting the ground. You should also read about becoming invisible to deer, and remember to keep you arms down at your sides when you are in the woods. Do not swim through brush and be as quiet as you can be, if you are not walking like a deer. In that case, you do not want the buck to watch you. He will be nervous if you walk like a human but he will overcome it once you are in your stand and the lure starts dripping into the D.I.E. scrape.

You are assured of many factors always playing out the same way with my DOMINANCE IS EVERYTHING system in place. I will mention a few of the most obvious ones here. If you follow my instructions to a tee and do not add anything to the system, it will always make the most dominant buck in that area take notice of your D.I.E. scrape and he will take it over. He will work over the rub and urinate in the scrape, or he will make a new scrape of his own within a few feet of the one you made. Then he will bed in the nearest available cover downwind of your stand. He beds close so he can be the first buck to get to the doe-in-estrus (you) when she arrives back at the D.I.E. scrape. He knows all does in heat go into estrus within a 2 or 3-day period and he is willing to wait for one of the does that are visiting your D.I.E. scrape to go into estrus. He also knows that does in estrus search for the dominant buck to breed. That is why the system works so perfectly. He is expecting a doe in estrus to visit the D.I.E. scrape during the daylight, and as soon as he goes to bed down you show up dragging her scent behind you. The doe in estrus is only there when you (the invisible doe in estrus) are there which is always during daylight. Thus, when you are there the dominant buck is there, and he is watching your area like a sniper. Always know that and stay as still in your stand as possible. He will only approach your D.I.E. scrape when all is quiet and he feels 100% safe.

Sometimes the buck will not take the scrape over. When this happens, it is a direct result of you setting the D.I.E. scrape up too close to his normal breeding or bedding areas. If he can see the scrape from his own bed, then he will not have to visit it to watch over it. I call that hunter error, when that happens. You can avoid it from happening by scouting the land and knowing where he is bedding and breeding, and then make a conscious decision to avoid hunting in any deer bedding or breeding areas with D.I.E., that way you will succeed at pulling the buck away from his comfort zone and make him hunt for you at your scrape. Once you use D.I.E., once or twice, you will see how it works and you will automatically avoid making hunter errors on set up day.

Know that the buck is not looking for a hunter, or a human. He is looking for a single doe in estrus, and at the same time, he is hoping he does not come face to face with the intruder buck that made the scrape. He is ignoring what is in the trees, and focusing on what is on the ground. You should not ever give him a reason to look up at you, then most of the time he will not, but when you are on the ground, it is a bit different. The dominant buck is bedded down nearby and he may see your movement as you walk in, but I am 99% sure that he will not be able to identify you as a human, not even if he is looking right at you. *Remember he is that close to you because he does not know you are there.* If he knew a human was a few feet from his core breeding scrape, he would wait until after dark to go anywhere near it. You will be invisible to every deer if you follow my instructions. You will be wearing full camouflage, which includes a facemask and gloves. To him you will look like a tree or a patch of brush if you are standing still. If you are moving then all he sees is a blur of brush as it moves with the wind. If the wind is not blowing do not worry, the buck will be convinced that any brush he is looking at (blurry or not) is really just a piece of brush and it can do him no harm. As you know, you must be scent free, that way the dominant buck will not be able to detect any human scent when he goes downwind of you to do a lip curl. All he will be able to detect are the natural scents of the woods, and the scent of each of the two invisible deer you brainwashed him to believe are in the area.

Many mature bucks fear bigger bucks, humans (whether they are hunters or not), and predators, but dominant bucks, monster bucks, and swamp bucks, they are different. They do not fear anything - not other bucks, not humans, and not predators! That is a very important fact that I think you should remember. I learned that from deer, and knowing that fact helped me formulate my **Dominance Is Everything** system into what it is today. Knowing that made me realize that it is impossible for a human being to intimidate the most dominant buck, a swamp buck, or a monster buck enough (with a physical manmade thing), that it would force the buck to leave the safety of his staging cover during daylight.

I have learned that messing with their minds is more powerful than messing with their other senses. Deer do not use their sense of reason very often. If they cannot make sense of it, they avoid it, but when they can make sense of it, that is when you have their full attention. D.I.E. gets the dominant buck's attention and he cannot stop thinking about the situation it presents him. He is drawn to the D.I.E. scrape, and he cannot ignore it.

Deer are set in their ways and they believe what they are taught to believe based on how they are able to detect and positively identify danger. When a human can overcome the three tests deer run on them (sight, sound, and smell) to try to detect them as danger, then that human does not exist in a deer's mind. That is a very powerful fact that I am proud to be able to prove to you.

If you are not a human but you make a noise in the forest, were you actually there? The answer is a tricky one. I would say a human was not there. Only the object that made the sound was there. D.I.E. hunters only make sounds with their feet on the way to or from their stand. If you walk like a deer those sounds are normal for all deer to hear, that is why I teach you to disguise your footsteps as the sounds of a deer (buck or doe) walking into the stand site in the morning, and the sound of a buck rushing out of the area at night. The only sounds you make in the tree stand are chewing or swallowing sounds when you eat or drink throughout the day, and I teach you to keep those sounds to a minimum, and to only eat or drink when you do not hear any deer moving around you. Becoming invisible to deer is easy, and using D.I.E. is easy too, the tough part is overcoming the things you may have already been taught, to allow yourself to hunt with D.I.E. as directed. The system does the brainwashing, so you do not have any hard work ahead of you. All you have to do is follow a few steps each day to be able to keep from being busted by the buck as he searches for you.

DOMINANCE IS EVERYTHING is a system I invented that brainwashes all deer into believing that a real pair of deer are breeding inside their territory. The herd is convinced that they are real because I behave like a deer. Deer are not afraid of other deer. I have said that before and I am sure you will read it again somewhere later on in the book. Deer cannot identify a D.I.E. hunter (invisible human) as a human—not ever!

Dominant bucks have approached my D.I.E. set up as early as one hour after I got in my tree stand on Day 1, and as late as the last 10 minutes before legal shooting time closed on Day 4. You never know when he will come to you, but you should always have faith that he will make it in on one of the four days of your hunt, as long as he never knows a human is there. When you pretend you are a deer, the buck reacts to your actions and begins to hunt you. He wants to meet your invisible deer. Keep up the charade as long as you have to, to persuade him it is safe to come in.

When hunting with this system, you are a deer whenever you step foot into the woods. The deer will think you are one of them. Your D.I.E. scrape, your behavior in the woods, your camouflage, and the way you covered your human scent will convince all the deer in the area, that there cannot possibly be any danger to them near the D.I.E. scrape, during the daylight or after dark. They never will locate your stand if you are up off the ground above their line of sight. Trust me your identity is that of a deer to them, the thought of you ever being a human being, just hanging out in their core breeding area never crosses their minds. Deer do not know you are a human unless you announce it to them. You are invisible on a D.I.E. hunt!

Deer do not know you are a human unless you announce it to them. You are invisible on a D.I.E. hunt!

When you pretend to be a deer—remember real deer do not sit in trees

The D.I.E. system transforms you into an invisible pair of breeding deer, and as a deer, you need to be briefed on what you can say to the dominant buck, and what you cannot get away with saying to him while you are in his territory. Deer talk to other deer, but always remember deer that are talking are not talking to a hunter in a tree. Never try to answer a calling deer on a D.I.E. hunt. Always remain quiet and make him guess as to which deer you are at the time.

If you do call to him only do it when he is not looking

There is a time and place to call to the dominant buck on a D.I.E. hunt. Later on I will show you when a good time to talk to him is, and also when not to try to communicate with him. You will also need to know why you can or cannot say certain things to the dominant buck. I have all the answers for you here, but because this concept is likely going to be new to you, I am first going to describe to you how to get in the head of the invisible deer that you are trying to represent, at the scrape site.

Look at this photo from a deer's perspective. A deer cannot see a human in this picture. I was invisible to deer while I walked like a deer!

Calling to the dominant buck is the only calling you will be doing. There is no need to call to any other deer, because you are only hunting one deer, the dominant buck, and he is the only one listening. Calling while you are invisible to deer is tricky, but it is easy to do if you follow these two rules:

Calling rule No. 1

It is important that you do not try to communicate with any buck, even the most dominant one if you know that he can see your scrape or your tree stand from his position.

Calling rule No. 2

Never talk to multiple bucks, let them talk to each other. They are converging at your stand site for only one reason and that is to find you (the invisible doe in estrus), so they can breed with you. When multiple bucks enter the area at the same time, no matter if it is day or night; they are not concerned with the whereabouts of the (invisible) monster intruder buck. He is one of them! Only the most dominant buck cares where that buck is hiding. Intruder breeder bucks only care about finding the doe in estrus and mating with her while she is still in estrus. They have to find her before any other buck does.

As I mentioned earlier, as soon as multiple bucks positively identify the doe in estrus' scent in your stand site, a buck breeding frenzy is underway. Every buck goes on a mission to find that doe, and the only deer that stands in their way, is the herd's most dominant buck. He has the earned right to breed that doe, and he will not relinquish his right without being physically removed from the top of the pecking order by a more dominant buck. He takes over the scrape, lays down a scent trail wherever he goes, and announces his dominance to the does that visit the area by making rubs and scrapes of his own. He beds down in the nearest available cover in order to keep other bucks out, and he makes it known that he fears no intruder! He is there to take a stand if he has to. There is no backing down. He is there to command the scrape, and to breed any does that visit it. As long as you convince him that you are not a human and that no human is there, he will behave the way I just described.

There is nothing like having two monster bucks fighting over the right to enter your stand site. It is a hair-raising experience! Monster bucks fight for the right to dominate a D.I.E. scrape! That is why I always hunt from a tree stand and only walk in or out the woods during daylight. It is not safe for an invisible deer (you) to be standing on the ground, in a dominant buck's core breeding area. Having one breeder buck within a few yards of me while I am in my tree stand is adrenaline pumping enough, but when more than one intruder buck showed up at the same time in 2009, I was thanking God, for helping someone invent tree stands. I could not imagine being in a ground blind waiting for a good shot opportunity, with those two magnificent racked bucks charging through the cover.

All the bucks that I have seen come to my set ups since 2000 have had huge bodies and large racks of antlers. Each one was on a mission with nothing but dominating on his mind. Their behavior in the area of the scrape always intimidates me because I think like a deer, and their pursuit of the invisible doe in estrus is always relentless. These bucks come here to fight for dominance of a doe in estrus. Each one is willing to go head to head with unknown challengers just to have the right to breed that day! They do not know a human is there. They will stop at nothing to find that doe! I believe that I would be at some risk of being injured by a breeder buck if I hunted from a ground blind with a dominant buck hunting pursuing me in the area. Not because he wanted to hurt me, but because I look like a bush, (I am invisible) and breeder bucks run through all types of vegetation in search of the invisible doe in estrus. When bucks are trailing a doe in estrus they trot through whatever cover is between them and the doe. They lower their nose to the ground and use their antlers to clear their path, just like a bulldozer. Time is of the essence! They need to find her now! Not later! For your safety I advise you to always hunt from an elevated tree stand, with its standing platform positioned a minimum of 10 feet off the ground.

At least one mature buck will come in on every D.I.E. hunt. If you are not busted, then you can count on the first buck being the most dominant, and in my experiences that buck has always had the biggest rack. He will be following the scent of the two invisible breeding deer and he will walk or trot into the area between you and the scrape if you let him. If you do not see him there then look for him to be staging (holding up) in light cover just downwind of your scrape. He will only come in when he knows it is safe.

Know that the buck expects to meet the two deer when he comes in. Once he is there, you need to attempt to either harvest him, or take his picture, because that may be the last time you may see him. He will not come back to the scrape during daylight if he figures out that there are really not any deer there. That is why I teach you how to role-play with the buck by calling to him. It helps convince the buck that the doe and the intruder buck are real deer, because not only can he smell their scent, but also he can hear their voices as they call out to him. Dominant bucks like to verify that a deer is a deer by hearing first, then scent checking, and finally by visually making contact, because he knows every deer in his herd except your invisible pair, you can count on him coming in close to take a look.

You should take the first buck you see, because he will always be the most dominant. I never wait for another buck to arrive. Although it is possible that another buck may come in, from my experience I know that the first buck to arrive on any of my hunts has always had the biggest rack of them all. He will always walk or trot in, showing off and posturing along the way. That behavior tells all the deer in the area, including invisible deer (you or me) that he is the boss and that he owns the territory. He is the most dominant buck.

If you pass on the first buck (the king) or miss your opportunity to shoot him, another buck could come in, but there are no guarantees. If one does show up he will be an intruder buck, and when he is within 35 yards of the scrape that buck will be the most dominant buck in the area of the D.I.E. scrape and rub at that time. It does not make him king of the herd. The king of the herd commands his territory at all times. He always walks or trots into areas he is unfamiliar with, he does not ever run into them. I find that non-dominant intruder bucks always run into the area of the D.I.E. scrape. I think it is because they know that they do not belong there, and they can smell the scent of both the doe in estrus and the real dominant buck in the area. Every whitetail herd has rules remember. No pecking order buck can go within 35 yards of the dominant buck when he is with a doe in estrus, unless he is challenging the king for his throne. Other bucks that come to a D.I.E. scrape are not pecking order bucks from the dominant buck's herd, they are intruder challenging bucks from outside his pecking order, and they show no allegiance to the king of the herd at any time.

In order for you to be able to pretend that you are a pair of breeding deer that are invisible to the king of the herd, you need to know what is going to happen when the buck comes in to find them. You also need to know that he is looking for two real deer, not a hunter in a tree stand. You need to be quiet unless the buck is leaving the area and he has not yet offered you a shot. If you do decide to make any deer calls always make them when the buck is facing away from you, and only make one sound each time. That means only one doe in estrus bleat, or one deep sounding (one-second long) buck grunt. Calling any more than that will get you busted. See the chapter on calling to learn what I know about calling dominant bucks in real hunting situations. Always remember to tell yourself that you are invisible to deer. I say it over and over in my mind (not aloud) while I sit in my tree stand. "I am invisible to all deer". It helps me pass the time, while I concentrate on staying motionless, scent free, and as quiet as I possibly can be, while the dominant buck is watching me, scent checking me, and listening for any sound I make.

Chapter 10

Becoming invisible to deer is easy—follow these steps

There are three steps you have to take in order to become invisible to deer. They are all equally important and invisibility cannot be attained if you do not follow the steps that I teach you here. Do yourself a favor and commit to becoming invisible to deer on your first hunt with my DOMINANCE IS EVERYTHING system. After you see the buck that hunts you, I am convinced you will understand why my system is as powerful as it is, that it brainwashes deer into believing its user is a real pair of breeding deer.

The three steps to becoming invisible to deer are:

1. You must wash your clothes in scent free laundry soap, and wash your body with scent free body wash.
2. You have to wear camouflage clothing from head to toe.
3. You have to learn not to behave as a human when you are in your hunting area.

In this chapter, I will teach you what I do to make myself invisible to deer. It starts with becoming 99% scent free. Then I discuss the importance of wearing good quality camouflage clothing, and finally how not to be detected (as a human) by any deer in the area. Although walking like a deer is preferred on a hunt, with D.I.E., it is not necessary for you to succeed, and at times, it can be too risky for you to attempt doing it. Always be safe when you hunt, and always avoid taking any unnecessary risks. There will always be another day to hunt if you concentrate on being safe while you are afield.

You must be 99% scent free: No exceptions!

My hat is off to you if you already know how to become scent free, and you have been hunting that way for some time. If that is the case, I am sure you know how important being 99% scent free is to the success of your deer hunts. It is impossible for a human to become 100% scent free so I do not ask that of anyone, but the fact of the matter is that in order to make the most dominant buck in any herd hunt you using D.I.E. you have to be 99% scent free before you enter the woods.

When you (a human) enter a parcel of land that deer live on, you really have entered the living room, dining room, kitchen, bedroom, hallway, front yard, backyard, or side yard of the most dominant buck in the area. That is the way he sees it. You are an enemy intruder in his home territory, and he does not ever welcome enemy intruders.

Every other deer in the herd will tolerate you (a human) being there, because it is not their job to maintain the security of the herd, it is the dominant buck's job. He knows some humans kill deer and he knows that any human that he finds inside his territory may be looking for him. When the dominant buck can sense a human presence in his territory he goes on alert, vacates the area the human is in, and informs all the other deer in the herd that a human is there. He protects his herd by telling them that all humans pose an immediate threat to their survival. His actions speak louder than his voice. Mature bucks immediately head for a swamp or some lowland cover to hide. They will go as far away from the threat as they can get without leaving their herd's territory. They run upwind when they are alerted, but they will not bed down on the upwind side of their territory during a crisis like this one, instead they run far enough to get away from the danger, then move left or right of it (at crosswind angles), and they funnel back into one of their core bedding areas. Dangers do not usually exist in all three of the herd's bedding areas at one time. They will surely be able to find a refuge, and when they do, they will remain there until after the human leaves the area, or after sunset whichever comes first.

The most dominant buck will not bed with the pecking order bucks. He is constantly aware of all threats, and he can sense when the threats are gone. He watches everything, and when you are in the area, he is watching you! When a dominant buck feels threatened by a human, he focuses on surviving the day, and puts breeding does in estrus on the back burner.

An invisible deer can walk through any part of a dominant buck's territory totally unnoticed during daylight, but there is no such thing as an invisible deer in the dark. Deer move to and from food and water sources at dusk and throughout the nighttime hours. I am convinced that one reason they do so is that they do not encounter humans as much at those times of the day. When they encounter a human their trip is immediately cancelled, and they have to fend for themselves and head for cover to conceal themselves from the immediate threat.

Deer can see in total darkness but humans cannot. We need to use electronic devices in order to see perfectly at night. If you were invisible to deer and you turned on a flashlight, you instantly become a human again, and you would no longer be cloaked by your invisible deer suit. Deer can identify a human when the human calls attention to his or herself. Never tell any deer you are a human on a D.I.E. hunt and they will never know. If they find out, then your dominant buck will only come in after dark.

It is very important that you only attempt to wear your invisible deer suit during daylight hours when you are using my system. **It is not safe to wear an invisible deer suit (walk like a deer) at night so do not ever do it!** You could be injured or even killed by someone or something that mistakes you for a real deer. There is nothing to gain by going to your stand in the dark. If you do you will be busted the minute you step one foot in the woods, and you would be putting your life at risk. Put your safety first when you hunt.

I designed the hunt part of my system to accommodate the need for a hunter to be safe while afield. I learned that the dominant buck would bed down near a D.I.E. scrape once he discovered that the doe in heat went into estrus, and she was visiting the scrape looking for him. That happens on Day 1 of your hunt, when all the deer in the herd first discover that a doe in estrus is at the D.I.E. scrape. He will always bed close to the scrape and allow other deer to pass by him while he is bedded, without confrontation. The thing is…he is expecting a doe in estrus and a buck at the scrape during the day, and he never is sure which one you represent when you get there, so he will never attempt to rush in to find out. That is if you arrive there after he has bedded down (in daylight). It is another story if he is active (on his feet) in the area when you arrive, as he will be if you fail to follow my instructions and you go in earlier than I tell you to. Then the fact that you are approaching his primary breeding scrape while he is there protecting it (in the dark), is viewed as a challenge. It is a night and day thing, nothing more. If you enter the land after legal shooting time opens like I do, the dominant buck will be bedded, and he will not pursue you while you make your way to your stand. I know the buck will bust you if you go in during the low light hours of the morning or even in the dark. I learned that the hard way. You should never go in the woods in the dark on a D.I.E. hunt. The buck will approach you close enough to identify you as a human, and he will avoid you for the rest of the time you are hunting that stand. You will be busted, and most of the time you would not ever know it. I know dominant buck behavior, so trust me when I tell you that you have to hunt with my system the D.I.E. way. It is the only way to use my tactics safely that will allow you to get 100% results. If you intend to hunt with D.I.E., you have to forget the way you used to hunt and do it the D.I.E. way.

It is only safe to pretend you are a deer during daylight, so that is the only time a D.I.E. hunter should ever be in the woods wearing an invisible deer suit. Each of the four days, we hunt from a few minutes after legal shooting time opens in the morning until a few minutes before it closes in the afternoon. You cannot enter the woods earlier than I instruct you to, or leave later than I instruct you to without taking a chance that the buck will see you and bust you.

Do not ever forget that D.I.E. is a system that you cannot change

DOMINANCE IS EVERYTHING is a name I gave to my system. The system uses tactics I developed that allow me to move around in deer habitat unseen by all the animals there. Achieving the state of invisibility has allowed me to discover a way to force mature dominant bucks, and intruder monster bucks to fight over the right to meet me during the rut. Of course, they have other intentions for the invisible doe in estrus (me) when they meet up with her, but I never let them accomplish their goals. I am only invisible to the buck that hunts me until I squeeze the trigger on my release or on my rifle, and that is always when the buck is less than 35 yards away. Once you fire your weapon all bets are off, sometimes the buck will not know a human is there even after you fire a shot, but other times he sees you shoot and he will do all he can to disappear fast. If you intend to harvest the buck, do your best to make a fatal shot on him, because if you only wound him he is smart enough to elude you. I have learned that the hard way and it is a tough lesson to learn. Once a dominant buck knows, he is being pursued by a hunter whether he has been shot or not, he will evade that hunter forever. Make your first shot count, because quite possibly it will be your last.

I recommend that you construct the D.I.E. scrape exactly the same way every time, then maintain it as directed, and leave it alone for 2 ½ days before returning to hunt over it. No one has ever failed when doing that. The dominant buck will find it by the time Day 2 of your hunt rolls around, unless you are busted before that. You commit to hunting over it for up to four days of the rut, only during daylight hours. You take your part and role-play with the buck by entering and leaving the buck's territory each day on a schedule that you set up ahead of time based on my recommendations. Once you are in the woods you pretend you are a deer (or not), and you get to your stand unseen by the dominant buck. At that point, you (the hunter) have become the hunted. When you hunt with D.I.E., you become part of the hunt. In the dominant buck's eyes and in his mind you are never his enemy (a human). Instead you are the most attractive and available doe in estrus in the county. Follow the steps I lay out for you, and prepare yourself to be amazed by the power D.I.E. has over the minds of the smartest bucks in the herd.

When you hunt with D.I.E., you become part of the hunt.

I will often times remind you of what "The Big Picture" is supposed to look like, so you do not get caught up thinking that you can hunt traditionally (the way you always have) and use my D.I.E. system at the same time. You simply cannot! It is one or the other and you have to make a choice. Sure, you could use some of my tactics to improve your odds of seeing a dominant buck on a traditional hunt, but why use only some of my tactics to succeed some of the time, when you can use all of my tactics and succeed all of the time. You need a game plan if you decide to hunt with my system, and once you put your D.I.E. hunt in motion, stick with it and see it through. Only using some of my tactics will not bring you a dominant buck every time, and more often than not, you will be busted by the buck because you will be granting him options. Every dominant buck that encounters a D.I.E. set up finds out fast that he does not have any options. He has to come in to uphold his hierarchy, and you can count on him doing so within four days.

In order to become an invisible deer you have to get prepared at home

Achieving total invisibility is not something a hunter can accomplish in the field alone, by spraying a human scent-removing product on themselves or on their gear. It certainly helps but there is more to becoming 99% scent free than that.

Before I walk away from my vehicle each morning, headed into my hunting area, I spray Scent Killer® 99% made by Wildlife Research Center® on my collar, my cuffs, around my ankles, under my hat, on my facemask, and around my waist. Human scent will disperse from those places so a person trying to become invisible to deer has to address the human scent issue. I have found that using that product alone is not enough. For me covering my clothes and gear with Scent Killer® 99% just adds the final changes to the process I use to become 99% scent free.

For the past 20 years, I have been 100% successful at not having any deer identify me as a human when they conducted scent checks or lip curls and were inhaling my scent. Deer inhaled the scent that left my body and drifted downwind to them, but no deer have been able to conclude that I am a threat to them or that a human was even there for that matter. All they can smell are the normal scents found in the area. They cannot tell that anything is wrong or that they might be in danger.

I have become invisible to deer, and the biggest part of it is overcoming a deer's sense of smell. I have a normal routine that I will share with you here. I always wash all my camouflage clothes with scent free laundry detergent (in cold water - gentle cycle) a week or two in advance to my D.I.E. hunt. Every morning before getting dressed for my hunt, I take a shower and I wash every inch of my body with scent free body wash and scent free shampoo. I even wash the washcloth I use and the towels I dry my body with in scent free laundry detergent, because I know what being busted by a monster buck feels like and I never want to experience that feeling again. The smell of scented fabric softener will give you away every time. Once I arrive at my hunting parcel, I spray Scent Killer® 99% all over my clothes as I mentioned earlier. I do it again two more times before I am ready to start waiting for the buck to arrive. One time is when I get to the base of my tree stand, and the other is after I settle into it. After the day comes to a close (if I have not had a chance at the buck yet) I use it one last time just before I leave my stand. Since I started this routine no deer has ever detected my presence in their territory. The do not have a clue that anything is there, not when I cover my scent like that.

I know of several products made by several manufacturers that work well together to make me 99% scent free. See the list below if you want to use the same products I use. If you do exactly as I do, you will always succeed on your D.I.E. hunts just as I have always succeeded at being hunted by the king of the herd on mine. Of course, you can continue using any products that have worked for you in the past, as long as they keep you scent free and prevent deer from identifying you by your scent. I am all for that. The point is a person has to be 99% scent free or they cannot expect the king of deer to come anywhere within 200 yards of them. Once you have that covered then there is nothing to worry about, you can hunt in any wind and not fear being detected.

Become 99% scent free or you will be busted! Those are the facts. Once you become 99% scent free, no deer can identify you as a human being just by inhaling your scent. To give yourself a 100% chance of being hunted by the most dominant buck with D.I.E., you need to be 99% scent free all day long. You can achieve a 99% scent free status if you make the effort.

I have used these products (without failure) to become 99% scent free.

SCENT FREE LAUNDRY DETERGENT:
Sport-Wash® (also called Sensi-Clean) by Sno-Seal™, an Atsko, Inc. product

Scent-A-Way™ Garment Wash by Hunter's Specialties®

SCENT FREE BODY WASH:
Sport-Wash® Hair & Body Soap by Sno-Seal™, an Atsko, Inc. product

Scent-A-Way™ Body Soap & Shampoo by Hunter's Specialties®

ODOR ELIMINATOR:
Scent Killer® 99% by Wildlife Research Center®

PERSONAL HYGIENE:
Scent Killer® Anti-Perspirant and Deodorant™ by Wildlife Research Center®

Scent-A-Way™ Anti-Perspirant - Model #01141 by Hunter's Specialties®

Scent-A-Way™ Lip Balm - Model #01130 by Hunter's Specialties®

I am sure there are other products that will work for you but I have not used any other products personally so I am not listing any of them here. Just be sure that deer cannot smell you when you deer hunt. If deer are acting skittish around your stand or if they are avoiding walking past you on a deer trail, it is likely that they can smell your human scent. Even if you thought you, were scent free you probably are not. All you need to do is purchase the products I use and you will not be detected on your D.I.E. hunts.

You only have one chance to outsmart the dominant buck

If you do not prepare yourself to be hunted by the king, and you expect the buck to ignore what his sense of smell tells him is lurking ahead, you are in for a wakeup call! If he hears you making noises in the woods unlike the sounds deer make; if he scent checks you, and knows you are not a deer; or if he sees you and identifies you as a human or another danger; then the gig is up! That buck has busted you, whether you were hunting or not! Once you are busted by the dominant buck you will not ever see him during daylight. He will go into hiding and will not enter any area you have been in, until after the sun has set.

Instead of being busted by the buck, let me teach you how to walk right by him, during daylight. I will show you how to make your way to the only room in his house where he wants to be. That location will be one you get to choose, it is where you decide to set up my D.I.E. system. It automatically becomes the dominant buck's primary bedroom and breeding area for up to four days. The buck will never know you are hunting him. The whole time he believes you are one of two real deer. I call them invisible deer because you make them up as you go. They never really exist, and he will never find them, that is if you are 99% scent free, he will not. If he smells you as a human, the invisible deer do not matter, because he will avoid you (the human) 24 hours a day from that point forward. Scent free soap smells like tree pulp to me. It is a natural aroma found anywhere there are trees or bushes. In my opinion there is no better scent a hunter can have then the smell of scent free soap (no scent at all).

More specifically how I use Scent Killer® 99% made by Wildlife Research Center®

Before I climb up into my tree stand, I spray it on my tree steps. After I settle into it, I take off the camouflage baseball hat that I wore in, I spray some Scent Killer® 99% in my hands and wipe it on my forehead, my ears, and my face (being careful not to get it in my eyes). I also spray it into my hair. I put on a knit hat and facemask or a full facemask. Most of the time my forehead sweats on the way to my stand and spraying Scent Killer® 99% in my hair seemed like the right thing to do to combat the human scent that I know is clinging to my forehead in the form of human sweat. So far, no buck has ever busted me by getting my scent, so I must be doing it right.

Wearing a full facemask is necessary for 100% success with D.I.E.

I always put on a full facemask before I enter the woods on a D.I.E. hunt and I do not go without one at any time, while I am in the woods. If the bucks sees the shine of your face you are busted and your hunt for that buck ends right there. I do not want my hunt ruined just because I did not want to wear a facemask that day. I learned the lesson the hard way, and I do not have to be told twice! I have four different facemasks, and I prefer to take all four along each day so I have a choice of which one to wear based on the outside temperature and whether or not it is raining or snowing. I like to wear thick wool ski masks, and thin facemasks made with materials like spandex or mosquito mesh. All of my facemasks are camouflage none of them are one solid color. Once I am settled in my tree stand on Day 1, I change my facemask from the mesh one to either a wool one or the spandex one, and I spray Scent Killer® 99% all over my head and neck again. When a big buck is pursuing you, you do not want the scent of a single drop of your sweat to give you away. I have never been busted doing it this way. If you do not wear a facemask, I expect you will be busted on at least some of your hunts. Why take a chance?

Be scent free and stay up in the tree

When I filmed wild deer during two ruts in 1991 and 1992, I would not let a buck get closer than 20 yards before I flailed my arms above my head and verbally shouted out "I am a man!" I did not worry about getting closer to does, but bucks in the rut are a different story. I prefer not to be on the ground when a buck approaches me during the rut. If I am above a buck's head in a tree stand, I have an advantage over him, and I know I am safe.

In 2009, I bow hunted from a tree stand that was 8 feet off the ground to the platform. A monster 10-point buck (See photos on pages 128 and 129) stood under my stand on Day 3 of my hunt and his antler tips were just 5-inches under the webbing on the stand. It made me a bit nervous and I have since then decided never to hunt from a stand platform that is less than

10 feet off the ground. I do not hunt above 20 feet. My ideal height range is 10–15 feet up. You do not need to be any higher than that. The buck that will be hunting you is not looking for you in a tree; he is looking for one of two deer on the ground. You will be invisible to him at any height, as long as you are above his line of sight. An alert monster buck's eye height is just about 5 feet off the ground, but his rack can go higher than 9 feet. At 10 feet off the ground, you should be in good shape. Prepare yourself for a close encounter with a massive racked buck. He will always be a mature buck and he may turn out to be a monster, you have to wait and see.

If I am on the ground working my way to my stand, scent free, dressed in camouflage from head to toe, and can see a mature rutting buck, he has my full attention. I know I am invisible to him, and because he cannot see me, I may be in danger. He thinks I am just a bit of brush, and if he wants to go somewhere, I know he will not care about pressing through some brush to get there. I have never been run over by a deer, and no deer has ever charged me, but I do not take chances when I am invisible to deer. If I thought my life was in danger, I would yell out "I am a man!" and flail my arms above my head. The buck would retreat, and my hunt would be over, but I would be safe and I could return to be hunted by another buck on another day. That is what I recommend you do if you are face-to-face with a mature rutting buck, and you have an uneasy feeling about it.

Dominant bucks know that human scent and odd aromas mean danger

You need to be 99% scent free when you scout, when you go out to set up the system, and on each day of your D.I.E. hunt. Of course, you cannot stay 99% scent free while you install a tree stand, but that will not matter. You will be out of the area for 2 ½ days after setting, the D.I.E. system up and your human scent will dissipate in that time. Deer will not fear you when you come in to hunt on Day 1 because of how I timed your return to the area. Your human scent is gone. When deer hunters enter the woods bringing foreign odors with them (such as whatever they ate for dinner, beer, gasoline, cologne, or perfume), they are jeopardizing the success of their hunt. If you take aromas from your house to the woods with you, the deer in the area are immediately alerted to your presence there and they see it as an intrusion. Never use scented fabric softener on your hunting clothes. Also using flavored mouthwash or regular toothpaste is not a good idea. I know from experience that dominant bucks can bust you if you make those mistakes.

Deer avoid all contact with humans whenever possible. They will change their normal behavior to avoid the area where they smell a human being. If you walk like a deer, "talk" like a deer, smell like the woods—or at least not like a threat—and keep yourself concealed in full camouflage so no deer can visually identify you as a human, then you will have mastered the art of being invisible to deer.

Wearing full camouflage is a must

Once you are 99% scent free, the next task to becoming invisible to deer is wearing good quality clothes with a camouflage pattern on them. Choose a camouflage pattern that matches the terrain that you walk through to get to your stand, as well as a pattern that will allow you to become two-dimensional to the deer when you are sitting up in your tree stand. A hunter who is standing still (not on a deer trail) or sitting down in their tree stand, and is scent free and in full camouflage has achieved the status of being invisible to every deer in the area. Make sure the fabric you are going to wear is waterproof, or if it is not waterproof plan on wearing a disposable rain poncho under it to keep yourself dry when it rains or snows. You need to hunt rain or shine, and you need to stay warm and dry to succeed on a D.I.E. hunt. If you are purchasing new camouflage clothing before your next hunt make sure the fabric is a soft fabric. Run your fingernails across it and see if it makes noise, if it does not make a sound then it is a good, quiet fabric. If it does make noise, when you wear it you will be making unnatural noises as you walk through the woods, and as you move through cover. Be careful not to give your identity (as a human) away to the buck by wearing noisy clothing. Avoid wearing noisy clothing whenever possible.

I used to have problems with this when I first started hunting, because my parents bought the cheapest clothes for me to hunt in when I was a kid. No disrespect to them. I know shopping for hunting clothes can be very expensive, and as a kid, I was lucky to have parents who were brought up in hunting families and promoted my becoming a hunter. I never complained about it, I just wore what they provided me with until I outgrew it, then I saved my money and I purchased my own hunting clothes. I purchased Mossy Oak® brand camouflage clothes that were waterproof and did not make any noise when I walked. I always wear soft, quiet fabrics that allow my body to move without making any unnatural sounds. Just keep in mind that cheap is not always quiet, and noisy clothes can get you busted.

Learning to react like a deer is a must

To be invisible to all deer when you are walking, you must know how to react like a deer. I want you to think about how the dominant buck reacts to the sounds of another deer (you) as it moves through the area. It is quite different from the way the dominant buck would react to the sounds of a human moving through the same area. If you are going to achieve the status of being an invisible pair of breeding deer, you need to be able to walk like multiple deer in the herd, that way your behavior will be persuasive and believable.

In 1993, I learned to walk like a deer. The combination of being 99% scent free, wearing full camouflage, and walking like a deer when I walked into areas where deer lived (were bedded), changed the way deer perceived my physical intrusion into their territory. I no longer was a threat to them. They immediately stopped sounding off alarms, and instead of fleeing when they noticed my movements, they walked calmly and nonchalantly over to me from the downwind side, to try to identify me. They were curious to see what type of animal I was, because they could not make out my physical shape, my facial features, or my intentions, from the behavior I was displaying. I was not pursuing them I was walking among them. There is quite a big difference.

When I walk among deer, I take my time. I prefer to act like a doe most of the time. Does are not threats to dominant bucks, and they attract all breeder bucks. Every mature buck wants to breed with does in estrus during the rut, and they will scent check every doe they meet hoping to find one that is in estrus or is very near going into estrus. I count on the most dominant buck to be the first buck to scent check my trail to my stand on Day 1, and on every other day that I hunt. As a new D.I.E. hunter, you will soon realize that the curiosity of a breeder buck is a wonderful thing for both you and me.

Becoming proficient at walking exactly like each deer in a herd, each with their own style and mannerisms took me only 15 minutes to master. Now I can mimic the way a deer of any age or sex within the herd—walks. If you always walk like a deer the same way, then the buck will figure you out. If he figures you out, you no longer will be invisible to deer. Keep him guessing with D.I.E.! Always send him mixed signals. Never tell him which deer you are. That way you will always be invisible to him.

Read **Chapter 11 "How to Walk Like a Deer"** in order to master the technique of walking like a deer. Your pace and the amount of pressure you exert as you touch your heel and toe down on the ground will determine which deer you are mimicking at the time. You can set your heel and toe down gently, but still making sure each one is heard as a separate step, and you will be walking like an adult doe, or a yearling doe. If you speed up your pace to a nonchalant gait, you will be a yearling buck, and if you slam your toe and heel down hard and walk briskly, you are certainly mimicking a monster intruder buck. If you walk in with someone else always pretend to be a doe and a fawn. Never try to be the dominant buck - it will get you busted! Never make any calls or rattling sounds when you are on the ground hunting with D.I.E., because the buck will come in and he will have the advantage. Get in your stand and wait him out where you are always in command of him.

Convincing you that you are invisible to deer is harder to accomplish than convincing the dominant buck that a human who is 99% scent free, in full camouflage, walking like a deer, and dragging the secret weapon doe urine behind him or her, is not a human. The most dominant buck in the herd, and any other deer that hears your footsteps, will look in your direction and catch a whiff of your scent trail, but they will be convinced that you are a real deer.

If I am in blaze orange camouflage, standing 15 yards in front of a buck, I can be invisible to him as long as I am not standing on a deer trail. You cannot be invisible to a deer, if you are blocking its view. In order to succeed using my DOMINANCE IS EVERYTHING system, you have to be scent free, in full camouflage, and act like a deer, all the while you are in the woods on the hunt. You have to keep up the charade until the second you successfully harvest the buck, or until you are busted by him, whichever comes first.

Look in the mirror: Do you see a human?

In order to be successful hunting with D.I.E. you need to look at yourself in the mirror at home before you go to your tree stand. If you look in the mirror and you see yourself as a human, you will need to stay home that day. My system needs you (the hunter) to believe you can pass for a real deer if a real deer tries to identify you. If you see yourself as being unidentifiable as a human to any deer that looks at you, scent checks the air for human scent, or hears you moving through the woods or while fidgeting in your stand, then you are ready to go to your stand. Wearing good quality camouflage is essential!

Here is how I want you to see your transformation from a human to a real but invisible deer. Go get a mirror, bring it back here, and then read on.

First, look in the mirror. What do you see? A human, am I right? Do you know why you see a human? It is because you look like a human to yourself and because you know you are a human. Now, cover your eyes and look in the mirror. What do you see when you look in the mirror with your eyes covered? You cannot see a thing, right.

Although you display the attributes of a human to yourself or to another person who looks at you, you do not display the attributes of a human to any person or animal that cannot see you. Do you follow me? If you are standing 10 feet in front of me but I am not looking at you, will I know you are there? Not unless you tell me! Remember, I said I am not looking at you.

Look in the mirror again and answer this question: What would you see if you were wearing a really good camouflage outfit that looked like the wall behind you and covered you from head to toe including your face (except for your eyes, your ears, and your mouth)?

I hope you answered that you would see a wall. What if you never made a sound and you stood up with your back against that wall while wearing your new wall camouflage? Now if someone not familiar with your house walked into that room, while you were dressed like that, and standing there motionless, what might they see?

I hope you answered, "Probably just a wall". Now carry this idea to the buck's home. Your camouflage outfit should match his "wall".

If you are completely hidden there still standing with your back up against the wall while wearing full wall camouflage, and you roll your eyes while a person or a deer glances in your direction, then what might they see?

I hope you answered, "Eyes moving on a wall".

I believe that deer are colorblind, that they can see only black, white, and gray tones. When you go shopping for camouflage to wear deer hunting, keep that in mind—and never roll your eyes at the dominant buck when he glances in your direction!

If you wear camouflage from head to toe, and you match your surroundings, then in a black and white world you can pass yourself off as a tree or a bush, a tag alder, or a vine wrapped around a limb of a tree. If you do not wear good-quality camouflage or you just wear solid colored clothing when hunting, you are not going to pass as a real tree, a bush, a tag alder, or a vine. You are going to look like a solid block of something (out of place) and a dominant buck will be able to identify you as a danger to him. If you continue to hunt wearing that sort of clothing, you will notice that some dominant bucks will know you are a human and others will just go on alert without knowing for sure, but it really does not matter because once you are busted, your D.I.E. hunt is over.

When you hunt with DOMINANCE IS EVERYTHING, you must always wear camouflage from head to toe. That applies to scouting day, set up day, and every day of your hunt. If you do not suit up appropriately and the buck never shows up on your four-day hunt, consider yourself busted! The only exception to this rule is on set up day. You do not need to wear a facemask on set up day but you should always wear a hat and gloves.

Being camouflaged (from head to toe) is only one of the three steps you have to take to brainwash deer into believing you are not a human. Becoming 99% scent free and learning to behave like a deer are the other two. In order to persuade deer to believe you are a deer, you have to think like a deer, walk like a deer, sound like a deer, and leave the same signs as deer would leave. Whenever you hunt with D.I.E., you can achieve all those tasks just by following the rules. You will always be invisible to deer, and they will believe you are one of them, from the first second you step foot into the area on Day 1 of your hunt.

Adolescent and mature deer see things differently

All yearling whitetail deer identify humans like this:

If it makes human noises, if it smells like a human, and if it looks like a human, then it is positively a human. Yearlings were fawns during the previous deer season. Many of them have never even seen a human. They do not know how to identify humans as danger. I consider yearling deer to be young and dumb, because they have not yet honed their skills for detecting danger, and escaping from it. That is the main reason that many yearling deer are harvested by hunters each deer season. The time it takes yearlings to realize that you (humans) are a threat to them, is much too long, and it will cost many of them their lives. I believe it takes most deer two years to master the skills needed to be able to avoid humans.

Mature whitetail bucks and does identify humans like this:

Mature deer have honed their danger detection skills and go about identifying humans and other threats to their survival in ways that are more expedient. They slip into nearby cover when they see a human, smell a human or hear a human. From the security of that cover, they analyze situations before reacting to them. It is survival of the fittest. The older a deer lives the smarter it becomes.

Every dominant whitetail buck identifies humans like this:

1. Do you smell like a human?

    First the buck will scent check you. If you do not pass his scent test by being 99% scent free, then you are an immediate danger to him. He responds to your presence by going on alert and leaving the area—that is if you do not succeed at changing his mind immediately. Smokers, beware!

2. Do you sound like a human?

If you pass his scent check but he can hear you making human noises, then he will leave immediately, offering no time for second chances. You have one shot at this; if you fail, you are busted! Turn off the ringer on your cell phone and do not use walkie-talkies with static. You have to be silent on your way in. That means no talking, drinking while you walk, or eating. Keep your mouth shut and pretend you are invisible. Invisible people do not make human noises. Once in the stand, you can get away with making some small noises like chewing food, but only for less than two minutes at a time. The buck that is hunting you will be trying to detect any unusual sounds that he can hear while he makes his way to your scrape. Sometimes he will call out to the doe by making *tending grunts*, or he will call out to the buck by raking brush. Do not fall for his attempts to get you to talk. Stay quiet in your stand. The buck is calling out to the invisible deer, not to a hunter in a tree stand. Do not respond at all. Invisible hunters and invisible deer do not make sounds. Always be aware of that and never tell him you are there. Just wait him out.

3. Do you look like a human?

After passing both the buck's scent test and his hearing test, the buck will still not be convinced that you are not a human, not until he conducts his sight test. He will move downwind of your set up and he will sneak in and attempt to look for the two breeding deer and for anything else that moves in the area around the D.I.E. scrape. If he sees you as a human, you are busted. Do not move around in your tree stand. Stay quiet for fifteen minutes at a time. Know that the dominant buck could appear within 35 yards of your stand during any fifteen-minute period. Push yourself to stay in the stand all day and only move when you are sure no deer are moving into, out of, or around your area. You should be able to sit for up to 3 hours without moving a muscle. If you cannot accomplish that, then do your best to make it one hour without moving and then take it 15 minutes at a time after that. When that buck is looking for danger, you have to allow him time to look, and not be in a hurry to pull him in. Once he believes it is all clear, he will walk in or trot in and stop in the open downwind or crosswind of you. You have to be patient.

Always walk through your hunting area with your arms down by your sides or in front of your legs. Do not extend them out in front of you unless you are falling. Never reach out and push any tree limbs or brush away from your face or chest when heading to your stand. Back up and walk around thick brush never swim through it. Yes, I said swim. When a person pushes brush out of their way and then enters the thick stuff to do it again, it looks as if they are swimming through the thick brush. Deer know the sound of people hurrying into the area and they will bust you if you do that. No deer ever push through thick brush (that makes noise) on purpose. They only do that if they are scared of something, then they head for cover and run into it no matter how thick or noisy it is, just to be able to hide in it. There is not a deer alive that is not alarmed when it hears another large animal running, or pushing its way through cover. Avoid doing that and you will not be identified as a danger to deer as you move through the woods on the way to your stand.

My theory is that while you are in the woods, you are being scent checked, you are being listened to, and you may even be under the dominant buck's surveillance. You must get to your stand in a calculated manner so you do not draw the attention of the dominant buck to you while you are moving. Go to your stand at the time I direct you to, and leave it exactly as I direct you, then the buck will not bust you on your way to or from your stand site. He will advance on your location once you are settled in your tree stand but not before that, if you do what I instruct you and nothing more. I have had a buck come in as early as eight minutes after I stopped moving around. You should be in your stand when you stop moving. Always do your best the first time so you will not have any regrets when the hunt is over.

Do your best and have no regrets

When you go into the woods each day of your hunt, you have to be 99% scent free, you must be wearing camouflage from head to toe, and you should walk like a deer as long as you are capable of doing it, and you have deemed it safe to do so. Be deliberate with your steps, and act like you know what you are doing, that way the bedded buck will not go on alert when he hears you walk in, because he reads your actions and he believes the deer you represent respects his presence there. He will be convinced that you are just passing through. Stay focused on getting to your stand without going downwind of the scrape. You have to enter the area from upwind and crosswind and take a different path each morning so the buck cannot pattern you. If you always stay upwind of the scrape, he will let you walk past him, and he will remain bedded as you do. The buck will ignore you until you get in your tree stand, or until the dripper hanging above the scrape starts dripping lure into the scrape (whichever comes first).

If you encounter the buck at the D.I.E. scrape or you see him standing between you and your tree stand as you make your way to it in the morning, then you need to hold up and wait where you are the second you see him. Never pressure the buck. He is looking for the two deer. Know that he has no idea a human is there. You are invisible to him right where you stand. He has not seen you, he cannot smell you, and he cannot hear you if you are not moving anymore. Wait him out, or you will be busted for sure. A situation like this one will be to your advantage if you ever wanted to shoot a buck from the ground. It is not my preference to do so, but if I am faced with a situation like that, I would be glad to have the chance. Because you are instructed to approach your stand from upwind and crosswind on Day 1 and from a crosswind on Day 2, Day 3, and Day 4, you will have the wind to your advantage each day as you make your way to the set up. In order to remain invisible to the buck you need to be upwind of him, and you are if you set it up as I directed. You want the buck to scent check the area to know there is no danger then he will proceed to go about his business of trying to find the doe in estrus before any other buck can find her. The dominant buck will always be downwind or crosswind of you when and if you ever see him while on your way in. Sneak off the path you were on and back yourself up against some cover of some sort, to break up the outline of your body. Do not push into the cover, just stand in front of it. Stay standing upright and point your weapon in the direction of the buck. Know that the buck will approach you from straight downwind if he is alerted to your presence, so move to an area that offers you a clear shot downwind

10 yards or more if there is one present. Now you have a decision to make. You can let the buck leave the area to bed down, and then enter the area quietly and get in your stand, or you can call to him as the doe in estrus and he will surely trot right over to find her, offering you a very close shot opportunity. It is your call to make.

Know that no deer can tell you are a human if you are scent free, standing still, in full camouflage, and not standing on a deer trail. Deer will look at you but they will not be afraid, so do not move or your will blow your cover. The buck will go straight downwind of you to do a scent check, before approaching your position. I have only gotten one chance with the dominant buck inside 35 yards on each of my hunts, but that is not to say he would never come back. There is still a lot to learn about the capabilities of my DOMINANCE IS EVERYTHING system. You are bound to face situations with dominant bucks that I have never faced. When you do, be sure you keep a clear head and know that he has no clue he is being hunted. You will be able to overcome any situation that he places you in, if you trust in your ability to remain invisible to deer. Do not worry about your meeting with the king of the herd. Look forward to it, and never forget the way it feels to be hunted by a king once you experience it!

Follow my instructions for walking like a deer and you can pass yourself off as a yearling buck, a doe in estrus, a fawn, or even an intruder buck. Remember, the buck that hunts you is going to check you out 100% of the time—before he comes in. He will always go downwind of your position to do that. If you convince him, you are a real deer and that no human is in the area, then he will come in. If instead he finds out you are a human, then you will be busted.

When a buck looks at you in the stand do not get nervous. The buck does not know you are a human, or that you might be a threat to him. It just means he is facing your direction. He cannot see you. When on a hunt with D.I.E. it is unusual for the dominant buck to look up at you in your tree stand, but if he does, just know that he does not have a clue a human is there. Realize that he is close to you because he does not know you are there! Stay calm and wait for him to look away before taking aim. The buck will always be looking around and checking the air for scent. He has to be on constant watch for an ambush. He has never been challenged in this area of his territory before and he will be very cautious because of it.

You are bound to get buck fever, and controlling it when the buck is in close is imperative. You cannot be invisible to deer if you are breathing heavy and your arms are shaking. I need to learn how to control buck fever better than I do, because it has cost me three monster bucks on my past hunts. I saw those monster bucks and I reacted too quickly. Once I rushed my shot and got a deflection while bow hunting, another time I overshot his back and only grazed his hide, and the third time I hit him poorly with a bullet in gun deer season and I never recovered the animal. Now I try to stay calm but that is easier said than done when monster bucks are in your midst. You will see. Know that a monster buck within 35 yards of you trusts the situation he is confronted with, and he has no clue a human is anywhere in the woods within 200 yards of him. No mature deer would ever approach a human, at anytime and especially during the rut.

The buck that hunts for you is not afraid of you or of anything else. He is the king of the herd at that moment and he is proud of it. Think about it, when a mature buck is afraid of something, it bolts out of the area fast. It covers a lot of ground as it heads for heavier cover, it does not stand out in the open like the bucks that come into a D.I.E. set up do. That is because on a D.I.E. hunt the human is invisible to the deer. Mature bucks know that uncertainty leads to danger and danger causes the death of deer. A deer goes on alert, if it feels its life may be in danger.

If a buck near your scrape is walking or trotting in, that is normal behavior; you can stop him with a grunt. If he looks at you, just hold still. Within forty-five seconds, he will lower his head and go about his normal business. That is when you will have a shot opportunity. Never tell any deer that you are a human, even if they ask. **Anytime a mature buck is moving toward you, he does not know you are a human.**

My D.I.E. system manipulates the minds of every whitetail deer in the herd so they believe that you are a real live deer whenever you enter their territory. That means from the second you step off the pavement and onto wild ground, you are in the territory of a dominant buck, and he and his whole herd are aware of you being there. Where you actually are physically standing does not matter. You could be at the roadside where you parked your vehicle (about to enter the woods), or standing in a grassy ditch ready to start walking into your hunting area. The exact place does not matter. What does matter is that you realize that the deer that live there are watching you. After you leave, they will scent check the area to see if you are gone, and then they will follow your tracks to the places you went while you were there. A deer can smell human scent for up to two days after the human left it, unless it rains or snows, then the scent is washed away. I learned that through trial and error.

If you are walking on a paved road, you are in the territory of humans, and the dominant buck that lives in the woods at the edge of the road hears you walking and expects you (a human) to be there. When you step off the road onto wild soil, you are in the home territory of a dominant whitetail buck, and he does not expect you (a human) to be there. If you continue into the buck's territory, walking like a human, the buck will positively identify you as a danger to him. Either he will hold up tight in his core bed or he will vacate it until you leave the area. He knows you are a human and that you do not belong in his territory. He will watch you to see where you go and he will investigate that place after you leave that day. You can count on that happening each time you enter the woods whether you are deer hunting or not.

The dominant buck is not nocturnal, but traditional hunters' behavior force him to move into open areas only at night or in lowlight conditions. If you refrain from going into your hunting area up until the day you scout for a stand site, the dominant buck will not know he is going to be hunted. I advise you to stay away from the property that you intend to hunt, as much as possible throughout the year, so the deer that live there do not know ahead of time that you are planning to hunt them during the rut.

The element of surprise is needed to fool a dominant buck into coming in close to your stand. Never tell a buck you are a human and that you are coming back. That is the message an installed trail camera gives the dominant buck after you install it. Remove any trail cameras now or as soon as possible so the dominant buck will discover your D.I.E. set up and expect a pair of breeding deer to be visiting it, instead of him discovering your human intrusion in his territory. He knows that no deer would ever breed near a human. The dominant buck will only come into a D.I.E. set up at night if you have trail cameras anywhere in his territory. It is a fact. I do all I can to avoid telling the dominant buck that he is going to be hunted, and I think you should do all you can to avoid telling him that too! If you use trail cameras you will not see the dominant buck within 35 yards during the day. He avoids the area because he knows a human was there and that they will be back to get what they forgot (the camera).

Your success with D.I.E., depends solely on your commitment to use it as directed

Again, success or failure with D.I.E. is not determined by whether or not you harvest the buck that came in on a D.I.E. hunt. Success is achieved when you use my system exactly as I direct you and you see a mature dominant buck or one of his challengers less than 35 yards away from you during daylight during the four-day hunt.

Failure on the other hand, it is the result of non-achievement, and it comes to those who make mistakes, whether those mistakes are intentionally made or not. Failure with D.I.E. means that for whatever reason you never saw a mature buck within 35 yards of you while hunting with my system. If you fail to see the buck then there is a reason for it. Sometimes it is your fault and other times it is not. If you do not see the buck, you were busted by him. You can prevent it happening to you again if you are willing to accept the fact that you were busted, and are willing to start over fresh with a new D.I.E. set up at a new location. Before you start over, you should re-read the chapters in this book regarding scouting, setting up and hunting, and then choose another 4 days to hunt. D.I.E. will succeed anywhere you place it. Being busted or not is determined by whether or not you do what I teach you.

I personally take pride in the successes that people who have used my system have experienced with it, and I want you to know in advance that I will be happy for you, when you become a successful D.I.E. hunter, whether you shoot the buck or not.

Chapter 11

How to walk like a deer

I know a way for you to walk among deer unnoticed, in broad daylight. I call it walking like a deer. I mastered it in less than five minutes, and it really works. You will be amazed. You can walk like any deer in the herd at any time. I will teach you how. I learned how to "walk like a deer" in 1991.

The combination of being 99% scent free, wearing full camouflage, and walking like a deer when I walked into areas where deer lived, together changed the way deer perceived my physical intrusion. I no longer was a threat to them. They never identified me as a human when I walked like a deer. They immediately stopped sounding off alarms, and instead of fleeing when they noticed my movements, they walked calmly and nonchalantly over to me from the downwind side, trying to identify me. They were curious to see what type of animal I was, because they could not make out my physical shape, my facial features, or my intentions. No deer can tell what I am when I am wearing my invisible deer suit and that makes walking among deer a whole lot of fun.

When I walk among deer, I take my time. I act like a doe 80% of the time. Does are not threats to dominant bucks, and they attract all mature breeder bucks. Any buck that wants to breed will scent check every doe he meets during the rut. Dominant bucks fall into that category of bucks. Their curiosity is a wonderful thing for you and me.

Mastering every deer's style of walking took me only 15 minutes. Now I can mimic the way a deer of any age within the herd walks and I can convince any deer that I am not a human being when I am walking like a deer. Whatever you do, never try to imitate a dominant buck when you walk like a deer. I tried it once and I learned rather quickly that the dominant buck stops hunting you if you try to tell his herd that he is not their king. He is the only deer that will not fall for it, and on a D.I.E. hunt, he is the only deer you are trying to brainwash. Walking like a dominant buck is not allowed on a D.I.E. hunt because it gets you busted. If you do it, he will know you are a human.

Outside of hunting season, walk like a deer to get close to them

On two separate occasions within a month of mastering how to walk like a deer, I was able to approach a bedded-down deer and poke it with a 3-foot-long tree branch, before either deer became aware that I was there. They knew something was there, but they assumed I was a deer, because I walked like a deer, and I moved at a deer's pace as I approached them while they were bedded down. I entered their bedding area by following a fresh deer track. I noticed the deer that left the track was exploring the area and taking its time as it moved into its bedding area. I moved at the exact pace that the deer that left the track had moved. I stopped when it stopped and I moved forward, and turned left or right when the tracks changed course. I remember that it took me 30 minutes to move less than 60 yards on both occasions. I was a deer in my mind, and my behavior told them I was a deer in their minds. Nothing is more amazing to me than being able to brainwash deer into believing I am one of them. I am sure you are going to love it too!

Once I learned how to get close to whitetails, I changed the way I hunted them. Now instead of wanting to sneak quietly into an area, attempting to get to my stand without being heard, I actually want the buck to hear me approach, but not as a human being, instead as an invisible deer. I know how to walk like a doe, a yearling buck, and an intruder buck. The steps are the same, but the cadence and the volume of the sound I make with my feet are different. You want the dominant buck to believe you are one of those three deer because each one of them are expected to walk into the core living space of the most dominant buck at anytime of the day. Your hunt will be the most fulfilling if you show up as one of the (three) deer that the dominant buck is expecting, and by doing so you will be consciously leaving your identity as a human at home where it belongs.

When you walk like a deer (Safety First)

I learned how deer approach different areas by watching my deer videotapes repeatedly. It is very important to know that the cadence of your steps has to be realistic when you walk like a deer. Never rush your steps; deer do not. They only hurry if they are afraid or unsure of their surroundings. On windy days, the buck's entire herd will move quickly from place to place. He will not rush though. His concern is not getting anywhere fast, it is getting where he is going alive! Remember, a dominant buck thinks about survival before anything else at all times. He is king there, and he will not run (when there are no humans in his territory) except to charge a challenger intruder buck in order to run him off, or to catch up with a doe in estrus. A dominant buck will always walk or trot if he is not alarmed and he will always posture when he moves. Posturing is a buck's way of displaying his dominance.

As a D.I.E. hunter, you need to know how to move through the woods unnoticed when you are hunting because a mature breeder whitetail buck is always waiting for you at your stand site. Do whatever is necessary not to spook him out of the area when you arrive. Walk in slowly and quietly, scanning the area for a big buck or a doe. I have never seen a doe within 35 yards of my tree stand on any of my hunts but others have.

Starting in 2001 and continuing through 2009, I walked like a deer (during daylight) on the way to my tree stand during archery deer season. On about 50% of my gun deer hunts—only when I am within sight of my tree stand—will, I walk into the area like a deer. I walk like a deer to my stand only in the morning during daylight, because I know the dominant buck thinks I am a doe in heat, and he expects me to show up in estrus at his scrape any minute. When I pass by his bed, he scent checks my scent trail (always from the downwind side). If I pass the scent test (which I always do), he will make his way to my D.I.E. scrape and rub. He will follow my scent trail, or go downwind of the strongest (2-inch wide) wind current that is coming off the D.I.E. scrape, before approaching the D.I.E. scrape from there. I will notice him most often when he is within 50 yards of me. I always sit still and keep focused on the scrape. He is on a mission to get to it, and I want to be ready when he gets there.

Safety is always the first priority. Assess whether you can safely walk like a deer (during daylight) where you decide to hunt with my DOMINANCE IS EVERYTHING system. In bow season, I have always hunted alone, on private land, so I have never had any issue with it being unsafe for me. When other hunters are not around, they cannot mistake me for a deer.

Walking like a deer can be more dangerous in gun season than in bow season, especially if you cannot control who hunts the same property you do, or if you are not sure if someone else is in earshot of you. Do not ever risk having a hunter mistake you for a deer. Always make a safe choice. When hunting near other hunters, walk like a human to assure your safety. If you master how to walk like a deer, continue to focus on all the mannerisms of it, except the way you put your feet down to make two deer steps instead of one human step. When I tell you to walk like a human, I want you to take human steps, but do everything else like you would if you were walking like a deer, so you do not call attention to your movement in the woods. That way any hunter who hears you move will know you are a human, but any deer that hears you move will want to get a visual on you before they will believe you are a threat to them. You must keep the herd guessing. Never tell them that you are a human. If you stop behaving like a human, they will never know you are one!

When I use D.I.E. during gun season, I tell everyone in my hunting party, where my tree stand is and I show them the routes I will take in and out of the woods that day. The routes are never the same. They vary depending on the wind direction. I make sure my fellow hunters know that I walk like a deer to my stand. I also instruct them not to come within 150 yards of my location, so they will not disturb the buck that is hunting my scrape or make him change his normal behavior.

Walking like a deer is not necessary for D.I.E. to work. The system works 100% of the time even if you walk in as a human. If you choose not to walk like a deer, the dominant buck will notice the lure at the scrape when the scrape dripper starts dripping (about 1 hour after sunrise) and he will come to the D.I.E. scrape sometime after that.

If you can safely walk like a deer to your stand, the dominant buck will oftentimes respond to the sound of your footsteps, rise from his bed, and come to your scrape before the lure starts dripping. That is why I do it. No one wants to be shot, or even shot at; never risk something like that! Be sure you do not walk like a deer if there is any chance that someone will shoot into your area when that someone hears a deer walking. The sound you make when you walk like a deer is identical to the sound a real deer makes as it walks through the woods. Be safe!

Never shoot your weapon without seeing your target clearly, and knowing what is beyond it.

The moose man taught me to walk like a deer

More than 20 years ago, I was watching TV and I saw a show about a man who made his own moose call. I cannot remember the name of his show, and I cannot find any reference to it on the internet, so I am unable to give him direct credit, but the credit is all his for my being able to walk like a deer. In his video he showed his audience, how he could intimidate a real bull moose with his behavior and he could command the moose to come in close enough for a bowshot. He put a hollowed out moose head that was made by a taxidermist, over his head and shoulders and he swayed back and forth. He grunted into his moose call and a giant bull moose answered him. Then he leaned forward and thrashed his fake moose rack into some brush raking it back and forth. In less than 5 minutes, a bull moose came charging in and stopped just 40 yards away. The moose profiled and postured showing off his huge rack and then the moose moved behind some cover and the man said he was going to walk like a moose to get the moose to come even closer. He did a weird step then another, and another. It sounded just like a four-legged animal was walking around, instead of the two-legged man that was really doing the walking.

That moose walked up to within 15 yards of the man, and that is when he said he was feeling a little uneasy because he did not have a weapon at the time. The man took off his fake moose head and flailed his arms at the moose yelling out "hey moose get out of here". The moose rambled off into the brush. 'Wow that was pretty cool, I thought to myself.' When the man summarized the encounter, he said that he never had used the moose-walk on any other animal except moose, but he believed it would work equally as well for any four-legged hoofed animals like deer, sheep, or antelope.

The first two times I walked like a deer—I could not believe my eyes!

I stood up and tried it right there in my living room. It was easy to learn and fun to do. The next day I tried it in the woods near my home. I found a doe and two fawns in a bedding area so I hid behind some tall yellow grass where they could not see me. I walked four or five steps like a deer, and then I heard them walking too. I could hear them coming toward me. I was downwind of them so they could not smell me. I stood there for a moment and a doe stuck her head around the grass and looked at me. I was literally four feet from that deer. She wheezed at me then turned around and trotted off, taking her fawns with her.

My second encounter walking like a deer was much more eventful. I had arrowed a doe on my family's property in New Berlin, Wisconsin in 1994. It was late in the day when I hit her. I lost her blood trail and I decided it was best for me to let her go for the night. She headed into a swamp on my neighbors land where I did not have permission to hunt. I stopped at his house on my way home, to ask if I could pursue my doe into his property in the morning. He said I could walk on it to try to find her but I could not hunt it. I thanked him and went home.

The next morning at sunrise I packed a gear bag with a knife, a rope, and a pair of gutting gloves (leaving my bow behind), then I walked down to the edge of the swamp where I had left off tracking the doe the day before. Her tracks led into some tag alder brush. I walked into the brush and out the other side following her trail, and making as little noise as possible. A few feet out of the brush, I found my arrow lying on the ground. Apparently, I hit her in the shoulder blade and the arrow had never gone through the bone. Not a good hit, and definitely not a fatal one either. There was no blood anywhere around, but there were plenty of deer tracks and they were headed off in all directions in that swamp. It was a core bedding area for bucks. I figured the doe was going to be ok, and our land was just 70 yards to the East, so I decided to go north a few more yards before heading back east to our land.

It was just about 8 a.m. on a December morning and the temperature was about 20 degrees. There was a brisk wind from the Northwest and I was walking straight north into the swamp. I thought it would be a perfect time to walk like a deer, because I knew all the deer in the area would be bedded down by then and it was likely I would be able to see one or two of them in that bedding area. We had 4 inches of fresh snow on the ground, and there was 1 to 2 inches of ice under the snow. I started walking like a deer and I was cracking through the ice with each step I took. I am 6'3" tall and I weigh 250 pounds, so when I walk like a deer I walk like a big heavy deer.

I walked like a deer for the next 30 yards stopping about every seven steps for just 20 seconds or so. The wind was in my face. I looked around and there was tag alder brush scattered every 10 yards or so. In front of me, I saw what I thought was the backside of a bedded down deer, just about 8 yards away from me. I snuck up on that brown patch until it was clear to me that it really was a deer. I had no idea if it was dead or alive because it never flinched as I approached it. I got 3 feet away from it before I stopped moving. It was facing crosswind with its head looking north but its chest and body was facing east. Its head and chest was behind a tag alder, therefore I could not see it, and it could not see me. I poked it in the rump with the arrow I had recovered 10 minutes earlier. Much to my amazement a buck stood up and took two jumps into the wind. He looked back standing broadside. He was a yearling 6-pointer, and at the time, I did not have the D.I.E. system. I would have liked to see a buck that close when I had my bow and I was on my own property, but it was as if Murphy's Law was in effect for me that day. The buck stood there looking at me for five minutes, then he took three jumps into the wind, and walked away heading into a thick patch of cover. Back then, I would have been proud to harvest that yearling buck, but now I would pass. Now I am strictly a dominant buck, monster buck, and swamp buck hunter. My motto is to let them grow, and they might become dominant in 3 or 4 years. I do shoot adult does for meat, but I prefer to wait until after I get my dominant buck.

How to walk like a deer (Step-by-step instructions)

Here are the steps to "walking like a deer":

Always move slowly but abruptly. Do not try to be quiet, the heel and toe of your boot each represent a deer's hoof impacting the ground, so make it known that you represent a four-legged deer and not a two-legged one. Deer know that the sound of a two-legged deer always means danger. Two-legged deer do not exist, so the sounds they hear must be made by a human.

Walking like a deer is as easy as counting from one to three.

When practicing, say the words aloud "one, two, three".

When hunting, say the words in your mind—not aloud.

If you are right handed I think it is easiest to start with your right foot first, and left handed people should start with their left foot first. If that is not comfortable for you, then make up your own mind, and do it the way you want to. The end result is not any different no matter which foot you start with.

Lift your right foot up 10 to 15 inches off the ground, tilt your toes to the sky (your foot will be at a 45-degree angle) then slam your heel down and say (one) keeping your toes still pointed to the sky.

On the count of 2, your heel is still down and you are holding that 45-degree foot position with your toes up.

On the count of 3, slam the toe of you boot down and say (three).

Then lift your left foot up, lift your toe and slam your heel down on 1, hold your toe up for 2, and slam your heel down on 3.

Your forward movement should only be minimal. When you step forward place the heel of your foot about 2 inches forward of the toe of your other foot. Do not stretch your legs out as a human does when they walk. You are not trying to cover a lot of ground in a short amount of time. You are trying to make the sound of four steps in the same space you used to make two.

I will use a ^ to represent a pause. Always pause one to two seconds between your steps. If you hear a deer walking nearby, stop all movement immediately. Try walking like a deer now or read on and try it when you have read it all. Just say the numbers aloud when you practice the steps, it is easier that way.

Speak the numbers out loud 1, 2, 3 ^^ 1, 2, 3, ^^ 1, 2, 3, ^^ 1, 2, 3, ^^ 1, 2, 3, ^^ 1, 2, 3,

                                        Right foot Left foot Right foot Left foot Right foot Left foot

Step 1 = plant your heel down and point your toes toward the sky on the count of 1

Step 2 = hold your heel still, and continue to point your toes toward the sky on the count of 2

Step 3 = slam the toe of your boot down so it makes noise on the count of 3

I recommend that you stand up right now (if you are capable) and try it out. You do not have to cover a lot of ground when you walk like a deer, but you have to practice for about 5 minutes before you really get the hang of it. If you watch a real deer walk in the woods you will see that it will hesitate between steps and you have to hold your toes up for the count of two, so that there is that same delay in the sound of the steps that you make. I love walking like a deer and I have made it a very important part of my **Dominance Is Everything** system because it works amazingly for everyone who uses it.

Your mission on your way to your stand each day is to convince every deer in the herd that you are a deer that is moving into the area of the D.I.E. scrape. **You should only choose to walk like a deer if you determine that it is safe for you to do so.** If not just walk softly as a human without making any noises that would call attention to your location. Deer do not know that quiet, scent free, camouflaged people are there. Invisible people do exist on a D.I.E. hunt. You get to choose if you will be an invisible human, or an invisible pair of breeding deer. Choose based on your safety. I am not there with you so I cannot determine when it is safe for you to walk like a deer or not. Your behavior when you hunt is 100% your responsibility. Whenever you walk like a deer and there are armed hunters in the area, there is some risk, so do not do it then. **NEVER TAKE A CHANCE WITH YOUR LIFE!** You only have one!

The only time I ever walk like a deer on a D.I.E. hunt is on the way to my tree stand each day of my hunt. I start walking like a deer, when I find the *first sign of deer,* or when I am 50 to 120 yards away from my tree stand whichever comes first. **IT IS NOT SAFE TO "WALK LIKE A DEER" AT ANY OTHER TIME!**

I stop walking like a deer when I get to the base of my tree stand. From then on, I am an invisible hunter, watching over the primary breeding scrape of the area's most dominant buck, while two invisible breeding deer approach it. Did I mention that I was an actor and that I was able to role-play with the dominant buck to make him believe that only the two invisible deer came in today? The invisible hunter is not anywhere to be found. He is invisible!

If you want to walk safely as a deer, then memorize the "NEVER DO" list, and follow the rules to hunt safely with the D.I.E. system. **Failure to follow my instructions could put you in harm's way. NEVER RISK YOUR LIFE WHILE HUNTING.**

Use common sense and be sure to take every precaution before you ever consider "walking like a deer" while hunting. You are hunting at your own risk, and I am not responsible for your actions. I am only telling you what I do, and how I do it so you can decide for yourself what you want to do. I know what has always worked for me so I am sharing those tactics with you.

You do not have to walk like a deer to get D.I.E. to work. It works without you walking like a deer! Ideally, you want the dominant buck to hear a deer coming in, or at least to not hear a human coming in. **THE CHOICE TO "WALK LIKE A DEER" OR "NOT WALK LIKE A DEER" IS YOURS TO MAKE.**

MAKE IT A SAFE CHOICE AND YOU WILL NEVER REGRET IT.

Pointers for getting where you are going in a timely manner

Walking like a deer is something special. You should only walk like a deer in the mornings on the way to your stand site. Start walking like a deer when you are within 120 yards away from your stand. If you are hunting deeper into deer habitat than 120 yards, then walk as quietly as you can as an invisible human until you get 120 yards of your stand, then start "walking like a deer". When you walk like a deer, you should pause every 18 to 26 (deer) steps, just like a real deer would. Each time the heel or the toe of your boot touches the ground you have made one deer step. Two deer steps equal one human step. Another way of looking at it is to pause after you switch legs 9 to 13 times.

When you pause, it is very important that you always pause on the count of 2, with your toes pointing up in the air. Wait 10 to 29 seconds before bringing your toes down on the count of 3, and then go another 18 to 26 steps, before pausing again. If you do, any real deer in the area that can hear your footsteps will believe that you are a real deer. They will remain bedded allowing you to walk right by them.

Waiting 30 or more seconds is not a good idea because the dominant buck is nearby listening and he knows that the sound of a deer stopping and hanging around the area near the D.I.E. scrape could mean trouble for him. Deer that pause for more than 30 seconds are usually looking for a place to bed down. You do not want the buck to think you are bedding down along the trail to your stand. You want the buck to believe you are going to bed down under your stand, near the scrape. That way he will wait for you to get in your stand before he approaches the scrape.

Dominant bucks move in on the location of deer sounds, within 4 or 5 minutes of the sound ceasing, so concentrate on making sounds with your feet similar to the sounds that real walking deer would make, at least until you start climbing up into your tree stand.

I mastered the timing of my pauses and cadence of the steps I use when "walking like a deer", by watching the behavior of real deer in the wild. If you do it the way I do then I know you will succeed. Changing the timing or cadence of your steps when "walking like a deer" will bring you different results. Follow my instructions exactly in order to expect success with my system. That is the D.I.E. way! No deviations.

The reason you should pause for 10 to 29 seconds is that all (walking) deer stop in an instant when they detect other deer in their immediate vicinity, and of course, they also stop when they detect danger. On a D.I.E. hunt you are not a human, you are a real pair of breeding deer that are walking into the core bedding and primary breeding area of the most dominant buck in the herd. In order to pull off the charade you need to behave the same way those two real deer would, as they enter the core living area of the most dominant buck in the territory.

All real deer can detect one another by scent, and when a deer detects another deer, they stop for a few seconds to make a decision. They need to decide which way to go from there. It is unheard of in the real deer world for any buck to approach a dominant buck while he is tending a doe in estrus, in his own territory, and that is in fact what you would be doing if you went downwind of your tree stand on your approach to it. That is why a D.I.E. hunter never approaches their tree stand from downwind. Following instructions will prevent you from being busted by the king of the herd as he waits for his next mate.

Any real deer in your position would be very nervous when they were within 35 yards of your D.I.E. scrape. They would stop, look, and listen for a few seconds, before proceeding into the dominant buck's territory. They would avoid walking toward the bedded buck, and they would avoid eye-to-eye contact with him. You do not know exactly where he is bedded, but you do know he is not upwind of your scrape. Be sure you go to your stand from a starting point that is at least 5 yards upwind of the scrape. That way you will not pressure the buck out of his bed, and whether you walk like a deer or not, you will be, assured that he does not know you are there.

Traditional hunters never pause like a deer, some of them never pause at all, and the ones that do pause always pause like humans. That is what gets them busted! There is a huge difference between deer behavior and human behavior. You probably understand now why dominant bucks do not show themselves to traditional hunters but why they will show up for a D.I.E. hunter every time.

Deer stop forward momentum while walking every 18 to 26 steps even if they do not detect any danger. They have to in order to determine that they are safe in their current surroundings. When deer are standing still, they conduct scent checks that help them determine which directions are safe for them to proceed into, based on the types of aromas they detect in the wind current. If it is not safe ahead, then a deer will stomp one of its front hooves on the ground. If something moves or if the deer just does not feel good about the situation then it will quickly turn around and retreat at a full gallop, heading for cover.

When you are pretending to be a deer on a D.I.E. hunt, you should be a confident intruder deer. Pause often and behave as a monster intruder buck, or as an intruder doe in estrus would. They both would sneak into the area, not calling attention to their movements. Do not make any sounds with your mouth, or your hands, only make sounds with your feet. Deer break brush as they walk over it, so you can do that too, but do not break large diameter trees or deer will know they are in the presence of a human, and they will go on alert. Small branches litter the ground in deer country and they are bound to get stepped on, so do not avoid them when you are "walking like a deer", but never go out of your way to make unnecessary sounds, such as purposely breaking brush.

The terrain in woods or in brush often changes every 15 to 30 yards, and deer that are not alarmed will always walk or trot through every change in terrain. They never hurry through terrain changes, so as a D.I.E. hunter you cannot either. Do not hurry to your stand, take your time like a real deer would. If you are wondering what you should do when you get to a hill and you need to go up it, or when you come to a clearing, or a logging road and you need to get across it, do not worry because I have the answers for you. Always think like a deer and do what a deer would do.

Practice walking like a deer

If you want to learn to walk among deer in the wild, in deer season and out of it, you need to start out by learning to read deer sign. The easiest way is to find a set of deer tracks in the woods and follow the tracks backwards to the deer's bed. Once you find its bed, you will find some feces nearby and you can determine if it was a buck or a doe just by analyzing its bed and its feces. Always start tracking a deer forward from the bed that it used the day before. Most of the time you will find a set of deer tracks leading from a food source to a bedding area. Do not follow those tracks forward to the place the deer is bedded now; instead follow them backwards to the bed the deer used the day before. That way you can tell where the non-pressured deer went as it walked toward its food source. You can learn from the habits of a non-pressured deer, but you cannot learn from the reactions of a deer that you pressure out of its bed. Deer do not behave normally when they are being pressured, and you will be giving up the element of surprise and turning in your invisible deer suit if you go to the deer in its current bed. Never pressure a deer, or walk into its current bedding area during hunting season, and it will never know a human is in its territory.

The best time to practice walking like a deer among real deer is after the rut when winter is upon us. Whether there is, snow on the ground or not does not matter. The fact that frost covers the ground in the mornings will be what sets that time of the year apart from the rest. You can track any animal that moves during darkness if you can see its tracks and having frost on the ground during daylight offers us humans the best view into the deer world that we can possibly get. Frost is better than snow for tracking animals (in my opinion).

Tracking deer on frost-covered ground allows you to learn everything about their movements all throughout the night. You can learn a lot from deer if you want to, but in order to understand deer you have to learn to think like a deer, walk like a deer, talk like a deer, and read sign like a deer.

Whitetail does, fawns, yearling bucks, and pecking order bucks all walk into and out of their beds unless they are pressured by an enemy, then they will gallop out of them. The dominant buck, monster bucks, and swamp bucks gallop into and out of their beds most of the time, so be alert and analyze the deer bed that you find, and the tracks coming out of it, so you can determine if you are tracking a buck or a doe before you start trailing it.

Follow the deer tracks as a deer not as a human. Act like you are a young buck and you need to do whatever the deer that left those tracks did in order to survive. If the tracks tell you that the deer was walking, then walk (like a deer). If the tracks show the deer was trotting then jog, and if the tracks tell you the deer was galloping, then jog faster or run. It is impossible to jog or run "like a deer", and you cannot jog or run like a human without being busted, so your only option is to jog or run like a deer with human legs.

Focus on staying upright and run or jog, while concentrating on not swinging your arms at all. Keep your hands down in front of your legs, so no deer will see you reaching forward or back. If you decide to run, only run in short bursts, and only run when a real deer would. Deer trot or gallop across clearings or up hillsides. You will need to jog up any hill that you notice deer run up. I try to avoid hunting with D.I.E. in areas where deer are running. I always set my D.I.E. scrape and tree stand up on the upwind side of a trail where deer are walking. I know walking deer are confident with their surroundings, and they are not afraid or looking to run into or out of the area. Scouting for a place like this gives me a distinct advantage over the buck when he does arrive. I can shoot a walking deer just as well as one that is standing still and getting a walking deer to stop with a grunt is much easier than stopping a running one. Running deer do not want to stop, the want to get to the other side of the danger. They will stop once they get there. I learned that from deer.

Whenever you are walking to your stand on a D.I.E. hunt, you must be aware that you are being watched by the dominant buck. I have said that before, and I will certainly say it again, because you are a traditional hunter until you hunt with D.I.E. as directed. I need for you to believe that what D.I.E. does for you is it makes you invisible to deer.

I think most traditional deer hunters assume that all deer can see, smell, or hear them as a human and that they have to be lucky to pass all the deer tests and not be identified. With D.I.E., it is different; the human rules do not apply to D.I.E. hunters. I have to teach you to think like a deer, and I need you to realize that no deer can see you, smell you, or hear you as a D.I.E. hunter. Once you realize that you are invisible to deer when you hunt with my DOMINANCE IS EVERYTHING system that is when you will trust that the dominant buck will approach a D.I.E. scrape during daylight even though you are there.

Always think about what the dominant buck must be thinking when he hears your move into his territory each morning. He will be where I tell you he is, and that is a given for every D.I.E. hunter, because the most dominant buck does not know that D.I.E. hunters exist. He is brainwashed to believe that D.I.E. hunters are a breeding pair of deer. We keep him guessing so he can never figure out which one we are at any given moment in time. He only hunts for deer that he cannot find.

If you think, it is impossible for a deer to hunt a human you are absolutely right! That is why you have to learn to stop displaying human characteristics when you enter the territory of the dominant buck. He is watching your scrape 24/7 and your stand is within 35 yards of it. He is the only animal in the herd that is destined to arrive at your stand within 4 days, and you can count on it happening if you trust me and trust in my system. *"Behaving like a deer" is necessary for a D.I.E. hunter, but "walking like a deer" is just an option.*

Always mimic the behavior of the deer that leave tracks in the area, and no deer will get nervous as you approach your stand site. When you see the deer tracks on the trail slow to a walking pace, then you must slow to a walking pace. If they stop, then you stop, and in less than 29 seconds, you start up again. Do whatever the deer did, and be sure to think about why the deer was running here, and why it walked there. Know that there is a reason for all the things a deer does, and a person with some time on their hands can figure out the reasons just by analyzing the time of day, the circumstance the deer was faced with, and the location that those tracks were made. To me tracking deer is fun, and finding them is even more fun, because once I find them, they do not know that I am a human, and they come in close to see what I am. Deer are not afraid of other deer, and I am an expert at convincing them that I am just another deer that is passing through their area.

Focus on learning to move like a deer

Now you know when to walk like a deer, but you still have to learn when to stop, and when to start again. You must practice walking, stopping and starting again, like a deer so you get it right. You can run or jog, to imitate a deer running or trotting but only do it when a real deer would be doing it, otherwise real deer will bust you when they hear you acting inappropriately.

Deer only run for four reasons.

1. Bucks and does run when their lives are in danger
2. When they are being pursued by another deer or a predator (such as a doe in heat)
3. A buck runs when pursuing a doe in the rut
4. All deer run when they cannot see ahead, which is the case when they climb a hill

Most mature deer that are running or trotting, will come to a stop with one of their front hooves off the ground. They do that so they can use their elevated hoof to try to detect danger. If they sense danger ahead, they will pound that hoof down loud and clear. The effort they make is most often rewarded when a human or a predator shows himself or herself by reacting to the sound of the pounding deer hoof. The deer picks up the movement of its enemy and it reverses course and high-tails it out of there! Deer know they only have a few seconds to flee the area before being attacked, or maybe even killed.

I teach you to walk like a deer, and pause like a deer, with the toe of your boot in the air on the count of 2, so you can pound your boot toe on the ground (resembling a deer pounding its hoof), if you see a human or another predator of deer nearby.

If you really want to walk like a deer, and have real deer believe that you are a deer, then you must behave as one of them the entire time you make your way to your tree stand each day, not just when it is easy for you to make deer steps. Whenever you walk like a deer, train yourself to think like one too!

If you do not see any humans or other predators of deer around, then start walking like a deer again by lowering the toe of your boot on the count of 3 in a normal fashion. You should lower your foot lightly; never pound it on the ground when there is not any danger nearby.

Only pound your boot toe down loud if you see a human or another predator, never pound it if you see a real deer. If you do see a real deer, stay still until it moves away or until it beds down. You can walk among deer that are bedded or walking away in front of you, but you cannot walk among deer that are approaching you in front. Remain still if any deer approach you and let them try to discover what you are. They will fail in their efforts and then you will be able to proceed on your way to your stand. Do not worry about the time, if you encounter a deer; just concentrate on not being identified as a human. Take all the time you need to accomplish that and you will not be busted.

After a pause on your way to the stand, look around without swinging your head or shoulders too much. If you do not see any deer, be sure to lower the toe of your boot softly so it makes the sound of the first step of your invisible deer, then take more deer steps and pretend you are doe as it picks its way through the available cover on its way toward the D.I.E. scrape.

Do not linger in one place for too long

Never pause in one place for more than 30 seconds or you risk the chance that the buck will become curious and try to discover why the doe in estrus (you) has stopped. He is expecting you to walk in any moment and he is prepared to follow you in right away. You do not ever want the buck to come to you while you are on the ground. You need to stay focused on getting to your tree stand and you should climb into it as soon as you get there. I believe you will be walking past the bedded down dominant buck as you go to your stand on Day 1 at least 50% of the time, and the odds that he is there watching you on Days 2, 3, & 4 are closer to 90%.

Look for the buck as you walk in, but do not veer from your path to search him out. When you are hunting using D.I.E., either the buck is watching you already on Day 1, or he has not found your scrape yet. If the latter is the case, he will surely discover it on Day 2 or Day 3. Do not let your guard down. Act as if he has already found it and he is bedded downwind in the nearest available cover. Believe he is watching you, and listening for you. If you believe it, you will act accordingly and the buck will not be able to identify you as a human. If he has found the scrape, he will be bedded downwind or at a crosswind of it and he could be within 10 yards of you at any time. Stay quiet, do not cough, or sniffle if you can help it, and get to your stand in an orderly fashion. **Do not "walk like a deer" all around the woods**. Deer are not active everywhere in the woods during the day. They are only active in and around bedding and breeding areas, which usually are in close proximity to a year round water supply. I teach you not to hunt where deer bed, or anywhere within view of deer bedding areas.

Never "walk like a deer" in the dark and only do it while you are entering the area, never when you are leaving it. You do not want the buck to follow you away from the area, do you? I surely do not.

My hat goes off to that moose man. Walking like a deer takes deer hunting to a new level. Bedded down dominant bucks do not know you are a human and they let you walk close to them without ever wanting to glance in your direction. It gives the hunter stealth, and the element of surprise. Deer cannot bust you if you walk like a deer. It actually attracts them to your area and it makes them believe there is nothing to be afraid of there. I made it a big part of my DOMINANCE IS EVERYTHING system and although it is not necessary that you walk like a deer for D.I.E. to work, I know it improves a D.I.E. hunter's odds of seeing a monster buck in the area if he or she walks like a deer while hunting with my DOMINANCE IS EVERYTHING system. Thank you Moose Man!

Chapter 12

The wind—check it, understand it, and adapt to it

Deer are always aware of the wind direction. That is the direction that the wind is coming from. Deer use the wind to their advantage at all times of the day and night. When the wind changes direction, the deer choose different rout°es to take to and from their food sources, their bedding areas, and their primary source of water. They make adjustments immediately, so they are always able to walk crosswind (with the wind hitting them in them in their ribs) or into the wind (with the wind in their face) as they move through their territory to get where they are going.

Mature deer of prefer to bed in the furthest downwind bedding area in their herd's territory. If deer bedded on the upwind side of their territory they would be in constant danger. No deer will ever walk with the wind hitting them squarely in the tail because they cannot sense danger that is upwind of them (with their nose, their ears, or their eyes) when they are in that position. If deer bedded on the upwind side of their territory they would need to be in that position (facing straight downwind) to run from danger that approached them in their bed. Deer prefer to escape danger that approaches them in a daytime bedding area, by first running directly into the wind for a short distance, and then by turning crosswind and hightailing it into one of their other two core-bedding areas. If they bedded upwind escaping danger would be nearly impossible without the deer having to leave the territory.

If a storm is sweeping up from the South, pushing its way through the area that you hunt, then the deer will be bedded in their northernmost bedding area. They can travel south, east, or west to get food and water, or to escape danger.

If a storm is approaching from the North, then the deer will move to their southernmost bedding area. They move as the wind direction is changing, that way they can escape danger if it approaches them from the North, the East or the West. They can move at crosswind angles to get to another bedding area if they are pressured out of that one, and they will be in position to travel at a crosswind to food and water.

Knowing which way the wind is coming from tells me and every other D.I.E. hunter where all the deer are bedded inside their territorial boundaries at any given time. That is because we look at the wind as being our friend. We are always thinking like a deer. We want our scent to travel downwind to the king of the herd, and we want to get his attention and make him come to us where we are, and not ask us to go to him where he is. We need the wind to send our message to the dominant buck. Swirling wind is all the better, because it tells all the deer in the neighboring herds that there is a doe in estrus looking for a mate near the D.I.E. scrape and rub. What could be better than that?

As you know does and fawns, pecking order bucks, and the dominant buck all have three core-bedding areas, and each of them is positioned inside the herd's territory in a strategic place that offers all deer a downwind bedding option regardless of the wind direction. There is always one bedding area to the North, one to the South, and the third one is either East or West of the center of the dominant buck's territory. If you drew them, out on paper they would lay out in a triangular pattern and none of them would be overlapping.

When the wind blows from the West (during the day), it carries the scent of every deer in the herd downwind to the waiting dominant buck. He beds on the East side of his territory when there is a West wind for that reason. With a North wind he beds on the South side of his territory, with a South wind he beds on the North side, and with an East wind he beds on the West side. **Dominant bucks do not bed with the rest of the deer in the herd, they always bed downwind of the other deer.**

My findings make sense so they are believable

When I teach this subject in D.I.E. seminars, I get many smiles from my audience and I see many people taking notes. Some people tell me that they never knew that the wind direction played such a major role in the daily lives of deer. They knew the wind was tricky to understand, and that deer prefer to travel at a crosswind or into the wind, but they had no idea that every deer in a herd had three bedding areas, or that deer used the wind direction to decide which bedding area to use each day. They had no idea that deer prefer to be in their furthest downwind bedding area during daylight hours, so their odds of surviving an encounter with a predator, are better than average. Most predators (including humans) approach deer bedding areas from downwind, and because the dominant buck is downwind of his whole herd all day, most predators cannot outsmart a dominant buck. He is the first deer to become aware that he is being hunted, and he escapes without incident. All mature deer think alike, and all D.I.E. hunters think like mature deer. Are you ready to become a D.I.E. hunter?

I love discussing the wind in my seminars, because people are floored at first when they hear me talk about how deer use it to make decisions on a second-by-second basis. After I explain what I know to them, they can see clearly how the wind protects deer from danger, and how deer adjust their positions so they always have an advantage over their predators, in ever-changing wind conditions.

The answers to most of the questions that traditional hunters have are floating around in the wind. All a traditional hunter has to do to understand whitetail deer the same way I do, is learn to understand the wind, and the shielding power it provides to animals. It helps them survive dangerous situations. Most every action that a traditional hunter takes inside a dominant buck's territory is viewed by the dominant buck as an intrusion. Humans act and deer react. Any human intrusion in the deer woods, forces deer into a dangerous situation. Mature deer (smart deer) use the wind to get safely out of those types of situations.

Have you ever wondered why deer move out of an area, and they stay away from it for days or weeks at a time? It all has to do with the direction of the wind. If the wind shifted when the deer disappeared then you have your answer.

Most of the people I teach my D.I.E. system to consider themselves to be hard-core buck hunters. They have a hundred or more acres to hunt, and they have record book bucks on their land but no matter what they do the big bucks almost always seem to outsmart them. They have a few Pope and Young bucks under their belt but they are seeing larger racked bucks on their property during the summer months than they see during the rut, and they are stumped as to where those huge racked bucks go when the rut is on. They have come to a D.I.E. seminar to learn what I do to make the king of deer hunt me, and I start out by asking them a few questions that I already know the answers to. I start out asking these questions to my average student who has 100 acres all to himself to hunt:

1. How many stands do you have on the property?
2. How many trail cameras do you have out?
3. How many stands do you hunt from during a four-day period?
4. What do you do if it rains or snows?
5. Where do you go if the wind switches directions?
6. Where are you hunting in relation to the dominant buck's primary bed?

Nine out of ten hunters give me the same answers, and I know right away, what their issues are. They are traditional hunters and they have never taken the time to think like a deer. I need to teach them how deer think, and why their behavior (as a human) in the territory of the dominant buck is seen as an intrusion in his house. I understand traditional hunting tactics, because I used to be a traditional hunter, but I no longer use any traditional hunting tactics, because I am now a D.I.E. hunter, and I am invisible to deer when I hunt. Traditional hunters cannot behave the way they do, and become invisible to deer. You probably are aware of that now. Furthermore, pursuing the dominant buck by pressuring him inside his own house will never bring the smartest buck in the herd to his front doorstep.

Most traditional hunters concentrate on their hunt, and what they can do to get more deer on their property, they hardly ever consider what the deer think of what they are doing. Deer avoid people remember, so the more activity you have on your property the more you are telling the deer that a human was there and that a human will be back. You are asking deer to start liking you because you are offering them food and shelter, but no matter what you do deer will always avoid you. It is their way of surviving encounters with humans.

Everything can change for you if you look at deer from their perspective. Allow me to show you some of the common problems that traditional hunters have, because they do not know how to use the wind like a deer, and therefore they are pressuring deer inside their core living areas.

Here are the answers I usually get to the questions I ask at seminar. You should be able to see why these traditional hunters are failing in all their efforts to see a dominant buck up close during deer season. Remember these questions are asked to my average student who has 100 acres all to himself to hunt:

1. **How many stands do you have on the property?** 10–15
2. **How many trail cameras do you have out?** 10–15
3. **How many stands do you hunt from during a four-day period?** 3 or 4
4. **What do you do if it rains or snows?** I go home to warm up.
5. **Where do you go if the wind switches directions?** I quit for the day, and hunt another stand in the morning.
6. **Where are you hunting in relation to the dominant buck's primary bed?** What? I do not know where the dominant buck beds. If I did, I would be hunting there.

After traditional hunters attend one of my seminars, some of them tell me that they are going to change the way they do things the next day. They want to be D.I.E. hunters, and some of them answer the questions like this when they leave my seminar:

1. **How many stands do you have on the property?** Ten to 15 now, but I am pulling them all out starting tomorrow! I will wait for Set-Up Day and put one in then as you say I should.
2. **How many trail cameras do you have out?** Ten to 15 now, but as of tomorrow I will not have any. I want the dominant buck within 35 yards during daylight, not his picture at 5 yards at night.
3. **How many stands do you hunt from during a four-day period?** I will only hunt from one as you say, and I will position it so I will not have to turn around in my stand to shoot.
4. **What do you do if it rains or snows?** I have warm clothes and a waterproof parka. I will stay in my tree until the buck comes in or until 5 minutes before legal shooting time ends.
5. **Where do you go if the wind switches directions?** Nowhere! The wind is my friend, because I am an invisible pair of breeding deer.
6. **Where are you hunting in relation to the dominant buck's primary bed?** As far upwind and crosswind of it as I can get, but certainly at least 80 yards away.

I am proud of those people because I know that I gave them what they came for. I gave them hope and I gave them the answers to all of their questions. I taught them how to use the wind like a deer, in every aspect of their hunt. I showed them the easiest way known to man to have a dominant buck, and a monster buck fight over the right to meet with you, as an invisible pair of breeding deer, and they became believers! I am proud of ever person that has ever come to a D.I.E. seminar, even the ones who did not follow my directions the first time. They will have the book this year and they will know what to do, to avoid being busted by the king of the herd.

Every experienced D.I.E. hunter would have answered those same questions exactly like this:

1. **How many stands do you have on the property?** None now, but I will have one in on Set-Up Day.
2. **How many trail cameras do you have out?** None, the dominant buck will not come in during daylight if I use any trail cameras, so I do not use them.
3. **How many stands do you hunt from during a four-day period?** Just one.
4. **What do you do if it rains or snows?** I enjoy the changing scenery, and stay put in my stand until 5 minutes before legal shooting hours close.
5. **Where do you go if the wind switches directions?** The wind is my friend, and I am invisible to deer, so I do not care which way the wind is coming from. I stay put in my stand and I watch my D.I.E. scrape and the 35-yard area downwind of it. That is where I will first catch a glimpse of the herd's most dominant buck.
6. **Where are you hunting in relation to the dominant buck's primary bed?** I am upwind and crosswind of it, at least 80 yards away. He has to move to a new location straight downwind of my D.I.E. scrape in order to hunt me. I would never take my hunt to the dominant buck. Since I started hunting with DOMINANCE IS EVERYTHING, the dominant buck and his challengers have been hunting me.

When I hear my customers telling me that they have never heard any of my tactics discussed before, I tell them I am not surprised, because I created my D.I.E. system based on my personal experience with deer. I see the deer herd the same way deer do, and I teach people how to understand whitetail deer behavior and how deer think. I have a gift, and I am sharing it with the world, because I am a generous person. I cannot make every hunter into a believer in D.I.E. but I have a chance to make you into a believer. I want you to focus on what I am teaching you, and not so much on what you have been doing differently all your life. You have to force yourself to hunt away from deer bedding areas, in order to have the king of the herd hunt you. Even though much of what I teach you sounds miraculous, my system does have its limitations. You cannot just place it anywhere and expect miracles with it. You have to use it as directed.

The wind does not lie—it only persuades

My D.I.E. system is capable of pulling the dominant buck and all of his challengers out of their beds during daylight. It brainwashes them to believe that you are an invisible pair of breeding deer. The wind on the other hand does not brainwash deer, it only sends messages to deer. No matter what, the wind does not lie, it only persuades.

When you hunt with D.I.E. you do not go into the house of the dominant buck, only a human would do that! You are a deer now, and you need to get used to letting the wind direction tell you where he is likely bedding. Trust the wind because it never lies. Set the D.I.E. system up crosswind and upwind at least 80 yards of his suspected bedding area. Do not try to see if he is there, instead trust the wind (as a deer would) and know he is there. Leave him alone when he is in his core living area and he will never know you are hunting him. Make sure you set up far enough away from his comfort zone that you are convinced that no deer frequent the area (during the day). There should not be any rubs or scrapes within view of your stand. Ideal D.I.E. set up locations are common and can be found on any property by a D.I.E. hunter who knows what to look for. Once you find a place like that, it will be obvious to you that you are in D.I.E. hunter's heaven! It will be tough for him to bust you there.

Remind yourself to think like an invisible pair of breeding deer. Hang out in his front yard, and send him messages telling him that you are waiting there to meet him. Do not take the messages directly to the dominant buck! You are not a courier, the wind is! Just concentrate on being patient and staying invisible while you wait for his arrival. Allow the wind to deliver the messages to him and he will show up in the flesh with his response. The D.I.E. system has never failed anyone who followed my instructions.

The wind will do all your talking for you if you let it. Let it tell him that you are a monster intruder buck and that you do not care that he owns the territory. It will carry the scents you put out to the dominant buck, telling him that you have already taken over a small piece of his territory, by making a D.I.E. scrape and rub, and that you have succeeded at attracting a doe in estrus to your location. Let the wind be the messenger that informs him that he has to come in and do something about it, if he cares about remaining the most dominant in his herd.

Do not ever expose yourself, as a human during this charade or your hunt will be instantly over. You need to play your part by doing what I teach you to do, nothing more and nothing less. Stay quiet when you are in your stand and let the wind and the D.I.E. system tell the story for you. Humans are enemies to deer but the wind is a deer's best friend. Which one would you trust the most if you were a dominant buck?

On Day 1 of your hunt, the wind sends the dominant buck a different message, it tells him that you are a no longer a monster intruder buck attracting does in heat. You are now a doe in estrus that has come to his primary breeding scrape (the D.I.E. scrape) looking for him so you can breed with him. He is not there when you arrive, so the wind tells him that you are only willing to visit his primary breeding scrape during daylight, and the rest of the time, you will be searching for a mature buck that will pay more attention to you than he does. The wind tells him that your estrus cycle is almost over and that you want to get pregnant. You cannot wait around for him. If he wants you then he will have to wait around for you. That he will do, folks! You can count on that!

On Day 2, Day 3 and Day 4 the wind tells the buck that the doe in estrus is walking in when you walk in, and that you are the doe. He wants to meet her, but he is leery of the monster intruder buck that made the scrape, so he takes his time coming in. He will always show up, if you always stay invisible to him. Just do your best and learn from your mistakes. Learning to correct your own mistakes makes you a better hunter.

The wind tells the dominant buck all of these things and more, when you are using Dominance Is Everything. I bet you can see now how powerful my system is, and why it will work to attract every dominant buck on earth during the rut, as long as the situation is the same no matter where a D.I.E. hunter sets it up. The beauty of my D.I.E. system is that D.I.E. hunters can set it up the same way every time no matter where they hunt whitetails, and when they do they can count on succeeding 99.99% of the time if they do everything right from the start. I cannot guarantee you success 100% of the time. I cannot even guarantee my own success 100% of the time, but so far, I have not failed to have the most dominant buck in the herd hunting me, on any of my D.I.E. hunts.

Anyone who uses my D.I.E. system as directed will be setting it up exactly as I would, if I was there. You can only expect to get the same results that Tom Earle and Matt 'Rhino' Rynearson have gotten with it, if you follow my instructions each time you hunt. They are the first two hunters in the world to learn how to make the king of the herd hunt them using my tactics. Each of them succeeded at seeing the biggest antlered buck of their lives on Day 1 of their very first hunt with my Dominance Is Everything system. Tom was hunting on public land in Walworth County Wisconsin in 2002 with a muzzleloader, and Rhino was hunting in Minnesota in 2008 on private land that he had never stepped foot on before, with his bow. I saw my first monster buck on private land in Waukesha County Wisconsin on my third D.I.E. hunt in 2001, a few weeks before I met Tom Earle, while I was hunting with my bow.

If the wind direction changes during your hunt, stay put, and let the buck adapt to it

That means you should continue to focus on the scrape, and keep an eye on the downwind side of the scrape. That may be a opposite direction than you were watching the day before, but it does not matter. The buck will always use the wind as his protector and he will be entering your area from downwind or crosswind 100% of the time. You will hear the buck's footsteps as he makes his way to you. Do not move your tree stand to adjust for changing wind directions; you will be busted if you do. Know that the buck is hunting you 100% of the time you are in the stand. He is watching you and scent checking you, he wants to meet you, and he will come in and offer his mating services to you if you let him. Be as still as you can until he offers you a shot opportunity. If you positioned your tree stand according to my tree stand placement instructions, you will always have a shot opportunity from your stand at an approaching buck no matter what direction he comes from.

During the four-day period when you hunt with D.I.E., the dominant buck goes on a mission to meet the doe in estrus and the intruder buck you present to him through the use of lures; he always will scent check your area before he comes in. You need to pass his scent test, and you will have to be 99% free of human scent in order to do it.

The wind carries scent downwind and crosswind

During your hunt with D.I.E., you will use specific lures at specific times to communicate with the area's dominant buck. You rely on the wind to carry each of these scents to the dominant buck; he will bed downwind of the scrape, moving closer and closer to it each day because the scent of the doe in estrus is prevalent.

To be able to keep track of the wind, I recommend you purchase a wind checker. I always use a product called Wind-Checker Model No. 581 made by Primos Hunting Calls. You really need to have one of these in your pocket in the tree stand, so you can always tell what the wind is doing with your scent. Wind-Checker is a scent free powder, and it works. I have hunted many times without it, but since I started using it, no buck has busted me. I can quickly determine which direction is downwind of me; that is where the buck will come from if he has bedded down in the nearest available cover. If not, he will approach from a crosswind or he will follow the scent of my dragline in.

A dominant buck will never walk with the wind blowing straight into his tail. No deer will ever do that. They prefer to travel at a crosswind, or quartering into or away from the wind. To you or me, crosswind would be with the wind hitting the side of our rib cage. Quartering away would be with the wind hitting the back of one of our shoulders, and quartering into the wind would mean the wind was hitting the front of one of our shoulders. Dominant bucks also like to walk directly into the wind. In that case, the wind would be hitting them in the nose.

Hunters who do not know the D.I.E. system think they have to walk into an area from its downwind side, but they are dead wrong. That is the biggest reason why most hunters hunting without my system, are busted by mature bucks, and they cannot get close to them during deer season. It is because dominant bucks bed on the downwind side of their herd and they face downwind in their bed. They see the hunter before the hunter can see them.

Always try to hunt from the upwind side of the dominant buck's territory. You are only hunting one to four consecutive days during the rut, so it will be easy for you to find out what the predominant wind direction is going to be on Day 1 of your hunt. Just check the local 7-day forecast on Set-up Day. Use the information you gather to make an educated decision on how to place your stand. Do not shift your stand in the tree at any point during the hunt. Always set it up with the wind hitting you on the back of your shooting shoulder, and point your toes to the scrape. That way the buck will always come in from the area in front of you, which is always going to be downwind or crosswind, and his goal is to end up at your feet in the D.I.E. scrape.

Once you install your tree stand on Set-up Day, stay away from it and within two days it will become part of the landscape. The human scent on it will be swept away with the help of the wind. Deer use the wind to detect human scent, and they can detect it for up to 48 hours after a human vacates an area, unless it rains. In that case, human scent washes away immediately. So does deer scent for that matter. That is why dominant bucks are most active in open areas on rainy days. They are out marking their territorial boundaries with fresh scent. Remember that once you step foot into a dominant buck's territory on Day 1 of your D.I.E. hunt, you are not a human anymore. You are an invisible pair of breeding deer, and invisible breeding deer do not adjust tree stands, they brainwash all deer into believing that they are hanging out in light cover behind a D.I.E. scrape, enjoying some quality time together. Check the wind, understand it, and learn to adapt to it as deer do, and you will feel like you are in a completely different world.

Chapter 13

Three lures that have never let a D.I.E. hunter down

I use only these three specific lures (table 1), three specific lure dispensing devices (table 2), and one specific scent-killer product (table 3) when I hunt with my system. I know they work flawlessly with each other to convince the king of any whitetail herd that a D.I.E. hunter is a breeding pair of deer. I used the exact same lures on my first hunt as I have for every hunt since. Everyone I teach my D.I.E. system to uses these lures, and those who followed my instructions have never failed to see the dominant buck within 35 yards on a D.I.E. hunt. Therefore, I instruct you to use these same three lures so you can be assured you will have the same success with D.I.E. as those who have hunted before you.

TABLE 1.   THESE THREE LURES HAVE NEVER FAILED A D.I.E. HUNTER

Brand Name	Active Scrape® Full Spectrum Scrape Scent	Still Steamin'® Premium Hot Doe Estrus Urine	Trail's End #307
The Name I give it	Multiple Does in heat & Bucks in Rut	The Doe in Estrus	The Monster Intruder Buck
Manufacturer or Distributor	Wildlife Research Center Inc.	Robinson Outdoor Products Scent Shield	Wildlife Research Center Inc.
Quantity Needed for a D.I.E. Hunt	4-ounce bottle	2-ounce bottle	1-ounce bottle

TABLE 2. EQUIPMENT NEEDED TO DISPENSE THE LURES

Name	Seal-Tite™ Scent-Dispensers	Key-Wick®	Ultimate Scrape-Dripper® or Magnum Scrape-Dripper®
Manufacturer	HME Products	Wildlife Research Center Inc.	Wildlife Research Center Inc.
Quantity Sold	Three per pack	Four to a pack	One
Quantity Needed	Six (2 packs)	Two	One or two
Use Instructions	I use scent dispensers. Use 3 with Trail's End #307 around the scrape on set up day. Swap the 2 on the sides of the rub out with doe in estrus on Day 1, and leave the 1 in back with #307 alone. Then use 2 - #307 & 1 doe in estrus in the stand.	Put two key-wicks in a large zippered plastic bag along with your dragline. Use one key-wick® for the doe urine and the other for the buck.	Having two is better than one because the buck can disable the first one and if that happens your scrape dripper will be nonfunctioning. I carry two on each hunt to guarantee my success.

TABLE 3. OTHER THINGS YOU SHOULD HAVE TO HUNT WITH D.I.E.

Name	Scent Killer® 99% The original	15 ft. Dragline	Dragline extension	A Large Plastic Bag that "zips"
Manufacturer	Wildlife Research Center Inc.	Various	Various	Various
Qty Needed	12 ounces or less	15 feet	4-5 feet	One
Use Instructions	Spray it on everything you touch.	½ to ⅝-inch diameter (new) soft nylon rope (without the braid showing)	¼ to ⅜-inch Hemp Twine	This will hold the dragline, the lures, and the key-wicks when you are not using them.

If you cannot find the brands I recommend for the scent wicks and scent dispensers, you can use whatever brand you are comfortable with, but always stick to using Wildlife Research Center Inc. brand Scrape-Drippers, because you can depend on them.

I know that all the products I use work 100% of the time, so if you are worried about it, just purchase the same items that I do and you will get good results. If you use any other lures, you are altering the D.I.E. system from the way I have uses it with 100% success—and your results will be altered meaning your success rate will be 99% or less. Therefore, you should always use the exact same lures in the exact same quantities as I have, in order to have 100% success.

I recommend that you use these three particular lures—I have not tested others

With my DOMINANCE IS EVERYTHING system, I use these three lures in very specific ways. The deer believe in the D.I.E. set-up, because I always make it the same way, and they always react to it in the same manner. If you cannot find one of these lures, please check back with me to see if I have any other options available to you. I am a distributor for the Robinson Outdoor Products Still Steamin'® Premium Hot Doe Estrus Urine. This urine is pure and it is collected from one single doe during her estrus cycle in the rut. I have been providing bottles of it to seminar attendees and I intend to do so in the future as long as I can continue to purchase quantities of it. I believe that my system will work with any pure doe in estrus urine that is collected from one single whitetail doe in estrus, but I am not sure of it. I intend to test other brand doe in estrus urines and other scents as they become available so I can personally recommend specific brands or bottlers to you and to my other customers in the future. This urine is in limited supply because it is pure urine. Please be sure to use the same products I use, if they are available. If not then look for another pure doe in estrus urine and try that. I cannot guarantee or even expect you to get 100% results from a product that I have never used before, that is why I do not recommend any other lures at this time. When and if I find other lures that work with my system I will be sure to make my findings public.

Every D.I.E. hunter that I have taught, that has killed a buck with my system has used these three lures exclusively, and I expect you to do the same.

My D.I.E. system is a system of brainwashing deer into believing that invisible deer are real, and I have been able to accomplish that feat by using these three products in the manner that I knew deer would be able to relate to them. I do not use them as directed by the lure and urine, bottling companies. In order for you to succeed using D.I.E., you need to use the lures the way I instruct you to, no matter what the label says. **Do not use the lures as the manufacturers' direct you to on the lure packaging.** That kind of behavior will get you busted! Using the lures in the manner the label directs you, while you are using DOMINANCE IS EVERYTHING will cause you to fail miserably. It will allow the dominant buck to figure out that, the D.I.E. system is not real, and that you are indeed a human.

My system is very precise, and in order for it to always sort out the bucks for you and bring in the most dominant buck, you must use the quantities of lure that I instruct you to use. Never add more and never use less. Always use the lures at the specific times I instruct you to, and use them in the exact sequence as I describe.

If you were to read the labels on the lure bottles you would see, that what I tell you the lures represent to the dominant buck, is quite different from what the manufacturers'

information on these lure labels tell you. I do not care what these lures represent to the non-D.I.E. hunters who purchase them, or to the manufacturers that make them. All I care about is how the deer that inhale these lures perceive their meaning on a D.I.E. hunt.

To me and to every other successful D.I.E. hunter (invisible deer) these three lures are what the dominant buck and the other deer in his herd believe they are. The Active Scrape is the scent of multiple bucks and multiple does in heat, during the rut. Trail's End #307 is the scent of the monster intruder buck that is challenging the king of the herd for the D.I.E. scrape, and the Still Steamin' Premium Hot Doe Estrus urine is just what the label says it is! In that case, it is no coincidence!

You see, it does not matter to any deer what the manufacturers say the lures are made of. Deer do not care about those kinds of things. When you hunt with D.I.E., you are the hunted and no longer the hunter that is because you are role-playing with the king of the herd, and he is convinced that you are a breeding pair of deer, not a human. Deer cannot read labels. So take my advice and do not read the lure labels. If an invisible deer lays down a scent trail and every real deer that inhales the scent of the invisible deer, believes the scent is authentic, who are we (humans) to stand in their way? Just let it be! Do not over-think what I am teaching you here.

When you think like a deer, you find yourself not asking as many questions that is because you are too busy analyzing real-life situations.

Do not read the lure labels

If you intend to understand my theories and want to learn how D.I.E. works you are going to have to ignore all material provided with the lures that you purchase for use with my system. The 'Scrape Hunting Techniques' book provided in the package with the Ultimate and Magnum Scrape-Drippers and a 4 oz. bottle of Active Scrape lure is loaded with someone else's views on how to use those products. That information contradicts the way I use the lures and the Scrape-Dripper with my D.I.E. system. My advice is to open the packages and take the lures out, and discard the packages and any books that come along with a lure. There was no book sold with the first Scrape-Dripper I purchased.

When I developed my system, a book was not available, so I never read it. I formulated the D.I.E. hunt using Active-Scrape, and Trail's End #307 lures, along with Scent Shield Still Steamin' Premium Hot Doe Estrus urine. I am not knocking the contents of Wildlife Research Center Inc.'s 'Scrape Hunting Techniques' book for use in traditional hunting, but if you read it before your first hunt with D.I.E., you will be confused and you will certainly mess up. Hunting with D.I.E. is very different from traditional deer hunting and you will be second-guessing yourself and coming up with all sorts of off topic questions if you read any of the data on the lure bottles or in the book that is included in their packaging.

To make it easy on yourself just label the Active Scrape lure (Buck and Does in heat), the Trail's End #307 (Intruder Monster Buck) and Scent Shield Still Steamin' Premium Hot Doe Estrus urine (Doe in Estrus).

I do not use the Scrape-Dripper as directed by the manufacturer either. First of all, I only use one at a time, and I speed up the way it dispenses lure so I can use it successfully with my D.I.E. system. I purge the dripper. I will show you how to purge the Scrape-Dripper to make it run out of 3 ounces of Active Scrape lure in less than 3 days. Their 'Scrape Hunting Techniques' book never says anything about that. I want you to use Wildlife Research Center Inc. products, but not as they direct you to. I need you to trust me and use the lures and the lure dispensing equipment only as I direct you. It is not my way—it is the D.I.E. way.

The Active Scrape lure dripping from a Scrape-Dripper makes all the mature bucks in the area into daytime visitors of the scrape, but the Active Scrape lure alone does not get the dominant buck's attention. What gets his attention is the fact that there is a territorial rub on a tree behind the scrape. He has to move in and take it over immediately.

I am the inventor of the D.I.E. scrape. Once the dominant buck owns a D.I.E. scrape he commands it on a daily basis for up to 3 days, but he is a busy buck during the rut and he will leave the area if a doe in estrus does not show up within 3 days. The timing of the lure change from multiple does in heat to just one doe in estrus is another one of my inventions. When the dominant buck gets one whiff of the Still Steamin'® Premium Hot Doe Estrus urine, he flips out and from that moment, forward the dominant buck will not allow any other bucks to enter the area, while he is around. He deposits his scent in the scrape and on the brush around it. No pecking order buck from his own herd will ever walk in within 35 yards of your stand. I have never seen one there anyway!

Active Scrape lure in a Scrape-Dripper brings a D.I.E. scrape to life

For 12 years, all the deer that have ever encountered my D.I.E. scrape (between Set-up Day and the first day of my hunt) have been brainwashed to believe it was a real scrape made by a real intruder monster buck, and that a doe in heat was visiting it each day along with the intruder buck. Active Scrape lure in the dripper makes all the deer in the area believe there are multiple breeder bucks and multiple does in heat visiting the scrape. The way I build my D.I.E. scrape is perceived by the dominant buck to be a challenge for his territory. I learned all my scrape constructing skills on my own while filming deer, and by making a dominant buck's scrape inside the territory of a dominant buck the D.I.E. scrape maker is always perceived as being a monster intruder buck.

Trail's End #307 is the monster intruder challenging buck

When I build the D.I.E. scrape, I apply Trail's End #307 lure on the rub and on the licking branch; it represents the scent of the invisible monster intruder buck. Those two places are where a real challenging buck would have left the scent of his glands, so every buck that encounters a D.I.E. scrape believes it is authentic. I also mask my human scent with Trail's End #307 whenever I am in my tree stand or when I am on the ground on the way to it. Wherever I am, the invisible monster intruder buck is. No deer can smell me as a human when I wash my body and my clothes with scent free soap and I pour a few drops of Trail's End #307 out along my walking path every 30 yards or so.

Scent Shield Still Steamin' Premium Hot Doe Estrus urine makes the king hunt you

Still Steamin' Premium Hot Doe Estrus urine is the doe in estrus in my D.I.E. system. On Day 1 of your hunt, you will only pour half the bottle (1 ounce) of the Still Steamin' Premium Hot Doe Estrus urine in the Scrape-Dripper, and it will take about two days to run out. That is the plan. It has to run out in two days or the buck will get wise to your set up and he will bust you. He will bust you because no doe can be in estrus longer than two consecutive days and he knows it. I do not want to take the chance of being busted so I only put 1 ounce of the doe in estrus urine in the Scrape-Dripper. The rest is used on the dragline into your stand each day. D.I.E. is set up so the dominant buck will pursue the invisible doe in estrus at the scrape for the first two consecutive days and then he will pursue you personally after that because you will be dragging the doe in estrus' urine in to your stand on a dragline on Days 3 and 4.

By dragging in the Still Steamin' Premium Hot Doe Estrus urine behind you and by pouring a few drops of Trail's End #307 out on branches along your trail to the stand each morning, you will keep the dominant buck guessing as to which deer you represent when you show up each day. He only hears one deer enter the area, but he gets the scent of both of them.

He will wait for you to climb your tree, but do it quietly because he does not know a human is climbing the tree. He thinks the doe is visiting the scrape, and that she is going to bed down in some cover upwind or crosswind of it within five or ten minutes. That is what a real doe in estrus would have done, and he thinks you are a real doe in estrus so he assumes that you would behave like a doe in estrus when you got to the scrape. After you settle in and sit still for a few minutes, he will make his move and attempt to come in and find you. Keep him guessing and he will not give up hunting you—not until he is within 35 yards of you on your downwind side—and by then you'll have him in your sights.

The Still Steamin' Premium Hot Doe Estrus urine is collected from one single doe during the rut. This urine gives your invisible doe a unique identity. It is her DNA. All mature bucks can lock onto the unique scent of a doe in estrus' urine and they do not forget about her for quite a few days. They each go on a personal mission to meet the doe as soon as possible. The only thing that stops them from pursuing her is when they meet a more dominant buck and he stands between them and the doe they are pursuing.

Every time a dominant buck gets near a D.I.E. scrape he gets the urge to freshen it (work it up). The dominant buck will search for the doe in estrus all day, every day for up to four days when you are using my D.I.E. system. On Day 1 of your hunt, he searches for the doe in estrus from the time you arrive there until you go home for the day. Once darkness falls, he gets worried that the doe has left the area again without looking for him, so he beds closer to the scrape, in hopes he will get to meet her the next day. You had better be ready in the mornings especially on Day 2 and Day 3, because those are the best days of the hunt for almost every D.I.E. hunter. The dominant buck is in a hurry to find the doe in the morning because he wants to get to breeding.

The Scrape Dripper is supposed to run dry during the hunt—DO NOT REFILL IT!

The Scrape-Dripper begins dripping lure about 1 hour after sunrise, and it stops an hour or so before dark. You can count on the scrape-dripper running out of Still Steamin' Premium Hot Doe Estrus urine on Day 2 or Day 3 of the hunt. The moment you step away from the scrape on Day 1 of your hunt should be the last time you ever go to that scrape. It is not okay for you to approach the scrape at any time after you have walked away from it on Day 1. I hope that is clear. The Scrape-Dripper is supposed to run dry; it has to in order for the dominant buck to believe the D.I.E. situation is a real one. He cannot find her at the scrape on Day 3 but her scent is still in the two scent-dispensers that you placed on each side of the scrape. Her scent lingers in the air, and so does the scent of that darn (invisible) intruder monster buck that originally made the D.I.E. scrape. He is still coming into the area each morning and leaving it near dusk.

If you have not gotten the buck by Day 2, you have to drag in the doe in estrus urine on Day 3 and Day 4. The dominant buck becomes very mobile on those two days. He has to find that doe in estrus immediately. He knows she is not coming over to him, so he is determined to go to her. You will see how eager he is to breed when you see him walk right in to your stand site. If you still have your buck tag on the morning of Day 3, it should be a really good day for you. Your dragline is the only source of the scent of the doe in estrus urine on Day 3 and Day 4 of a D.I.E. hunt. That means the buck will be hunting you first and focusing on the scrape second. If he hears you enter the area he will not wait long to approach the D.I.E. scrape. When the dominant buck comes into the area he will scent check the D.I.E. scrape from a distance of 30 to 100 yards, and he will always be downwind of it. If he smells the doe in estrus and does not sense a human in the area, then he will do a lip curl. You must always be ready for him.

Getting vocal with the king is an option after Day 1

I never call to the buck or make any unnecessary sounds from my tree stand on Day 1 of my hunt. I want the buck to feel that he is as safe coming into the area while I am there as he was the day before, on the last day of the waiting period. I assume he visits the scrape on a daily basis and that it is just a matter of time until he comes in during daylight. It is just a matter of less than four consecutive days to be exact.

You can be vocal with him on Day 2 and Day 3 by making one single doe in estrus bleat at random times during the day. Keep those times spaced three or four hours apart and only make one doe in estrus bleat. He will not bust you if you make sure that no deer are moving around within hearing distance of you before you call. If he responds to you grunting then keep up the conversation until he is nearing your location. Once you can see him or hear him approaching stop calling completely and let him come in within 35 yards. He always will. The wind and the lures set the stage for your behavior in your stand. Remember to pretend you are one of the (invisible) deer at the scrape when and if you ever decide to talk like one. Otherwise sit back, relax, and let these amazing lures, the signs of the intruder buck at the scrape, and way that your behavior going to and from the stand is perceived, do all the work for you. The DOMINANCE IS EVERYTHING system is brainwashing the buck to believe his next mate is just a few yards ahead.

Let D.I.E. bring the king of the herd to you! Be patient, and have faith that the buck is on his way!

The king will hunt you every time

I know the dominant buck will try to trail me in on the 2nd or 3rd morning of my hunt if I didn't shoot him on Day 1 because by then he has been to the scrape at least one time since I introduced the scent of the single doe in estrus to him. He locks on to her scent and he waits for her to return. I am the doe in estrus in the morning when I walk to my stand on Day 2, Day 3, and Day 4 and he knows it. He can approach the scrape during the day and only expect to find the doe in estrus there, or he can wait for nightfall and I can tell him the intruder-challenging buck was back. I am the doe on the way in, and the buck on the way out. It does not take him longer than one 24-hour period to figure that out, and he wants to meet the doe in estrus without any interference from the intruder monster buck so you can be confident that he will always be coming in during the day if you did not see him on Day 1.

Chapter 14

Get into the head of the most dominant buck

Although deer lures and doe in estrus urine are powerful attractants that help D.I.E. hunters brainwash deer, there is more needed to succeed on a D.I.E. hunt than just laying down some believable scent. **You have to get in the head of the dominant buck and intimidate him.**

I find that the best way to do it is by making a D.I.E. scrape. A D.I.E. scrape is a territorial scrape with a rub behind it and a licking branch over it. Scout to find a good place to set up a D.I.E. scrape. Look for a heavily used deer trail that leaves *semi-open cover* and heads at a crosswind into thicker cover, but make sure that the thicker cover is not a deer bedding area. Scout it out to make sure. If you do not find any deer beds in it, then it will be exactly what you are looking for.

I always start my scouting trip at the furthest upwind water supply that I can find. Walk the water's edge both upstream and downstream. Closely inspect all heavily used deer trails that cross the waterway. At least one of those trails should be a one-way trail at the point where the deer enter the water to cross it. *One-way deer trails* are used during daylight by many deer, and during the rut, you can be assured that the dominant buck will all be accustomed to using one-way trails on a daily basis. If you cannot find any one-way deer trails to set up on, then search for a deer trail in an area where deer are walking or trotting single file out of a clearing and into some mixed cover. There should be some large 3½-inch long or longer deer tracks on that trail. Always try to set up a D.I.E. scrape on the upwind side of the deer trail and never cross the trail for any reason during your hunt. If you can find a place to set up like that then you will be hunting the same way I do. It is not necessary for you to set up along a deer trail, but when you do, you are assured that the deer in the herd will discover your system is there on the very first night that you set it up. The sooner the dominant buck finds it the sooner he starts commanding it, and the more aggressive his behavior gets toward the other bucks in his herd. You want the buck to get aggressive because it keeps him interested in the D.I.E. scrape both day and night. He loses sleep over it, and he cannot wait to meet your invisible pair of deer. He wants to breed with the doe and make the intruder buck go away.

Always think about the buck that is hunting you, and concentrate on what he is going to be thinking as he makes his way to your D.I.E. scrape. The buck has to believe a doe could be bedded behind the scrape (upwind or crosswind of it), otherwise the buck will be unwilling to approach it. I tell you to build it up against some cover because if you do not the buck will not take over the scrape, and he will not rush to come into the area within 35 yards of it. If you find yourself having to build the scrape in a place that does not offer a lot of nearby cover, you should know not call to the buck during your hunt from that stand. If you do, you will be busted immediately. The good news for folks that have to deal with less than perfect set up conditions is that if you build the D.I.E. scrape as directed, then the buck will still come in no matter where you build it, as long as you stay invisible to him. The buck will hold up downwind of the D.I.E. scrape, in whatever available cover there is nearest to it. In the case, that nothing is there for him to hide in then he will come directly from his primary bed in the area. If he can see the rub on the tree behind the scrape from his hiding place (because you placed it out in the open with no cover behind it), then he will hesitate within 35 yards of you in whatever cover is nearby.

Be sure you never install a D.I.E. scrape in the middle of a field because the dominant buck will not show up. He will never come in if he can see that there is not a real deer standing near the D.I.E. scrape, or if he is sure there are no doe could be bedded behind it, or off to either crosswind side of it. You should always take those things into consideration when you are setting up the D.I.E. system.

You need to make the scrape on the edge of something. Some brush, a fence line, a tree line, or a change in cover. If you build it on the edge of something every time then the buck will have to come in close to see the rub and the dirt in the scrape. He wants to see if a real deer visited it while he was away. That is what you want him to do. If you find a good place to set up, stand at the base of the tree you expect to sit in and check to see if you would have a clear shot to the scrape. You also want to have an opening straight down in front of you and straight downwind of the pawed up dirt in the scrape. If it all looks good to you then that is a perfect spot for you to install a tree stand and build a D.I.E. scrape.

The dominant buck will always come in, if you let him, but if you make it too easy for him he might hold up in cover and refuse to come out. It is always up to you to decide where to set the D.I.E. system up on your hunting property. Which four days of the rut to hunt with it is your choice as well. Those two aspects of the hunt do not affect the outcome. Once you learn to use the system, the whole hunt is up to you to plan and see through.

My job is to teach you a straightforward approach to setting the D.I.E. system up the right way, every time. I always go about setting up the same way no matter where I am hunting or when I am planning on going. I always set up in an upwind corner of the property where no deer are bedding, breeding, or feeding, and the D.I.E. system has brought a monster buck in for me on six of my last eight hunts.

Make the buck come in close to see past the rubbed tree and the scrape and make sure you will be able to see his whole body clearly; when he gets there. He will stop wherever you grunt one time to him, and he will continue looking forward (behind the scrape) unless he knows where your grunt came from. If you have to trim out shooting lanes then you are in cover that is excessively thick! The only trimming I do is in the tree I am sitting in, and on the ground in front of my scrape. Unless I have to cut a vine, off or move some dead branches out of my area. I try to leave as much natural vegetation in the area as I can, so the buck does not know a human was there. Look for area of open terrain that is 30 or more yards long and 5 or more yards wide, with cover on at least two sides. Sit on one side of the clearing and build the D.I.E. scrape on the other side. You will be shooting to the outside edge of the *thick cover* on the other side of the clearing. Try not to cut any more brush than you have to. Dominant bucks know their area and they know when something changes in it. If a tree that was there yesterday is no longer there today, he will notice that being gone. Remember he has to feel safe before he will come in. I always make it my focus to keep the element of surprise on my side. I never try to alert the buck to my being there as a man, at the same time I try to convince him that I am a pair of breeding deer.

Always scout your property 10–14 days before you want to be in your stand. Make sure you are hunting inside some light cover. Build a D.I.E. scrape with the rub and scraped up dirt facing the direction that you think the biggest deer will come from. Check the tracks in the area and assume that the deer that made them like to walk in the direction they were going when they made the tracks. Always build the scrape up against some semi-thick cover. You should be able to see into it about 5 yards but not much further than that.

Hunt where you can get into the area without making too much noise along the way. You should only "walk like a deer" when you get within 120 yards of your stand and only on your way in, never on your way out. Sometimes I hunt closer to the road than 120 yards, when I do I make sure that there is a deer trail on each side of me before I set up there. The dominant buck will not feel comfortable having to approach a D.I.E. scrape from downwind if there are not any deer trails on that side of your stand.

On Day 1 you do not want the buck to hear you until you get near the scrape (within 50 yards of it), so walk quietly until you get that close, then make your steps a little more pronounced to get his attention. Trust that he is near and that he is downwind of you at all times. He will always assume that you are harmless to him if you walk like a deer, place your heel, and toe down softly. On Day 1, you must always enter the area from an upwind and crosswind direction (making an arc) from your starting point at your vehicle, and ending up just a few feet upwind or your D.I.E. scrape.

On Day 2, Day 3, and Day 4 (if you need any or all of those days) you will not go to the scrape, instead you just go directly to your tree stand. I keep a small bottle of #307 in my right hand all the way to my stand. I have mastered being able to open it, pour a few drops out, and then close it with just my right hand.

When you walk to your stand, do not reach out to move branches or tree limbs, deer do not reach out—not ever! Because you are walking like a deer, the only real deer that is bedded down nearby is the most dominant buck and he will stay bedded and let you pass by him.

When the dominant buck is trailing you, or when it first discovers you moving through its territory, he stays back at first because he is not sure what you are. It is impossible for him to smell you because you washed your clothes in scent free soap, then you washed you body with scent-free body wash. You are as close to being a scent free human as anyone can get. If you followed my directions, you also sprayed your collar, cuffs, waistline, and your boots with Scent Killer 99% before you stepped one foot in your hunting area that day, and because you are using Trail's End #307 as a masking scent, you have covered all your bases. As long as you do not release any foul odors or make any humans sounds on your way to your stand, you will be able to slip into it undetected. Keep your arms down at your sides and if you come into thick brush do what a deer would do, back out, and go around it. Do not push through heavy brush or thorns. The only time a real deer would do that is if it was running from danger, so if you do it you will be sending out an audible alarm to all the deer in the area that there is something for them to worry about in the area. They will freeze in their tracks and then go on alert. I teach you to go into brush on purpose when you leave the stand 4 minutes before closing time, so the buck will do just that. He will stop right in his tracks and allow you to slip out of the area undetected by any deer. The charade has to go on until you get the buck or until your fourth day of hunting is over, whichever comes first. Never give the buck a chance to see you as a human. Always do what I teach you, to be able to keep the dominant buck guessing.

Yes, all those little things matter to deer. If you never thought of them now is the time to start thinking about the noises a human makes as he or she enters the woods. Deer are listening, to every sound they can hear, so do not make any sounds that would be abnormal for deer in that area to hear, and you will be welcomed by the herd.

You will be walking into the dominant buck's home territory and entering his house during the early morning light 45 minutes to 1¼ hours after legal shooting time opens. By coming in later than traditional hunters do, you are allowing the dominant buck enough time to get to his bed uninterrupted. He hears you come in but your behavior has him believing you are a late arrival to the bedding area (a yearling buck or a doe in estrus perhaps). Do not be too late getting to your stand or you could be busted, the buck is waiting downwind of the scrape for a visitor there. Never tell him which deer you are. You must always keep him guessing with D.I.E.!

Chapter 15

You are pretending to be a doe in heat, going into estrus

Here is my theory on how a doe's heat/estrus cycle works and how it times out.

It is important for you to understand how the heat/estrus cycle of a whitetail doe works, so you can relate to the way the dominant buck will be behaving as he approaches a D.I.E. scrape. He thinks you are a doe in heat, at first and once he smells the scent of the doe in estrus that you put in the dripper on Day 1, he knows you are a doe in estrus. Everything you do in deer country gets noticed by the deer that live there, that is why it is so important that you always set up the D.I.E. scrape and your tree stand the same way every time. My system convinces the deer that you are one of them, whether you are in the woods or not. D.I.E. will do all the work for you, as long as you use it as directed.

Deer believe in what they can make sense of, and all deer believe a D.I.E. scrape is the primary breeding scrape of the most dominant buck in the herd. By sunset on Day 1 of your hunt, that is exactly what your D.I.E. scrape will have become. I designed my D.I.E. system to duplicate a real-life situation that deer have to deal with year after year during the rut. This one situation is so believable that every deer that encounters a D.I.E. scrape reads it and reacts to it the same way. D.I.E. scrape is a real scrape to real deer, because it is set up where a real scrape of this sort would be. You will fail if you put it too close to deer bedding because no intruder buck would ever go to the dominant buck to start trouble with him in his core living area. The D.I.E. scrape attracts does in heat and does in estrus on a continuous basis. They commit to it just as they would if it was real.

Which intruder buck moved in and made the D.I.E. scrape does not matter to the deer in the general population of the herd, the answer to that question only matters to the dominant buck. He is the only deer that owns the property and he has to find the maker of the scrape in order to show him the way out of the territory as soon as possible. That is why the buck keeps coming back, before the doe at the scrape goes into estrus.

I have the D.I.E. hunt timed out so you are the buck that made the scrape on set up day. You are one of many does in heat that visit it, during the waiting period, and you become one single doe in estrus, that is accompanied by a intruder monster buck, on Day 1 of your hunt. Day 2,

Day 3, and Day 4 you are both the buck and the doe. You are the doe on the way in, and the buck on the way out. You keep him guessing until he gets enough guts to show himself to you.

The dominant buck commands the area and keeps his pecking order bucks away from it. He expects the doe to be in estrus for 1 to 1 ½ days, and he expects to find her near the scrape during daylight. He will search for that one single doe in estrus from the second he identifies her scent as being that of a doe in estrus, until he finds her or until she goes out of estrus whichever comes first. Normally that would be after two days, but it is not a normal situation. In the case of a D.I.E. hunt there are two matters that the dominant buck has to attend to which make him hunt the D.I.E. scrape and the D.I.E. hunter for up to four consecutive days. He has to breed the doe before any other buck does, but he also has to run the invisible monster buck out of the territory. Because the dominant buck is not the only buck that is interested in finding the doe to mate with her, he has to bed nearby and wait for her to return. His competitors are not afraid of him, and each will take his turn trying to dethrone the king. They have racks of antlers almost as big as, or bigger than the dominant buck, so he has his work cut out for him. The closer you set up to a herd boundary the more competition the buck has at the D.I.E. scrape. He looks for her all night, and when he does not find her near the scrape at night as he normally would, he gets concerned and he backs off a bit. When he backs off, other breeder bucks move into the area from other herds, and monster bucks move in with hopes of finding the doe in estrus before the dominant buck resumes searching for her. Monster bucks do not always move into the area, but if they already live in that area and they can smell the scent of the pure doe in estrus urine at the D.I.E. scrape, nothing will stop them from coming to meet the doe.

On Day 3 and Day 4 you are the only fresh source of the doe in estrus' scent, and every buck in a half mile radius wants to be your mate. They know that the doe has to be bred by the end of the day on Day 4 of your hunt or she will no longer be in estrus. They will not wait for her estrus cycle to end. Sit still and your king will come to dominate his scrape. The rest will stay away while he is there. He will be the biggest racked buck that you will see, and you had better take him if you want to shoot the king, otherwise you may go home empty handed. Remember other bucks want to come in, but nothing is guaranteed. The dominant buck has a 35 yard bubble around his body that no buck can go into without showing subordination to him. You may witness a buck fight but I would not count on it. Just remember what you are there for and concentrate on reaching your goal each day.

Be aware that all bucks will follow a doe in estrus for up to 2 days but never more. They know that no doe could be in estrus longer than that. Once the dominant buck is working your D.I.E. scrape, he will advance to it within 48 hours during daylight. You can never tell for sure which day and at what time (during your hunt) the dominant buck first inhaled the scent of the doe in estrus, dripping out of the Scrape-Dripper, but you do know that you will have his full attention for up to 2 days from the first moment he did. That is why a D.I.E. hunt could be over in one hour or it could take up to four whole days, because the dominant buck comes in when he believes the doe in estrus is waiting for him nearby the D.I.E. scrape. You are the doe in estrus, and you need to hunt all day, each day so the buck believes the doe in estrus and is searching for him at the D.I.E. scrape. If he knows she is there, then he will come to meet her. Be careful and enjoy being hunted by the king of the herd!

The dominant buck controls what his herd members do inside his property boundaries, but he cannot control what any bucks from other herds do, and he certainly cannot control every non-ranking buck. During the rut intruder, challenging bucks compete with the dominant buck for does in estrus, but his pecking order bucks do not, they yield to the dominant buck in their herd, and give their doe in estrus to the dominant buck if he asks for her. It is a pretty sweet deal that the dominant buck gets; it is no wonder why all pecking order bucks want to be dominant!

A D.I.E. scrape can only be set up one way and that is the way I teach you to do it. The dominant buck in the area will take it over most of the time, but not always. He will come in within 35 yards of it during your 1 to 4 day hunt, as long as you never let him know a human is there. I always set D.I.E. up and hunt with it the same way, and the buck that hunts me always comes into my area the same way. Stay consistent with your D.I.E. set-ups and you will be rewarded for your efforts.

Pretending you are a real doe in heat is easy as long as you do not ever have to be there. The Scrape-Dripper convinces the herd that you are multiple does in heat that are visiting the scrape from set up day until Day 1 of your hunt. On a perfect hunt, you are not there when the buck finds the D.I.E. scrape, rub, and starts being brainwashed. The D.I.E. scrape and the way you set it up against some type of edge of cover, does all the persuading that you need it to do, to convince any bucks in the area that in order to find the doe they have to walk right up to the scrape and look at her.

The way I set my system up persuades the dominant buck and the other breeder bucks to behave as they normally would if they found a primary breeding scrape of a dominant buck, and it had the scent of some does in heat in it. They search for the does in heat, but they cannot find them anywhere, so they come back. The dominant buck will not allow other breeder bucks to keep coming back because he intends on becoming the mate of every doe that visits the D.I.E. scrape, and once he takes it over it becomes his primary breeding scrape instantly. He runs off every buck that approaches the scrape during the night, and he beds down close to it during the day so he can cut off any intruder bucks before they can get to his doe. When 3 days pass since he first caught a whiff of the doe in heat's scent at the D.I.E. scrape the dominant buck assumes that at least one doe should be in estrus. When he hears you walk in he is hoping you are the doe. The dominant buck has been waiting for her, but he is not sure if it is the doe or the buck that he heard walking in, because your behavior keeps him guessing. He is short tempered because no buck has a right to enter the invisible 35-yard bubble he has established with his scent around the D.I.E. scrape. He moves in close and commands the area for up to 4 consecutive days. He has to or he will lose his dominance, and we both know that he is unwilling to give that up without losing a fight first!

At first, even the most dominant buck in the herd shows subordination to the invisible monster intruder buck that made the D.I.E. scrape. He does so, by not entering into the 35-yard bubble (of the invisible intruder buck) around the D.I.E. scrape during daylight until he thinks the intruder buck is physically there. The sound of your footsteps as you make your way to your stand is what triggers the dominant buck to move in. He immediately stops acting subordinately and dominates the scrape for all to see. That is why I named the book "Dominance Is Everything… To A Monster Whitetail Buck!" because it truly is! Dominant and monster bucks display their dominance when confronted by a challenger, and whenever a doe in estrus is nearby. A D.I.E. scrape puts dominant bucks and monster bucks in both of those situations at the same time. It guarantees an invisible D.I.E. hunter that he or she will meet the king of the herd within 35 yards of a D.I.E. scrape while on a hunt. The D.I.E. system should make sense to you now.

Understanding a doe's heat/estrus cycle will help you understand why my system works every time, and why I believe that only a human could mess it up. I believe the duration of a whitetail doe's heat/estrus cycle is 3 ½ to 4 consecutive days in length. A doe is in heat for the first 2 ½ days, and then she goes into estrus for the last 1 to 1 ½ days of her heat cycle. When a doe is in heat she is unwilling to breed and cannot get pregnant, but when she is in estrus she is willing to breed, and able to get pregnant.

A doe in heat is an attraction for all mature breeder bucks. She will parade around showing off to every buck she encounters, hoping a mature buck will take notice of her being in heat, and will follow her until she goes into estrus. Then they will mate and she will become pregnant.

Dominant bucks know that does in heat are not willing to have sex (with any buck) before they go into estrus, so dominant bucks do not chase does in heat. Chasing does not lead to mating. A dominant buck's ability to time his entrance into the area downwind of a doe in heat that is going into estrus (right at that minute) leads to mating.

Lesser bucks are willing to follow does in heat, but dominant bucks are not! Every mature buck knows when a doe is in heat it means that in less than 3 days she will be in estrus and the strongest buck that is with her at that time will be allowed to mate with her. Just having the highest rank does not mean he gets the doe, a dominant buck has to beat all other bucks in order to get the doe. Every mature buck is interested in mating with every doe in estrus that he can find, but as long as there are multiple bucks interested, there will always be a need for a pecking order. It is the buck's way of sorting themselves out according to rank, and dominance. Buck dominance is the deciding factor that bucks use to determine which one of them has earned the right to breed, and which other bucks need to fight for that right on a doe by doe basis. Dominance Is Everything to every mature buck!

Pecking order bucks chase does in heat because they have to compete for breeding rights. Chasing goes on during daylight hours and after dark and deer usually chase in a core breeding area, they will chase any doe that does not yield to them. When does are in heat they run and get chased, but once they are in estrus they stop and allow the most dominant buck in the area at the time to mount them for breeding.

Every dominant buck knows the rut well, and he knows he is being watched by at least one of his enemies at all times. His survival is more important to him, than chasing does in heat. When he senses a doe in heat is nearing estrus he trails her but from the security of downwind cover. He watches her as she runs from pecking order bucks, and when he senses that she is in estrus, he charges out of cover heading straight into the wind on approach to the backside of the doe in estrus. Any pecking order buck will yield to their king, but an intruder buck may stand and fight. It does not matter to the king, he will fight over the doe, and he is confident that he will prevail every time.

If the dominant buck is not around when a doe goes into estrus, the strongest pecking order buck will have the right to breed that one doe. Any buck can challenge him, but left unchallenged a lesser buck will breed. Does in estrus stand still and wait for a buck to mount them, they do not run away. Therefore, if you see a doe running from a buck she is likely only in heat. Any doe in heat is nearing estrus, and any doe that has gone out of estrus is not of interest to any buck anymore.

A dominant buck will always protect himself from danger by waiting for the sun to set before heading out into the open, in areas where he is pressured by humans. At a D.I.E. scrape, the dominant buck has no idea he is being watched, by a human. You are invisible to him. A dominant buck stays in downwind cover until a doe in estrus can be located (you arrive) then he moves crosswind until he is straight downwind of the doe's location (the D.I.E. scrape). He will do a lip curl, which helps him verify that the doe is in estrus, and then if he is like most other breeder bucks he will call to her to let her know he is on his way. That is what to expect a dominant buck to do when he discovers your D.I.E. scrape. First, he takes it over, then he fights to dominate it, and finally he waits downwind or crosswind of it for a doe to go into estrus. He expects one doe to come back to the scrape to breed with him. You are the doe in estrus that he is seeking, and you only approach the D.I.E. scrape (his primary breeding scrape) in the daytime. He is not used to breeding during the day out in the open, but he is willing to do it! He will make his way to your stand site, the whole time he will be looking for one of those two deer that he knows come in everyday, but always elude him. Stay still in your stand, that way you can count on the dominant buck showing up while you are there.

How the dominant buck goes from doe to doe during the rut

I am a firm believer that does go into estrus sometime on the third day of their four-day heat cycle. The estrus period of a doe's heat cycle only lasts 24 to 36 hours and it is a continuous period when a doe will mate with any buck. Does visit core dominant buck scrapes while they are in heat so they can get the attention of the dominant buck before they go into estrus. That way the doe is likely to be bred during her first heat/estrus cycle. Does that do not succeed in getting pregnant during their first heat/estrus cycle go back into heat/estrus 26 to 30 days later. If they are not bred the second time around, then they will not give birth to a fawn the following spring.

Every whitetail deer herd is structured so the most dominant buck gets to breed with the first doe that goes into estrus. He stays with her, and mates with her as often as she will allow him to while she is "hot" (in estrus). When she goes out of estrus, he leaves her, and goes on a mission in search of another doe that is ready to breed. If there is only one doe in estrus at any given moment in that herd, you can be assured that the most dominant buck is the one mating with her.

He has earned the right to breed with every doe in his territory. He will stay with a doe in estrus for up to 1 ½ days. It depends on how far she was into her estrus cycle when he met up with her. Once she goes out of estrus, he walks his territorial boundaries in search of other does in estrus, and at the same time, he inspects his territory for any intrusions that might have been made in the past two days when he was mating with the previous doe. Whenever he is without a mate, and he comes upon another happy pair of breeding deer, he breaks them up and takes the doe in estrus for himself. When more than one doe is in estrus at the same time, then the next highest-ranking pecking order buck can breed too. When multiple does go into estrus, multiple bucks in the pecking order get to breed at the same time. The order in which they are allowed to breed is the pecking order. Non-dominant bucks can breed too, but in order to be successful they have to be alone with the doe.

The higher a buck ranks in the pecking order the more breeding he will do during the rut. Breeding rights start at the top, and work their way down the pecking order. The only time that all mature bucks have a right to breed is when there are as many does in estrus as there are bucks in the pecking order. Otherwise breeding the herd's does is a job for only the strongest bucks in the herd. The most dominant buck leads that group.

In the pre-rut, the most dominant buck is the first buck to breed. That is because there is only one doe in estrus when the rut starts, and the king of the herd has earned the right to be her mate. No pecking order buck will confront the king while he is pursuing any doe in estrus, including the first doe in estrus of the season. Once one doe is in estrus, the rut has officially started! Pecking order bucks show the dominant buck the respect he deserves. Pecking order bucks breed according to their rank in the pecking order. Lesser-ranked bucks yield to higher ranked buck all year long. That is why there is a pecking order, so herd bucks are not always combating one another during the rut. When you see two bucks fighting over a doe in the rut, one of them is usually an intruder from another herd. They are not both pecking order bucks. Pecking order bucks yield to one another. Intruders rarely yield, because they have nothing to lose and everything to gain. Intruders try to steal what they cannot have.

Pecking order bucks are not interested in fighting the dominant buck for the first doe in estrus, they follow him around at a distance of more than 200 yards, watching him and waiting for him to commit to the doe. Once he does, they know it is safe for them to start chasing other does. Once the dominant buck is committed, it is the #2 ranked buck's turn to find a mate. Pecking order bucks are subordinate to their king. They will not attempt to fight with him after the rut starts unless they believe he is wounded or worn out and that they can overtake him. Only intruder bucks, monster bucks, and swamp bucks, will fight a dominant buck for a doe in estrus, and they are willing to do it whenever they find him with one. Those bucks do not owe allegiance to any buck.

Knowing that was a fact, I set up my first D.I.E. scrape attempting to challenge the dominant buck over a doe in estrus within 3 yards of my tree stand. The only difference between a real situation and the situation that D.I.E. puts before the buck is the fact that breeding pair of deer in the D.I.E. system are always invisible. All that matters to me as a D.I.E. hunter is that the most dominant buck is convinced they are real. So real that he is willing to quit chasing real does in heat just to hang out downwind of my D.I.E. scrape, for a few days, while I mess with his mind. He will allow me to enter the area as one of those two deer, without coming in to greet me, because he is not sure which one I am. Once I am settled in my stand, he makes his move and comes in posturing and displaying his dominance for all creatures to see!

A whitetail doe's 4-day heat/estrus cycle:
1. Day 1 The doe is in heat
2. Day 2 The doe is in heat
3. Day 3 The doe is in heat ½ the day, and in estrus the other ½ of the day
4. Day 4 The doe is in estrus all day

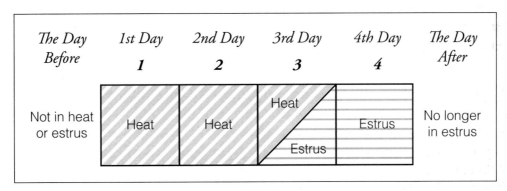

FIGURE 14 The 4 days of a whitetail doe's heat cycle.

When a doe is in heat, the dominant buck checks in on her at night but he will not stay with her. While she is in heat, he will never break out of cover for her, unless she just went into estrus and another buck is attempting to mount her to breed. Then he will come out to run the other buck off, and commence breeding the doe in estrus. Does in heat are not yet ready to breed but many of them will be mounted by bucks against their will regardless of that fact. Pecking order bucks are impatient and many times, they do not wait for a doe heat to go into estrus, instead they chase the doe until she yields from exhaustion, and then they attempt to mate with her against her will. I say attempt, because a doe in heat will run out from under a buck if she can. Does-in-heat visit dominant buck scrapes so the dominant buck will become aware that they are nearing estrus. Does-in-estrus seek out the dominant buck, monster bucks, and other mature bucks to mate with, so the pecking order bucks will leave them alone. Does do not want to be mounted until they are able to get pregnant, and that time comes when a doe is in estrus.

When a doe goes into estrus, she will breed with any mature buck she can find, but most does actually seek out a mate by going to the primary breeding scrape of the herd's most dominant buck. There the doe urinates in the dirt in the scrape, just in front of the rub. The dominant buck is always nearby and he identifies the doe by the scent of her urine. He knows she is in estrus and is willing to mate with him. Having a doe in estrus show up at your doorstep willing to breed, I believe is every buck's dream! Now all he has to do is follow her scent and find her so they can breed, before another breeder buck gets to her first.

The only thing that could possibly delay a dominant buck's approach to his next mate is a threat on his life or the risk of exposing himself to a risky situation. The most dominant buck is always more concerned with his safety than he is with breeding, and he may actually wait for the sun to set before he joins his next mate. In the meantime, the doe in estrus may be pursued by other large racked bucks, and a breeding frenzy will be underway in no time. When the dominant buck does finally get to her, he will have to fight monster intruder bucks, and win his fights, just to win back the right to breed with her. Every dominant buck knows when a doe in estrus comes to meet him that the only thing that matters is being sure he is the only buck that will be breeding with her that day.

Dominant bucks are set in their ways. They will not adjust their schedules for anything except a doe in estrus or a challenge by another buck for a doe in estrus. I knew that when I put my system into play the first time. I knew that D.I.E. was going to be near perfect for me because it offered the most dominant buck the right to remain dominant in his herd, and it gave him the opportunity to command the D.I.E. scrape, rather than having to fight me for it. I let him take it from me and I never touch it again. What I did not know was that I could keep his attention at a D.I.E. scrape for up to four days, even though a doe is only in estrus for 24 to 36 hours at the most. I know now why that is possible. It is because the dominant buck does not always find a D.I.E. scrape on set up day. Sometimes he does not even find it during the 2 ½ day waiting period. He might find it for the first time, after dark on Day 1 of my hunt, after I have gone home. Because he walks his territorial boundaries once every (3 days) 72 hours, I am assured he will find it within 3 days of the time I construct it. Whenever he comes in, I am assured that he will take over my scrape, and he will command an area that stretches 35 yards in every direction from my scrape and 35 yards in every direction from my tree stand. No deer will be allowed to enter that area if you set it up as I do. Only the two invisible deer and the dominant buck are allowed to live there, all the other deer must stay out or else!

Whenever the dominant buck finds my D.I.E. scrape and rub, he believes the doe just came into estrus, and that she will be pursued by all the breeder bucks in the area until she goes out of estrus. He has to find her, breed with her, and stay with her until she is out of estrus or he loses his hierarchy, and he will no longer be the king of the herd. In a dominant buck's mind, there is no reason to quit. He will hunt her down until he finds her, or until he is convinced that she never existed. For me that means I will always see the herd's king because I am an expert at keeping him guessing, and I will never allow him to believe that she never existed. How about you? Do you have what it takes to role-play with the king of the herd? Keep reading and you will be a master at it by the time you finish reading this book.

A dominant buck will always trail a doe in heat from the security of downwind cover, and he will only go to her if she is in estrus, if it is dark, or if another buck is attempting to mount her. He will search for with does in estrus, but does in heat are not his focus during the daylight hours, which are the only hours a hunter can see to shoot a deer. The D.I.E. scrape is saturated with the scent of multiple does in heat, from the time you build it on set up day, until Day 1 of your hunt when you return to it and change the lure from does in heat to one single doe in estrus. Day 1 of your hunt is the third day of a doe's heat cycle. It is the day that a real doe in heat, that visited the dominant buck's scrape on set up day, would be going into estrus. He is expecting her arrival and he welcomes the sound of her footsteps approaching the D.I.E. scrape on Day 1. He assumes that you are back to search for him to mate with you. DOMINANCE IS EVERYTHING has been a flawless system. It has worked every time a D.I.E hunter has left the D.I.E. scrape alone for 2 ½ days before returning to hunt over it. It will work for you too!

The picture you paint for the dominant buck is a pretty one

When you are in your tree stand the (invisible) doe in estrus is upwind or crosswind of the scrape. When you are gone (at night), the doe is gone, and the scrape-dripper has shut off as well. Every dominant buck in the world will be convinced that the Still Steamin'® Premium Hot Doe Estrus Urine is urine from a real live doe in estrus, because it is urine from one real live doe in estrus. I recommend that you give that bottle of pure doe in estrus urine a name! It has a unique DNA signature, one the dominant buck has never smelled before. I like to name her Sally.

Sally arrives at the D.I.E. scrape on Day 1 when you arrive there, and she stays nearby while you wait for the buck to wake up and smell the scent of her sweet perfume. All day long, the Scrape-Dripper drips depositing Sally's pure urine in the scrape. At the end of Day 1, the Scrape-Dripper shuts off with a 10° temperature drop. If you did not see the buck, you go home for the night and the buck gets more anxious to meet Sally the next day. On Day 2 starting about an hour after sunrise (with a 10 degree temperature rise) Sally's scent starts dripping into the D.I.E. scrape again, and you guessed it you arrived there and got in your tree stand 15 minutes or so before her scent started dripping. Here we go again. When you are there, Sally is there, when you are gone, Sally is gone. The most dominant buck wants to mate with Sally, but you do not know when he is going to lock on to her scent so you have to become Sally each day as it was the first day. Eventually he will come. He has come in within four consecutive days, for every D.I.E. hunter before you. This is no different. He is on his way! Trust in the power of the system. D.I.E. is going to rock your world!

Whenever he comes in he is not afraid or looking for a hunter because you are invisible to him, he thinks he is alone, and he will make his way in without any urging. If you do not get him on Day 1 or Day 2, you should know that the hunt stays the same for Day 3 and Day 4 but the mindset of the dominant buck is a bit different. On Day 3, you are being hunted full time. The scrape is being hunted too but the big attraction is you. He will come to your stand first on Day 3 and 4 and then head to your D.I.E. scrape. That is because the Scrape-Dripper ran out of Sally's urine late on Day 2 or Early on Day 3. It is supposed to run out. Do not make any efforts to refill it or you will get busted 100% of the time. Trust me!

You are the hunted, mainly because you are dragging in the only fresh sign of that doe in estrus on Day 3 and Day 4. Your dragline is doped up with her urine, and you drag it directly to your tree stand with you. The D.I.E. scrape is meant to dry up on Day 2 or early in the morning on Day 3, and when it does if you have not seen your buck yet, it is ShowTime!

I am pumped right now telling you this. These are the guts of my DOMINANCE IS EVERYTHING system. Without the role-playing, or the existence of the D.I.E. scrape, you would just be deer hunting traditionally, now you are being hunted by the king of deer with D.I.E.! It does not get any better than this!

I for one am not satisfied just seeing any buck when I hunt whitetails. I need to see the most dominant buck in the area, and my DOMINANCE IS EVERYTHING system has performed at 100% for me during on each of my past 11 hunts with it. I will never hunt mature, dominant, and sometimes monster whitetail bucks in any other manner, at any time in my future. DOMINANCE IS EVERYTHING to every D.I.E. hunter too! Take it from me I am hooked!

I used to have questions about deer and what made dominant bucks tick, but not anymore. Now I have a clear understanding of everything that I need to know in order to get close to monster bucks on every hunt I go on. I found the answers to my questions by videotaping deer in the wild for 16 months straight. I have over 500 hours of footage that I witnessed first-hand. I learned what I know by watching the tapes repeatedly. I saw bucks displaying their dominance on those videos. It did not matter how old the buck was at the time. Whenever the rut was on, the bucks were constantly displaying their dominance and I could see the ranks of the bucks in the pecking order. I knew which buck was dominant by his behavior, and by the other buck's behavior toward him. Learning how the buck pecking order works and how a whitetail herd works were both crucial in the development of DOMINANCE IS EVERYTHING (my role-playing) system. I have mastered a one-of-a-kind system that you and I can get the same results from no matter where we hunt with it! That is amazing!

God blessed me with the passion to enjoy the time I get to spend with deer and other animals, the will to press on, no matter how tough the task before me is, and the determination to always do my best and have no regrets. I have given this system my all for the past 13 years and I am now willing to share it with every man, woman, and child that would like to learn how to use it. I am far from being done hunting dominant whitetail bucks. It will take me a lifetime to get sick of having monster buck fever. Once you have it you cannot get over it. You will surely see what I mean when you hunt with my DOMINANCE IS EVERYTHING system for the first time.

Chapter 16

The 4 continuous phases of the whitetail rut

All mature whitetail deer take part in the mating season, also called the rut, in one way or another. The rut has four stages that coincide with one another. They are the preliminary rut, the chase phase, the primary rut, and the late rut. This is how I see the rut, and what goes on during it:

1. **Preliminary Rut,** (called pre-rut), starts when the dominant buck makes his first primary breeding scrape and the first doe that goes into heat visits it. He would have already made numerous rubs along his territory boundaries a few weeks before the pre-rut began. This is the period when the first doe in heat goes into estrus and the dominant buck exercises his earned right to breed with her. I believe multiple bucks and multiple does are mating during the pre-rut, but only after the dominant buck breeds with the first doe. The rut starts when deer are having sex. Therefore, the rut is on within 4 days of the beginning of the pre-rut. In every herd, the dominant buck and his highest-ranking pecking order bucks get to breed with the first few does that come into estrus. More than one doe will go into estrus during the pre-rut, but they do not run and chase to show off. Does search for their king and he mates with them, until there are too many does for him to handle at one time. By then the chase phase is upon us.

2. **Chase Phase,** when multiple does are in estrus at the same time. You will see multiple bucks chasing multiple does in daylight during the chase phase. I am 100% sure that the highest-ranking pecking order bucks have been mating for a week already when the chase phase begins. During the chase phase, multiple does are in heat and in estrus. Breeder bucks are chasing does in heat, and some are breeding with does in estrus. When you see a doe being chased, she is in heat (nearing estrus). Does walk around when they are paired up with a buck. They only run when bucks attempt to mount them and they are not yet in estrus. The highest-ranking bucks in the herd, monster bucks, swamp bucks, and the dominant buck are all coming out in daylight now, to get to does in estrus, and for that reason I call it the best time to hunt with the D.I.E. system.

3. **Primary Rut,** when the largest number of does, are in estrus at the same time. During the primary rut, almost every pecking order buck gets a chance to breed. Sometimes yearling bucks will get an opportunity to breed during the primary rut. Some does are in heat

while others are in estrus, and all breeder bucks are pursuing them wherever they go. During the primary rut, the most dominant buck sometimes leaves the area for up to 2 days, in search of a doe in estrus. He will always return to walk his territory boundaries on the third day. The primary rut is an all-out breeding frenzy in the deer world. Intruder breeder bucks are roaming and dominance of the herd can change from buck to buck multiple times in a week. The fights you witness during this period of the rut are sometimes to the death, and more often than not, they include an intruder buck as a combatant.

4. **Late Rut,** when the rut is approaching its end, and only few does are in heat at the same time. Much like the pre-rut, the dominant buck is the primary breeder in the late rut, but his pecking order has shifted now, due to some of the bucks in it being killed by predators or hunters.

Intruder bucks pursue every doe they can find and pecking order bucks group back up in their bachelor group to prepare for winter's weather elements. Yearling bucks are accepted into the bachelor group of the pecking order during the late rut, and they spar with each other to determine their rank. This is the time of year when the herd becomes tight-knit. They rely on each other for their safety.

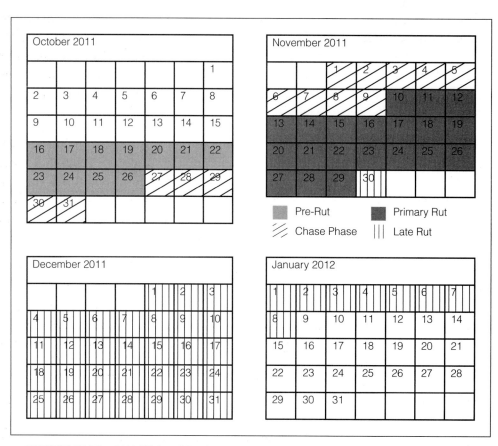

FIGURE 15 The 2011 Whitetail Rut in Wisconsin (Pre-Rut, Chase Phase, Primary Rut, Late Rut).

Every mature buck outside the pecking order is fighting for every doe he finds that is in estrus. Bucks in the pecking order are yielding to the dominant buck. Lots of yearling does go into heat in this period, also does that were not successfully bred during their first cycle come back into heat now. Fawns born earlier the same summer go in heat and in estrus for the first time during late rut too. Many does will go into heat during late rut, but not all at once like the primary rut. D.I.E. will pull the breeder bucks to you like a magnet, during late rut.

It is a great time for a D.I.E. hunter to be in the woods but it is much tougher to stay warm in your tree stand, than it is earlier in the rut. Monster bucks roam in search of does in estrus. I love hunting in the late rut with D.I.E. because no matter where I set it up, the biggest racked bucks within a half-mile fight over the right to command it. It is your last chance to meet the king of the herd before deer season ends and bucks shed their antlers.

The calendar on the previous page shows the upcoming rut (2011) as I see it, for the State of Wisconsin. These dates will be the same in coming years, because the rut is very predictable, contrary to what most people believe. Later on in this chapter, I explain how to determine when the rut is on in any part of the United States of America or in Canada. The rut is on when deer are breeding. It is as simple as that. Scout to determine if the rut is on. That is the only way I know to be 100% sure of it.

The following descriptions **(Pre-Rut, Chase Phase, Primary Rut, and Late Rut)** coincide with the dates on the calendar above. No matter where you hunt, there are four phases of the rut and deer are mating during every one of them. In Wisconsin, these dates are valid, in other states you need to be the judge of the dates. You should read this section even if you do not hunt in Wisconsin. I made extra comments about each phase that will help you understand the best times to use the D.I.E. system.

Pre-Rut, I believe it runs from roughly from October 16 through October 26 here in Wisconsin. It could start any day between October 12 and October 16, but I am sure that the rut is always on by October 16. It is a 10–14 day period when the first one, two, or three does go into heat in each herd here in Wisconsin. Dominant bucks are marking their territories with rubs and they make at least one primary breeding scrape somewhere inside their territory during this time.

I do not prefer to hunt with D.I.E. during the pre-rut because I do not want the dominant buck to know that my system is make-believe. My belief is that he has to breed with a few does before he finds a D.I.E. scrape in order for it to be something he is interested in bedding down near and protecting. I do not want the first doe in heat or in estrus that he encounters to be an invisible one. The dominant buck has to get used to the routine of the rut before he meets the most exciting doe that he has ever met. I do not want him to give up on the system, and walk away from it for a real doe in estrus, and by refusing to hunt with D.I.E. prior to October 29 each year; I have always been able to succeed with it. I do not know if D.I.E. will succeed in the pre-rut with 100% success, because I never hunted with it then, and neither has anyone else, due to me giving them advice not to. Why change a single thing when I already have a system that has never failed? If you want to be 100% successful with D.I.E., you should wait to hunt with it until the pre-rut is over. Non-ranking monster bucks keep to themselves during the pre-rut. I think it is out of respect to the king of the herd.

Chase Phase, I believe it runs from roughly from October 27 through November 9. I love hunting the chase phase. If I have four consecutive days off during this time period, you can expect that I am sitting in my stand being hunted by the king of deer. Dominant bucks have already bred two or more does when this time arrives. They are actively breeding and protecting their mates from intruder bucks. They will establish dominance wherever there is a doe in estrus. It is the best time of the rut to hunt with D.I.E. because the dominant buck is always home. If you hunt in this period, your odds of seeing the buck that ran the herd all summer are the highest! Hunting the chase phase gives you the best odds of seeing a monster buck on a D.I.E. hunt! Do not pass up an opportunity to hunt during this period.

Primary Rut, I believe it runs roughly from November 10 through November 29. The largest numbers of does are in heat and they all go into estrus during this two to three-week period. All mature bucks are pursuing does. The whole pecking order is in a breeding frenzy. Even some immature bucks (yearlings) are breeding now, because a dominant buck is with a doe in estrus nearly all the time. He cannot keep up with all the does in estrus. Wisconsin's gun deer season falls into this period.

Late Rut, It runs roughly from November 30 through January 8, but it may go up to 4 days longer. I saw a doe in estrus on January 12 2010, and the rut was still on, but I cannot prove the rut would still be on every year at that time. Late rut is the time when does that went into estrus in November and early December and were not successfully impregnated come back into estrus for the second time. Adult does that were born late in the summer months go into estrus during this period too, and do not forget that this is also the time when fawns born the previous May and June go into estrus for the first time. I do not think doe fawns can get pregnant, but I have seen bucks chase them and attempt to mount them as late as January 12. The rut ends when the very last doe in a herd goes out of estrus. In Wisconsin that is on or after January 8 each year.

D.I.E. works anywhere deer live as long as the rut is on

I am absolutely sure that the DOMINANCE IS EVERYTHING system will work in any state of the U.S.A. where whitetail deer live and in Canada. I am not familiar with the dates of the whitetail deer-hunting season in other parts of the country or in Canada, so I will not specify which dates would work the best for hunters using my D.I.E. system in any of those places, but I am happy to help you determine when the rut is on. When it comes to knowing whether the rut is on, I recommend that you use these simple tests. They are in no apparent order.

- If you stand on the downwind side of a doe bedding area (never stand in the bedding area), and you take a deep breath through your nose, if the air has an aroma similar to that of black licorice, then at least one doe is in heat.
- When you find a doe track in a scrape, she is certainly in heat, but she could be in estrus.

- If you see a doe with her tail half-cocked, and she is not defecating, then she is in estrus. It looks like she lifted her tail and hinged it in the middle. She also arches her back whenever she is standing still. It is a signal to all the area bucks that she is ready and willing to breed. You will know it when you see it.
- If a buck has his nose up a doe's hind end, then that doe is either in heat or in estrus. I call that situation "a doe with a buck in tow".
- If bucks are still raking saplings to intimidate each other or they are seen fighting, then they are still sexually excited and looking for mates.

In all of the above cases, you can be sure that the rut is on!

In Wisconsin, the rut is on from the time the first doe goes into estrus in the pre-rut in mid October, until the last doe is bred in the first or second week of January. Deer are mating in every part of Wisconsin during that time. Just because people do not see bucks chasing does, does not mean that the rut is over. The rut has nothing to do with what people see. It has to do with when deer mate. Most deer mate in heavy cover (cover you cannot see through), and most people have never witnessed a pair of deer mating. In two years of filming deer, that is the one act I never caught a pair of deer taking part in. I have seen bucks mount does, but they were never able to complete the task, maybe because I was watching. They mate wherever the doe is when she goes into estrus. It is not usually out in the open and they do not intend on letting any humans watch.

I have had 100% success with DOMINANCE IS EVERYTHING on hunts that began as early as October 29th and as late as December 24. I have personally hunted with my system in late October; early, middle, and late November; and middle to late December—all with 100% results. Does are in estrus and breeder bucks are mating with them through January 8 here in Wisconsin. I can assure you they will respond to the D.I.E. system up until then.

As I already stated, an important fact about adult does that do not get bred successfully the first time that they go into estrus, is that they will go back into estrus a second time 26 to 30 days after their first heat cycle. What I did not tell you, is why it is important to know that as a D.I.E. hunter. Here is the answer. When I developed DOMINANCE IS EVERYTHING I originally had to decide how much Still Steamin' Premium Hot Doe Estrus urine (collected from one single doe) I should use in the Scrape-Dripper, and how many drops I was going to put on the key-wick® tied on the dragline. I also took into consideration the amount I used in the three scent-dispensers I installed on Day 1 of my hunt. After allocating half of the bottle of urine to the Scrape-Dripper, keeping enough to use on the key-wick® that I dipped it in the bottle each morning at the first sign of deer, and two or three drops in each of 3 scent-dispensers, there was over a ¼ of the bottle of doe in estrus urine remaining. Retaining that left over pure doe in estrus urine could be the difference between bagging your dominant buck, or not having 100% chance of doing so, while hunting the same property, from the same tree stand, and while using the same scrape. I always date the bottle of urine when I open it, and I name the doe by writing her name and the date on the label. If I missed the dominant buck when he came in, or if I had to leave unexpectedly during my hunt for work or a family emergency, I could return in 26 to

30 days and resume my hunt for that same buck from the same stand, granted he never saw me as a human.

Once the dominant buck breeds with all the does he can find inside his herd, he will roam (leave the area) searching for other does in estrus in other dominant buck's territories, and he will come back to look for the does that he pursued earlier in the rut, that he never found. He knows those does by their unique scent, and he knows they will return to his scrape looking for him when they go back into heat. He will remember the scent of your D.I.E. doe and he will pursue her once again at your scrape 26 to 30 days later.

Every doe goes into heat each year at the same time she did the year before. If this is the doe's first year of life then the doe (fawn) will go into heat 6 months after it was born. From then on, it will be one year after that for the rest of the doe's life.

The buck that works your scrape and follows you around the woods when I hunt with DOMINANCE IS EVERYTHING, will give you his undivided attention for no more than four consecutive days. After that, he will know either he has been had, or he will figure out that the doe you represent could not possibly be in heat or estrus anymore, and then he will give up. The scrape goes cold (is ignored) and all the other deer lose interest in it as well, starting on the fifth day. There is no Day 5 with the D.I.E. system.

When you set up the D.I.E. system and hunt with it on Day 1, you start to bully the dominant buck that lives there. You do not stop pushing him around until your hunt is over or up to four days later (whichever comes first). I do not expect him in on Day 1. I have only seen one buck on Day 1 and he busted me, so I always teach people that you will likely see him on Day 2 or Day 3, but if not then it will be Day 4.

Your actions speak louder than words. You built the scrape and it made him believe you are a monster intruder buck that is willing to fight him for dominance of any does that visit the scrape. You tell him through your daily visits to the area that this unique doe in estrus is ready to breed. He sees your repeat visits to his primary breeding scrape, as an invitation from the doe in estrus. She is inviting him to mate with her. Are you sending him mixed signals? The answer is no. You are always two deer, and you have to be in order to keep him guessing! The Scrape-Dripper does a good job of brainwashing the dominant buck into believing the doe was there just before he arrived each day, and he never gets wise to your D.I.E. set up being manmade. He is hooked on the scent of the one single doe in estrus, and he will stop at nothing to meet her the next time she comes to the scrape. That will be when you walk in. It is the only time the doe in estrus is in the area, and that happens to be during broad daylight during your four-day hunt with DOMINANCE IS EVERYTHING. Imagine that!

Just when the dominant buck thinks, he has the situation all figured out, you go and switch it up on him—or, so he thinks! He makes his way to the scrape each day shortly after you arrive there. He calls out to the doe over 50% of the time. She (you) will never answer him, so he gets it in his head that she is playing hard to get. That must be because she has found the monster intruder buck (you) first! He believes she is with that buck, and they are breeding in the cover upwind of the D.I.E. scrape. He gets the feeling that they are not leaving his territory until the doe is out of estrus. That only gives the dominant buck a day or two at the most to find her and breed with her, but first he has to find the invisible monster intruder buck, and run him out of the territory! Good luck with that! It can never happen because that intruder buck is invisible.

Do you see how the buck can easily be fooled into believing the situation that my D.I.E. system places before him is real? Do you see that it is up to you to be committed to coming in, climbing into your tree stand, and observing the area around the scrape each day? You may call it deer hunting because you are armed and licensed to kill a deer, but I call it being hunted by the king of deer, because he has no clue I am ever there when he hunts for me. You are not a buck hunter if you are not pursuing the buck. He is the hunter and you are the hunted. You are one who is hunted by dominant bucks. You are a D.I.E. hunter!

Timing your hunt

If you are planning a hunt with D.I.E. this fall or winter, plan to set it up after the rut has been on for 11 days or more. Wisconsin hunters that means October 27 is the earliest you should be setting D.I.E. up. Do not scout the land for dominant buck and monster buck sign until the rut starts. That means Wisconsin hunters can scout after October 16. If you want 100% odds of seeing the king of deer on your hunt with D.I.E. then never hunt it without waiting 2 ½ days between set up day and Day 1 of your hunt. Hunting with a shorter waiting period will still bring the dominant buck in, but he will not always be the first buck you will see. When you wait the 2 ½ days, the dominant buck is always the first buck to walk or trot in. I like a sure thing, so I always wait the 2 ½ days.

How the rut works from the dominant buck's point of view

Not all bucks fight, but the ones that do, fight for dominance. When they win a fight, they win something. Losers do not win anything they lose something. Bucks have a pecking order so that they know which buck is boss in the herd and how many mature breeder bucks are in the ranks behind him. The pecking order is not a set thing. The pecking order changes when bucks are killed, when a ranked buck fights another buck within the ranks, and when an intruder buck from another herd wants to join this herd. An intruder buck has to either fight the dominant buck for the whole herd or fight with a few pecking order bucks to determine where he will rank in the pecking order. Intruders just passing through a herd's territory do not have to fight with herd bucks, but if they decide to bed down and stay a day or more during the rut, then they do.

Intruder bucks are not members of the area's herd. For that reason, they do not rank in the buck pecking order in that herd. Some of them belong to another pecking order in a neighboring herd. Intruder bucks roam into other territories in search of does in estrus, to breed with them. They are called intruders because they do not live in the area they are seen in, they wander in looking for does in estrus. I call all mature bucks that are away from home at the time, roaming intruder bucks. Dominant bucks become roaming intruders and so do monster bucks, but only during the rut. The sex drive of a breeder buck cannot be stopped without a bullet or an arrow. The only natural way it stops is when the rut ends. At that, time bucks concentrate on surviving the winter and escaping their natural predators until the rut starts again the next fall. Bucks live to breed and to be dominant! Does that sound familiar?

A dominant buck will not allow any lesser bucks to breed in his home territory when he is without a mate. He will patrol the area on a daily basis looking for does in heat, and does in estrus. When he finds them, he tries to prevent them from hooking up with bucks. That type of behavior from the dominant buck ticks off many lesser bucks, and they choose to become roaming intruders in other herds during the rut. He is constantly watching the other bucks and keeping them in line. They hate him for it and he gets the reputation of being the herd's bully buck! Lesser bucks have to get away from the dominant buck in order to find a doe in heat or better yet, a doe in estrus that they can have all to themselves. Many lesser bucks succeed in finding solo does in estrus and they get to breed with them, but they risk having to pay the price if her king is waiting nearby. All mature bucks will fight if another buck of equal or lesser size or rank gets in his way, but the most dominant buck will only fight another buck, in order to uphold his dominance.

If you have ever hunted more than one day from a tree stand that was set up between two doe bedding areas during the rut, you likely saw multiple 2 ½ to 4 ½ year old bucks working in and out of those bedding areas during the rut. The reason they did not stand around waiting for a doe in heat or in estrus to join them there, is because none of them were the most dominant buck in that area at the time. They were trespassers, intruders or mature lesser-ranked pecking order bucks. They have to keep moving so the dominant buck will not catch them inside one of the core doe bedding areas. If he caught them there, he would kick their butts for just being there, and if they had a doe in tow, he will run them off and steal the doe away.

Only the dominant buck has the earned right to breed. He can go wherever he pleases, whenever he wants to, inside his herd's territory. All the lesser bucks in the herd have to show subordination to him, and none of them will ever make direct eye contact with him. Inside the pecking order, there is only one-buck law that is upheld by all the mature bucks within its ranks, and that is **no buck shall ever look directly into the eyes of the most dominant buck, unless that buck intends to challenge the king for dominance of the entire herd**. When a pecking order buck takes on the king, it is not just for one doe, it is for the whole territory. The challenger must be willing to fight to the death in order to become the king of the herd, because the dominant buck will not ignore any challenge from any buck unless he is totally exhausted, badly wounded, or dead. Dominant bucks are like U.S. military troops, they set out on missions with the intent on winning every battle they are involved in, and they focus on seeing their mission through to completion. Every dominant buck I have ever seen was an expert at being stealthy and cunning. They are combatants with aggressive behavior toward their peers. They are relentless in their pursuit of (you) as the invisible doe in estrus that is frequenting the D.I.E. scrape and (you) the invisible monster intruder buck that never leaves the doe in estrus' side. The dominant buck will pursue you while on his mission to uphold his dominance of the herd. You should expect to see him walk or trot in, and posture right in front of you, during every single D.I.E. hunt.

While the lesser bucks are roaming and trying to avoid the dominant buck, they often happen to meet some pretty does in estrus. Of course, they are attracted to those does, because it is obvious to the bucks that those cute does are willing to party. The sweet smell of their doe in estrus perfume is tough to top for a mature whitetail buck. It is alluring and a doe that smells like that is hard to come by. Mature bucks know what to do when they find a doe like that. They need to win her affection, and they had better do it fast or they risk another buck showing up with the same doe on his mind. My system plays with the minds of mature bucks, and makes them fight over (me) the invisible doe in estrus at the D.I.E. scrape. Does do not care which buck breeds them, as long as he is big and strong. Then again, if no big and strong bucks are around at that moment, the does lower their standards and any mature buck will do. I am convinced that the mindset of all mature bucks and does during the rut is just as I described it above. Can you see yourself being able to think like a deer now?

I developed my **Dominance Is Everything** system so I could brainwash the most dominant buck in the area into believing that overnight, a sweet looking doe showed up to see him. But before she could ring his door bell and ask him to come out to play, another buck, from a neighboring herd, snatched that 'hot doe' up and took her away. When you set up my system and hunt with it on Day 1 of the hunt, you start to bully the dominant buck that lives there, and you do not stop pushing him around for up to four days. The timing of your actions, speak louder than words. The D.I.E. system makes him believe you are an intruder buck that is willing to fight him for dominance of the scrape, and for the right to breed with any doe that visits it.

Your actions hit home with the buck, and because he has never backed down from a challenge before he is not about to start now. He knows he has to put an end to you being in his territory, so he goes on a mission to rid the area of you (the invisible monster intruder buck). You do not quit either, you (the invisible hunter) go home at closing time but right after first light when all normal deer are in their beds or just bedding down for the morning, here you (the invisible monster buck and doe in estrus) come! You are back! He is extremely angry! It is Day 2 and he will not have you (the invisible monster intruder buck) push him around another day. That is why he comes in, and because you are invisible to him, he never knows a human is there.

When he is coming toward you do not try to shoot him on his way in. Believe me when I tell you that he does not know you are there as a human. He has no clue you are in a tree watching him, and if you can calm your nerves and stay still as he approaches your location, you will see how comfortable the dominant buck is when he gets within view of the scrape.

The place you decided to make the D.I.E. scrape and rub is indeed inside the dominant buck's territory. He is king there, and he will display his dominance over every deer in the area, as he makes his approach to the scrape. He will achieve that, by posturing all the way in. Grunt one time if needed to stop the buck, or just take your shot.

The secret to success with the system is playing your part as the intruder buck by using Trail's End #307 lure as your cover scent, and by never talking to the buck when he talks to you. If he grunts to you with tending grunts, do not make buck sounds back to him. Stay quiet and he will come. He is trying one last time to get you to show him the doe's exact location. Do not make a sound if he is close to you. You are invisible to him. Stay that way. You can wait him out and you will always win the waiting game. He will always come in during daylight on one of the four days in order to dominate the D.I.E. scrape.

Chapter 17

Stay away from the land until you need to scout it

Knowing how a dominant buck lives his daily life during the rut, helps you put yourself in his mindset so you can think like the dominant buck. It allows you to analyze the way that you were perceived by the king of the herd, when you entered his territory on past hunts. It is important to look at your past hunts from the dominant buck's perspective so you can easily see what you did that you made it easy for him to pattern you when you entered or left the property. Remember that you were an intruder in the dominant buck's house, anytime you entered the property in the past without becoming invisible to deer ahead of time. Thinking like a deer is not that hard to do, if you know how to go about it. The more you hunt with my system the more you will understand why the dominant buck has been able to avoid you on most of your past hunts. You will become aware of the little things that you have been doing that gave your location away to him.

Whatever the reason for the buck avoiding you, it all comes down to you telling him that you were a human, or him identifying you as a threat to his survival. Once you refrain from announcing your arrival as a human entering into the territory of deer, the outcome of your hunts will change immediately for the better.

I developed the D.I.E. system so it runs like a well-oiled machine. You should only enter the woods in the home territory of the dominant buck 3, 4, 5, or 6 days out of the year, if you want to go one-on-one with him in the rut. Start with 3 days, and if you need four then go for it. Five if need be, and six if he holds out and makes you hunt all four days. How long it takes to meet the dominant buck one-on-one depends on your behavior in the area and the way you role-play with the buck. You need to keep him guessing, not ever telling him which of the two invisible deer you are, and he has to be convinced that your set up is a real situation before he will come in. When both of you get what you want, that is when you will meet on common ground.

In order for a dominant buck to want to live on a property, he has to be unmolested there 24 hours a day, 7 days a week. Leaving the woods wild is always a good idea. I think a person should make an effort to avoid going out on their hunting land during the summer and the early fall, before their scouting trip. The only exception is farming. If you are a farmer and you have to manage your crops, then go ahead and do it. Deer get used the sounds of a tractor. Farming the land will not bother the deer at all. There is a dominant buck in every herd, yet most deer hunters have never seen one. I know the reason is that traditional hunters pressure deer just by walking around in their hunting parcel to pass time. If you pressure deer then they will go where they need to in order to avoid making contact with humans. Traditional deer hunters force deer to move away from their tree stands, their ground blinds, and their tower stands.

By always hunting with D.I.E. the same way, a D.I.E. hunter can infiltrate the territory of any dominant buck, for up to six days each season, without scaring that buck off, and without making him feel pressured by a human presence inside his territory. A D.I.E. hunter is invisible.

The six days a D.I.E. hunter can be in the territory of the dominant buck are:
1. Scouting Day 10 to 14 days before Day 1 (of the hunt)
2. Set Up Day 3 days prior to Day 1 (of the hunt)
3. Day 1 (of the hunt) The third day after Set Up Day
4. Day 2 (of the hunt) Follows Day 1 if needed
5. Day 3 (of the hunt) Follows Day 2 if needed
6. Day 4 (of the hunt) Follows Day 3 if needed

Also see Figure 1 in Chapter 1 on page 18.

My advice for anyone who reads this book is to cease from going into areas you know deer bed on the property you want to hunt, to look at deer, to track deer, or to scout for deer. Only go into area where deer live when you have to. I want the deer in the herd I intend to hunt, to be surprised to find my scrape. I do not want them to expect to see a human there sitting in a tree stand! If you like to track deer (like I do) then track them on some public land that you do not hunt deer on, that way you will not be telling the whole herd that a human was there, and that he or she is coming back!

To be successful with my system you need to follow my instructions; and the first instruction I have for you is to leave the buck's territory alone until your scouting day. If you have trail cameras installed right now on the land you are going to hunt with my system, I advise you to go pull them right now! Seriously, it is that important! Put the book down, go out and pull your trail cameras (and their supports), then come back and pick the book up again so we can move on.

Trail cameras kill the deal. The smartest buck in the herd (the most dominant buck) will not come in 100% of the time during daylight if you use a trail camera anywhere on your property while you are using my D.I.E. system. Using trail cameras forces the dominant buck to visit the area only after dark. Your element of surprise is gone before you even show up to hunt.

The dominant buck knows you were there and that you (a human) will be back! So far not one D.I.E. hunter using my system, has ever succeed at seeing the dominant buck during daylight, within 35 yards of their stand, with one or more trail cameras installed in the area. The dominant buck is a lot smarter than most people think. I have never used a trail camera and I have the buck approach my stand site during daylight on every hunt. If your land is trail camera free then you are all set to meet the dominant buck! If not then remove the cameras for success with D.I.E.!

Once you have had a successful hunt, setting the scrape and the stand up will become second nature to you. Trust in the system and adapt to it, do not try to make it adapt to you. You have been well trained to prevent the dominant buck from patterning you. No deer will know you are a human on a D.I.E. hunt unless you announce it to them. Stay out of the dominant buck's territory in the off-season and allow him to live there in peace.

I consider the rut to be "The Big Dance"

When the rut ("The Big Dance") is in full swing go out there and call the dominant buck out with D.I.E., he will never expect a visitor with two legs to be impersonating a sexy four-legged doe in estrus. Use the ticket that God gave you (brainwash him with D.I.E. and your invisible deer suit) to get into the big dance (the rut), and be sure to take a front row seat (hunt within 35 yards of the D.I.E. scrape) so you do not miss the action. You are destined for many dances (great hunts) with majestic monster bucks, as long as you keep your identity (as a human) a secret from all the deer that want to dance (breed) with you (the doe in estrus), at a D.I.E. scrape during the rut.

What deer see and what people see

I have included some photos of me snowshoeing in Wisconsin's Kettle Moraine State Forest near Whitewater, Wisconsin in 2009. The photographer that captured these images was Scott Anderson of Brookfield, Wisconsin.

What whitetail deer see.

What a human sees. All that matters to a D.I.E. hunter is what deer see.

Here are more examples.

What deer see.

Again, this is what a humans sees.

Here I am wearing my fall camouflage, and this is what deer see.

Again, this is what humans see. Deer do not look for humans, unless humans announce to the deer that they are there.

After viewing the photos, I am sure that you can see that a deer could not visually identify a human as a danger to them if the human hunter was motionless, and wearing full camouflage. When a hunter is sitting still in their tree stand, they are two-dimensional to all deer that look up at them. That means that deer do not see depth. It is as if they are looking at a photograph. If you wear a facemask, a hat, gloves, and a full camouflage outfit, no deer can identify you as anything other than a bunch of tree limbs unless you move. Do not move, not even one eyeball and the deer will never see you. A deer will only stare at you for less than 45 seconds. If you can stay, still and you do not look in the deer's eyes, within 45 seconds the deer will lower its head and go on with its normal behavior. If you never sat in that tree before, the deer should not look up there at all, but if a deer does look at you, always know it does not see a human in a tree. If it did, it would have run away before then.

Chapter 18

Scouting

21 Questions to help you see "The Big Picture"

Before you hunt with DOMINANCE IS EVERYTHING, you need to see "The Big Picture" on the property you are going to hunt. Seeing "The Big Picture" means, you can see the deer herd from the deer's perspective. Answering these 21 questions will help you see it.

1. Can you map out your land? Mark all scrapes with rubs behind them, all buck rubs (rubbed all the way around the tree), and all heavily used deer trails.
2. Where is the nearest source of water? Is it a lake, a river, a ditch, a pond or a water-filled rut on a logging road?
3. Where are the heavily used deer trails? Are there any one-way trails on this property?
4. Are there any deer tracks longer than 3 ½ inches (tip of the toe to back of toe pad), and at least ¾-inch wide (each pad)?
5. Where have you sat during past deer hunts, and did the deer look at you in the tree?
6. Do other people have access to this property? Where do you park your car when you are on the property?
7. If yes for #6, then can you prevent them from accessing it when you are hunting there with D.I.E.?
8. What time of day have you seen deer while hunting and what are they doing when you see them?
9. What direction does the prevailing wind come from?
10. Where is the nearest core doe bedding area? That is where five or more does, fawns, and yearling bucks bed together.
11. What about lowland? Is there any? Where is the nearest swamp in relation to this property?
12. Is there available cover either in the lowland or around it for deer to hide?
13. Are there any roads inside your property boundaries? Old unused logging roads count too.
14. How many acres do you have at that location? How big of an area, are you describing on your map?

15. How do you access the property when you hunt it now? Is it by foot, by ATV, or by car or truck?

16. Can you enter it from more than one direction? If so, which one(s) north, south, east, or west?

17. Are there high wolf numbers or other predators of deer in your area? If yes, do they live where you are hunting?

18. Are there any farm fields, food plots, bait piles, oak stands, or other places deer congregate to feed on this parcel of land?

19. Has a buck ever looked up at you when you were in a stand on this land?

20. How many other people are on this land during your 4 days of hunting? How far away from you will they be?

21. Do you have permanent stands on the property? Permanent stands are stands that you leave in the woods year round.

The answers to the 21 questions will paint the big picture for you. Once you can see the big picture on a property, you will know if it is a good place to use D.I.E. or not. Although DOMINANCE IS EVERYTHING does not fail to brainwash the most dominant buck in the herd into believing your D.I.E. scrape was made by an intruder monster buck and is being visited by a doe that he has never met before, but that is not enough for any person to succeed using the D.I.E. system. You need to become a deer in the deer's mind. You have to take part in the role-playing part of the hunt. You have to brainwash every deer in the herd into believing that there is not a human being in their midst—not ever!

In order to see the big picture you need to analyze what the deer are doing on the property before you go out there to hunt them. If you hunted there last year, or if you walked the land before, then you will be able to answer these questions. If not, then plan to find the answers on your scouting day.

Question 1, *"Can you map out your land? Mark all scrapes with rubs behind them, all buck rubs (rubbed all the way around the tree), and all heavily used deer trails."*

The answers to this question tell a person where deer are bedding and where deer are the most at peace on the property. Scrapes are meeting places for does in heat and in estrus to meet bucks that want to breed. All scrapes made with a rubbed tree behind them, and a licking branch over them, are being maintained by the most dominant buck, and he can only maintain one at a time, so these are the most important scrapes on any property because they give up the location of the bedded dominant buck during the day. The dominant buck beds straight downwind of the rubbed up tree that stands directly behind the scrape. He watches the rub in daylight and in the dark. When a deer stands in front of the rub, it blocks his view of it. That is when the buck rises to his feet and scent checks the scrape to see which deer is there.

I do not use this knowledge to pursue the buck in his bedding area or at one of his primary breeding scrapes. Instead, I look for it so I know where his furthest downwind bed inside his

A core breeding area, the same one Bullwinkle was breeding twin does in. Read about Bullwinkle on page 387.

territory is during the rut. He will be in that bed when he is watching his primary breeding scrape, once I find it and I verify that the wind is hitting the backside of the tree that is rubbed, then I know the dominant buck is bedded downwind of that rub right then at that moment in time. It gets very exciting for me then, because I know where he is and how I am going to go about pulling him hundreds of yards upwind and crosswind to my location. The buck will end up taking a heavily used deer trail for the last 20 steps to my D.I.E. scrape.

All buck rubs that are rubbed all the way around the tree, tell you that two or more mature bucks are constantly fighting for that particular piece of breeding territory. If you find a scrape with a rub behind it and a smooth rub goes all the way around the tree, then two or more bucks are challenging each other for breeding rights to that scrape. It is an ongoing grudge match. Odds of a monster buck hunting you are 50% higher in places like that. Remember to stay at least 80 yards away from all buck sign made on 2-inch or larger diameter trees.

Heavily used deer trails are located in transitional areas, and setting up the D.I.E. scrape on the upwind side of a heavily used deer trail that leads into cover is one of the best set ups a D.I.E. hunter can have. **The reason is deer literally walk through terrain changes (transitional areas).** If they walk there then they are at peace there, and if they are not threatened there then they you can be sure that they use that trail during daylight hours as well as at night. If there are large deer tracks on the trail, then mature deer use it, and the dominant buck uses it too. If you are able to set your D.I.E. scrape on the upwind side of a heavily used deer trail, and you are able to position your stand upwind and crosswind of that, at whatever your best shooting distance is (under 35 yards), you would be making your fellow D.I.E. hunters (including me) jealous. Setting up on a one-way trail is even better if you can find one.

Question 2, *"Where is the nearest source of water? Is it a lake, a river, a ditch, a pond or a water-filled rut on a logging road?"*

The answers to this question tell a person where the deer get their water. Dominant bucks, monster bucks, and swamp bucks all live near water, and they go to water twice a day (during daylight). I am not sure how many times they go to water in the dark. Hunting with D.I.E. upwind and crosswind, or just crosswind (no closer than 80 yards) from the upwind edge of a cattail marsh with some standing water in it will up your odds of seeing your dominant buck early on in the hunt, rather than later in the four days. Give the buck privacy when he is in his core bedding area (swamp). Hunt him in a new area where he is not familiar with the bedding options. Make him come to you upwind and crosswind of his normal bedding area. I like to be 80 to 250 yards away from his normal bedding area. Water is life to all deer, and to all living things. Hunt over a creek or a near a river crossing whenever possible, because the sound of the water nearby will muffle any sounds you make when you move around in your tree stand. I want you to stay as still as you can, so he will never be alerted to your presence.

Question 3, *"Where are the heavily used deer trails? Are there any one-way trails on this property?"*

The answers to this question tell a person where the deer like to travel and which way the wind is predominantly coming from at that time of year on the parcel. You can tell which way the wind normally comes from when deer use any heavily used deer trail just by analyzing the direction that the deer head on the trail. Unpressured deer travel at crosswind angles. When they are in danger, they head straight into the wind and they normally run. When you analyze a deer trail, measure the size of the tracks on it, note which way they were headed, and then walk the trail in both directions to see what type of cover the deer were coming out of and heading into. Find out if the deer were walking or running on the trail when they made those tracks. If they were running then the wind was hitting them in the face at the time. The next question to answer is; which direction is the wind coming from at that moment? Is it hitting you in the face when you stand in those deer tracks? If the answer is yes and if the tracks are fresh then those deer might have been running away from you. You can learn a lot from analyzing deer tracks on trails.

One-way deer trails are found in areas where there are three or more types of cover (terrain changes) in a 30 or 40-yard stretch of the trail. It is common to see one-way trails at water crossings, going up slopes, and heading from a field edge into cover that is too thick to see through. One-way deer trails are not rare, they are easy to find, if you look for them. They are only one-way for 30 or 40 yards, the rest of the time they are two-way trails. Many people walk right past these trails and never consider how easy they are to hunt.

Deer normally run across open areas and slow to a trot before walking into cover. Look for one-way deer trails where running deer slow to a trot. I have always hunted on the upwind side of a one-way deer trail, because with my system you want your scent to carry to the deer and the deer walk on the deer trails, so being upwind of the deer trails makes the most sense to me.

Scouting

What a heavily used deer trail looks like, with snow on it.

This is the start of the One-Way deer trail that I set my D.I.E. scrape upwind of in 2006, and 2009 when I was hunted by monster bucks. Notice the dirt showing through the snow. That is the result of deer trotting on this trail. Behind me there is a small incline, and the deer had to trot on this section of the trail in order to feel safe.

No deer will go the wrong way on a one-way trail. Not even the most dominant buck. If you can get your hands on an aerial photograph of your hunting parcel, and the land that borders it, I am sure you will be able to pinpoint multiple locations that are worth scouting for one-way deer trails. I use the internet to help me narrow down the herd's primary bedding area locations, before I ever get there. You can see deer trails, terrain changes, and water sources from an aerial photograph and if you have the internet, it is free to download it. Search your county website and look at the land data, or go to googlemaps.com and search for it there. Heavily used deer trails show up on satellite photographs. They are like super-highways for deer. You cannot miss them. Set a D.I.E. scrape up on the upwind side of any heavily used deer trail you can find. Setting up on the downwind side can get you busted. Not all the time, only some of the time, but why take any chances of being busted.

Question 4, *"Are there any deer tracks longer than 3 ½ inches (tip of the toe to back of toe pad), and at least ¾-inch wide (each pad)?"*

Take a tape measure, a pen, and some paper along with you when you scout. Write down all the buck sign you see. Then map it out later when you get home. Any deer tracks longer than 3 ½-inches are made by a mature deer. If they are ¾-inch, wide on each toe pad at the rear of the track then the deer is at least 2 ½ years old. These are just my observations. If you see, fawn tracks on the trail do not set up on it. Fawns travel with their mothers. Wherever you see a fawn walking around during the day there is likely a core doe bedding area nearby. I do not want anyone who hunts with D.I.E. to set up in or near a core doe bedding area. That is not how my system works. You need to get as far away from doe bedding and from fawn tracks as you can in order to make the king of deer pursue you. Bigger tracks mean bigger deer, and bigger deer mean monster bucks. Splayed toes on the front hoof tracks indicate the buck was displaying dominance. There is only one buck that displays his dominance with every step that he takes, every day that he is dominant, and that is the most dominant buck in the herd.

Scout to find dominant buck tracks. Look out in the open where he will be posturing. This track was made in the middle of a harvested cornfield in late October during the pre-rut.

Questions 5, *"Where have you sat during past deer hunts? Have deer ever looked at you in a tree stand?"*

The answers to this question tell a person where they can set up D.I.E. and where they cannot. D.I.E. will not erase the memory of any deer that saw you in a tree. If you were busted in the past, do not try to hunt from that tree stand with D.I.E., instead make sure you choose a new location, and install a new portable stand on set up day. I use a chain-on or a belt-on style stand with 3-foot long (belt-on) ladder steps. You can use a ladder stand, a climber stand, a chain-on, or a belt-on stand with 100% success. I have not tested it from a permanent stand so I cannot tell you it will be 100% from one of those, but if you do decide to try it from one I recommend, that you do not use one that you installed less than one year earlier. Well-established stands may work, but I cannot be sure. I know portable stands always work.

Deer only look into trees for humans, when humans tell deer they are in a tree. Do not ever set up and hunt from a tree stand where a deer busted you in the past. You will be wasting waste 4 days of your life, and you could have been successful somewhere else if you would have just set up a new stand as I directed you to. I am not saying that you will fail if you hunt out of a pre-existing stand. What I am saying is that anyone that does is lowering the chance of seeing the buck from 100% to less than that. Is it worth it? Not to me!

Question 6, *"Do other people have access to this property? Where do you park your car when you are on the property?"*

If other people have access to the property, you need to talk to them and tell them you need 7 days to yourself in the area. Four days of the hunt and three days leading up to it. You need 150–200 yards all the way around yourself to be free of any people, vehicles, and domestic animals from set-up day through the day you get your buck. Without having the land to yourself you have the chance of being busted by someone or something else interfering with your set up or your stand. I would rather not hunt with D.I.E. on a parcel where I will be interfered with. If the dominant buck sees anything that is not normal in the woods there, he will lock up and not come in to you during daylight.

It can happen if a another person comes in during your waiting period and sets up a stand near your set-up, not knowing you are hunting there and when you come into the area to hunt all of a sudden there is another hunter in your spot. It happens, and the only way you can avoid it is by pre-planning and telling the other people to stay out for the week you will be there. If you are hunting public land, get away from the parking lots. Hunt a half mile or more upwind of the lot so you are hunting a different king than the other hunters are hunting.

Where you actually park your vehicle matters. Park it where it cannot be seen by a deer that is standing under your tree stand, or making his way to your stand site. The dominant buck will follow your scent around after you leave each day, and if he sees you get into your vehicle and drive away, you will be busted. Park your car away from your location and if hunting public land, be sure to park on the opposite side of the street, from the land you intend to hunt. It will throw passersby off your trail.

Question 7, *"If yes for #6, then can you prevent them from accessing it when you are hunting there with D.I.E.?"*

If you cannot be alone when hunting with D.I.E. your odds of seeing the most dominant buck will be less than 100%. To me that is reason enough not to use it in places where I cannot be alone. It has always brought the most dominant buck to me, and I have always been alone on my hunts, so why change anything now. Use your judgment and give it your all.

Question 8, *"What time of day have you seen deer while hunting here and what are they doing when you see them?"*

This question takes for granted that you have hunted this parcel before, or that you at least drove past it and saw a deer feeding on a field nearby. If not, then you cannot answer this question, but if so, what I am looking for is a timeline for deer travel. Does and fawns go straight from bedding to food in the late afternoon.

Doe trails from bedding to food sources are straight lines so it is not hard work to estimate where doe bedding areas are. All you need to do is note the location where you first saw a doe entering a food source. Draw her body on a piece of paper. Draw an oval for her body and a circle for her head, then draw the outside edge of the food source, and identify the edge of cover she came out of when she entered the food source. Now draw arrows describing what the wind direction was that day and then look at the drawing. Take your pencil and draw a straight-line right through the middle of the doe from her nose to her tail, and extend that line through the rear of the deer for 100–200 yards. Somewhere in that direction, 100 to 200 yards or more is a core doe bedding area. Do not go there to check it out, just trust me that they bed in that direction.

You should set up 150 yards or more away from doe bedding areas, always upwind and crosswind of them. You want the scent of the lure in your D.I.E. scrape to drift past the edge of the core doe bedding area so every buck in the herd will smell it as they pursue does in and around the core doe bedding area. The scent will drift more than 300 yards so do not ever crowd the deer. Deer will avoid you if they can sense you.

Never hunt so close to doe bedding that you can see bedded deer. If you can see deer lay down you are too close. You should always know you are in a doe bedding area or on the fringe of one if you see does, fawns, or yearling bucks from your tree stand. Hunting from there with D.I.E. may allow the dominant buck to bust you. Heading crosswind of a doe bedding area will put you in the pecking order buck's bedding area, and going downwind of the does puts you in the bedroom of the king of the herd.

With my system, you need to be invisible to all the deer, and in order to achieve that you have to hunt far away from the places that you know they bed. Trust me on this. Go upwind and wait for the king there. He will come.

If you hunt too close to bedded deer he will still come, but only after dark or near dark. He will hold up in cover inside the bedding area or near your stand but he will not come in because he can see you enter and leave the area and he is sure you are a human. You will be busted! Move away from doe and buck bedding, and make him come to you. Deer leave food sources in the morning are going to water and then to bedding.

Question 9, *"What direction does the prevailing wind come from?"*

As I said before, deer check to the wind before taking a single step. On your scouting day, you need to know which way the wind should be coming from on Day 1 of your hunt. That way you will look at your tree stand options over by analyzing which tree will provide you the most cover in. You are only using one tree stand, and one set up location with this system. It is a fixed stand that you never shift or relocate, no matter what the wind direction is.

> Always point your toes toward the scrape (both right and left-handed shooters).

I have my set up instructions down to a science. If you are a right-handed shooter, always keep the wind to the back of your right shoulder, or hitting you in your right cheek. If you shoot left-handed then always keep the wind to the back of your left shoulder or hitting you in your left cheek. Having the wind hit you squarely in the center of your back is ok too, but setting up facing other directions will allow the buck to hide behind cover and not offer you a clean shot opportunity.

Always point your toes toward the scrape (both right and left-handed shooters). Those of you who do not do this will find yourself faced with a dilemma when the buck comes in. Over 50% of the time the buck will hold up behind cover (inside 35 yards) if you point your toes right or left of the scrape. I found this out the hard way and now I never change my set-up. I stick to what works every time and I get 100% results on every hunt. If you do exactly what I teach you then you will succeed too.

Here I am at deer height pointing to the deer trail that the 17-pointer came running in on in 2009. One of my scrapes is in front of my knees, and a Scrape-Dripper is hanging up in the tree over my left shoulder. Bucks always quarter to the rub. They never approach it head on.

If deer tracks are fresh when you scout at 10 a.m. in the morning then those tracks were made as the deer went to bedding. Non-pressured deer like to enter bedding areas from downwind or crosswind, and they exit bedding areas from crosswind, not straight into the wind. Deer bedding areas are secluded areas and the deer hide there. You will never find a deer trail that runs from the downwind side straight through the middle to the upwind side of a doe bedding or buck bedding area. Adult deer are not dumb, and they would have to be in order to

This is what a big buck trail looks like, it happened to be the one the 17 pointer was on when I shot him.

This is the view that the bucks had when they got to my scrape. I was sitting up in the cut out spruce tree.

make a trail like that. One their enemies could follow right through the middle of their bedding area. That will not ever happen, so do not even look for it. Stay focused while scouting, setting up, and hunting with D.I.E. and use the wind to help you understand what the deer are doing on your hunting parcel.

Question 10, *"Where is the nearest core doe bedding area? That is where five or more does, fawns, and yearling bucks bed together."*

This is the most important question you should ask yourself. Once you know where the core doe bedding area is, you will know where to set up D.I.E. (Upwind and crosswind at least 150 yards of course). Now do not get me wrong, D.I.E. can be set up anywhere within 35 yards of a deer track and it will work 100% of the time, but I have figured out how to get bucks to compete for me and my invisible doe in estrus, and the differences have to do with where I set the system up. The closer you follow my advice when you set up, the better your odds are of seeing a monster buck hunting you.

All mature bucks pursue does in estrus and every doe in heat goes into estrus at some point during the rut. Knowing does and bucks spend 80% of the daylight hours in or around their bedding area, and dominant bucks go to water twice a day in daylight should make you want to hunt 150 to 200 yards upwind or crosswind of a known doe bedding area nearby a water source if possible. If you do that all the deer in the herd would know about your D.I.E. scrape the first night that you set it up. That way the location of the D.I.E. scrape get the bucks fighting over the right to breed the invisible doe in heat when she comes into estrus. That will happen when you show up to hunt of course.

Question 11, *"What about lowland? Is there any? Where is the nearest swamp in relation to this property?"*

Mature bucks live in lowland areas near water. Dominant bucks, monster bucks, and swamp bucks live in water whenever they have a chance. You need to know where water is in order to guess where the dominant buck lives. Once you know that you can strategically work out the details about where to set up in order to pull him a couple hundred yards from there to your location. You are going to love scouting for your hunt! Do not worry if there is not any water on your land, just find out where the deer in the area are getting their daily water from, and hunt as close to that as you can, while making sure you are not hunting in or near deer bedding areas.

Question 12, *"Is there available cover either in the lowland or around it for deer to hide?"*

If the water source is out in the open without cover around it then the deer use it mostly at night. Most year-round water sources have flowing water, and they are found in wooded or grassy areas. Does like to bed on dry ground, unlike pecking order bucks, they like to bed on the outside edges of swamps. Dominant bucks bed in the wettest end of a swamp. Again, do not go into buck or doe bedding areas when scouting or hunting. Most doe bedding areas are 400 or more yards apart. Hunting between them is ok, but always sit upwind of any deer trails in the area, if you can. It helps you stay invisible. Deer will expect humans to be on their downwind side. You are not a human, so stay upwind.

There I am in the ultimate tree stand hunting over the ultimate set up.

This was my view to my D.I.E. scrape(s) and rubs, in 2009 I modified the system and used two rubs and scrapes, instead of one.

That was me showing Dick Ellis - Editor of *On Wisconsin Outdoors* magazine, what a D.I.E. rub and scrape look like. I just recovered the 17-pointer, that is the reason for the grin.

Question 13, *"Are there any roads inside your property boundaries? Old unused logging roads count too."*

Roads are obstacles for all deer. Old logging roads will have scrapes on them and you should scout old logging roads first. Look for crossing trails, tracks, rubs, and scrapes, and do not go off the logging road until you walk its entire length through your property. You can learn a lot about the herd from walking the easiest traveled path. Deer will not usually bed within 40 yards of a road made for vehicular traffic, for that reason you will only see signs that deer crossed a road like that. If you have a county road running through your property, hunt upwind of it at least 100 yards to have the best chance at having a dominant buck feeling comfortable with your choice of stand and set up location. Hunting too close to a road (that cars travel) will get you busted.

Question 14, *"How many acres do you have at that location? How big of an area are you describing on your map?"*

When you look at "The Big Picture", you should realize that a dominant buck's territory is generally about ½ mile long and ½ mile wide but they can be smaller or larger based on how many total deer are in the herd, and how many mature bucks are in the pecking order. You should hunt only a 5 or 10-acre piece of your property. There is no need to hunt it all. All you need is one stand and more than one way to get to it. If you have to walk in the same way each day then you will have to walk in making different trails each day so the buck cannot pattern you. The more options you have the better it will be for you.

Question 15, *"How do you access the property when you hunt it now? Is it by foot, by ATV, or by car or truck?"*

I want you to make as little impact on the land as possible when you hunt with D.I.E., do not drive an ATV in a mile or more unless you have to. Just hunt where you want to and make sure you do not walk more than you have to on your way into your stand. Hunt in a tree as close to the road as D.I.E. will allow you to. That way your hunt is fun and easy and you do not have any trouble getting the buck out of the woods. It is a win-win situation for you.

Question 16, *"Can you enter it from more than one direction? If so, which one(s) north, south, east, or west?"*

Ideally, you want to be able to walk into your stand site from both the East and West, if you have a North or South wind, or from the North and South, if you have an East or West wind. Having options is a necessity, because sometime during a hunt, you will be busted and when you do, you will need a second tree stand and D.I.E. scrape location. Plan and find two spots for D.I.E. at least 80 yards apart from one another and make sure your tree stand will be situated in different types of trees so the dominant buck does not figure out what type of tree you will be sitting in the second time. He will look for humans in any tree of the same type as he busted you in, if he ever does bust you.

Question 17, *"Are there high wolf numbers or other predators of deer in your area? If yes, do they live where you are hunting?"*

I ask this question only because I am aware that deer vacate the whole area when a pack of wolves moves into it. I witnessed that first hand when I was hunting whitetails in Northern Wisconsin in 2009 during our state's gun deer season. Deer are a big part of the diet of wolves, bears, and mountain lions.

When you are hunting with D.I.E., you are asking the dominant buck to show himself during daylight, within 35 yards of your tree stand. You are telling the buck that a monster intruder buck entered the area before him. He analyzed the area and was able to determine that this spot was the safest place he could find to breed the area's does in estrus, so he made a primary breeding scrape (a D.I.E. scrape) in the area. You are also telling him that every does in estrus feels safe within 150 yards of your stand in all directions.

If you know there are high numbers of predators in that area, then do not set the D.I.E. scrape up there.

To ask a dominant buck to leave the safety of his bedding cover during daylight in the rut, is a tall order for a buck in normal everyday life, but as you know the most dominant buck has to come to the D.I.E. scrape, in order to uphold his hierarchy, so he does so without fail.

In this case, you are asking him to come in and show himself when not only humans are hunting him, but wolves, bears, and possibly mountain lions too. He knows they are hunting him but he does not have a clue that you are, so your odds of success are still 100% if you are not busted. The D.I.E. system has not ever failed anyone who followed my instructions, but hunting with it in places where four legged predators are taking up residence nearby is not smart. If you have, many wolf tracks on your property try to hunt far away from them, so the buck will not be skittish as he approaches your stand site. If it were up to me, I would make it as easy as I could for that buck to get to my scrape. If it meant choosing another property to hunt, where deer were not being harassed by predators, then so be it. It is your call to make.

If you use D.I.E., the dominant buck will come. Just use common sense when setting up so that the dominant buck will believe that these two deer are really feeling safe coming into this area each day. Do not set it up where deer would not feel safe and never set it up in wide-open areas. There has to be some cover that would hide a bedded doe within 5 yards upwind of the scrape. If your set up location offers at least that much cover, then it will convince the most dominant buck that he should pursue the doe in estrus there.

Question 18, *"Are there any farm fields, food plots, bait piles, oak stands, or other places deer congregate to feed on this parcel of land?"*

All deer congregate at food sources. It is there that they can see one another on a daily basis. They all eat something while they are there, but that is not why food sources are important to a hunter using D.I.E.; the primary food source is another location that you need to stay away from with my system. Many deer congregate there and almost every time I have seen a food source during the rut I have found a scrape with a rub behind it along one outside edge of the food source. I want you to focus your efforts on the outside fringes of the buck's territory, not inside his core areas. Treat his food source as his living room and dining room combination. His bedding area is his bedroom, and his water source is his kitchen. Heavily used deer trails are his hallways, and the road you park on is in his front yard, his side yard, or his back yard.

You want to call the buck out into his yard to discover a primary breeding scrape made by a monster intruder buck. You want him to believe this buck just snuck in there to try to attract some of the area's does, and that this buck is bigger, stronger, and smarter than he is. You do so by playing mind games with this one buck, the king of the herd. You cannot play a trick on one deer if all the rest know about it, because some of them will give you away. That is why I never hunt where deer congregate, because too many eyes are on my stand site there, and because it is not normal deer behavior for any intruder buck to build a core dominant buck scrape inside the core area of the reigning dominant buck. It is not believable to the dominant buck, and although some customers of mine will inevitably do it, they will see that the dominant buck is no dummy. He will not take over your D.I.E. scrape if you build it too close to his bedding area, a doe bedding area, or on an active food source. You have to pull him away from places like that. Install the D.I.E. scrape on the edge of cover, where the buck has to approach it very closely in order to see into the cover upwind or crosswind behind the scrape.

Question 19, *"Has a buck ever looked up at you when you were in a stand on this land?"*

This is important to know because deer form habits of looking into trees of the same type that they once busted a human in. Real deer know when to look up for a human in a tree, and they know it because the human told the deer that he or she was there. Many humans blow calls for the heck of it, as if to pass time in the tree stand. I know that anytime a human calls three or more times consecutively, he or she is giving their location away to all the deer in the woods. Deer can hear calls more than 200 yards away.

Do not ever continue to hunt from a tree after a deer busts you there. Move to a new stand location all together. It is over for you there. Never tell a deer that you are a human in a tree. They do not ask so why are you telling them. Always know when you blow a grunt tube or a doe bleat that the dominant buck is the only deer listening (when you hunt with D.I.E.), and know what you are going to say to him before you say it. If he is talking to you (as a deer) then be quiet, and wait him out. Talking to him from a tree, as a deer is impossible, so do not ever do it. You cannot convince a deer that his challenging intruder buck is 15 feet up in a tree, so never make more than one grunt out of a tree stand. That is one grunt in a day, not in an hour. Read Chapter 24 "How to talk like a deer".

My advice for consistent success with D.I.E. is to remain 100% quiet. Do not talk to the buck until he is within 35 yards and you want to stop him for a shot. Then grunt one time and do it loud. He will stop in his tracks and he will always look straight upwind. If you want to call more often, know what you are saying, and when it is safe for you to say it, otherwise you will be busted more often than not.

Question 20, *"How many other people are on this land during your four days of hunting? How far away from you will they be?"*

Public land hunters, you do have a choice where you hunt. You have just as much choice as a private land hunter when it comes to hunting with my system. You have to be alone. No person should be within 150 yards of your stand or your scrape and no one should have access to it. You need to be alone in the woods with the deer. They can see other people but they cannot see you. A dominant buck will not show up under your stand if he can see another person moving within his view from your scrape. It is hunter error if you are busted for being too close to other people. No matter where the nearest hunter is to you, always make sure they either know where you are ahead of time or that you move away from them a half mile or more for your safety. Never purposely, hunt next to other hunters. Never walk in on the same trail as others do, and never talk to anyone when you are in the woods, in the stand, or when you leave. The dominant buck will hunt you from set up day until you take him or until 4 days of hunting passes by (whichever comes first). Do not go out of your way to be busted. Wear full camouflage and stay scent free. Do everything as I taught you and do not worry about what the next person is doing. Other hunters are not invisible to deer, because they do not know how to be, but you are. Stay focused and the buck will work his way past them to get to you. He will be avoiding all humans all day long. That does not change, what changes is the fact that he doesn't know you are a human so he comes to you instead of avoiding the area you are in. Get ready for an amazing hunt where you are "the hunted" and the king of the herd is the hunter!

Question 21, *"Do you have permanent stands on the property? Permanent stands are stands that you leave in the woods year round."*

I ask this question so you are aware that all deer can see permanent stands and that your element of surprise is gone if you hunt from one of them. I cannot say that you will fail hunting from a permanent stand, but I can tell you that I never hunted with D.I.E. from one. On set up day, I have always placed my tree stand in the area within 35 yards of my scrape. I hunt out of sight from any permanent tree stands. If you find yourself staring at a bunch of stands on your property when you scout, I would advise you to remove one or two of them as soon as possible so deer will feel comfortable walking in that area during daylight. Hunting from a permanent stand would be ok if you were sure that deer were not going on alert in the area of the stand. You have to be quiet in your tree, and you cannot be seen moving around. If a deer sees you as a human at any point during your hunt, you are busted, and you only get one chance at this with each dominant buck. Any deer seeing you gets you busted, even if the deer is not the dominant buck. Use your judgment, but know that the way I have hunted with D.I.E. has never failed, so trust that my way will work for you if you follow it as I direct you.

Guidelines for scouting without overdoing it

You do not have to be alone on scouting day or on set up day, but the fewer people you take in the woods with you the better. I like to keep it to just me and one other person. If you are going in with another person, always instruct him or her not to talk to you in any lengthy conversations while you are near any known deer bedding areas or immediately after you jump a deer from its bed. If you jump a bedded deer, it will watch you and it will try to figure out what you are. You do not want it to do either of those things when you scout so if that happens to you my advice is turn around and walk away into some cover. Act as though you never saw that deer and never look at him or her again that day. Avoid pushing that deer any further, but note the place you jumped it from its bed. Also, note the time of day and the current wind direction. Analyze why the deer was bedded there, and figure out if it was a monster buck, a lesser buck, a juvenile buck, or a doe.

I like to scout between the hours of 10 o'clock a.m. and 2 o'clock p.m. This is a scheduled time I have personally chosen for my scouting because I know most deer are bedded down at that time of the day, and those that are not bedded are holding tight in cover where I will not likely bother them. I do not scout heavy cover, I scout open areas and terrain changes, where a buck would likely travel to or stage in late in the day. I want to avoid spooking the dominant buck, so I stay away from his bedding area. Do not press through swamps or lowland areas. On scouting day always walk with the wind in your face or at a crosswind, to give the buck a comfort zone upwind and crosswind of his bed, in case you jump him and he has to elude you.

Do not try to find a dominant buck on your scouting trip. Instead, try to find out what else is around his hiding place. Use the answers to the 21 questions to help you figure out where the dominant buck likely beds and then stay away from that area completely. Try to find a trail that leads into semi-light cover of some sort. Once you find that look for a tree stand location.

Every hunt with **DOMINANCE IS EVERYTHING** has a 'big picture' and you have to become part of it in order to succeed with my system—not as a hunter, but instead as an observer. I want you there within view of the scrape, watching for the buck and waiting patiently for him to arrive. You have to want to be there too. It is not up to me if you remain in the tree all day, it is your call to make. If you get out of the tree before closing time, your odds diminish to less than 50% that he will come in for you during daylight. Just look for a comfortable tree to put your stand in. Look when you are scouting. Look to put your back into the wind when you are sitting in the tree. I set my stand up so the back of my shooting shoulder is in the strongest wind, on set up day. I know the wind will change during my hunt but when I set up this way the wind never affects my hunt in a negative way. I never want to face directly into the wind, because the buck will come from behind me then, and the North wind is cold in the fall. I do not want to get cold.

I know deer season is open already when you are out scouting so you may be tempted to take your bow or gun along with you. I do not see any harm in doing that, but I personally have never taken my weapon along on a scouting trip. I really want to experience the thrill of the hunt when the biggest buck in the territory is hunting me at my stand site. I am not interested in shooting any deer on my scouting trip. Hunting with **DOMINANCE IS EVERYTHING** is adrenaline pumping and there is no forgetting that feeling once you experience it. It is worth the wait to be hunted by the king of deer.

When you see big deer tracks on the property and the rut has started, that means a big deer (buck or doe) is frequenting the area right then, today, not last week or last month. Scouting during the rut allows you to see where the dominant buck is hanging out, and that assures you that you can move away from his core living areas and pull him to you with the D.I.E. system. It is imperative that you pull him to you and do not get tempted to go to one of his living areas you would be making a hunter error if you hunt near his core living areas.

Scouting for a D.I.E. Set Up location

You are in charge of where you set the D.I.E. system up, but use some common sense and do not put it in an open field with no cover around. Give the buck enough cover to stage in, within 80 yards of your stand, that will allow him to bed down in it and feel safe there. He will leave that cover to come to you. Because the wind can change and it often does during a D.I.E. hunt, you should look around your potential set up location before setting anything up. Make sure that there is ample staging cover on two or three sides of the location you want to put the scrape. If you only have cover in one direction then do not set it up there. One direction is only 90° of a full circle around you.

In order to have the best chance that the dominant buck will move into the area downwind or crosswind of your set up to bed down and wait for you, the buck has to have at least two bedding and staging areas to choose from. They need to be in different directions so the buck can bed nearby no matter what the wind direction. Remember he is going to want to bed within view of the scrape, downwind or crosswind of it, just the same.

Always make sure you think like a deer when setting up. If you were him, where would you likely stage with a north wind, a south wind, an east wind, or a west wind? If you can answer those questions by standing, where you want to make the scrape and pointing out his staging areas, then go ahead and mark that location on your map as a great location to be hunted by the king of the herd. If not, then keep looking.

The place you decide to install a D.I.E. scrape has to be realistic to a monster buck. It has to make sense to him. I prefer to have an opening (an area with no staging cover) leading to it on a crosswind or upwind and crosswind side. Try to find a place with an opening on the side that you will be entering the area from, when you walk to your stand site each morning.

I have had huge success hunting with D.I.E. in a situation like this. It leaves the dominant buck with two or three patches of cover to choose from to bed or stage in, when the wind is normal. For instance, when the wind is from the Northwest, An opening on the north end of the area will give you an easy way in, without having to cut out any walking lanes. I never trim a path to my stand, if it is too thick, I move out of the cover to the edge of it. Hunting too deep in cover will allow the buck to hold up on the outside edge of it, where you should have set it up in the first place. I had that happen to me once. The buck lived on, that day. Set up on the outside edge of cover, not in it. The scrape and rub behind it has to be on the outside edge facing out, and you should be at a crosswind of it, the distance of your best shot at less than 35 yards, sitting in your stand just a few yards upwind or downwind of the scrape. I prefer to be 10 yards crosswind of it and 2 to 5 yards downwind of it. That way the buck is walking in parallel to my scent and it is drifting past him off to one side. I am 99% scent free and I do not worry about being identified as a human by the buck, but I do not locate my stand where he will be coming head on to it either. I take precautions to be sure my scent, will always drift parallel to the scent that is leaving the D.I.E. scrape, and I mask my scent by placing three scent dispensers in the tree with me. One has doe in estrus urine (Still Steamin' Premium Hot Doe Estrus urine) in it, and the other two have the buck lure (Trail's End #307) in them. Any deer that is downwind of me believes a buck and a doe are mating upwind of them. Those are the only lures I use.

Analyze the area that you want to set up in, and look at how you would approach the stand on each morning of the hunt. Work out a written scenario on a pad of paper as if you had to hunt all four days, it will help you see the big picture there. I recommend that you do that. Know how you will approach the stand each day ahead of time, and figure out a plan B in case the wind shifts on you, so you can get to the stand without having to go downwind of the scrape.

If you set up in an area where there is an opening upwind and at a crosswind angle of your stand you can be sure the buck will not bed in your path to the stand, even if the wind turns and your path happens to be downwind that morning. If there is not any cover for him to bed in without being seen, then he will not be bedded there. Planning ahead like that will help you avoid being busted on the way into your stand, no matter what the wind direction is.

Your odds of seeing a monster buck increase if you set up 80 to 200 yards away upwind and crosswind from the wet end of a swamp or a buck staging area. Bucks stage at crosswind angles of their bedding areas. Look for staging area rubs. I cannot say it enough, always move upwind and crosswind, from the active rutting buck sign, or from a doe bedding area so you will not be busted. You want to get away but do not go too far away. Always hunt at least 80 yards away from the nearest edge of their bedding cover and always angle away (go upwind and crosswind) from it before setting up.

The further you set up away from live deer, water, and a core bedding area, the longer it will take the buck to get to your location. That is not a bad thing. I am just stating a fact. He will still come in, but it will likely be late in the afternoon. I do not want to sit in a stand for 4 days if I do not have to. Anytime I have set up 80 to 200 yards from the nearest edge of a core doe bedding area, I have only had to hunt a maximum of 3 days to get my opportunity at the most dominant buck there.

I randomly set up my D.I.E. scrape the first three times I used it, and I hunted over it only part-time. I had a mature buck hunt me each time, but the only time it was a monster buck was on my third hunt, when I went in during daylight just after sunrise. On my first two hunts I got in my stand after 2 p.m. and stayed there until I shot a mature buck just after 4 p.m., but neither of those bucks were the most dominant. I learned that it takes more hard work and dedication on the D.I.E. hunter's part to see the most dominant buck face-to-face, especially if he is a monster buck. You have to sit in your stand all day according to my scheduled times in order to be hunted by the king of deer. It is not that tough, but it is not easy either. It takes a special effort from you, to harvest a dominant buck with my system. The system does do miracles, but you have to be there, all day or until the dominant buck arrives in order to be part of the hunt, otherwise, the system will collapse, and you will send the herd mixed signals, making them aware that the whole situation was a hoax.

I am showing you one way to build the scrape and one way to install a tree stand, because the way I do it, I never fail. You have endless opportunities to set the system up wherever you want to, and succeed with it there. I am trying to explain the best way I can, how I choose a set up location, so the deer that discover my D.I.E. scrape believe it is authentic. There are very few reasons why a buck can bust you, and I believe I know what each error a hunter can make is. Take my advice, forget how you hunted your whole life, and give my system a shot, you will be surprised at what it is capable of in the hands of a trained D.I.E. hunter.

Do not use it as an addition to your way of hunting. Replace your way of hunting with the D.I.E. system. That is how I became successful with it, by diving in headfirst! You get to make choices when you set up and when you hunt, and they are ones that will determine whether or not your hunt is flawless. You can have a dream hunt with D.I.E. every single time, but you have to become a believer in **Dominance Is Everything** and have some faith in the system and how you are behaving differently, before you head to your stand, not only after you see the system work. Have faith in your ability to set it up correctly and to hunt over it all day, while the dominant buck is hunting you, and you will not regret it.

Time your scouting trip for consistency

I scout roughly 2 weeks before I plan to hunt an area because I do not want the deer in the area to remember our meeting when I come back. All my human scent will disappear from the area within one or two days, and if it rains that night, it is all gone right away. All deer are alerted to human scent, but not all deer see it as a danger because not all deer have ever seen a man or a woman before. Only deer that have been hunted, shot at, or chased by a human being have a fear of them. When I scout, my concern is not whether a deer will be afraid of me or not, instead my focus is on spending only as much time as I need, in the area I am going to set the D.I.E. system up in, to gather the data that I need in order to outsmart the most dominant buck there. That means I look for doe bedding areas, rubs, scrapes, tracks, trails, possible tree stand and D.I.E. scrape locations, and all water sources. You should find two spots where there is a tree that is suitable for making a D.I.E. scrape in front of it, and where your tree stand will be within 35 yards of the scrape. I prefer to hunt 10 or 15 yards from my D.I.E. scrape so I can hit the buck when he comes in. I am more accurate at 10 yards than I am at 35 yards. After I get all the information I am looking for, I get out of there. I do not try to find any deer. I know where they are based on the wind, the tracks, and the rubs. I avoid going into wetlands, or near buck bedding areas. I do not want to jump a buck, I just want to find buck sign, and look for tracks that are 4 inches long or longer that the toes are splayed and the dew points are down. Those are the tracks of my herd's king. Once I find out where he is, I move away quickly so I do not disturb him in his sanctuary. The less he knows about me the better.

Do yourself a favor and look for a set up location that is easy for you to access from upwind. Always plan ahead, look for changes in the wind direction during your 4-day hunt, and know which 4 days you are going to hunt before you go out to scout. You should time your scouting trip to be 10 to 14 or more days before you plan to be in your stand on Day 1. Your whole hunt revolves around Day 1 of your hunt, so when you are planning your next D.I.E. hunt start by pulling out a calendar and deciding which day on the calendar, you will become the hunted! Make that Day 1, and mark the next three consecutive days as Day 2, Day 3, and Day 4. Then go back from Day 1 three calendar days and call that set up day. Look at Day 1 again and move back from it one more time, but this time move 7 to 14 days back and circle those dates on your calendar. If you could have a perfect D.I.E. hunt you would want to take your scouting trip on one of the days you just circled. The rest of the year, you should stay away from the deer as much as possible. That is if you want to have the king of the herd hunt you in the fall.

You can scout anytime after the rut has started, and you will get accurate information. Remember that your human scent will stay in the woods for up to 48 hours, and deer can detect it. The main thing is that you do not hunt in the stand and expect to see the king of the herd if human scent is still lingering in the woods. I use the waiting period as the time I need to rid the area of all human scent. He will watch your every move whenever you are on the property before the hunt, during the hunt, and after the hunt. You get to make all the decisions; the dominant buck does not have a choice. He is coming in because he has to, in order to remain being the most dominant. Your behavior in his territory determines if he comes in during the day or at night. If you avoid pressuring him in is living space and do not use trail cameras on your land, then he will come during the day, if you refuse to use D.I.E. as directed then you will not see him during the day, he will only come in after dark, because of your behavior.

If you wash your body from head to toe in scent free body wash and shampoo, and you wash your clothes in scent free laundry detergent that keeps fabrics free of scent and U-V Brighteners you are on your way to being invisible to deer. If you wear full camouflage from head to toe including a facemask and gloves, and you spray down everything you touch with Scent-Killer 99% then he will come. If you do all those things, you will be invisible to deer when you are standing still or sitting down.

If not then you messed up. If you mess up then he will be watching you after your D.I.E. hunt from the privacy of his kingdom, but if you get it right the first time, by following the rules for using D.I.E. as directed, then you will be watching him as his head and rack adorn your living room wall.

I wish you the best on your D.I.E. hunts. Always be safe and enjoy your time with the king of the herd. If you fail, dust your pride off, figure out what you did wrong and don't make the same mistake twice, then go back out there for another four days. Hunt from a new location, install a new stand in a new area, and build a new D.I.E. scrape and rub. Failure is only temporary. I been busted many times, but the system has not ever failed, the buck came in every time. How many days did you hunt each season when you were a traditional hunter? I expect that you hunted more than 4 days! Do not think the season is over if you make a mistake, because it is not. You can move a quarter mile away and find success there with the system.

Take notes when you scout, so you can remember what you find

It is very important to take notes when you scout your hunting land, mark down all deer sign that you find. I recommend that you draw an outline of the immediate area on a piece of paper, also draw out the property borders. Then walk into the woods and note (by drawing a mark) where you first find any deer sign. It does not matter if it is a trail, a track, a rub, a scrape, a deer bed, some droppings, or a real deer, all that matters is that you write down what you find and where you find it. Take notes and document all the deer trails that you come upon, especially the ones that you cross. Draw out their direction of travel. Use arrows to show which way the deer are traveling on that trail, and note how wide the trail is. Take a tape measure with you. An eight-inch wide trail is a doe and fawn trail, a two-foot wide or wider trail is used by the whole herd running up a hill, crossing a creek, or bunching up and bursting from cover. A buck trail will be heavily used but there will not be any fawn tracks on it. Dominant buck trails are narrow on the ground but they are widest 3 to 5 feet off the ground. They have to be in order to have room for their massive racks as they run through the woods. Look for room on that trail for a buck to have a 33-inch wide rack, knowing that he runs through cover with his head about 36-inches off the ground. His rack would be 3 to 5 feet off the ground if he was walking or trotting. He will use a trail where his rack will not be hung up on brush as he moves down the trail. Look for *big buck trails*, they are out there, and when you find one try to find a place to set up a D.I.E. scrape on the upwind side of one.

Inspect the tracks on the deer trails. Are the deer walking? Are they running, or are they trotting? Deer run (gallop) for a reason. Figure out the reason and follow the trail to the place where the deer slow down to a trotting pace, and then follow their tracks until you can see where they slowed to a walking pace. Deer sometimes run because they have to climb a hill, or because they were being pursued by a predator (a human) or another deer. A running deer is a frightened one. Deer run because they are not safe in that area at that time of the day. They usually run across open areas to get near some cover, then they stop outside that cover and scent check it, before walking into it.

You would do yourself justice with D.I.E. if you set up your D.I.E. scrape on the outside edge of the cover that they were walking into. Then set your stand inside the cover a few yards, and face the scrape. It is a perfect set up because deer do not look in the woods to see danger when they are outside of it. You should hide 10 yards inside the woods, not on the edge of it, and because you are scent free, and in full camouflage, the deer will not know you are there. See Figures 16–19 on the following pages.

Deer trot when they are in a hurry to get somewhere or when they are unsure of danger, and they walk when they are not threatened. As a D.I.E. hunter you want to hunt where you are within view of a deer trail that deer walk on. If they walk there, then they are at peace there, and that means you will know you are invisible to the deer if they are walking around you, or walking in front of you. Your shot opportunity will be at a walking buck or one that is standing still, and your hunt will be more enjoyable.

Always make an effort to think like a deer when you are scouting. When you find a deer track stop and ask yourself "If I was a deer, when would I have made these tracks? Which way must the wind have been coming from? Where was I coming from? Where was I going? Was I walking, trotting or galloping? Was I safe when I was here? Why or why not? Where would I be now? Is this a buck trail or a doe trail? Could I be the dominant buck? What room of the dominant buck's house is this spot on the trail in?" Answering those questions will tell you where the whole herd is. It is easy. Analyze what you know and figure out (make an educated guess) for what you do not know. It will make you a better hunter.

Then become a (scouting) D.I.E. hunter again and figure out where the dominant buck is bedded in relation to the spot that you are standing. You should be able to figure it out, just from finding one deer trail and analyzing it.

Deer travel at crosswind angles when they are at peace. All deer head into the wind when they are at risk, and bucks go into the wind when they are pursuing a doe in heat or in estrus.

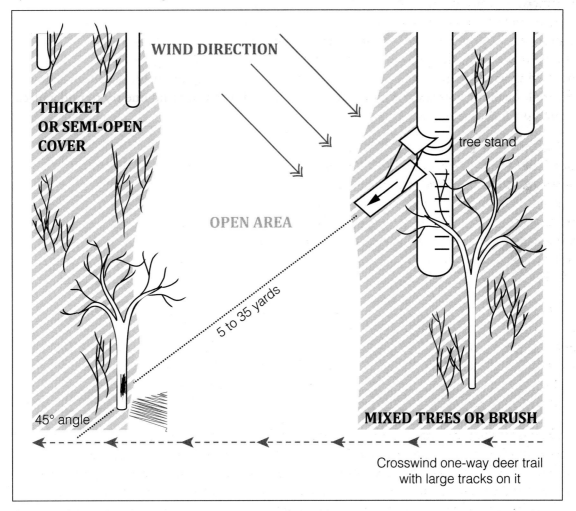

FIGURE 16 This is the Ultimate D.I.E. set up for a right-handed shooter. Notice the one-way deer trail. Rub the tree at a 45-degree angle to the deer trail so it faces downwind and crosswind at the same time. Then the buck cannot miss seeing it, and he will not be looking at you.

Does, fawns, and yearling bucks all walk the same trails. I call them doe trails. You will find fawn tracks on those trails. They go from a food source to a water source in the morning, then from water to bedding within the same hour as they left their food source. They stay bedded most of the day, only standing up to eat, to get water, to defecate, or to shift their bedded position due to a wind change, or a shadow being cast off their body. Then in early afternoon, they go straight from bedding to food, and stay there most if not all night. Pecking order bucks run anywhere does in heat or in estrus go, because they have to compete for breeding rights. Dominant bucks run from immediate danger and they run to a challenger if they know where he is, otherwise they walk, and at times, they trot. They are kings. They walk *stiff-legged* everywhere. They trot if they are concerned about getting somewhere fast or if there is a doe in estrus in front of them.

If it is daylight, you can presume the dominant buck is in his bed or out getting water near his bed. If it is a doe, she is in one of her three core bedding areas. I would bet she is in the one

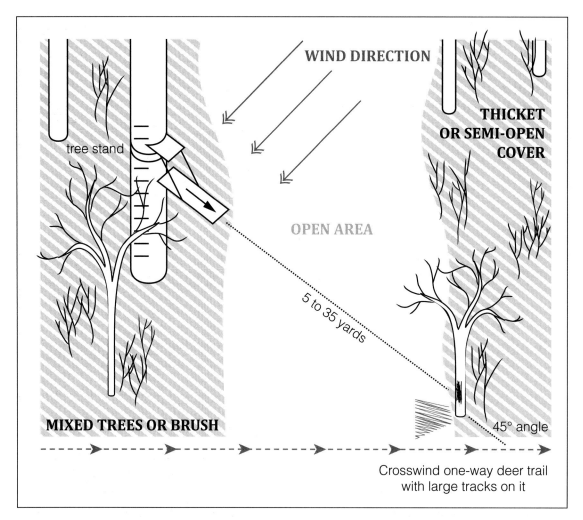

FIGURE 17 This is the Ultimate D.I.E. set up for a left-handed shooter. Notice the one-way deer trail. Rub the tree at a 45-degree angle to the deer trail so it faces downwind and crosswind at the same time. Then the buck cannot miss seeing it, and he will not be looking at you.

that is furthest downwind at the time. Check the wind and determine which way it is blowing. Point to downwind and know that she is over that way somewhere. The dominant buck is bedded downwind of the does, fawns, and yearling bucks, and the pecking order bucks are bedded upwind and crosswind of the does, fawns, and yearling bucks. Yearling bucks are kicked out of doe bedding areas when their mothers go into heat, and the pecking order bucks will not accept them in it until the late rut, so yearling bucks always bed off on their own in random places between the does and the pecking order bucks. Dominant bucks will not bed near does and fawns or near yearling bucks, because those deer are the least educated and he would be at risk of being killed if he was with them in daylight. He beds downwind and crosswind of his does at all times. Here in Wisconsin it is common for him to bed 100 to 350 yards downwind or crosswind of his does.

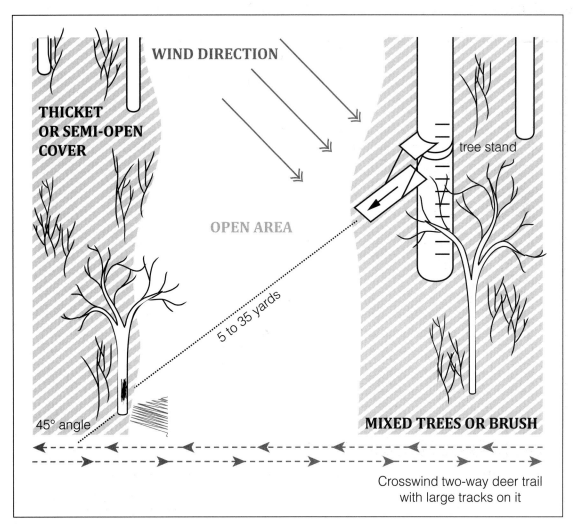

FIGURE 18 This is my preferred way to set up D.I.E. for a right-handed shooter. This one is the same as Figure 16 except there is two-way traffic on the heavily used deer trail. Rub the tree at a 45-degree angle to the deer trail so it faces downwind and crosswind at the same time. Then the buck cannot miss seeing it, and he will not be looking at you.

Inspect every deer trail you find, and discover which deer are using it. Look for deer tracks, specifically large deer tracks, and if you find some, measure the length of the tracks. The toe length of each side of the deer's hoof should be 3 ½ inches or longer and the width of each toe on a mature deer will be three-quarter inch or wider. On a monster buck here in Wisconsin the hoof length will often be longer than 4 inches, and the width of each rear pad of the hoof will be one inch or wider. The longer the hoof print the bigger the buck, but sometimes a large track can turn out to be the track of a mature doe. Buck tracks tend to be wider than doe tracks. You do not need to figure out if the tracks are from a buck or a doe, just find big hoof prints. The biggest tracks on your property will do.

I know that where there is a mature doe during the rut, there is always a mature buck that will pursue her once she is in estrus. Therefore, when you find some extra large deer tracks

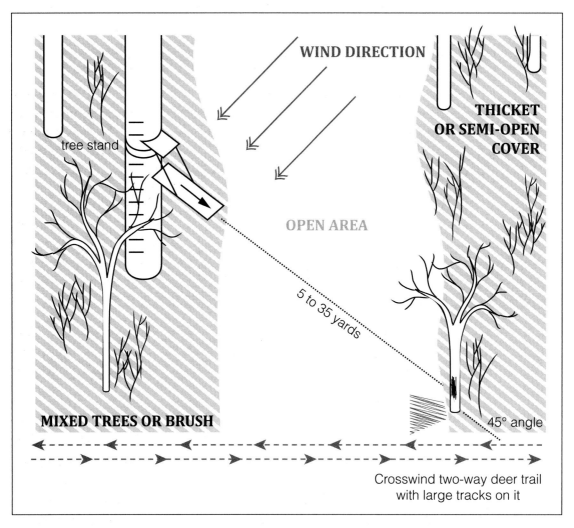

FIGURE 19 This is my preferred way to set up D.I.E. for a left-handed shooter. This one is the same as Figure 17 except there is two-way traffic on the heavily used deer trail. Rub the tree at a 45-degree angle to the deer trail so it faces downwind and crosswind at the same time. Then the buck cannot miss seeing it, and he will not be looking at you.

in your area, they were potentially made by a monster buck. Note which direction the tracks are heading and analyze when the tracks were likely made. Look at the terrain and see where they are coming from and where they are headed, and you will know what time of day the deer would have come to that point in the trail. Check the wind direction to know when the deer made the tracks. The same direction means today, a different direction means at least two days earlier.

Use all that I have taught you to see the big picture on your hunting property. It will make you more aware of deer travel patterns; and I am sure it will make you a better hunter. Knowing what a deer is likely to do before it does it, will help you make better decisions on where to place your tree stand and where a deer will feel comfortable walking around during the day. All deer move during daylight hours. Hunt upwind and crosswind of their normal daylight activity zone and be sure you cannot see them when they are in their beds. Give them the space they need in their sanctuaries and the dominant buck will surprise you and show up at your stand not knowing you are hunting him.

The most productive spots to encounter monster bucks are near water

I look for places near but at least 80 yards away from core doe or dominant buck bedding areas, lowlands, and then the wettest end of a marsh or swamp. Not many predators want to run into tall grass, trudge through muck and then swim in water to get to their prey, that is why you will find that the biggest and oldest bucks in the territory live in or near a swampy area whenever there is one available. Good solid live trees big enough to hold a 250 pound man (like me) are not always easy to come by near a swamp, a creek, or a river, because of all the flooding that occurs in places like that. Most of the trees will be dead in the swamp, but that is ok because you should never enter any swamp before or during a D.I.E. hunt. If you do, you will roust the mature buck that calls that place home, right out of his sanctuary. He will not come back until you have given up and no longer go into his core bedding area. He has willpower to live. I f you do not roust him then he will come to you. Instead, scout for trails with large tracks on them leading into and coming out of lowland areas.

Dominant bucks are what you are in search of, so dominant buck sign is what you look for when you scout. **The D.I.E. system consists of four distinct steps in a brainwashing process, and each of the steps is of equal importance. You must concentrate on all of them in order to make the buck hunt you every time.**

You should keep all four of these steps in mind when you are scouting for a place to set up:

1. *The D.I.E. scrape has to be a surprise to the dominant buck.* You need the element of surprise. To accomplish it you must scout and find a place where a dominant buck frequents then you hunt on the upwind side of it. Look for a place where there are no buck rubs within 80 yards of the tree stand. If you cannot find that then try to locate at least one heavily used deer trail. If it is a one-way trail, that is even better. If you like to hunt field edges try to hunt within bow range of a corner of the field. Build the scrape within 10 yards of the corner and hunt away from the corner as far as you prefer to shoot. You

should try to find at least one core doe bedding area or if you do not have one on your land, at least know which direction you would have to go to get to the nearest one. Look for tall grass and thorn type brush patches (ultimate big buck cover), and make notes of all these things on your pad of paper.

Look for buck droppings. They are not all single droppings like the droppings of does. In every pile of buck droppings, there will always be a clump of 5 or more droppings that are stuck together. The bigger the diameter of each dropping is, the older the deer was that left them.

Look for fresh tracks with splayed toes, those are the tracks of the most dominant buck he postures 24/7 so he leaves no doubt among the pecking order bucks that he is their king. Write down which direction they are traveling.

You should find two or more rubs made on trees that are 2 inches in diameter or larger. That rub is maintained by the king of the herd or one of his competitors, (never a pecking order buck). Analyze the rub and know where the dominant buck is in relation to it. If the rubs are not on your land, do not worry. Just know where the nearest rubs are to your hunting location. He lives where his fresh rubs are, and every three days he walks past each one of his fresh rubs to refresh it.

Do not ever touch any real rubs or real scrapes. Try not to make any impact on the normal lives of the deer in the area. It is all right to install a D.I.E. scrape in any dominant buck's territory and call the whole herd's attention to it, but never mess with one of the dominant buck's own territorial markers on a D.I.E. hunt. In a whitetail's world, if an intruder buck messes with a dominant buck's scrape he is trying to take over the territory. You do not want to take over anything, all you want is to let the buck know that you are a very pretty doe and you are on a mission to have him as your mate. That way he will take over your scrape and make it his own. He has to re-establish his dominance there and then and he has come in daily to maintain it. If you leave his scrapes, alone you will have the upper hand on him, because he will not be looking for a human. He will only look for a pair of invisible deer at the scrape. Humans are the number one culprits for messing with real buck rubs or scrapes and dominant bucks know that, so you are putting him on alert if you mess with any of his sign.

If you hunt with D.I.E. in more than one area in his woods at the same time, you will have him continually running back and forth. You can only be in one place at a time, so do not confuse him with multiple scrapes, multiple stands, or multiple hunters. Keep it simple - one hunter, one stand, one D.I.E. scrape, and one dominant buck. Never use two set ups. That will likely end in disaster and you will wise up the buck.

To make it a surprise you need to consider all the sign and always set the stand up to only benefit you. Give yourself an open view to the scrape, look for staging cover for the buck to hide in just downwind of the scrape, and look for a good tree that has a licking branch 5 to 7 feet off the ground within 35 yards of your stand. Make sure you wait to rub the bark off that tree, when you come in on set up day. Do not do anything to the woods now, just find two set up locations and take notes.

When you get home log onto the internet, go to www.googleearth.com, search for your hunting location. If you have any meadows or a crop field there, you will be able to see deer trails running through them from looking at the satellite photographs. I scout my hunting land this way and I can see trails that lead into swamps that I never knew were there before I looked on the web. Satellite imagery is incredible and if you have the internet, you can use it free.

2. *The buck works the D.I.E. scrape and makes it his own primary breeding scrape.* The dominant buck finds the D.I.E. scrape and is intimidated by it so he works it up, urinates in it, he sometimes rubs the tree, and he licks the licking branch. Instantly it is not a D.I.E. scrape anymore, now it is the primary breeding scrape of the herd's most dominant buck. The dominant buck will visit that scrape at least once a day now, and he will continue to do so as long as he has competition at that scrape.

Make sure when you scout that you choose a site for the scrape that is the shortest distance away from your stand. You should only want it to be out as far as you can accurately shoot, but never farther than 35 yards away, regardless of if are you bow or gun hunting. The system brings him within 35 yards because you always place the scrape within 35 yards of your stand and you always follow my instructions. There is no option for you to put it out further than 35 yards from your stand, and no reason for it either. If you are accurate at 30 yards then set it out there. If you are better at 10 or 15 yards then figure on setting it up like that, and if you like to shoot straight down (I would like to meet you) then plan on setting the scrape up on the tree next to the one you are going to sit in.

Do not change anything in the woods on scouting day. Just draw out some scenarios to choose from and maybe take a few snapshots with a digital camera. Take photos of your tree stand choices and of the 2 to 4 inch diameter sapling or tree, you are going to build your D.I.E. scrape under. I do not putting ribbons on the trees because I believe the dominant buck is smarter than humans are. I believe both deer and humans know that a ribbon on a tree was placed by a human as a marker of some sort. It tells me that a human was there and that he or she will be back, just as a trail camera does. Deer know when people are in their woods and they remember you for two days because you leave your human scent behind (when you are not scent free) so why leave them a reminder of their encounter with you. Take a photograph of the tree and keep the ribbons in your pocket, use a GPS to find your tree stand not thumbtacks. You are a daytime hunter now, you do not need to use a flashlight until you have hit your buck and are tracking his blood trail. I may be particular, but I am an expert at hunting with my DOMINANCE IS EVERYTHING system. You cannot be an expert if you make all kinds of mistakes, and never learn from them. I want to be invisible to deer 100% of the time I am in the woods, and I am invisible when I do not tell deer I am a human and I will be back. Ribbons, permanent tree stands, bait stations, trail cameras, and other human items like those tell the smartest buck in the herd that you are a human and that you will be back. The other deer do not seem to care about those things, but why should they? They do not run the herd or have to maintain a safe place for other deer to live. They just have to eat, drink, mate, and sleep. A dominant buck has to do all that and dominate, and in order to accomplish his duty he has to survive all human encounters. He will avoid you and any other human he encounters. Make a choice!

Become 100% invisible and expect to see a miracle, or continue to hunt as you always have and take what comes along. The choice is yours.

3. ***You arrive at the scrape on Day 1 of the hunt and you tell him you are a doe in estrus.*** When Day 1 rolls around you are the doe in estrus, and he believes that you are a real doe. You are one that is willing to breed with him as soon as he comes in. When you scout you need to make sure you have some available cover nearby. Of course, you need to leave him some downwind cover anywhere from 20 to 120 yards downwind of the scrape so the buck can stage in it before coming in. Also you need to have some cover upwind of the scrape as well, so he cannot see the entire area around the D.I.E. scrape without coming in close and standing within bow range of you.

   On scouting day, stand where your tree stand will be and look toward the scrape location. Think through the first day of your hunt and figure out where you will enter the land, how you could walk in with the wind to your back, or with it hitting you upside the head, and then figure out whether the sun will be blinding you at any time of the day if you sat there. I try to hunt as close to the road as I can, so the buck will only hear me walking like a deer for 50 to 120 yards. I do not want to walk like a deer more than 120 yards. That is too long. I want him to stay within 120 yards of my scrape the whole time so I start dragging the doe urine behind me when I am less than 120 yards from my tree stand, or my scrape.

   When you step onto the property you are going to hunt on Day 1, you walk quietly and slowly like a man until you get to the first sign that a real deer was there. A track, a trail, a rub, some droppings, some browsed off brush, or a scrape. Remember it is daylight and the legal shooting hours have been open for more than 20 minutes. As soon as you find the first sign of deer, you have entered the home territory of a dominant whitetail buck. You will stop there for 30 seconds to one minute and prepare a dragline, and then you can start walking like a deer (if it is safe to do so). Walk in an arc toward the scrape and stay on the upwind side of it, walk in any loose cover that you can walk through. You do not want your jacket to catch on brush, but you do not want to display yourself out in the open either. Try not to enter the area the same way twice. Even if you just walk a few feet to one side of where you walked the day before, that is better than walking in the same exact tracks.

4. ***You leave the area and he thinks he missed you so he beds down close and waits to hear you walk in the next morning.*** Your odds of seeing the buck get better by the day. He is behaving nocturnally before he finds your scrape and each time he comes back to it he comes earlier and earlier because he believes the two deer were there a minute before him and that he was too late again. He will come in during daylight as soon as he is able to figure out that he will only be able to find the doe there then. Keep the faith and wait him out.

Chapter 19

Set Up Day

In order for my system to perform to its full potential it has to be set up, and hunted over the same way each time. The reason why the dominant buck is first to come in is because I give him 2 ½ days to find the set up and to take it over. The longest it has ever taken a dominant buck to find a D.I.E. scrape has been 3 ½ days. That means that the king will have found your set up and will be hunting you by the morning of Day 2 of your hunt, on every hunt. The waiting period of 2 ½ days is proven to make the D.I.E. system flawless for all those who have waited that amount of time, before returning to the area of the scrape to hunt it. For those who wait, 2 ½ days the first buck in has been the most dominant buck in the herd every time. That cannot be said for the hunters who crammed the set up and waited less than 2 ½ days, or did not wait at all. Those hunters see multiple deer in the area. I prefer to work with a flawless system so I am always rewarded for my patience. I will wait the 2 ½ days from set up to Day 1 of the hunt, every time I hunt with D.I.E., as long as I can coordinate the time to set up 2 ½ days in advance to my hunt.

Here are the set up rules to live by for 100% results with D.I.E.

1. Wait 2 ½ days after making the set up, before you come back to hunt.
2. Choose to set up at the stand site that you know is the furthest downwind of the two set up locations you scouted. That way if you are busted by the buck and you move to your secondary location for the rest of your hunt, the buck can make sense of the doe's move. Make sure it is off in a crosswind direction. It shows the dominant buck that the pair is moving away, and by moving crosswind, it brainwashes the buck to believe, that the doe and buck are not afraid of the human intruder that he busted during the day. The dominant buck will more than likely show up bright and early the next morning at your new stand site. Be ready for him.
3. Make sure there are large deer tracks on a trail that runs at a crosswind to the current wind direction.
4. Scout the property to know where the deer are bedding, where they are feeding, and where they find water. You can hunt near their water source but you should avoid hunting with D.I.E. near their bedding and feeding areas, because deer are at home there. You want to

pull the dominant buck from his bedroom and his living room or dining room out to his front yard or his side yard to your location. Then he will not know you are hunting him. Know which room in his house you are hunting. You want to stay out of his bedrooms (bedding areas), and the living room (food source), because deer congregate there. Hunt in a hallway leading into a room, not in the room itself. Deer always walk through doorways at the end of hallways. That means you should follow a deer trail from a food source, a water source or a bedding area, to where that trail enters into a different type of cover. Look for a place on the outside edge of the new cover to set up. That is where every D.I.E. hunter will have a dream hunt. Look for a heavily used deer trail, and stay upwind of it. Shoot downwind or crosswind toward the trail or toward the scrape. Whenever possible build the scrape on the upwind side of that trail.

5. Always place your tree stand upwind and crosswind of a core-doe bedding area, or a core-dominant buck bedding area, but never in one. Do not enter a swamp (where the dominant buck lives). If you cannot find a core-doe bedding area, just focus on choosing the tree that will provide you the most cover for your stand. Passing deer should not be aware of your presence.

6. Figure out where the buck will likely stage, and make sure you give him a staging area if it is at all possible. He will always come from downwind or crosswind so look for a stand site that offers staging cover downwind of your scrape.

7. Always face the scrape. That is his destination and he will be coming in to re-fresh it at least once a day after you arrive as the doe in estrus on Day 1. If your toes are facing the scrape then the buck will always be in front of you when he makes his final approach to the scrape.

8. Concentrate all the while you are in the stand and know that the buck will come in for sure (often between you and the scrape). He is on a mission and he has to show up in order to remain dominant.

9. Hunt on the edge of something. Whether it is a tree line, a drainage ditch, a creek, a field edge, a fence line, a clearing, or a thicket does not really matter, as long as your D.I.E. scrape is on the edge of something. You need to have the buck think that a doe in estrus could be bedded upwind of the scrape within 5, 6 or 7 yards. The wind is bound to change direction sometime over your four-day hunt, and when it does, it will switch to come out of a direction that is at least 90 degrees in another direction. You ideally want to have some staging cover at least 180 degrees around the D.I.E. scrape (on its upwind side). That makes the set up believable.

10. If you want monster buck potential you should scout for core-buck and core-doe bedding areas. If you find one or more on your parcel, situate your stand upwind and crosswind of all of them. You need to pull the buck out of his bed, or out of a core-doe bedding area, by way of scent dispersal at your scrape site. You do not want him to see your scrape from his current bedding area, or from any of his current breeding areas. Do not hunt within view of any real scrapes or real rubs if you can help it, and if you find any do not tamper with them. If your hunting land is riddled with rubs and scrapes and you need to set up within

view of a rub or a scrape you are going to have to stay super still in your stand, in order for the buck not to notice you there. The system is not 100% successful in bringing a buck in during daylight if you go to the buck's core-living areas and hunt him there. That is exactly what you are doing in a case like this one. It is your choice where you use it of course. I personally do not care to hunt a property if I cannot get at least 80 yards away from active buck sign. I have had past hunts where I set up right next to existing rubs and scrapes and the dominant buck would talk to the doe from his downwind staging cover but he would not come out. On each of those hunts the buck outsmarted me, because I took my D.I.E. scrape to him and set it up where he knew the best places to hide and watch it. He never had to come out, because he could see all around my scrape all day long. He waited until dark to come in and I had to figure a way to get out of my stand with a monster buck running back and forth under my stand all night. If you go to the buck, you are hunting traditionally. I do not hunt that way anymore. I scout further upwind and eventually I find an area that gives me the advantage over the buck. The biggest advantage I have is fact that he has to come to me because I am what he wants, (a doe in estrus looking for a mate) and I am not going to him. The dominant buck will approach the scrape and take it over if you make him travel 80 or more yards to get to your stand site. I concentrate on having 3 or more types of cover between my stand and the buck's bed. You cannot command him if you go to his front door and ring his doorbell. I like to honk the horn from across the street to get his attention.

11. Whenever possible install your stand upwind and crosswind of a core-buck or a core-doe bedding area, while trying to avoid the pecking order bucks. Never go straight upwind. If you do not have a bedding area on your parcel, then install your stand upwind or crosswind of a deer trail. Set up so you have a shot downwind and crosswind to the scrape and make sure there are no real scrapes within immediate view of your D.I.E. scrape. He will not come to your scrape if he can see it from one of his own scrapes.

12. Set your stand upwind and crosswind of your scrape and always at your most comfortable bow shooting distance, or 35 yards away (maximum) for gun and bow hunters alike.

13. You can face any direction in your stand except directly into the wind. If you do that, the buck will always be coming in behind you. I have not been busted in a tree since I started sitting in my stand with the wind hitting me in the back of my shooting shoulder. I always face my toes to the scrape. Check your 5-day forecast and set up for the expected wind direction on Day 1 of your hunt. Do not second-guess the wind. Set your stand up so you are facing the scrape, and make sure that the strongest wind current is hitting you in your shooting shoulder or in the middle of your back.

14. Your best shots are always at the scrape and downwind of it. To succeed 100% of the time I always sit facing downwind or crosswind to the scrape, where I can see it and shoot toward it comfortably. I am a right-handed shooter and I sit facing WSW when the wind is coming from the North. The wind would have to be from NNW for me to face south. A left-handed shooter should face SSE with a North wind, and face south with a NNE wind. If you do that then you will never have a bad shot-angle to the buck. He will always come in from downwind of the scrape.

Choose the best stand site and expect to be hunted there

Every DOMINANCE IS EVERYTHING set up consists of a tree stand being installed, and the D.I.E. scrape being constructed within 35 yards of it. Always start with your tree stand location. It is the most important thing to consider. Depending on how good you get at analyzing your area's herd, you may be able to set the system up and predict the bucks every move, as I am able to do. I know exactly where the buck will bed, where he will want to stage, and finally where he will go to scent check me before coming in within 35 yards. I have not been wrong since 2000.

The best advice I can give you on stand location is choose a spot where you are concealed and comfortable, where you cannot be positively identified as a human by a buck that looks up at you, and where your tree stand platform is above the buck's line of sight. That means your stand platform should be 10 to 20 feet off the ground. I do not advise anyone to go any higher than 20 feet up. Remember, never *skyline* yourself in your stand. Use common sense and sit in the *shadow line*. Try not to face directly into the sun, whether you wear glasses or not, facing the sun makes you squint and deer can see you in your tree stand whenever you move your head. Avoid making any unnecessary movements while you are in the stand. Remember you are always being watched.

Setting up the same way every time will bring you consistent results

Build the D.I.E. scrape up against cover with the pawed up dirt and the D.I.E. rub facing an opening 10 yards long or so. That way you do not have to trim any shooting lanes to be able to shoot to it. Make sure you can approach your stand from upwind and crosswind without having to cross deep water and without traipsing through thick patches of brush on the way in. Trimming a branch or a few limbs is ok, but do not clear the forest or move any dead logs from the area, on set up day. The time to do those things is in winter after your hunt when you have time to prepare for the next hunt. Choose a scrape location at a downwind and crosswind angle from your tree stand, and always point your toes toward the scrape as you sit in your tree stand. The buck will come from downwind or crosswind 100% of the time and he will always offer you a clear shot opportunity as long as you grunt to stop him when he is in the clearing. If you do not point your toes to the scrape you will have a difficult time seeing the buck if the wind reverses direction during your hunt. That will never be a problem for a D.I.E. hunter that faces the scrape.

Remember to make sure the wind hits you on the back of your right shoulder or in the center of your back for right-handed shooters, and on the back of your left shoulder or in the center of your back for left-handed shooters. Never clear shooting lanes out behind you when you are hunting with a bow. If you were gun hunting, it would not hurt to have a shot opportunity out of your tree stand on the upwind side, but I do not trim anything out behind me. That way I have good cover back there and I never am tempted to look back. The dominant buck will come in within 35 yards of you every time, so make sure that you can shoot downwind and crosswind of your stand up to 35 yards. Hunting in too thick of cover is a mistake you should avoid. Remind yourself that the king of deer is coming and he does not know you are there, so he would prefer to walk out in the open where he believes he is safe rather than walk into a trap in thick cover. Put yourself in his mindset and you will see how easy this is going to be for you. The buck will come to the scrape if you let him.

Position your scrape paralleling a heavily used deer trail

I like to position my scrape with the rub and the pawed up dirt facing my left or my right (crosswind) on the upwind side of a major deer trail with large deer tracks on it, preferably going in only one direction. I place the scrape 2 to 3 yards at the most away from the trail, always on the upwind side (toward me). Deer only travel directly into the wind when they are worried about something, if they are fleeing a bad situation, or if it happens to be a buck that is pursuing a doe in heat or in estrus. Otherwise, all deer walk at crosswind angles. Therefore, although it is not a 'Never Do' rule, and my system will work no matter where you put it, I will never place my D.I.E. set up next to a trail that is headed straight into the wind. Look for a heavily used deer trail. The leaves on it will look like crushed corn flakes or the dirt on it will be dug deep in the ground. If it is within 15 yards of water, the tracks will be fresh and the trail will be very defined and muddy. I love hunting in places like that. Tree lines on the edges of water crossings often offer perfect D.I.E. set up locations.

Install a D.I.E. scrape on the outside edge of cover

I place my stand only 10 to 20 yards from the scrape and I always place the scrape on the edge of something, usually on the edge of a terrain change, where semi-open cover transitions into thick cover. Thick cover is cover you can only see 10 to 20 yards into, that is thick enough to make a buck think that a doe in estrus could be bedded down in it within 5 to 7 yards behind the scrape.

When you build the D.I.E. scrape, you are constructing a man-made (mock) scrape, and you are pretending to be a "monster intruder breeder buck" that has come from over a mile away to take up residence at the very place you decided to rub the tree and build the scrape. I call the place where your tree stand and your D.I.E. scrape can both be seen at the same time your **'stand site'**.

The dominant buck will be aggressive and committed to coming in

Real intruder breeder bucks do not fear meeting the dominant buck, nor do they seek him out on purpose. They simply try to avoid him while they dart in and out of cover, seeking does in estrus. In real life, intruder bucks are able to accomplish their goals at least some of the time. They only want to breed with the doe and be gone. They rarely try to take over a dominant buck's territory. The D.I.E. scrape you are building is an exact replica of a dominant buck's (core) primary breeding scrape. Each herd only has one dominant buck at any one time, as you know. The dominant buck that will be hunting you is bedding downwind of his own primary breeding scrape and he is meeting does in estrus there, before he meets the likes of your D.I.E. scrape. Once he finds your scrape, he abandons his and moves into the area to command yours.

Concentrate on making him come over 100 yards to you if possible

If you did not know, a dominant buck cannot be in two places at once, he has to take over your D.I.E. scrape immediately in order to keep his hierarchy in place. Once he does that he goes back to what he was doing, which I assume was looking for a doe in estrus in his core breeding area, but he has to deal with the pressure of other breeder bucks swarming the area around your scrape. All mature bucks are drawn to the scent of a doe in heat because they all know she will be in estrus soon. Then she will allow whichever buck is with her at that time to breed with her for up to a day or a day and a half. Every buck wants to breed, and until now, the dominant buck was busy breeding in his own core breeding area.

The presence of a D.I.E. scrape inside his territory is a challenge and he will never walk away from a challenge from another buck. You need to be placing the set up out of view (upwind) of all buck breeding and bedding signs. That means you cannot put it where you see a scrape or a rub, or some beds, or heavy amounts of deer feces. Never bait with this system either. You want the buck to leave his normal living area and come to you upwind or crosswind at least one hundred yards away. If your property is small and you cannot move 100 yards from his sign, then go as far away from it as you can get. He will not take over a scrape that he can see from his normal bedding or breeding area, so know ahead of time that you will fail to make the buck come to you in daylight if you set it up too close to his active sign. Never hunt a property with D.I.E. that you cannot follow all the rules on. Never set D.I.E. up in a deer bedding, or breeding area, you will fail if you do. The system will perform and bring the most dominant buck in within 4 days but placing the scrape too close to his living space forces him to hide from the human who placed the tree stand. He will come at night only, because a human is near. When you install a tree stand near dominant buck habitat, he notices it immediately and he avoids you. By installing the stand out of his view 150 or more yards (preferably upwind and crosswind) of his living space, he will never notice the tree stand, because he is more interested in the D.I.E. scrape. He knows that no intruder buck would ever breed under a tree stand, and if you build it right next to him, he knows a human was there to put it in. Please use common sense and never take the D.I.E. system to the buck. Trust my advice. I invented this system and I know its boundaries. It is not capable of making a dominant buck into an idiot! He is smarter than both you and I. I really believe that. Hunt away from him and you will succeed. This is not anything like a traditional deer hunt. You will have no doubts with D.I.E. if you use it as directed.

He knows if he takes over the scrape and stands guard over the area (by bedding downwind of it for a few days), the intruder buck should stay away, or come in and fight, and business will be back to normal for him in a few days either way. What he does not know, is that the Scrape-Dripper is emitting the scent of multiple bucks and does into the dirt of the scrape and that it is only doing so during daylight. He soon finds out that the buck that made the scrape (identified by the scent of #307 lure) is not going anywhere. Since the dominant buck took over the scrape, and the intruder does not attempt to retake the rubbed tree, so the dominant buck is the commander of the scrape. We mess with his mind though by leaving the scent of the intruder buck (Trail's End #307) lingering in the area, because you placed a scent dispenser 5 yards behind the scrape on set up day, and you will not remove it until your hunt is complete. It will keep him guessing!

D.I.E. brainwashes the most dominant buck

The dominant buck is being brainwashed by the D.I.E. system to believe that deer that are not really there, truly are! He revisits the scrape two or three times a day in an attempt to get rid of the intruder buck that made it, that is the only way he can get the scent of the buck out of his territory. As long as the #307 is lingering in the area, the dominant buck is convinced his position at the top of the pecking order is at risk of being lost. He cannot have that happen, so he gives up on living (bedding) in his core bedding area for the night, and he moves temporarily into the area downwind or sometimes crosswind of your D.I.E. scrape the second night after he locates your scrape.

When he thinks the intruder buck is gone (on the third day after you made the scrape), the buck lets his guard down a bit and goes back to his core area, thinking he has won. The scent of the #307 around the scrape is very faint after three days, and the (invisible) intruder buck never showed up to fight the king when he was there (which is what would of happened if the situation was real), so the king thinks he is victorious. He usually leaves at first light on Day 1 of your hunt, and you arrive about one hour after he has gone. That is why most hunters using D.I.E. do not see the buck on Day 1. It takes him all day before he comes back to scent check the scrape in most cases. In less than 10 % of the cases, he is still there and you could possibly see him in the morning on Day 1.

Once the buck scent checks the scrape on Day 1 of your hunt, he will confirm that there is a single doe in estrus in the area and that she indeed visited your D.I.E. scrape, which became his core dominant buck breeding scrape the minute he took it over. All lesser bucks in the herd have steered clear of it since then, and the only threat the buck has at the scrape is the threat from intruder challenger bucks that visit it at random times at night and during the day. You can probably guess that the dominant buck has to move back to the area immediately so he can find the doe in estrus and breed with her before any other buck can. Therefore, he moves back in. Now you are in the tree, and depending on how good you are doing at staying motionless, scent free and quiet in your stand, the buck may or may not attempt to approach the scrape during daylight, that day.

Give him staging cover or he will be hesitant to come in

I told you the whole scenario so you would know that the buck that hunts you would come into and go out of the area as he pleases and that he wants to travel crosswind whenever he can. If you know where he is likely bedding before you set up, you can predict the path he might take when he is on his way to you. He is going to want to stage downwind of your scrape for at least 15 minutes before he makes his way in when he finally does come in, so be sure to leave him some light cover at least 50 to 100 yards downwind of your stand that he can stage in. If you have a water source nearby, it is a definite plus, so always look to sit near a water crossing if you have the option. Remember not to sit downwind of the deer trails. You need to sit upwind and crosswind of them. No matter what, do not sit downwind of a major deer trail. The dominant buck's normal travel patterns are to run on the downwind side of deer trails and to crisscross them at certain points. I want you to sit upwind of the deer trail so the buck can get wind of all of the scent at the scrape and around your D.I.E. set-up, including the scent of the lures you deposit along your trail on the way to and from your tree stand.

As I noted earlier in this chapter a dominant buck cannot be in two places at one time, but at this point in a D.I.E. set up I am sure he wishes he had a twin. His job being king of the herd requires that he stays within 200 yards of your D.I.E. scrape until he finds the doe in estrus and breeds with her, (that is as long as he is not currently tending a real doe in estrus) or as long as he has to in order to uphold his rank as king.

Because I am an expert at setting D.I.E. up, the bucks that hunt me have always bedded within 50 yards of my stand, but that may change someday due to my need to hunt different areas in the future.

He is aware of the constant real threat of intruder breeder bucks (monster or not) that are constantly on the move during the rut. They travel from place to place without regard for herd hierarchy, and they show no fear of getting beat in a head-to-head battle for the right to breed any doe in estrus that they encounter. The dominant buck that hunts you just wants to get this whole thing over with, and he is determined to do it before the doe goes out of estrus. Once four days in the tree passes, your hunt is over, if it had not ended already. No dominant buck will ever commit to finding a pair of invisible deer for more than 4 days in a row. He would rather revert to being a nighttime breeder, and if you miss your shot opportunity at him or if he busts you during the hunt that is what he will surely do.

Guess where he lives—do not attempt to go there

The dominant buck that manages your hunting property may or may not live (bed) there. Where he lives only matters to a D.I.E. hunter for one reason, we guess where he lives so that we know where he is coming from when he approaches our D.I.E. set up for the first time. If you always set it up (the same way) upwind and crosswind of the place that you guess the buck has his core bed, then you can judge the results of your hunts the way I have over the years. On your scouting trip you should try to find at least two of the three core doe bedding areas and the primary water source the deer use on your property or adjacent to it. I know that the most dominant buck's primary bed is always located downwind of every doe bedding area in his territory, and deer herd's main water source is either in the buck's bedding area or upwind and crosswind of it.

Draw it out and show all bedding and water sources—you'll find him that way

A dominant buck never wants to bed upwind of the place where his does are bedding. The dominant buck will bed downwind of all 3 core-doe bedding areas 99.99% of the time. That means that hunters who hunt with a predominant NW wind, can safely presume that the dominant buck is always bedding down south, southeast, or southwest of core-doe bedding, and either south, east, or west of his primary water source. As you know, the wind can switch to a different direction in very little time. That is why all deer have multiple bedding areas. They need to stay downwind of any expected danger, so they can identify it before it can threaten them.

> *The dominant buck will bed downwind of all 3 core-doe bedding areas 99.99% of the time.*

I know dominant bucks always have three or more core beds and each one is in a different type of terrain usually 300 to 500 yards or more apart. Does always have three core bedding areas, two will always be inside a dominant buck's territory, and usually the other one is on the fringe of two dominant bucks' territories, but he could have all three in his territory. Does can come and go throughout the year from herd to herd. Whitetail bucks do not gather does up in harems, as bull elk gather their cows during the rut. In the whitetail deer world, DOMINANCE IS EVERYTHING, no matter where a breeder buck is, he can breed with a doe in estrus as long as he is the most dominant buck in the area at that time.

Pecking order bucks are not of interest to a D.I.E. hunter

You may ask why I do not ever talk about the pecking order of bucks. I do not because they are not important when it comes to locating a place to set up the D.I.E. system. Pecking order bucks always bed out of sight of the dominant buck, and although they are free to walk through the area he is bedding in, they never have the right to remain there. Wherever the dominant buck lives, you can be assured there are no pecking order buck beds within 100 yards of it.

I believe that every dominant buck I have ever seen came from a bed that was located 100 yards or more away from all the other deer in the herd. I do not believe that any dominant buck will bed with a pecking order buck during the rut. In fact, I have only seen dominant bucks bedding with other deer after the rut was over, from the last week of January, all of February, and March. The only exception is if the buck is being pressured by hunters then he will bed with a swamp buck or a non-ranked monster buck. The dominant buck still beds off by himself but within view of the rest of the deer in his herd. When the dominant buck and the pecking order bucks do not have antlers (Jan, Feb, and Mar), they assemble in tighter groups and live through the winter months together. I only know this to be true in Wisconsin where I did my research. Because pecking order bucks are forced to stay away from the dominant buck during the rut, and because the dominant buck is drawn to protect the D.I.E. scrape, I never concern myself with the whereabouts of the pecking order bucks while I am hunting with my system.

If you give the system the 2 ½ days to set up (the Waiting Period), and you stay away from doe bedding areas and only hunt upwind and crosswind of them (like I do) then you will not likely see a pecking order buck on any of your hunts. Dominance of the scrape is determined before you even go to the stand on Day 1 of your hunt, when you allow the herd to have 2 ½ days to fight over it. I have never seen a pecking order buck within 100 yards of my D.I.E.

scrape while I was hunting over it, on hunts when I had waited the full 2 ½ days to hunt it. Just for the record, pecking order bucks bed in transition areas with deadfalls to break up their outlines and they bed 40 to 80 yards apart from each other. With D.I.E., you need to forget about the pecking order bucks and focus on scouting for the signs of the king of the herd. Then hunt as far upwind of his bedding area as you can without leaving his territory. Also, always shift your stand site off in a crosswind so you are not straight upwind of his bed. It will help you to know he is leery of any scent that is constantly blowing (drifting) into his bed. If possible, I want the scents of my D.I.E. set-up to be first detected by the king of the herd when he is walking between two doe bedding areas.

Always build the D.I.E. scrape in a place where there are no other buck rubs or scrapes within view of it. If you can see a real rub or scrape from your stand or from the ground under the stand, then do not set up there. If you do you will be taking the D.I.E. scrape to the buck's breeding area, and that is a big mistake for a D.I.E. hunter. You need to avoid making mistakes that will cause the buck to figure out you are a human. An intruder buck would never make a dominant buck primary breeding scrape in the same room of the dominant buck's house that the dominant buck is living in. When you find rubs and scrapes, move upwind at least 80 yards and crosswind at least 30 yards, and set up where there is not any active dominant buck sign. He has to leave his house to get to a D.I.E. scrape. If you do not move away from his sign, you are not asking him to come to you; instead, you are going to him. Traditional hunters have been going to the buck forever. D.I.E. hunters do not go to the buck! We make him come to us!

> *Traditional hunters have been going to the buck forever. D.I.E. hunters do not go to the buck! We make him come to us!*

Hang the Scrape-Dripper up above your head if possible and make sure you try to hang it from a branch that will allow it to get some sunlight. That way it will activate on a routine basis. The Scrape-Dripper is a tool that makes the dominant buck pattern the lure flow (in the scrape) until he is convinced that the invisible pair of breeding deer has been visiting the scrape every day, but just a bit earlier than he has been going there. It helps brainwash him to believe this breeding pair of deer have invaded his territory and they are continuing to meet daily at the scrape even though he has made his presence known there (by taking over the D.I.E. scrape). He is in command of the area the entire time he is hunting you, that I am certain of, and he will remain there looking for you as the doe in estrus and the intruder monster buck, as long as you do not ever go back to the scrape. Let him manage it. Stay away from it after you replace the Active Scrape lure with Scent Shield Still Steamin' Premium Hot Doe Estrus urine on Day 1 of your hunt. He will hunt for those two deer for up to 4 days straight. Part of the hunt is letting the buck take his territory back, and letting him command the D.I.E. scrape. If you fail to stay away, he will bust you and your hunt will be over immediately. So do not ever get out of your tree stand unless you shot the buck or it is the end of the day and you are going home. Never go back to the scrape. That is a big never. Leave the lure alone there and focus your hunt on the buck that is coming in, not on the Scrape-Dripper and what it is doing or is not doing.

The area leading up to the scrape (downwind of it) should be wide open for at least the first 10 yards, and the scrape should be set up against some cover that is thick enough to hide a bedded down deer, but not so thick a deer wouldn't walk into it. The buck comes in close when he is convinced the doe in estrus is at the scrape. Once he is close enough to see the rub on the tree, he knows that the doe is not in sight. He then looks over the area and calls out to her by making multiple tending grunts. He is expecting an answer from her. You are not a real doe in estrus on the ground, you are an invisible doe in estrus in a tree, so do not talk to the buck when he calls out for the doe. Otherwise, he will know you are a hunter in a tree, and you will be busted. At that point, your hunt will be over, and that buck will go back to breeding the real does in that area only at night.

It is a strict system but it gets results

My rules are strict because my system is a method, and the 100% results I have achieved come from following all the instructions on every hunt with D.I.E., not just following some of the rules. Stay focused on your purpose and wait the buck out when he gets vocal, then he will be oblivious to you being there as a human, and you will be hunted by the king of deer.

Once he is ticked off enough (usually within the first two days of finding the scrape), the dominant buck will visit the scrape during the heat of the day. It is usually in the morning just after sunrise on Day 2 or Day 3 of your hunt, and of course you are there as the doe in estrus to greet him. Believe me, this is the precise way I that developed D.I.E., it is a believable situation that most deer have seen before, that is why it makes the king of deer hunt the user of the system.

I teach you to build the scrape, and then I show you how to use the three lures methodically with my system. I then step it up a notch and I teach you how to act like a deer (on the ground) and how to be invisible to deer (in your tree stand). Then I show you the brilliant way I brainwash the most dominant buck with the scrape, the scent, and the timed use of the Scent Shield Still Steamin' Premium Hot Doe Estrus urine collected from one single doe, both at the scrape and being dragged in behind the hunter every morning. Dragging the Trail's End #307 out each day keeps the buck guessing where the intruder monster buck is all day, and it keeps the dominant buck bedded as you approach your tree stand. What more could any buck hunter want? I take it a step further, and tell you that you can make him respond to you if you know how to call or how to use a decoy and rattling antlers; all of which are not at all necessary for those of you who do not care to use them. Then the final stage of the hunt is finally here it is the time when the buck puts you to the tests. I showed you how to pass his scent check, his hearing test, and his viewing test, and the best way to do those things is to stay still and wait him out. Then the decisive moment is at your doorstep. The minute your herd's king approaches your stand site and makes his daylight attempt to come in and find the doe in estrus, he does so while you are there waiting for him. I never get used to that moment. It is truly amazing!

I believe this kind of hunting has been gifted to me by God, and each time I experience a monster buck hunting me I thank God for allowing me to learn what makes dominant bucks tick and how to get close to them. I believe in miracles, and many of the people I will teach my

DOMINANCE IS EVERYTHING system to, will surely believe in them too, once they see the amazing majestic behavior that the dominant buck displays as he makes his way into a D.I.E. set-up. There is only one word that I can use to describe the feeling I get when I see a dominant buck for the first time as he comes into my stand site looking for me (as an invisible pair of breeding deer), and that is "unbelievable".

The dominant buck is brainwashed from the minute he lays eyes on the D.I.E. scrape, which could be as early as set up day. He does not know that a human can make a dominant buck scrape, that a human can gather up doe in estrus urine and bottle it, or that a human can walk like a deer. He does not know these things because I never told him and I teach you to never tell him. Dominant bucks do know lot of things about traditional hunters but they know nothing about a hunter using DOMINANCE IS EVERYTHING. That is what gives my readers and me the advantage over the king of the whitetail herd. It is what sets my style of being hunted by the most dominant buck apart from the traditional style of hunting for mature bucks.

Hunting with D.I.E. vs. hunting without D.I.E. is like night and day, there is a drastic difference. The most dominant buck does not know you are hunting him, and he could not imagine that any deer is capable of outsmarting him and eluding him forever, that is, not until he meets a D.I.E. set-up. To him these invisible breeding deer are real and they are there. They walk in each day and they leave the area at night. They tell him they are there and then they disappear before his very eyes. How do they do it? He will never find out if you follow my instructions. He has never seen an invisible deer, and neither have I for that matter, but both he and I believe in them. He does not believe in miracles, but I certainly do! My question to you is, do you?

Do not think like a traditional hunter anymore—you are a D.I.E. hunter now!

Traditional hunters are human and they cannot help but display human characteristics that deer notice. They cannot change what is natural behavior to them without being trained to mimic the behavior of deer, and until they read my book they will never know how to be invisible to deer like you and I. They walk like humans, they talk like humans, they swim through cover like humans, and they think like humans. Once you become a seasoned D.I.E. hunter, your traditional hunting tactics will become a thing of the past. If you ever used a call, a decoy, or some rattling antlers, just for the heck of it, you will never do those things again. Am I alone here? I think every deer hunter has blown a deer call just to see what might happen. I ask my customers in my seminars and I have not met a person yet who has denied doing it. A D.I.E. hunter has a reason to talk to a deer and when he or she does, they know what they are saying and which deer is listening (that would be the most dominant buck).

Traditional hunters bait deer to get them to come in but that can only be a hit or miss proposition for the hunter. Bait is not powerful enough to sort the bucks out for a traditional hunter. Many of them use trail cameras because their friends tell them to or because they want to see what they are missing, and they do not know that the trail camera is forcing their biggest trophy buck to move away from their property, and telling him that a human is there and will be coming back. I am glad I never used a trail camera. I hunt the herd's king and he hunts me. I like it that way. I do not know why so many people think that using a trail camera helps them get a monster buck. In my world (the D.I.E. world), I know better. I have a system that has never failed anyone, and it forbids its users from placing trail cameras, because I formulated it without using trail cameras. It works exactly the same way every time you use it. There is really no need to look at photos of the bucks in the area to size up the herd before you hunt them. Just know this…whichever buck is king is the one that will be hunting you, and if he is overthrown then the victor will hunt you. All you need to do is stay away from the woods and not let the deer know you are coming before you get there. Follow my instructions and it will be easy for you.

Traditional hunters hope for a king—D.I.E. hunters will see one in < 4 days

Not all traditional hunters bait deer or use trail cameras, I am sure of that, but all traditional hunters are dreamers and they hope for success. D.I.E. hunters are being hunted by the king of deer, they do not hope, they expect it, and D.I.E. performs miracles for them. In my opinion, trail cameras are toys not tools. Pull your trail cameras now if you have any installed on your hunting property. Trust that what I teach you is entirely the truth and trust in the system. DOMINANCE IS EVERYTHING is a tool, and it never gets dull or worn out. It is a miracle system that I believe I am blessed to discover, and able to teach the world about. I do not believe it can ever fail.

Deer hunting cannot get any better for a D.I.E. hunter

I have not met a person yet who has given the D.I.E. system their all on a hunt and has not gotten 100% results from it. Everyone who harvested a buck using D.I.E. has claimed they followed my instructions to a tee, and they boast that they will never hunt for whitetail bucks any other way in the future. Some of them tell me they cannot wait for next hunting season, so they can hunt with D.I.E. again. I am sure you are going to love hunting with my system, because no dominant buck will ever have a clue that you are there, and no matter where in the world you decide to hunt whitetail deer, if there are deer in the area, then their king will come in looking for you. He will never know you are a human, a person with many skills. He will only see you as a tree branch or a bush, a part of his secret world. He will not be afraid of you, because to him you will not even exist.

That is what is so amazing about my inventing this system. When you hunt with D.I.E., you never interfere with the dominant buck's normal behavior. You leave the buck completely alone in his sanctuary (core bedding and breeding areas) so he can run his herd normally and he is not alerted to your human presence inside his territory. You can learn to predict the buck's actions from the minute he discovers the scrape, until the second you fire your shot or click the shutter on your hand-held camera. Dominant bucks always react the same way to a D.I.E. set-up, that's because they cannot see you, do not hear you make any human sounds, cannot smell you, and they have a never-ending desire to dominate every deer they come in contact with, in the rut and out of it. You can count on them to come in and try to find the doe in estrus if you can remain invisible to them.

Using a portable tree stand is the best bet

I used to set up the system in a different area every year, but I have recently learned that it will work in the same location year after year if that location still allows the hunter total concealment, and an open shot to the scrape. Ask yourself, "which tree gives me the most cover and the most protection from the wind, rain, and/or snow?" Once you have found a tree that offers you all those things, make the decision to hunt from it. It does not matter if you like to sit in a tree line, in a woodlot, in a pine plantation, or on the edge of a field. What does matter is that you always consider the wind direction when you are hunting, and use it to your advantage. A dominant buck will not approach you or your stand site from upwind. He will come in, either on a crosswind or from straight downwind. So make sure that when you set your stand up that you have a clear view downwind and at a crosswind to your scrape. If you are not sure of which direction the prevailing wind will be coming from on your hunt, just call the local TV station and ask the weatherman which direction the prevailing wind comes from in your area at that time of the year.

Where I hunt in Wisconsin, between October 16 and the end of December, the prevailing wind comes from the Northwest. It brings cold temperatures and lots of snow. As a Wisconsin hunter I appreciate having snow on the ground when I am deer hunting because it is easier for me to track the buck after I hit him. Snow also silences my approach to the stand, and the dominant buck's approach to me. I always sit still, face forward, and look for the deer by moving my eyes, and focus on not moving my head very much. There is never a need to look back for him. He will come in to the area right in front of me and all I have to do is wait there patiently for him to arrive. You should do the same.

If you currently hunt from a ground blind or from a tower stand, you may want to let a friend take over your ground blind or the tower stand this season. I have never hunted with my D.I.E. system from a ground blind or from a permanent stand, so I do not know if it will work from either of them 100% of the time.

The first time you hunt with it, make sure you do not change anything. Hunt from a portable tree stand that you place on set up day. The slightest change can ruin your chances of success. I cannot stress that enough. Follow my instructions and a dominant buck will come in every time. Change them even one bit and failure is a possibility.

You can choose where you hunt and where you will sit or stand to wait for him. If you see a mature deer track, then you know a deer was there recently and I assure you a mature breeder buck will be happy to visit that spot, especially if you are offering to set him up with a good looking blind date (with an invisible doe in estrus) when he gets there.

How a dominant buck will behave on his way to your stand site

A dominant buck prefers to have a lot of open space in front of him at all times during the rut. They will walk in posturing all the way, as they approach your D.I.E. scrape. They know the area better than you do, and they know what has changed since they were there last. If you cut out some brush a day or two before, they will take notice. They will stop on their approach to the scrape and analyze the situation. They need to give it a scent check before proceeding.

Give every buck that approaches your stand the time he needs to analyze your presence there before he comes in. He will likely be approaching from downwind or at a crosswind of you. He will come in deliberately showing off his rack and he will be looking for an intruder buck and a hot doe at the same time. Do not let yourself get over anxious, and do not ever turn around in your stand to see him. If you do, he will see you. His focus is on your stand location and on the scrape, which should be out in front of you. His goal is to make sure he is safe from predators before proceeding to the scrape. If he happens to cross your scent trail (that you made on your way in that day), he will scent check you and if you pass that test, he will proceed to come in. If you fail the test he will hold up in cover, or he will retreat to a downwind position. Sometimes he will follow you in and walk right underneath your tree stand (if you remain motionless and let him come in). Other times he will hold up in cover for 20 or 30 minutes without moving. You have to wait him out. If you wait, he will come.

If a buck is coming in and stops abruptly, stay still and wait him out. You need to outlast him. You must OVERCOME THE URGE and DO NOT LOOK anywhere but directly in front of you. If you give up and move at any time while he is near you, he can bust you. Tell yourself its mid-day and this dominant buck is coming in. Always assume it is the most dominant buck in the area. The smartest buck on the planet is what I think he is! He saw something that looked a bit different to him just before he stopped. Maybe he saw your tree steps or a ladder, maybe he smelled the doe in heat urine you put out, or maybe he smells a real doe that came through that area before you got there that morning. Whatever he saw, it did not scare him away. It just stopped his momentum. He is still overly anxious to meet the doe in estrus. Therefore, you need to stay still and not call, or rattle, or do anything at that point. If you make any sounds or movements, the buck will pinpoint your location and he will retreat.

If the sound of him walking has stopped and he is behind you, he will always be downwind or crosswind of you. You have to wait him out. You can do it. He does not have a clue that you are there! This is a DOMINANT BUCK and he is the king of all the deer in the area. He is not afraid of anything. Not predators, not people, and not any other deer either. All you have to do is sit still and be ready to draw back or raise your rifle when he gets under you or in front of you. Your best shooting lane is right in front of you and you know he is on a mission to approach the D.I.E. scrape.

By the time, you think of all that stuff, the buck will likely start walking again, heading in a beeline to your scrape. You will see his massive rack as he passes you by. Gun and bow hunters should behave the same, wait for him to get in front of you to take the shot, that way he has already looked over the area, and has ruled out the chance that a human is there. He just walked through there so he feels 100% safe. It is as if he is in his own bedroom now. If you jumped out of the tree, he probably would not run, because he would not know what you were. Do not jump out of the tree for me! You already passed the tests, he did not see you, smell you, or hear you, so you do not exist to him. You are not even there! The DOMINANCE IS EVERYTHING hunting system makes this all possible for you, and now you are in control of this hunt and the buck is at point blank range.

Remember to watch the buck that hunts you, when he is in front of you, and try to learn all you can from him. If he is behind you, just listen for him to move again, and do not turn around to check him out unless he is moving at the time. Once you see him, focus on how you will get your weapon ready without him seeing you or hearing you. Take a well thought out shot, and make it count.

Make sure there is always at least 15 yards of open space in front of you. Since you will always be facing the scrape head-on, with your toes pointed toward the rubbed tree that is behind the D.I.E. scrape, the area between you and the scrape should always be wide open. If it is not clear, either trim it out if you own the land, or move the set up to a better area that offers easier shooting if you don't. I learned this the hard way twice. You would be smart to take my advice and forget any thoughts that might cross your mind about the buck looking up and seeing you. Because you put this tree stand in on set-up day, the buck that dominates this area is already familiar with the changes you made to the area, and he could care less of what is going on in your tree stand. He only wants to meet and breed the doe in estrus.

When deer look, at you they only see the pattern (printed) on your clothing and they see it in black and white, and shades of grey. If you are camouflaged in a tree that allows your human shape to be covered up, deer cannot possibly identify you as a human, granted you do not make eye contact with the deer. He will see you as part of the tree. Whitetail deer are colorblind and even though you may know that, try looking at it from their perspective instead of just ignoring that fact. Your hunting buddy can see the colors you wear, but I believe a deer cannot. You may stand out to a hunter but not to a dominant buck, not if you are in camouflage from head to toe and sitting still as he approaches you. **DOMINANCE IS EVERYTHING** makes a buck look for a deer on the ground with four legs and a tail, he will not look up in a tree for anything. If he looks in a tree and you know you did not move do not worry, in 45 seconds or less he will look away and go about his business. Remember he would not stand still within 200 yards of a human if he knew one was there. You are invisible to him even if he is staring right at you.

The D.I.E. scrape has him brainwashed. It keeps his focus on the scent of the doe in estrus and the monster intruder buck upwind of his position. He is not looking for a hunter at all. He thinks you are a deer. Stay still and remember never to make deer sounds while you are in a tree, if there is a chance that any deer could be looking in your direction or if a deer is within 50 yards of you. The deer will pinpoint the location of the source of the sound and bust you—Being busted stinks!

It has happened to me many times while I was learning to master this system. You can overcome being busted, but sometimes it means hunting an area where the buck that busted you is not king. Keep focused while on your hunt because you may only get one chance at the dominant buck in your area. Keep that in mind when you start the hunt and do your best to be patient. You have to be more patient than the buck. Remember, he is the hunter on this hunt and you are the prize he is hunting for.

Nothing is more important than making sure that your view to the scrape is not obstructed by anything. It does not have to be completely open, but do not construct your D.I.E. scrape in heavy cover, or in an area where there is heavy cover between your stand and the scrape. That type of set up will spell disaster for you. If you cannot see the scrape from your stand, then you will not get a clean shot at the buck when he comes in to work it. Trust me that he will come in to it, even though you are there. If you stay still and control buck fever, you will be fine and he will be close enough for you to get an easy shot.

Always build the D.I.E. scrape on the edge of something. I wrote that enough times that you should be brainwashed by now if you read it aloud. Putting it on the edge of heavy cover is fine but then you should hunt it from an opposite angle so you are not sitting in the heavy cover. You should always face the scrape. I like to put my D.I.E. scrape on the edge of a heavily used deer trail, or at least within deer sight of that main trail. The normal view a deer has is from 2 to 5 feet off the ground.

Put yourself in the buck's shoes and crouch down while you are standing next to the heavily used deer trail. Then, look slightly downwind and crosswind 20 yards or so, to where you want to place your tree stand, if you can see the tree stand in your view then that will be a good place for the scrape. Next, go to the place your stand will be, and look back at the place you want to put the D.I.E. scrape. If it is open from you to the scrape, (I mean wide open) then you are in a good place. If the heavily used trail has tracks going only one way on it, then you are in a perfect position to control the dominant buck's behavior. I shot the 17-pointer on a one-way deer trail like this. I knew where he would be headed and where I could stop him with a grunt for an easy shot. It panned out the way I expected, and I got him. You have to be patient and have faith in the system, even if you miss the dominant buck, stay in your stand and wait for the next one to come in. You may even see the same one again, but you will likely have to be extra quiet and extra still to get the one you missed to come back.

If you find a one-way trail near a core buck breeding area, you just upped the odds of that dominant buck actually being a monster buck by 50%! Do not overlook hunting anywhere from 80 yards to 150 yards away from a core buck breeding or bedding area if you get the opportunity to do so. It may land you a monster buck!

Setting up the stand on set up day

Placing the tree stand in a good location is the most important step on set up day. You need to dress accordingly so you do not work up a sweat when you are putting in your tree stand. It is ok to sweat a little on set up day, but attempt to control the amount of human scent you let out in the area while you are there. Only put in one tree stand, I have only used portable stands so I recommend you use a portable stand that you never installed in that tree before. I have used belt-on, and chain-on style stands. You can use a climber or a ladder stand and expect success too. A belt-on or chain-on stand will not make any sound once it is installed, and not making any manmade sounds when climbing the tree is advantageous for a D.I.E. hunter. I recommend you use some screw in steps if possible for the first 6 feet and then use climbing sticks above that. Climbing up steps makes very little sound and I have found that the dominant buck cannot pinpoint my location, if I am quietly climbing my tree.

To have 100 % success with D.I.E. you should choose your tree stand location by following these guidelines:

1. Predominant wind direction to your back or hitting you in the back of your shooting shoulder.
2. Staging cover for the buck to hide in downwind or crosswind within 50–70 yards.
3. Preferably a water source within 100 to 200 yards.
4. A heavily used deer trail, downwind of your stand within view

Make sure to have enough cover upwind of your tree stand for you not to be seen by the buck as he approaches your stand from downwind.

It is very important that you plan the events of set up day. Start now by memorizing these three steps that will help you learn how to analyze the set up. Look at it from the buck's point of view. **Today is set up day and you want to accomplish the following 3 tasks:**

1. Go into the woods without calling attention to yourself. Not letting the public know you are there, and all the while not letting the deer know you will be back. Do not talk, urinate, spit, or cough near your stand. The dominant buck could be listening and you do not want him to hear you making any more human sounds than are necessary. If you need to trim branches out of your shooting lane, cut them off above the 6-foot mark, then they will be above the deer's line of sight. Setting up during daylight between 10 am and 2 pm is the best. Most deer are bedded at that time of day. Always hunt upwind or crosswind of a bedding area if you want a chance at a monster buck. Anywhere will do for the dominant buck, but monster bucks tend to stay close to their bedding areas for safety.
2. Position a tree stand so you have a good clear view inside 20 yards to a D.I.E. scrape which you will make today. If hunting with a gun, sit at a crosswind and walk in from upwind to your stand. Make sure you cut a shooting lane upwind of your stand, on your drag trail in. The buck will likely follow you in when he arrives, and you will be able to shoot him while he sneaks up on you if you are sitting at a crosswind angle. Bow hunters should leave their back trail as natural as possible, because he will likely notice your movement while you shift your body to look behind and he will bust you. I concentrate on looking at the scrape, and what is downwind of it. I know the dominant buck is coming and he always is focused on getting to the scrape so I face toward the scrape, at all times. If the buck follows me in, he will come to me first and then head to the scrape, giving me a quartering away or a broadside shot most of the time. Trim all brush out of your way and set up your safety strap today. Hang up a bow or gun holder on a heavy tree limb and lower the string that you will use to bring your weapon up in the tree, to the ground.

3. Climb up your tree and attach your safety harness to the tree trunk above you. Sit in the stand and shoot at a target in the scrape. Know how much your arrow lifts and how many inches you need to aim low to hit your target dead on. You will only get one chance at the buck in the scrape if you let him get to it. You are responsible for hitting your target. I am leaving that part up to you.

Equipment and things to remember when preparing to set up

On set up day, you are there to install your portable tree stand and construct a D.I.E. scrape no matter if you are hunting on public or private land. Public land hunters should remove their stand before going home if the law requires it. Once you install your tree stand in a tree that will keep you concealed at all times, and keep you dry in bad weather, you are ready to build your D.I.E. scrape. After you build a scrape before you dope it up as I instruct you to do, you should set up a target and take a few practice shots to your scrape (inside 35 yards) with your bow. Bow hunters need to make sure they compensate for arrow lift. Gun deer hunters, should never fire a gun anywhere near your set up location until you have the buck in your sights. You should practice shooting at a gun range.

Because the D.I.E. system is so versatile, a hunter can place his or her stand within 35 yards of any real deer sign, and it will work. Then you construct the D.I.E. scrape within 35 yards of your stand. The buck comes within 35 yards of your stand on a D.I.E. hunt. He is usually much closer than that to the scrape. If there are not any trees suitable to hold your tree stand, I recommend you hunt a different property with it. It is dangerous to hunt from the ground with my system. The buck is coming in looking for love, and you are invisible to him. I do not advise anyone to hunt from the ground with D.I.E. because you could get injured by the buck when he advances. Get up in an elevated tree stand where you are safe, wear a safety harness and stay alert. Make sure your body shape is never silhouetted in the sky while you are in your tree stand.

You can pick any tree for a stand but it should always offer you all these advantages:

1. **Use only one tree stand and install it on set up day, never earlier.** The element of surprise is lost if the buck you are seeking is already aware of your stand location. If you have permanent stands on your property, do not use them while hunting with D.I.E., you will be better off to install a hang-on stand in a new tree that overlooks a main trail. Make sure you are at least out of direct view of any permanent stands. You can hunt from permanent stands but I cannot verify if they will work every time or not? I have never hunted from them with my system.

2. **Your tree stand must have a clear view directly to your D.I.E. scrape.** If you cannot make a clean shot to the scrape, you may miss the one opportunity you are going to get to shoot the buck. His focus is always on the scrape or on the scent of the doe in estrus on your dragline that you took in if you used one in the morning. If that is the case, he will

follow you in or he will go to the scrape, it all depends on where he bedded down in the morning that day and whether or not he heard, you walk in "like a deer".

3. **The location of your D.I.E. scrape must be within 35 yards of you when you are in the stand.** Both gun and bow hunters should use this same rule. Bow hunters, if you place the scrape further away than 35 yards you risk the chance that the buck will approach it from the far side and never offer you a shot. Gun hunters, you risk the chance that you will not see the buck clearly through whatever cover is between you and him and that you might get a deflection when taking the shot. Nevertheless, to get the buck in close make the D.I.E. scrape as close to you as possible without giving your stand location away to any deer. Know the buck is staring at the scrape as you come in each morning and he is anxious to walk in if he sees a doe or if he smells a doe in estrus entering the area. If he only smells Trail's End #307, then he will not immediately follow, at least in my experience they have never followed me immediately. I think it has to do with the buck urine in it. Bucks will not rush in were another buck is without first doing a scent check to try to identify the buck. If he can positively identify the buck, then he knows if it is a buck under him in the pecking order or not. He is not threatened by a buck of lesser stature. Yes, dominant bucks are this smart. I have learned to respect them enormously.

4. **Your D.I.E. scrape should be located on the outside edge of something like a tree line, the edge of a woodlot, a logging road, a pine tree plantation, a thicket, a farm field, etc...** Do not put the D.I.E. scrape in the middle of a field or in the middle of the woods with no trails or changes in terrain. The buck needs to feel safe there, in order to approach your stand site (D.I.E. scrape and stand location) during broad daylight. When bucks proceed into a change of cover they do so walking or trotting, not running (unless they are threatened). You want the buck to walk or stand still. It is a lot easier to stop him when he is listening to his surroundings, as he would be if he was walking or trotting. When dominant bucks run, they are trying to get somewhere else fast, and they do not pay much attention to what is going on around them. You can move in your stand unseen by a running buck or trotting buck, but not one that is standing still, or walking.

5. **The tree must offer you a safe place to stay without the risk of falling out.** You do not have to go 20 feet high in your tree stand to get a chance at a monster buck. All you need to do is stay motionless while he approaches you, and let him walk in to you. I sit just as high as I need to in order to be sitting above any deer's line of sight. I do not prefer to sit on the top of any high hills, because I would be silhouetted there. Have a friend go with you on set up day, ask him or her to stand at the scrape and crouch down, and look at you with their head 4 to 5 feet off the ground. Ask them to ignore what you are wearing and any colored items you may have with you, and then tell you if your body can be seen as that of a human when you are sitting or standing up in your stand. If they think it is easy to make out your body shape then that is not a good choice for your stand location. No deer will be looking in the trees when you use D.I.E. if you have never hunted from this stand before. Once you take a buck from that stand, pull it out immediately or within 24 hours of the harvest date. Do not hunt in that stand until the following season, at the earliest. If any buck identifies you as a person while you are in your stand, you will know

because he will run away. If he is not running then he is not sure what you are yet, just stay still until he looks away before you move a muscle.

6. **It should be easy to climb to your platform and the tree should offer you a place to hang up your weapon and your gear.** Comfort is #1 in a tree stand you are going to be staying in all day. Always be sure you wear a safety harness and cinch it up snug so it will hold you if you were to lose your balance or fall out of the stand. Nobody wants that to happen but bad things can happen to good people. I never sit in a tree without a safety belt or harness attached to me securing me in my seat. Make sure the tree you decide to hunt in is big enough in diameter to hold you and that it is a live tree. If it has live leaves on it that would be a good sign that, it is alive. If you think, you are going to work up a sweat while you climb into your tree stand I would not sit there. The buck that is hunting you will smell you if you are perspiring a lot and you should try to avoid getting sweated up at all costs. Spray your skin and clothing often with SCENT-KILLER 99%.

7. **The stand has to be set up 2 ½ days before the Day 1 of the hunt.** You should always (100% of the time) install the stand at the same time you set up the scrape and trim your shooting lanes (on set-up day). Never hunt from an existing stand unless you do not want to rely on the outcome of the hunt. I have never hunted with DOMINANCE IS EVERYTHING from an existing stand, because I believe the dominant buck may live on the land I am hunting. If he does not bed there then he at least travels through there once every three days all year long. He has seen this stand and he knows humans made it and go into it. That is too much information for a dominant buck to have on my whereabouts already. He has to be convinced unmistakably that I am not there, that no person is there, I do not even want the thought to cross his mind that it is possible for a human to be there. Thus, my firm belief is that a D.I.E. hunter needs the element of surprise, and they should do whatever they can to be sure deer do not know they are coming or that they hunted from that tree before. You can hunt from permanent stands, but never make it a location where deer have seen you before. I have limited data on using D.I.E. with permanent stands. I can state the fact that no one has ever failed because of they got busted in a portable stand. If all you can do is hunt from a permanent stand then that is your call, but I would not count on the system working for you 100% of the time because you are not following the directions. The system has to be used the same way every time in order to get 100% positive results every time. Enough said. Public land hunters and climber tree stand users are ok to install the stand each day and remove it each night.

8. **If possible, there should be some available cover downwind of the D.I.E. scrape for the buck to bed down in.** It does not have to be downwind of the scrape but if it is then it will be a plus for you. Take into account the fact that dominant bucks always stage before heading out into open areas in early and late afternoon. The buck naturally wants to stage downwind of any area he is likely to be headed to for the early part of the night; that would normally be a feeding area, but now it is a breeding area (your D.I.E. scrape). Give him that consideration when choosing a stand site and you will see him approach you in the morning hours, most of the time. If you know there is available cover in the area you want to hunt, why not use it to your advantage. Nine times out of ten, the dominant buck will bed down in the cover that you have set aside and left unmolested for him.

9. **Always place your stand upwind and off to one side of the staging cover.** Your stand can be anywhere from 35 yards from the cover or up to 250 yards away from it, as long as the buck that is going to bed there will not be able to stand up and see clearly to the rub behind your D.I.E. scrape or to your tree stand. If he sees you, he will never come in, and if he can see the rub from his position, he will know that no deer could be there during the day. By walking "like a deer" when you are nearing the scrape on your way in, he hears you as a deer during the daylight so he will not be able to figure out it is a trap, even if he can see the scrape from his hiding place. Available cover means at least 5 square yards of tall grass or a thicket that would hide a bedded buck during the daylight.

10. **Pick your stand first and make it a comfortable place to stay all day.** On scouting day, you should locate one or more stand sites on the parcel. These places should be able to accommodate a tree stand. On set-up day, build a D.I.E. scrape 3 to 35 yards slightly upwind and mostly crosswind of your tree stand. There must be some cover downwind and on at least one crosswind side, for the buck to stage in. I prefer to set up on a heavily used deer trail because those trails are used all day long by deer, but it is just a personal choice. If you build a D.I.E. scrape on the upwind side of a deer trail the buck will walk the trail when he is near the scrape, and knowing that allows you to predict his movements in front of you while you are in the stand.

11. **Always start by finding a good stand site.** I look for buck sign like rubs, scrapes, and core beds first. If I find any of them, then a mature buck is in the area. Never hunt within view of a real buck rub, scrape or bedding area. Chart the deer trails and I note which way the trails are heading and at what time of day or night I think deer are traveling on them. Draw arrows on your sketchpad showing the direction of the trails. Make sure to label North, South, East, & West on your sketch. Then draw arrows showing the prevailing fall wind direction. Jot down where the wind is coming from that day. You never want to hunt closer than 80 yards to the upwind edge of bedding cover. You do not have to move 80 yards upwind of the bedding area, you could be 80 yards left or right of it and only 2 or 3 yards upwind of it. It is up to you.

12. **Mark the nearest water source on the map if you know where one is.** Know that the buck that hunts you is going to go downwind of your scrape to scent-check you every time before he will approach your stand site. Figure out where the nearest available cover is downwind of your probable stand and stay away from it. Do not ever walk through it. Just imagine if a buck were standing in it. Go to the upwind edge of it and think about this question. Would he be able to see a real doe if she was bedded within 5 to 7 yards upwind or crosswind of the scrape? If the answer is yes, that is *not* the best place for you to choose to set up. If the answer is no, then you are in a great spot for a close encounter with a dominant whitetail buck.

13. **It will not hurt to hunt there even if the buck could see the scrape from his bed, because the system will work no matter where you put it.** A dominant buck that can see the scrape from his daytime bed will not come in on his own without first hearing doe bleats or buck tending grunts, which make him believe the pair of deer are in the area around the scrape again. Rattling antlers will bring the dominant buck out of his bed to your location too, but do not let him see you or you will be busted. **Later on in Chapter**

24 – How to talk like a deer I teach you which sounds I make and I explain the calling sequences I use that always bring me success.

14. **Try to locate a heavily used deer trail that heads into thicker cover or follows the edge of thick cover.** If there is a main trail or two within 20 yards of you, that is good. I say 20 yards mainly because it is my easiest shot with a bow. If you are a better shot at a different distance like 10 yards or 30 yards, then use that as your guide, and expect the buck to travel the heavily used deer trail on his way into the scrape if his staging area is downwind of that trail. Set up with an easy shot to that trail and build the scrape just off to one side of the trail 3 to 6 feet from it. Make sure the back of the scrape has a 2 to 4" diameter tree that you can rub. Later in this chapter, you will learn how I build a D.I.E. Scrape.

15. **Dominant bucks stick tight to cover and if your D.I.E. scrape looks normal to them, you have better odds of seeing multiple mature bucks at the scrape.** Seeing the most dominant buck is a given, but seeing more than one mature buck at the scrape at one time is always just a chance. My archery hunt in Wisconsin in 2009 was the first time I ever saw three bucks come to the system, and they all were there in a 3-hour window. If you build the D.I.E. scrape where you find the most big buck tracks, where multiple bucks are splaying their front hooves, you are on the border of a territory. If you can hunt upwind of a trail full of tracks like that, you are inviting all mature bucks to meet the doe in estrus and they will come in at all hours of the day, especially if the scrape is built near water, and adjacent to a core bedding area. I seek those types of places out on the property I wish to hunt because I want a monster buck and I have seen monster bucks on 6 of my 11 hunts. All of those 6 bucks were 160-inch bucks or bigger and at least two of them, I am sure, were pushing over 200 inches. All of them came into an area where I sat in a tree outside a core dominant buck bedding area, on the outside of a cattail marsh, and each time the buck approached me walking in on wet ground. Most of the times when hunting, I could not see the buck until he was standing still straight downwind of me within 20 yards. These giant bucks just appear sometimes. It is amazing.

Some helpful hints to think about

No matter what weapon you are using, always make sure you do not build the scrape farther away from you than 35 yards. That way, the buck will always come in from downwind or crosswind of it and you will be able to shoot him at less than 35 yards. Building the scrape farther away than 35 yards of you takes the buck's focus off you, and you do not want that! You need his full attention while you are in your stand so he thinks a real doe in estrus is there and he makes a move to come in to meet her.

As a rule, I do not even turn my head around toward my back when I hear a deer approaching. Anytime I hear a deer approaching my stand from behind me, it has always continued on its path, whether it was under my tree or to the side of it, they all have walked out in front of me dead center. That deer has always turned out to be a dominant buck or an intruder buck (never a lesser buck, a doe, or a fawn). I have the utmost faith in my DOMINANCE IS EVERYTHING system and you should too. Count on the buck going downwind of you and the scrape before he comes in. Position yourself in your stand so your most comfortable shot is directly to the scrape. Do not move around when the buck is approaching unless he is running in or he cannot possibly see your movement. If a bird or squirrel sees your movement, it will sound an alarm to the buck, so watch all creatures around you and do not move if they are watching you. Your hunt will be over if the buck becomes afraid of your area or of you.

My favorite set up will work well for any D.I.E. hunter who hunts when there is a Wind from the North or Northwest. In a Northwest or a North wind, I always face toward a heavily used deer trail. I sit 10, 15, or 20 yards north of the main trail and then from there I go 5–10 yards east and place my stand. That way the D.I.E. scrape is always at a crosswind to me. In that instance, I am facing my tree stand platform toward the SW. The sun will not be in my eyes, the buck will bed down to the NE, E, or SE, and he will never see me when I go to the stand during the hunt. The series of photos that you see here show you what an ultimate set up should look like.

Always walk into your stand site from upwind or crosswind of it, and always keep your eyes open for the buck. Do not walk into the wind when you use D.I.E. (NEVER). With DOMINANCE IS EVERYTHING you have to believe the buck is downwind of the stand but bedded down close enough to the D.I.E. scrape that he will smell the urine when it starts dripping around 8 o'clock a.m. Central Time.

Note: If you came in with the wind in your face, you would alert the buck to your presence and he would likely evade you, because he is on alert to anything in the area that is coming from the downwind side. He will expect you to be a buck and he will watch your every move. Traditional hunters methodically enter their hunting area from downwind, and nearly all of them get busted by the dominant buck on their way in.

You should never walk into the wind with the wind in your face on a D.I.E. hunt. You are a deer and deer only go into the wind when they are afraid or pursuing something. You are neither so do not walk into the wind on a D.I.E. hunt. You can do it when you scout and you should do it then so any deer you jump will be jumping out of their beds and you can document which way they run from you. They run to one of their other two bedding areas, so that is the easiest way to find all three core doe bedding areas, but never walk into the wind on a D.I.E. hunt because the buck is bedded downwind of you and he will bust you as a human.

When you come in from upwind, he cannot smell you (as a human) because you are scent free. He cannot see you because he is downwind of you and he will be watching downwind until he hears you walking like a deer, and by then you are at the stand site. You are invisible so you could walk in from either crosswind without being busted.

Remember when I said dominant bucks travel either crosswind or into the wind? Well with me sitting crosswind of the stand at less than 20 yards, I have a one in three chance he will want to walk in from behind me, and I prefer it, because I use a dragline on the way in. I dope it up with doe in estrus urine, and no buck can ignore that. When he winds me, he follows me in like a lost puppy that sees his master.

In this set up you, want there to be some type of bedding area downwind or crosswind of the scrape even if it is more than ¼ mile away. It is a flawless set up because a dominant buck's travel pattern is very predictable. He will always approach the scrape from the S, SE, SW, or NE. You are 20 yards north of the actual deer trail and his focus is on your D.I.E. scrape as soon as he can see clearly to it. Before he can see the scrape, his focus is solely on the area under your tree stand, because he heard you walk in (like a deer), and he is looking for that deer. If he is looking in your direction, assume he is searching for the doe in estrus (you). If he stands back in the brush, and rakes brush, then he thinks you are the intruder buck.

Photographers should set up according to the hand they use to click the shutter. If you are right-handed then set up whenever possible with **Figure 18, page 263 Chapter 18**. If you are left-handed use **Figure 19, page 264 Chapter 18**. When you set up with the wind hitting you on the back corner of your shooting shoulder and the buck comes in while you are sitting in your stand, you will have a clear shot at him, without ever having to stand up. You can stand up if you want to but you will not have to. He will come in from downwind or he will follow your trail in (at a crosswind). He does not have any other options. A dominant buck will never approach a 'hot' scrape from upwind.

Either way he will think he is alone because he will not see you or your tree stand directly in front of him as he makes his way in. Your tree stand platform will be positioned above his line of sight off to his right or left (upwind of him), when he is entering the area, and eventually (if you let him go to the scrape) he will be upwind of you. If he is upwind of you (looking upwind for the doe in estrus), you can take aim without being noticed, as often as you would be, if he was downwind of you looking upwind.

When you are a D.I.E. hunter sitting within 35 yards of a D.I.E. scrape you are invisible to the whole herd. Out of sight is out of mind to an incoming deer. The dominant buck is on a mission, he wants to get close to your scrape so he can look for the bedded doe in estrus that he believes is bedded in cover upwind or crosswind just a few yards away from the scrape.

The buck may see your ladder or your tree steps but those things will not bother him. He sees those types of things everyday (in his line of sight). The tree stand platform and the movement that deer can see on the platform is what deer worried. Keep your tree stand platform above the deer's line of site and you can sit in it and not be noticed by any deer, there is no need to hunt from 30 or 40 feet up. Deer hunting is not supposed to be life threatening! Dominant bucks do not look for humans near their core breeding scrapes. They only build these types of scrapes in areas that humans are never seen. Most people have never seen a scrape made like the D.I.E. scrape (a dominant buck's core breeding scrape), because most people never knew where to look to find one.

The biggest advantage for you setting up like this is that you never need to adjust your stand position. The buck is hunting the two deer at the D.I.E. scrape. He is not interested in hunting humans, he cannot smell a human, hear a human, or see a human, so a human is the furthest thing from his mind when he enters the area.

The wind can shift up to 90-degrees to your left or to your right, in a matter of hours and setting up this way guarantees that you never have to adjust your position in the stand. The buck is coming directly to the scrape, or first to your stand and then to the scrape. Keep focused on the scrape with your toes pointing toward it and you will love the results of your hunt. How you set up, has everything to do with how safe the buck will feel when he gets there!

Equipment you will need to construct a D.I.E. scrape and to set up your tree stand on set up day:

1. **A portable tree stand** – It is very important not to place your tree stand in the woods until set up day, and then always install your stand before making the D.I.E. scrape and rub.

2. **Tree steps, a ladder, or strap on climbing sticks** – Self-explanatory

3. **A safety harness to attach in your tree stand** – Sit in your tree stand and set the height of your safety harness so you cannot fall out if you lean too far forward. Then, when you get down out of the stand, leave the top part attached to the tree. I wear my safety harness over my bibs but under my parka, and I have it on when I get to my land. If you do what I do, when you get up to the stand, all you do is attach the part hanging down from above you in the tree to its counterpart near your neck line, and you are all set to hunt without making a whole lot of noise in the tree when you get there. You are hunting at your own risk, so always be safe and control your movements while in the stand.

4. **A tool belt, a backpack, or a fanny pack** – Carry your Scrape-Dripper the Active-Scrape, and the Trail's End #307 lure bottles in a safe manner where they cannot be banged together or broken on the way to your stand. Never open any lure in the woods while you are setting the system up, unless you are standing right over the scrape. You only want scent originating from the scrape on set up day. Do not drag scent of any type in with you on set up day. You want to be a human on set up day, not a deer.

5. **Three Seal-Tite scent dispensers washed clean and scent free with new cotton in each of them** – No scent dispensers go up in the tree with you on set-up day. You should pour 3 or 4 drops of Trail's End #307 in 3 separate scent dispensers and place them in a triangular fashion around the scrape. One on each side of the rubbed tree 4 feet away and the third one 5 yards behind the scrape at *hand height*.

6. **A heavy carpenter's hammer, a tire iron, or a nail puller or a toothed saw** – I use a 22 oz. carpenter's hammer or a toothed saw to make the rub behind the scrape. I never use an antler. I want it to look nasty, not clean. I want the dominant buck to be puzzled when he finds it, not expect it. A hammer claw does a good job on a tree.

7. **A friend or significant other for safety and for help with the set up** – Make sure your friend is scent free and does not yell out in the woods. You can talk on set-up day but keep your voices down. On set up day, you should behave as a human. There is good reason why you should not act like a deer. Because he will come to you if you act like a deer, but he will stay away and out of eyesight of you if you are a human, because you are a potential danger to him. Always know a dominant buck is watching you when you are in your hunting land. If he is not physically, there at that moment it does not mean he cannot figure you out. He will come in as soon as you leave and he will try to figure out what

went down there while he was away. Keep that in your mind all the time on set-up day. Be quick about it! Get the stand set up first, then build the D.I.E. scrape, and finally practice a few bowshots to the trail or to the scrape, right out of your stand. If you encounter a deer or two when you get to the area, that is ok, just make sure you ignore them and do not look at them. They will go away and when they do, you can commence in setting up the system. Never hunt from the stand on set up day for any reason. Get out and let the system work for you. Go home and watch the weather, know where the wind will be coming from on Day 1 of your hunt and plan your approach to your scrape that morning. Do not go out to your stand before you are hunting it on Day 1—not for any reason.

8. **A handsaw and a knife** – When you are in your stand looking to the scrape, you should be able to shoot unobstructed directly to it. If you cannot, then you need to trim a shooting lane. If you own the land or have permission to hunt there then you can clear a lane with the owner's permission. Only cut the stuff in your way, and only cut the overhanging parts of vines off. If you cut the base of a vine and pull it out of a tree the buck will notice that and he may figure out a human was there. You could be busted before you even start hunting the stand. If you are hunting on public land, you cannot cut down brush and trees legally, so you will have to take other measures to get clear shooting. I recommend you hunt in a tree that offers you a backdrop to your upwind side. A dominant buck will never approach from upwind of you, so you do not have to worry if deer can see you from upwind of your stand. Make sure you only hunt as high as needed to get out of the eyesight of oncoming deer. Hunt near a main deer trail and never right above one. Stay 10 yards or more away from the trail and place your tree stand upwind of it. I know this is opposite of how you used to hunt, but that is why it works. With DOMINANCE IS EVERYTHING, you want a deer to smell you and to hear you but not to see you, but if he does see you he still will not know, you are a human so it is all good! Everyone I know has been taught to walk into the wind to approach deer but that is bad advice when we are talking about sneaking up on a monster buck. He is looking downwind while he is bedded, so if you approach from there, you will jump him up all of a sudden or he will see you and slip away in heavy cover. With my system, you always approach your stand site from upwind or crosswind because the buck will not be there. It gives you an opportunity to get to your stand without alerting him to your presence as a human. He will become alerted to the presence of the invisible pair of deer when the Scrape-Dripper starts dripping each day. That is usually 1–2 hours after sunrise.

9. **One empty Scrape-Dripper either new or cleaned out and human scent free** – Just make sure you have both parts to it—the bottle and the nozzle. Sometimes the nozzle will loosen up and fall off if you are hand carrying it to your stand. So be prepared and put it in a plastic zipper bag with the Active Scrape lure and the #307 lure. You only need one Scrape-Dripper for a normal hunt. If you are busted by the buck, you can use two Scrape-Drippers to get the buck to follow you to a new location. I found that worked on my bow hunt in 2009 after the dominant 10-pointer busted me in my stand on Day 2, I moved and built a double scrape set up on Day 3 and the 10-pointer walked right under my tree stand the next morning on his way to meet me. I was trying out two drippers for the first time. They worked well together but I do not know enough about using two

drippers to promote you to use them full time yet. I tried something new, and it worked. Using two drippers can keep the buck's interest elevated. I recommend this for gun season or to use if you are cramming the system. Cramming the system is using it as directed except, instead of waiting 2 ½ days to hunt, you only wait 1 ½ days or only ½ day before hunting over the scrape. When a D.I.E. hunter crams the system with a 1 ½ day waiting period it still brings in the most dominant buck within four consecutive days, but he is not always the first buck to come in. With a 2 ½ day waiting period the dominant buck is always the first buck to come in, and with only a ½-day wait, the system is not 100% for the dominant buck at all. It has been only 33% successful for me with a ½-day wait. I use it for gun season that way. I advise you to use only one dripper when you set the D.I.E. scrape up. I prefer only to use one and I have had a dominant buck hunt me each time I used the system. I only tried two Scrape-Drippers on one occasion and it worked, but on that occasion, I moved my stand because the buck busted me. It pulled him into the new area the next morning. It was incredible! Using two Scrape-Drippers will be ok as long as they are within 3 yards of one another, each on their own scrape. One is filled ¾ with Active Scrape lure and the other with ½ bottle of the Still Steamin' Premium Hot Doe Estrus urine.

10. **Camouflage clothing, a hat, and gloves (no facemask required on set-up day)** – Dress light because you are bound to break a sweat on set up day. <u>Always wear gloves and always wear some sort of head covering</u>. If you are sweating, then wipe your sweat with a handkerchief and put it in your pocket.

11. **(Optional) a digital hand held camera is nice to have** – I like to take pictures of my view from my stand and the view to my stand from the scrape. I started this habit in 2009 when I was hunting the same tree I had hunted a couple years before. You should become familiar with your surroundings and figure out where a buck can approach you from, before the time comes that he makes his appearance at the D.I.E. scrape. Do not use trail cameras to monitor deer when you want to hunt with D.I.E. on your property. However, having a digital camera in your backpack is ok. Do not take pictures with sound or flash activated on your camera after set up day. The buck is watching your area and listening for signs of danger. The sound of a camera shutter is a sound of danger, as is a cell phone ringing or vibrating. Silence your cell phone before going in the woods.

12. **A spray bottle of scent-killer 99%** – Spray Scent-Killer 99% on everything you or your friend touches.

13. **Montana brand doe decoy** – Before you build the scrape, set the decoy (without any stakes) in a bedded-down position within 5 yards behind the rubbed tree. The decoy should be in the brush upwind or crosswind of the scrape. You have to make sure that when the dominant buck is in the staging cover nearest to the scrape, he could not possibly see if a doe was bedded down behind the scrape. I use a Montana doe decoy because it works well and if I need one to get the buck to come in on Day 3 or Day 4, I have one that I know works. To check, walk downwind to the nearest available cover, squat down to about 3 feet off the ground (a bedded-down buck's approximate vision height), and face the scrape. If you can see more than an ear of the doe decoy, do not build the scrape there. In order for the dominant buck to come in within 35 yards of you every time, you need to

make sure that the scrape is within 35 yards of your tree stand and that the cover is thick enough behind the scrape to hide a real doe that is bedded down. You want the buck to have to stand up in the nearest available cover downwind of the scrape to see the rubbed tree. He will stand up every couple of hours while he is hunting you. He does that so he can view the scrape and the rub and so he can conduct a scent check of the area. He is waiting for two deer to arrive there. If a real deer is visiting the scrape, the dominant buck will not be able to see the rub; the deer would block it. That prompts him to do a scent check and come in. Warning: Never get out of your tree during your hunt and approach your scrape. If you do, the dominant buck will stand up and stare at you, thinking you are the doe visiting the scrape, and you will be busted. If you remain in your tree and trust that D.I.E. has brainwashed him to believe the deer were there when he was not looking, he will come in that day or the next as soon as he knows it is safe.

14. **Your bow and a target** – Take a broad-head target out to your stand with you and take your bow. Shoot two or three arrows into the target at your scrape before you leave the set up.

15. **The 1 oz. bottle of Trail's End #307 lure and the 4 oz. bottle of Active-Scrape** – You need these two bottles of lure for the initial set up of the D.I.E. scrape. Remember to throw away the packaging and the book that comes with the scrape dripper and the Active-Scrape. D.I.E. hunters use these products differently than the manufacturer recommends. Always do what I teach you to do with the D.I.E. lures in order to have the D.I.E. story make sense to the entire herd.

Scrape-Drippers made by Wildlife Research Center Inc. are great for D.I.E. hunters

I purchased a Scrape-Dripper made by Wildlife Research Center Inc. The first time I implemented using it over a D.I.E. scrape, I constructed it next to a main trail in my hunting area in 1998, and it made the bucks in my area visit my stand site during daylight. The Scrape-Dripper has the power to transform nocturnally acting bucks into daytime breeders in as little as two days, if you hang one over a D.I.E. scrape, and pour in 3 ounces of Active Scrape lure, which is also made by Wildlife Research Center Inc.. Do not forget to purge it the way I teach you. That makes it drip right away. All the breeder bucks in the area take notice of it and attempt to search for the does in heat around the D.I.E. scrape. From the minute you leave the area on set-up day until you return the morning of Day 1 (of your hunt), the D.I.E. scrape is working toward firing up all the area bucks for you. This Ultimate Scrape-Dripper is a miracle product in my opinion.

It is part of my DOMINANCE IS EVERYTHING system, but it is only a part of it. It is one of the tools I use to make the most dominant buck in the area aware that an intruder buck has infiltrated his territory boundary, and is setting up shop there. When you arrive at the scrape on Day 1 of your hunt you are bringing in Still Steamin' Premium Hot Doe Estrus urine, and you are replacing the Active Scrape lure in the Scrape-Dripper with the Still Steamin' Premium Hot Doe Estrus urine. Now your hunt begins! Every living breeding buck in the area will now try to visit your D.I.E. scrape and will run through the area searching for the invisible doe in estrus. From that moment forward, the dominant buck will be hunting you.

Do not use drippers as the manufacturer suggests—listen to my advice to succeed on a D.I.E. hunt

I do not use the Scrape-Dripper as directed. I modify the way I use it. I purge the Scrape-Dripper when I am ready to leave the scrape, so it starts dripping immediately, that way it will be completely empty in 2 to 3 days. I would say any buck hunter who has never used a Scrape-Dripper over a D.I.E. scrape is missing out. You absolutely need one of these products on every hunt you have with my D.I.E. system. In bow season 2009, I used two!

What it **cannot** accomplish is making the most dominant buck hunt for you. You need to accomplish that task on your own by reading this book and understanding your part in this hunt with my DOMINANCE IS EVERYTHING system.

Dominant bucks are territorial deer that will not tolerate intruder bucks of any age making territorial breeding scrapes inside their territory, or attempting to breed with does in estrus inside their territorial boundaries. Every subordinate buck in the herd will chase a doe in heat, but they do not all get to breed with does in estrus. Dominant bucks, monster bucks, and swamp bucks, are the primary breeders in the herd, and chasing is not breeding. When a doe is in heat, she does not allow any buck to breed her. Dominant bucks, monster bucks, and swamp bucks have been around a few more years than the pecking order bucks and they know it is not safe to chase a doe in heat out of cover in daylight during the rut. They will not waste their time chasing does in heat. Once a doe is in estrus it is another story. A doe goes into estrus at the end of her (4-day heat/estrus cycle), and all bucks go crazy for her. Every buck in the herd will pursue a doe in estrus. It is as if they are mesmerized by her beauty. They stand behind the doe and stare off into space. It is uncanny. I believe I can make any buck that catches the scent of the doe in estrus follow me just by dragging Still Steamin' Premium Hot Doe Estrus urine in behind me each day. I have not seen a mature buck yet that can cross my drag trail and keep on going, every buck that cuts my scent trail follows it to my stand. This is pure doe estrus urine, and nothing is more intoxicating to a mature breeder buck than this stuff. They believe there is a doe in estrus ahead and they want her bad! Little do they know it is me, and that I am in a tree watching them approach—surprise!

Again, it is just my theory that a doe's heat and estrus cycle is only 3 ½ to 4 days long. I came up with my theory by seeing how the bucks reacted to my D.I.E. system when I was hunting them. I have seen it happen 11 times in a row now. I can control the dominant buck when I am in the woods as the doe in estrus. I can call him and he will come to see me, but I cannot pull him in on command when just the Active Scrape lure is in the Scrape-Dripper, even with Trail's End #307!

Having Active Scrape lure in the dripper tells all the bucks that there are does is in heat visiting the scrape. The dominant buck is leery of going out in the open during daylight, and he will never chase a doe in heat. He is holding out for one of those does to go into estrus. I am going to be his next date, but before I show up as a deer, I set up as a successful D.I.E. hunter. I always build my scrape in a clearing, so the buck will always offer me a wide open shot opportunity, and I know the dominant buck and monster bucks are fighting each night for the right to dominate a doe in estrus. They think they hit the jackpot when they get a whiff of my D.I.E. scrape on Day 1! The dominant buck will go anywhere he has to in order to breed a doe in estrus, and he does not wait a second longer than he has to, to make sure it is safe where he is going. He has better things to do that waste time with a doe in heat that he cannot see. The D.I.E. scrape and D.I.E. rub are the most powerful tools a deer hunter can have, they are almost as powerful as loaded weapons, but the D.I.E. scrape, the D.I.E. rub and the D.I.E. system are not weapons they are tools, heck they are the whole dang toolbox! Anyone can succeed with my system. It is a great system that brings the king of deer to anyone who follows the instructions. It is going to come in handy for hunters who want to hunt in multiple states each year, especially when you hunt land that is unfamiliar to you, like public land.

A D.I.E. scrape is owned by the buck that made it (invisible intruder buck-you), until it is taken over by the real live dominant buck in the area. You can be assured he will take it over if you build it away from his normal breeding and bedding areas. Because the Scrape-Dripper is dripping Active Scrape for nearly 3 days straight, and it only drips during daylight (from 8 a.m. until 3 p.m. at my D.I.E. scrape), the first mature intruder buck that finds it will work it up and take it over. Then other intruder bucks will fight for the right to breed the does that they believe are in heat and are visiting the scrape. As the dominant buck makes his rounds of his territory boundaries (once every three days), he will find the D.I.E. scrape and he will work it up and take it over. Sometimes he will make his own scrape right next to it, or he will destroy the overhanging licking branch you had above the D.I.E. scrape, if he is furious!

If you were to set up on an existing scrape, you would not be able to get the upper hand on a buck and make him hunt you. The main reason is the dominant buck makes his scrapes in areas where he can bed down and watch them from the safety of his staging cover. All existing real scrapes that I have found have had some staging cover downwind or crosswind that offered the dominant buck a view of the rubbed tree (behind the scrape). The staging cover has to be thick enough to hold the buck when he is bedded, and open enough that the buck can pass through it on his way to the scrape, when he decides to come to it. That is what staging cover is. It is a safe place for the dominant buck to stage until it is safe to travel out in the open. He will stage when a doe in estrus is at his scrape if it is daylight at the time. If you find a real scrape, analyze it and figure out where the buck that made it will be staging at that very moment. Set up D.I.E. upwind 150 or more yards and crosswind 30 or more yards from the nearest scrape, for success.

You cannot use one of the buck's existing scrapes, if you do, when the buck beds downwind of it, he will be in a safe place where you cannot see clearly to get a good shot at him, and he will be watching you mess with his scrape. It is like you watching a person plant a bomb under your car, then you see them go hide in the bushes waiting for you to go for a drive. Really, that is why you do not get good results when you mess with setting my system up on or near a real buck scrape. You get the same result you get when you plant a trail camera in the woods, and then try to hunt near it. The dominant buck knows that camera is a human object and if he stays where human, scent is that, his life is in danger. He will avoid it for as long as it is there.

With the D.I.E. system, you have to keep him guessing. First, you scout and locate an area for your set up. You want to shoot to a main trail or to a clearing, and you want to be hidden in your tree stand 10 to 15 feet off the ground. I prefer to put the scrape in front of my toes as I sit in the stand. You have to know what the prevailing wind direction is before setting up. Find a transitional area or a creek crossing, and make your D.I.E. scrape within 20 yards of you. I like to make it 5 or 10 yards away from me. As long as no deer can see you in the tree, you can build the set-up anywhere and the buck will come. Which particular tree does not matter, what matters most is that you are alone there and that your hunt cannot be interfered with. Then find some staging cover if you can. The buck will want to stage crosswind or downwind of the scrape 50–70 yards away. Make sure he cannot see your scrape or the rub behind it from the staging cover. Picture a doe decoy at the scrape and look around to make sure he cannot see any deer at the scrape if he is further than 35 yards away from it. That assures you he will come in close to investigate the scrape each day. It is very important that you do not set the D.I.E. scrape up on top of a real scrape. Pick a new tree to rub and make a scrape under it, in a place where there has never been a scrape or a tree rub before. If you can see a real rub or scrape you should not hunt there. You need to go upwind or crosswind of that area and pull the buck to you. He will come in close if you make him explore the area. Do not sit in real thick terrain. The buck will not come into thick brush to work a scrape during the day. He will not be safe there. Once your second hunt with D.I.E. on this property comes along, you can hunt the same stand and use the same scrape, as long as you were not busted there before. Once you are busted somewhere, be sure you never hunt in that spot again.

In real life when a dominant buck finds a scrape (one that he did not make) in his territory, his first instinct is to take the location back. He works the scrape and makes it his own. He then stakes it out waiting for the next buck that comes along to attempt to work it up. That buck usually is the one that originally made it, and the dominant buck knows that so he hangs around the area (within a ½ mile of it is my guess) so he can scent check this particular scrape again 12 to 24 hours after he first took it over. If no intruder buck challenges the dominant buck at that scrape in a day or so, then the land under the scrape is the property of the dominant buck again. However, if an intruder breeder buck works up the scrape after the dominant buck took it over, that means trouble with a capital T for the dominant buck. Then he has a territory dispute he has to settle. Whenever the dominant buck is threatened by an intruder buck, the dominant buck will hold his ground and wait for the intruder buck at the scrape. Count on the dominant buck bedding down on the downwind side of the scrape and coming in to freshen it on a daily basis until he feels the doe would be out of estrus. That means, hunt until you see the buck or until the end of Day 4 and then pull the set up and the stand.

Your goal as a user of D.I.E. is to set up your tree stand, construct the D.I.E. scrape, apply the lures the right way on set up day, and to get it all done between the hours of 10 a.m. and 2 p.m. That way no deer will see you set it up. They are bedded down between those hours and you are setting up at least 80 yards upwind and 80 or more yards crosswind of any deer bedding areas, so you will be good to go. I just want you to stay away from live deer. How far you go is up to you, but if I were you, I would always try to get 80 yards away from the nearest edge of cover that I thought a big buck was bedded in or that I knew he would bed in once he smelled the scent of my single doe in estrus urine. Hunting too close will get you busted. Setting up less than 80 yards away from bedding cover is not advised, it is too close to deer bedding.

How to make a D.I.E. scrape and a D.I.E. rub

First, install your tree stand facing the tree that you are going to rub behind the D.I.E. scrape. Then you build the scrape and make the rub behind it. Start rubbing the tree 20 inches off the ground and rub it 12 to 15 inches high. Rub it smooth in the middle so it shines in the night but leave the bark shredded on the top and the bottom so it is an obvious territorial challenge being made by an invisible monster intruder buck. Next, take the leaves off the first 15 inches of the licking branch. Hold the tip of it in one hand and peel the leaves and small twigs off the main stem by pulling them back toward the tree trunk. Then break the tip of the licking branch off 3 to 6 inches back from its tip. Make sure you choose a live branch for a licking branch. A dead one will not work. Strip the bark off the first inch of the licking branch. To do that you should use gloved hands and pinch the tip of the branch with one of your thumbs, your index finger, and your middle finger from the same hand, then dig your fingernails into the bark through the glove and pull your hand away from the tree (keeping your fingers in a pinched position). The bark will peel off the tip. If you want to break the licking branch, and let it hang (or not) you can snap it back a few inches from the tip. It does not matter how you do it as long as you make sure that it gets done.

Next, make the scrape by standing in front of the rubbed tree. Face the tree the same way you expect the deer would be facing it when they walk down the nearest deer trail. Call that the front of the D.I.E. scrape, and the front of the D.I.E. rub. Rub the tree behind the scrape on the downwind side, or at a 45-degree angle of the downwind side, to make the D.I.E. rub authentic. Then paw up the ground as a buck would, by either using a hammer claw or the toe and heel of your boots. Claw up the dirt or kick it back, in an effort to remove all vegetation and debris from it. Use only your boot or a tool like a hammer claw to move the dirt, do not use your hands or a real deer hoof (from a dead deer). Rubber boots and clean metal tools will not leave any scent in the dirt.

I never use a real buck antler or a smooth bladed knife to make the rub. I always use a hammer claw or a crosscut saw, because they rip the bark better and you want to be sure to leave the tree with the appearance that it was ripped up at the top and bottom of the rubbed area. Only rub the front of the tree, and try to use a 2 to 4 inch diameter tree to make a D.I.E. rub on behind the scrape. Only rub the front of the tree, and only a 2-inch wide and 15-inch high area of the front of it, no matter if the tree is 2 inches, 3 inches or 4 inches. The rub has to face the direction you guess that the buck will come from, so the rub and the scrape both face the oncoming deer. If you asked me, I would say face it downwind and crosswind so the buck always sees it no matter where it is. That would be at a 45-degree angle to straight downwind. See Diagram 15 below.

Now you have made a manmade replica of a dominant buck's primary breeding scrape. It becomes a D.I.E. scrape when you walk away from it, but you have to dope it up first. It will become a real dominant buck's scrape when the dominant buck finds it and takes it over. From that point forward, you are not to go anywhere near the scrape and never refresh the lures, not for any reason. My system is flawless, so do not mess it up by over thinking how it works. Just trust me and let it work for you without disturbing it. Once the dominant buck owns it, he will be hunting you. Count on it.

Applying lure in and around the D.I.E. scrape is done methodically

You will need to take the Active Scrape and Trails End #307 along on set up day.

To dope up the scrape with lure you should always start with Trail's End #307. After all, it represents the intruder challenging monster buck that made the scrape, so it is fitting that his scent is left with his work of art, so all the area bucks will become familiar with his scent as they discover his scrape. Building the D.I.E. scrape is the start of the D.I.E. brainwashing process.

Always set the scrape up the exact same way. Once your stand and scrape are both installed then shoot to the scrape with your bow. Make sure you will not miss the buck when he arrives there. On over 50% of your hunts, he will go to the scrape if you let him. When you are done shooting to the scrape, then you are ready to dope the system up with lure.

Step-by-step lure use process

Always start doping up the scrape by placing the exact amount of Trail's End #307 lure that I instruct you to, in precisely the following locations.

1. Pour Trail's End #307 lure down the face of the rub that you made behind the scrape, on a 2 to 4 inch diameter tree. Let the lure drip from the bottle and make if run down the rub from the top of the rub to the bottom, before you stop pouring it.

2. Break off the tip of the licking branch, hold the bottle of Trail's End #307 up to the tree limb, and dip the tip of the limb into the bottle. Trail's End #307 should be dripping off the first one to two inches of the licking branch.

3. Pour a nickel-sized amount of Trail's End #307 into (3) scent dispensers (with clean cotton in them) and place them at your hand height in the following locations. Hand height is the height your hands are when you are standing up with your arms extended at your sides, with your fingers pointing to the ground.

    a. Place one open scent dispenser with Trail's End #307 in it 5 yards behind the scrape.
    b. Place one open scent dispenser with Trail's End #307 in it 4 feet to the left of the scrape.
    c. Place one open scent dispenser with Trail's End #307 in it 4 feet to the right of the scrape.

Now you are done with the Trail's End #307 for set-up day. Close up the bottle and put it in a zippered plastic bag so you will not get it on your clothes or hunting equipment. I keep it in an outside pocket of my backpack. You will need it again on the way to and from your stand each day of your hunt, which will begin in 2 ½ days.

Finish doping up the scrape by placing the exact amount of Active Scrape lure that I instruct you to, in precisely the following locations.

1. Open the package the scrape dripper came in and take it out. Throw any book that comes with it in the garbage or give it to someone who never intends to hunt with my D.I.E. system. If you read it, your mind will be messed up for sure. What I teach you to do with the Scrape-Dripper, the Active Scrape lure and the Trail's End #307 and what the manufacturer Wildlife Research Center Inc. teaches you to do with them are two opposite things. You bought my system to use it so do what I teach you and discard the book if there is one, before reading it. Listen only to what I tell you and my system will work for you. No one else knows it better than me.

2. It is a good idea to count the amount of turns it takes for the nozzle on the Scrape-Dripper to fall off, before you fill the Scrape-Dripper with lure. Each Scrape-Dripper is different. Some will fall off in ¾ turn and others in 1 ½ turns. You need to know that ahead of time so you will not open it too far by accident and lose all of the Active Scrape as it spills out on the ground in the scrape. If that happens, you will still have ¼ bottle left that you can add to the dripper. Originally, I had you saving the last ¼ bottle so you could dump it in the dirt of the scrape before you leave the area, but if it spills when you are purging it, then put the last ounce in the dripper, and purge it again. That way the system will still work.

3. It is also a good idea to have a back-up Scrape-Dripper in case the first one might become dismantled by a buck or in case the first one freezes up on your hunt. Then you can swap the second one out in place of the first and you will still be in business. I always have an extra Scrape-Dripper in my backpack on my hunts.

4. Active Scrape lure is only used in the Scrape Dripper and in the dirt under the licking branch. Here are specifics about how to use it. Pour ¾ of the bottle (3 oz.) of Active Scrape lure in the Scrape-Dripper. Tighten the nozzle so it is *snug* and tie the Scrape-Dripper up in the tree above the scrape about 6 or 8 feet off the ground if possible, using the string that is provided. You want it to drip about 2 or 3 feet out in front of the rub, so hang it over that spot. Try not to hang it on the licking branch, instead choose a branch above it. Bucks work the licking branch over, and it is possible the dominant buck will break it off before you come back to it on Day 1 of your hunt.

5. You need to purge the Scrape-Dripper so the Active Scrape starts dripping immediately. *Purging the dripper* is a procedure I came up with on my own. It makes the dripper emit one ounce of lure per day instead of it taking 4 or 5 days to dispense the same amount (as the manufacturer of the Scrape-Dripper suggests its users do). You put 3 ounces in the dripper on set-up day and then you purge the dripper losing a little bit, so in reality the scrape dripper will likely drip with Active Scrape lure for just 2 ½ days from the moment you leave it. That is exactly when I want it to run out. That is the same day you will be coming back to begin hunting over the D.I.E. scrape. You are setting the stage for a one to four act play. The length of your charade will depend upon which day the buck decides to show up. My purging procedure must be followed in order to make the king of deer believe the D.I.E. scrape is really being visited by more than one real doe in heat, and that one of those does goes into estrus at exactly the same time a real doe would have. Purging the Scrape-Dripper releases the air bubble in the dripper and allows the lure in it to flow out immediately (without having to wait for a 10° temperature rise). It will still de-activate

with a 10° fall in temperature (at sunset), and it will re-activate again when the outside temperature rises 10° again the following morning (about 1 to 1 ¼ hours after daylight).

Scrape-Drippers are designed to make all visiting breeder bucks return to the scrape during the day, and the particular Scrape-Drippers I instruct you to use do exactly that. The Scrape-Dripper makes the deer in the area aware of the existence of the D.I.E. scrape from the moment you walk away from it on set up day. That is when the brainwashing of the area's herd begins. The bucks scent check every area before they move into it and when they go downwind of this area they smell Active Scrape and Trail's End #307 in the same vicinity as one another. They are drawn to the scrape by the lure. They investigate it but do not take it over. Only the most dominant buck can do that. The dominant buck takes it over by working it up, and from that moment forward, it belongs to him.

He takes the D.I.E. scrape over because I taught you to make a challenging intruder monster buck scrape. A scrape with a rub behind it can only be made by the king of the herd. That is the type of scrape you made. The real king of the herd has to take it over. He does not have a choice.

To purge the Scrape-Dripper, first loosen the nozzle very slowly in a counter clockwise direction until the air bubble is released. You will know when that is, because the lure will shoot out. That is what you should expect, so stand back away from it so the lure does not get on your clothes. As soon as it shoots out, turn the cap back toward the snug position. Only make it *finger snug* this time. That is not tight, but not opening by itself either. Loosen the cap one more time until you see a droplet of lure form on the tip of the nozzle. Then leave it that way so it will continue dripping drop by drop. If it seems to pour out every time you loosen it, then tighten it finger snug and loosen it 3 or 4 notches on the cap. You will see the grooves on the cap above the nozzle. I call them notches. Just make sure it has a drop on the tip of the nozzle when you leave it, and it will work correctly.

6. Pour the remaining ¼ bottle (1 oz.) of Active Scrape lure straight down in the dirt under the Scrape-Dripper.

Now you are done with the Active Scrape lure for the entire hunt. Close the bottle and put it in a zippered plastic bag so you will not get it on your clothes or hunting equipment. When you get home, throw the empty bottle of Active Scrape in the garbage. You are done with it.

The following series of photos show you how to make the D.I.E. scrape and rub according to the DOMINANCE IS EVERYTHING standards. You must make it just like I do to get the results I have gotten.

When scouting you want to sit in the shadow line whenever possible (deer do not look for danger in the shadow line), at the height of the brush line.

Set Up Day

Scout to find a buck trail that heads into semi-open cover. If you cannot find a buck trail find a trail with big deer tracks on it.

Follow the big deer tracks, or walk on the trail through one type of terrain into another. Find where another deer trail crosses his path, and look for cover upwind and crosswind of the intersecting trails to set up in. Stay more than 30 yards away if possible (both stand and scrape) from the intersection, and always hunt on the upwind side. The focus is not on the intersection it is on your D.I.E. scrape and rub off to one side 30 or more yards from the intersection.

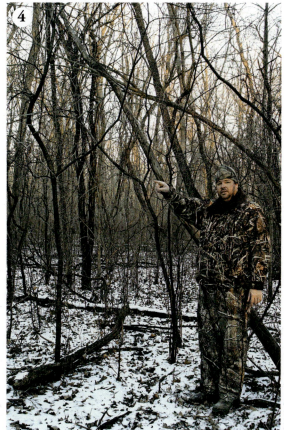

Find an area where you can only see 20 or 30 yards before the cover gets too thick to see through (when you are standing up), and where you can only see 5 to 10 yards (at deer eye-height). Make sure the deer tracks show you that deer are walking in that place. Look for a sapling 2 to 4 inches in diameter on the upwind side of the deer trail, that you can make a D.I.E. rub on and a scrape in front of. Make sure it has a licking branch.

5

Decide which side of the tree to rub. Make sure that you rub a side that is at a 45-degree angle to the trail. The deer should be able to see it from (10 yards away) when they are approaching it. The wind was from the Northwest and I was facing west. Make the rub face the palm of my hand. I am standing on the leaves that I will kick out of there later, and my left hand is over the buck's trail. In front of me and behind me are crosswind directions. I will sit in a tree (in this case an oak) behind my right shoulder, 20 yards back and 12 to 15 feet up to my stand platform. My toes will face the rubbed part of the D.I.E. rub, then I will be facing the way the buck tracks came from. He will come from that way again, once every 3 days.

6

The rub should only be made between my fingers. Start rubbing from the bottom up at 20 inches off the ground. Make the D.I.E. rub 12 to 15 inches in height. Always rub the side of the tree that the buck tracks tell you he came from.

Using a toothed saw is best but a hammer claw will work. Rub it 1-2 inches wide but do not rub it clean. It has to have shredded bark hanging off it at the top and the bottom. Just take the first layer of bark off. There has to be some staging cover within 120 yards of the front of the rub for it to be a realistically constructed primary breeding scrape made by a monster intruder buck.

This photo was taken looking northeast. The wind was coming from the Northwest (from the left of the scene). The deer trail is South (downwind) of the D.I.E. rub just 3 feet away. The rub is at a 45-degree angle to the deer trail on the side the buck approaches the tree rub from. He cannot miss seeing it, or smelling the scent of it from the trail he normally walks on.

When the dominant buck sees it, he will stop in his tracks for a moment.

I am standing upwind of the scrape, facing the same direction I would be facing if I were in my stand (in the oak tree) on Day 1 which you can see is behind my right (shooting) shoulder. Notice that I set the scrape and rub 10–15 yards downwind of the cover. In this instance I had to build the scrape here so I could sit in my stand facing Southwest. Whenever I hunt with a North or Northwest wind I point my toes straight Southwest and build the D.I.E. scrape 10–20 yards in front of me. I have 100% success seeing monster bucks when I set up like that. I always set the scrape up crosswind of my stand. That way the buck is focused on it, and not me. The deer trail is always downwind of my scrape. It is my personal preference. You can do it how you like. I consider this a set up on the edge of cover. Getting closer to the cover would have been better but I didn't have that option here.

Place 3 scent dispensers out at hand-height. One to the left of the scrape (4–5ft), another to the right (4–5 ft), and the last one you should place 5 yards behind the scrape. You should keep your lure in a sealable plastic bag. I am pointing at the Scrape-Dripper that I hung over my scrape. Hang the dripper 12 to 36-inches away from the tree trunk, on a tree limb.

I am pointing out the one-way buck trail downwind of the D.I.E. rub and the soon-to-be D.I.E. scrape.

Set Up Day 309

I am pointing toward my tree stand.

I am pointing at the licking branch, that is hanging over the scrape, nearby the trail.

I am pointing at the Seal-Tite scent dispenser 4-ft off to the left of the scrape.

To make the scrape, face the rub and kick back the leaves and debris on the ground under the dripper. Make the pawed up area into a trapezoid shape. The front at the tree base should be 18-24 inches wide, 3 feet front to back on each side, and 4 feet wide at the front.

Use ¾ bottle of Active Scrape in the Scrape-Dripper (3 oz.), and the rest (1 oz.) goes in the dirt of the scrape before you leave the area.

Tighten the nozzle snug and tie the Scrape-Dripper above the pawed up area.

Grab a hold on the bottle with one hand and the nozzle with another. You are going to purge the dripper. Doing so will make it start dripping right away.

Loosen the cap slowly, (purge) until some lure shoots out.

Shut it off quickly but only finger snug (not snug) see glossary for definitions of terms.

Loosen again but only slightly, until it shoots out a second time. Then turn it off again, only finger snug.

Loosen it a final time only 3 or 4 notches (ribs on the collar of the cap), so that only a drop of the lure appears on the tip of the nozzle. Now the dripper is purged. You will need to purge the dripper again on Day 1 of your hunt, when you come to hunt and you change out the lure to the single doe in estrus.

Use only 3 or 4 drops of Trail's End #307 in each of the (3) scent dispensers placed around the scrape on set up day.

Set Up Day 311

Be sure to leave the bark shavings on the ground and do not remove any ground cover behind the D.I.E. rub.

Pour #307 on the trunk of the tree starting at the top of the rub, until it drips down the face of the rub to the bottom of the shaved area.

Peel the bark from the tip of the licking branch and dip it in Trail's End #307. This is the last step for setting the D.I.E. scrape and D.I.E. rub up the right way. Be sure you pour the last ounce of Active Scrape in the scrape before you leave the area.

This is the view the dominant buck will have when he discovers my D.I.E. scrape and rub within 3 days of the time I constructed it. The arrow points at the rub and scrape. Assume the buck will travel the same path if the wind is the same and if he never knows a human is there.

After setting up, you must go home for the 2 ½ day waiting period in order to have 100% odds of success on each hunt. If you were to hunt it right away your chance of getting busted is at least 20% where as it is 0% if you wait 2 ½ days first. Only return on Day 1 of your hunt. Do not watch the scrape from your car or yard, if you do the dominant buck could be watching you. If he sees you on the land between set up day and Day 1 of your hunt you just threw you 100% odds of success in the trash. Use it as directed and have faith that it works exactly as I say it does, and you will see results.

The following three photos show you what to do with the lure in the Scrape-Dripper when you arrive at the scrape and rub on Day 1 of your hunt.

Approach your scrape from upwind and crosswind, making an arc to the scrape from your car. Stand on the upwind side of the scrape and trail, and do not cross in front of either of them. Take the Scrape-Dripper down off the branch you tied it to on set up day and pour any left over Active Scrape lure straight down into the scrape.

Pour ½ bottle (1 oz.) of Still Steamin' Premium Hot Doe Estrus urine (collected from one single doe) in the dripper as directed.

This is the invisible doe in estrus' pure urine. If you opted to use the scent dispensers around the scrape then you should take the two that are on the left and right out now, and replace them with two new ones with the same doe in estrus urine in them. Leave the one 5 yards back behind the scrape alone (it has #307 lure in it). That one tells the dominant buck that the invisible intruder buck still frequents the area even though he is no longer dominant of the D.I.E. scrape. Do not go near that one for any reason.

You have to purge the Scrape-Dripper again on Day 1 after you change the lure from Active-Scrape to Still Steamin' Premium Hot Doe Estrus urine. Then leave it until your hunt is over. Never walk up to the scrape after you walk away from it on the morning of Day 1 of your hunt. If you break this rule the buck will bust you everytime.

Chapter 20

The Waiting Period

Dominant whitetail bucks are active all day long during the rut, they are keeping an eye on all the does in the herd, and at the same time, they are watching the pecking order bucks as they harass does in heat on the outside edges of doe bedding areas. If you see multiple mature bucks during broad daylight, those most likely are pecking order bucks from the same herd. None of them is dominant there. The dominant buck will always be cautious and not make public his whereabouts. He is a survivor, and the only places a dominant buck will frequent during daylight without a doe in estrus nearby are areas that offer him cover to hide in. Those include his core bedding, core breeding, and core staging areas, all of which are within a few yards of a water source. In order to outsmart him with D.I.E. you have to leave him alone when he is in his core living areas, and allow him to take a few days to discover your D.I.E. scrape and rub. Do not push it on him by taking it to him; you must make him come to your hiding place to find it! You should not attempt to make the king of deer into your puppet; the D.I.E. system will do that for you. What you need to do is set up the D.I.E. system and leave it alone for 2 ½ days, before returning to it, that way the dominant buck and all the other deer in his herd will be able to discover it on their own.

The dominant buck is king of the herd, and he walks his territorial boundaries once every 72 hours (3 days). He will find the D.I.E. scrape, and when he does 99% of the times, you will not be there. That is the way I want it to be, and by the time you fully understand this system you will want it to be that way too. That way the buck is in his own element, and he fears nothing when he is working the scrape. He takes it over and he beds downwind of it just like he would if it was his own. He will let his guard down just enough for a D.I.E. hunter to have the advantage that he/she needs to harvest him. The more you allow the king to have his way, the more confident he gets with the situation, and the easier your shot opportunity will be once the buck comes in and you are there waiting for him.

Other bucks will find the scrape too, but I do not focus my hunt on them because they do not dominate the scrape as the most dominant buck does. He is the buck that hunts you! He owns the territory and he has to be the one to take it back! The other bucks are trying to get to the doe in estrus, but they do not care about the territory. The dominant buck will be the first one in if you give him 2 ½ days to find it, take it over, and own it before you come in to hunt over it.

If you do not wait the 2 ½ days, your odds are less than 100%, and the most dominant buck will most likely not be the first buck you will see. I have crammed the D.I.E. system (set it up with a shorter waiting period than 2 ½ days), and I succeeded at seeing the heaviest buck I ever saw in my life, so I know it works, but only some of the time. I am one out of three for seeing the king of deer, when it comes to hunting with less than a 2 ½ day (standard) waiting period. On all of my crammed hunts, I waited at least at least 16 hours before I returned to hunt over my D.I.E. scrape and rub. If you cram the system you should expect to see other bucks (less dominant), and maybe some does in the area of the scrape. In order to speed up the response time of the most dominant buck I prefer to hunt on a heavily used buck trail when cramming the system. Normally I would look for a one-way trail, away from heavy cover, but in this case, you would want to be just outside the doe bedding area by about 80 yards, wherever you see large deer tracks on the trail. That is a buck trail and pecking order bucks use it all day long. If the pecking order bucks find the scrape first, then they will urinate in it, and it will really tick off the king of the herd, once he finds it. The reason it takes the king up to three days to find it is because he is busy mating with does in estrus. He will be far away from the scrape for up to two days, while he finishes up the breeding he is doing with a real doe in estrus. When he makes his rounds on the third day, he is looking for intrusions, and he will find the scrape. He will take it from whichever buck is maintaining it at the time.

I will introduce the invisible pair of breeding deer to the herd on Day 1 of my hunt when I come in to hunt over the scrape, but Day 1 of the hunt has not come yet, and therefore no deer are breeding at the D.I.E. scrape either.

The remainder of the hours left in set up day, and the two whole days that follow set up day, collectively make up "the waiting period". The first day after set up day is a day that you need to stay out of the property. You will be staying home the second day too. By doing so, you are investing in the future success of your D.I.E. hunt. The king of deer has not failed to come in for any D.I.E. hunter who waited the entire 2 ½ day waiting period before going in to hunt. Use it as directed and you will be joining our ranks.

On set up day, the goal is to intrude into the front yard or side yard of the dominant buck, build a scrape and a stand, and dope it up. That tells the dominant buck that he has some competition for that one piece of his territory where the D.I.E. scrape is. He is not being challenged face-to-face by the maker of the scrape, when he is near the scrape so he takes it over, and goes back to his business as usual. After a few hours, he realizes that he has to come to the challenger instead of waiting for the challenger to go to him. This challenger is nowhere to be found, because you are the challenger and you are at home waiting for 2 ½ days to pass by.

Normally the intruder buck would get the doe and get out of there with her, but in the case of a D.I.E. scrape, no buck can get the doe. Again that is because you are the doe, and you are at home for the waiting period. In order for the system to always perform as I have had it perform, you need to give it 2 ½ days of peace and quiet. You pop into the herd's territory for less than 4 hours on set up day, and you are out of it until the third sunrise that follows your exit. That is Day 1 of you hunt! That is the day that the entire herd is introduced to the sweetest smelling doe in estrus that they have ever met!

What bucks do when they discover the D.I.E. scrape

Most pecking order bucks will find the scrape after dark the same day that you build it (**Example A**). Every mature buck is attracted to a D.I.E. scrape because of the doe in heat lure dripping in it, and they will be drawn to it once the doe in heat goes into estrus (that is when you are hunting over it). When you set it up you have to give the breeder bucks enough time to find it, work it up, get into a few fights over it, and then dominate it. The winner of the fights is the most dominant buck. He earns the right to stick around and wait for the invisible pair of deer to come back (**Example B**).

When the most dominant buck in that area takes over the D.I.E. scrape, he stays in the area to guard the scrape from all (real) intruder bucks and to confront the (invisible) monster intruder buck if and when he ever does locate him. I can tell you right now, that the dominant buck never meets the monster intruder buck, because I made him up in my head. He doesn't exist, but thanks to Trail's End #307 lure, you have the dominant buck believing that he does! The dominant buck identifies the scent of the Trail's End #307 as the scent of the invisible intruder buck. The aroma from the Active Scrape lure dripping into the pawed up dirt of the scrape makes him believe that there are multiple does in heat that are visiting his scrape during the day, but the Trail's End #307 lure was put out on set up day. It doesn't drip during the day so the dominant buck believes that the intruder buck is a monster buck, because he doesn't come out in broad daylight like the does do. As long as you can keep him guessing where the two deer are, then you are going to have fun with this system.

Example A: What a pecking order buck does when he first finds the scrape:

1. He finds it at night. Active Scrape lure is damp but was left hours ago. The scrape is "cold", the dripper is not dripping in the dark, and that tells the buck that the does were not there after dark. He has to come back earlier if he wants to meet any of the does.
2. He is curious to see where the does that left their scent behind actually went.
3. He works the scrape (paws up the dirt, and urinates in it).
4. He wanders around the area, into and out of bedding areas searching for the does in heat that Active Scrape lure tells him are urinating in the scrape during the day.
5. He tries to find one of the does and tries to avoid encountering the dominant buck.
6. He leaves the area when a more dominant buck arrives—unless he wants to fight, and that would be only if he thought he was capable of winning, so it is unlikely to happen.
7. If he fights the dominant buck and beats him, then he will rub the tree behind the scrape and nibble on the licking branch. He will stay there to dominate the scrape and he will be hunting you. If he never fights or he gets beat, then you will see a different king.

Example B: What the dominant buck does when he first finds the scrape:

1. He finds it at night (most often). Active Scrape is damp, but was left hours ago. (The scrape is "cold".)
2. He runs off all intruder bucks and fights for dominance there.

3. He gets mad and rubs the tree behind the scrape enlarging the rub you made. Sometime he rubs it all the way around.
4. He paws up the scrape, works the licking branch, and deposits his scent on it.
5. He urinates in the D.I.E. scrape, making it his own real primary breeding scrape.
6. Often he thrashes the branches above the scrape and breaks them off.
7. He may make another real scrape 3 to 5 feet away from the mock scrape.
8. He might tear up all the brush in the area of the scrape with his antlers.
9. All night he searches the area for the buck (you) that made the scrape.
10. He runs his territory boundaries, and freshens many of his scrapes and rubs.
11. He checks the core doe bedding and breeding areas, looking for you, as the challenging monster intruder buck.
12. He sticks as tight to the scrape as he can and beds downwind in cover.
13. He stands up in his bed every few hours to scent check the scrape and to watch for motion in front of the rub.
14. When he smells the doe in estrus for the first time (on Day 1, Day 2, Day 3 or Day 4 of your hunt) he will make his way to the scrape to freshen it, and he will be yours for the taking.

Below is a summary of what I believe the dominant buck thinks when he finds a D.I.E. scrape. The buck finds the scrape during the night and the Scrape-Dripper already stopped dripping before he got there. The scrape is "cold" now, but he can still smell the scent of does in heat in the scrape, and he is anxious to rid the area of the intruder buck that made that scrape inside his home territory. He cannot identify a specific doe, so he searches the doe bedding areas for any doe in heat. He knows the buck that made the scrape only by his scent, the scent of Trail's End #307.

Every single time a dominant buck finds your D.I.E. scrape for the first time (as long as he did not see you build it); he will behave in this manner. If the buck has not tore up the area around your scrape, rubbed the tree behind it, or left a track (with splayed toes) in the dirt under the rub by the morning of Day 2, then believe me when I tell you that he can see your scrape from his normal bed. You set it up too close to real deer. It is not a believable situation if you take it to the herd. You need to make the most dominant buck leave the herd to come to the scrape.

You are forbidden to go to the scrape on Day 2, Day 3, and Day 4, so make a judgment call from your tree stand the morning of Day 2. Did he rub it or not? Do not go to the scrape to find out, or you will get busted 100% of the time. Do not just assume that you are busted if you cannot see the rub enlarged. Sometimes the buck will be unsure of himself and he will not rub the tree or work the licking branch at all. Usually you will hear the buck grunting or raking brush sometime on Day 1, or right away in the morning of Day 2, just a bit downwind of you. If you hear a buck talking to you then do not move. Just wait for his arrival. If he is talking to you, he does not know you are there. Do not call to him or he will know you are a human in a tree stand.

On the other hand, if you have not heard any deer walking or grunting, or bleating, the area is quiet and no other animals are coming near you, then all the creatures in the woods know a human is there. Setting up too close to real deer sign can get you busted like that. It happened to me once before I learned my lesson. The buck will not come to you if he knows a human is there, and in this case, he would know you were a human because you went to his doorstep and announced it to him.

If the buck doesn't work up your scrape, it could mean you set it up too close to his living quarters. If that was the case, you can still succeed from there by chance but certainly not 100% of the time. Check the 'Never Do' list and move the stand, the scrape and the lure upwind and crosswind at least 100 yards to get the buck to come to the doe there.

If you decide to move because you think you were busted do not move until 10 o'clock a.m. or later on Day 2 of the hunt. If you do not see that the rub you made on set up day is enlarged, and the buck did not make another scrape next to yours with a rub behind it, and a licking branch over it, then the odds are high that the buck knows there is a human in the area. Maybe you were interfered with. I never quit hunting my first stand choice unless I know for sure I was busted. You will see the buck running away from you if that is the case. Then you should move to your second location but do your best not to pull your stand out before 10 o'clock a.m. or after 2 o'clock in the afternoon. The four-hour window from 10 a.m. until 2 p.m. is when most deer are bedded, and if you know where your second stand site location is then you have plenty of time to move there and get the scrape and rub set up in the new location before 2 in the afternoon. When you do move, make sure you are not talking as you go. To whom might you be talking? I do not know, but some people talk out load as they move through the woods after being busted by a buck, and I want to be sure I tell you that he will bust you in the new stand too if he hears you talking. You have to set up quick, spray down with Scent-Killer 99% and then sit in the stand for the rest of the day if you are able. If not just, come in the next morning (Day 3) on time, doing everything the same, but going to the new stand location. The buck will hunt you there. I have never had it fail when I moved on Day 2 of a hunt, after being busted.

After the dominant buck has done all the things I stated in Example B, he has just finished a long night running his territory boundaries looking for you. He is tired and mad at that invisible buck (you). He wants to get back to his bed where he can get some rest, but he first has to deal with that darn intruder buck (you). "Where is that buck?" the dominant buck thinks. When the sun is just rising on the first day after set up day, you are at home (not there) but the dominant buck is there. Example C shows how his day pans out.

Example C: What the dominant buck does the next morning after he finds the scrape, during the waiting period:

1. He could not find you (the buck) at night, so he returns to the scrape at sunrise or a little later to scent check it.

2. The scrape is not fresh; it's "cold". He figures the monster intruder buck has not been back, so he beds nearby downwind in cover, waiting for you to return as the buck.
3. About 1 to 1 ½ hours, later the temperature rises 10 degrees and Active Scrape begins to drip into the soil in the scrape. Active Scrape is the scent of multiple does in heat and at least one buck in the rut.
4. He can smell the Active Scrape. He is curious but cautious, so he scent checks the area for any danger.
5. He goes to the scrape, but stops along the way to grunt and rake brush. The lure convinces him, "They were here. It's hot." He works the scrape and stakes it out, marking brush in the area and getting vocal if any other bucks come by.
6. He checks the doe bedding areas and comes back to bed down even closer in thick cover.
7. He scent checks the scrape again about noon, and it smells sweet. He checks, and the scrape is "hot"! Where are those does in heat? He cannot find any of them!
8. Night falls and he gets up, and goes to the scrape again. The Scrape-Dripper has stopped dripping lure. Now the scrape is "cold" again.
9. He runs his territory boundaries again, this time focusing only on nearby bedding areas and heavily used doe trails. He may visit some real does to check for any in estrus, but if he cannot find any, he will be right back in his new favorite place come sunup, waiting for the intruder buck to come back or for one of the does to show up in estrus.
10. He thinks about it. When he went to bed in the midday, the invisible pair of deer (the scent of the Active Scrape) must have been there: they had to have been because their scent was fresh then. He now believes he is on to you (the invisible intruder buck). He believes you are coming back in the morning, so he beds down within 35 yards of your scrape. He gets up from time to time to get some water, but then he moves back to the scrape again. He moves closer each time, but he stays in the nearest available cover. He literally could be 5 yards from the D.I.E. scrape. That's okay. You have a plan—and that plan is to stay home one more day.

This buck is the smartest buck in the herd, and the king of all deer in the area, and so he must do a lot of thinking. I think at this point a light bulb goes on in the buck's head and he thinks something like this: "They must be in this together!" The does must be coming into estrus now, because their scent is again dispersing at the scrape telling the most dominant buck that those does are searching for him. Every doe in heat goes into estrus within 3 days and the dominant bucks has always responded to my D.I.E. system when I changed the doe in heat, into a doe in estrus on the third day after set up day. That day is called Day 1 of the hunt.

In reality, the scrape is now saturated with nearly 3 ounces of Active Scrape. In a single day, about 1 ounce of Active Scrape lure drips out of a Scrape-Dripper when you purge it the way I teach you. You put 3 ounces in the dripper, so it should run dry on the third day. Trust me on that!

The buck never sees the Scrape-Dripper. He really thinks that breeding deer are in the area and he is missing seeing them. He gets very cautious now because he cannot figure this thing out. He still checks in with his herd and looks for real does in estrus until you come in to hunt the scrape. For two whole days, he cannot find a doe in estrus, but he keeps looking because he does not believe in invisible deer, or invisible humans. If there is deer scent on the ground and it is pure, then a deer must have been there.

You come in on Day 1 and 90% of the time, you will not be meeting the buck that day, but you do not let that statistic get you down, you are there to introduce the doe in estrus to the herd. You know that a D.I.E. hunt can change in a minute if a breeder buck locks on to the doe in estrus' scent. Any day in a tree stand being hunted by the king of deer is a good day to be alive, so you sit there and give it your all. Day 2 and Day 3 are the days most bucks make their appearance. If you sat all day and then went home as I directed you to, the next day would be better for you. The odds of seeing the king on Day 2 are 50%!

The next time the dominant buck comes in, he will scent check the scrape and he will know that you represent one single doe in estrus. Most of the times the buck first finds the scent of the doe in estrus it is at night on Day 1 of the hunt after you went home for the day. That is when he starts hunting you. He runs his territory boundaries again looking for the intruder buck and marking his rubs. He has to keep his rank as king, and that means he must patrol his home turf and run out any intruder bucks before they breed with any of his does. Your intruder buck is really in for it when the dominant buck catches up with him.

The dominant buck has earned the right to breed with the does in his home territory, and the D.I.E scrape is in his territory. That is why he takes a personal interest in finding the invisible doe before the invisible intruder buck does. Again—both of those deer are you, and you are at home during the 2 ½ day waiting period instead of being there. You have to be at home; otherwise, this stuff would never happen. I am sure that if you saw this going on, you would try to shoot the dominant buck before he got a chance to hunt you. That is why I set it up with a 2 ½ day waiting period, so the deer can get accustomed to the stand and scrape, and not fear that a human is there. Deer can scent check and identify human scent for up to two days after the human has left the area (without rain) and you will be away from the area for nearly 3 days when you first come back to it. That works out perfectly for you.

You cannot shorten the waiting period and have 100% success with D.I.E.

Brainwashing the buck takes ½ to 2 ½ days. Let him enjoy his last two or three days on this planet. DOMINANCE IS EVERYTHING works for you because the dominant buck is unaware of any human ever sitting in your tree stand and he is unaware that a human is coming in. His head is spinning. What he used to count on is not predictable anymore, but the dominant buck will not stop pursuing the doe in estrus once she arrives, until she would normally go out of estrus or until his competing bucks give up, whichever happens last within 4 days. I can tell you from experience that the king of deer will always show up within 3 days of the time he identifies the doe at the scrape as being in estrus. The earliest that can happen is on Day 1 of your hunt, when you arrive at the scrape and change the lure in the dripper to that of the single doe in estrus. A dominant buck could be on his way to you at that moment.

The dominant buck is uncertain now. In the past, anytime he saw a challenging rub or a scrape with does visiting it inside his territory he could always find the buck and the does in heat—because they stayed around in the area by the scrape. I would be willing to bet that he has never had to deal with an intruder monster-challenging buck that came to his territory and made a dominant buck's primary breeding scrape there. I think I am the first one ever, to put any buck in this exact circumstance as my **Dominance Is Everything** system does. He is frustrated because he cannot find them, and that is because they really do not exist. He hasn't figured that out yet. If you stay away from the land for the full 2 ½ day waiting period, like I instruct you to, he will not ever figure that out during your hunt, and he will keep pursuing the doe and avoiding the buck until you meet him face-to-face on your four day hunt. You are going to love the first hunt you have with D.I.E.!

D.I.E. can fool the dominant buck with the Active Scrape dripping for up to three full days, but not any more than that. I prefer to fool him with it for the afternoon of set up day and then two whole days, resulting in a 2 ½-day waiting period when the hunter should stay out of the area. The buck will never hunt for the hunter without the user becoming the doe in estrus and visiting the scrape that the dominant buck has taken over. He is not going to commit until that doe shows up, so you have to hunt on Day 1 or your buck will be wise to the set up. (Example D) shows the dominant's buck next experience.

Example D: What the dominant buck does the second morning of the waiting period, while he is waiting for you to return:

1. He had another long night. He approaches the scrape and works it in the dark.
2. It is not fresh; it's "cold". He knows the monster intruder buck has not been back, so he beds nearby. Once the dominant buck works the scrape, you leave it to him. He owns it after that.
3. About 8:30 a.m. the temperature increases 10 degrees and Active Scrape drips, or maybe not. Maybe the dripper is empty. The buck goes to the scrape anyway because he is being taunted by the pecking order bucks in the area.
4. He can smell the Active Scrape and he does a lip curl: No doe is in estrus yet.
5. He goes to the scrape. It's "hot". He works it and hangs out again.
6. He checks doe bedding areas, and then comes back to bed down nearby again.
7. He scent checks the scrape again about noon and it smells sweet. He checks, and it's "hot"! How could he keep missing these does? He is convinced that at least one of them was just there a minute before him.
8. He goes for water. When he comes back, he checks it again, it's "hot" but no deer!
9. Night falls again. He gets up and goes to the scrape, but the Scrape-Dripper has shut down again. Now the scrape is cold again.

A dominant buck is a very aggressive buck and he will stop at nothing to find and breed with any doe in estrus that is visiting one of his scrapes. A dominant buck makes his own rules. By teaching other hunters the D.I.E. system and having them hunt on public and private land in Wisconsin and Minnesota, during gun and bow season, I have learned that this scenario plays out wherever you set up the D.I.E. system. The buck is hot (mad) when you show up on Day 1 of your hunt, because you have to show up or he is going to give up. That is your cue to show up. I hope you find his front hoof print in the dirt of the scrape, because that tells you that he did indeed have at least one night like the one I just described to you. You should stay alert and watch the scrape constantly. He will slip in undetected if he can.

Anyone could buy a Scrape-Dripper, use it as I directed you to and get these results from it if they were not there near the scrape hunting it during the first 2 ½ days. If you were there, the buck could not act in his normal way and he would not have established this pattern of checking the D.I.E. scrape, in a routine.

The DOMINANCE IS EVERYTHING system is what makes the buck hunt you, not the just the Scrape-Dripper dripping Active Scrape for three days. The Scrape-Dripper makes the usually night time active dominant buck into a daytime breeder, and it ticks him off because he is king, and the D.I.E. scrape is a territorial challenge to his authority within his herd boundaries. Using the Scrape-Dripper is part of my D.I.E. system, a much-needed part, but not the main factor.

The rub behind a scrape, with a licking branch hanging over it intimidate the dominant buck because they are in his territory. The pecking order bucks are aware of the threat that the dominant buck is dealing with. Challenging bucks from other herds see the existence of that scrape as a chink in the armor of the dominant buck, and they may come charging in at any moment to fight him for rights to the territory or for the rights to breed with the invisible doe in estrus. I believe intruder bucks are out for themselves, but they sometimes end up in the same place at the same time eyeing up the same doe in estrus, and if that happens all hell breaks loose. It happened to me in 2009 with the buck on the cover of this book, and what a hunt that was!

Choose to hunt with OPTION 1 or OPTION 2

There are two ways to make the D.I.E. system work. Both get the same result, but dragging in the Still Steamin' Premium Hot Doe Estrus urine collected from one single doe, seems to attract more bucks to the area of the scrape than not using a dragline does, and more bucks mean more competition for the dominant buck. All that competition keeps the odds high that the dominant buck will be a monster buck. Dragging out Trail's End #307 lure keeps the dominant buck's focus on the scrape, and off of you. Choose which option you want to use and stick with it all 4 days - do not mix it up. They both work 100% but not part of the time. You have to stick with only one option for the whole 4 days of the hunt. I always choose OPTION 2. I used OPTION 1 on all of my hunts prior to 2001, and since then I only use OPTION 2, because I have seen 6 monster bucks on 5 hunts using OPTION 2, and I only saw 1 monster buck in 3 hunts using OPTION 1. Each time I had the dominant buck hunting me.

OPTION 1 makes the buck hunt the scrape only

You do not become the hunted—the scrape is the attraction to the buck

On set up day, you set up the D.I.E. scrape according to the normal set up instructions. You wait the 2 ½ days and return to the scrape on Day 1 of your hunt with intentions to hunt all day or until you take your buck. You do not use a dragline. On your way in use the Trail's End #307 as a cover scent, by pouring a little bit out of the bottle and onto branches and brush 3 feet off the ground as you walk into the area in the morning. Do not over use it. Only pour out 1 or 2 drops in three or four places along your trail on your walk in. Do not use any of it on the way out unless you think you have lost your scent free status while in the stand.

When you arrive at the D.I.E. scrape on Day 1, empty the contents of the Scrape-Dripper into the dirt in the scrape, and open the 2 oz. bottle of the Still Steamin' Premium Hot Doe Estrus urine collected from one single doe. Pour ½ of it in the Scrape-Dripper, purge the dripper, and leave it alone. Get in your tree stand and stay there all day. When you leave at the end of the day, walk out, as a human but do not tell any deer you are a human. When you walk to the scrape in the morning, walk like a deer if it is safe for you to do it. The only reason for not walking like a deer on the way to the stand is if you fear another deer hunter might mistake your footsteps for a real deer and shoot at you through the cover. This can be a real problem and you should never risk your life to walk like a deer. If you have any risk of that happening, NEVER walk like a deer in that area. You should always verify that no other hunter is hunting within sight of you before you set the system up, and if you cannot be sure, you will be safe then do not walk like a deer. Walk softly as a human instead. If you cannot be alone the buck will not come in, so do not expect success if someone else is in your area.

If you choose to hunt with option 1, the results will be very much like this: A dominant buck will search for the doe in estrus, and his focus will be on the D.I.E. scrape the entire time. He will approach during daylight, at least one of the four days you set out to hunt him. He will come in within 35 yards of your position, and if you set up on the edge of something as I instruct you to on set-up day, you will have a clean shot to him, and an opportunity for a wall hanger buck.

OPTION 2 makes you the "hunted" and the scrape is also an attraction

The dragline defines your identity when going into and coming out of the area

With Option 2 you have more responsibilities because you are role-playing with the dominant buck, by becoming the two invisible deer that you introduced to him at the D.I.E. scrape 2 ½ days earlier. When you hunt with Option 2, you become the invisible deer not only at the scrape but also on the way to it in the morning on Day 1 and on the way out of the area, at the end of each day of your hunt. When Day 2 rolls around, if you have not harvested the buck, go directly to your tree stand, get in it and prepare for the buck to arrive. Avoid going to the scrape.

Day 1 starts by you pulling a dragline behind you with Still Steamin' Premium Hot Doe Estrus urine on it, that way you enter your hunting area in the morning as the doe in estrus. Your every move is being watched by the dominant buck, and when he gets your scent, you will become the center of his attention for the next 2 or 3 days.

When you get to the D.I.E. scrape on Day 1, change the lure to the doe in estrus urine exactly the same way as you would for Option 1. Empty the contents of the Scrape-Dripper (Active Scrape) into the dirt in the scrape, and open the 2 oz. bottle of the Still Steamin' Premium Hot Doe Estrus urine collected from one single doe. Pour ½ of it in the Scrape-Dripper, purge the dripper, and leave it alone. Get in your tree stand and stay there all day. When you leave at the end of the day you should walk out as the intruder buck dragging the #307 on your dragline (tie on a fresh key-wick), and walk out like a human, but do not tell any deer you are a human. Never go back to the D.I.E. scrape after you put the Still Steamin' Premium Hot Doe Estrus urine in the scrape dripper. If you do, you will be busted instantly.

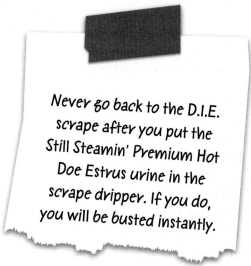

Never go back to the D.I.E. scrape after you put the Still Steamin' Premium Hot Doe Estrus urine in the scrape dripper. If you do, you will be busted instantly.

Once the scrape is dripping with Still Steamin' Premium Hot Doe Estrus urine, you have now become an attraction to him—A very hot attraction to him at that! You have now identified yourself as a doe in estrus, and one that he has never had the privilege of meeting or mating with before. He will likely rise from his bedded position, and head toward the trail you walked in on. There, he will scent check your trail, identify you as a doe in estrus, and come walking in like he owns the joint. The rest is history.

Chapter 21

'The Rundown – Step-By-Step D.I.E. Hunt Instructions

In order for you to have a successful hunt or photography session with D.I.E., first you need to see the 'Big Picture'. The 'Big Picture' is how the herd in your area relates to the terrain there, and how they avoid danger there. If you scout the way I teach you, then you will see the 'Big Picture', you will understand what your herd is doing now, and how the dominant buck will react to the D.I.E. scrape once you set it up there. In order to see the 'Big Picture' a person has to know the rundown. I have summarized the duties that every D.I.E. user has to fulfill before, during, and after the hunt, in order to achieve 100% success with my system. Just for the record, I call it a hunt whether you kill anything or not. Here is the rundown.

1. Plan your hunt. Make sure you have a strategy ahead of time. Set up in a good place that you found on your scouting trip and make sure you have a back up location identified before you leave the woods on scouting day. Set up in a place that makes sense to the system, where the deer do not sleep, eat, or breed. Planning your hunt and your strategy will help you avoid hold-ups and prevent you from being busted by the buck that hunts you. Not planning could result in a failed hunt and the only errors made will be your own.

2. Know your capabilities with your weapon, mainly how accurate you are at varied distances or odd angles. If bow hunting, shoot to the scrape on set up day and also shoot down in front of your tree (within 5 yards of it), to make sure you can hit the buck if he stops underneath your stand or in the scrape. Always give yourself the best odds of making a clean kill, by setting the D.I.E. scrape up crosswind of your stand just as many yards away as you are most accurate shot range (always less than 35 yards). Either the buck will come in from downwind of the scrape or he will follow you in. Stay alert and know that you have the upper hand on a D.I.E. hunt.

3. Practice your calling at home or in the car, not in actual hunting situations in your stand. Learn to make both buck tending grunts and doe in estrus bleats. Learning to wheeze wouldn't hurt you either. Know which sounds you are making with your calls or with your voice and only make them when the buck is not looking in your direction and when the sound would be appropriate to make. Never make more than one grunt or doe in estrus bleat. You have to keep him guessing!

4. Wash all your hunting clothes and your under-garments in scent free laundry detergent without UV-brighteners. Do not use any fabric softeners. Deal with any static you may get. Deer will not care.

5. Wash your entire body with scent free body wash, use scent free antiperspirant, and lip balm, if you use any at all—I do.

6. Wear camouflage clothing with tree limb and leaf patterns on it from head to toe, so all your body is covered except your eyes, mouth, and nostrils. Always wear a full-face mask, gloves, and a hat or ski mask. Spray your outer clothing with Scent Killer® 99% made by Wildlife Research Center® Inc. 14485 Azurite St NW Ramsey, MN 55303, or a similar product that you have never been busted by a deer using. You need to be invisible to deer, without it, you could be busted!

7. Learn to walk like a deer. Make the sounds of four legs instead of two. If you want the buck's attention when you walk in to your stand in the morning on Day 1 of your hunt, snap a twig under your foot near the scrape (not near your stand). Only walk like a deer when it is safe to do so.

8. Do not add anything to my D.I.E. system. Do not display behavior other than the behavior I teach you to display. No using other scents or lures, no dumping out leftover food or drink around your stand, and no urinating or defecating on the ground around your stand site or within 100 yards of it. In addition, absolutely no trail cameras allowed.

9. Practice sitting still in a stand from daylight to dark just one day if you can (before your actual hunt). I did it and I learned a lot. Set up your stand outside but far away from your hunting land. If you have a nice tree in your back yard, that will do. Practice staying still for 15–30 minutes at a time, and then moving only slightly if you have to. Then go another 15 to 30 minutes. Once you hunt with D.I.E. you will see that from the time the buck gets out of his bed, until the time he gets within 35 yards of you can be anywhere between 8 minutes and 45 minutes. Just do your best not to move unless you have to, and then always move your eyes before you move your head. You will never need to turn around in your stand if you set up with your toes facing the scrape, as I teach you. Only chew food or drink fluids for two or three minutes at a time or the buck can bust you. I learned that the hard way, so you will not have to. Never look a deer in the eyes.

10. Only go up in your tree stand as high as you need to in order to get out of the line of sight of any approaching deer. In my opinion, 10 feet up is the lowest I would sit, and 20 feet up is the highest. Those heights are how high your standing platform should be. Sitting higher can get you busted and is not as safe. Always wear a safety belt and attach it above your head in the tree. Always load your weapon as soon as you pull it up in the tree and do that as soon as you get safety belted in. The buck can approach as soon as your feet stop making sound on the ground. I have only hunted from trees but my system will work even if you are on the ground. It will be harder for you there because the buck will see you moving and you are in danger of being run over if you are in full camouflage, so I do not advise it. Hunt at your own risk, but always put safety first when hunting with D.I.E. Hunt alone but keep a cell phone with you on silent, so you can call for help if you ever need it.

11. Scout during the rut 10 to 14 days before the first day that you want to be in your stand. The rut is on then and the dominant buck has made his core dominant buck scrape upwind of the place he is bedding. That is where he will be meeting his first few does in estrus.

12. Check the wind, and find out which direction it is coming from before you enter the land (at the road). Also check it at the base of your tree stand, and then again, once you settle into the stand after you load your weapon. When setting up, check the wind by the scrape and set out three scent-dispensers with Trail's End #307 in them. One goes upwind behind the scrape 5 yards, and the other two go on each side of the scrape 4 feet away at hand-height off the ground. Do not place any scent in your tree on set up day. On the first day of your hunt, you will place some Trail's End #307 and some Still Steamin' Premium Hot Doe Estrus urine in your tree, around your body, as directed.

13. Walk in a different set of footprints each time you enter the woods to hunt. Day 1 - you always enter from upwind and crosswind looping to the scrape and arriving there on its upwind side. Day 2 - go straight to the stand from a crosswind or upwind angle. Day 3 -do the same thing as Day 2 but go 6 to 10 yards away from the trail you took in the day before. Day 4 - go crosswind if possible and head straight to the stand. Get in fast that day because the buck will be eager to meet you.

14. Always watch the scrape, the area downwind of it, and of you. No matter where you are, he is there watching your scrape and the area around it from downwind. Always enter the woods at the times I specify and if it is foggy that day, wait until you can see to shoot 20 yards or more. Never walk in while you cannot see 20 yards ahead. It is not safe for you there then. Think about it. The buck could be within 20 yards of you and you would not see him. That is why you should wait to go in until you can see 20 yards. In heavy fog the temperature is rising and the dripper is going to start dripping so do not hesitate any longer than you have to, get in there at a brisk pace when you can safely.

15. On Day 1, start walking into the territory of the herd 20 minutes after legal shooting hours open. Drag a key-wick dipped in Still Steamin' Premium Hot Doe Estrus urine behind you on a 12 to 15 foot long heavy ½" nylon rope. On Day 1 always walk in a looping direction, from upwind and crosswind making soft footsteps so you do not alert the buck to your being at the scrape until you are done doping it up. You want to be the doe in estrus that day, and she would move in quietly. After you switch out the lure, make louder steps "walking like a deer" to your stand. On days 2, 3, and 4, always make deliberate steps pounding your heel and your toe on the counts of one and three. You are making the sounds of the intruder buck with your feet but you are laying down the scent trail of the doe in estrus with the dragline on those days. See I told you that you could pull off being two deer at once!

16. When you get to the scrape on Day 1, do not cross the deer trail if there is one on the downwind side of the scrape and do not stand in front of the rubbed tree. Spend less than 8 minutes dumping the Active Scrape lure out and getting the Still Steamin' Premium Hot Doe Estrus urine into the Scrape Dripper, then hurry to your stand walking like a deer, and climb the tree. Know you are being watched so hurry up when at the scrape. You are invisible to him, but he will not wait long before scent checking the scrape and if all is

well, coming in. Always purge the dripper before leaving the scrape on set up day and on Day 1 of your hunt.

17. Once you get into your stand there is no getting out of it until closing time, unless you shoot your buck. Then you should go, and retrieve your trophy. Take a photo of you with your buck and submit it to me via email or mail a copy to me, and write a brief story about how you used my DOMINANCE IS EVERYTHING system to get him. With your permission, I will then post your story on my web site: **www.dominanceiseverything.com**. If you email your results, please email them to me at **mydiehuntresults@gmail.com**. The first 100 testimonials I get from the users of my system will be written (published) in my next book titled "DOMINANCE IS EVERYTHING… The Big Picture on Public Land!" Whether you shoot the buck or not, if you tell me the story of your first successful hunt with or without photos, I will post it publically with your written permission.

18. If you do not see the buck on Day 1 of your hunt, then you are going to have to hunt on Day 2, but first you have to get out of your stand without being seen on Day 1. Climb down 4 minutes before legal shooting hours close and step 10 feet or so upwind of your stand. You are done walking like a deer for the day. Drop the dragline with a new key-wick tied to it (dipped in #307) and jog into the nearest brush you see ahead (upwind) of you. Break some branches there. That will hold the advancing buck up, so he will not follow you. Now walk fast and steady like a human but keep your hands by your sides as you work your way out to your car or your home. Do not talk at all until you are out. Tomorrow is another day.

19. On Day 2, start walking into the territory of the herd 29 to 34 minutes after legal shooting hours open. That way the buck will not be able to pattern your approach to the area. Go in at a crosswind to your stand dragging the Still Steamin' Premium Hot Doe Estrus urine and pouring a few drops of the buck (#307) out every 30 yards. Calling is ok if you make just one note and space it 4 hours or more apart. Hunt until 4 minutes before legal shooting hours close. If you do not see the buck, then you will have to hunt on Day 3. Drag the buck (#307) out the same way you did on Day 1 after your hunt. Always close the scent dispensers that are up in the tree with you before you leave each night, that way the buck only smells the scent of the two deer at the scrape at night and in the area around the scrape and stand during the day when you are there. It forces him to come in during the day to meet the breeding pair of deer.

20. On Day 3, start walking into the territory of the herd 10 minutes after legal shooting hours open. That way the buck will not be able to pattern your approach to the area from the time you got there the day before. Go in at a crosswind again but this time from another angle. Go directly to your stand dragging the Still Steamin' Premium Hot Doe Estrus urine and pouring a few drops of the buck (#307) out every 30 yards. Calling is ok if you make just one note. Rattling will work if you do it as instructed. Hunt until 4 minutes before legal shooting hours close. If you do not see the buck, then you will have to hunt Day 4. Drag the buck (#307) out the same way you did on Day 1 and Day 2 after your hunt. Always close the scent dispensers that are up in the tree with you before you leave each night. Open them again when you get in the stand in the morning.

21. On Day 4, start walking into the territory of the herd right when legal shooting time opens or within 5 minutes after it opens. That way the buck will not be able to pattern your approach to the area from the time you got there the day before. Go in at a crosswind again but this time from another angle. Go directly to your stand dragging the Still Steamin' Premium Hot Doe Estrus urine and pouring a few drops of the buck (#307) out every 30 yards. Make deliberate steps with your feet today. Make sure you can hear your footsteps and make sure not to stop more than 5 or 10 seconds at a time every 18 to 26 deer steps as I have taught you. Always walk like a deer on the way in (if it is safe) and always jog out for the first 10 yards and walk briskly the rest of the way like a human when you leave. Communicate with the buck if he hangs up in cover. If he grunts wait until he is done and give him one doe bleat. He will show up. If he rakes a tree or makes a scrape while you watch, call to him with the doe bleat again. If he comes in with a doe but does not offer you a shot, then call with a buck grunt but only one grunt and make it deep sounding. He will come to your stand then. Calling is ok if you only make just one note. Rattling will work too if you do it as instructed. Hunt until 4 minutes before legal shooting hours close. If you do not see the buck by that time on Day 4, then you were busted by him at some point during the hunt. If you were busted you would know it.

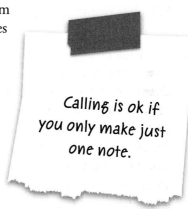

Calling is ok if you only make just one note.

The number one reason for hunter failure (being busted) is failure to remove trail cameras from your hunting property. I never used a trail camera on any of my D.I.E. hunts and in order for you to succeed; you need to hunt the same way I do.

The 7 ways a D.I.E. hunter has failed are:

1. By hunting while trail cameras were in place on the property
2. By setting up inside deer bedding areas
3. By quitting early. Getting out of the tree stand before the buck comes in or before the day's hunt is over. Also not returning to your stand to finish a hunt. I made that error twice. Both times the buck was hunting me, but I had to leave to work a day job.
4. By moving in the stand too much
5. By not pulling your weapon up
6. By being interfered with
7. By missing the shot

The easiest mistakes to fix are the ones you have not made yet. Those are numbered 1 through 5 above. Numbers 6 and 7 are two are things a deer hunter cannot always control. Shooting practice will help a hunter who misses a shot (7) and hunting on property that other people do not frequent will help a hunter that has been interfered with on a D.I.E. hunt (6).

There is a right way and a wrong way of doing everything. I found it difficult to write certain parts of this book because I had to discuss the wrong ways. The ways I was busted and the ways Tom and Rhino were busted by kings of the herds. We harvested some nice bucks with D.I.E. but I am sure there are going to be thousands more in a year or two. We were the pioneers who led the way for you to follow in our footsteps. I am very proud of Tom and Rhino, for being dedicated D.I.E. hunters, and for keeping my system, a secret for nearly 14 years combined. I couldn't be happier to see this book through to completion. It has been a long journey and I hope you feel that my story was worth the wait.

I am giving you all the information you need to use my **Dominance Is Everything** system the right way. It is up to you to show me what you have learned. When you succeed with D.I.E. I want to know about it. Please share your D.I.E. hunting stories with me so I can post the D.I.E. hunter's statistics on my website so future customers can see what the system is all about and how it works for people all across America and Canada.

I am giving you the best training I have given any D.I.E. hunter. I have showed you the way and have warned you of the wrong way. I have done my job to the fullest. I hope that you hunt with D.I.E. uses it as directed, at least the first time you hunt with it. If you do your best when you hunt with D.I.E. as I do, then you will be assured some happy endings to your hunts and a story to tell every season. I like to hunt with no regrets!

22. Never hunt on Day 5 because there isn't a Day 5. The stand site is a ghost town on Day 5, and rightfully so. Bucks figure out that the doe was not real and the whole herd is banned from going to that stand site anymore for a few days. It is off limits to all deer. We can only brainwash the king of deer for up to 4 days with my D.I.E. system. He will stay clear away from the scrape on Day 5. You will see if you ever waste a day to find out. I always saw my buck in four or less days so I have never hunted Day 5 but one of the other people I taught tried it, once. He agrees with me that Day 5 is a great day to remove your scent dispensers the dripper and your tree stand from the area. No deer will be there to see you remove it on the fifth day. Do not hunt from the same stand for more than 4 consecutive days.

23. If you got your buck, another buck is dominant within 2 hours, but that buck has to mark his territory first. If you have a friend or a family member who wants to hunt from your stand, after a D.I.E. hunt do not let them. Pull your stand and give the area a day to rest. Otherwise, you will be wising up the herd. They will be able to pattern you, and they will bust you. Deer remember to stay away from places they encountered humans in the past. No doe would be in heat for more than four days, and hunting from a stand for more than four days allows deer to figure out that the D.I.E. system is not real. You can hunt from the same tree and use the same scrape a month later or a year later, but I would not do it a day later. Pick another stand and scrape site on the property for your friend and they will have 100% odds from that place. I have not tested putting another trained D.I.E. hunter in my stand after I took my buck, so I am not as convinced that it would work 100% of the time, as I am convinced that setting it up in a new area 100 or more yards away would. Get out of view of your old set-up if you are putting in a new one.

24. Remember the king of the herd can change with the outcome of every dominant buck fight, or if the dominant buck is killed or wounded by a hunter, a predator, or a vehicle collision. DOMINANCE IS EVERYTHING to all mature breeder bucks. You will see a mature breeder buck at your scrape if you follow all my instructions. No one has ever been able to prove me wrong, and over 30 people have hunted successfully with it prior to the date this book was published. The D.I.E. system is as real as it gets!

25. In gun season and in bow season you always need to be sure it is safe to walk like a deer and that you are alone where you are hunting. If other people are near you do not use D.I.E. on that hunt, and never walk like a deer when other people are around (to be safe).

26. Always use the lures as I direct you to. Do not refill any lure bottles or dispensers except those with you in the tree. Never stop on your way in or out to re-dip the key-wick. It is not necessary. I have never done it and I have never needed to. Do not change a thing if you want to succeed all of the time. If you have issues during your hunt, try opening up this book again, to see where you went wrong. If you think you did everything right, but the buck still busted you, check the 'Never Do' list to make sure you didn't miss something. I am available to my customers but certainly not 24 hours a day. I know my system works exactly as I teach it, so you should be able to work through your issues on your own. In case you cannot, then you might want to take in one of my seminars so I can teach you how to use it personally.

27. Never ignore the D.I.E. rules. It works anywhere there are no trail cameras on the property you are hunting. As long as you are alone there and you are never interfered with, or the hunting area isn't interfered with, and when you are willing to follow all of my instructions, you will have success. If you want to see your herd's king then you need to commit to do what D.I.E. requires of you - nothing more and nothing less.

28. Always build the D.I.E. scrape exactly the same way each time you hunt with DOMINANCE IS EVERYTHING—No exceptions!

Here is the timeline of an entire hunt with D.I.E.

Here is the timeline of an actual hunt with **Bob J. Mercier's DOMINANCE IS EVERYTHING** system. You can set it up anytime as long as the rut has been on (when deer are breeding) for at least 10 days, and you can use it successfully until the last doe in estrus goes out of estrus. The whole rut is open to you and you can succeed whenever you use it. I find the first week of November (in Wisconsin) to be the most exciting week a buck hunter can be in the woods. I do not always hit the buck when I take a shot, but my hunts are still 100% successful.

For the sake of saving space in the following diagram, I abbreviated the following sets of words:

I abbreviated the words **"AFTER LEGAL SHOOTING HOURS OPEN"** to be ALSHO

I abbreviated the words **"BEFORE LEGAL SHOOTING HOURS CLOSE"** to be BLSHC

TABLE 2.

October 20	**SCOUTING DAY** Scouting Hours 10 a.m. – 2 p.m. Scout when you can (one time only), 10-14 days before Day 1 of your hunt	Scout for rubs and scrapes, find doe bedding and pick 2 different set up locations upwind and crosswind of the deer sign. Setting up on the upwind side of a trail is an excellent choice. Less than 120 yards into the woods is even better. Make sure there are deer trails 360° all the way around you.
October 31 Halloween	**SET UP DAY** Set Up Hours 10 a.m. – 2 p.m. Take a friend along	Set up your tree stand first and face it directly to your scrape. Position yourself so the wind hits you in the back of your shooting shoulder. Then build the D.I.E. scrape and dope it up. Practice shooting (bow) to the scrape. Go home.
November 1	**WAITING PERIOD** Day 1 of 2	Stay away from the land and the stand site completely. The buck has to find the scrape and take it over and this is his time to do it.
November 2	**WAITING PERIOD** Day 2 of 2	Stay away from the land and the stand site completely. The buck has to find the scrape and take it over and this is his time to do it.
November 3	**Day 1 of your hunt**	Start 20 minutes ALSHO. Go arching to the scrape dragging the doe urine and pouring the buck (#307) out every 30 yards. Change the dripper to doe, and get in your stand. Stay quiet all day. Hunt until 4 min. BLSHC. Drag the buck (#307) out.
November 4	**Day 2 of your hunt**	Start 29 to 34 min. ALSHO. Go crosswind to stand dragging the doe urine and pouring the buck (#307) out every 30 yards. Calling is ok if just one note. Hunt until 4 min. BLSHC. Drag the buck (#307) out.

November 5	**Day 3 of your hunt**	Start 10 min. ALSHO. Go in upwind & crosswind to the stand but on a different angle dragging the doe and pouring buck every 30 yards. Calling is ok if just one note. Rattling or decoying is ok. Hunt until 4 min. BLSHC. Drag buck (#307) out.
November 6	**Day 4 of your hunt**	Start 1 to 5 minutes ALSHO. Go in upwind & crosswind to the stand but on a different angle dragging the doe and pouring buck every 30 yards. Make loud steps so the buck will respond to you. Calling is ok if just one note. Rattling and decoying work. Hunt until 4 min. BLSHC. Drag the buck (#307) out.

Chapter 22

Freezing temps require you to modify your D.I.E. hunt

When you are hunting in cold climates in late November, December, and early January you may experience problems with the Scrape-Dripper freezing up. First of all you should know I am not affiliated with the makers of the Scrape-Dripper, therefore I do not know the answer to how to make a Scrape-Dripper work in freezing temperatures. You may want to contact the manufacturer 'Wildlife Research Center Inc.' and ask that question of them. I use a common sense approach to working with frozen Scrape-Drippers and I still achieve 100% success with D.I.E. as long as I always do it this one way. I will share my experiences with you here so you can overcome this obstacle if you ever encounter it on your hunt.

The first time I experienced a frozen Scrape-Dripper, I pulled the D.I.E. set-up out and I chose a warmer 4-day period to hunt, but that is not always an option. The weather gets colder as fall progresses into winter, and sometimes a person decides to press on and finish the hunt because they do not have another four-day period to hunt. In cases like that, you can still make it happen, but you need to change your tactics on Day 1 and Day 2 of your hunt. Day 3 and Day 4 stay the same. You never go to the scrape on Day 3 or Day 4 even if a dripper is frozen. That is because the dripper is (normally) empty on Day 3 and Day 4 anyway, so just stay away from it.

If the temperature where you hunt drops below 32 degrees, prepare to encounter a frozen Scrape-Dripper by purchasing two Scrape-Drippers before your first hunt. That way you can hunt with D.I.E. anytime during the rut including during cold weather. There is only one time that a D.I.E. hunter will ever be at the scrape to discover a frozen scrape dripper, and that is in the morning on Day 1 of your hunt. When you open the cap on the Scrape-Dripper if you find that the Active Scrape is slushy, or that the bottle has ice crystals in it, you need to swap it out with a new one. Take that frozen dripper home with you and thaw it out after your hunt on Day 1, so you can use it on Day 2 again, that is unless you harvested the buck on Day 1. On the morning of Day 2 bring the clean and dry dripper back to the D.I.E. scrape and replace the one you hung in the tree on Day 1. Again, only add ¼ of the Still Steamin' Premium Hot Doe Estrus urine to the new dripper. This is the only instance in which I will advise you to approach the scrape the same way on Day 2 as you did on Day 1. Arch your way into the scrape on both of those days, but do not walk the exact same path. Be sure you purge the Scrape-Dripper each time you put a new one in so you can verify that it is dripping before you climb into your tree stand. Once you get in the stand, do not get out until the end of the day. Anytime you get down you could get busted, so I do all I can to stay in the stand until I get my shot at the buck.

If the lures freeze you should replenish the scent dispensers

If you used scent dispensers (using them is optional) as directed, you would have three scent dispensers in a triangular pattern around the scrape and all of them would have Trail's End #307 in them when you arrived there in the morning on Day 1. Replace the two scent dispensers on the sides of the scrape with two new scent dispensers and pour a nickel-sized drop of the same doe urine that you used in the Scrape-Dripper, into each of these two scent dispensers. The nearby-bedded buck will be able to smell that urine within a few minutes, so add the urine to the scent dispensers last. Then get in your stand as soon as you can.

If you did not place any scent dispensers out on set up day, I strongly advise you to use them now because of the freezing temperatures. Anything you can do to help the scent drift throughout the area while you are in the stand would be a good thing. Place one scent dispenser on each side of the scrape about 4 feet off to each side. I put them at hand height.

You can top off the two scent canisters on Day 2 if you want to, it will help you get the scent of the doe in estrus out to the bedded buck. **Caution: There is also one scent dispenser placed 5 yards behind the scrape and it has Trail's End #307 lure in it. You placed it there on set-up day. That scent dispenser should never be topped off.** Leave it there so the dominant buck can still smell a hint of the presence of the challenging buck that made the scrape.

Do not ever challenge the dominant buck at the D.I.E. scrape after set up day. Adding more #307 lure to the scrape would be a challenge to the most dominant buck. So never do it. He owns the scrape on Day 1 of your hunt and he has to remain unchallenged by your invisible buck in order for him to believe that the situation that D.I.E. presents him with is a real one. The brainwashing ends if the buck figures out that a human is hunting him.

My next statement only applies to this one scenario of having a frozen Scrape-Dripper. I never want anyone who uses D.I.E. to approach the scrape after the morning of Day 1, for any reason! This is the only exception to that rule.

If you have to deal with a frozen Scrape-Dripper, then you have to visit the scrape before going to your stand on each of the first two mornings of your hunt. Be sure you keep the time you spend there to a minimum, and be sure not to make any noises while standing there that will call attention to yourself. Normally you want to move your feet to get the buck's attention when you are at the scrape but not in snow or on frozen ground. The buck can be bedded as close as 5 yards downwind or crosswind of the scrape, but most likely, he is 35 to 50 yards away on Days 1 and 2. If he sees you there on the ground, you are busted.

If the dripper is frozen when you get there on Day 1 you will have to swap it out and come back once more the morning of Day 2 to replace it again. You can never be sure how far away he is, so it is very important that you walk in arching towards the scrape on Day 1 and Day 2.

On Day 1, always start from upwind and crosswind of the scrape and work crosswind in an arching direction so your final approach to the scrape is from straight upwind. Stagger your approach time the next day so you enter the area at least, 7 to 15 minutes later on Day 2 than you did on Day 1. That will prevent the buck from patterning you on your approach. On Days 3 and 4, go directly to your stand and avoid the scrape completely. By that time, the buck is hunting you and not the scrape, although he still has to visit the scrape each day, his response to your set up is triggered when you arrive at your stand, instead of when the dripper starts dripping.

The more briskly you walk like a deer and pound your heel and toe, the more eager the buck will be to get to your scrape that day. He can hear you walk in and he is listening for you to arrive (as a deer). By approaching in the arching direction from upwind, he will not hear you until you are at the scrape. Walk softly and do not linger at the scrape. Never cross the deer trail if there is one near the scrape, unless it is necessary, and if you have to, then do not stand on the trail for even one second. The dominant buck is watching that trail and the scrape 24/7 from the time he scent checks the area on Day 1. That is because he locks into the scent of the doe in estrus. He focuses on looking for a body mass that blocks his view of the rub on the tree, or one that stands on the deer trail. If your body blocks his view of the rub behind the scrape, you will be busted. So, always come in quiet and once you are there, stand off to the upwind side of the scrape. That way you will not block the buck's view to the rubbed tree behind the scrape. Count on him always being downwind or crosswind of the scrape and of your stand.

Each day you should approach the stand quietly walking like a deer (granted you determine it to be safe). Keep your toes facing straight forward. If you want to walk loudly, then point your toes out away from your body. In this case, you want to go to the scrape as quietly as possible, so you should keep your toes pointed forward and set your feet down softly. You need to get in your tree stand unseen by the buck each day. That way you are invisible to all the deer in the area.

He will scent check the scrape one or two hours after sunrise and he will often make his entrance at that time if all is quiet and peaceful in the area. You do not want the sound of your footsteps to trigger his arrival if you are dealing with a frozen dripper, but otherwise you do. You may need time to replace a frozen dripper with a dry one and you will have the time (3 to 5 minutes) when you approach your stand from an upwind angle arching towards the scrape.

When you get there, each morning on Day 1 and Day 2 (only), you need to swap out the frozen dripper and install a warm Scrape-Dripper with just ¼ bottle of the Still Steamin' Premium Hot Doe Estrus urine in it. D.I.E. is designed to keep the buck guessing, and part of that design is how the scrape is maintained. On Day 3 and Day 4, you do not want any doe urine dripping into the scrape. You only want it on your dragline as you walk to your tree stand. Completely avoid going to the scrape on Day 3 and Day 4, on all of your D.I.E. hunts if you want to succeed 100% of the time.

Do everything normally on set up day. Just pack a second Scrape-Dripper in your backpack, and be ready to remove the frozen dripper from above the scrape and replace it with the warm one from your backpack, if needed on Day 1 or Day 2. If you take a frozen dripper out on Day 1, then thaw it out at home, rinse it out with water, and dry it out with a blow dryer. Pack it in your backpack for use on Day 2 if needed.

Warning: After setting the D.I.E. system up, never go to the scrape or the stand site until you intend to hunt it on Day 1. Even if you think the Scrape-Dripper is frozen, do not go back to it before the morning of Day 1 or the buck will bust you 100% of the time. When you originally set the system up you added Active Scrape to the Scrape-Dripper as directed. Do not go back to the scrape for 2 ½ days, if you want to have 100% odds of seeing the most dominant buck within 35 yards during the day. I am going to assume you are on Day 1 of your hunt when you first discover the Scrape-Dripper is frozen up. You would realize this when you open the dripper to dump out the Active Scrape and you notice it is iced up under the nozzle. The best thing for you to do is to replace the entire dripper with a new one and put ¼ bottle of the Scent Shield Still Steamin' Premium Hot Doe Estrus urine in the new dripper instead of the normal ½ bottle of urine. Take the frozen dripper home and thaw it out. Be sure you bag it up so you do not get deer lure on your clothes or in your vehicle.

Plan for the worst case scenario, and you will be prepared

If you do not have two Scrape-Drippers, you really should purchase a second one before the season so if and when it freezes, you will still be in business. I have six of them. I only use one or two at a set up, but I bought more in case I lose the nozzles. On numerous occasions, I have come back to my set up on Day 1 of the hunt, only to find the scrape was torn to shreds and the branch that the dripper was tied to was broken off and was laying on the ground in the scrape. The buck got furious with the licking branch and the branch the dripper was tied to, he broke them down with his rack. The nozzle for the dripper was missing and because it is black, I can never seem to find them on the ground near the scrape. Even if I did find it, having debris inside the tube would hamper the way the lure comes out of it, and then I could not use it with confidence. You are better off having an extra Scrape-Dripper in your backpack on Day 1, than not having one. That way you are ready for anything.

Do not give up if the buck is still hunting you

If you are stuck with one dripper and it is frozen up yet you do not want to quit, you can make the most of your hunt by hunting day by day the best you can. You will have to drag the Still Steamin' Premium Hot Doe Estrus urine in with you to your stand each day and then drag the Trail's End #307 out of the area when you leave. The odds of success will be 50 to 99% if your Scrape-Dripper has frozen up and is not dripping, as long as you drag the lure in and out. Many hunters will experience a frozen dripper if they choose to hunt in winter. I intend to hunt the late rut for the next two seasons with my bow so I can experiment with new tactics while hunting in snow on public land using my system. To me, having 50% odds of meeting the king of deer is better than having zero odds. If I find myself on a hunt and I am facing an obstacle, I "take the bull by the horns", so to speak. I would much rather try to overcome it and continue hunting with D.I.E., than quit and pull the system out. If the buck has not busted me and the buck worked the scrape before the morning of Day 2, I will hunt the full four days even if I get a freeze up. In that case, the buck is hunting me and I am determined to wait him out. I know that I will get a close encounter with him if I toy with his mind and taunt him, messing with his dominance at the scrape. It will not matter if there is scent dripping in the scrape or not. Immediately make your choice to finish your hunt, or to pull out, either way do it with no regrets.

Wearing snowshoes helps keep you invisible

Remember you are invisible to all deer if you are in full camouflage, you are quiet, motionless, and you are 99% scent free. If you have mastered being invisible to deer then you needn't worry about them identifying you as a human by your tracks in the snow. I have learned that deer cannot identify snowshoe prints as being made by a human. If there is snow on the ground (no matter how deep it is) wear snowshoes when you walk into your stand site, and drag the Scent Shield Still Steamin' Premium Hot Doe Estrus urine in behind you starting at the first sign of real deer. Any mature dominant buck, monster buck or swamp buck that finds that trail will follow it in close to your location and then he will go downwind of you and do a lip curl, and a scent check. If you pass his tests, he will approach the scrape.

Chapter 23

"SAFETY FIRST" while gun hunting with D.I.E.

Up until 2006, I never used my DOMINANCE IS EVERYTHING system during gun season because I felt it would be too dangerous to "walk like a deer" when other people were armed in the woods. What changed in 2006, is that I decided to tell my entire hunting party that I was going to walk out to my D.I.E. stand site in broad daylight, and that I would be making the sounds of a deer walking (for the last 120 yards) as I approached my stand. They agreed not shoot into my area for any reason, and also not to conduct any deer drives near my stand. Each person in my hunting party agreed to stay away from the area until I got my buck, and they all guaranteed me that they would never shoot at a deer without first seeing it clearly, and then making sure the shot was in a safe direction (away from fellow hunters). Their promises were good enough for me, so I set out on my first gun deer hunt with D.I.E. feeling safe about hunting during gun season with it. On that hunt I encountered the largest racked, biggest bodied buck that I have ever seen in my life! I wish I could have a second chance at that majestic king of deer, but I cannot. I rushed my shot and I missed the vitals on that monster buck at 15 yards. I lost him to two other hunters from outside my hunting party, that both unloaded their weapons on him after he left my area. I tracked his blood trail for a mile until I saw signs that two people were trailing him ahead of me. I could tell I had hit him in the front leg and that it was not a fatal shot. I felt sick and disappointed in myself because I knew better than to rush a shot at a standing deer. I do not know if they ever caught up with him. When I first laid eyes on him, he was standing broadside just 15 yards away. He snuck in behind me at 9 o'clock in the morning on Day 2 of my hunt. The wind had shifted its direction 180 degrees from the day before, and was now coming from the Southeast instead of the Northwest. I messed up that day by not using a scent checker to identify the prevailing wind as soon as I settled into my tree stand. Checking the wind is a necessity for every D.I.E. hunter. Do not assume that the wind direction is the same as it was a few hours ago. It changes often, sometimes more than once a day and you have to know what direction the wind is carrying your scent in order to know where the buck will be coming from. Then you can see him make his move into the area.

If I had only done what I teach you to do, I would have succeeded at harvesting a monster 300+ pound 5+ year old record-book buck with main beams as big as my forearms. Instead, I rushed my shot and hit him poorly in one of his front legs. In hindsight, I regret taking that shot all together. Monster buck fever is real folks! Let me tell you! I surely was suffering from a bad case of it that day.

My D.I.E. system is as safe to use in gun season as it is to use in bow season—as long as you do not "walk like a deer" on your hunt during gun season. You do not have to walk like a deer to have the D.I.E. system work. All you need to do is get in your stand without being seen by any deer in the area, and without being positively identified as a human. Walking like a deer makes the most dominant buck hunt both you and the D.I.E. scrape, but just walking in silently as a human will bring him in too.

Public Land Hunters Beware! Walking like a deer makes you a target and doing so on public land could get you shot during gun deer season, if you hunt around people who do not hunt safely. I do not want anyone to get hurt while hunting with D.I.E., so I advise you to never risk your safety, your life, or the life of others when deer hunting with DOMINANCE IS EVERYTHING. Never "walk like a deer" during gun season unless you are 100% sure that there are no other people in the area (within a half mile) around you.

If you are not sure, it is 100% safe, never assume it is, and if you do walk like a deer in gun season, know that you are doing it at your own risk. When in doubt, go without! Your safety is #1 when hunting. Never take a chance with your life. You only have one!

Choose one of these 3 OPTIONS before going GUN DEER HUNTING with D.I.E.

OPTION 1 = Do not use D.I.E. during gun season at all. (That's the safest way)

Choosing OPTION 1, keeps you safe to hunt another day, but it takes away your opportunity to become hunted by the king of deer. I personally would rather not hunt for bucks on a property if I could not use D.I.E. safely there. It has been a sure thing for me and hunting traditionally is not exciting for me anymore. I want to be hunted by kings, but that is just me.

OPTION 2 = Use D.I.E. but opt out of "walking like a deer" during the hunt.

If you choose Option 2 and you hunt with D.I.E. but do not walk like a deer, you will still get the results you seek, as long as you are not busted by any deer as you make your way to the stand each day. Go to your stand the same way as I directed you to if you were walking like a deer, instead this time, just walk as a human. Walk slowly and softly instead of making abrupt deer hoof sounds. If you do it correctly the dominant buck will hunt the scrape, he just will not be hunting you. Another thing you need to do differently on a gun hunt is not drag in any Scent Shield brand Still Steamin' Premium Hot Doe Estrus urine to the stand in the morning. Instead, drag in a key-wick dipped in Trail's End #307. The #307 will act as your cover scent, and when the dominant buck gets a whiff of it, he will be convinced that you are the intruder buck that originally made the scrape. He will stay bedded while you pass by his location and soon after you get in your stand, he will move downwind of the scrape and attempt to find you there (as the intruder buck).

When you hunt with D.I.E., you never want to call attention to yourself as a human. In this case, you will not be dragging the doe in estrus urine behind you because that would get the attention of the dominant buck, and it would make him pursue you on your scent trail immediately. If he did that, he would not hear the sounds of a doe walking into the area instead he would hear the sounds of a human walking in. That is the reason why walking like a human and dragging the scent of one single doe in estrus will get you busted. When you are busted, your hunt is over and the buck wins. That is why I never drag the doe in estrus urine when I am walking like a human. It is a different story when you drag in the Trail's End #307 and you walk quietly as a human. The dominant buck still gets wind of your scent as the intruder buck, but he does not follow it right away. He lets you get to your tree stand before he advances. That is what you want him to do in that case. Use the #307 if you are gun hunting and decide to walk like a human, that way you are not at a higher than normal risk of getting hurt. Always be safe.

OPTION 3 = Continue to hunt with D.I.E. as you would on a bow hunt.

Walk in like a deer and drag the Scent Shield Still Steamin' Premium Hot Doe Estrus urine to your stand in the morning, but first verify that you are the only hunter in the woods at the time, and that your life is not in any danger. You must be 100% sure that no one will mistake you for a real deer if they hear you walking like a deer. If you are not the only hunter that will be in the woods, you need to talk to the other hunters ahead of time. Tell them how you will be acting and why. Tell them to stay away from you, and tell them not to shoot in your direction. Tell them where you will be walking in and where you are planning to walk out each day. Check in with the other hunters if they are members of your hunting camp, and make sure they know where to look for you if you do not come back after dark. You should be at the road or in your yard within 20 minutes after legal shooting hours close. Staying any longer will get you busted.

With all three options, you should never walk like a deer in the dark. If you do, you could be killed. I am not kidding. A dominant buck is capable of running through you (because you are invisible to him) or worse yet another hunter could mistake the sounds of your footsteps for those of a deer and shoot you. You should never go into the woods "walking like a deer" in the dark or while you are unarmed. It isn't safe to walk like a deer at any time unless all of the following statements are true: you can defend yourself, you can see what is coming toward you, and you know there aren't any other people in the area while you are there.

Never risk your safety when gun hunting with D.I.E.

I have hunted with D.I.E. during gun season for three consecutive seasons now, and each time I had the most dominant buck hunting me. I will certainly do it again, but I will make darn sure that my life is not in danger before I walk like a deer on any hunt. Up until now, I have always hunted on private property for my gun hunts, and the members of my family are safe hunters, so I have not been in any danger on any of my hunts, but I never take anything for granted. I will never attempt to hunt with D.I.E. if there is a chance I could be mistaken for a real deer (by a human). You need to have a conversation with every deer hunter in your hunting party before you go into the woods. Let them know exactly where you will be hunting, and tell them that you will be making the sounds of a deer, the same sounds a deer makes as it walks through the woods headed toward its bedding area. First, ask them nicely to stay out of the area then tell them to stay away! They must stay at least 150 yards away from your stand site the whole time you or any of your D.I.E. set-up gear (tree stand, scrape, and Scrape-Dripper) is in the woods. That is from set up day until you get your buck, or until the end of Day 4, whichever comes first. If they refuse to stay away, I recommend that you do not use D.I.E. at that location. You will get busted and wise up the dominant buck to the system, not to mention your life could be in danger. It is imperative that you take these necessary precautions to avoid becoming a victim of a shooting accident.

I do not advise anyone to walk like a deer if it is possible that another human being could hear the sound of your footsteps, or if you know that another person is nearby and you know that they cannot see you (whether they are armed or not).

People get excited when they hear a deer approaching, and if they hear you walking like a deer they will not know you are a human, unless you tell them ahead of time. Never risk your safety or risk your life when deer hunting. Never "walk like a deer" in gun season, unless you are 100% sure there are no other people in the area. If you do it, you are doing so at your own risk.

I am not responsible for your decisions or for your actions, only you are. So please be careful and do not ever put yourself at risk of being hurt or killed while deer hunting. It is not worth it. Always promise yourself to put your safety ahead of your urges to gun hunt using DOMINANCE IS EVERYTHING. It is what is required of you.

I keep warm in my stand in winter as I wait for the buck. My facemask is off so you know who I am.

©2010 Robert J. Mercier (self-portrait)

Do not forget that DOMINANCE IS EVERYTHING works all throughout the rut, in both gun and bow seasons here in Wisconsin. I do not know when the rut is on in your neck of the woods, but you can be sure that D.I.E. will bring the king to you, if deer are mating in your state or province when you hunt with it. If you can bear the elements that Mother Nature unleashes in winter I think you will enjoy a winter hunt with DOMINANCE IS EVERYTHING.

Chapter 24

How to talk like a deer

Let me start off by saying, you never need to use a deer call or a doe decoy in order to make the dominant buck hunt you with my system. This system is self-sustaining, but if you want to be able to talk to the buck when he is near you, then you need to have a call or a voice like a deer to do it. I have mastered the use of both.

What I knew about calling bucks prior to inventing D.I.E.

I used a buck grunt call on my deer hunts ever since I started bow hunting in 1993. The first time I bought a call I read the instructions on the package, and then I practiced with the call. I thought it sounded good to me, and I was all set to go monster buck hunting, or so I thought. I went deer hunting and I did what the calling instructions told me to do. They said make three long grunts into the call if you see a big buck, and it will be as if you had challenged him to a battle. If he is willing to come in, he will likely charge in at that very second. The instructions also stated that if there was not a big buck around, I should never make the three long grunts in succession, because it may scare away any lesser bucks that are in the area. I had bought this call so I would be able to call in a big buck, and I thought it would be as easy as that.

I had never been face to face with a mature buck during daylight while I was hunting, so I assumed that every deer I heard walking through the woods prior to shooting time, had to be a big buck. I used to go to my tree stand each day about an hour before legal shooting time so I could settle in my stand and give the deer a chance to get used to me being there, near their bedding area, before sunrise. I was a traditional deer hunter back then. I hunted according to what I was taught by other people, and I tried new things based on how many of the people I knew were using the stuff.

One morning during gun season, hunting in Northern Wisconsin, I was sitting in my stand near a core doe bedding area and I heard a deer walking slowly towards me. It was about 50 yards away and upwind of me. Shooting hours had not opened yet and it was still too dark to see. It stopped walking when it got close to me, so I started assuming that it had to be a monster buck. I knew they were nocturnally acting deer and that monster bucks were smarter than me, so I figured I had to be really lucky to just happen to see one, and even luckier than that to be successful at shooting one. I pulled my grunt call from my coat and I blew it making three long deep sounding grunts. The deer responded by wheezing and it trotted out of the area. I figured that deer must have been a lesser buck; otherwise, he would have stood his ground instead of running away.

A few minutes later, another deer came trotting into my area and it put on the brakes in about the same place the first one had stopped. I was not wearing any scent free clothes, but I did wash up with soap and water earlier that morning. Now I know better, but I didn't then. When this deer stopped, I still could not see it in the early morning light, and I did not want it to run away as the last one did so I decided to make two short grunts instead of three long ones. I didn't have a clue what two short grunts meant to a buck, or even if my grunts sounded real to that buck or doe, but I thought, it was worth a try to see if that deer would respond to me. I was wrong! There was never a vocal response from that deer, and again it trotted away into the bedding area downwind of me.

Now what? What was I doing wrong? Maybe I did it all right and those deer where does or fawns and they only sounded big to me. I thought it was possible that they were not alarmed from the sounds I made and that they would come back later in the morning to see what I was. I found out the hard way that a hunter should never blow a grunt call unless they are sure of what they are saying and to which particular deer they are saying it to. If you are experiencing these types of problems when you blow your grunt call, it is probably because you do not have an idea of what a grunt call was made to do.

Was it the call, or was it the caller that had really failed? I will tell you sincerely I believe it was a little of both. I didn't have any experience at that time using deer calls, and had never studied what sounds a human could make with a deer call that would really attract deer. Like many other hunters, I had only heard some buck grunts at a distance and I was not sure if the sounds I heard were really being made by a real buck or another hunter blowing a deer call, because I had never actually seen a buck grunting while one was within view of me. The only sounds I knew deer made were fawn bleats, snorts and sneezing. I called it blowing but I now call it wheezing. I was not sure which deer were making the sounds, and I had no clue as to why they made them. Sure, I had a lot to learn—do you? If not, then I commend you, but if you do have a lot to learn about calling dominant bucks then I think you will really appreciate reading the way I explain it to you throughout the rest of this chapter.

That buck grunt call was supposed to make me a better hunter, and I knew I had to practice with it so I would be ready to step up to the plate with a monster buck, when I finally would encounter one. Getting practice with the call was not the problem. The problem was that the instructions were too vague, and I was trying to find out what sounds I could make with it that would attract a buck to me, instead of scaring them away from me. I used that call for three gun seasons and three bow seasons. I only harvested 2 bucks in those six years, and neither of them ever heard one grunt out of me!

I only had one monster buck within view of me in all of those six hunts combined. I was bow hunting on our 12-acre parcel of land in New Berlin. I was new to bow hunting, and at that time, I didn't use any lures. A 12-point monster buck came out of some tag alder brush and started eating on the soybean field about 80 yards straight upwind of me. I was well hidden in a 30-foot pine tree and that buck could not see me. I pulled the grunt tube (buck call) out of my jacket pocket, and I blew three long deep grunts towards him. He was grazing on soybeans and he barely took notice of me. He looked up in my direction and then he put his head back down and ignored me all together. I was using a Carry-Lite full body buck decoy, and I had a real 8-point rack of antlers on it, and a real tail. The monster buck's rack was twice as big as the rack on my decoy.

The decoy was positioned under my stand facing NW quartering away from me, and the monster buck was straight ahead of it about 70 yards away facing me. The wind was from the North and it was opening weekend in the Wisconsin Archery Deer Season, which falls on the second weekend in September. When he heard the sounds of my grunts, he did not move one inch. He just fed there for the next 3 hours, staying more than 65 yards away from me at all times. When it got dark and legal shooting hours closed, I cased my bow, climbed down from my tree stand, picked up my decoy, bagged it up, and then I went home. The buck stayed on the edge of the field watching me pick up and ship out. I could not scare him away. It was as if he was taunting me saying you are not smart enough for the likes of me! He was right! I was as green as green gets, and he was a monster buck that was going to live out the rest of his life without ever being threatened by me. Up until that day, I never saw any monster bucks face to face while I made grunts, and because he was so smart and didn't fall for it, I decided to stop using the grunt tube indefinitely. It was back to waiting patiently for a buck to happen along the main trail again. That is all I knew I should do to see a buck back then. Boy, have things changed for me since I started hunting with DOMINANCE IS EVERYTHING and you will see plenty of changes as you start using my system too.

What a grunt call was made to do

Grunt calls are made to imitate the real sounds of bucks during the rut so a hunter can make the sounds while hunting and pass himself or herself off as a real buck. I did not understand deer vocalizations back then, not like I do now anyway, and for that reason, I know now that I was just out there making noises that could not be deciphered by any deer, therefore they never believed that I was one of them. Blowing a deer call just for the heck of it, or because you are bored when you are using my DOMINANCE IS EVERYTHING system, will cause the dominant buck to become alerted to the presence of a human when he hears your second note. You are much better off not calling at all until the second you want to stop the buck for the shot. When that time comes you should not yell, whistle, or bark like a dog to stop the buck, because those are human sounds and dog sounds and you do not want him to know that a human or a dog is there in case you miss him. You would want another shot opportunity, wouldn't you? Instead, you should call with your mouth or a grunt tube and make one blast of a grunt like an intruder buck. He will be expecting that, and he will stop to see where this buck is before he takes another step. I like to wait until the buck is near my scrape because I have a clear shot there, but if you are gun hunting you can take him whenever you can successfully hit him with a fatal shot. Do not chance a poor shot, because you will likely miss him, and the buck will know you are there and your hunt will be over. I like to make the grunt with my mouth to stop the buck. I say "NNNaahh". The bucks have all stopped in their tracks to that sound, and they look straight ahead, because they never know where the sound is coming from. On most of my hunts with D.I.E., the buck stands broadside of me when he stops, and on 90% of my hunts, the buck has been within 15 yards of me. Close encounters with monster bucks give me "Buck fever" baby! I suffer from a severe case of it!

I highly recommend a Grunt Snort Wheeze call made by M.A.D. Calls.

I highly recommend a Grunt Snort Wheeze call made by M.A.D. Calls even though it has been out of production for a few years now. I have used this call with 100% success, on all my D.I.E. hunts. I call it the voice of the herd. This one call can mimic the sound of every deer in the herd. It has been very convincing to the bucks that have hunted me, and I will not go to my stand without it. There is a 'Big Picture' with regards to calling and using decoys in conjunction with D.I.E., and I will paint that picture for you here. You should know that it is ok to use a grunt tube with D.I.E. but you need to know when to do it, and how to do it.

There are only 3-buck sounds you should make from your stand. The others will not work with the system. The three sounds are tending grunts, dominant buck growls, and rattling antlers. You should become familiar with all of these sounds and if you choose, you can use them successfully with my DOMINANCE IS EVERYTHING system. I have tested each of these sounds while hunting dominant bucks and I found I could use them all without changing the outcome of my hunt for the worse. **I choose to use a Grunt, Snort, Wheeze call made by M.A.D. Calls. It can make fawn bleats, doe in estrus bleats, buck grunts from yearling bucks, mature bucks, and monster bucks, and it also makes a snort and a wheeze**. I love it!

Follow my directions and the eyes of the most dominant buck in the area will not be on you as a hunter blowing a grunt call. If you do this right, the dominant buck will not look for you with his eyes; instead, he will hunt you and seek you out by listening to the sounds of your voice. Your voice will be the voice of a monster intruder buck that is attempting to mate with the doe in estrus (at the D.I.E. scrape), smack dab in front of your stand. The sound of your voice or your call will bring the dominant buck in for battle.

The only time you should ever make any deer calls when you are using D.I.E., is when you are actually sitting in your tree stand scent free and completely concealed. Calling from the ground is dangerous, because the buck will charge in and you will be surprised to say the least. You should be in your stand where you have a better view of the area, and where you are safe before calling on a D.I.E. hunt.

On Day 1 of your hunt, after you settle into your stand, make some grey squirrel barks. I like to make 14 to 17 of them in a row and then I shut up and put the call away. Squirrels often go into hiding when a person climbs a tree, but if you can bark like a squirrel, real squirrels will answer you, and they will tell all the animals in the woods that you are just a big squirrel not a hunter climbing a tree. The excitement level of the birds and animals in the area calms down almost immediately. I make squirrel sounds because I know it works to relax deer and to get them to go off alert status right away. When deer hear any sound that they cannot positively identify, they go on alert. That means the #1 priority of that deer is to find out what made the sound, before it does anything else. Then it will decide if it will stay in the area and conduct business as usual, or leave the area immediately. They always decide based on what the source of the sound is, but our goal is not to be seen by the buck so we have to distract him with sounds that do not attract him in any way. Do not make coyote yelps because he will leave, but squirrel calls, crow calls, or turkey yelps will work. If you get in your tree without shaking it, then you do not have to do any calling.

I have had success using a Montana brand whitetail doe decoy

I have had 100% success using a Montana (brand) doe decoy on my hunts. The decoy is collapsible so it fits inside my backpack or inside my jacket. It can be assembled in less than two minutes and the deer that see it lock up on it and charge into the area. They are alarmed that the doe is there. They have never seen her before, and they know that she is expected because they have been scenting her urine in the area for the entire time you have been there. Placing a silhouette type Montana Brand doe decoy out at your scrape will bring your buck in. You had better not fall asleep in the stand or you may have to purchase a new one when you wake up. Both bucks and does will come to a Montana doe decoy. The only time I ever see does come to it is if I am cramming the D.I.E. set up and I do not wait 2 ½ days for the dominant buck to take it over. If I am hunting first thing the next day after I build the scrape, I like to use the decoy. If you want to communicate with the buck that hunts you, then calling, decoying, and rattling are the ways you can do it. I have used all three of these tactics in conjunction with my set up and I have always gotten 100% positive results with them. I have yet to see a deer avoid my Montana doe decoy.

I recommend using a Montana brand doe decoy at your stand site when there is snow on the ground, as long as you are not at any risk of being shot when you are placing or picking up the decoy. Set it up when you arrive and take it down at night just before you leave. Using a Montana Brand doe decoy will settle the buck down and he will have his mind set right from the start that the doe is at the scrape whenever you are there.

Most dominant bucks will think a Montana brand doe decoy is a real deer the first time they see one, because from a distance, a picture of a doe looks exactly like a real doe to a deer. Remember what I said about deer only being able to see two-dimensional. That means a deer can see the height and width of an object, but in order to see the depth of something, deer have to get close enough to walk around the object they are trying to evaluate. Bucks walk toward one another at quartering angles so they can size up their opponent's body mass and rack size. A deer cannot tell that Montana brand decoys do not have depth until the deer gets right up next to the decoy, or until the deer views it from straight on. By then you will have a close shot opportunity so it will not matter anyway. Montana brand decoys are silhouette decoys made of cloth. They look real—from every angle except from straight on in the front or straight on in the back.

Carrying full body deer decoys out into the woods can be very dangerous, I used to use one but I was really nervous when I did. I always had to tell my hunting party where I would be walking and that they should be aware that I would be carrying a full-bodied deer under my arm. Boy and I glad I do not have to worry about doing that anymore. I will not hunt with D.I.E. if there will be any other hunters within 150 yards of me while I will be hunting nor will I use a decoy there. That is because the dominant buck will likely bust me if I am not alone, and using a decoy is not safe when other hunters are in the area. Someone could mistake the decoy for a real deer and shoot at it. I do not want to be shot at, so I avoid ever putting myself at risk of it happening to me.

I use a Montana Doe decoy on some of my D.I.E. hunts. It is a color silhouette decoy, and it will work on any day of the hunt as long as the buck cannot see it from his staging area. I started using a Montana brand doe decoy during gun season, and I love the results. I put it up against some thick brush crosswind of my stand about 10 yards. I face it to the scrape or at a crosswind, and I try to keep its tail end towards my right side whenever possible. When it is set up that way, the buck can only see it from two directions, and since the other one is backed by tree trunks and brush, the buck only has one way he can approach from, and that would be from crosswind of it. That is where I am. I set the decoy between my scrape and me and keep its shoulders facing the scrape. If a buck comes into the scrape from the opposite crosswind side he will be head-on to it, and he will never see it. I want it that way. That guarantees me that he will not see it until he is on his approach from downwind of me, and when he locks onto the decoy from there, he is all mine. I can easily shoot to the scrape from my tree, and I can hit any buck that is there with a fatal shot.

When a buck sneaks up behind you, he is concentrating on everything he can see. Using a doe decoy does not threaten him and it helps you keep him brainwashed, because you are able to distract him from looking at your tree, your ladder, or tree steps. He focuses on the trail you walked in on and on the decoy at the scrape. Once the buck sees that decoy he is distracted and he will posture and walk in slowly, always approaching the doe decoy from the rear. If you set it up as I do, you will have a quartering away shot to the buck's vitals. I have never had a buck approach the decoy yet but I have used this decoy and I have had the buck come in within 35 yards of it while I was there. When I saw the monster buck, he was straight downwind of the decoy doing a lip curl, only 15 yards downwind of me. I rushed my shot and hit him in the front leg. I lost that buck because of a rushed shot. Monster buck fever gets the best of me and I do not always take a deep breath first. My instincts are to shoot fast while I have the buck in my midst, but I do not have to shoot fast at a standing buck! I made a bad call on my shot that year and I will forever regret it. The buck lived to see another day.

Are you a beginner at calling, decoying, and rattling?

If you have never used a deer call or a decoy before, or if you used them but did not get good results from them, then this chapter is going to be valuable for you. If you use calls on every hunt you go on, you are like me and you may or may not agree with my calling techniques. What I would like to point out in this chapter, is that I built this system around the idea that the hunter has to become an invisible doe in estrus in order for the dominant buck in the area to take notice. With that in mind, you also need the dominant buck to think that there is the real threat from one or more mature intruder bucks coming to the scrape to steal his hot doe away. You can remain silent and let the lure tell the story, or you can tell the story to him personally and watch him come in. I prefer to tell him the story. I call to him as both an intruder-challenging buck and as a doe in estrus. I am able to do that because I am a seasoned hunter using the D.I.E. system and I know which calls to make and when to make them.

I talk to one deer and he happens to be the dominant buck. I know he is listening to every sound in my vicinity and he will come in as soon as I tell him that I (the doe in estrus) am there. You can call to the buck. I talk to him, but do not just call and call and call. He is listening and he wants you to tell him you are there. Then put the call away and wait for his arrival. Overcalling will get you busted. If you are busted you have to move everything, so try not to get busted, and your present location will work for you.

A dominant buck is in charge of every deer in his territory. If you talk like a deer, know he is listening. He is always within hearing distance of you when you are in your tree stand, so always know what you are going to say before you say it. Always talk directly to him and convince him you are not in a tree, but that you are a real deer on the ground closer to the scrape than he is. If you see him coming in, then stop calling and get ready for your shot. If you do not stop calling, he will pinpoint your stand and locate you. Never let him do that! Avoid being busted!

Knowledge is power when imitating real buck grunts

Before I started hunting with my D.I.E. system, I never considered what a mature buck was physically doing at the very second when he let out a grunt or a series of grunts. I didn't know why whitetail bucks grunted, what they were saying, which deer they were communicating with, or how they reacted to the sound of another buck grunting. I thought hearing a grunting buck was a good thing and that I could call one in if I grunted back when I heard a grunt. All those things are true, but when I grunted back, I didn't know how many deer were listening to me and I did not have any clue as to what I was actually saying to them. I was scaring them away without even knowing it. How would you like it if someone walked up to you and started lecturing you about politics and scolding you in a foreign language that you couldn't understand a word of except for all the bad words they said? I am convinced that is how deer feel when a hunter blows a new call they are unfamiliar with and the deer are within hearing distance of the call. The only expertise I had in calling deer was that I was an expert at scaring monster bucks away from my stand. I accomplished that by blowing my buck grunt call in all the wrong ways and at all the wrong times.

At that time in my bow-hunting career, I had many issues. I didn't know it then but I now can clearly see now that my hunting tactics were a mess. I made poor choices. One of my biggest problems was that I wanted to break the silence and talk to the deer, but I didn't know how deer talked to each other, what their language consisted of, or how to understand the sounds real deer were making. I just blew air into the call and I got nothing out of it. Blowing a call is not the same as calling in a buck or a doe. In order to call to a deer you need to be a deer, at least in theory, and just having a call does not make you a caller. It is very important that you never make any calls during a deer-hunting situation, unless you know which deer you are calling to, what you are saying to that deer, and in what tone of voice you are saying it.

Do not ever call just to make noise or because you are bored

Do not just blow your call because you are bored, or you hope a deer will hear you and come to see what is going on. Only young deer (yearlings or fawns) will likely fall for that type of noise. They are very naive because they have always been followers. They are not in charge of leading any other deer into and out of cover, and they have not lived long enough to reach maturity yet. Once a deer becomes mature, it has to survive situations of danger all on its own. When a buck or doe turns 2 years old that time comes for them. They get smarter every day that they are alive, all deer do. Deer for the most part are not vocal animals. The only times I hear them make sounds are when they are faced with a situation. If they are not near another deer or facing a situation, then a deer will not make any sound with its voice. As a D.I.E. hunter, you should live by the same rules deer do. Stay quiet unless you find yourself in a situation with a real buck. Situations can occur when two or more deer meet at the same location, when a deer encounters one of its enemies, when a deer discovers a D.I.E. scrape and rub, or when a deer is frightened for its life.

The only reason I have to call to the dominant buck is to get him to stop holding up in cover and to ask him to show himself to me out in the open between my D.I.E. scrape, and me if he is the most dominant buck in the herd. On all my hunts with D.I.E., the dominant buck has brought it, when I called him out!

The number one reason young deer (fawns and yearling bucks and does) fall to hunters is they do not know how to use the survival skills that they were born with. Those skills keep them safe, they help them make well thought out decisions such as where to travel, where not to travel, and when it is safe to travel. Young deer are basically, young and dumb. Do not ever call to more than one deer at a time, otherwise they will surround you and pinpoint your location, and the only thing you will succeed at is being busted in your tree stand.

It is ok for you to talk to the buck that hunts you, if you see him walking at a broadside angle to you, or if he is 100 yards away or more, as long as he is on the move. Do not call to a buck that is standing still. I do not advise you to talk to any deer unless you have heard its voice and you know where where it. Do not call if he can look right at you from his position, or if he can hear the sounds of your footsteps. Never call if he is with a doe in estrus. The only reasons to call to the buck on a D.I.E. hunt are to announce that the doe in estrus is at the scrape looking for the dominant buck, or to grunt him away from his doe in estrus if he brings one in with him to the D.I.E. scrape. I have wheezed at numerous bucks (one time only) after I took my shot, and I got a deflection or I missed. Wheezing gets his attention and he turns around to come back to the scrape. If you have a rifle or a gun of any sort, making a wheeze can be a blessing for you if you miss him somehow with your first shot.

You can talk only to mature bucks when you hunt with my D.I.E. system. Never start a conversation with a dominant buck. You will be giving him your caller ID if you do. The last thing you want to do is tell him which deer you are, and where you are calling from (10 to 20 feet up in a tree). Both of which he can figure out if you talk to him, when he is able to pinpoint your location. If you do not know where he is, do not call. He may be right underneath your stand, and you will be embarrassed, to say the least, if you see him flagging his tail within 20 yards of you. When in doubt, do without, is what I say.

You can opt out of making any calls

If you would rather not make any deer calls, that is fine with me. The D.I.E. system works without making any calls, but you might want to learn to make a single buck grunt with your mouth to stop a walking buck for a standing shot. It is up to you.

If you want to call to the buck—learn to master these three calls

They are:

1. The doe in estrus bleat
2. The mature buck tending grunt
3. The wheeze call

1.) **The doe in estrus bleat** is a soft doe call that can be made by using a M.A.D. GRUNT, SNORT, WHEEZE call. Pull the call out of the hard clear plastic chamber and roll the black O-ring down the reed towards the high pitch end. It should be within 1/2' to 5/8" from the end of the call. Then put it back in the clear chamber and stretch the black plastic bellows out as far as you can. Talk into the call from your diaphragm saying "yeah"! Talk softly because the doe in estrus is sweet on the buck and she wants him. She is not at all aggressive. You have to make convincing doe in estrus bleats if you speak for the doe. Only make one call (yeah) then stop for the rest of the day. Do not call with a doe in estrus bleat any more than one time each day. The buck will always be trying to pattern the sound the doe makes, so he can look right at the doe and identify her before he commits to coming in. You cannot afford to let him find you in your stand, so do not call again that day, and do not call the next day at the same time of day. If you haven't made any sounds in your stand at all during your four-day hunt, you are in good shape when the buck shows up. I do not to talk to any deer but the dominant buck and I do not make a sound with either of my deer voices until I know where the buck is and whether or not he is coming towards me.

The only exception is when I have less than 4 consecutive days to hunt. If that is the case, I know I am not going to see the buck on each hunt, so I call to let him know that Sally is here waiting for him, and I ask him to hurry to meet her, before another huge buck finds her first. When your odds of seeing the buck are less than 100% you can mix it up a bit, because you have nothing to lose, but there is still a time and a place to make a call, and in that case, it is only as soon as I am settled in my stand. I make one or two doe in estrus bleats in an upwind direction so he cannot pinpoint my location. It has worked for me, so I know I can do it.

2.) **The mature buck-tending grunt** is made with the same call. First, pull the call out of the hard clear plastic chamber and roll the black O-ring up the reed towards the low pitch end of the call. Stop it 1/4" away from the end. Then put it back in the clear chamber and stretch the black plastic bellows out as far as you can. Cup your hand around the end of the black tube, and talk into the call from your diaphragm saying huh, hugh, huh, huugh, etc… Make 6 to 9 grunts and stop. Put the call away. If he is near, that is all he needs to hear and he will come into fight within an hour or two. Keep looking downwind.

3.) **The wheeze** is a sound made by all deer when they are frightened by a sound, a movement, an odor, or the sight of something they cannot identify as safe, or that they can positively identify as dangerous to their well-being. Every hunter should have a wheeze call and know how and when to use it. You should have a wheeze call so you can wheeze back when a deer wheezes at you. That way the deer thinks you are another deer and it will not continue making a fuss about you being there. That is unless it saw you without your invisible deer suit on, then you would be positively busted (identified as a human) anyway. Nine times out of ten, when a deer wheezes and I wheeze back the deer will relax and come to me to see which deer I am. The only time I ever hear bucks wheeze is when I miss them with an arrow and the arrow was close to the buck body. He will wheeze because he senses danger, but he does not know a human is hunting him, even after I shoot. Sometimes I get another shot. To make a wheeze, use the same call again and first look at it. Notice, there is an empty chamber on the call that has a curve to it. That is the wheeze chamber. All you do is take a deep breath and huff into that chamber one time. If the deer that wheezed at you wheezes back, then do it once more. Match the deer wheeze for wheeze until they stop wheezing. Reacting to a wheeze with a wheeze will take deer off alert status, and give you another chance to outwit them. Once you get back home that day figure out what you did wrong. If you did not wash in scent free soap before the hunt, that is what triggered the deer to wheeze at you. If it saw you, then your camouflage is not adequate; if you broke a twig under your foot then avoid doing that in the future, and if you walked in from downwind, and approached the area with the wind in your face, then you have to go back to the front of this book and start reading it over. You had to be busted by that deer. Never walk into the wind when you are walking like a deer, or at any time during a hunt with D.I.E., or you will fail and not see the dominant buck. Never wheeze for the heck of it. Wheeze only in response to a buck or doe out of sight wheezing at you. If they are in view do not wheeze or they will see you in the tree.

What to say to the buck if he holds up in cover

From time to time, the dominant buck will hold up in cover within 35 yards of your tree stand, and you will feel helpless for a minute or two. If that happens to you and he does not offer you a clear shot, you have to become a deer and talk to him. Do it as he walks away from you, not when he is standing in clear view of you, but only call to him if there is ample cover to hide a bedded down deer directly behind your tree stand. Your set up day is important not only for the set up but also for the hunt, because you need there to be some cover under your tree in order to allow you the opportunity to call to the buck. If you do not have any cover under your tree then you will get busted if you make any deer sounds while you are in your stand.

You have to do different things in different situations in order to keep him guessing. If the buck made his way to your stand site and hung up inside 35 yards but he has a real doe with him, then it is likely he will not come right to the scrape. He will walk around there for a minute or two, physically looking for one of the two (invisible) deer. When he is convinced they are not there, he will walk off with his doe into some nearby cover, and they will breed in that cover. He keeps his doe in estrus at his side while he investigates the invisible doe in estrus at your scrape.

You need to use common sense and figure out that the only sounds you are allowed to make in the tree are tending grunts, doe in estrus bleats, and a wheeze but only when necessary. In this case, the dominant buck brought a doe in with him. That means she is in estrus now, but he has to check in on the D.I.E. scrape so no other bucks take it over while the invisible doe in estrus (you) is there. Remember, he heard you walk in earlier in the day. You can get that buck to wheel around doing a 180-degree turn by waiting until he is 50 yards away and then blowing one deep sounding tending grunt in the opposite direction than the buck is headed. Point the call away from the buck when you make the grunt. Carry the note 4 or 5 seconds, and only do it one time. If you do this, the buck will come running in and stand front and center between you and the scrape nine times out of ten. If he tries to leave again then make a doe in estrus bleat just one time. It should work. He is looking for the two deer you represent and he can smell their scent, but without visually seeing them within a minute or two of arriving at the scrape in daylight, the dominant buck will leave the area.

You have to mess with his mind, his eyesight, his nose, and his hearing. Make sure you keep him guessing! If he comes in downwind and stages there, and then he starts doing repetitive tending grunts in your direction, either you should stay quiet or you should make one or two doe in estrus bleats (but never make three). He will come in immediately for the doe in estrus if he believes she is all alone. If you are in the open and there is not ample cover in your area that could possibly hide the deer you are pretending to be when you are calling, then I advise you to stay quiet the whole time. Never make any deer sounds if there is absolutely no way for the buck to believe there could really be a real doe or a real buck under your tree or within 5 yards upwind of it. You could get busted that way, so avoid calling when you are in the open. Never call when you know the buck is in close and he is staring in your direction. The system brings him in but it is your job to toy with his mind if he doesn't offer you a shot, so he will come back to the scrape and posture there for you. Do not be afraid to talk to the buck. Just do not overdo it and never call if you think he will know you are in the tree making the calls.

Practice makes perfect

When you buy a call from a store and start practicing with it, you will likely question every sound the call makes. Do not question it, just learn what you need to know about it, and only make the three sounds that are safe to make while you are hunting during the rut. If you practice all the sounds your call can make, you are wasting your time. Most of those sounds, when coming from you, will scare bucks away instead of bringing them in running to you. You cannot just make any deer sound on a D.I.E. hunt. You can only make the three I mentioned earlier in this chapter. If you made fawn calls for instance, you would be busted instantly, because the dominant buck does not hang out and breed with fawns in the area. Blowing a call too loudly will also get you busted. If you cannot talk softly to a deer and you yell at them through your call, you will not be able to get them to respond to you in a positive way. Deer shy away from the unknown, so let it be known that nothing is in your tree. To accomplish that, all you can do is sit quietly there.

When I put my M.A.D. GRUNT, SNORT, WHEEZE call on the lanyard and around my neck in the morning, before I enter the woods, I have just become a whole herd of deer. I say that because that one call allows me to mimic every voice within a deer herd. That one call may be as miraculous as my D.I.E. system. To me, having that call with me is as important as having my bow and my 1 oz. bottle of Trail's End #307 lure. If I forget my M.A.D. call at home, I honestly turn around and go to get it. If you do not want to use that particular call, that is up to you, but you should have deer calls with you that allow you to make the sounds of a (soft) doe in estrus bleat, a doe bleat, buck tending grunts, deep sounding growls from a monster buck, a snort, and a wheeze. I bought this call because it does all that, and more. It can make a yearling buck grunt, and any age doe bleats too; including fawn bleats. We are not hunting does here, so there is no need to make any fawn bleats while you are hunting with DOMINANCE IS EVERYTHING. Fawn bleats attract does, yearling bucks, and predators. None of those animals has ever been sighted by me, while I was hunting with my system.

Each time you make a deer sound in a hunting situation you have to become the deer you are trying to represent with your call. I know no one else ever told you that, but no one else, before me, ever hunted the way I do, as one of the deer in the herd. Trust me that your world is going to change for the better, at least while you are hunting with my D.I.E. system, if you practice being the deer that you are telling the dominant buck you are, he should believe you. I am not just a man blowing a buck grunt call. When a buck hears me grunt from my stand, I am a monster intruder buck and I am breeding with a doe in estrus, right smack dab in the middle of a different dominant buck's home territory. By doing so, I am challenging the dominant buck to come out and beat me up if he can! I put myself into the head of the (invisible) monster intruder buck, and I become a monster intruder buck, before I even make a grunt, the grunts I make are then more genuine than the sounds a person makes just blowing a call. I make the sound come from my gut (my diaphragm) and it makes the sound that comes through the call sound like a buck's real voice. I treat deer as if they are smart animals, and I show them respect when I am in their world. The dominant buck will not tolerate any other buck breeding his doe. Respectfully or not, and I count on that!

You need to put yourself in the buck's place, and look at you (the hunter) from inside the buck's head. You need to try to figure out what the buck is thinking at the very moment that you want to talk to him. That way, you can speak to him in his language and he might believe you are a real deer; instead of him busting you in the tree, knowing you were an inexperienced deer hunter making fake grunts to him and teaching him how to find you.

Playing mind games with a dominant buck takes skill

Having been successful with getting close to deer in the wild when I filmed them, I thought I would start applying those tactics to my bow hunts on my parent's 12-acre parcel in New Berlin, Wisconsin. I could not legally hunt deer there with a gun (if you wondered). The hard part was, I had to stay inside our property boundaries, and the buck I was seeking did not. I had to learn to use the wind the same way a deer does so I could get close to him without allowing him to discover me before I got to my stand. That was a near impossible task, but I achieved it.

I needed to get into his head so I could confuse him, arouse him, and intimidate him. I knew that if I could accomplish those things all at once, I would be communicating with him mentally, and I would not have to do any more calling or decoying. I set up the DOMINANCE IS EVERYTHING system as a first attempt to accomplish those tasks, and what I accomplished was nothing short of a miracle. I developed an amazing system that gives any person who uses it correctly, the power to go into character and role-play with the most dominant buck in their area. Thus convincing him, you are many deer all at once.

By using my system, the dominant buck does not have the upper hand on the (D.I.E.) hunter. The (D.I.E.) hunter calls all the shots and can push the buck away or pull him in at any given time. Better yet, the hunter can wait for the buck and let the buck think he is alone. I think being quiet in the tree is the best way to hunt with my system. You cannot mess up if you do not make any deer vocalizations. No matter who you are, or what your deer hunting achievements have been up until now, you will have to change the way you think about your quarry, and you will have to understand that the mind games I have taught you to play with the king of deer are only part of the "Big Picture".

There is a "Big Picture" that every D.I.E. hunter has to envision and clearly understand. In order to succeed with my DOMINANCE IS EVERYTHING system you must place yourself inside the story, role-play with the dominant buck, and adapt to the situation that the amazing D.I.E. system presents you with during your hunt. The DOMINANCE IS EVERYTHING system does not adapt to you. If you are able to see "the Big Picture", I am sure you will have the faith needed, and the willingness to commit (as a D.I.E. hunter), to following the instructions and seeing your hunt with D.I.E. through to completion. The dominant buck in your area has no clue you are hunting him at any time during your hunt, and he will never let you down if you do your best to stay unseen by him while you visit his world. I hope you have a cozy tree stand and I hope the buck comes in during the first 3 days for you. If not, it will be the Day 4 You can count on it!

Rattling antlers work at certain times

I am not against you rattling from your tree stand, but a word to the wise—do not overdo it. The dominant buck is hunting you. That means he is looking intently for you as if you were his target and he is a sniper. He can pinpoint every sound you make in the stand, and he will try to discover what is making the noises he hears. He is hunting you remember. He does not automatically trust that rattling coming from 15 feet up in a tree can be the sound of real deer fighting. You have to persuade him of it.

I would advise you not to rattle during your hunt, but if you do decide to rattle, do it for a reason; to get the buck to come to you, not just to make a sound like a buck. If you overdo it, the buck will hold up because you gave him too much to think about. Rattling everyday in the stand is not good. Too much of a good thing gets old quick. A little calling and rattling is better than a lot of it. When in doubt, go without is sound advice.

Everything you do while in the stand can mess the hunt up for you, so I recommend you sit quietly and observe the hunt the first time you use the system. Get a feel for it and succeed at it before you go and make mistakes by calling or rattling at the wrong times, or in the wrong manner. The buck will come in no matter if you call him or not, so why take a chance.

Chapter 25

D.I.E.—a system that allows you to role-play with the king

You should only walk like a deer on your way into your stand (far away from all deer bedding areas). Do not ever try to get into deer bedding areas walking like a deer while hunting with my system. Oh no, never do that! You could be killed. When I said I walked like a deer into bedding areas, that was back when I was filming deer from 1991–1994 and I was unarmed back then. The forest I was walking in was off limits to any hunting, and no one was allowed to discharge a weapon in the whole county then. It was safe for me to walk like a deer there. It is not safe for you to walk like a deer when you are hunting if there is any chance another person could hear you and not see you. Do not take risks with your life. Make sure it is safe before you walk like a deer.

You need to walk like a deer on the way to your tree stand, which should be upwind and crosswind of deer bedding by 150 yards or more (whenever possible). You walk like a deer so they are not alerted to the sounds of a human walking into their territory, and so that all the deer in the area are convinced that you are one of them. Deer are not afraid of other deer. When they hear a person walking like a deer they remain bedded down as you walk in, and you can walk right past bedded down deer. If you do it right, only one deer will be within hearing distance of you then. That would be the most dominant buck or a monster intruder buck that challenged the dominant buck to a fight over your D.I.E. scrape (the night before) and has apparently beat him. Either way, only one big buck is hunting you each day. He will come to you wherever you set up the D.I.E. scrape as long as you followed my set up instructions. I have never seen the system fail.

Never walk into a known buck or doe bedding area on purpose while bucks have antlers on their heads. I have lived by this policy ever since I invented the DOMINANCE IS EVERYTHING system. My thought process is that if I leave the bucks and does alone in their bedding areas, they will not have a clue that I am hunting them. I hunt upwind and crosswind of those bedding areas, sometimes as close as 80 yards away and other times as far as 400 yards away, in order to make the most dominant buck come to me where I am. I want him to give up bedding where he is comfortable (lives), and I want him to come to my area and bed down where I tell him. An area where I have the upper hand with him, where I am easily concealed in my tree stand, and where I can get in and out of it without having to walk through the entire property alerting all the deer there to the fact that a human is in their midst. There, I can wait patiently for him and I will always know which way he is coming from and where he is likely bedded as I walk in. What I have done on my hunts with D.I.E. has always worked, not only for me but for the other two men I have taught my system to, prior to going public with it in October 2010.

You know the dominant buck will be bedded in the nearest available cover downwind or crosswind of your stand and that he will come in from downwind or crosswind every single time. You are familiar with the nearest available cover downwind and crosswind of your stand because you chose the set up location based on where that cover was in relation to the prevailing wind and to the location of your D.I.E. scrape. The hunt is planned and so is the dominant buck's visit. He doesn't know that, but that is because it is a surprise! You can expect the buck to react to the set up exactly as I tell you he will. Stay hidden and always be ready. The buck can show up at any time and you may get bored but you should stay in your tree, because every minute that passes takes you a minute closer to your meeting with the king of the herd. If you have faith in DOMINANCE IS EVERYTHING, you will never regret it.

Traditional hunters usually push deer out of their bedding areas so that they can get a clear shot at them. I was taught to hunt that way, but I do not care to do that anymore. Now that I have D.I.E., I have transformed myself from being "the hunter" to being "the hunted". I do not hunt deer traditionally anymore, nor do I ever intend to again (not while I have a buck tag to fill). Do not get me wrong, traditional hunting is fine if you want to kill does or pecking order bucks, or if you do not want to hunt the king of deer with D.I.E., but once you learn to use my system, everything changes. I do hunt traditionally for does when I want to put some meat on my table or in the freezer, but there is no reason for me to give up hunting with D.I.E. ever, it has always been a sure thing for me.

The only times I ever think it is alright to walk into deer bedding areas are in late February, all of March, and all of April, and I do so in order to look for shed antlers. I do not push deer out of their bedding areas at any other time of the year. DOMINANCE IS EVERYTHING works whether you walk like a deer or not, but I have found that the dominant buck will hunt both my D.I.E. scrape, and me if I walk like a deer on my hunt. If you do not walk like a deer, the dominant buck only hunts the D.I.E. scrape. He will not hunt for you. The fact is that the dominant buck will come in within 35 yards of you no matter what, and sometimes the dominant buck turns out to be a monster buck.

If you do walk like a deer (I would) the dominant buck will hear you arrive in the morning. It triggers a breeding frenzy at your stand site. All the mature bucks in the area fight over the right to dominate the doe in estrus that you tell them just arrived there. When you arrive on Day 1, it is the first day that the doe is in estrus and the intruder monster buck is there with her. That is what the dominant buck believes anyway, and when you leave just before dark, then they are gone. When you come back on Day 2, the doe in estrus is back and it is the last day the buck believes she could be in estrus so he makes every effort to come to the D.I.E. scrape that day. The only thing that will stop him is a human or another danger that he identifies in the area of the scrape. The buck should come in during the first, second, or third day, but there is a fourth day just in case you need it. The system has never failed to produce the buck within 4 days of hunting as long as the hunter gave the D.I.E. scrape 2 ½ days to set up.

The reason the hunt lasts from one to four days is because no one can tell which day the dominant buck will find the D.I.E. scrape. That buck does not know that the invisible pair of deer are there, so your first day hunting is not always his first day of pursuing the doe in estrus. If he finds the D.I.E. scrape on your set up day then he will come in (hunt you) on Day 1 and Day 2. If it takes him until the first day of the hunt for him to find it, then he will come in on Day 2 or Day 3, and if he is with a real doe in estrus on set up day, then he will stay with her for one or two days to breed. The dominant buck will leave a doe as soon as she is out of estrus, and then he will always run his territory boundaries to see if anything (an intruder buck, a predator, or a human) has moved into his territory while he was away (focused on breeding his last doe). On this trip around his territory, he may find another real doe in estrus, and if he does, he will stay with her to breed for one to two days. Whether he finds another doe in estrus or not, the dominant buck runs his territory boundaries every 2 or 3 days (during the rut), and you can count on him locating your D.I.E. scrape before daylight on Day 2 of your hunt. Even though a doe is in estrus for less than 48 hours, the buck will still follow her scent at your D.I.E. scrape for up to four consecutive days. That is because other bucks find the doe's scent at different times, when they are without a mate and they come to the D.I.E. scrape in search of the doe in estrus (you), the same way the dominant buck did a few days earlier. Those intruder bucks do not know which day the doe went into estrus. They have not even met her yet! They will pursue her at your scrape for one to two days too. Then the hunt will be over, because all the bucks in the herd will give up if none of them can find her in less than 4 days time. No doe would be in heat or estrus longer than that! Word travels through the herd that the doe in estrus is nowhere to be found. They will fight for her when they all know she could be real, but they will walk away never to come back once they know she is not. The dominant buck stays in the area and constantly keeps his senses focused on the D.I.E. scrape because he is pressured by the other breeder bucks in the area, and because there is always a chance that the intruder monster buck that built the scrape will come back. That is only a thought in the dominant buck's mind, and we let him believe that by using Trails End #307 lure as a cover scent, and as the scent of the buck at the D.I.E. scrape, on the D.I.E. rub, and in a scent dispenser 5 yards behind the D.I.E. rub, when we built it.

Every mature breeder buck that discovers the scrape after you start hunting it, believes the doe in heat just went into estrus that day, so you should expect them to pressure the dominant buck, at the scrape each night constantly. All mature bucks are attracted to the scent of a doe in estrus and because the doe is inside his territory boundary, he is the buck that has to stay there until she comes back. If he left, the other bucks would breed her there and he would not be in control of his herd or that part of his territory anymore. Because the buck believes the doe in estrus really exists, he is willing to fight for his right to breed with every doe in his herd. The thing that makes him anxious to come in early in the day is the threat of the neighboring herd's bucks coming back each night. He just wants to meet the doe and to mate with her so the other bucks will back down and leave him alone there. The more determined you are to be that doe, the more determined he is to meet you. After four consecutive days, he will give up if you have not shot him, and he will tell all the other deer in the area to abandon the scrape as well. It is a like a ghost town around your scrape on Day 5. That is why there is no Day 5. No deer believe there could possibly be a doe in heat or estrus for that long. Do not hunt on Day 5 or you will be BUSTED! Day 5 is a perfect time for removing your stand and scrape from the woods. No matter which day you shoot your buck you need to pull out the stand and the scrape. Always leave the area as you found it until you get your next buck tag. Then you can move back in and set it up again, the same way you did on your last hunt with D.I.E. (as long as you were not busted in that stand).

Do not try to out-think my system. It works exactly the way I have it set up. Just believe in it and it will perform for you. I learned what the system was doing to the dominant buck after I succeeded hunting with it. I always analyze my hunts so I can try to make sense of the dominant buck's actions. Trust what I tell you and believe in it and you will be able to use my D.I.E. system the same way I do. When you get busted, (everyone does eventually) go back to the book and figure out what you did wrong. Correct it and pick another 4 days to hunt, choose another tree stand location, and buy some new lure, then go at it again. The system works every time, at least up until now it always has. You can hunt with D.I.E. successfully as long as you believe in it. Non-believers will look for excuses to have it fail. I wrote the book to give you proof that my system is real and that it does what I say it does.

It was ground breaking when I learned that deer could not tell what I was. It was 20 years ago when I was filming them and not hunting them. I learned to walk like a deer and I entered a core-doe bedding area on one of the deer trails the led into it. I was only armed with a video camera. That's when deer started walking towards me instead of just ignoring me altogether. I wasn't feeding them; I was playing with their minds. I was brainwashing them into believing I was one of them. I didn't act like a human, I didn't smell like a human, and I didn't look like a human. Therefore, I couldn't be a human. I walked like a deer, I talked like a deer, I moved through cover at a deer's pace, and I only traveled through my hunting area at times of the day that deer were not apt to be moving. That convinced the real deer that I was one of them, and they never looked in my direction as I approached them, not until I was only 3 or 4 feet away from them. Then they would stand up and look surprised. I immediately froze in my tracks of course, and by doing so, the deer never went on alarm. My being in full camouflage, 99% human scent free, and the fact that I was inside the deer bedding area was enough proof that I was invisible to them. The deer stayed relaxed and tried to figure out what I was instead of sounding an alarm. It is amazing wait until you see for yourself how close you can get to deer in the fall and winter.

Role-playing with deer is fun because a person can play many parts without having to change clothes or having to talk to deer. It is all in the way you walk. When you are a deer in the minds of deer, then you are welcomed into the herd. You belong there just as much as they do. The first time that I got 3 feet from a bedded down 6-point buck I had achieved greatness. I have been able to get that close to two other deer in my life, one was a doe and the other a 10-point buck. I approached him in his bed while I was hunting, before I invented my system. An amazing feeling comes over you when you know you are invisible to deer. Folks, you will get that same feeling for the first time when your area's dominant buck comes into your stand site looking for two deer (you represent) that are nowhere to be found. DOMINANCE IS EVERYTHING has given me special powers, and after reading my book you will have these powers available to you too. You have the power to talk to deer through your actions and to make them look for you as a deer. Who other than a D.I.E. user can do that?

When I began hunting with DOMINANCE IS EVERYTHING, I only hunted a few hours in the afternoon each day and I was successful at having a mature buck come in within 35 yards of my stand, each time I set it up. I wanted desperately to be able to convince mature bucks that I was one single doe in estrus and I was able to do it with Scent Shield's Still Steamin' Premium Hot Doe Estrus urine. It wasn't until November 2001, when I found out, I was being hunted by the king of deer. That was the first year I sat in my stand all day. The king of deer always beds downwind of the scrape and waits for you to come in. He expects a "hot" doe of course, and at the time it was a problem for me to know how to pretend I was one, but it didn't take me long to figure out that I should walk like a deer and enter the woods after daylight so the buck wouldn't get out of his bed as I walked in. I knew the king of the herd was the last buck to go to bed in the morning, and that he galloped into his bed instead of walking into it. I knew I could wait forty-five minutes to one hour after daylight to arrive at my stand and the buck would not be hanging around the scrape anymore. That would allow me to get into my tree stand without disturbing him at the D.I.E. scrape. I knew just how to do it. I decided to walk in as if I was an adult doe, because all deer in any herd will accept the presence of an adult doe. That got me in there without a hitch, but the buck came in within 5 minutes after I got there and he busted me when I was standing in front of the D.I.E. scrape (changing out the lure). I had to change the lure from a breeding pair of deer to just a doe in estrus. I needed to get in there without calling attention to myself then I would have the five extra minutes it takes to change the lure at the scrape on Day 1, without the buck advancing on my position. The next bow season I decided to walk in like a yearling buck on Day 1, and I was successful at pulling that off too. That time, the dominant buck stayed bedded until about an hour after I settled into my stand. He wasn't sure which buck I was but I was sure he was not threatened by me entering the area. He got interested in finding me after I stopped making noise at the scrape, and by that time, I was safely up in my stand. That is what you can expect the buck to do.

One time I tried to be the most dominant buck throughout the whole hunt. That was not a good choice at all. Everything got messed up real fast when I told the herd that their king was an invisible buck! All the pecking order bucks showed up in the area and they were all trying to establish dominance at my scrape. The biggest problem was they all came in at night, and they all avoided it during the day. Even the king of the herd was confused. I think they knew it wasn't real because the real dominant buck was there with them. They know their king, so do not ever try to become their king. You'll just make things difficult for yourself. Just try to fit into the herd by becoming a deer that is outside the pecking order. Pretend you are a yearling buck on Day 1, the doe in estrus on Day 2, and when the third day of your hunt rolls around, if you haven't seen him yet then you can be the monster intruder buck. If you need Day 4, then show up as the breeding pair and get vocal as soon as you settle in your tree stand. Tell the buck that both deer are there on Day 4, and always remember to drag out the Trail's End #307 when you leave your stand so the buck thinks that the intruder was there the whole day too. I have every kink worked out already so you do not have to wonder what to do; just do what I tell you, sit back in your stand, and wait for the dominant buck to show up. It is as easy as that.

There can only be one dominant buck in every herd at any one moment in time. If you act as the dominant buck, you are challenging his hierarchy, and he will be on to you as a human. Dominant bucks know how challengers behave when they are in the dominant buck's territory and no person would know how to behave (like a deer) to convince the dominant buck that he is no longer dominant of his own herd. The two things D.I.E. cannot do, are change the way a real dominant buck forms his pecking order, or interfere with how he keeps the pecking order bucks in the ranks under him. Those are skills that only a real dominant buck is capable of displaying for all to see. He does that by posturing and displaying his dominance.

My experimenting with becoming the dominant buck taught me that I have a limit to what I can do with my invisible deer suit. I can be a yearling buck or doe, an adult doe, a fawn, or an intruder buck (from another herd) but I can never be a pecking order buck or the dominant buck when I become an invisible deer. It was after learning those facts that I decided never to be a dominant buck, or a pecking order buck, but instead I always had to be a deer he was not in control of. I would call him out to breed with a "hot doe" (a doe in estrus). That is a doe in her heat cycle but she is ready and able to be bred at that very moment in time. I was not done there. At the same time I would tell him I was a monster "intruder buck" (a challenging buck from another herd), that had brought this doe in heat with him from a herd (over a mile away). Although the doe was in heat when the (invisible) pair arrived, she was going into estrus within a few days. That is when I showed up and started hunting overlooking the D.I.E. scrape. I showed up as the doe in estrus. Her scent filled the air and all mature bucks took immediate notice of my location. Then the games began. The dominant buck had to move in close to the scrape to protect it from the (invisible) monster intruder buck, and when he believed there was nothing nearby the scrape that can threaten his survival, he decided to come in and work up the scrape, all the while keeping an eye out for the "hot" doe.

I set up the D.I.E. system for the first time in 1998, and I didn't have a name for it back then. I just called it my secret system. I knew I could convince all deer that I was one of them by behaving the way deer behaved, and by leaving signs that deer were in the area instead of leaving signs that a human was there. Learning which deer I was supposed to be when the buck arrived took some getting used to. I now know how to make the first move, but back then, I would wait for the dominant buck to come looking for me as both deer. You will know which deer he is convinced you are, by observing how he postures when he moves into the area. I have hunted with D.I.E. with both gun and bow and I have had the king of deer hunt me every time I have set it up. I have taught it to two men who have proved it works in states other than Wisconsin, and on both public and private land, and I am convinced it will never fail because all deer believe the D.I.E. set up is a real life situation that they have to deal with. You become part of the hunt, and the dominant buck comes to you. It is a fun way to hunt mature bucks.

The system only works when deer are mating and that is from October 16 through January 8 in Wisconsin. Trust me that there are deer mating everyday between those dates in the state of Wisconsin. It doesn't matter if there are any does in heat or in estrus in your area at the time, the most dominant buck will be convinced that there is one single doe in estrus if you set up the system as directed and give it your all. For the sake of respecting that the dominant buck is not stupid, I do not advise anyone to set the system up before October 27 each fall. I want to be sure that the dominant buck has had sex with at least two does before he meets the D.I.E. system. That way he will be convinced that the signs and the scents that he discovers in the area are real signs made by real deer. He will be brainwashed to believe that the doe in heat and her boyfriend are real, and that he must wait for the doe to go into estrus. He will wait near the D.I.E. scrape and rub. He must breed with her before he can return to his normal bedding area. He comes in determined to find her as soon as possible. Waiting until October 27 to set up D.I.E. has always worked for me, so I believe there is no reason why you should rush to set it up before then. If you do want to hunt with it between October 16 and October 29, then you are heading into uncharted territory. It may work but I cannot prove that it will be 100% successful for you. All I can tell you is that I have had 100% success with it on every hunt when I stick to October 27 as the earliest set up day. That makes my first day in the stand (Day 1 of the hunt) October 30. I think you should do what I have done, that way you have your best odds of always succeeding.

D.I.E. succeeds at bringing in mature bucks, within 35 yards of your stand during the first three days of the hunt over 92% of the time. I am the only person who ever had a buck come in on the fourth day. I structured the D.I.E. system into a four-day hunting period to make sure that it never failed. Sometimes the dominant buck is not at home (in his territory) when you set the system up, and in those cases it will take him 3 or 4 days from set up day just to find your D.I.E. set up. Once he finds it, he instantly locks into it. The buck only hunts the D.I.E. scrape for two days straight, and then he hunts for you the other two. I set it up that way so the buck cannot figure you or the system out. We have to keep him guessing. That way he will never know where you are or which deer you are at any given time. It makes him frustrated and aggressive and he always shows up within the four-day hunting period.

By analyzing the 11 times I hunted with D.I.E., I have been able to prove that doing certain additional things will raise your odds of seeing a monster buck on your hunt to more than a 50% chance. Walking like a deer as you walk toward your stand is one of those things. Using a dragline like I use is another. Using six scent dispensers on your hunt helps too. Setting up on a one-way trail helps, and so does setting up over water or near water in an area offering cover. Being able to make a doe in estrus bleat helps, and so does the ability the hunter has to role-play with the buck by announcing that there is a buck fight at the scrape. Setting up on territorial boundaries is dynamite, and making sure you are set up, upwind and crosswind of core deer bedding and/or breeding areas helps immensely. Monster bucks do not exist in every herd, but they are more common than you can imagine. You can scout for monster buck sign if you know how to read rubs and scrapes. You can learn about monster buck behavior from reading what I have written about them. Once you are hunted by a monster buck with D.I.E. you will never quit hunting with it. I am pretty darn sure of that!

The DOMINANCE IS EVERYTHING hunting system only attracts only mature bucks to your stand site. Once the most dominant buck finds the scrape, he takes it over and makes it his own primary breeding scrape. You will only see mature bucks come to the scrape and none of them will be pecking order bucks from the same herd as the dominant buck. I am assuming that you set the system up away from all buck territorial sign, and away from buck bedding and the core breeding area. You can set the scrape up anywhere and face it in any direction and the dominant buck will come to it, but you can get busted if you just throw the set up in, and do not pay attention to the prevailing wind direction. People that use D.I.E. will see how versatile it is once they set it up the first time, and I know everyone will be thankful they have learned it, but for me, there is more to using it than just putting it in the woods. You can learn from the system, and you can get more proficient at encountering monster bucks (3 ½ year old or older bucks that have huge mass on their antlers) on your hunts with D.I.E. if you take notes on your hunts. I write down everything I do each day so I can remember what worked good, and what got me busted. It will help you make better set up decisions in the future.

In this book and at my seminars, I teach people how to set up D.I.E. for the best odds at a monster buck. I want you to know that the more you plan your hunt the better your odds are of seeing a monster walk in. All the planning you need to do is to scout and to choose your stand location wisely. Those two things give you the biggest advantage over a person who just crams the system and hunts over it. If you do your homework, the best hunts of your life will come while you are hunting with **Dominance Is Everything**. I am sure many state record bucks will be harvested using my system and many more "big buck contests" will be won with entries that were brainwashed by my system. It is my hope that everyone who uses D.I.E. will appreciate it and be thankful to me for sharing it. I know I am blessed to have been the one to invent it, and I am looking forward to teaching it to each and every one of the people who reads the book, attends a seminar, or hires me to show them how it works on their hunting property. I want to teach it to 100,000 or more people in my lifetime. I think if I could accomplish that, I will have experienced another miracle!

I learned all I know about the rut, dominance, rubs, scrapes, lure use, calling, using decoys, and rattling from the deer that hunted me. I also learned how to aggravate the most dominant buck so much that he will stop at nothing to get to the D.I.E. scrape during daylight (while you are in your tree stand). Deer are amazing animals, and although each whitetail buck has a different rack, and a different set of friends, I am confident that every dominant buck will react the same way when he encounters a D.I.E. scrape (no matter where in North America he calls home). Take my D.I.E. system into your hunting parcel and see what it does to your herd's king. You will see what power D.I.E. gives its user to brainwash the king of deer into believing in invisible breeding deer. Get ready for the most exciting hunt of your life, and remember when you hunt with D.I.E. you need to hunt alone, in daylight, and only during the rut, in order to have the most dominant buck hunt you! Keep him guessing with D.I.E.!

Role-playing every day is important—stay with it

I cannot stress enough the fact that if you do not trust the system to work, you will fail in seeing a dominant buck. Because you let your mind wander back to the old way you hunted, and you will have thoughts about changing something, or maybe you will quit early one day and give up. Do not go in early, as you used to before you were taught to hunt with D.I.E., doing that will kill your hunt with my system. This system has nothing to do with the old way you hunted. You need to overcome those thoughts or you will be bound to fail. This hunt is only 4 days long. You will not likely have to hunt all four days, but you have to leave that up to the buck. When he comes in, that is the last day of your hunt. Unless you miss your shot or you get busted, then you have to hunt the next day. That goes on for up to four days and then you are done.

Most people that will use my system are going to love it, because they will succeed at getting the dominant buck in their sights and there is no forgetting that feeling. They will be hooked. I should say you are going to be hooked! You have to hunt up to 4 consecutive days in order to role-play with the buck that hunts the scrape and hunts you. If you are not there, then the doe in estrus is not there and neither is the intruder buck. You have to pretend you are both of them and you have to bring them into the area everyday in order to get the dominant buck's attention, and in order for him to want to seek them out at the scrape. That is where the doe's scent is coming from. The DOMINANCE IS EVERYTHING hunting system makes the king of the herd stay focused on you. Please take my advice and do whatever is called for. Stay focused on the fact that destiny has brought you and the dominant buck together and he is on his way to see you every minute that you are in your tree stand. Sit still and wait for him to arrive. I know that some hunters get impatient waiting to see a deer. I used to too, but not anymore. With my system, you are only hunting one buck, the most dominant one in the area, and now you have him hunting you. Trust me your patience will pay off. He will decide which day to show up, and you have to be committed to be there to meet him. It is as simple as that.

The dominant buck could come in on the first day of the hunt, and then you would not need the other three days you took off from work. For me, he usually comes in on day two or day three, within 3 hours of my arrival to my stand. You have to go in on time on Day 1 and stay all day to set the stage for the second day's hunt. On Day 2, you are brainwashing him all the while you are there, and you are setting the stage for the third day. If you haven't seen him on Day 3, you should be really pumped because he is going to come in on Day 4. Believe me on this! You have to role-play that you are an invisible doe in estrus, wandering around the area of his primary breeding scrape on a daily basis, but you just keep eluding him. Call to him with doe in estrus bleats if you want to. They help. He loves the attention that the doe is giving him, and when he cannot stand to wait around anymore, he will trot in to look for her. He will head directly to the scrape and attempt to freshen it up. You will not let him do that—will you? It is as easy as that!

Chapter 26

Always live by the rules—here are the "NEVER DO" lists

"NEVER DO" list for Walking Like A Deer

1. Never walk like a deer in the dark.
2. Never walk like a deer when another deer hunter/person can see or hear you.
3. Never walk like a deer if a deer is watching you.
4. Never walk like a deer for practice while you are on your hunting land.
5. Never walk like a deer during your scouting trip.
6. Never walk like a deer on set up day.
7. Never walk like a deer if you do not want deer to follow you.
8. Never walk like a deer if your personal safety will be in jeopardy.

"NEVER DO" list for Scouting & Setting Up

1. Never use any trail cameras on the property if you intend to hunt with D.I.E. there.
2. Never bait deer and use D.I.E., or hunt where you can see someone else's bait.
3. Never walk to your stand site in the off-season, if possible.
4. Never spend any more time in the woods than is necessary.
5. Never let more than one other person scout or set up with you.
6. Never chase deer while scouting.
7. Never walk through a core doe or buck bedding areas.
8. Never disturb a real buck's scrape or rub.
9. Never yell out while you are in the woods unless you need help.
10. Never leave your cell phone ringer on while in the woods.
    (Set it to silent only—not to vibrate.)

11. Never wear cologne or perfume when in the woods.
12. Never wear solid colors into the hunting woods, if you can avoid it. Deer will see you.
13. Never hunt from an elevated stand without wearing a safety harness.
14. Never pull a loaded weapon up into a tree stand (always unload it first).
15. Never place a tree stand before set up day.
16. Never place a tree stand between a road (vehicles travel on) and the first sign of deer.
17. Never prune any tree limbs before set up day.

"NEVER DO" list for Days 1, 2, 3 and 4 of your hunt

1. Never park your vehicle where you can see it from your stand or your scrape.
2. Never hunt within view or earshot of another hunter. (Stay at least 150 yards apart).
3. Never hunt with someone else using D.I.E. within half a mile of you. Two hunters need to use D.I.E. in two different places. Otherwise, you may both attract the attention of the same dominant buck. (I have not tested two D.I.E. set-ups near each other).
4. Never tell any other hunters you are using D.I.E. (They likely will try to investigate your stand site, and could ruin it for you).
5. Never hunt with D.I.E. in a wide-open area. It will not be believable to the deer.
6. Never assume you will have 100% success without using lures that do what these do:
   - Wildlife Research Center's Active Scrape.
   - Robinson Outdoor Products' Still Steamin' Premium Hot Doe Estrus Urine.
   - Wildlife Research Center's Trail's End #307.
7. Never set the scrape further than 35 yards away from the nearest deer track.
8. Never touch/alter the rub or the scrape after set up day.
9. Never urinate in the D.I.E. scrape or do anything else to it—ever.
10. Never refill any lure in the Scrape-Dripper after it runs out.
11. Never waste time getting into your stand each day. Once you are there climb up.
12. Never climb out of your stand until you shoot the buck or 4 minutes before closing time.
13. Never stay in your stand past the end of the shooting hours. Get out and go home.
14. Never throw food or garbage out of your stand.
15. Never smoke or chew tobacco in your stand.
16. Never walk more than 5 yards downwind of your stand or your scrape during the hunt.
17. On Days 2, 3, and 4, never go to the scrape at all.
18. Never leave your stand or scrape-dripper in the woods past Day 4 of your hunt.
19. Never walk with your weapon perpendicular to your chest or legs.
20. Never doubt the power of the DOMINANCE IS EVERYTHING system.

Chapter 27

Cramming the D.I.E. system (optional)

I have learned through the years that the system can be modified, and I can still get great results, but I have not done enough research on those modifications yet to convince me that they will always work for you. Anytime you modify the D.I.E. system you change the system's results from being a sure thing, to a being a mere chance. If you cram the system you are taking a chance that you will not see any deer on the hunt, and on the flipside, you have a chance to see a monster buck. If you ask me, there is a time and a place for a crammed D.I.E. set up, but only if it is not possible for you to hunt for up to four days. Never turn down an opportunity to hunt with D.I.E., because you will be amazed at what you can learn from deer when they do not know they are being hunted.

If you do not have four consecutive days to hunt deer this fall but you can arrange to be in the woods for at least 2 or 3 days, then setting D.I.E. up is still worth a try. You will have to cram the hunt in a two-day period instead of a four-day period. You will have to set up during daylight, the day before you hunt, and you will skip the waiting period. These modifications will lower your odds of seeing a dominant buck at your stand because it pressures the buck to show up now or never, and the smartest buck in the herd sometimes will prolong his visit to the 3rd or 4th day, which is 'like never' to a 2-day hunter. If he lives there he will likely show up, but if he doesn't bed around there, he will likely hold up in heavy cover for a day or so before coming in.

D.I.E. is not 100% if you cram it because of the timing. The doe in heat just appears, and the doe in estrus is there before you are. Those things are not normal to the deer, but the power of D.I.E. isn't normal either so let's run with it. On a normal 4-day hunt, the use of the lures is timed out so the buck is mesmerized by all that is going on around the scrape from set up day, until Day 1 of your hunt. He finds the scrape and takes it over while does in heat are visiting it, then you show up as a single doe in estrus that is escorted by a monster intruder buck, that no real buck can seem to find. It all makes perfect sense to the herd, because you come in from upwind of them and they expect to see intruders coming in from crosswind angles. You surprise the dominant buck and he takes his time figuring the D.I.E. scrape and rub out, before committing to going to it during daylight. Every part of a typical D.I.E. hunt is in harmony with the others.

Now you want to speed the system up (to cram it) because you do not have four days off during the rut. That is quite all right, the system still works if you cram it, but not with 100% results. You can never know when the dominant buck will find a D.I.E. scrape, and if you have only two days to hunt and he does not find it in that amount of time then you go home with a lesser buck or with nothing at all. In order to better your odds that it will be immediately on set up day, rather than 1, 2, or 3, days later you set up the same way but you keep the scrape close to you (within 20 yards) and place it in mixed cover, near a core doe or core buck bedding area if you have that option. You still need to stay 80 yards away so you are not pressuring the deer when they are in the bedding area, but you are close enough there to see them come and go in as well. Build the D.I.E. scrape and rub in an obvious place near a major deer crossing. Stay upwind of everything if you can. Upwind of the bedding area, upwind of the deer trail, upwind of the D.I.E. scrape and rub and of course crosswind too. Conceal yourself high enough in a tree to be hidden from any approaching deer's line of sight, and stay still.

If you gun hunt and only have two or three days to hunt, you need to rush the set up and get your stand in, in a very quick manner. This is how you should build the mock-scrape(s) in a rushed time frame, so you can hunt in the stand the next morning. **Note: You only should set up this way if you do not have a four consecutive day buck hunt planned, and there is no way for you to be in your stand for more than 3 days.** This set-up does not give you 100% results, and for that reason, I do not advise you to use this set-up, unless you do not have any other option and you wish to give my theories and my system a try. It is your choice.

This sped up version of D.I.E. has had its place in my repertoire but I never attempt it during bow season, only in gun season. I feel the dominant buck may become wise to all the other hunters in the area during the gun deer season, and because I cannot control who else may be hunting nearby my location, I sometimes choose to cram the system rather than not using it at all. If the buck is naturally comfortable in the area you set up in, then he will walk right in on Day 1 or Day 2, because you are laying down the scent of the hot doe in estrus urine on set up day. Sometimes it is worth it to have only a 1 in 3 chance to see the most dominant buck during your gun hunt, even though it is just that...only a chance.

To rush the system, do a quick scout and locate a core doe or core buck bedding area. Set up your tree stand within view of the nearest available cover that is downwind of your stand. Sit on the upwind side of deer bedding and face downwind and crosswind keeping the back of your shooting shoulder facing the wind. Keep the D.I.E. scrape(s) close to the tree stand. Only put in one stand.

You can cram the D.I.E. system with one D.I.E. scrape and rub or with two. I find that two Scrape-Drippers dripping different lures works great to get every mature buck in the area worked up into a breeding frenzy, and they give the dominant buck a heck of a tough time 24/7. He has difficulty upholding his dominance at the scrapes, and it has resulted in multiple bucks showing up on my one hunt using two Scrape-Drippers set up the way I describe here. If you want to use two Scrape-Drippers, it is ok, but always set these things up the way I tell you to—no variances please. If you use two Scrape-Drippers, rinse both of them out with water and air-dry them with no cap on before using them (unless they were new).

Making two D.I.E. scrapes

Build two D.I.E. scrapes, there can be one on each side of a deer trail (the way I did it), or you can put them right next to each other on only one side of the trail preferably the upwind side. If you only have one of the two trees you chose for a D.I.E. rub offering you tree a licking branch, then you will be hanging both drippers from the same tree (with the licking branch) but from different branches above the scrape. Set up in a 2 to 4-inch diameter sapling like you normally would.

If you find two trees to make two rubs on, and each one offers you a licking branch 5 to 7 feet off the ground then you should not hang the two drippers in one tree, only hang one in each tree. In this case, the two trees should be less than ten feet apart. Make one rub on each tree behind each of the scrapes. Dig up the soil under the licking branch with a hammer claw or the heel of your boot to make the scrapes.

Do not use a real antler to make the rub(s), and do not use a real deer leg to make tracks in it in the dirt. You will mess my system up if you do either of those things. You do not want the buck to try to identify the invisible buck (you) that made those mock scrapes. You do want him to notice the scrapes, but you do not want him to hunt down the buck. You want him to work the scrape and take it over right away, that way he will bed downwind of it, and he will wait for the doe in estrus (you) to return to the area the next morning. Never leave any boot prints in the mock-scrape(s), and always wear gloves.

Next, pour half the bottle (2 oz) of Active Scrape lure on the ground (in the dirt of only one scrape), and then pour the rest of it into only one Scrape-Dripper. Tighten the cap on the dripper so it is snug but not super tight, just so none of it comes out, then invert it and tie it to an overhanging branch 5 to 7 feet above the mock scrape that I call the D.I.E. scrape.

Then get out your secret weapon, the Still Steamin' Premium Hot Doe Estrus urine, and pour half the bottle (1 oz.) into the other Scrape-Dripper. Tighten the cap on the dripper so it is snug but not super tight, just so none of it comes out, then invert it and tie it to an overhanging branch 5 to 7 feet above the other D.I.E. scrape.

Unscrew the top of the Scrape-Dripper just enough so a little lure pours out into the scrape, and then turn the cap snug again. That will prime the pump so to speak. Then open the cap just a quarter turn in a counter clockwise direction, until you see a drop of lure or urine clinging on the tip of the black rubber tube. Always make sure the dripper(s) are dripping before you leave the set up. If it never drips, no buck will be there looking for the doe. Once you have the scrape(s) built, cut your shooting lane and get the heck out of the woods. I always dream that night that a monster buck is out there under the moonlight working up my scrape.

Only one D.I.E. scrape

If you only use one D.I.E., scrape then pour all the Active Scrape lure on the ground in the dirt of the scrape, and hang the Scrape-Dripper up with a half of the bottle of Still Steamin'

Premium Hot Doe Estrus urine in it. Keep the other half bottle so you have enough left for use on the scent wick on your morning dragline.

When you rush a set-up, you can hunt it the first morning after, but a few things will be different. First of all, the deer that you will see in the area will be bucks, does, and fawns, (basically the whole herd) because you threw out 'waiting period', and on the morning of Day 1, the buck most likely hasn't found it yet. Once he finds it, he will work the scrape up and rub the tree behind the scrape. You should only rub about a one-foot high area on the tree, start 20-inches off the ground and move the jagged saw up 12 to 15 inches from there, only rub the tree on the side that faces downwind or crosswind. If there is a main trail there, face the rub towards the trail, so any deer traveling the trail will see it head on.

Like I said before, the buck may not have found it yet and if he hasn't, you need to know that he is going to be more nervous now with you there than he would've been if you had left the scrape alone for 2 ½ days before hunting over it. You should focus on watching the downwind side of the scrape at all times, but keep your body facing the scrape itself. If you need to stand up to look downwind, that is ok, but always move slowly. Try not to make any sudden movements, including turning your head left and right. Take 30 or more seconds to turn your neck and head to view the area. If you are turning your head left and right in a second or two, you are moving it too quickly. Slow your movements so deer cannot see you move.

You can modify the D.I.E. system if you only have three or less days to hunt, but the results are not predictable. The buck that hunts you is more likely to identify you as a person, and he is more likely to wait for Day 3 or Day 4 to show up. With all those negative possibilities looking you in the face, it is totally up to you to make the choice to use the 'crammed' version or not. I do not prefer to hunt with the crammed version of D.I.E. (shorter version), but I have used it on three gun deer hunts. On all 3 hunts I had a dominant buck working my D.I.E. scrape within 2 ½ days after set up, but only one buck ever showed himself during the two day hunt when I was there. Therefore, the odds of success for a 2-day hunt have been 33% successful for me. I do not want a dominant buck on private property to be wise to my set up, so I only cram the hunt into a 2 day period when that is all the time I have to be on the property. If I have four consecutive days available to hunt, then I always choose to use the system in the normal fashion. It has never let me down when I have 4 days to hunt.

You cannot determine which day or at what time the dominant buck will approach your mock-scrape, but you can predict which direction he will come from. He will always scent check the Still Steamin' Premium Hot Doe Estrus urine so you will always know he is going to be downwind of the D.I.E. scrape and he will come in close if you let him.

In order for the DOMINANCE IS EVERYTHING system to produce a mature breeder buck 100% of the time, you need to be able to hunt four consecutive days there is no way around that. I have crammed the set up process and eliminated the waiting period on each of my last three gun hunts, and I saw one monster buck on one of those hunts. Both of the other two hunts were going well when I had to return suddenly to work. I will try to set up ahead of the season this year, so I can make my hunt with a gun as fruitful as my last one with a bow was.

The system is unpredictable when you rush the set up and do not role-play with the buck. I wanted to show you that there are options with my system, but if you choose to use any of them, you could be reducing your odds of seeing a trophy buck. **DOMINANCE IS EVERYTHING** is a sure thing if you work it the normal way. For me, having a 33% chance of a Monster buck coming within 35 yards of me during gun deer season is a lot better than having a 0% chance of it. I use it regardless of the time it takes to set it up and tear it down, even if I can only hunt with it for one day. I am not done testing new ways to use my system, but the time has come for me to share it with you and anyone else who wants to experience a hunt of a lifetime.

Chapter 28

Important lessons to avoid being busted

One of the men I taught my D.I.E. system to told me that he messed up big time (the first time he used it), by not pulling his weapon up into the tree with him as soon as he got his safety belt on. He told me that a monster 12-point buck came walking in within a few minutes of him getting into his stand on Day 1 of his hunt in 2008. He tells me that the 12-pointer was a Pope and Young 180+ inch buck, and it was likely the biggest buck he ever had come within bow range. The bruiser buck was walking directly down the tree line that his stand and D.I.E. scrape were set up on. He said by the time he got his facemask and his gloves on, that the buck was only 40 yards away and walking in at a steady pace. He waited for the buck to stop in some cover, but he didn't stop, he just kept coming. He was determined to get to the pair of breeding deer within that minute. When the buck stopped he was within 10 yards, and that D.I.E. hunter was about to be busted with his bow dangling on a rope at the base of his tree. He decided he had to try to get his weapon up so he started to pull his bow up slowly. I asked him, "What did the buck do?" He told me that the buck caught his slow movement in the tree as he was trying to bring his bow up. At that point, the monster buck turned around, and trotted away. That humbled D.I.E. hunter was Matt "Rhino" Rynearson, a Wisconsin Pro Staff hunter. I agreed to teach D.I.E. to Rhino because he is a pro hunter and I wanted the public to hear his testimonial that my system doesn't fail. Rhino will tell you that D.I.E. is a miracle dominant buck hunting system that he will not stop using. He continues to hunt with D.I.E. season after season, in multiple states of our great nation.

Rhino texted my cell phone (from his tree stand) that morning at about 10:30 a.m. His text message said something like this, **Just got busted by a monster 12-point at 10 yards! Will he come back?** I replied, **"What do you mean you got busted? NO"**.

I had told Rhino everything he had to do in order to succeed right out of the gate with my system, and apparently, he made a mistake somewhere. I was eager to find out why he was busted, so I called him. That is when Rhino told me he was up late the night before and overslept on the morning of Day 1. The buck was right on time coming to the D.I.E. scrape but Rhino was 3 hours late. That was the first reason why he was busted; and not pulling his weapon up right away was the second reason. Rhino definitely was suffering from monster buck fever, and he was reluctant to move out of the area, but I told him it was over for him there and that the buck knew he was a human so he had to go somewhere else and hunt another king. The hardest part for him to handle was that he had done the set up, waited the 2 ½ days, got in his stand unseen, and the system worked; but he was busted on his first day. That must have hurt. He had to pull his stand out of an ideal location where he had the dominant buck hunting him, and move it to a new location and hunt another dominant buck there. Not only that, but he had to trust me that I knew if he stayed there and waited for the buck to come back, that he would be wasting three days in his tree stand. Once you are busted, it is over for you there. I know that very well.

I told him to move at least a quarter mile upwind and crosswind towards the direction from where he entered the woods. There he was instructed to set the system up again. I didn't know it at the time but he decided to use trail cameras at his new location. When I trained him to use my system, I advised him against the use of trail cameras. He asked me if it was all right to use them with D.I.E. and told him that I never tried using one. I had succeeded every time I hunted without a trail camera so I did not want him to use one, because I could not give him any odds of succeeding with them. Rhino was a promoter of trail cameras at the time and he told me he wanted to try them sometime with my system. I thought having a trail camera in the woods would give the bucks and all the other deer in the area a chance to put 2 and 2 together and tell them that the trail camera was put there by a human and that the human would be back when they came in to get the pictures. I told Rhino that placing a trail camera near a D.I.E. scrape would be like telling the smartest buck in the territory, that you were there to do him harm, and that you would be back; then ask him to stick around waiting for you to kill him. I did not think that was a smart thing for an invisible hunter to do. I still feel the same way. No one who ever used a trail camera anywhere on the property they hunted with D.I.E. on has ever seen the dominant buck during the day. The trail camera kills the deal, so take my advice and do not ever use them with my system.

With **DOMINANCE IS EVERYTHING**, a hunter needs the element of surprise. Using a trail camera, takes away that element. Rhino waited 2 ½ days after setting up the D.I.E. scrape in his new location, then for the next four days, he hunted it but he didn't see any deer within 35 yards of his stand during daylight. He called me and told me he saw two large racked bucks on his trail camera at night but nothing during the day at the scrape. I told him I never used trail cameras and that one of those bucks would have visited the scrape if he hadn't told them that a human was there (by placing the trail cameras). The dominant buck will still come to the D.I.E. set up because he has to, but he will do it after dark if he knows a human (a deer's #1 enemy) is there.

Rhino pulled that stand out and moved again to another new area that was over 100 yards away on the edge of a field. There he set the system up again but this time without trail cameras. This was the third time in 2 ½ weeks that Rhino was hunting with my system. There he successfully harvested a 7 ½ year old 10-point buck with his bow at less than 15 yards. The local hunters in the area told him that they believed it was the most dominant buck in the area, and that they had never gotten close enough to shoot him when he was in his prime or at any time before.

I included this story in the book so that you would realize how important it is to set up my system exactly as I tell you. The D.I.E. system does not fail, only hunters who do not follow instructions do. Rhino was not the first person to learn a lesson the hard way with DOMINANCE IS EVERYTHING, and he will not be the last. It has taken me 12 years of trial and error to get this system mastered so anyone can use it. I was busted by bucks many times in the beginning, but now I know a sure fire way to avoid that from happening, and I am showing you the way that the system works every time. Just follow my instructions and you will be fine.

Do as I say and the dominant buck in the area will come into your stand site and will offer you a easy shot opportunity, during broad daylight, always within the four-day hunting period. Please do not use trail cameras with my system. Do not worry about what your buddies are doing. If you intend to hunt with D.I.E. this fall and you expect the system to work for you, then you have to abide by all the rules and the first one is, do not use any trail cameras. Pull them out and leave them out year round where you want to hunt with D.I.E. Do not make excuses for them, just get rid of them, and hunt the way I teach you to hunt. If you never used a trail camera then you can disregard all the lessons I am trying to teach those folks that do.

Have faith in the D.I.E. system

Every dominant buck is set in his ways, and the older he is, the more educated he is. His life revolves around the rut. His priorities are set in order just like those of a monster buck. Most important is his survival, then breeding, and finally socializing with other deer. There isn't any part of his being that says he should be curious, ignorant, easily persuaded, naive, or willing to take chances with humans.

Dominant bucks are methodical. They live their lives like my DOMINANCE IS EVERYTHING system is structured—in a very methodical way. Every step they take is well thought out and planned. They do not guess, they decipher and plan. One wrong move on his part and his hierarchy is over, not to mention that the king is dead. They cannot afford to take chances with humans, so they never allow humans to get close to them—not ever! Most human beings never see the most dominant buck while they are hunting deer. I mean when they have a weapon and they are pursuing deer, not just driving by a field near dusk looking for the area's king. The king of the herd avoids all contact with humans, and rightfully so.

Human hunters hunt him every fall, and they will not stop pursuing him once they catch a glimpse of him in their sights. I used to hunt like that. I would follow the biggest deer track I could find and I thought I could tire that huge buck out and eventually catch up to him and kill him. It never happened. Monster bucks and dominant bucks are smarter than most hunters are. I know they are smarter than I am. The dominant buck has a will to survive, a will to remain dominant, and most of all a will to keep humans from entering into his own private world. If he did that, then it would be trouble for him and he wouldn't be safe, not even in his own bedding area.

I invented my own way of hunting mature bucks because I was not able to be successful hunting traditionally. I call my system the D.I.E. WAY, and when I first put it in action, I did it for a chance to get a large racked mature whitetail buck. Right from the start, it has produced much more than that for me. When I taught it to Tom Earle of Palmyra, Wisconsin in 2002, and to Matt "Rhino" Rynearson of West Allis, Wisconsin in 2008, I told them that the system hadn't failed for me so I felt that if they did what I did, they would have the hunt of their lives with it every year they used it. Well to this day, it has not failed anyone, and both Tom and Rhino attest to it being the best way they know of to attract dominant and monster bucks to the stand site of a deer hunter, a nature lover or a photographer.

Chapter 29

My secret to 100% success—I always keep him guessing!

Hunt with D.I.E. by becoming an observer, and forgetting you are a hunter. Do not move in close to the buck and look for him, instead move away from his core living areas and make him look for the two invisible breeding deer (you). Take for granted the fact that the dominant buck will be looking in your direction the entire time he is making his way to the D.I.E. scrape, and know he will always be in staging cover before he begins making his approach. Knowing those two things are true, you can understand why you need to sit motionless for at least 15 minutes at a time in your tree stand to allow the buck to approach. I have seen dominant bucks cover 350 yards of open ground, walking at a steady pace, while on a mission to meet the pair of invisible deer, and the bucks got to the scrape within 15 minutes. The longer you can sit motionless in your tree stand the better off you will be.

The dominant buck's way of thinking sets him apart from all other deer. He is in charge of his own world, he reports to no deer, and he does not fall for hunter's tricks like the young and dumb fawns and yearling bucks do. He is in no hurry to get anywhere. He has all the time in the world, and whenever he decides to leave the safety of cover, he conducts a scent check, a hearing test, and a visual scan of the area he is entering into, long before he arrives there. In the case of a D.I.E. hunt, you are not there as a human, so be sure that you never give him any ideas that a human is there. Stay scent free all day by spraying down with Scent Killer® 99% whenever your bare skin becomes becomes exposed to the air.

The area where you are hiding is the area the dominant buck is testing. He will constantly be testing the area upwind and crosswind of himself for danger. You have to pass all three tests in order for the buck move in your direction. If he keeps coming, that means he does not know that any human is there. If he were convinced that you are not a human and that you are not a threat, why would you ever want to tell him anything different? When the buck is feels safe he will come in posturing and showing off as if he owned the place. There is no mistaking a dominant buck's behavior as he makes his way to a D.I.E. scrape. If you drag the pure doe in estrus urine, behind you on a dragline each morning (like I do) then the buck will be making his way to you first and to the scrape second. Know that you are invisible to him every second that he is within 200 yards of you, even if he is walking away. He is just living his life the way he usually does. Do not get too excited and shoot before the buck offers you a fatal shot opportunity. He is in no hurry. So why should you be?

Before the dominant buck makes his final approach to your stand and the scrape, you will hear him grunt on over 50% of your D.I.E. hunts. When you hear him grunting it is a good thing, it means that he is straight downwind or at a crosswind and he is close enough to see the scrape. He is just outside the 35-yard (invisible) bubble, that the D.I.E. scrape has surrounding it, and he is convinced that at least one of the two (invisible) breeding deer is there at that very moment.

On six of my eleven D.I.E. hunts, I witnessed the dominant buck staging in light cover, 35 to 80 yards away downwind of me, while he called to the doe in estrus. Each time, the buck was standing still, staring at the scrape, with his neck stretched straight forward, as if he was preparing to do a lip curl. He made a series of tending grunts (ranging from 5 to 30 grunts) to let the doe in estrus know that he was downwind of her, that he had checked the area out, and that it had passed all three of his tests. He was telling the doe that it was safe for her to come out and breed with him, right there and then.

What you do in response to his calling will determine whether he will advance on the scrape, or not. The only thing an invisible (human, deer, and hunter) can do is observe, so that is what you should do. Do not call to him. Just watch and learn. If you call to him (as a human, a deer, or a hunter) you will be busted instantly, even if he cannot see you, because calls can be tracked. Do not call to a buck when he is standing still, or he will pinpoint your location and he will bust you. As an experienced D.I.E. hunter, I never call to a buck that is facing in my direction.

If you refrain from calling then the buck will attempt to get the attention of the intruder buck by raking brush or making a scrape. Do not reply to the dominant buck no matter how vocal he gets. That is how you remain invisible to him. After he is through talking to the invisible deer, he will approach the scrape in an attempt to look for the doe in estrus and to command the D.I.E. scrape. That is when he will walk out into the open, and offer you a shot opportunity. Stop him with a grunt, and make your shot count.

Getting busted stinks—avoid it happening to you by not breaking any rules

The three most obvious causes of being busted on a D.I.E. hunt are:

1. **Making the buck aware that you are a human being (his enemy)**
   There are many reasons why deer can identify a human as a dangerous enemy, but there are no reasons why a D.I.E. hunter should ever be identified as one. A deer should never be able to see you, hear you, or get your human scent. I have taught you how not to behave in ways that deer know humans behave. By behaving like a deer instead of a human, you are never telling any deer that you are a human, and you are giving them the impression that you are a deer.

Review this list often so you can put forth your best performance when you are role-playing with the herd's most dominant buck. Avoid making these human gestures on your D.I.E. hunts and you can avoid being busted.

You can be busted by the king of the herd *if you*:

- Do not become 99% scent free and invisible to deer
- Place a trail camera anywhere inside his herd boundaries
- Go to or from your stand in the dark
- Walk into the property from a public parking lot
- Walk down the center of an active logging road
- Rush to your tree stand, or swim through brush on the way in
- Use a walkie-talkie with radio static, or allow your cell phone to ring
- Set up too close to deer bedding or breeding areas, or to real buck sign
- Fail to use the three lures as directed
- Fail to wait the 2 ½ days of the waiting period before hunting
- Get out of your tree stand before the end of the day
- Walk in from downwind of the stand or the scrape
- Arrive at your stand earlier or later than instructed
- Set up in a stand where deer have looked at you before
- Go back to the scrape for any reason after you leave it the morning of Day 1
- Do not pull your weapon up in the tree stand and load it

2. **If you tell him that he is being hunted and that you are coming back**

I strongly advise you to follow all the instructions, that I provide you with in this book, so you can have a hunt of a lifetime with my DOMINANCE IS EVERYTHING system, instead of having a frustrating memory of a hunt gone bad, and a story that no one wants to tell, about the dominant buck that outsmarted you.

You are setting yourself up to be busted if you:

- Use any trail camera(s) inside the territory of the dominant buck
- Spend too much time in the woods near active deer sign
- Place multiple hunting stands on the property
- Talk aloud within 120 yards of the stand
- Continue walking when you encounter a deer
- Lay down bait and construct a D.I.E. scrape and rub near it
- Move around in your tree stand too much or too often

- Eat or drink in the stand for more than 2–3 minutes at a time
- Do not wash your body and hair with scent free soap before each hunt
- Do not become 100% invisible to deer
- Leave your stand before the buck comes in, or the end of the day arrives
- Make any human noises, or start up a vehicle within 120 yards
- Park your vehicle in plain sight of your tree stand
- Call too much, or rattle too much, or place a decoy poorly
- Set up in the open where a buck can see the rub from >35 yards away
- Fail to live by the NEVER DO rule lists
- Set up and/or hunt within 150 yards of another hunter
- Set up further than 35 yards away from a deer track

3. If your hunt is interfered with he will stop hunting you

As you know, it is impossible to control what other people do when they deer hunt. We can only control our own behavior, and because America is a free country, public land means just that, it is open to the public. Many people enjoy walking around in the wild enjoying all that nature has to offer. I am one of those people and I would guess you are too. There are going to be times during your D.I.E. hunts when you see a person walking, or driving a motorized vehicle within 200 yards of your stand site, or maybe you see a domesticated animal run through the area. If any of those things happens, you were just busted and you have to quit hunting from that stand for the rest of that four-day hunt.

I call it being interfered with. Outside elements can cause a dominant buck to lock up and return to becoming a nighttime breeder again. All of my hunts that have been interfered with have ended with the buck never coming in during the four days. I have had 3 of those bad experiences, and each one taught me a tough lesson. Dominant bucks only go where it is safe, and if they see a human they will avoid the area until the human is gone, and then until the human's scent is gone (2 more days). That human can be anyone.

If there is any disruption within 200 yards of your stand site from the time you set the scrape and stand up, until the end of the fourth day, consider yourself busted, and pull the stand and scrape out immediately. If you have deer within view of you, wait for them to leave and then pull the set up out. If you do not quit, then you will waste every day you are in the stand.

I have never seen a deer from my stand after being busted. The dominant buck stops hunting the scrape during the day, and he tells the rest of his herd to avoid the area completely. As the leader of D.I.E. hunters everywhere, I think it is my duty to tell you that your hunt is over if it is interfered with. If you find yourself in that situation all you can do to succeed is pull the stand and the scrape out and move to a different property to hunt with the system. Go where you will not be interfered with. If you want to stay on that property, then talk to whoever interfered with you and ask them to stay out of the area while you set up and hunt with the system again. Pick a new stand site for success. Be sure to move at least 80 yards upwind and/or crosswind of the spot you were busted. If you do not have 80 yards left to go before you are at your property line, then wait a week for things to calm down, and try it again from a spot nearby your first stand.

After installing a D.I.E. scrape and rub, you have to be invisible to deer at all times whether you are in your stand or not. When a human or an animal interferes with your hunt, they take your ability to be invisible away from you. The dominant buck avoids all dangerous situations and the area around your scrape just became one. You should know you have to quit if you are busted, no matter what the cause was. You can start over somewhere else. The dominant buck still has to breed and he is still willing to fight all intruders, whether you were busted inside his territory or not. Remember to always think like the buck, see what he sees, and know what he is thinking before he even thinks it!

If you are busted you cannot succeed on that hunt. All you can do is adjust your schedule, pull out the stand and scrape and leave the area as he did. If you can hunt another part of that property without being interfered with there, go ahead and do that, but wait at least 72 hours before you go back into the area. Allow your human scent to dissipate, and the memory of your doe in estrus to drift from the dominant buck's mind, before you go back to set it up again with a new set of lures. Start out at the beginning again, with the set up day, and the waiting period, then go back in but this time you will be a doe in estrus with a different name.

If you find yourself standing up in your tree stand staring off at the backside of a retreating dominant buck, know that you are not alone. I have been in your shoes before, and so has Tom Earle (the first person I taught D.I.E. to). I do not know if it ever happened to Rhino. Having a D.I.E. hunt interfered will happen to many D.I.E. hunters at least once, so if it happens to you, know that it is something you cannot control and that it is not your fault. Being busted stinks, but there is always tomorrow. Get up, brush your pride off, pull your tree stand, and set the system up again in a new area that is completely out of view of the area where you were busted.

If you were busted by the buck, and you know for sure, that he saw you as a human, then you need to move right away. Choose a different type of tree to place your tree stand in, because the buck will be looking for humans in every tree that resembles the one you were in when you were busted. My advice to you is to move in an upwind and crosswind direction from your first set up location. Always avoid making contact with the buck (avoid walking downwind of your scrape) and always respect the fact that you are in the home territory of the most dominant buck in the herd, whenever you are on that property, even when you are not hunting deer.

Succeeding is easy when you have faith in the system

Remember when you hunt with D.I.E., you are a breeding pair of deer, and only you know that they are invisible. Be sure to wait him out, and when you do see him making his entrance toward the stand site, let him come in close before you attempt a shot. Once he is within 35 yards the D.I.E. system has done its job, and you are still invisible to him. Never tell him that you are a human sitting in a tree. The secret to success with D.I.E. every time is always keeping him guessing!

Chapter 30

Stories of my most memorable hunts with my D.I.E. system

Bullwinkle—A 12-point monster buck that got away

D.I.E. changes everything! Because DOMINANCE IS EVERYTHING to a monster whitetail buck, the D.I.E. system makes the dominant buck check in at the D.I.E. scrape at least once a day while you are hunting. The buck will come in during daylight only one time that I know of. Even if he is with a real doe in estrus he will come away from her and come to you, or he will bring her with him to your stand site, because he has to when D.I.E. is set up in his territory.

During the chase phase in 2006, I witnessed a 12-point monster buck I named Bullwinkle leave two real does in estrus (I believe were twins), to visit my D.I.E. scrape during daylight while I was there. I got him to come to me after two days of watching him chase that pair of does in and out of cover, about 130 yards downwind of my stand. I decided to put on a play for him in hopes he would feel he had to come to me immediately to uphold his territory.

I successfully pulled him away from those two does (at least one was in estrus) by making the sounds of a buck fight (over the invisible doe in estrus) at my scrape. I called and rattled to get his attention away from the does he was mating with, and although he took his merry time getting away from them Bullwinkle galloped in with less than 10 minutes left on Day 4 of my hunt. Deer vocalizations are sometimes a very good thing when hunting with my D.I.E. system. I could not believe my eyes at the time but it happened and I will tell you about it here and now.

Here is the story

In 2006 during my Wisconsin bow hunt I had a 12-point monster buck (I named Bullwinkle) hunting me. He is the most massive racked buck I have ever seen in my life, still to this day. His rack was at least 36-inches wide inside. His main beams were 3 or more inches in diameter at their bases. He was mating with two does in estrus about 130 yards away from me during my D.I.E. hunt. My D.I.E. scrape was set up and I was hunting in the same tree, as I was when I harvested the 17-pointer in 2009. The made a D.I.E. scrape and rub, there were no real rubs in that area. I was facing a one-way deer trail. This heavily used deer trail only had deer tracks heading West on it. The buck was to the East of me for 3 days. Each day starting on Day 2 of my hunt the buck came out of heavy cover and staged in a tall grassy area along a drainage ditch on our 12-acre parcel. I could not see the buck's entire rack until he came in with 10 minutes left in the day on Day 4 of my hunt. He was hanging out in staging cover downwind of my stand and as his luck would have it there were two does about the same size allowing him to mate with them on the same days. I watched as he chased those two does in and out of the cover for 2 ½ days of my hunt. The buck showed up on Day 2 of my hunt straight downwind of my stand and he was running up and down the drainage ditch making 20 or more tending grunts each way as he went. The ditch was the best breeding area on our land, and I knew it but there were no trees in it large enough to hold a tree stand so I was never able to hunt it. I hunted off our widest water source where I knew all deer frequented during the day at that time of the rut. I was hunting in a transitional area, where deer were at ease and they could find water and cover within 5 yards of me at all times.

The buck staged in the SE corner of our land each night before dark, and he showed up with these two does three days in a row. I looked with binoculars and I could see the two does were about the same size. I figured they were yearling twins, and that they went into estrus at the same time each year so the dominant buck could manage to keep them together where it would have been unlikely for two does born at different times to be in estrus at the same time. He was straight downwind of my D.I.E. scrape and he stayed there all day long. When night approached, he stopped chasing them and came down the ditch grunting towards my set up. I tried to call him on Day 2 with a buck grunt and he did not budge from the cover. On Day 3, I used my Montana doe decoy but he never gave me a look-see. On Day 4, I made loud sounding footsteps as I "walked like a deer" in that morning all the way (100 yards) to my tree stand and he stayed with the does again. Then it hit me! I needed to role-play with him, because he could not see my scrape from his position, but he could smell the scent of the doe in estrus and the intruder buck in the area, it was the only thing I didn't try yet that I thought might work. I thought it over and came up with the ultimate game plan to get him jealous of the invisible intruder buck shagging tail on the invisible doe in estrus at my scrape. I decided to make it a buck fight and to be aggressive. What did I have to lose? It was Day 4 and this buck was having sex with two does for over half my hunt, right in front of me.

First I analyzed the situation from a hunter's perspective

It was three hours before shooting time was going to close and I saw the two does run out of a brushy tree line to the SE of my position. The wind was from the WNW and the deer were getting the scent of my set up all day long. I raised my binoculars and looked. The does looked to me as if they were both yearlings. They both had their tails up, half-cocked and drooping over. From what I know of deer these does where in estrus. It was November 4, 2006 and that was Day 4 of my 4-Day hunt. I heard buck grunts coming out of the tall grass where the does where. The buck was running through some tall yellow grass along the drainage ditch and he was very vocal, letting out constant short bursts. They were tending grunts. Good news for me. I knew he was a breeder buck and he was downwind of me. My D.I.E. scrape was 'hot' for 3 days and this was my 4th and final day. He knew where my scrape was but he was with two real hot does, in the same area. I could not blame him for staying with them instead of coming over and staking out my stand site for an invisible doe.

Next, I analyzed the situation from the perspective of a invisible pair of deer

He was most dominant buck in the area, he brought the does to a staging area straight down wind of me, and he was tending both of these 'hot' does (does in estrus) for multiple days. It all made sense. I thought about the circumstances of what he was doing and I guessed what I should do. I figured I had to try to tell him that the invisible doe was really here right now and that another buck was here and attempting to breed her. That was a good plan so I pulled my M.A.D. Grunt Snort Wheeze call out of my jacket and I proceeded to make doe in estrus bleats with it. They were too quiet; the buck was not reacting to them, so I put the tube inside the bellows chamber and tried again. The result was much better. It amplified the sound so it would carry across the field. I figured if I could hear him grunting then he could hear the doe in estrus bleats.

He just kept chasing the two does in and out of the grass. When they ran onto the field, he waited and when they jumped back in the cover, he chased them around grunting the whole time. It was great fun for me to witness it but I wanted to see the buck. I thought about getting out of my stand and going downwind of the buck, so I could sneak up on him maybe even "walking like a deer" to get close, but it was only a thought. I always remind myself to stay in the stand from start to finish each day. I know the buck will come. It was tempting to go but I waited and stayed put. I wanted to give the system the chance it deserved. I wanted to see if Day 4 was needed, for a hunt with D.I.E, up until that day the dominant buck always came in on Day 1, Day 2, or Day 3.

I had my rattling antlers with me in my backpack and I had them rigged so I could lower them to the ground and make them rattle from down there. I decided to pull them out and initiate a fighting sequence. When I was filming deer in 1992 I noticed that dominant bucks would run in at a dead run, for a buck fight over a doe in estrus in the area. I knew it was late in the season to be rattling but this had to be the dominant buck and if he knew about my D.I.E. scrape and rub, then he knew I represented a doe in estrus from Day 1 of my hunt. I decided to make it sound as if the doe was still here but now two big bucks were here too. They were fighting over the doe and they would not quit until he came in. I lowered the rattling antlers and I let out 3 aggressive buck grunts, then some doe bleats and some tending grunts. I slammed the antlers together on the lower limbs of the green spruce I was sitting in. I was a one-man band! The buck stopped chasing and stopped grunting for a few minutes. I smashed the antlers together for 3 minutes and stopped, letting out three long dominant grunts after that. Then I stayed quiet.

I looked at my watch and it was two hours before closing time and the buck was not coming. The does started darting in and out of the cover again and I could hear the buck running through the grass back and forth. I slammed the antlers together repeatedly pounding them on the ground and making the sounds of hoofs stomping. Then I stopped and put all my calls and antlers away. That was enough for me. I did some loud tending grunts and packed it in. I figured the buck had to have heard that, and I did not want it to sound like it was too good to be true so I ended it. Every buck fight ends with on buck vocally announcing his win and the other retreating from the area.

The sun had already set and the cardinals and chickadees where starting to fly into the spruce tops around me. I know that time of the day very well. That meant I only had 20 minutes of legal shooting time left. I left those 20 minutes in the hands of God. Looking back, I think I prayed from my stand that God would bring that buck to me. All of a sudden, he came across the field at a full gallop. He ran straight to my tree. I mean he ran through thick briars and underbrush and stopped within 1 foot of the trunk of the tree I was sitting in. I never do cut the lower limbs out on the tree I sit in (I like to keep my tree base as natural as I can on the lower 8 feet), so I could not shoot. I looked down though and there he stood! He took three deep breaths, I saw the steam coming out of his nostrils, and then he backed out of the brush and ran downwind to the main trail. I had my scrape on that trail. He trotted up the 4 ft. incline near my stand and he came down the other side, his hooves splashed in the creek, while his head cleared the green spruce trees. I was sitting in that row of trees straight north of him only 10 yards away. My shooting opportunity was 4 yards past the spruce trees on the other side of the waterway, and my scrape was a yard or two past that. I am a lung shooter with my bow.

I grunted to him one time with my mouth, while I drew my bow back. He stopped in his tracks facing my D.I.E. scrape, with his front hooves in the water of the creek and his back hooves still on solid ground hidden under the canopy of green spruce trees. Darn he stopped too soon I remember thinking! I did not have a clear shot at any vitals except his neck, and I was not going to shoot him in the neck with a bow. I had a bad experience in the past with a neck shot and did not want to risk losing this monster buck the same way I lost a 10-point 140-class buck in the past. He displayed his huge rack and stood still for nearly a minute while I was at full draw. He turned his head toward me and lowered his rack as if to challenge the buck that grunted to him. That is when I was amazed to see his gargantuan rack and body. The inside of his main beam was blocking the perfect shot I wanted right behind his shoulder blade. His rack was massive. It had to have been a 36-inch inside spread, and the mass was enormous. The buck's body was huge and he was solid muscle. I remember leaning out of my tree allowing my safety belt to hold me as I swung out to get a better angle on his ribs. His hind end was still under the pines and I was kicking myself for grunting so soon. Just one more step and he would have been broadside and wide open. I could not hold it any longer so I leaned forward and aimed for a spot right behind his shoulder two ribs back (lung area). He had swung his head around and was facing my D.I.E. scrape when I let the arrow fly. It deflected 6 feet away from me and stuck in the gravel between his legs. No way! I could not believe it. That buck was 10 yards broadside but his whole body from the 2nd rib back, was covered by spruce branches, because I grunted too early and I stopped him 3 feet earlier than I wanted too. He ran into the woods upwind of my scrape, one minute before closing time. He wheezed at me about once a minute for 15 minutes straight. I refused to get out of my stand until he shut up. I think he was laughing at me. I know he did not see me and I had my chance at him but I missed.

You are probably laughing right now and I deserve it but I tell you it hurt. To miss a buck of a lifetime at 10 yards! I had trouble sleeping many nights after that. The next day I pulled my stand and packed it in for the bow season. I am a Realtor here in Wisconsin and I had many families depending on me to sell their properties at that time. Getting 4 consecutive days off away from my job is tough sometimes, and in 2006, we had a booming real estate market. I had to go back to work. The buck lived on, and I have a great story to tell, about another one that got away, but that God brought to my doorstep so I could admire the magnificent animal in my midst. I suppose if I would have fatally hit each buck I has come into the D.I.E. system while I was watching over it, then this book would have 11 success stories in it and I would not be writing all of these lessons I learned. This book would have been shorter for sure.

The moral of this story is you can intimidate any dominant buck even if he is a monster buck. You can call him out of whatever he is hiding in, but you have to use your head and make the situation feel real to the dominant buck. When he comes in is up to him entirely, but if you are patient and you wait until 5 minutes before legal shooting time closes each day before you leave your stand, then you are assured the buck will show up for you. If you have a doe decoy, a doe in estrus call, a buck grunt tube, a set of rattling antlers and a lot of patience, you are as prepared as I have ever been for your next encounter with a monster buck on a D.I.E. hunt! Even when a dominant buck has a live doe in estrus with him, or maybe two, you can intimidate him with a territorial dispute near the D.I.E. scrape and rub that you make when you set up the D.I.E. system. All dominant bucks need to keep their dominance in their home territory, and that need to remain dominant of all the bucks in the herd, was Bullwinkle's only weakness that day. Every dominant buck has the same weakness and DOMINANCE IS EVERYTHING takes advantage of it. D.I.E. gives the advantage to the hunter who uses my system. Go get him and send me the photos. Keep him guessing and he will keep hunting you.

My 2009 Wisconsin bow hunt for the 17-point buck

On November 5, 2009, I finally accomplished the goal of harvesting a monster buck with my bow, and it was the most amazing hunt with DOMINANCE IS EVERYTHING that I ever had! I got buck fever again but this time my arrow flew true and I have the 17-point non-typical buck on the cover of this book to show for it. The buck was indeed hunting me. It had nothing to do with luck when that buck showed up and took on a contender just 50 yards downwind of me. After he beat his opponent in a head-to-head battle, he came charging in attempting to steal the doe in estrus from the most dominant buck in the area. The herd's king was a huge racked 10-pointer with an estimated 18-inch inside spread, and 15-inch G2's and G3's. I missed the 10-pointer 2 ½ hours earlier at point blank range right under my tree. His antlers were only 5-inches under the platform of my stand a minute before I released my arrow. I overshot his back and grazed his right shoulder. The buck did not see me and walked into the woods upwind of my scrape.

A few hours later this 17-point monster intruder buck and another intruder buck that I never saw the rack on, showed up at the same time. They fought and the one that won was the 17-pointer. He then charged the scrape and I grunted one time with my mouth. He stopped right where I expected him to stop. He was just an intruder buck hanging out downwind and crosswind of my D.I.E. scrape at 7 o'clock a.m. that morning, but at 9:30 a.m. when I shot him with an arrow at 10 yards he surely was the most dominant buck at the scrape at that time. The king had left the area to soothe his wound, and two intruders took advantage of his absence.

He is the sixth biggest buck I have ever have ever seen while hunting with my **Dominance Is Everything** system. I admit that I am not as good of a shot with my bow as I want to be. I am sure that most deer hunters would say they have never missed 5 huge whitetail bucks in their lifetime, much less in five consecutive bow hunts. Although it is tough to get over a missed shot, I do not let the missed opportunity stop me from hunting dominant bucks. It is too darn exciting to be hunted by the king of deer! Once you see what I mean and I am sure you will agree.

The thing I have going for me is that I have invented a system that turns the tables on dominant bucks. The deer hunter becomes the hunted. The D.I.E. system has never failed to make the most dominant buck in the area hunt for the hunter. You can have 5 dominant bucks come to you in five attempts if you use the D.I.E. system as instructed. My **Dominance Is Everything** system will change the way you hunt bucks if you try it, or at the very least, it will give you another option. The system makes it easy for a hunter to succeed at getting close to dominant whitetail bucks during the rut. Hitting them successfully is totally up to you.

Summary

I have hunted with D.I.E. for 11 seasons now. On every hunt, I followed the same set up procedure, and on each hunt the most dominant buck in the herd (at that time) was indeed hunting me. When I invented the D.I.E. system, I was just a man who loved to hunt deer and sought out the most elusive deer of them all, a monster whitetail buck. I knew that monster bucks were real from the time I was a kid and I first saw one. Ever since that day, I have been mesmerized by the capabilities of escaping danger that all old monster bucks possess. It has become my life's work to learn to outsmart the king of deer. I have mastered all a person needs to know to bring the king of the herd to their stand site while they are hunting him. Repetition has paid off for me and repeating my actions when setting up my D.I.E. system will pay off for you too.

Trust me that I know D.I.E. better than anyone in the world does. Trust me that I have taught you well, and trust in yourself that when you commit to hunting up to four consecutive days with DOMINANCE IS EVERYTHING, you will be rewarded with a hunt of a lifetime. My system is miraculous! It is well thought out and proven, and more importantly, it is believed by all whitetail deer to be real. When you hunt with D.I.E., you become the hunted, instead of being a hunter. The most dominant buck believes you are one of the pair of deer that he has been sensing for the past few days in the area around your stand. He knows he is the king and he fears no deer in his herd and no other animal in his territory. He has to find you (the pair of breeding deer), and he has to find you fast, before it is too late for him to make a difference in the lives of those two (invisible) deer.

There are many amazing aspects of a going on a hunt with DOMINANCE IS EVERYTHING. It is unlike any other way of hunting deer. Hunting with DOMINANCE IS EVERYTHING puts an end to your using any traditional hunting tactics that every D.I.E. hunter knows get hunters busted. You will not be going to your stand in the dark, or leaving it after dark. You will not be making deer drives, forcing deer to leave their sanctuaries. You will not have to shoot at running deer. You will not see fawns and yearling bucks walking through your area. When a deer comes in, it is the most dominant buck. If you can hear, two deer walking toward you do not turn around. Be confident it is the dominant buck and a doe in estrus is coming along with him.

You will retire all trail cameras you used on that property (if you used any). Trail cameras are not tools they are toys. Cameras do not help you get close to a dominant buck, the actually hamper your chance of seeing one during the day from a stand near the camera location. DOMINANCE IS EVERYTHING is a tool, and you now own the right to use it. Mature bucks fight over the right to breed your (invisible) doe, and the most dominant buck in the area shows up every time. Now you can be invisible to deer without buying special clothes to wear. All you need is good camouflage, to be scent free, and to walk like a deer when it is safe to do so. There is no more walking over a quarter mile to get to your stand (unless you only have walk-in access). In addition, there is no more having to hunt longer than 4 days each season for a mature buck. D.I.E. frees up your weekends and by doing that, you will have the opportunity to hunt across the United States and Canada if you want to.

For me, the things I am proudest of are the lessons I have taught in this book. It has taken me 30 years to learn all I know about whitetails, and until now, I was not sure how I was ever going to teach the world how to hunt with my system. This book, my seminars, and my private (½ day one-on-one) lessons are the answer. Throughout the book I have taught you what makes mature bucks tick, and more importantly how to outsmart every herd's dominant buck during the rut. Knowing how to hunt with D.I.E. will change the way you look at the deer from now on.

No longer will a mature buck be just a nice buck, now you will always wonder when you see a buck whether he is the most dominant or not. If you take my advice and walk out in the woods in late winter when the snow still covers the deer trails and the ground is still frozen enough for you to walk safely, then you will see the big picture. You will know what your herd did all winter, and you will know what to expect of them next fall. Dominant bucks fill my dreams, and adventures into the territory of the most dominant buck in the North American herds, await me.

There is no mistaking the mannerisms every mature dominant buck exhibits as he comes into a D.I.E. set-up, looking intently upwind (behind your mock scrape) for a lonely doe in estrus, which he is convinced has been seeking him out to breed. He will be posturing and moving slowly and cautiously with confidence, many times dragging his front hooves on the ground and becoming very vocal with his grunting and growling. Dominant bucks all behave the same way when they find the D.I.E. set-up. They react to it as a territorial intrusion. Those types of aggressive signs of dominance from other bucks in the area are not ever tolerated by the king of the herd. He has to come to the scrape to maintain it and to make sure no other breeder bucks get an idea to take it from him. He commands the area and as each hour passes, he gets more eager to meet the (invisible) pair of deer you represent to him. He will only advance on the scrape and into your area after you arrive, and he will never know you (a human) are there. That is what I thank God for the most. The fact that every hunter who uses D.I.E. as directed, is always invisible to deer. That by itself is a miracle. Being invisible to the king of deer is incredible. Always knowing that monster bucks are alerted to your presence and that a monster buck may be the one that hunts you, should get you excited to get out and hunt with **DOMINANCE IS EVERYTHING**.

I am a method hunter, not a hunter of chance. My method of brainwashing the most dominant buck to believe I am a deer is all any buck hunter needs to know to be able to have a close encounter with the herd's king at any given time during the rut. Knowing what I have taught you about whitetail doe's breeding cycles, and how mature breeder bucks respond to a D.I.E. set-up, you should now be on board as a true believer in the capabilities you will have when you commit to hunting with **DOMINANCE IS EVERYTHING**! My system is unique, and the way I use it is a method that the deer respond to the exact same way, no matter where in the world you set it up. Why hunt trophy mature whitetail bucks any other way? **DOMINANCE IS EVERYTHING**... To A Monster Whitetail Buck! Are you a believer?

Glossary

Bachelor buck groups A group of bucks that all belong to the same herd that hang around together while the buck's antlers are growing. Bucks in the herd break up into bachelor groups starting in the spring and staying together through the summer. When the rut arrives in the fall bachelor buck groups break up and bucks fend for themselves. Not to be confused with pecking order bucks that hold rank, a bachelor group of bucks could consist of all yearling bucks, all mature bucks, or some of each.

Big buck trail A trail that a buck with a 33-inch wide rack of antlers can walk down without getting his antlers snagged up on tree limbs or vines. Big bucks travel on the downwind side of heavily used deer trails. These trails are always in cover. Hunting with D.I.E., and setting up so you are shooting to a D.I.E. scrape made on the upwind side of a big buck trail is an excellent set up to have.

Breeder buck A mature buck no matter if he holds rank in a pecking order or not.

Busted A buck busts you when he identifies you as a threat to him. It means he saw you move, heard you make a human noise, or smelled human scent on you. You can be busted and the buck does not know you are a human, or he can positively know you are a human. If he knows you are a human your D.I.E. hunt is immediately over in that stand. If he does not know then you can move to your D.I.E. set up to second stand site location and finish your hunt there.

Challenger buck Is a buck that is challenging a more dominant buck to a fight. A more dominant buck will never start a fight with another buck of lesser rank. Challengers are bucks that want something the buck they are challenging has, such as a higher rank, a herd, a choice food source, a territory, or a doe in estrus. Dominant bucks are often challenged, but they are never challengers.

Core-bedding area Does & fawns & yearlings, Pecking order bucks and the Dominant buck each have core-bedding areas of their own. I have found that they each have three core bedding areas in a dominant buck's territory. A core bedding area is a preferred bedding area where the deer bed routinely depending on the wind direction and the weather. There are 9 total core-bedding areas in every herd.

Core breeding area An area with a canopy over heavily used deer trails. A place where the mature bucks run after does in heat and in estrus. Most often, it is an area where the brush is thick on the outside but opens up once you enter the area. It is a tough place for a human to get into without making a lot of noise, due to thorns, mud, water, or some tall grass. Breeder bucks run up and down or left and right through their core breeding area, chasing does in estrus and breeding with them. This is an all day meeting place for mating deer. If you squat down (at a deer height) inside a core breeding area you will see how easy it is for a big racked buck to run in there, but by standing up (as a human) it looks pretty tough to get through.

D.I.E. rub A special rub that only a person using DOMINANCE IS EVERYTHING knows how to make. Robert J. Mercier invented it in 1998. There is nothing like it in the real world. The rub is made on a 2 to 4-inch or larger diameter tree, it is commonly made 2 inches wide, and it has a shredded appearance (similar to a territorial rub), but it is wide enough in the middle to shine like a beacon for all deer to see (similar to a smooth rub). The unique characteristic is that the D.I.E. rub is not torn down to the smooth live tree trunk. It is left looking rough, only the outer covering of bark is removed. No whitetail buck in real life leaves a rub looking like that behind a scrape. All rubs behind scrapes are smooth in real life. A D.I.E. Rub is made on a tree behind a D.I.E. scrape and it makes dominant bucks move in and take it over. When they rub it they go all the way around the tree sometimes, and when they leave it, it no longer has a shredded appearance. It will be rubbed smooth. It becomes will be the primary breeding scrape of the herd's most dominant buck.

D.I.E. scrape A special scrape that a D.I.E. user constructs within 35 yards of his or her tree stand on a D.I.E. hunt. D.I.E. scrapes are made exactly the same way every time. They have a D.I.E. rub on a tree behind them, the ground is pawed up in the scrape and they have a licking branch hanging over them. D.I.E. scrapes are the focus of every dominant buck that encounters them. They must be constructed exactly as directed in this book.

Doe in estrus A doe that is 2 to 2 ½ days into her heat cycle goes into estrus. Estrus is the 1 to 1 ½-day period when a doe will allow bucks to mount and breed with her. Estrus is part of a doe's heat cycle. It is the last part. A doe seeks the dominant buck when she is in estrus and he seeks her too. All bucks will breed with a doe-in-estrus because she will let them, but once a dominant buck is breeding her he will stay with her and fight other bucks if he has to in order to dominate the doe and keep his right to breed with her.

Doe in heat A doe that is at least six months old, that is nearing her receptive period (estrus) during the rut. I believe does are in heat for 3 ½ to 4 consecutive days, and they go into heat at the same time each year. A doe-in-heat attracts all bucks, but she is not able to get pregnant if she is bred while in heat. She has to go into estrus to be able to get pregnant. I do not think does in heat want to get bred.

Doe trails Heavily traveled trails that whitetail does (of all ages), fawns, and yearling bucks use on a regular basis. They travel in open areas and through thick cover. A doe trail travels in very straight lines and goes through mixed terrain, mainly on the downwind side of clearings. Not in the clearings, just in the cover on the downwind side of it. Doe trails are only as wide as a deer's body in most cases.

Dominance The way a whitetail buck displays his strength towards other bucks in the area. The most dominant buck displays his dominance by posturing, raking brush, grunting and growling, making rubs, making and maintaining scrapes during the rut, and by fighting if necessary. He spreads his toes on his front hooves when he walks 24 hours a day and 365 days a year. Dominance is earned it is not granted. Bucks rank in the pecking order by their strengths and their ability to win fights with other bucks. DOMINANCE IS EVERYTHING to all mature bucks. Being dominant earns bucks the right to breed.

Dominance Is Everything Also referred to as the D.I.E. system. Is a system I (Robert (Bob) J. Mercier, New Berlin, Wisconsin invented in 1998 that makes the most dominant whitetail buck in the herd seek out two breeding deer at a man-made scrape (D.I.E. scrape) that the user of the D.I.E. system makes. The buck will always approach during daylight within 35 yards or less of the user's tree stand, within a 1 to 4 (consecutive) day period that the user gets to choose during the rut. The two deer the dominant buck is looking for do not exist in real life, they are invisible, but he does not know it. He will seek out the pair of deer for up to 4 days, at which time he figures out he has been misled. The user of the system is the breeding pair of deer and they have options to role-play with the buck if they want to.

Dominant buck The highest-ranking buck in the pecking order, he is #1. He is the king.

Dominant buck's primary breeding scrape A name I give the D.I.E. scrape once it is taken over by the most dominant buck, and any scrape you find in the wild that is made like it but the rub behind it is rubbed smooth not ripped or shredded. They are hard to find, because the dominant buck only can maintain one of them at a time. You know that he is maintaining a scrape if the rub is fresh and the scrape below it is freshly pawed up and damp with urine. The dominant buck leaves a single track (made by one of his front hooves) in his primary breeding scrape and there is always a chewed-off licking branch above the scrape. When you find one of these in the wild, you know that the king of the herd's favorite breeding zone is right there.

Dressed weight The weight of a deer after it has had its entrails (guts) removed.

Finger snug A looser setting (than snug) for the cap of a Scrape-Dripper, but still not allowing the lure or urine to flow out of the Scrape-Dripper. The cap has to be finger snug when it is inverted hanging over the scrape, so you can purge it.

First sign of deer The first sign of deer is the first track, rub, scrape, a bed impression, some droppings, or browsed vegetation that you see as you enter a piece of land from human civilization. When you find the deer sign you are at the first sign of deer. Deer do not spend time in areas you do not find any deer sign, so when you pretend you are a deer on a D.I.E. hunt, you cannot drag lure in or pour lure out between your car or your house and the first sign of deer. If you do you will be identified by deer as being a human.

Hand height The height your hands are at when you are standing with you arms down at your sides. If you bend your wrist up, that is hand height. I made the phrase up.

Heavily used deer trails Well-beaten trails you see in the woods as you walk through your hunting area. These trails are used primarily by does, fawns, yearling bucks, and some low ranking pecking order bucks. A deer trail is dug into the soil more than a couple inches, and that deer travel on all day long.

'Hot' doe A doe in estrus that is willing to breed with any buck.

Intruder buck Is a mature buck from another herd that may or may not hold rank in that herd's pecking order, or a mature buck that lives inside this herd's territory but does not hold rank in the pecking order. Intruders roam wherever they want to in search of does in heat and in estrus. They owe no allegiance to any dominant buck when they are out of their herd's territory and they do not fear losing fights. They are fighters, and many of them are monster bucks. Some of them are swamp bucks.

King of the herd The most dominant buck.

Lesser bucks These are non-dominant bucks of all ages. If he is not dominant then he is less than dominant. Thus, he is a lesser buck.

Lip curl Only bucks one year old or older do lip curls. It is done only during the four phases of the rut. A buck does a lip curl by standing still and stretching his neck out in a straightforward direction or in an upright pose. First, he exhales and then he inhales deeply and in the process, he curls his upper lip back under itself, so it touches his front upper teeth. A buck does a lip curl when he catches the scent of a doe in heat or a doe in estrus. He can analyze the scent of a doe's urine and determine whether she is in estrus. The dominant buck has done a lip curl downwind of my D.I.E. scrape or on my back trail where I dragged in the doe in estrus urine that morning, on over 50-percent of my hunts. It is normal behavior for a breeder buck to do a lip curl from a position 10 to 50 yards downwind of the scent of a doe in estrus before he approaches the doe to breed.

Mature buck A 2 ½ year old or older buck (also known as a breeder buck).

Monster buck Is a buck that has a rack of antlers that is so massive in main beam diameter, tine length, and spread that a person exclaims overwhelming joy when they see it. If you cannot fit your hands around the main beam of a buck's rack, he is likely a monster buck.

Monster intruder buck An invisible buck that you are telling the herd, made the D.I.E. scrape. On every hunt with DOMINANCE IS EVERYTHING is scent is Trail's End #307 lure.

Neutral buck A mature buck that does not hold rank in the buck pecking order. Such as non-dominant monster bucks, swamp bucks, and retired dominant bucks. They do not care about being the king of the herd.

One-way deer trails A deer trail used by both bucks and does that are travelling in only one direction. Check the tracks on trails and you will find one. They are commonly found where deer are moving through 3 or more types of terrain in less than 40 yards. Do not overlook water crossings and roadway crossings. Deer use one-way trails 24 hours a day.

Pecking order bucks Mature (2 ½ year old or older) bucks that rank lower than the dominant buck and live within his herd. They show subordination to the dominant buck whenever they encounter him. Each one holds a rank lesser than the one above him. They all want to become the most dominant buck someday, but many of them never accomplish it. They rank #1, #2, #3, #4, #5, etc…

Posturing A physical display of dominance and sheer muscle that all bucks display when near a challenging buck. The dominant buck postures on every step year round.

Purging the dripper Every Scrape-Dripper must be purged in order to activate it so it will drip immediately. I discovered my own way to make the Scrape-Dripper drip on the timeline of a real doe in heat that eventually will go into estrus. I purge the dripper when I add lure to it so it will become the live deer immediately at the D.I.E. scrape, instead of having to wait for a 10° temperature increase to get it to start dripping.

Rut Is the mating season for deer. In the whitetail deer world the rut is the most exciting time of the year. Deer of all ages breed. Doe fawns and yearling bucks breed too. The rut is a period of time that deer are actively breeding. In Wisconsin, the rut starts by October 16 and it runs through to January 8 of the next year. These are not the exact dates but represent what I have learned and can prove to you are the dates that the rut is on in Wisconsin. It may turn on earlier or shut off later, but the rut is always on (deer are mating) between those dates.

Scent check All deer do scent checks. They go downwind of a place or a thing they are unfamiliar with and they raise their head and nose up high in the air and inhale deeply. The scent that the wind carries downwind to the deer's senses is inhaled by the deer and they analyze it to determine what lies ahead.

Semi-open cover cover you can see 40 yards in when you are looking at it from a deer's perspective, 3 to 4 feet off the ground.

Shadow line The northwest, northeast, southwest, and southeast sides of a tree trunk are in the shadow lines. A phrase I made up to mean the sides of a tree that do not get direct sunlight at any times of a day. If a person sits in a shadow line, the sun does not cast their shadow out away from the tree as it would if they sat on the north, south, east, or west sides of a tree.

Skyline To show your body form in the sky. To not be concealed in the tree stand. To sit in open cover where deer see you and are alerted to you being there.

Snug The tightest position you put the Scrape-Dripper nozzle and cap in so it is tight, and can be hung upside down, without leaking any lure or urine out.

Staging Dominant bucks, and most mature bucks stage (hold up) on the edge of cover before heading into any open area during daylight. It is their way of avoiding hunters and it is the best way I know that allows them to stay in charge of every situation. When a buck is staging, he is waiting for something. Usually he waits for sunset, but sometimes he is waiting for a challenging buck or for a doe in estrus. All dominant bucks will stage before they come into your D.I.E. set up. They stage in medium to light cover. Always downwind or crosswind of the place they are trying to get to, and always nearby one of their core bedding areas. Staging bucks are smart bucks.

Stand site the place where you can see your tree stand and the D.I.E. scrape and rub at the same time.

Swamp buck A mature 3 ½ year old or older buck that does not rank in the pecking order, that lives alone in a swamp or lowland area, and that has a coat that is darker than average deer, sometimes even black.

Tending A mature buck tends (mates with) a doe in estrus by staying with her as long as she is in estrus.

Tending grunts Are short bursts of air (sounds) that mature bucks make when they see a doe in estrus, are chasing, or following a doe in estrus, or when they are nearing the location of a doe in estrus and they can smell her scent. I believe a buck making tending grunts on his way to a D.I.E. scrape is saying, "Hey baby, here I am! I can smell you but I do not know where you are hiding. Come out so we can get together."

Territorial rub A dominant buck makes territorial rubs to mark his core living space boundaries. They are on trees that are at least 2 inches in diameter. Most common are 4-inch to 8-inch diameter trees. Hard or soft bark does not matter. These rubs are shredded. In most cases the bark is not removed entirely from the tree. The rubbed side of the tree faces one of the 3 dominant buck's core bedding areas.

"The Big Picture" Seeing your area's herd from their point of view. Knowing where the deer bed, breed, find water and feed. Knowing how to get into your property without telling deer a human is there, and watching deer and learning from them, instead of just looking at them. Seeing the big picture allows you walk among deer, and to communicate with them on their level (a deer-to-deer level).

Thick cover cover you can only see 10 to 20 yards into at a deer's height.

Transitional cover Two or more types of terrain within 50 yards. They can be as simple as two different types of vegetation. Bucks stick to the edges of cover. You will always find big deer tracks in transitional cover.

Walking stiff-legged The way a dominant buck walks when he is within view of a challenger, or near one of his territorial boundaries, no matter what time of the year it is. During the rut, the dominant buck walks stiff legged all day long as he makes his rounds through his territory. Non-dominant bucks do not walk stiff-legged unless they are being challenged.

Yearling bucks Immature bucks that are 1 to 2 years old. They do not hold rank in the pecking order. They are too weak and inexperienced to be able to command a herd.

Hunting Notes

# Hunting Notes

Hunting Notes